The African Diaspora in the U.S. and Canada at the Dawn of the 21st Century

A Global Academic Publishing Book

The African Diaspora in the U.S. and Canada at the Dawn of the 21st Century

edited by

John W. Frazier, Joe T. Darden, and Norah F. Henry

State University of New York Press

A Global Academic Publishing Book

Published by
State University of New York Press, Albany

Printed in the United States of America

For information, contact State University of New York Press, Albany, NY
www.sunypress.edu

Library of Congress Cataloging-in-Publication Data

The African diaspora in the United States and Canada at the dawn of the 21st century / edited by John W. Frazier, Joe T. Darden, and Norah F. Henry.
p. cm. — (A Global Academic Publishing book)
Originally published: Binghamton, N.Y.: Global Academic Pub., 2009.
Includes bibliographical references.
ISBN 978-1-4384-3684-5 (pbk. : alk. paper) 1. African Americans—Race identity. 2. Blacks—Race identity—Canada. 3. African Americans—Social conditions. 4. Blacks—Canada—Social conditions. 5. United States—Race relations. 6. Canada—Race relations. 7. African diaspora. I. Frazier, John W. II. Darden, Joe T. III. Henry, Norah F. (Norah Fox) IV. Title: African diaspora in the United States and Canada at the dawn of the 21st century.
E185.625.A385 2010
305.896'073—dc22

2010041945

10 9 8 7 6 5 4 3 2 1

Acknowledgments

We are grateful for the opportunity to edit this volume. Our deepest thanks are extended to our chapter authors, who represent both native-born and foreign-born people of the African Diasporas in the United States and Canada, as well as other ethnicities from various ethnic backgrounds from around the world. We thank the authors for their perseverance in writing and rewriting their manuscripts to meet the recommendations of the editors and reviewers. We also thank the anonymous reviewers for their time and insights that improved the overall quality of this volume.

We also express our gratitude to Dr. Sylviane Diouf, Curator of Digital Collections at the Schomburg Center of Rutgers University, and photographer Joshua Norman, for permission to reproduce their original materials. Thanks are also due to Mr. Kevin Heard and the GIS Core Facility at Binghamton University, who produced original maps and improved others throughout this volume. We also thank Ms. Lisa Eldred, Michigan State University, for editorial assistance.

This volume would not be possible without the support of many individuals, but we are particularly thankful to the staff of Global Academic Publishing, including Mary Beth Willis, who offered the initial encouragement for this volume. The text was guided from inception to completion by Ms. Lori Vandermark, whose constant attention, encouragement, diligence, and cheerful outlook are gratefully appreciated. We also thank Jennifer Winans for typing, Matthew Tynan for graphics and other support, and Amanda Stone for marketing efforts.

John W. Frazier　　Joe T. Darden　　Norah F. Henry

Contents

Section 1:
An Introduction

Chapter 1

An Introduction to the African Diaspora in the United States and Canada at the Dawn of the 21st Century

NORAH F. HENRY, JOE T. DARDEN, AND JOHN W. FRAZIER

Approximately four centuries ago the first African set foot in North America, yet it is impossible for any text to capture the complete Black experience on the continent. As the 21st century begins, the persistent legacy of Black inequality and the winds of dramatic change are inseparable parts of the current African Diaspora in the United States and Canada. It is an onerous task to embrace both dimensions in a single text, especially given the two distinct cultural histories and separate policies of two very different places. Despite the challenges these differences pose, it is worthwhile to explore the common experiences and problems shared by these two neighbors. In addition to providing a better understanding of Black experiences for other scholars, we hope that our collective effort will contribute to a dialogue among scholars and contribute to the informed and difficult decisions of policymakers of both countries.

We emphasize geographic concepts in this text. For students who only memorized the mundane facts of grade-school geography, this work will come as somewhat of a surprising and new educational journey. College geography is more theoretical and conceptual. It suggests that the facts are less important than the context in which they occur. For example, the total tons of fish caught by Norway are important only within the context of fishing as an economic activity, and as a part of the human-environmental interface. Conceptual thinking examines subjects within broader thematic structures, including the physical environment, spatial location, human-environmental relationships, regional studies, place, and movement. In fact, these are the broad themes of the discipline of Geography.

Each theme has numerous concepts that foster understanding of particular relationships. For example, within human-environmental relations, cultural landscapes occur when an ethnic group modifies an area's appearance and structure to reflect its presence there. Similarly, movements occur in various ways and for a variety of purposes. Thus, immigration and migrations that reshape countries, regions, and places are of importance to geographic inquiry. This volume continues that thematic tradition as we consider the African Diaspora in the United States and Canada. The themes and concepts of this chapter will be apparent throughout this text.

The African Diaspora in the United States and Canada, increasingly complex in recent decades, illustrates the persistence of inequalities and spatial isolation for many of African descent, despite the growth of the Black middle and professional classes. These, in part, explain the Return Migration to the Southern U.S., and new suburban and other settlements by the African Diaspora in various North American regions. Another part of the explanation is increased African and Afro-Caribbean immigration and refugee populations that contain diverse socioeconomic characteristics. These, too, add to the complexity (both social and spatial) of the intricacies of the African Diaspora in the United States and Canada.

The persistent racial legacies expressed through institutional and individual White-majority behaviors mark both Canadian and American landscapes and continue to restrict equal access of people of African descent to basic resources. At the same time, liberalized immigration policies and labor needs rooted in globalization have attracted an increasing number of ethnically and socio-economically diverse African and Afro-Caribbean ethnic groups to both nations.

This volume represents the work of social scientists from geographic, historical, sociological, and political science perspectives, from Canada and the United States, including African-Americans and Canadian Blacks, African immigrants, Afro-Caribbean immigrants, and Whites. In addition to the general themes indicated earlier, these essays reflect a special emphasis on place. This concept is as old as Geography itself, but has experienced a bit of a renascence in recent years. It also has been the subject of increased attention in other disciplines (Hayden 1999; Frazier, Margai, and Tettey-Fio 2003; Wiese 2004; Frazier and Tettey-Fio 2006). The place perspective, while recognizing the influence of global processes and the importance of theory, argues that place itself influences experience and the formation of particular landscapes and other geographic patterns. The attributes of a place, in conjunction with global and regional forces, create the final and unique experience and expression of culture and ethnicity.

This volume also examines the roles of institutional forces that work at various geographic scales to support and to hinder those of the African Diaspora in both nations. Institutions have been equally important in both countries because they helped shape historical Black experiences and locations within the context of Anglo-dominated societies. Specifically, federal, regional and local policies supported by White-dominant institutions regulated Black immigration and created spatial and social segregation on a racial basis and reinforced ethnic isolation and inequalities, which have persevered over centuries. These are undeniable dimensions of the African Diaspora in the two nations as we enter the 21st century. Their persistence requires our attention and vigilance, despite institutional efforts to level the playing field in housing, employment, and immigration policies. This is especially true because national efforts are implemented in a local context, within the support or constraints of place. On the other hand, supportive institutions in some cases have eased immigrant and refugee adjustments to very new places. Among these are the refugee settlement programs (VOLAGS) that have resettled Blacks in various locations. At other times, ethnic institutions, such as ethnic churches, have played significant supportive roles for various Black immigrant groups.

Another aspect of the Diaspora in the United States and Canada is the tremendous variety of recent changes brought about by the rapidly increasing Black immigrant populations. These have contributed to an increasingly *diverse* Black population in both ethnic and economic terms. The types of immigrants and their settlement locations, of course, vary from place to place, as do the circumstances of their arrival, and the socioeconomic status (SES) of the group. The specifics about ethnicity, ethnic identity, refugee status, and other characteristics lead to differing mixes of Black ethnicities and classes in United States' and Canadian communities. In addition, the local racial/ethnic settings vary place to place, such that Black immigrants may encounter native Blacks of a particular SES, or none at all. Where Black natives and foreign-born do meet, their associations range from mutual support to competition that may result in "distancing" (Vickerman 2001). Thus, the complexities of SES differences, racial and cultural histories and identities, economic opportunities, ethnically supportive institutions, and political environment, create intricacies in experiences, attitudes, and settlements that are difficult to unravel.

In both nations, Black immigrants have found that not only has access become easier in recent decades, but also that they are free to move about without non-economic regulations or restrictions. As a result, and especially in the United States, Black secondary migration has complicated our understanding of migration behavior and settlement choice. This is true in Gateway Cities and in regional patterns, such as the well-established "Reverse" migration of Blacks to the American South. They also complicate relationships with non-Blacks in some communities and with native-Blacks in other places.

All of these processes and relationships are evolving as we begin a new century, yet their coverage by social scientists has been scant. They beg our attention because they are newer and changing parts of American and Canadian fabrics still unknown, but that require understanding that will guide our individual identities and well being. We must unweave one dimension of this fabric: the persistence of racism and racial inequalities that is rooted in our separate but similar cultural and political histories and in expressions of our human geographies. Similarly, we must get a better grasp of the changing Black dimensions of our national, regional, and local identities that are influenced by global and national practices, but are crafted by the uniqueness of places in which we live. We must grasp the macro- and micro-dimensions of processes and their local expressions. If we do, we may have a better understanding of our past and future and a basis for dialogue within and between our nations about issues old and new. Such an understanding may also stimulate young people to become activists in seeking greater equity in our societies and the generation that mandates needed changes. Indeed, changes are needed if we are to address the common problems and issues still faced by people of African descent in the 21st century.

COMMON PROBLEMS AND ISSUES AFFECTING THE BLACK EXPERIENCE IN CANADA AND THE UNITED STATES

We present here the common problems and issues faced by people of African descent, whether they reside in Canada or the United States, within the context of the following themes and concepts:

A. place and its attributes;
B. ideology of the dominant group and the historical legacy of slavery;
C. immigration policy and its impact on immigration;
D. differential incorporation;
E. residential segregation;
F. socioeconomic neighborhood racial inequality;
G. racial inequality in the social structure;
H. the impact of anti-discriminatory public policies.

A. Place and its Attributes

In terms of place, both Canada and the United States share a North American border. The two countries differ significantly in terms of total population and the number and percentage of people of African descent. Canada's total population was only 33 million—i.e., only 11 percent the size of the 285 million people in the United States in 2001 (Statistics Canada 2003; United States Bureau of the Census 2006). In both places (Canada and the United States), the sense of place in terms of "belonging" for people of African descent has been shaped by their demographic minority status among an overwhelmingly White majority population. In both countries, there is color stratification. In Canada, the White majority ancestry groups consist of British and French populations and their White Canadian offspring. At the next rank are Whites from other European countries and their White Canadian-born descendents. Together, these White Europeans constitute 65 percent of Canada's total population aged 15 years and older (Statistics Canada 2003). In the United States, the predominant European ancestry groups are German, Irish, English, and Italian. These groups, along with other European groups and their American-born descendents, constitute 74 percent of the total population of the United States.

In Canada, Blacks (used interchangeably in this volume with "people of African descent") comprise 2.2 percent of the total population, whereas in the United States, Blacks are 12.4 percent of the total population (U.S. Bureau of the Census 2006). In Canada, Blacks are the third largest visible minority (i.e., non-white, non-European racial/ethnic group) behind the Chinese and South Asians. In the United States, on the other hand, Blacks are the second largest racial/ethnic minority group after Hispanics, who constituted 14.8 percent of the total population in 2006 (U.S. Bureau of the Census 2006).

B. The Ideology of the Dominant Group and the Historical Legacy of Slavery

In order to fully understand the experiences of people of African descent in Canada and the United States, one must understand the role of ideology and the historical legacy of slavery. As a concept, ideology is a belief by which one group of people carves out a certain vision of how things ought to be (Gyekye 1997). Political power is used to bring about this vision. Through political power, ideology is translated into an explicit program or action (Gyekye 1997). This action can either include or exclude people who are not members of the dominant White group.

Ideology is a key characteristic of any socially or politically organized nation. The ideology of the dominant group is critical to understanding immigration policy, differential incorporation of Blacks and other immigrant groups, their spatial distance from the White population and their level of residential segregation, neighborhood socioeconomic inequality, and overall racial inequality within the social structures of both countries.

Ideologies of the Dominant Group in Canada and the United States

In Canada and the United States, the dominant group, i.e., the White population, has maintained two opposing ideologies: (1) the ideology of democracy, and (2) the ideology of White supremacy. Democracy emphasizes equal access to housing and neighborhoods without regard to race and, if enforced fully, would lead to the following social and spatial outcomes, namely, racial residential integration, racial occupational integration, and ultimately overall racial equality (Darden 2004).

Throughout the history of Canada and the United States, the ideology of democracy has **not** been implemented fully due to a very powerful opposing ideology; i.e., the ideology of White supremacy. This ideology has varied in time and region in both Canada and the United States. It has also been influenced by certain historical economic circumstances, such as slavery in the Southern region of the United States and in the Atlantic region of Canada (see chapters 3, 4 and 8). White supremacy often increases as a country's unemployment rate rises and there is an increase in competition for scarce jobs in a declining economy. Such increase in White supremacy may be reflected in increased anti-immigrant sentiment against people of African descent and other immigrants of color.

Unlike democracy, which emphasizes equal access to opportunities without regard to race, White supremacy ideology believes that, in any relations involving White people and people of color, the White population must have the superior position and competitive advantage through any means necessary (Rose 1969). When White supremacy ideology becomes stronger than the ideology of democracy, it leads to the following racial and spatial outcomes—racial residential segregation, racial occupational segregation and persistent overall racial inequality (Darden 2004).

In order to maintain the superior position and competitive advantage, Whites (the dominant group in Canada and the United States) have created and maintained a racial hierarchy that treats groups differently based on skin color. Usually, the lighter skinned people, or those with features most like whites, are treated less harshly and receive less discrimination in housing, jobs, and education. Such differential treatment has had social, spatial, and economic consequences on various racial (visible) minority groups leading to racial stratification and differential disadvantage (Darden 2003).

According to Pulido (2002, 2006), "people of color in the U.S. have distinct experiences of racism based on their histories, immigration, economic incorporation, current economic status, and the interaction with whites." [sic] The differential experiences create the racial hierarchy, which refers to a particular configuration of racial/ethnic positions, with some groups occupying either more privileged, or more subordinated locations than others (Pulido 2002). A similar pattern has been found in Canada (Darden 2004). Thus, the racial hierarchy, according to Pulido, is maintained via distinct race-based actions that have taken various forms of domination, subordination, and exploitation by Whites and various forms of specific resistance by racial minority groups. Such race-based actions by Whites as discrimination in housing and jobs, combined with exclusion from White neighborhoods, have class consequences as well (Darden 2003).

C. Immigration Policy and its Impact on Immigration of People of African Descent

Prior to the 1960s, both Canada and the United States had racially restrictive immigration policies favoring European immigrants. Thus, few people of African descent (whether from the Caribbean or Africa) entered Canada or the United States as voluntary immigrants. Therefore, one should not underestimate the importance of a country's immigration policy in shaping the racial/ethnic composition of immigrants.

As this volume will show, voluntary immigration of people of African descent to Canada and the United States is primarily a recent phenomenon. In Canada, once the racial restrictions were lifted, immigrants from the Caribbean and Bermuda increased steadily, reaching a peak between 1971 and 1980. Fewer immigrants from the Caribbean and Bermuda entered Canada from 1991–2001. However, immigrants from Africa increased steadily from 1991–2001, exceeding immigrants from the Caribbean and Bermuda for the first time. Africa, not the Caribbean and Bermuda, is now the number one source region for Black immigrants to Canada (Statistics Canada 2003); (see also chapter 3).

In the United States, the number of immigrants from Africa nearly tripled during the 1990s. The number of Blacks from the Caribbean increased by over 60 percent (Logan and Deane 2003). In 2000, Blacks from the Caribbean numbered 1.5 million, which was larger than the number of Cubans and Koreans. Africans exceeded 600,000. In Canada and the United States, people of African descent settle more often in the large metropolitan areas. As they continue to arrive, they are faced with issues of differential incorporation, residential segregation, and persistent socioeconomic neighborhood racial inequality.

D. Differential Incorporation

Differential incorporation is a concept in which the White majority differentially incorporates some non-white, non-European groups into the mainstream society to a greater extent than other groups (Henry 1994). Incorporation is conceptualized on the basis of equal access to the rewards that the economic and political systems in Canada and the United States generate and distribute (Breton et al. 1990). Differential incorporation is also conceptualized as a two-way process. One process relates to the *internal characteristics* of the minority or immigrant group.

The focus of the internal-characteristics process is on the group's strengths and weaknesses, both economically and politically, and its cultural values, in other words, the group's social capital as measured by education, skills and experience. Each immigrant group possesses a quantity of social capital, and arrives in their new country with that social capital. The other process involves *the external forces* imposed on the minority or immigrant group by the White majority group, despite the internal characteristics of the minority or immigrant group. Racial discrimination is a major form of these external forces (Darden 2004; Lieberson 1980).

This volume shows the strength and persistence of racial discrimination as a force affecting the process of incorporation. Blacks, whether in Canada or the United States, are more likely than other racial minority groups to report experiences of discrimination and a lack of incorporation because of their racial and/or ethnocultural characteristics (see chapter 3).

E. Residential Segregation

Within the conceptual framework of differential incorporation, the residential segregation of Blacks from Whites is a way for the majority group to maintain neighborhood socioeconomic racial inequality. Black residential segregation in both Canada and the United States is due less to the unequal socioeconomic status between Blacks and Whites (Darden 2003; 2004) and more to subtle racial discrimination, racial steering, and white avoidance of neighborhoods with a certain percentage of Blacks (see chapter 3).

The mechanisms to carry out such discrimination include institutional actions in the housing market. For example, real estate brokers may show prospective White and Black home buyers houses in different neighborhoods. Similarly, lending institutions may grant or deny mortgages to Blacks and Whites differentially, regardless of creditworthiness criteria. These actions make it difficult for Blacks to have access to better-quality neighborhoods (Massey and Denton 1993). Thus, the White majority group keeps its spatial distance from Blacks and secures its dominant and superior position over them by accessing a disproportionate share of the high-quality neighborhoods' resources and rewards, including housing (Darden 2003).

In the process of gatekeeping neighborhoods along racial lines, the differential incorporation concept also suggests that many Whites avoid those neighborhoods with a certain percentage of minorities or a certain minority group. The avoidance is usually more pronounced when a certain minority group is large in number or when the minority group is Black (Darden 2003). Inversely, Whites would be less likely to erect residential barriers if a minority group represents only a small number of residents. In other words, the smaller the number of minorities in the neighborhood, the less likely it is that institutional barriers will be erected. The reason for this social phenomenon is that the size of the minority group matters in creating a threatening situation for Whites who want to maintain dominance (Blalock 1967). The outcome of the actions of the dominant group is differential spatial separation and race and class inequality (as expressed by Pulido 2002).

Thus, it can be argued that a major reason Blacks in Canadian metropolitan areas have a lower level of residential segregation on average than Blacks in American metropolitan areas is due to the higher percentage of Blacks in American metropolitan areas (see chapter 4). Unlike metropolitan areas in the United States, where the average Black percentage may reach 20 percent or more, the percentage of the Black population in Canada ranges from 0.2 percent to 6.6 percent. The average percentage of Black is 1.7 percent in census metropolitan areas (CMAs) in Canada. However, the lower level of Black residential segregation does not ensure a lower level of socioeconomic inequality in neighborhoods occupied by Blacks and Whites in Canada compared to Blacks and Whites in the United States.

F. Socioeconomic Neighborhood Racial Inequality

The neighborhood living conditions of Blacks in comparison to Whites in Canada are similar to the neighborhood conditions of Blacks and Whites in the United States. Blacks in Canadian CMAs usually live in lower quality neighborhoods in comparison to Whites (Galabuzi 2006). However, due in part to their smaller numbers, few if any of the neighborhoods can be described as slum-ghettos in the American sense of the word (Murdie and Teixeira 2003). Nevertheless, when it comes to neighborhood socioeconomic inequality between Blacks and Whites in Canada and the United States, there are generally more similarities than differences. In both countries, Blacks are less able than other groups (White and non-White) to translate their socioeconomic gains into comparable neighborhood quality. In other words, in both Canada and the United States, the attainment of neighborhood qualities among Blacks is not related to their levels of education and income (Fong and Gulia 1999).

G. Racial Inequality within the Social Structure

This volume addresses the question of whether Blacks in Canada have achieved more racial equality than Blacks in the United States (see chapter 3). Based on socioeconomic indicators, it is demonstrated that Blacks in Canada and Blacks in the United States face similar socioeconomic inequalities. Racial inequality is the norm. Whether Canadian-born or foreign-born, and whether American-born or foreign-born, Blacks on average compared to Whites have higher unemployment rates, lower percentages of high-income earners ($100,000 or more), a lower percentage of households with bachelor's degrees, and a lower percentage of Blacks compared to Whites in high-level occupations, i.e., management and professional occupations (see chapter 3). As racial discrimination is a factor in the persistent inequality, this volume examines how the two countries compare in the area of anti-discrimination public policies.

H. Similarities and Differences in Anti-Discrimination Public Policies

Although racial discrimination has been documented by researchers in both countries, the reaction to such findings has generally been different at the public policy level. Most Canadian policy makers (unlike most policy makers in the United States) are more likely to *deny* that racial discrimination is a problem. It has been a long tradition in Canada that racial discrimination is not a practice that occurs in Canada. If and when it does occur, it is merely an isolated incident and not systemic, as it is in the United States. Although not factual, this myth remains among a large segment of Canadians (Darden 2004).

Both the public policies toward and the life experiences of Canadian and U.S. Blacks influence the content of this work. Although focused on seemingly disparate groups, the policies and influences coalesce and represent an historic and ongoing set of circumstances that constitute a significant history and geography for the Black Diaspora. It is to this significant history and geography that this work responds.

THE ORGANIZATION OF THIS BOOK

This volume presents the experiences of Black native-born and Black immigrants from Africa and the Black Caribbean (Afro-Caribbean) amidst the backdrop of the historic international migrations, and the current influx, that has brought more than two million Africans and Afro-Caribbeans to the United States and Canada. The organization of this volume employs both regional and place approaches, within a thematic framework. The book is divided into four sections. Section 1 is the introductory chapter that introduces the major concepts and provides an overview of the Black immigrant experience in Canada and the United States. Section 2, *Perspectives on the African Diaspora in Canada,* illustrates the issues faced by people of African descent in Canada. In the five chapters in this section, Darden and Teixeira, Mensah and Firang, Darden, Teixeira, and Jones present the historical context for Black Canadians and the wide range of current issues facing Black Canadian immigrants, including immigration restrictions, inequality in the economic sector, the internal characteristics of early and more recent immigrants, government policies regarding ethnicity and race, and their impact on the social and spatial mobility for people of African descent.

Chapter 2, by Darden and Teixeira, provides a historical summary of Canada's Black settlement and discusses Canada's current policy of multiculturalism and retention of a group's ethnic identity. This approach is different from the United States' stated goal of assimilation. Focusing on unemployment rates, income inequality, and educational, occupational and residential segregation, Darden and Teixeira illuminate disparities between Blacks and Whites, which affect the lives of both foreign-born and Canadian-born Blacks.

In chapter 3, Mensah and Firang examine the employment structure, opportunities and equity for Anglophones and Francophones in Montreal and Halifax. They provide a summary of differential employment histories, restrictive immigration policies, language differences, and demographic and ethnic composition of immigrants in two different Census Metropolitan Areas (CMAs).

Examining race and equity issues in Toronto, Darden presents a persuasive argument in chapter 4 that Blacks have faced racially restrictive immigration policies that limited their settlement in Canada. Once permitted to immigrate (after racial restrictions were lifted) Blacks have faced institutional and social restrictions that impeded equity in employment and resulted in underemployment, higher unemployment, greater poverty and a poorer quality of life compared to European immigrants.

Teixeira also uses Toronto as a pertinent locale in chapter 5 to examine recent immigrants and housing issues. Examining recent immigrants from Angola, Mozambique, and the Cape Verde Islands, all groups with Portuguese cultural associations, Teixeira reveals that for these recent immigrants, their Black color influenced their limited ability to relate to local White Portuguese populations. Thus, "Blackness" is a consideration in whether support structures and social institutions in Toronto provide equal assistance to new immigrants.

Concluding this first section on the Black experiences in Canada, Jones' discussion of Jamaicans in Toronto in chapter 6 provides insight into race, location and social mobility for a subgroup of Caribbean Black immigrants. Attracted to Toronto, as an alternative to Miami or New York City, recent Jamaican immigrants have been assisted by earlier Jamaican immigrants who set up social networks that facilitated integration into the community. The point based Canadian immigration policy, which stresses education and skills for entry over the United States' family re-unification based policy, has created more skilled, educated Jamaican immigrants in Canada compared to recent Jamaican immigrants in the United States.

Section 3, *Perspectives on the African Diaspora in the United States*, examines both the native-born Black and immigrant Black populations. Blyden and Akiwumi provide an effective introduction to this section in chapter 7 by presenting the issues facing both U.S. native-born and immigrant Blacks at the beginning of the 21st century. Included in their presentation is the controversy over the term "African Diaspora," as well as the "Americanization" of most resident immigrants of African descent. They provide information on the increasing numbers and origins of recent Black immigrants to the U.S. and a range of their experiences. Focused on residential choice and settlement issues, Blyden and Akiwumi also identify the major metropolitan areas of the new immigrants, as well as their loss of status and the resulting discrimination that they suffer, as they make the transition from former country to new. The new environment creates new roles and expectations for African immigrants, and old customs must frequently change. Being transnational immigrants, however, a switch back to former customs is expected when they return home, but is not always an easy transition. Especially for students who returned home with high educational attainment, their ideas about people, social responsibility, and social justice may have changed, as well as their willingness to express their ideas. Returnees have not always been welcomed by their governments. Finally, the sustained importance of the place of origin is revealed in the practice of "remittances" sent home. The remittances continue to play an important role in contributing to economic development initiatives.

Following this overview, the next subsection (*Theme 1: Persistence of Inequalities*) contains four chapters examining the experiences of native-born Blacks in four American metropolises—Austin, Atlanta, Detroit, and New Orleans.

Skop, in chapter 8, provides a view of segregation, marginalization, race and public policy in racially divided Austin, Texas. Acknowledging the importance of politics and institutional forces in influencing racism, Skop explains the importance of space in gaining economic and political rights and strength. She reveals the institutionalized aspects of race inequalities and space, and the importance of recognizing highways and other infrastructures as barricades that separate races and reinforce isolation.

Bullard, in chapter 9, also indicates the importance of public policy in the Atlanta metropolitan region for Blacks seeking economic improvement. Chapter 9 provides insight into the roles of transportation and redevelopment issues in inequalities. Amidst tremendous population growth, much of which has been minorities, foreign born, and refugees, the city has created plans that ignore the needs of a changing spatial structure of the local populations. With a bi-modal income structure, Atlanta's policies related to residential location, employment and transit facilities have impeded the advancement of Blacks and low-income residents. Redlining and predatory lending have been important issues affecting the social and spatial mobility of Blacks.

Examining different issues in Detroit, in chapter 10 Darden also details the importance of public policy and "challenges the traditional view of the characteristics of Blacks in the suburbs." He notes that an excess of governmental boundaries results in greater socioeconomic stratification of places (municipalities) that seems to rank municipalities by their level of "desirability." Socio-economic status, race and residential segregation are important concepts in this chapter. More importantly, however, is a concept coined by Darden called "geographic racial equality." This concept identifies those municipalities where Blacks have achieved equal education, income and education as Whites. Such places exist in metropolitan Detroit, America's most racially segregated metropolitan area.

The final chapter in this native-born Black experience section examines the impact of Hurricane Katrina on residents of New Orleans, a predominantly Black city. Rawlings uses New Orleans and Hurricane Katrina to examine issues of equity and public policy in chapter 11. The overriding themes here are of race, place, policy, and displacement for a native-born Black population.

The second subsection of Section 3 (*Theme 2: Perspectives on Recent Black Immigrants*) examines Black immigrant experiences from the recent as well as the more long-term immigrant perspective. This section begins with Frazier and Harvey in chapter 12 addressing the out-migration of Black migrants, both native and foreign- born, from America's largest gateway, New York City. Besides the internal migration discussion, the major topics they reveal are economics, culture, and ancestral niche as they relate to perceived opportunities at particular places that attract both groups. Black destination choices vary between native-born and foreign-born Blacks, which are another focal point of this chapter. Clearly, distance decay is a factor for both native-born and foreign-born Blacks, who show some different preferences based upon birth location but respond to opportunity measured in various ways.

In chapter 13, Boswell and Sheskin examine Black populations in Miami and New York City and illustrate the fallacy of considering Blacks as a homogeneous population. Their settlement theme provides examples of race, ethnicity and class issues when examining African Americans, West Indians as a group, and Haitians, Jamaicans and sub-Saharan Africans as separate ethnic groups.

In chapter 14, Frazier uses Broward County, Florida and its recent Jamaican immigrants to examine socioeconomic characteristics, settlement patterns and compare them to New York City's patterns. Ethnicity and cultural landscapes play significant roles in this chapter (14), as do Jamaican occupations and images of African-Americans. Changes in migration patterns between Miami-Dade and Broward Counties and the overall social and economic status of Jamaicans in Broward result in emerging settlement patterns that are more complex and differ from those reported for New York City and Miami.

Chacko's study of Ethiopians in the District of Columbia in chapter 15 illustrates the importance of ethnicity and cultural cognition, as well as the importance of informal networks and institutions. She reveals the importance of churches in preserving culture and the impact that level of education has on attitudes toward pluralism.

Akiwumi and Estaville's work on Somalis in Maine, chapter 16, also deals with cultural cognition and sensitivity, ethnicity and cultural identity, and the importance of institutions. The role of public policy, technology and culture in the Maine Somali group presents an interesting cultural contrast of a group that values its cultural identity, but also desires assimilation.

In chapter 17, Scott examines the two waves of Liberians in Minnesota and the differences between them. He, too, draws the distinction between ethnic groups and color as he discusses settlement, residential location, cultural similarities, and the roles of food and language in differentiating culture groups.

Chapter 18 focuses on Ghanaians, in Cincinnati, Ohio. Yeboah illustrates the push and pull factors characteristic of international migration that play a role in this post-1980s African immigration. However, cultural niche, economic adjustments, stepwise and direct migrations and connections to the homeland are important for this late 20th century immigrant group. The economics of "remittances," the Diversity Immigration Lottery, and changes in U.S. immigration policy are important for this group of immigrants.

Ofori, Tettey-Fio, and Frazier focus on ethnic groups and ethnic small-business issues and the closing of the Bronx Terminal Market in chapter 19. They explore in this case study how the public policy issue of gentrification combines with cultural cognition and ethnicity, and with general economic principles. Under the circumstance of forced closure and limited time frame, the importance of co-location, public official roles in providing assistance to small ethnic businesses, and accessibility are revealed. The case study indicates the importance of the combined roles of ethnicity, economics, and geography in preserving ethnic small business opportunities.

The book concludes with Section 4, a final chapter that summarizes the findings and presents conclusions. Viewing the whole fabric woven by these discrete chapters, we see intricate patterns of the African Diaspora in the United States and Canada. New African immigrants and native-born Black residents face common experiences. Despite differences in origin, regional residence, and timing of immigration, native-born Blacks and African and Caribbean Blacks face many of the same issues and also experience conflicts between themselves. Social and economic status, level of education, occupation and other economic factors, residential preferences, discrimination and relocation patterns, business-relocation assistance, national immigration policies, race, community organizations, and other factors coalesce to produce the environments in which people of African descent in the United States and Canada live in the 21st century. Taken as a whole, they inform us of the complexity of constantly changing experience. After all, human geography and its societal groups are an unfolding set of stories. Thus, we must examine each story and relate it to the whole. The experiences and places presented in the following chapters contribute to these understandings.

Section 2:
Perspectives on the African Diaspora in Canada

Chapter 2

The African Diaspora in Canada

JOE T. DARDEN AND CARLOS TEIXEIRA

THE CONCEPT OF DIASPORA

The word "diaspora" is derived from the ancient Greek "diaspeiro," which means "to sow or scatter from one end to the other" (Vertovec 2006, p. 5). According to Vertovec (2006), a diaspora is commonly defined as a self-identified ethnic group with a specific place of origin that has been globally dispersed through voluntary or forced migration.

An important aspect in the study of the diaspora of any group is the extent to which the group has become integrated into mainstream society, as measured by certain socioeconomic indicators including educational attainment, income, occupational equality, unemployment, and homeownership and residential segregation. Within any diaspora (ethnic, national, or local) the members are highly diverse and complex (Vertovec 2006). The African Diaspora is no exception. The African Diaspora in Canada provides an excellent subject of study because Canada has become a multi-racial, multicultural society due in large part to the diasporas from Asia, Africa, and the Caribbean.

THE AFRICAN DIASPORA IN CANADA

According to the 2001 Canada census, 18.4 percent of the population had been born outside Canada, the highest proportion in 70 years (Statistics Canada 2003a). Blacks (used interchangeably in this chapter with "people of African descent") are the third largest visible minority group after the Chinese and South Asians. Statistics Canada (1997, p. 97) defines a "visible minority" as a person (other than Aboriginal) who is non-Caucasian in race, i.e., non-White in color. Visible minority and racial minority will be used interchangeably in this chapter.

At the top of the social structure are the British and French populations and their White Canadian-born offspring, which comprise nearly half (46 percent) of Canada's population (15 years and older). In the second, or middle tier, are the other European groups and their White Canadian-born descendents, accounting for about 19 percent of those aged 15 years and older. Together, these White European groups comprise 65 percent of Canada's population aged 15 years and older. In the third, or lowest tier, are the people of non-white, non-European descent, who account for 13 percent of the population aged 15 years and older. People of African descent, representing 2.2 percent of Canada's total population, constitute one group among the 2.9 million people aged 15 and older in this third tier. The remainder of this tier consists of those of mixed heritage (15 percent), including some of European and non-European origins (Statistics Canada 2003c).

Understanding the African Diaspora in Canada requires understanding Canada's policy of multiculturalism, which became the official policy of the federal government in the 1970s. Multiculturalism was supposed to distinguish Canada from the United States. Rejecting the notion of a single Canadian culture, federal assistance was promised to "(a) assist minorities in maintaining their cultural identity; (b) foster full and equal involvement in Canada's social and economic institutions; and (c) encourage harmonious links through the elimination of racism and discrimination at all levels of society" (Elliott and Fleras 1990, p. 64). Since the 1970s, many Canadians have boasted about Canada's cultural "mosaic" that encourages each ethnic community to retain its culture and language, and its superiority to America's more assimilationist and nationalistic "melting pot" (Darden 2004, p. 84).

The attitudes of the White Canadian majority towards the immigration of people of color into Canada also play a role in understanding the African Diaspora. Hawkins (1988) notes that, during the 1980s, the Canadian public did not accept the idea that national development depended on immigration. Indeed, in 1986, 58 percent of a sample of 1,020 Canadians polled believed that Canada should take fewer immigrants. Moreover, 72 percent believed that Canada was taking more than its fair share of refugees (Hoskin 1991).

Some researchers began to relate Canada's lack of support for more immigrants to the racial composition of those who were arriving (Reitz 1988, p. 119). These immigrants, most of whom were people of color, were expanding Canada's mosaic to include races, religions, and cultures that were new to Canada. Not surprisingly, an opinion survey showed growing opposition to the rising immigration (Angus Reid Group 1991).

Despite a generally high level of education and skills, the Canadian public as a whole did not readily endorse the large number of immigrants from non-European countries. Criticisms ranged from the fear of job competition to the fear of "problems" that immigrants of color might bring. Among the fears mentioned by most White Canadians, however, was the fear (associated with White supremacy) that the continuous increase of immigrants of color would undermine the White Anglo-Saxon Protestant character of Canadian society (Elliott and Fleras 1990). This fear was intensified by the fact that the White Canadian population, although still large, was aging and was not being replenished by younger newcomers from Europe (Knowles 1992). The trend at that time clearly had implications for Canada's changing demographic character.

Thus, Canada began to realize that more attention had to be given to "immigrant integration." Thomas (1990), of the Strategic and Planning and Research Immigration Policy Branch, viewed integration as a bidirectional process involving accommodation and adjustment on the part of both migrants and the host society, and distinguished it from assimilation, which implied the complete absorption of the migrant minority population into the dominant culture or society. Integrated individuals, according to Thomas (1990), are able to participate fully in all aspects of their societies. A key question was whether immigrants of color, i.e., Canada's "tolerated immigrants," would be able to participate as fully in all aspects of society as White Immigrants, i.e., Canada's "preferred immigrants."

To many White Canadians these immigrants of color presented a growing dilemma. How could Canada adjust to a sizeable population that was different racially and culturally from the traditional, White European population? What programs (if any) should be developed to encourage or facilitate the smooth integration of the immigrants?

CONCEPTUAL FRAMEWORK: CANADA'S RACE AND NATIONALITY STRUCTURE AND DIFFERENTIAL INCORPORATION OF IMMIGRANT GROUPS

Canada's immigration policies, employment practices, occupational segregation, educational attainment, income inequality, homeownership rates, residential segregation, and overall socioeconomic inequality between groups, including people of African descent, are best understood within the context of Canada's race and nationality structure. Moreover, the two predominantly White groups (upper and middle tier) have engaged in a process of differential incorporation, bringing some non-European groups into the mainstream to a greater extent than other groups. However, despite a growing interest in "visible minorities" in Canada, geographers have accomplished very little research on the Black Diaspora and its impact upon Canada (Mensah 2002; Darden 2004; Owusu 2006). People of African descent represent an excellent sample population to study the processes of incorporation into an increasingly complex and diverse Canadian society. This chapter examines the extent to which people of African descent have been incorporated into mainstream Canadian society.

Canada, like the United States, is a predominantly White society where the ideology of White supremacy is deeply ingrained in the culture (Darden 2004). The ideology of White supremacy argues that in any relations involving people of color, the White race must have the superior position (Rose and Associates 1969, p. 68). In Canada, like the United States, White supremacy evolved as an ideology to provide privilege to those with White skins, providing an entry point or passage through which Canadians of British, French, and other European ethnic groups competed with one another and with non-European groups for residential space, jobs, prestige, and power. Such competition has resulted in a society deeply stratified by class, and above all, color (Darden 2004, p. 4) because with few exceptions, those ethnic groups considered "White and European" have stood above the groups of color. As in the United States, phenotypical and physical features have been used in Canada as a symbolic indicator to determine a group's access to resources, property, and power (Bolaria and Li 1988).

In general, the greater the difference (skin color, nationality, language, religion, and culture) between the White Canadian majority groups and the non-White, non-European groups, the greater the barrier to integration into the mainstream. Thus, racial discrimination is a major barrier faced by non-White groups in general, and by people of African descent in particular, and may be a factor in explaining why, given such a long history in Canada, Blacks have not become more integrated. It is within this conceptual framework that the African Diaspora in Canada is described and explained.

Data and Methods of Measuring Indicators of Inequality

Using data from Statistics Canada, reports of the Ontario Human Rights Commission, Canada Mortgage Housing Corporation (CMHC), and previous studies, we analyzed several indicators, including the spatial distribution of people of African descent, their comparative unemployment rates, income inequality, educational attainment, occupational inequality, residential segregation, homeownership, and overall socioeconomic inequality, within the context of immigration and settlement patterns in provinces and census metropolitan areas (CMAs) throughout Canada. Canada's CMA differs slightly from the metropolitan area in the United States, although the delineation methodologies are similar. For example, the critical population threshold of 50,000 is lower in the United States. In Canada, a CMA is formed by one or more adjacent municipalities centered on a large urban area known as the urban core. The census population threshold of the urban core is at least 10,000 to form a census agglomeration and at least 100,000 to form a CMA. To be included in the CMA, other adjacent municipalities must have a high degree of integration with the central urban area as measured by commuter flows derived from census place of work data (Statistics Canada 2002). Toronto, Montreal, and Vancouver, Canada's largest CMAs, are examined in greater detail via indicators of discrimination in employment and housing to assess the strength of external forces that may prevent full incorporation. The chapter concludes with a discussion of public policy implications.

BLACKS IN CANADA: THE HISTORICAL AND GEOGRAPHICAL PATTERN

While the mass media in Canada tend to portray the Canadian Black community as a cohesive and largely homogeneous group, in fact it is characterized by high heterogeneity. Canadians of African descent include not only the Canadian-born, but also Blacks from the United States, the Caribbean, South America and Africa.

The historical experience of Blacks in Canada begins with slavery in Nova Scotia, with Black slaves helping to build the city of Halifax (Smith 1899). In 1749, when Halifax was founded, the census reported 104 slaves in a total population of 3,022 (Riddell 1920). Black slaves were bought and sold with newspaper advertisements in the *Halifax Gazette* (for examples of ads see Smith 1899, p. 10). Indeed, according to Grant (1973), slavery was an accepted institution in the provinces of Nova Scotia and New Brunswick.

Black slaves were also brought to Nova Scotia by Loyalists during the period of 1783–1791. Instead of field laborers, according to Walker (1992) many slaves from Virginia and the southern colonies were Blacksmiths, tailors, carpenters, and bakers. Black Loyalists, in search of the "promised land" in the north, started to arrive in Nova Scotia in 1783. These Black Loyalists were runaway slaves who deliberately sought the British and offered services to the Loyalists against the American colonists (Walker 1992, p. 18). As free Blacks started to arrive, it created a problem for the slave owners as Black slaves and free Blacks observed the conditions of each other, causing Whites to impose discriminatory measures against free Blacks in 1783. These acts in Canada had the effect of "keeping the *Black* man in his place" (Walker 1992, p. 392).

Discrimination against Blacks in employment and housing in Nova Scotia continued into the next century. Blacks were viewed as a source of cheap labor, were often exploited (Walker 1992), and occupied the lowest social and economic positions in the vertical mosaic (Pachai 1993, p. 31). The Black Loyalists were not provided with land promised by the British, and were often discriminated against when trying to find housing in White areas. Over time, Black communities became geographically separate and distinct from White communities as Blacks began to locate on the fringes of White communities or in all-Black neighborhoods (Rawlyk 1968; Walker 1992, p. 393). Black schools were separate from and unequal to White schools, and Blacks, economically dependent on Whites, were marginalized (Clairmont and Magill 1999).

School segregation became official policy in 1865, when the legislative assembly of Halifax authorized separate Black and White schools by law (Saney 1998). This policy was not abolished until 1954 (Pachai 1993, p. 30), the same year the U.S. Supreme Court ruled that separate schools were inherently unequal and unconstitutional in the landmark case of Brown vs. the Board of Education — Topeka (1954). As was the case in the United States, racial segregation of schools continued after the decision. According to Pachai (1993, p. 30), separate and unequal schools continued to provide Blacks in Nova Scotia with poor education long after *de jure* segregation had ended (Winks 1969, 1980).

While major concentrations of Blacks settled early in what would become the Atlantic provinces of Canada, and particularly Nova Scotia, important populations of Black settlement can be found across the landscape of early Canada. As Walker (1999, p. 145) notes, "African Canadians participated in the original settlement of almost every region of Canada." Black slaves were present at the foundation of Montreal, Halifax, and virtually all the Loyalist communities. In New France (Montreal and Quebec), most were urban domestic servants. Over time, the close proximity of Canada to the United States was to have a profound impact upon Black settlement in Canada, for with the passage of the Abolition Act of 1793 in Upper Canada, runaway slaves who arrived in Upper Canada were considered "free." As a consequence, in the years prior to the American Civil War the numbers of American Blacks settling in Ontario communities, such as Amherstburg, Buxton, St. Catherines, Windsor, London, Chatham, and later Toronto, increased rapidly. While no official data were kept on the numbers of American Blacks arriving in Canada at this time, it is estimated that before 1850 there were some ten thousand Black American fugitives living in Canada, a number that increased by approximately twenty thousand in the decade between 1850 and 1860. This wave of immigration put strains on the Upper Canadian economy of the time, and there were increasing levels of discrimination and segregation against Blacks in Upper Canadian schools and public areas (Mensah 2002, pp. 49–50).

The history of Black settlement was different in Western Canada. The first Black settlers arrived in Western Canada from California at the end of the 1850s, and were mostly skilled and literate Blacks — not fugitives from slavery as in Eastern Canada — who were dissatisfied with the increasing racism and discrimination in California. Many of these settled in Victoria and on Vancouver Island, where they found the "closest approximation to equality for Canadian Blacks in the nineteenth century" (Mensah 2002, pp. 51–53). The Prairie Provinces were the last areas of Canada to attract Black settlement, as it was not until the early 1900s that they arrived in large numbers in these areas. For example, in 1909 some two hundred Black immigrants settled in Saskatchewan from Oklahoma, and another three hundred settled in Alberta in 1910. While these settlers were mostly farmers, their communities faced considerable challenges as prairie governments and civic groups continually campaigned to frustrate Black settlement in these provinces (Mensah 2002, pp. 51–53).

In general, racial segregation and discrimination were "facts of life" for most Blacks living in Canada until the second half of the twentieth century. In 1871, the Canadian census reported 21,496 Blacks (referred to as Negroes) at the time (Mensah 2002; Walker 1999, p. 148). By 2001, the number of Blacks had reached

662,210 (Statistics Canada 2003a). Canada's Black population in the contemporary period suggests how increasingly important the contributions of the Black Diaspora have been to the transformation of the Canadian social and cultural landscape in recent years.

BLACKS IN CANADA: THE CONTEMPORARY PATTERN

The contemporary pattern of Black settlement in Canada reflects the radical transformation in Canadian society that arose due to changes in Canadian immigration policies in the 1960s. While the policies prior to this period were largely discriminatory against non-Europeans, in the 1960s altered Canadian policies and increasing prosperity in Western Europe marked the beginning of a sharp decline in European immigration and a substantial increase in immigration from Asia, Africa, the Middle East, the Caribbean, and Latin America. This trend towards the "internationalization" of Canada's immigrant population has continued, so that by 2001 almost 80 per cent of Canada's recent immigrants were from non-European countries. Regarding immigrants of the Black Diaspora, in particular, the reasons for their migration and settlement in Canada are complex and diverse. Indeed, reflecting the heterogeneity of this community, the "push/pull" factors that contribute to the decision to migrate differ widely among many Black immigrant groups. For example, most Blacks from Africa and the Caribbean "come for a better standard of living" (Mensah 2002, p. 67). However, ethnopolitical conflicts have contributed to an influx of refugees from Africa, including from such countries as Ethiopia, Ghana, Nigeria, Somalia, South Africa, Sudan, Uganda, Angola, and Mozambique. Interestingly, despite the continual increase of immigrants and refugees from Africa over the past two decades, today "Canada has no immigration policy for Africans" (Opoku-Dapaah 2006, p. 72). These facts, together with the long delays and reduced immigration prospects for Africans seeking entry into Canada, in contrast with groups from European countries, have led to most Africans in Canada arriving as "refugee claimants" (Mensah 2002, pp. 72–73).

Black Settlement Patterns

In contrast to the United States, Blacks in Canada have always been a very small percentage (less than 3 percent) of the total population. In fact, Blacks comprised less than 1 percent of the total population until 1981, and increased only to 2.2 percent in 2001. Blacks represent the third largest visible minority group in Canada behind the Chinese and South Asians.

In 2001, at least 62 percent of all Blacks in Canada resided in Ontario. Moreover, 97 percent of all Blacks in Canada lived in five provinces: Ontario, Quebec, Alberta, British Columbia, and Nova Scotia (Statistics Canada 2003a) (See Figure 2.1). On the other hand, 88.1 percent of the total Canadian population lived in these same five provinces. While historical factors account for much of this high concentration of Blacks in a few provinces, language also influenced Black immigration and settlement in Canada. For example, French-speaking North Africans and Haitians from the Caribbean select the French-speaking province of Quebec to settle and live, while English-speaking Blacks mainly favor Ontario and the other English-speaking provinces.

Blacks in Canada are urban oriented, and are attracted mainly to Canada's largest CMAs. The Toronto CMA had the largest number (310,500) and the highest percentage (6.6 percent) of Blacks in 2001. As a consequence of increasing immigration from around the world, including Africa and the Caribbean, Toronto is today Canada's most culturally diverse metropolis, with its Black community mirroring the heterogeneity of migrant communities in Canada. Toronto was followed by Montreal, which had 139,305 Blacks, representing 4.1 percent of the total population. Ranked third was Ottawa-Gatineau, followed by Vancouver. These two CMAs had 38,185 and 18,405 Blacks, respectively (Table 2.1). Although Blacks represented 3.6 percent of Ottawa's population, Blacks represented a very small proportion (0.9 percent) of Vancouver's total population. Together, these four CMAs are where 76 percent of all Blacks in Canada resided in 2001 (Statistics Canada 2003a).

In Canada as a whole, and in these four CMAs in particular, most Blacks are immigrants. The exceptions (CMAs where the majority of Blacks are Canadian-born) are Halifax, which has the highest percentage of Canadian-born Blacks (91 percent), and Windsor, with 60 percent. The two remaining CMAs where Canadian-born Blacks exceeded Black immigrants are London and Oshawa. In both CMAs the Canadian-born Black population was 52 percent in 2001 (Statistics Canada 2003a).

Figure 2.1.
The Spatial Distribution of the Black Population Across Canada, 2001.

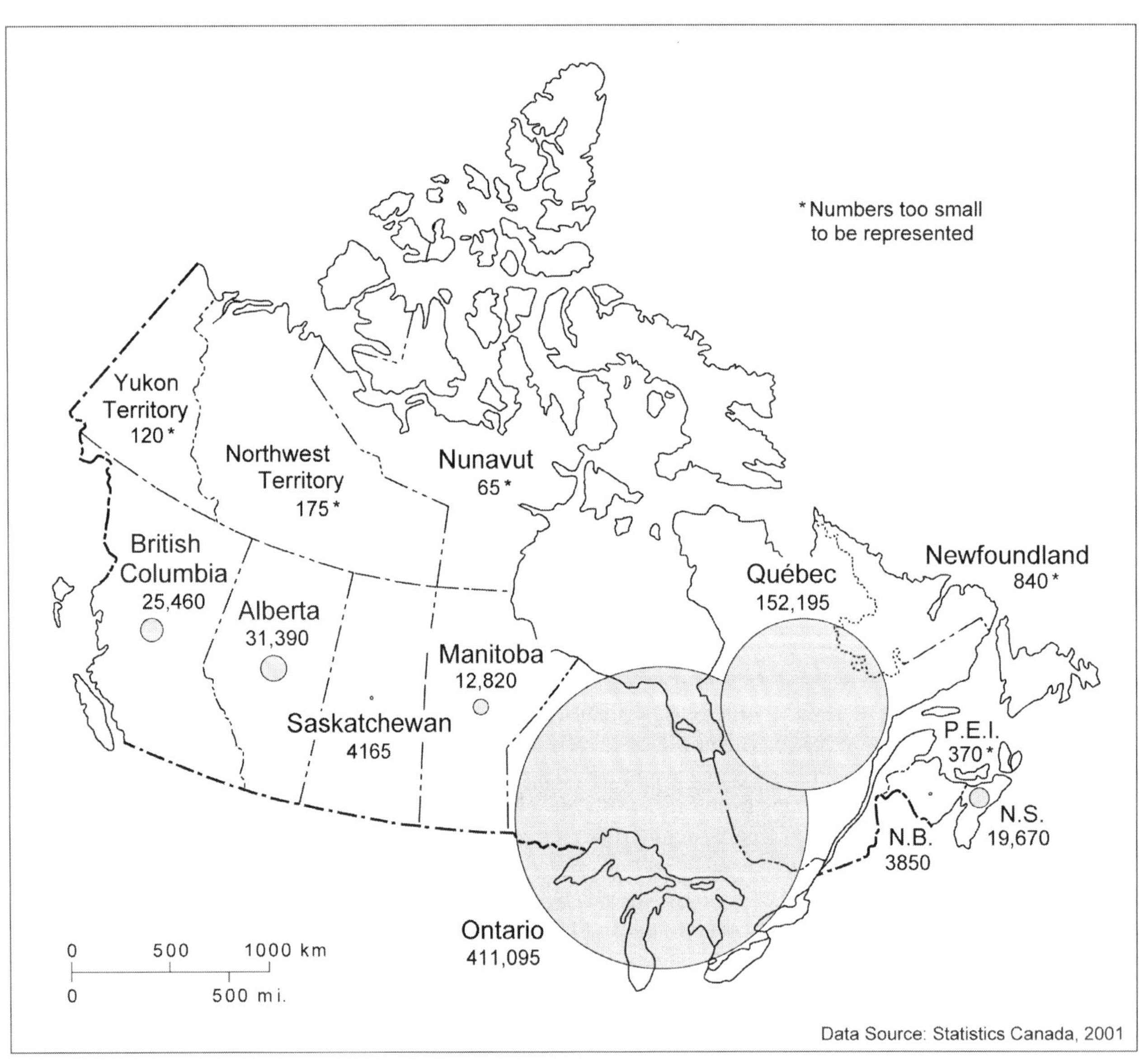

Table 2.1.
Spatial Distribution of the Black Population in Canada by Census Metropolitan Area.

Census Metropolitan Area	Total Population	Black Population	Percent Black Population
Toronto	4,647,960	310,500	6.6
Montreal	3,380,645	139,305	4.1
Ottawa-Gatineau	1,050,755	38,185	3.6
Vancouver	1,967,480	18,405	0.9
Edmonton	927,020	14,095	1.5
Calgary	943,310	13,665	1.4
Halifax	355,945	13,085	3.7
Hamilton	655,055	12,855	1.9
Winnipeg	661,725	11,440	1.7
Windsor	304,955	8,125	2.7
London	427,215	7,610	1.8
Kitchener	409,770	7,345	1.8
Oshawa	293,550	7,180	2.4
St. Catharines-Niagara	371,400	3,840	1.0
Quebec	673,105	3,640	0.5
Victoria	306,970	2,180	0.7
Regina	190,020	1,580	0.8
Saskatoon	222,635	1,520	0.7
Saint John	121,340	1,440	1.2
Greater Sudbury	153,890	1,075	0.7
Sherbrooke	150,385	1,040	0.7
Saguenay	153,020	985	0.6
Trois-Rivieres	134,645	515	0.4
Thunder Bay	120,365	440	0.4
St. John	171,105	350	0.2

Source: Statistics Canada (2003a). 2001 Census of Population. Census of Canada Catalogue Number 97F0010XCB2001003.

Spatial Distribution of Blacks in the Toronto, Montreal and Vancouver CMAs

Figures 2.2, 2.3 and 2.4 show the spatial distribution patterns of Blacks in the Toronto, Montreal and Vancouver CMAs. In Toronto, pockets of Black concentration have been identified both in the inner city (e.g., Scarborough, Etobicoke, North York), as well as in the suburbs (Brampton and Mississauga) (Figure 2.2). The spatial distribution of Blacks in Toronto was quite dispersed by 2001, but included distinct concentrations in certain cities/neighborhoods of the Toronto CMA. In part, the "island" (Caribbean) and/or "region" (Africa) of origin may explain the formation and maintenance of multi-nucleated residential patterns among Toronto's diverse Black community.

However, housing affordability (rent and/or prices) also seems to determine the decision of many Blacks to settle in the suburbs in lower standard apartment complexes (Skaburskis 1996). As a result of these factors, we can see the concentration of large numbers of Black families in neighborhoods such as Jane and Finch, Regent Park, and Bathurst Heights, where subsidized housing provided by the Metropolitan Toronto Housing Authority (MTHA) is available (Murdie 1994). Black Africans, such as Ghanaians and Nigerians, have concentrated in North York and Brampton, while Somali refugees, a group that faced major barriers on arrival, have tended to live in crowded conditions in high rise apartments, particularly in the City of Etobicoke and often in close proximity to Toronto's international airport (Murdie and Teixeira 2003).

Figure 2.2.
The Spatial Distribution of the Black Population in the Toronto CMA, 2001.

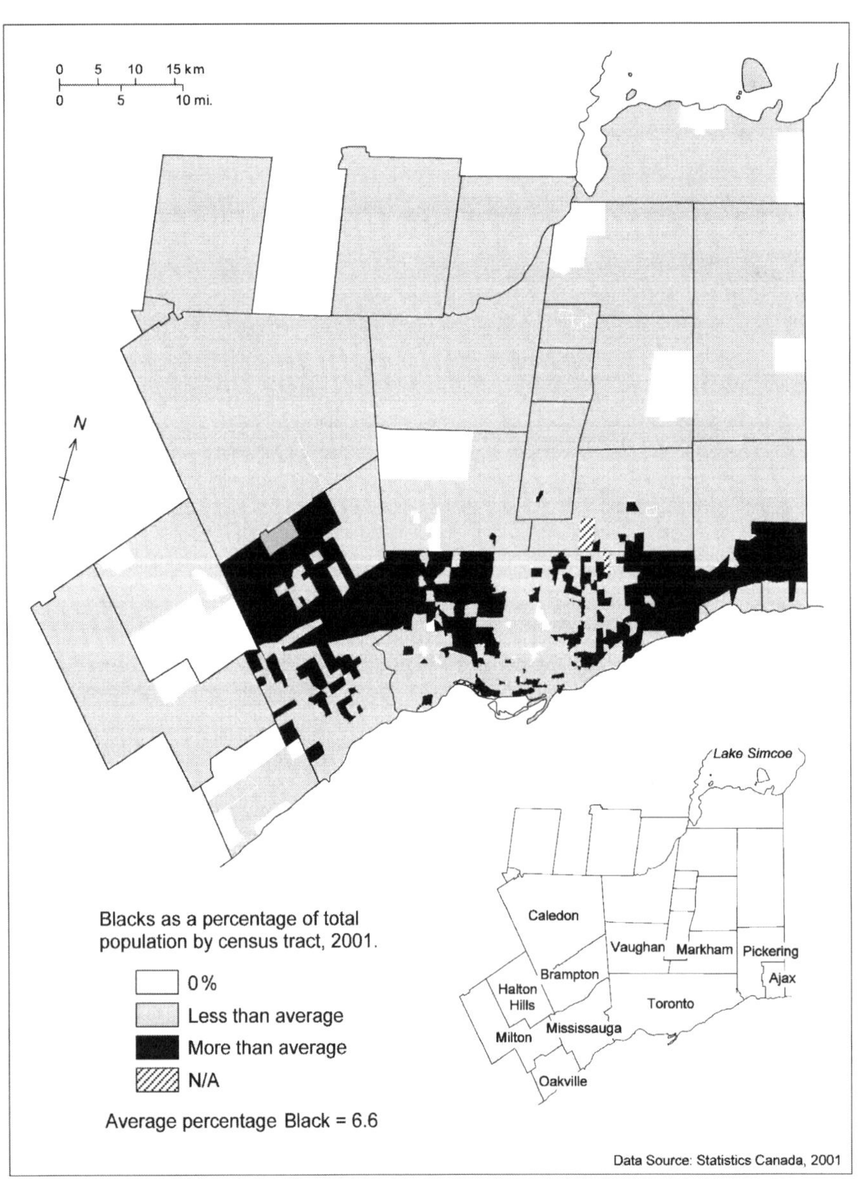

The spatial distribution of Blacks in Montreal is presented in Figure 2.3. The Black population displays clear residential preferences for certain area/neighborhoods, notably on the Island of Montreal. Few Blacks chose the suburbs of Montreal as places to live, such as Laval (north of the island) or South River (south of the island). In general, they are over represented, particularly in the central part of the island of Montreal, in a perimeter (geographical area) running from Cote-Saint Luc-Hampstead-Montreal Ouest and the neighborhood Cote-des-Neiges to Cartierville. Most Blacks living in this geographical area are French-speaking immigrants from North Africa. In contrast, Caribbean immigrants, particularly those coming from Haiti, are mainly distributed along the Rivière-des-Prairies in the east part of the island of Montreal (Rivière-des-Prairies, Montreal-Nord Est and Montreal-Nord Ouest) and St. Michel (Apparicio et al. 2006). As in Toronto, "island" and/or region of origin in Africa partially determines where Montreal's Black immigrants reside. Other factors such as affordable housing (to rent and/or buy), proximity to French-speaking communities and the existence of strong ethnic networks of contacts that characterize some of these Black communities may help explain this group's complex spatial distribution in a bilingual and divided city — West (English) and East (French) Montreal.

Figure 2.3.
The Spatial Distribution of the Black Population in the Montreal CMA, 2001.

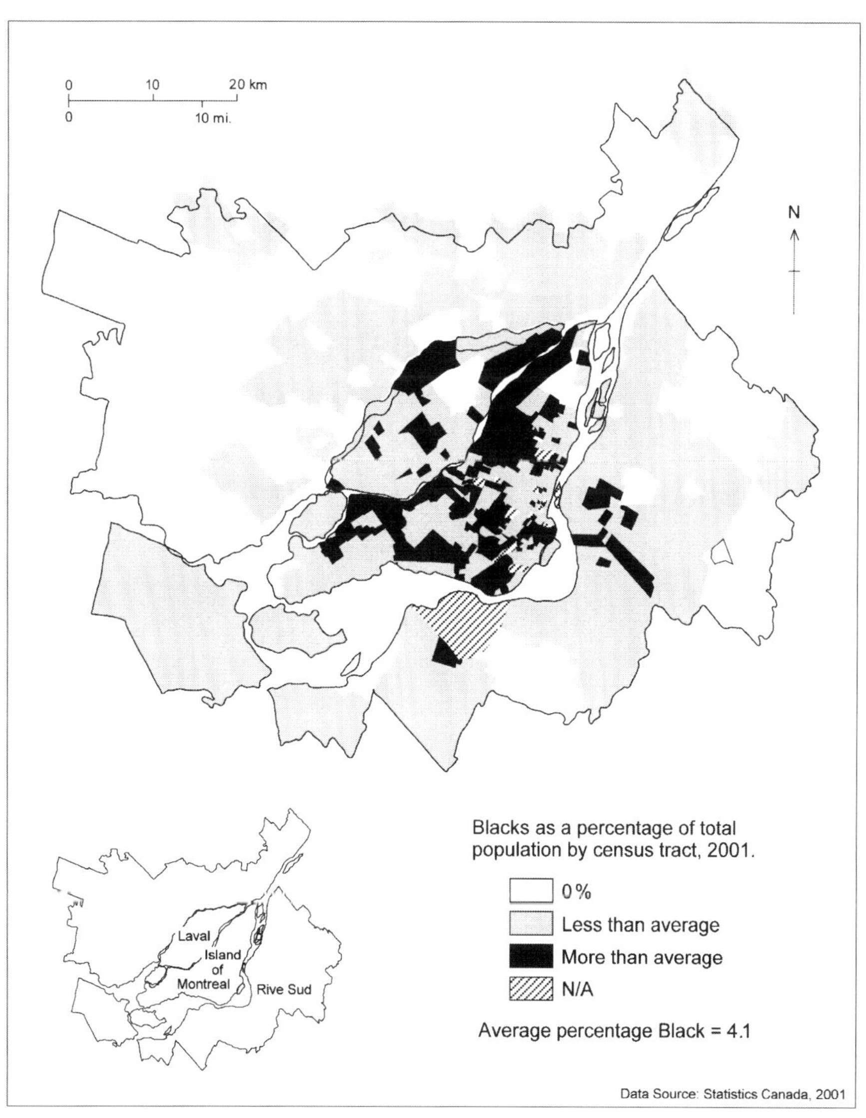

In contrast, the spatial distribution of the Black population in Vancouver is more dispersed (suburbanized) over a wide range of communities (Figure 2.4). Some of these areas are the same areas/communities where other visible minorities, including new immigrants, reside (e.g., Burnaby, Richmond Coquitlan and Surrey). However, in general, Blacks in Vancouver are more suburbanized than their counterparts in Toronto and Montreal.

In sum, the residential patterns of Blacks in these three main CMAs vary, reflecting relatively low levels of segregation, and moderate levels of suburbanization. Perhaps the evolution of these Black neighborhoods of concentration has been due to a combination of different "forces," including lower household income (compared to the income of Whites), compounded by housing supply, cost, and discriminatory constraints. It is important to note that none of these neighborhoods of concentration is a "ghetto" in the sense of the large-scale ghettos with *majority* Black populations in certain neighborhoods of American cities (Darden 1981; Murdie 1994; Ley and Smith 1997). This is due in large part to the relatively *small* percentage of Blacks in Canada CMAs compared to the relatively *large* percentage of Blacks in most American metropolitan areas (Fong 2006; Darden 2004). Also, as noted by Bourne and Rose: "Diversity in Canadian CMAs has Suburbanized" (2007, p. 264).

Figure 2.4.
The Spatial Distribution of the Black Population in the Vancouver CMA, 2001.

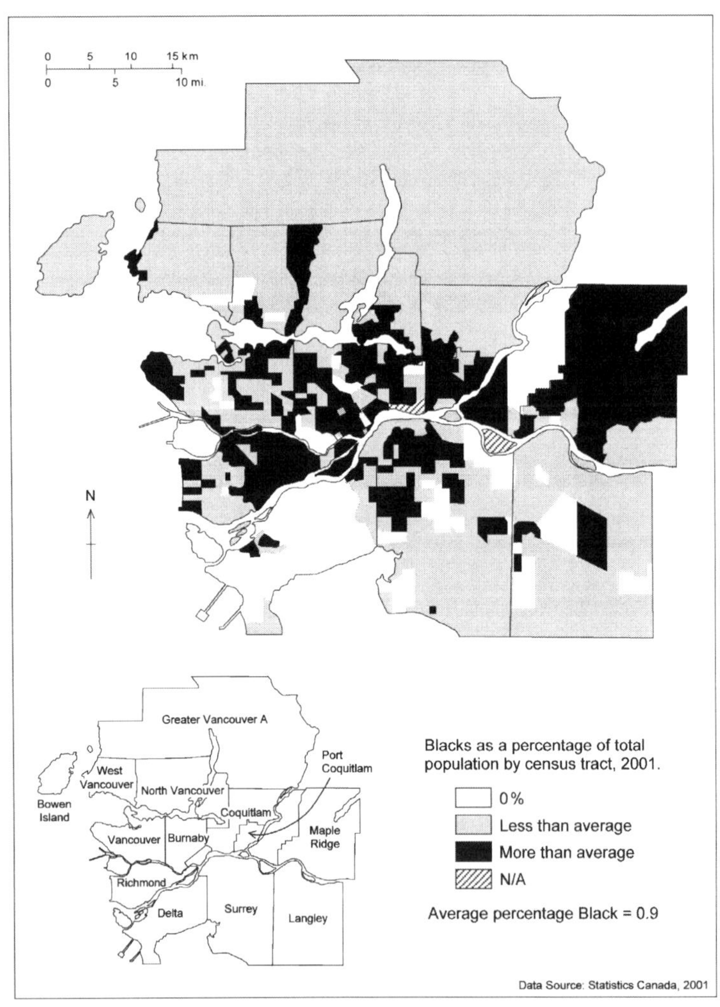

CHANGES IN THE BLACK POPULATION BY PERIOD OF IMMIGRATION TO CANADA

Before 1961, immigrants from the Caribbean and Bermuda and immigrants from Africa represented 0.8 percent and 0.5 percent of all immigrants to Canada, respectively, due to Canada's racially restrictive immigration policy (Darden 2004). Once the restrictions were lifted, immigrants from the Caribbean and Bermuda increased each period, reaching a peak of 91,475 during 1971–1980. Fewer immigrants from the Caribbean and Bermuda entered Canada from 1991–2001. However, immigrants from Africa increased steadily, reaching 139,770, or 7.6 percent of all immigrants from 1991–2001 (Table 2.2), and exceeding immigrants from the Caribbean and Bermuda for the first time. Africa, not the Caribbean and Bermuda, is now the number one source region for Black migrants to Canada (Statistics Canada 2003c).

Table 2.2.
Changes in the Black Population by Period of Immigration to Canada.

Place of Birth		Period of Immigration				
	Total Immigrants	Before 1961	1961–1970	1971–1980	1981–1990	1991–2001
Caribbean and Bermuda	294,050	6,990	42,740	91,475	68,840	84,005
Percent of Total Immigrants	5.4	0.8	5.7	9.8	6.6	4.6
Africa	282,600	4,635	23,830	54,655	59,710	139,770
Percent of Total Immigrants	5.2	0.5	3.2	5.8	5.7	7.6
Total Immigrant Population	5,448,840	894,465	745,560	936,275	1,041,500	1,830,680

Source: Statistics Canada (2003a). 2001 Census of Population. Census of Canada Catalogue Number 97F0010XCB2001003.

People of African descent, Canadian-born and immigrants, constitute a visible and increasing part of Canada's racial/ethnic diversity, thus their incorporation into Canadian society may be measured through employment/unemployment rates, income inequality, educational attainment, occupational inequality, residential segregation, and home ownership.

THE INCORPORATION OF PEOPLE OF AFRICAN DESCENT INTO CANADIAN SOCIETY

Unemployment Rates

The unemployment rate for the total Canadian-born population (age standardized 25–54) was 6.0 percent in 2001, compared to 7.9 percent for Canadian-born Blacks. Among the total foreign-born population, the unemployment rate was 7.0 percent compared to a foreign-born Black unemployment rate of 9.6 percent. Thus, whether Canadian-born or foreign-born, the Black unemployment rate was at least 1.3 times the rate for the total population (Statistics Canada 2003c; Milan and Tran 2004). The Canadian literature shows that Blacks quite often experience difficulties integrating within the workplace due to racism in their search for employment.

They also encounter unequal treatment, such as non-recognition of credentials obtained in their country of origin, and the requirement of Canadian experience as the pre-condition for skilled jobs (Opoku-Dapaah 2006). The unemployment rate of people of African descent varies, however, by ethnic origin. Statistics Canada (2002) defines ethnic origin as the ethnic or cultural group(s) to which an individual's ancestors belonged. Ethnic origin is not tied to language, citizenship, or nationality. Statistics Canada reported more than 200 different ethnic origins in the 2001 census. Selected ethnic-origin groups of people of African descent reveal how close these groups are to the total population on the indicator of unemployment. The unemployment rates range from a low of 7.1 percent for Guyanese and Barbadians (similar to other foreign born) to a high of 26.1 percent for Somalis. On the other hand, the unemployment rate for Somalis (overwhelmingly refugees) was 3.7 times the rate for the total foreign-born population.

Racial Inequality of Incomes in Canada

Racial inequality of incomes, measured by comparing the percent of Blacks compared to Whites in the "high earners" group ($100,000 or more in 2001), and including the immigrant status of the racial groups (Canadian-born or foreign-born), reveals the unevenness in the overall distribution of income between Black and White households. The Index of Dissimilarity ranges from "0" (no inequality) to "100" (complete inequality) (for computation of the index, see Darden 2004).

In 2001, the racial gap in median household income was evident regardless of immigrant status. When all Black households were compared to all White households in Canada, the results revealed that 12.7 percent of all Black households earned $100,000 or more, compared to 18.2 percent of all White households, a difference of 5.5 percentage points in favor of White households. The gap between Canadian-born Blacks and Canadian-born Whites narrowed slightly. The data show that 13 percent of all Canadian-born Black households earned $100,000 or more, compared to 17.9 percent of all White Canadian-born households, a difference of 4.9 percentage points. When Black immigrants are compared to White immigrants, the data show that 12.8 percent of Black immigrant households earned $100,000 or more compared to 19.9 percent of White immigrant households, a difference of 7.1 percentage points, and the highest gap among high income earners. White immigrant households have a higher percentage of households earning $100,000 or more than the White Canadian-born households. Black immigrant households do not differ in earnings from the Black Canadian-born households. An examination of the income inequality between Black and White households in the largest CMAs — Toronto, Montreal, and Vancouver (71 percent of Blacks in Canada live in those three CMAs) — revealed income disparities at the urban level.

Toronto Census Metropolitan Area

In Toronto, 16.1 percent of all Black households earned over $100,000 in 2001, compared to 33.7 percent of all White households, a difference of 17.6 percentage points. The Index of Dissimilarity between Blacks and Whites in earned incomes in the Toronto CMA was 23.9.

When the Black Canadian-born population is compared to the White Canadian-born population, for 2000, the data show that 16.2 percent of all Canadian-born Black households were high income earners, compared to 36.5 percent of all White Canadian-born households, a difference of 20.3 percentage points. The Index of Dissimilarity between the income distribution of Canadian-born Blacks and Whites was 27.5.

Comparing Black and White Immigrants, the data show that 16.4 percent of all Black immigrant households earned $100,000 or more compared to 26.6 percent of White Immigrant households, a difference of 10.2 percentage points. In Toronto, immigrant status does matter in racial differences in income inequality. The Index of Dissimilarity between Black and White Immigrant households in income distribution was 15, i.e., much lower than the Index of Dissimilarity for Black and White Canadian-born households (27.5) in the Toronto CMA.

Montreal Census Metropolitan Area

In Montreal, 6.4 percent of all Black households earned $100,000 or more in 2001 compared to 16.9 percent of White households, a difference of 10.5 percentage points. The percentage of all Canadian-born Black households earning $100,000 or more in Montreal was 7.4 percent in 2000, compared to 17.1 percent of Canadian-born White Households, a difference of 9.7 percentage points.

What is the importance of immigrant status? When the Black Canadian-born population is compared to the White Canadian-born population in Montreal, does the income gap get smaller? Similar to Toronto, immigrant status does matter in influencing racial inequality in incomes. In 2001, fewer Black immigrants (5.8 percent) compared to Canadian-born Blacks (7.4 percent) were among the high earners. Among White Immigrants, 14.6 percent were in the high earner category, which was more than twice the percentage of immigrant Black households (5.8 percent).

The Index of Dissimilarity between all Black and all White income distribution in Montreal was 21.5. When the Canadian-born Black population is compared to the Canadian-born White population, the Index of Dissimilarity results were similar, i.e., 21.4. However, when Black immigrant household income distribution is compared to White immigrant household income distribution, the Index of Dissimilarity was much lower, declining to 13.7.

In other words, the income inequality gap between all Black and all White Canadian households was no different than the inequality gap between the Canadian-born Black and White households. However, the income inequality gap between Black and White immigrant households was much smaller than the gap for all Black and all White Canadian households.

Vancouver Census Metropolitan Area

In Vancouver, 12.2 percent of all Black households earned $100,000 or more in 2001, compared to 24.7 percent of all White households, a difference of 12.5 percentage points. Among Canadian-born Black households, the percentage of high-income earners was 14.4 percent compared to a White Household percentage of 25.4 percent, a difference of 11 percentage points. The Index of Dissimilarity was 16.3.

Among Vancouver's Black immigrants, 10.3 percent earned $100,000 or more, compared to 21.2 percent for all White immigrant households, a difference of 10.9 percentage points. The Index of Dissimilarity between the Black and White Immigrant household distributions was 16.7, which was nearly identical to the Index of Dissimilarity between the Black and White Canadian-born households of the Vancouver CMA.

In sum, *race, place and immigrant status* matter in determining differences in incomes among households in Canada's three largest census metropolitan areas. Analyses of 2001 census data revealed that regardless of place (CMA), Blacks have a lower percentage of households earning $100,000 or more compared to White households. The income gap varies, however. There is greater income inequality between Blacks and Whites in the Toronto CMA, and less in the Vancouver CMA.

Immigrant status also matters in explaining income inequality. The racial difference gap is widest between Canadian-born Blacks and Canadian-born Whites in Toronto, followed by Montreal. The gap is smallest in size between Black and White immigrants in Montreal and is largest in Vancouver. The results show that it is important to examine racial differences in income in Canada (given its high immigrant population) by comparing the Canadian-born households separately from immigrant households.

Educational Attainment

Educational attainment, measured here by the percentage of households with at least a bachelor's degree (including master's and doctorate degrees) revealed that of Black Canadian-born households in Canada in 2001, 10.4 percent had a bachelor's degree or higher compared to 13.6 percent of White Canadian-born households, a difference of 3.2 percentage points. Black immigrant households had achieved a higher level of education (13.2

percent) than Canadian-born Blacks. However, there was still a gap between Black immigrant and White immigrant educational attainment. The percentage of White immigrants in Canada with a bachelor's degree or higher (17.6 percent) was 4.4 percentage points greater than Black immigrants.

Toronto Census Metropolitan Area

Educational attainment differed in the largest CMAs. In the Toronto CMA, 10.8 percent of Black Canadian-born households had a bachelor's degree or higher level of education in 2001 compared to 24 percent of White Canadian-born households, a difference of 13.2 percentage points. Among Black immigrant households, that percentage was 10.2 compared to 18.4 percent for White immigrant households, a difference of 8.2 percentage points.

Montreal Census Metropolitan Area

In Montreal, 10.2 percent of Canadian-born Blacks had a bachelor's degree or higher level of education compared to 16.5 percent of White Canadian-born households, a difference of 6.3 percentage points. Among Black immigrant households 13.5 percent had a bachelor's degree or higher compared to 20.7 percent of White immigrant households, a difference of 7.2 percentage points.

Vancouver Census Metropolitan Area

The Black population in Vancouver is very small compared to the Black population of Toronto and Montreal. Does the size of the Black population matter in the difference in educational attainment between Black and White households? Among the Canadian-born Black households, 11.7 percent had a bachelor's degree or higher compared to 18.4 percent for White Canadian-born households, a difference of 6.7 percentage points in favor of Whites. Among Black immigrant households, 17.5 percent had a bachelor's degree or higher compared to 21 percent for White immigrant households, a difference of 3.5 percentage points.

In sum, the gap in educational attainment was greater among Canadian-born Black and White households in the Toronto CMA. The gap was smaller between Black and White immigrant households in the Vancouver CMA.

Occupational Inequality

Occupational equality is another socioeconomic indicator of incorporation into the mainstream **and a key ingredient for financial well being.** Statistics Canada ranks occupations according to a classification system into 25 hierarchical categories. The highest category, the most prestigious and generally best paid occupation, is that of management. The tasks, duties, and responsibilities involve decision-making and influence over other workers. This is followed by professional business and finance. At the bottom of the occupational hierarchy are manufacturing, utilities, and laborers. We will focus on the top occupational categories (management and professional business and finance) in order to determine the representation of Blacks and Whites at the top.

In 2001, 8.2 percent of Canadian-born Black households held occupations in the top category, compared to 12.1 percent of White Canadian households, a difference of 3.9 percentage points in favor of Whites. Among Black immigrants, 7.7 percent of households were in the top level of occupations, compared to 15.5 percent of White immigrant households, a difference of 7.8 percentage points (Table 2.3).

Toronto Census Metropolitan Area

Of Canadian-born Black households 9.4 percent were in the top level occupations in the Toronto CMA in 2001, compared to 18.4 percent of White Canadian-born households, a difference of 9 percentage points. In fact, Canadian-born White households were almost twice as likely to hold high-level occupations as Canadian-born Black households.

The percentage of Black immigrant households with top level occupations was 8.3 percent, compared to 17 percent for White immigrant households, a difference of 8.7 percentage points. Thus, White immigrant households were twice as likely to hold high level occupations as Black immigrant households in Toronto.

Table 2.3.
Socioeconomic Characteristics of the Black Population in Canada and in the Largest Census Metropolitan Areas (CMAs).

	Canadian-Born			Immigrants		
Place	Income Inequality[1]	Educational Attainment[2]	Occupational Inequality[3]	Income Inequality[1]	Educational Attainment[2]	Occupational Inequality[3]
Canada						
Black	13.0%	10.4%	8.2%	12.8%	13.2%	7.7%
White	17.4%	13.6%	12.1%	19.9%	17.6%	15.5%
Toronto CMA						
Black	16.2%	10.8%	9.4%	16.4%	10.2%	8.3%
White	36.5%	24.0%	18.4%	26.6%	18.4%	17.0%
Montreal CMA						
Black	7.4%	10.2%	5.4%	5.8%	13.5%	5.4%
White	17.1%	16.5%	13.3%	14.6%	20.7%	16.9%
Vancouver CMA						
Black	14.4%	11.7%	9.3%	10.3%	17.5%	12.3%
White	25.4%	18.4%	14.8%	21.2%	21.0%	17.5%

Source: Computed by the authors from data obtained from Statistics Canada 2006. Public Use Microdata Files (PUMF). Ottawa: Minister of Industry.
1. Percent of total Black and White households earning $100,000 or more
2. Percent of total Black and White households with a bachelor's degree or higher level of education
3. Percent of total Black and White households in management, professional business and finance occupations

Montreal Census Metropolitan Area

Among Black Canadian-born households in the Montreal CMA, 5.4 percent held top-level jobs, compared to 13.3 percent of White Canadian-born households, a difference of 7.9 percentage points. It shows that White Canadian-born households were 2.46 times more likely to hold top-level jobs than Black Canadian-born households in the Montreal CMA. Black immigrants, like the Black Canadian-born, had 5.4 percent of their households with top-level occupations, compared to 16.9 percent of White immigrant households, a difference of 11.5 percentage points. In other words, White immigrants in the Montreal CMA were 3.1 times more likely to hold top-level occupations than Black immigrants.

Vancouver Census Metropolitan Area

Among Black Canadian-born households in the Vancouver CMA, 9.3 percent held top-level occupations, compared to 14.8 percent of White Canadian-born households, a difference of 5.5 percentage points.

Among Black immigrant households, 12.3 percent held top-level occupations, compared to 17.5 percent of White immigrant households, a difference of 5.2 percentage points in favor of Whites.

In sum, occupational inequality between Black and White households varied by CMA. The occupational gap was widest in the Montreal CMA between Black and White immigrant households. The gap was smallest in the Vancouver CMA between Black and White immigrant households. Whether they were Canadian-born or immigrant, a lower percentage of Black households in the Montreal CMA had achieved high level occupations than those in Toronto or Vancouver. In fact, Black immigrant households in Vancouver were more than twice as likely to hold high-level occupations (12.3 percent) than Black immigrant households in the Montreal CMA (5.4 percent) (Table 2.3).

We conclude our findings on incorporation of people of African descent in Toronto, Montreal and Vancouver by stating that racial equality has not been achieved for either Black Canadian-born or Black immigrants. By examining residential segregation and neighborhood socioeconomic inequality and homeownership in the next sections, we expect similar forms of racial inequalities.

Race Matters in Occupational Achievement

These findings based on 2001 census data are consistent with past studies of occupational inequality based on race. Based on a study of Black occupational achievement in Toronto and controlling for education and experience, Darden (2005) revealed that race matters in predicting the probability of occupational status of Blacks and Whites. Education and experience being equal, the marginal effect of race for Whites' chances of having a professional or managerial job was 17.3 percent positive compared to a negative marginal effect of 8.3 percent for Blacks having the same job.

Blacks often face racial discrimination in the Canadian labor force. In the face of such barriers/constraints, some of them try to go into small business in order to have more "control over their own destiny." However, even in this sector African and Caribbean immigrants in Toronto (as well as in other major Canadian cities) experience institutional discrimination (such as limited access to credit) as a major impediment to their participation in self-employment (Henry 1994).

Residential Segregation

The extent of residential segregation is another indicator of incorporation of a minority group into mainstream society. Residential segregation has consequences for a group's access to quality schools, housing, recreation, shopping, jobs, and health care facilities, and affects quality of life. Thus, the issue of segregation raises important research questions about social exclusion and the ultimate integration of visible minority groups, including Blacks.

One of the continuing debates in the literature on immigrant groups in North America, including Blacks, concerns the forces — structural and cultural — that contribute to the spatial concentration or dispersal of these groups. These forces are complex in that they are experienced in different ways by different minority groups. In the case of Canada's major "ports of entry"/gateway cities for immigrants and refugees — Toronto, Montreal and Vancouver — both structural and cultural forces appear to play a role in sustaining the spatial concentration of these groups and in defining these cities' changing ethnic and racial geography. Several interrelated questions arise from this: Is immigrant (or visible minority) residential concentration increasing or decreasing overtime? Are residential concentrations good or bad? Do immigrants (or visible minorities) want to live in ethnically/racially mixed neighborhoods, or do they prefer to concentrate in neighborhoods primarily occupied by their own group? What are the roles of urban gatekeepers (for example, landlords in the private and public rental sectors, real estate agents, mortgage lenders) in limiting neighborhood and housing choices? Do Blacks pay more for housing? In this regard, past studies suggest that there exists considerable evidence that race matters in Canadian housing markets, and that Blacks are in a disadvantageous position when looking for and locating affordable and good quality housing (Fong and Gulia 1999; Darden 2004).

Unlike research on residential segregation of Blacks in the United States, which has a long history, research on Black residential segregation in Canada has been more recent (Balakrishnan and Selvanathan 1990; Fong 2006). While most past studies have measured the level of Black vs. White residential segregation, we expand the analysis to include the residential segregation of Blacks of different ethnic origins from Whites. We limited the analysis to those Black ethnic origin groups with a population of at least 2,000 and to Canada's three largest CMAs.

Little variation exists in Black residential segregation for the Toronto and Montreal CMAs. The Index of Dissimilarity between Blacks and Whites was 48.7 in the Toronto CMA, and 49.4 in Montreal. Blacks in Vancouver had a lower level of segregation with a Dissimilarity Index of 36.7 (Table 2.4). Examining specific groups within the Black populations of these CMAs reveals some differences. For example, in Toronto, Jamaicans and Trinidadians/Tobagoans were slightly *less* segregated from Whites than were Blacks of African ethnic origin, with an Index of Dissimilarity of 48.5 for the former, and 50.3 for the latter.

Table 2.4.
Residential Segregation and Homeownership Rates in Canada's Largest Census Metropolitan Areas, 2001.

Census Metropolitan Area	Index of Dissimilarity* Black vs. White
Toronto	48.7
Montreal	49.4
Vancouver	36.7

*The Index of Dissimilarity ranges from "0," indicating no segregation, to "100," indicating complete segregation. The higher the index, the greater the degree of residential segregation.

Homeownership Rates.

Place	Black Canadian-Born	White Canadian-Born	Ratio	Black Immigrants	White Immigrants	Ratio
Canada	45.8	73.4	1.60	41	75.9	1.85
Toronto CMA	43.3	75.3	1.73	42.6	75.2	1.76
Montreal CMA	37.3	62.4	1.67	30.3	62.5	2.06
Vancouver CMA	42.2	66.5	1.57	40.7	66.5	1.63

Source: Computed by the authors from data obtained from Statistics Canada, 2006. Public Use Microdata Files (PUMF). Ottawa: Minister of Industry.

In the Montreal CMA, Jamaicans were *more* segregated from Whites than Jamaicans in the Toronto CMA. The Index of Dissimilarity between Jamaicans and Whites in Montreal was 70.7. Montreal Jamaicans were also more segregated residentially than Blacks from African ethnic origins with a Dissimilarity Index of 59.7. Haitians, the largest Black group in Montreal, had a slightly lower Index of Dissimilarity at 56.6. The most highly-segregated Black group in Montreal was of Trinidad/Tobago origins with an Index of Dissimilarity of 79.8.

In Vancouver, Jamaicans and Blacks of African origins experienced about the same level of residential segregation, with indexes of dissimilarity of 45.7 and 44.6, respectively. The most segregated Black group (Trinidadians/Tobagoans) had an Index of Dissimilarity of 66.8.

Residential Segregation and Neighborhood Inequality in the United States and Canada

The research on Black residential segregation in Canada's largest metropolitan areas suggests that Blacks are generally less segregated than Blacks in large metropolitan areas in the United States. Also, Blacks in Canada seem to be more suburbanized than their counterparts in the United States. There is no evidence, however, that the reasons for such differences are due to Canada's greater racial tolerance or Canada's lack of racial discrimination in housing (Novac, Darden, Hulchanski, and Seguin 2002; Darden 2004). The reason is more likely due to the fact that Blacks are a very small percentage in metropolitan areas in Canada. Because of small numbers, Fong (1996, p. 22) acknowledged that Blacks are less likely to become the target of discrimination in housing. Also, Blacks are not the largest visible minority group in many Canadian metropolitan areas. In other words, there has been less of a need by Whites to restrict the small number of Blacks from White neighborhoods.

Both of these factors tend to reduce residential segregation. The largest visible minority group constitutes the greatest threat and is usually more residentially segregated from the White majority. In the United States, for example, where the Black population is small in Sunbelt metropolitan areas, Black residential segregation is as low as the levels in Canada (Frey and Myers 2002). Also, the least Black-White segregated metropolitan areas are in Texas, California, and Florida, where Blacks are not the largest racial minority group. Larger and more visible minority groups tend to increase residential segregation. This is the situation of the Chinese, the group that is the most segregated in Toronto.

Finally, Blacks are over represented in council or public housing in both Canada and the United States, but council or public housing in Canadian metropolitan areas is more spatially dispersed compared to a concentrated pattern of location in most large American metropolitan areas. These factors may explain why Blacks in Canadian CMAs generally are less residentially segregated than Blacks in the United States. There is more evidence to suggest that these factors, as opposed to differential degrees of racial discrimination in housing, explain the difference. The evidence suggests that racial discrimination in housing in Canada is not significantly different than racial discrimination in housing in the United States (Darden 2004; Novac, Darden, Hulchanski, and Seguin 2002).

Despite the low levels of Black residential segregation in Canadian metropolitan areas (CMAs) compared to the high levels in the United States, the situation of Blacks is similar in terms of neighborhood characteristics where most Blacks reside. Blacks in Canadian CMAs usually live in the lower quality neighborhoods (Galabuzi 2006; Darden 2004; Kazemipur and Halli 1997). In Toronto, for example, a higher percentage of total Black households occupy neighborhoods with lower socioeconomic characteristics, whereas a higher percentage of White Households compared to Blacks occupy neighborhoods with the higher socioeconomic characteristics (Darden 2004). We argue that residential segregation by race receives its importance when it is measured within the context of racial inequality by neighborhood socioeconomic characteristics. In other words, it is the consequence of residential segregation, not the pattern, which makes social justice, equal opportunity and racial equality of interest. To be sure, the two are related, but the focus must be on racial inequality by socioeconomic characteristics of neighborhoods if public policies are to be implemented to address the problem. In other words racial residential segregation in and of itself is not an issue in the absence of social and economic consequences related to disadvantages and deprivation. There is a recent study of residential segregation conducted in five countries, including Canada (Johnston, Poulsen and Forrest 2007). The authors concluded what was already well known, that is, that Blacks in the United States are more segregated than other groups. What was more important in the study, however, were their conclusions that "the degree of segregation in cities of the five countries (including Toronto) is a function of common processes of *discrimination*, *disadvantage*, and *self-segregation*.

Each operates differently in terms of the intensity of their outcomes in different types of places" (Johnston, Paulsen, and Forrest 2007, 732).

We also argue that researchers should focus less on how to measure segregation. By doing so, they often omit the more important question of the social and economic consequences of the segregation and racial inequality of neighborhood characteristics due to discrimination, which denies justice, opportunity, and racial equality. An exception is Hulchanski's 2007 study entitled "The Three Cities within Toronto: Income, Polarization among Toronto Neighborhoods, 1970–2000." Hulchanski's excellent study reveals that the proportion of low and very low-income neighborhoods increased from 19 percent to 50 percent since 1970. Moreover, socioeconomic characteristics of neighborhoods follow a racial pattern. In city 1, where Whites are disproportionately located, income increased 20 percent or more since 1970. However, in city 3, where Blacks are disproportionately located, income decreased by 20 percent or more.

However, none of these areas can be described as a "ghetto" in the American sense of the word (Murdie and Teixeira 2003; Ley and Smith 1997). In contrast to the large American ghettos, which are typically located in the inner cities, these Canadian areas exist in both the inner city and the surrounding suburbs, are dispersed rather than compact, and often are situated adjacent to middle-class or stable working-class neighborhoods. Nevertheless, concern has been expressed about these pockets of poverty that are associated with poorly maintained private-rental complexes and public housing developments (Murdie and Teixeira 2003).

Many Black Torontonians of African and Caribbean origin believe that a subtle, but pervasive, pattern of prejudice defines their lives in the city (Mensah 2002). Racial discrimination seems to be the major barrier preventing the integration of Blacks in Toronto. A survey by the *Toronto Star* revealed that Blacks (both Caribbean and African), more than any other group, felt discriminated against (Carey 1999). The survey indicated that racism was a major concern for 71 percent of the Blacks interviewed, and only 4 percent of the Caribbean and African Blacks interviewed thought that their neighborhood displayed racial harmony. Furthermore, only 24 percent of Blacks compared to 65 percent Torontonians stated they were homeowners, and half of the group thought they had less access to loans and credit than other groups. For most immigrant groups including Blacks, race seems to increase the odds for living in poverty (Kazemipur and Halli 2003, p. 20). As one study (Kazemipur and Halli 2003) notes, "Compared to Whites . . . Blacks whether immigrants or native-born, have a much higher likelihood of living in poverty, even after controlling for their education, age and full/part-time nature of the job. . . . This effect of race . . . calls for further attention." Clearly, for Blacks in Toronto, whether in housing search or business, race and racism matter (Darden 2004 2005; Darden and Kamel 2000).

According to Myles and Hou (2003), Blacks tend to live in neighborhoods surrounded by the worst environments. As in the United States, there is evidence of a color hierarchy to neighborhood quality in Canada. The median neighborhood income of the average Black family is only 79 percent of the average White family (by comparison, Chinese families earn 91.7 percent of the average White family's income) (Myles and Hou 2003; Darden 2004).

Given the smaller size of the Black population in Canadian metropolitan areas and the smaller number of very poor neighborhoods, the Black experience generally may be somewhat less harsh in Canada. However, similar to the United States, Blacks with incomes and education levels comparable to White immigrants not only live in poorer neighborhoods, but also show no improvement in attaining the same quality neighborhoods as Whites (Fong and Wilkes 1999).

A previous study of Blacks in Toronto revealed that Blacks are less able than other groups to translate socioeconomic gains into spatial outcomes (Fong and Gulia 1999). The authors found that the attainment of neighborhood quality among Blacks is not related to their levels of education and income nor their proportion in the census tract. There was no consistent, statistically significant effect of any factor on Black's attainment of neighborhood quality. Thus, more than other groups, Blacks in Toronto may face problems of translating their socioeconomic status into desirable neighborhood qualities.

Myles and Hou (2003) concluded that for Blacks to become truly integrated, they need a combination of higher income, educational achievement, and home ownership. These factors are associated with a substantial increase (10 percentage points) in the number of White neighbors that is matched by a corresponding decline (–7 percentage points) in the number of Black neighbors (Myles and Hou 2003).

Homeownership Rate Differences

In Canada, like other predominantly White societies, homeownership provides owners with a stake in the system. It is also perceived as an "indicator of social status and a source of personal autonomy" (Agnew 1981, p. 75). There is a growing awareness among Canadian scholars of the cultural importance some immigrant groups attach to homeownership, which represents an important economic factor in the real estate markets of Canada's major cities and its suburbs. The evidence suggests that, over time, some immigrant groups achieve rates of homeownership equal to or exceeding those of the non-immigrant population (Murdie and Teixeira 2003; Haan 2005). Access to housing has become one of the primary routes for immigrants' social and economic integration into the host society, and settlement in the suburbs represents for many the achievement of the "Canadian dream" (Ray and Moore 1991; Murdie and Teixeira 2003).

In contrast, tenants are more likely than homeowners to be viewed as an unsettling "out-group" with a lack of social esteem (Agnew 1981, p. 75). Black tenants are less likely to be seen as an integrated part of society than homeowners, and more likely as a transient group dependent on their landlords (Balakrishnan and Wu 1992). Economically speaking, federal, provincial, and municipal policies are less likely to favor tenants and more likely to favor homeowners (Backer 1993). For example, the lack of federal and provincial commitments to affordable housing during the 1990s resulted in today's Canada having the smallest non-market housing sector of any major Western nation, except for the United States. Relatively few new rental units have been built in Canada's most multicultural cities (Toronto and Vancouver) since the mid 1990s, and rents for existing units increased at approximately twice the rate of inflation. Thus, for many new immigrants such as Blacks, these economic factors are aggravated by barriers such as discriminatory practices in the private rental market.

Scholars have concluded that race remains an important barrier to equal treatment in Canada's housing market (Danso and Grant 2000; Murdie 2002, 2003; Murdie, Chambon, Hulchanski and Teixeira 1996; Darden 2004; Hulchanski and Shapcott 2004; Darden and Kamel 2000). More studies, comparing within and between minority groups, and within and between Canadian cities, are needed. Further research is also needed into housing discrimination by the diverse urban social gatekeepers involved in the production and allocation of housing, which may contribute significantly to the restriction of immigrant minorities' access to affordable rental housing and homeownership. Moreover, the audit method should be used to measure such discrimination (Novac, Darden, Hulchanski and Seguin 2002).

Racial Differences in Homeownership Rates in 2001

Our examination and analysis of the most recent data from Statistics Canada show that, whether Canadian-born or immigrants, most Blacks in Canada are *not* homeowners, while most Whites in Canada do own their homes. Homeownership among Blacks ranges from a low of 30.3 percent in the Montreal CMA among Black immigrants, to a high of 43.3 percent among Canadian-born Blacks in the Toronto CMA (Table 2.4). White immigrants in Montreal were twice as likely as Black immigrants to own their homes. White homeownership ranged from 62.4 percent among White Canadian-born households in the Montreal CMA to 75.3 percent among White Canadian-born households in the Toronto CMA. The least racial inequality in homeownership rates was between Black and White Canadian-born households in the Vancouver CMA, where the Black Canadian-born rate was 42.2 percent compared to 66.5 percent for White Canadian-born households. The differences in rates revealed a ratio of 1.57, i.e., Whites were 1½ times more likely to be homeowners than Blacks (Table 2.4).

Evidence of Racial Discrimination as Barriers to Full Incorporation

Despite the multicultural and anti-discrimination policies developed by Canadian federal, provincial and municipal governments, Blacks still face significant barriers in locating and obtaining housing, with discrimination being the most formidable barrier. However, while discrimination and prejudice are recognized as barriers to equal access in the housing market (Darden 2004; Novac, Darden, Hulchanski and Seguin 2002), the actual role of discrimination in Canada's housing market remains largely unstudied. In general, few studies in Canada have attempted to account for the underrepresentation of Blacks and other visible minorities in the housing market (rental and homeownership) by using the audit method to measure racial discrimination, which is the most effective method and is widely used in the United States (Darden 2004; Novac, Darden, Hulchanski and Seguin 2002).

Reitz and Breton (1994) have documented that racial discrimination in Canada is as prevalent as racial discrimination in the United States, however, Canada's *response* to racial discrimination has been distinctly different. Unlike the United States, Canada more frequently denies that racial discrimination is a problem (Darden 2004), despite the continuing revelation of evidence of discrimination.

In 2002, Blacks were more likely to report feeling that they had been discriminated against or treated unfairly by others because of their ethno-cultural characteristics. Nearly one-third (32 percent) of Blacks, or 135,000, said they had these experiences sometimes or often in the past five years, compared to 21 percent of South Asians and 18 percent of Chinese (Statistics Canada 2003b). The pattern suggests that perceived discrimination varies among visible minority groups. It appears that the perceptions of discrimination are greater among those with darker skins. This is consistent with the ideology of White supremacy, in which lighter-skinned groups, i.e., those with features most like Whites, are treated less harshly and receive less discrimination (Darden 2004, p. 10). Indeed, skin color (as opposed to ethnicity, culture, language, or religion) was the reason given by 70 percent of those stating that they had been discriminated against. This percentage was higher than the percentage for any other reason.

CONCLUSIONS AND POLICY IMPLICATIONS

This chapter examined the African Diaspora in Canada from the conceptual framework of differential incorporation, evaluating to what extent people of African descent, i.e., Blacks, have been incorporated into the mainstream Canadian society, a predominantly White society where the ideology of White supremacy is ingrained in the culture. To assess racial inequality, unemployment rates, income inequality, educational attainment, occupational inequality, residential segregation, and home ownership rates, and evidence of racial discrimination as a barrier to full incorporation were examined.

After analyzing the most recent census data available, we conclude that *race* and *place* matter in the process of incorporation, which supports previous research. On all indicators, racial inequality was evident. Whether Canadian-born or foreign-born, Blacks had higher unemployment rates, a lower percentage of high-income earners ($100,000 or more) and a lower percentage of households with bachelor degrees or higher educational attainment. Also, a lower percentage of Blacks compared to Whites held high-level occupations, i.e., jobs in management and professional work.

Canadian Blacks generally have a lower level of residential segregation from Whites than U.S. Blacks, due in part to their small numbers. However, similar to Blacks in the United States, the neighborhoods where most Blacks reside are of lower quality than the neighborhoods where most Whites reside, resulting in a lower quality of life for Blacks compared to Whites. Finally, while most White households (whether Canadian-born or foreign-born) are homeowners, most Blacks are renters. Racial inequality varies to some degree between census metropolitan areas.

These differences by race, as revealed by the socioeconomic indicators, are influenced by racial discrimination. Canada, unlike the United States, is more likely to deny that racial discrimination is a problem and has fewer *strong* anti-discrimination policies in place to address the problem (Darden 2004). Moreover, those anti-discrimination policies that are in place are generally weaker than the policies in the United States. As immigration of Blacks to Canada continues, the key question Canada will face is whether the country will continue to deny that it has a problem of racial discrimination or will it face the problem and introduce stronger legislation.

Acknowledgments: The authors would like to thank Robert Janke for extracting and preparing the Statistics Canada data and Carolyn King for preparing the maps. Their assistance is greatly appreciated.

Chapter 3

The African Diaspora in Montréal and Halifax
A Comparative Overview of "the Entangled Burdens of Race, Class, and Space"

JOSEPH MENSAH AND DAVID FIRANG

... the facing of so vast a prejudice could not but bring the inevitable self-questioning, self-disparagement, and lowering of ideals which ever accompany repression and breed in an atmosphere of contempt and hate — W. E. B. Du Bois[1]

INTRODUCTION

Canada, like most immigrant-receiving nations of the West, is home to many visible minorities, some of whom have arrived only recently, while others, including the African Diaspora, have a long history in this country. In 2001, some 13 percent of the Canadian population belonged to a visible minority group. It is estimated that by 2017 roughly one in every five people in Canada could be a visible minority (Statistics Canada 2005). The African Diaspora is the third largest visible minority group in the country, surpassed only by Chinese and South Asians. Unsurprisingly, the African "community" exhibits extensive diversity in country of origin, with some born in Canada, many others born in Africa (the ancestral epicenter of Blacks), and still others hailing from the Caribbean, United States, and other parts of the world. As a corollary, one finds a wide range of linguistic, religious, socio-economic, and spatial patterns among the African diasporic communities across Canada.

While some general accounts of the history and the sociology of Africans in Canada do exist (Walker 1980; Williams 1989 and 1997; Tettey and Puplampu 2006), it is only recently that some researchers (e.g., Mensah 2005) have begun to tease out the cultural and socio-economic variations within and between Africans in different parts of the country, and it is to this scholarship that the present chapter seeks to contribute, using Montreal and Halifax as case study areas. More specifically, we compare the historical backgrounds, cultural diversity, socioeconomic characteristics, and the contemporary immigration patterns of members of the African Diaspora in Montreal and Halifax to discuss Africans' level of achieving socioeconomic mobility, the settlement and incorporation problems they face, and the extent to which social and economic mobility of these Africans is influenced by race-, class-, and space-induced discriminatory practices.[2]

The urban tilt in our analysis reflects the urban character of the African Diaspora in Canada, which for the purposes of this paper, is broadly defined as *Black* Canadians.[3] "Blacks" and "members of the African Diaspora" are used interchangeably here. We employ 2001 census data, the most recent available at the time of this writing. The italicizing of *race* in our subtitle mirrors our recognition of, and our angst over, the paradox of race — a concept that is as unreal as it is consequential in the daily lives of Africans in Canada.

In consonance with intersectional theory, we realize that *race* is not the only axis along which human suppression is enacted. In some contexts, gender, class, disability, sexual orientation, or permutations of these social axes, may be more consequential, however, the constraints of class, gender, etc. are epiphenomena, reducible to the burdens of racial discrimination. Another impetus for giving primacy to *race* concerns not only the extreme dehumanization engendered by racism, but also the cunning subtleties of race-based discrimination in Canadian society. In our view, it is high time we brought *race* (and its *–ism*) to the fore and confront it squarely. Winant (1997, p. 27) could not have put it any better when he noted that "the mere fact that basic racial questions are at once so obvious and so obviously unanswered suggests how urgent is further theoretical [and empirical] work on race." Although numerous race-related issues confront African Canadians, the socio-economic and physic sequelae contribute the greatest burdens because they persist on a daily basis.

HISTORY

Most Blacks in Halifax are third-generation Canadians or beyond, with some even tracing their ancestry to the era of slavery (Milan and Tran 2004). Former New England residents brought the first major group of Black slaves to Halifax and other parts of Nova Scotia around the mid-eighteenth century, after the expulsion of the Acadians. The Black population in the region rose with the arrival of Black Loyalists in the 1770s, and later with the arrival of the Maroons[4] from Jamaica. At the beginning of the American Revolution in 1776, there were already some five hundred Black slaves in Nova Scotia, and this number tripled as White Loyalists who supported the British fled during and after the five-year Revolutionary War, taking their slaves with them (Clairmont and Magill 1973; Walker 1980). Another major wave of Black immigration to Nova Scotia occurred between 1813 and 1815, when several African-American war refugees settled in towns such as Halifax, Hammonds Plains, Beechville, and Lucasville. In fact, the British encouraged Black slaves to desert their United States masters in return for settlers' status and land. It is estimated that some 3,600 Black American slaves were brought to Canada around this time, with many of them settling in Halifax and other parts of Atlantic Canada (Mensah 2002). The well-known Black settlement of Africville was created in 1842 out of the Black refugee community planted near Halifax (Boyko 1998; Clairmont and Magill 1999).

In 1899 another group of Black immigrants from the United States came to work in the steel mills of Cape Breton and Halifax. This relatively small group of immigrants was gradually replaced by a larger pool of Black immigrants from the Caribbean by the 1920s (See Table 3.1).

Table 3.1.
Blacks in Halifax and Montreal by Immigration Status and Period.

Immigration Status & Period	**Canada**		**Halifax**		**Montreal**	
	All Canadians	*All Blacks*	*CMA Population*	*Black Population*	*CMA Population*	*Black Population*
Total Pop.	29,639,035	662,210	355,945	13,085	3,380,645	139,035
Non-Immigrants	23,991,905	297,985	329,605	11,910	2,724,200	56,845
Immigrants	5,448,480	344,255	24,385	945	621,890	70,215
Before 1961(%)	16.4	1.3	18.4	4.2	13.3	1.5
1961–1970 (%)	13.6	10.6	16	8.5	14.4	8.3
1971–1980 (%)	17.1	24.1	18.4	12.7	17.1	29.5
1981–1990 (%)	19.1	25	16.5	16.4	20.6	27.1
1991–2001 (%)	33.6	40.6	30.8	57.7	34.6	42.1
Non-Permanent Residents	198,645	19,970	1,950	235	24,555	6,235

Source: Statistics Canada, 2001 Census of Canada Catalogue # 97F0010XCB2001044.

In Halifax, and elsewhere in Nova Scotia, these Black pioneers tilled the land, worked the mines, cleaned homes, and built roads and other structures, some of which still exist. Like their counterparts across Canada, these Blacks were promised good arable land-grants which never materialized, forcing many into destitution (Milan and Tran 2004; Frances 1973; Winks 1971). The tightly-knit community of Africville — just on the outskirts of Halifax — became the hub of the Black presence in Eastern and Atlantic Canada (Clairmont and Magill 1999; Boyko 1998). With time, a number of deleterious urban facilities, with negative externalities, including an infectious disease hospital, a slaughterhouse, and a garbage dump, were located near Africville. In addition to this blatant environmental racism, the residents of Africville had no potable water or sewer services by the early 1960s. Living conditions in Africville degenerated to a point where many non-residents perceived it as a slum area — a perception which culminated in the bulldozing of the entire community for the sake of urban beautification. The residents of Africville were eventually relocated into public housing projects in and around Halifax. Today, Halifax is home to more than 13,000 Blacks, most of whom are Canadian-born. Inside the Halifax Census Metropolitan Area (CMA), resides the bulk of the Black population along the peninsula that extends into the Halifax Harbor.

As with Halifax, the history of Africans in Montreal is a long-standing one, going back to the days of slavery in Canada (Williams 1989). Some historians (e.g., Walker 1980; Tulloch 1975) believe that the prosperity of the New England colonies, which was commonly attributed to the hard work of Black slaves, led to a demand in New France for the importation of Blacks. Williams (1989) reports that about 1,132 Black slaves and domestic servants lived in and around Montreal as early as 1685. Notwithstanding years of popular denial, it is now generally acknowledged that the enterprise of slavery persisted in major Quebec cities such as Montreal, even after the 1759 conquest brought Quebec under British control (Boyko 1998; Williams 1989). According to Boyko (1998, p. 158) "the article of capitulation, signed after the fall of Montreal in 1760, guaranteed the continuation of slavery in the colony." While some of the Black pioneers in Montreal, and elsewhere in Quebec, were used for agricultural, shipbuilding, and mining purposes, the vast majority worked as domestic servants for the elites — i.e., the city administrators, doctors, prelates, and the merchant class.

With the establishment of the Union United Church in 1907, the Universal Negro Improvement Association in 1919, and the Negro Community Center in 1927, scholars such as Williams (1989) commonly trace the beginning of a genuinely viable African diasporic community in Montreal to the three decades between 1900 and 1930. During this period, most Black women continued to work as domestic servants, while most Black men found employment in the railway sector, as porters and cooks. Even then, Montreal, like Halifax, not only exhibited a perceptibly segregated labor market, but also a segregated residential pattern, with most members of the African Diasporic community residing in the city's West End. World War II brought some changes to the employment circumstances of Blacks in Montreal, with more Black women gaining employment beyond domestic services into the burgeoning war-related factories; and many Black male porters of the Canadian Pacific Railway getting unionized, with some improvements in their working conditions (Williams 1989).

The 1960s saw the introduction of French-speaking Haitians into Montreal's African Diasporic community. The first wave of Haitians to Montreal — made up mostly of political exiles, scholarship students, and professionals working in health services, education, and social services — numbered in few hundreds per year. During the early 1960s, Quebec initiated extensive education reforms under its Quite Revolution,[5] and many Haitian scholars and professionals found teaching, nursing, engineering, and other professional positions in Montreal and other cities in Quebec. The second major wave of Haitians to Montreal occurred in the early 1970s involving thousands of both skilled and unskilled workers, with many entering the city's burgeoning plastic and textile industries. Unlike the first-wave Haitians, this group involved many illiterates, some of whom spoke only Creole French, and, consequently, had problems adjusting to life in Canada. Montréalers were not prepared for the presence of such a large number of Blacks among them, especially with some venturing beyond the city's West End into traditional White neighborhoods for housing. And, as with Blacks in Halifax, it was just a matter of time before anti-Black racial problems surfaced, especially in the city's taxi industry where many Haitian men were employed (Lampkin 1985). Today, Montreal is home to the second largest African Diasporic community in Canada, after Toronto. Four percent or nearly 140,000 of the 3.3 million people in Montreal are Black, with most of them living in and around Montreal-Nord, LaSalle, St. Leonand, and Pierrefonds (See Table 3.2).

Table 3.2.
Generational Roots of Blacks in Halifax and Montreal (%).

	Canada		**Halifax**		**Montréal**	
Generation	*All Canadians* *N*=23,901,360	*All Blacks* *N*=467,095	*City Population* *N*=289,855	*Black Population* *N*=8,990	*City Population* *N*=2,761,210	*Black Population* *N*= 100,685
1st Generation	22.4[1]	71.4	8.9	12.0	22.4	75.8
2nd Generation	16.4	18.5	9.4	7.1	10.7	20.3
3rd Gen. & over	61.2	10.1	81.7	81.0	66.8	3.9

[1] Percentages do not add up to 100 due to rounding.
Source: Statistics Canada, 2001 Census of Canada Catalogue #.97F0010XCB2001044.

CONTEMPORARY IMMIGRATION

Even though the African Diaspora has a long history in Canada, it was only after the introduction of the "point system" of immigration in the 1960s that Africans began to arrive in Canada in significant numbers (Mensah 2002). For most contemporary African immigrants, the move to Canada is attributable to the *push* exerted by the ethnic conflicts, political instability, and the harsh environmental and economic conditions in several African source nations, on the one hand, and the understandable *pull* of Canada, as a well-to-do nation, with relatively conducive immigration and refugee policies and programs, especially since the late 1960s. Unlike the Black fugitives, slaves, and loyalists of the 18th and 19th centuries, many of whom settled in rural farming communities, the contemporary African Diaspora in Canada is overwhelmingly urban, with nearly half of its members living in the nation's largest metropolis of Toronto.

Table 3.1 indicates that a large proportion of the Black immigrants in both Montreal (42.1 percent) and Halifax (57.7 percent) came after 1990; the comparable figures for the entire CMA populations of Montreal (34.6 percent) and Halifax (30.8 percent) are evidently smaller. Whereas a mere 1.3 percent of the entire Black population now in Canada trace their period of immigration to pre-1961, the corresponding figures for Blacks in Halifax and Montreal are 4.2 percent and 1.5 percent, respectively. However, by 2001, many of the older immigrants had died, thus, focusing on "the period of immigration" alone gives the erroneous impression that the Blacks Diaspora in Canada is a recent phenomenon.

Table 3.2 provides data on the generational roots of Blacks in Halifax and Montreal. Clearly, a far larger proportion of the Blacks in Halifax (81 percent), compared to those in Montreal (3.9 percent) has roots going back to the third generation and beyond. Thus, even though both Montreal and Halifax have a long-standing Black presence, the latter has a larger proportion of Blacks who trace their generational ties to the city. The City of Halifax (together with its adjoining city of Dartmouth) is often seen as the historic hub of the Black Diaspora in this country, home to more "indigenous," or non-immigrant, Blacks than any other Canadian city (Mensah 2005).

Black immigrants from different parts of the world have affinity for different Canadian cities for reasons of geographic proximity, historical ties, language proficiency, and the usual cumulative causation and network effects of immigration. As shown in Table 3.3, the top five source countries of African immigrants to Halifax include Nigeria, South Africa, Ethiopia, Sudan, and Uganda, in that order. All of these countries, with the notable exception of Ethiopia, are officially Anglophone. Even in Ethiopia where the official language is Amharic, English is not only the most important foreign language, but also the medium of instruction in the nation's secondary schools. Contrast this with the situation in Montreal, where none of these countries made the comparable list. In fact, with the exception of Ghana and Mauritius, all the top 5 source countries for Africans in Montreal have French as their sole or co-official language.[6] Even in the case of Mauritius one finds the unusual situation where English is the official language and the language taught in schools, but French dominates the public sphere, as *lingua-franca* among the many different ethnic groups in the country. A similar pattern emerges for Caribbean immigrants. The bulk of the English-speaking Caribbean immigrants head to Halifax, just as Haitian immigrants, in particular, head for Montreal. Jamaicans are, indeed, the leading Caribbean immigrants in all major Canadian cities, with the notable exception of Montreal, where Haitians top the list of immigrants (Mensah 2005).

Table 3.3.
Top 5 African and Caribbean Ethnic Origins[1] in Halifax and Montreal, 2001.

Rank	Halifax		Montréal	
	African Origin[2]	*Caribbean Origin*	*African Origin*	*Caribbean Origin*
1st	Nigerian	Jamaican	Congolese	Haitians
2nd	S. African	Barbadian	Ghanaian	Jamaican
3rd	Ethiopian	Trinidadian-T	Cameroonian	Trinidadian-T
4th	Sudanese	Guyanese	Zairian	Barbadian
5th	Ugandan	Cuban	Mauritian	Dominican

[1] The rankings of ethnic origins are done by population size. Also, the rankings are approximations, since many of the categories used in the Census overlap; a good example is the overlap between the ethnic categories of *Black, Ghanaian, Akan* and *Ashanti* — a typical Ashanti may very well belong to the other 3 categories.
[2] North Africans, including Libyans, Algerians, Moroccans, Egyptians, and Tunisians are excluded, as the Census categorizes them as Arabs.
Source: Statistics Canada, January 21, 2003. 2001 Census of Canada, Catalogue # 97F0010XCB2001001.

While source country of immigrants is important in illuminating ethnic make-up of the Africa Diaspora, we must interpret the data with caution, for not all the people from these nations are Black. Few truly mono-ethnic or mono-racial nations exist due to heightened inter- and trans-national migration, and intercultural mixing worldwide. Jamaica (and most Caribbean nations) provide a good example. After the abolition of slavery, several Chinese and East Indian indentured laborers were brought to the area to work on the sugar plantations. Many of these laborers brought their families and remained in the region permanently following completion of their contracts. Centuries of inter-racial mixing has yielded an ethno-racial potpourri of immense proportion in that part of the world. Similarly, people from the leading African source countries are not of uniform ethnic and racial identity. South African immigrants, in particular, are just as likely to be Black as they are to be White.

In addition to the ethno-cultural diversities attributable to Blacks from the leading source countries of Africa and the Caribbean, the "indigenous" Black population and contemporary Black immigrants from other sources (e.g., the United States, Latin American, and Europe) contribute to diverse populations. Despite the enormous ethno-cultural diversity, some striking features of the African Diaspora in Montreal and Halifax remain, including the preponderance of the "indigenous" Black population in Halifax, and the overwhelming presence of Haitians in Montreal.

Blacks are by far the largest visible minority group in both Halifax and Montreal, and their presence is hard to miss *across* both cities, despite their spatial concentration in specific residential neighborhoods such as St. Leonard and Montreal-Nord in Montreal and along the harbor in Halifax (and the adjoining city of Dartmouth). Blacks constitute more than half of the visible minority population in Halifax, and a third of a similar population in Montreal. As with the general Canadian population, and many other visible-minority groups in Canada, Black women outnumber Black men in both Montreal and Halifax (Table 3.4). This imbalance results, in part, from the historic female-specific Caribbean Domestic Schemes, by which the Canadian government actively recruited young Black women from places such as Guadeloupe, Jamaica, and Barbados to work in Canadian homes as live-in nannies. The first such program is traced to 1910, when some 100 Guadeloupian women were recruited for domestic work in the province of Quebec (Mensah 2002). A common pattern of immigration among Caribbeans then (and, even now, to some extent) was for the women to come first under the Domestic Scheme, and once settled, send for their spouse and children, if any. There are indications that the situation is normally reversed among African immigrants in Canada, with the men coming first and later getting their partners and children to join them (Mensah 2002). Thus, one has to be careful not to lump all Black groups in Canada together in interpreting their sex ratio. In addition, the usual imbalance in life expectancy, favoring women, contributes to the imbalance.

Table 3.4.
Sex Ratios of Visible Minorities in Halifax and Montréal.

Group	Canada		Halifax		Montréal	
	Total Pop.	*Sex Ratio*[1]	*Total Pop.*	*Sex Ratio*	*Total Pop.*	*Sex Ratio*
Total Canadian Population	29,639,035	97	355,945	93	3,380,645	94
Total Visible Minority Pop.	3,983,845	95	25,085	92	458,330	98
Chinese	1,029,395	94	2,440	105	52,110	90
South Asia	917,075	103	2,345	111	57,935	114
Black	662,210	91	13,085	85	139,305	89
Filipino	308,575	74	480	55	17,890	65
Latin American	216,975	95	410	71	53,155	95
E.S Asian	198,880	98	715	142	39,570	99
Arab	194,680	119	3025	107	67,830	121
West Asian	109,285	113	330	100	11,580	120
Korean	100,660	93	457	75	3,760	93
Japanese	73,315	83	335	68	2,295	66
Visible Minority *n.i.e.*[2]	98,920	92	980	106	6,785	107
Multiple visible minority	73,875	98	465	119	6,115	101

[1] Sex Ratio is estimated as the number of males per 100 females.
[2] *n.i.e.* refers to those "not included elsewhere"
Source: Statistics Canada, 2001 Census of Canada Catalogue #95F0363XCB2001004.

Socio-cultural Background

Educational attainment, official-language proficiency, and religion affect both visible minorities and the general population in Halifax and Montreal and influence race-based socio-economic exclusions that members of the African Diaspora might face.

Table 3.5 illustrates that the educational level of Blacks in Montreal is generally better than their counterparts in Halifax. For instance, while 29.9 percent of Montreal's Black population had less than high school education as of 2001, the comparable figure for Halifax stood at 41.3 percent. The proportion of Blacks with university degrees is also higher in Montreal than in Halifax. The educational attainment of Blacks in Montreal is similar to others in the city. However, a careful look at Table 3.5 reveals that even Blacks in Montréal are under-represented among the city's university graduates, especially when compared with other visible minorities.

Table 3.5.
***Educational Attainments of Blacks and Visible Minorities in Halifax and Montréal* (%).**[1]

	Halifax			**Montréal**		
Level of Educational	*City population* N=289,855	*Visible Minority Pop.* *N=18,045*	*Black Population* *N=8,990*	*City population* *N=2,761,215*	*Visible Minority Pop.* *N=343,050*	*Black Population* *N=100,685*
Less than high school	26.3	29.8	41.3	28.2	28.3	29.9
High school only	9.6	9.7	9.2	16.1	13	12.5
Some postsecondary	11.5	13.5	11.8	9.7	12.1	13.8
Trade cert/diploma	12.8	8.5	11.7	9.3	7.4	10.2
College cert/diploma	16.2	10.5	13.3	15.1	13.4	15.7
Univ. below bachelor's	2.6	3.1	1.9	3.8	4.6	4.2
University degree	21.1	25.0	10.8	17.7	21.2	13.7
Bachelors degree	14.8	16.6	7.1	12	13.8	9
Univ. cert. above Bachelor's degree	1.7	1.6	0.72	1.8	2.2	1.4
Master's degree	3.8	4.6	2.7	3.3	4.1	2.6
Earned doctorate	0.81	2.2	0.61	0.65	1.1	0.73

[1] Figures include only people who are 15 years and over.
Source: Statistics Canada, 2001 Census of Canada Catalogue # 97F0010XCB2001045.

Within Halifax, Blacks have far *lower* educational backgrounds than other visible minorities and the general Halifax population. In fact, Blacks have more than a ten-percentage-point deficit, relative to other visible minorities, and to the general Halifax population, in terms of university degrees; the figures for the lowest echelon of education are equally unfavorable for Blacks. Overall, Haligonians (i.e., the people of Halifax) seem to have a slightly higher educational attainment than Montrealers, thus, the educational deficit of Blacks in Halifax, relative to their counterparts in Montreal, demands attention. National data indicate that "Canadian-born Blacks are just as likely to be university educated as others born in Canada" (Milan and Tran 2004, p. 6). Historical analysis, shows that Halifax contains more indigenous and 3rd generation (and beyond) Blacks than Montreal (and in fact, than any other major Canadian city). Thus, one can reasonably speculate that Blacks in Halifax would have a fairly comparable educational background to other Canadians in Halifax and elsewhere, in the absence of any entrenched, anti-Black inequity in the city's educational system. Blacks' under-achievement in education requires an empirical and racially-informed study of Halifax's educational system.

Members of the African Diaspora exhibit a wide diversity in mother tongue, given the numerous polyglot African, Caribbean, and other countries from which they hail.[7] Of Canada's two official languages, English is by far the most prevalent among the African Diaspora in Halifax. As shown in Table 3.6, English is more common among Blacks in Halifax (94.2 percent) than among the general Halifax population (88 percent), or other visible minorities (89.3 percent). Expectedly, French-only ability among Blacks in Halifax is virtually zero. Conversely, French is the dominant official language among Blacks in Montreal, with as high as 42 percent of them declaring proficiency in French only.

Unlike official-language ability, religion typically has very limited bearing on immigrants' employment prospects in Canada.[8] The African Diaspora in both Halifax and Montreal emanates from a wide range of countries, resulting in pluralistic religious background. While some profess faith in "Eastern religions" such as Hinduism and Buddhism, the overwhelming majority of Blacks are Christians, just like the general population in these two cities.[9] For instance, as many as 73 percent of Blacks in Halifax are Protestants, and approximately 13 percent are Catholic (see Table 3.7). The Christian population in Montreal is equally high, but the Catholic-Protestant split is nearly equal (36.9 percent Catholic, 35.9 percent Protestant). Also, unlike Halifax — where the proportion of Africans of Islamic background is miniscule (1 percent) — the African Muslim population in Montreal is quite moderate (4 percent). At the same time we must note that the proportions of Black Muslims in both Halifax and Montreal compare very well with the corresponding figures among the general populace in both cities.

Table 3.6.
***Official Language Ability of Blacks and Visible Minorities in Halifax and Montreal* (%).**

Official Language Ability	Halifax			Montreal		
	City population N=355,945	*Visible Minority Pop. N=25,090*	*Black Population N=13,085*	*City population N=,3380,645*	*Visible Minority Pop. N=458,330*	*Black Population N=139,300*
English only	88.0	89.3	94.2	13.3	21.3	14.6
French only	0.1	0.04	0	37.9	29.2	42.0
English & French	11.5	9.3	5.7	53.0	43.4	42.1
Neither Eng. nor French	0.2	1.6	0.1	1.5	6.1	7.7

Source: Statistics Canada, 2001 Census of Canada Catalogue # 97F0010XCB2001044.

Table 3.7.
***Religious Affiliations of Blacks and Visible Minorities in Halifax and Montréal* (%).**

Religions Affiliation	Canada		Halifax		Montreal	
	All Canadians N=29,639030	*All Blacks* N=662,210	*City Population* N=355,945	*Black Population* N=13,085	*City Population* N=3,380,645	*Black Population* N=139,305
Catholic	43.6	2.7	37.2	12.9	74.5	36.9
Protestant	29.2	41.1	45.4	73.0	6.2	35.9
Christian Orthodox	1.6	1.7	0.8	0.6	2.8	0.6
Christian n.i.e.	2.6	9.3	1.4	1.5	1.1	4.6
Muslim	2.0	7.8	0.9	1.1	3.0	4.0
Jewish	1.1	0.2	0.4	0.1	2.6	0.2
Other religions	3.4	25.1	1.0	0.3	2.2	10.2
No affiliation	16.5	12.1	12.9	10.5	7.6	7.7

n.i.e.= Not included elsewhere
Source: Statistics Canada, 2001 Census of Canada Catalogue # 97F0010XCB2001044.

Employment and Income Characteristics

While human capital theorists indicate that educational attainment influences employment prospects, *ceteris paribus* (Krahn and Lowe 1998, pp. 112–13), there is more to the employment outcomes of visible minorities than educational qualifications (Li 1998). Taken at its face value, the human capital theory predicts poor employment outcomes for members of the African Diaspora in both Halifax and Montreal, primarily because of their relatively weak educational backgrounds. Following the same logic — and, thus, limiting our independent variable strictly to educational qualification — one would also expect other visible minorities in both Halifax and Montreal to do better, employment-wise, than the general populations in these two cities. Additionally, one would expect the African Diasporic community in Montreal to have better employment outcomes than their counterparts in Halifax. However, the situation is neither unilinear nor straightforward.

Members of the African Diaspora in both Halifax and Montreal are relatively worse off in terms of employment and income levels. For instance, whereas the unemployment rate for Halifax as a whole stands at 7.2 percent, the rate for the Black population is nearly double (13.2 percent), it is also some two percentage points higher than the rate for other visible minorities in the city. The situation is even worse for Blacks in Montreal, where the unemployment rate for the city is 7.2 percent, while that for Blacks stands at a whopping 17.2 percent (and that for other visible minority is 15.6 percent). A striking feature of the data in Table 3.8 is the uncanny upward gradation of most of the "positive" or favorable variables (notably, labor force participation rate in Halifax and the percentage of people with full-time employment in Halifax) from Blacks, through other visible minorities, to the general population. However, when it comes to the "negative" or unfavorable variables, one finds a downward gradation, still starting from Blacks, through other visible minorities, to the general population. Good examples in this regard include the rate of unemployment, the rate of government transfer payments, and the incidence of low-income in both Halifax and Montreal.

Table 3.8.
Employment and Income Characteristics of Blacks and Visible Minorities in Halifax and Montreal.

Employment and Income	**Halifax**			**Montréal**		
	City Population N=289,855	*Visible Minority Pop. N=18,045*	*Black Population N=8,990*	*City Population N=2,761,215*	*Visible Minority Pop. N=343,045*	*Black Population N=100,685*
Labor force ppt. rate (%)	67.8	60.0	59.3	65.7	63.3	66.2
Unemployment Rate (%)	7.2	11.4	13.2	7.2	15.6	17.2
Employed full-time (%)	63.2	53.1	51.4	60.8	53.5	54.9
Incidence of low income (%)	11.7	34.1	37.6	17.6	40.4	40.7
Gov't transfer payment (%)	10.8	14.2	20.5	12.2	16.7	19.4
Median family Income ($)	22,986	14,749	15,160	21,888	14,547	15,110

Source: Statistics Canada, 2001 Census of Canada Catalogue # 97F0010XCB2001047.

Table 3.8 suggests that members of the African Diasporic community in Halifax are relatively better-off, economically, than their counterparts in Montreal. The difference in unemployment rate, incidence of low income, and median family income are all telling. To the extent that Africans in Montreal are generally better educated than those in Halifax, one cannot rely much on their respective human capital for prescience here. Even the fact that other visible minorities are usually sandwiched between Blacks and the general population, as we just saw with the preceding gradation, goes against the human capital theory, as other visible minorities were found to have fairly similar, if not better, educational attainments than the general populations in both cities. To be fair to the human capital theorist, though, one has to acknowledge that other visible minorities in both cities have lesser official language abilities, which would obviously undermine their employment outcomes. Understandably, linked to the poor employment and income levels of Blacks in both Halifax and Montreal is their over-representation in processing and manufacturing occupations and their under-representation in management positions (Table 3.9).

Table 3.9.
Occupational Backgrounds of Blacks and Visible Minorities in Halifax and Montréal (%).

Occupation	Halifax			Montréal		
	City Pop.	*Visible Minority Pop.*	*Black Population*	*City Pop.*	*Visible Minority Pop.*	*Black Population*
Occupation — Not applicable	1.5	4.4	5.4	2.7	7.3	7.7
All occupations	98.5	95.6	94.4	97.3	92.7	92.3
Management occupations	11.4	11.3	7.8	10.6	7.2	3.6
Business, finance and administration	19.6	16.8	20.3	20.1	14.3	16.3
Natural & applied sciences	7	5.8	2.3	7.3	7.9	4.5
Health occupations	6.4	6.3	4.8	5.4	6.4	10.5
Social science educ. gov't service & religion	8	10	9.8	8.1	5.5	6.3
Art, culture, recreation and sport	3.2	2.7	2.3	3.9	2.3	2.3
Sales and service occupations	27.5	32.3	33.8	22	23.1	22.2
Trades, transport & equipment operators	11.9	7.1	8.8	12	8.6	9.1
Occupations unique to primary industry	1.2	0.60	0.93	0.70	0.3	0.3
Unique to processing, manufacturing & utilities	2.2	2.7	3.6	7.5	16.8	17.1

Source: Statistics Canada, 2001 Census of Canada Catalogue # 97F0010XCB2001046.
Percentages do not add up to a hundred due to rounding.

Entanglements of Race, Class, and Space

It is clear from the preceding paragraphs that Blacks in both Montreal and Halifax have restricted employment and income circumstances. While relatively poor educational background is undoubtedly a causal factor, the more fundamental issue becomes one of why the educational backgrounds of Blacks are poorer in the first place, especially in Halifax where the overwhelming majority of Blacks are third-generation Canadians and beyond.

It would be disingenuous to discount the subtle and not-so-subtle anti-Black racism in any account of Black poverty, unemployment, and underemployment in Canada. Other visible minorities in Canada face the canker of racial prejudice, as well. However, we contend that the situation with Blacks is patently unique, and, arguably, more damaging for two interrelated reasons. First, Blacks in Canada, as in the United States, are the only people whose ancestors were forcibly removed from their homelands and enslaved in this part of the world. While some are quick to point out that this enslavement occurred centuries ago, its consequences have contemporary manifestations — at least, in terms of persistent negative stereotypes and mythologies — which undermine Blacks' pursuit of a fair share of the proverbial pie in Canadian society. Second, Blacks tend to serve as the discursive polar opposite of the dominant group (i.e., Whites) — primarily, as a result of the racial stereotypes and prejudices of the past — and, consequently, bear the worst forms of skin-color racism and all the negative connotations that "Black" conjures in both the sacred and secular discursive formations in the West (Mensah 2002). The socio-economic and psychological burdens that "Blacks" have to endure, as the designated polar opposite of "Whites," are as numerous as they are onerous. And, as Harper Lee had Atticus say to Scout in *To Kill a Mockingbird*[10]: "You never really understand a person ... until you climb into his skin and walk around in it."

The skin-color racism faced by Blacks in Halifax and Montreal (and, indeed, elsewhere in Canada) is so stealthy and so class- and space-entangled that one is often at a loss to identify the right entry point for its analysis. For a variety of reasons — some personal, others structural; some social, others economic; and some impelled and others voluntary — Blacks in Halifax and Montreal often find themselves in rundown, racially segregated housing in census tracts with high poverty rates (Mensah 2002; Kazemipur and Halli 1997). While such places may provide some social capital for the settlement and integration of new Black immigrants, these same neighborhoods inadvertently feed into the marginalization, pauperization, and the eventual ghettoization of the African Diasporic communities in some parts of our cities. Counter-intuitively, such rundown neighborhoods are not cheap to live in. Indeed, residents tend to pay fairly similar prices for their housing as do "their affluent neighbors, a few streets over" (Preugger, Cook, and Hawkesworth 2004, p. 124). Also, it is not uncommon to find residents of such rundown neighborhoods paying more for auto and residential insurance, grocery, and other urban facilities, because of the relative dearth of these facilities in poor neighborhoods. But for the lack of economic wherewithal, many Blacks would move out of such neighborhoods. Yet, we must also note that many other Blacks take solace in the social network and the sense of belonging such neighborhoods often engender for the racially oppressed. And, as many who are in "a Black skin and walk around in it" would attest to:

> The probability of experiencing racial hostility . . . increases as one moves from friendship settings to such outside sites as the workplace, where a Black person typically has contacts with both acquaintances and strangers, providing an interactive context with greater potential for discrimination. (Feagin 1997, p. 367)

Still, the sheer concentration of Blacks in specific urban neighborhoods — e.g., in the area bounded by the Harbor, North Street, Robie Street and Cogswell Street in Halifax; and LaSalle, St. Leonard and Montreal-Nord in Montreal — exacerbate the social and economic problems of Blacks (See Figures 3.1 and 3.2). This is not only because of the longstanding overlap between race and class in Canada, or what John Porter called *the vertical mosaic*, but also because racism itself is often spatialized through residential segregation and other forms of spatial injustices in the location and allocation of urban resources and their externalities.

As the number of Blacks in specific neighborhoods increases, the available resources dwindle through the suburbanization of non-Blacks as well as the Black middle and upper class. This, in turn, feeds into the depletion of the Black neighborhood's tax base for education, health care, and other social services. With time, the neighborhood becomes crime-ridden and economically depressed, with minuscule employment opportunities, if any at all. The only resources that do not seem to be in short supply in such neighborhoods are the apparatuses of police surveillance and race-based profiling, harassment, and, sometimes, brutality, once the image of a Black crime area solidifies in the mass media and the collective mind of the public (Tator and Frances 2006; Wortley and Tanner 2003 and 2004).

Even so, it is when Blacks venture beyond their immediate residential environment into the world of mainstream education, employment, and the like, do they encounter pervasive racism in all of its subtle and not-so-subtle forms. There are even some indications that the ambiguities surrounding the assessment of immigrants' qualifications and credentials in Canada are often exploited to discriminate against Black immigrants in the job market. In a shrewdly planned and executed experiment, Esses et al. (2007) found that a Black South African immigrant, for instance, bears a greater risk of having his or her skills discounted in Canada than a White South African immigrant with similar qualifications, giving some credence to propositions about Canadian *credentialism as racism*. Such downward mobility-producing credential evaluations and other forms of racial discrimination, which push many Black parents into dirty, dead-end and low-paying jobs, feed into Black children's disillusionment about formal education, with thoughts of any concordance between education and employment finding little, if any, resonance among them. In Montreal, in particular, one finds many well-educated Blacks who cannot find employment beyond taxi-driving, and even here, until recently, there were insidious anti-Black discrimination by members of the public who refused to ride taxis driven by Haitians, and by dispatchers who declined to send Haitian drivers to customers (Hamilton 1990/91).

Figure 3.1.
The Distribution of Blacks in the Halifax CMA.

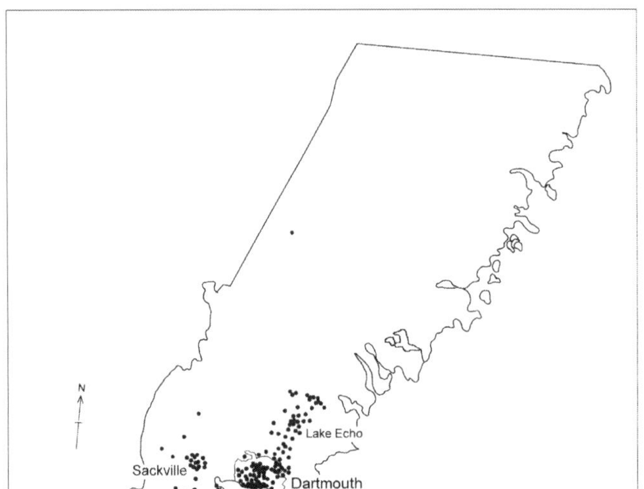

Figure 3.2.
The Distribution of Blacks in the Montreal CMA.

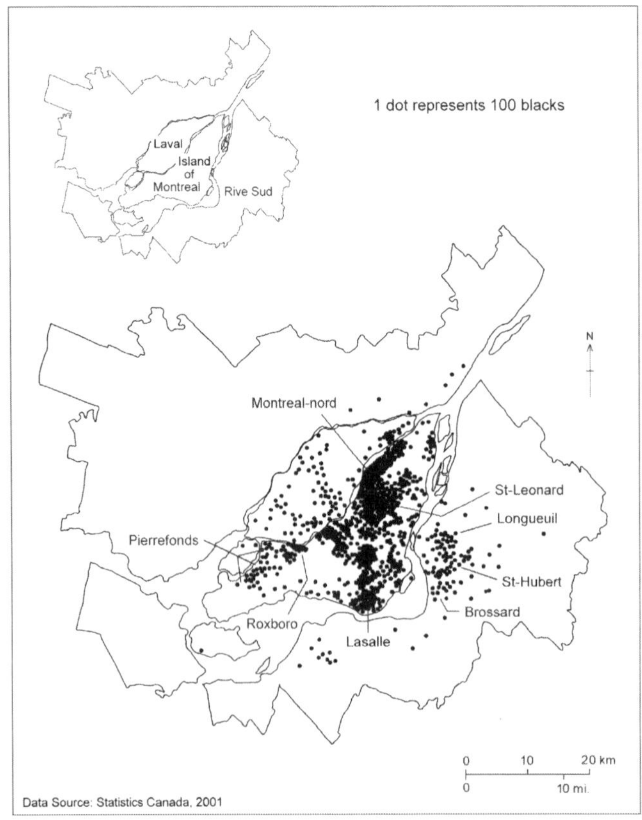

The virtual omnipresence of the stigma of being Black in a White society — and all the psychic, emotional, and socioeconomic burdens that entails — undermines the integration of Blacks into mainstream society, be it in Halifax or Montreal. For instance, Blacks are often followed around, albeit stealthily, in stores; discriminated against in education, housing and employment; and routinely racially-profiled and harassed by the police, especially when driving, yielding the now common intertextual word-play of being arrested for "*driving while Black*." Simply put, Blacks often have to think and strategize about possible responses to racial situations over which their White counterparts hardly ever need to worry, compelling Blacks to develop what some call a "second eye" reminiscence of Du Bois's notion of a "double consciousness." With this "second eye," or a "second antenna" — invariably colored by personal and group experience — many Blacks are constantly assessing situations to see whether infractions are perpetrated against them because people are simply rude/unconcerned, or they are done to them just because they are Black (Feagin 1997). Rather than offering Blacks a genuine self-consciousness, this second-sight just sap their energy, constantly compelling them to react to situations thrust upon them by the outside world. This is how Du Bois (1997, p. 49) put it:

> The second-sight . . . yields him [sic] no true self-consciousness, but only lets him see himself through the revelation of the other world. It is a peculiar sensation, this double-consciousness, this sense of always looking at one's self through the eyes of others, of measuring one's soul by the tape of a world that looks on in amused contempt and pity.

The intricacies of the psychic and socio-economic burdens wrought on Blacks by racial oppression, in general, and the dynamics of this double-consciousness, in particular, have so far escaped the analytical gaze of Canadian social scientists, but the need for more research in this area can hardly be overlooked any longer.

SUMMARY AND CONCLUSION

Blacks have been in both Halifax and Montreal for centuries, with some tracing their roots to the era of slavery in the New World. In both cities, the waves of Black immigration have historically been tied to labor demands in such areas as domestic work, mining, agriculture, and the railways industry. Notwithstanding the long-standing history of the African Diaspora in both Halifax and Montreal, we saw that it was only after the introduction of the "point system" of immigration in 1960s that members of this Diaspora came to Canada in significant numbers. And for reason of geographic proximity, historical ties, official language ability, as well as the network, institutional, and cumulative causation factors implicated in international migration, we noted that Blacks from different countries tend to be drawn to different Canadian cities, with Montreal and Halifax attracting more Black Francophone and Black Anglophones, respectively. Blacks form the largest visible minority group in both Halifax and Montreal, and their physical presence is simply hard to miss, especially in neighborhoods such as Montreal-Nord and LaSalle in Montreal and in the peninsula that extends to the Halifax Harbor in Halifax.

Unsurprisingly, we noted some similarities among the two Black Diasporic communities under consideration, especially in terms of their long-standing history; their spatial concentration in specific city neighborhoods; the preponderance of women amongst them; and their predominantly Christian religiosity. Still there are some major differences worthy of note, lest one falls into the homogenizing tendencies of many previous studies. For instance, whereas Montreal attracts most of the Francophone members of the African Diaspora, Halifax has more affinity for Anglophones. Also, the African Diaspora in Halifax is far more "indigenous," than the one in Montreal, with many members of the former having roots that are traceable to the third generation and even beyond. Moreover, we noted that even though Haligonians, as a whole, have slightly better educational attainments than Montréalers, the opposite is true when one zeros in on members of the African Diaspora in both cities; still, we found the employment chances of Africans in Halifax to be relatively better than their counterparts in Montreal. On the whole, the African Diasporic communities in both Montreal and Halifax exhibited poor employment and income backgrounds than other visible minorities, than the general population, in their respective cities, prompting us to look into the entanglements of race, class, and space in Canadian society for some preliminary explanatory insights.

Acknowledgement

We would like to thank Ms. Carolyn King (Cartographer at the Department of Geography, York University, Toronto), for making the two maps included in this chapter. We are also indebted to the Ghana Institute of Management and Public Administration (GIMPA) for hosting Professor Joseph Mensah during his sabbatical in Ghana — when this chapter was finalized.

NOTES

[1] This quote is from an excerpt from W. E. B. Du Bois's *The Souls of Black Folk,* in Diana Kendall (ed. 1997), *Race, Class, and Gender in a Diverse Society: A Text-Reader,* p. 52.

[2] We refer to these as "the entangled burdens of *race*, class, and space," in our sub-title.

[3] This is a self-identified, ethno-racial designation commonly used in the national census as one of many categories of the nation's visible minority population; this definition facilitates the use of empirical data from the national census.

[4] The Maroons were descendants of fugitive Jamaican slaves who engaged in a series of battles against the British for their independence. Many believe the Maroons were slaves from the famous Ashanti tribe of Ghana, well known for their fierce battles against British imperialism in the Gold Coast, now Ghana (Mensah 2002, p. 48).

[5] With the election of Jean Lesage's Liberal Party in 1960, Quebec moved in a new direction commonly referred to as the Quite Revolution in Quebec's history. As part of the Revolution, the government took a more nationalistic stance and created a more powerful civil service that allowed Francophones access to the middle and senior positions often denied them in the private sector.

[6] Cameroon has English and French as co-official languages, while Ghana is officially Anglophone.

[7] With more than 600 different languages spoken across Africa alone (de Blij 1993), it would be unreasonable to expect any linguistic uniformity among continental African immigrants, in particular. While the linguistic diversity among Caribbean immigrants is not as overwhelming, there is still no doubt that the African Diasporic communities in both Halifax and Montreal are patently multilingual. It is only by way of Canada's official languages could we bring any semblance of homogeneity to the exceedingly heterogeneous world of languages among the African Diaspora in this country.

[8] The language-employability relationship seems to have changed in the post-911 era, most notably for people of the Islamic faith.

[9] Canada is a largely Christian country (77 percent), with 43.6 Roman Catholic and 29.2 percent Protestant. The majority (54.8 percent) of Blacks in Canada also are Christian, with Black Protestants being the largest group (41.1 percent). Just under 3 percent of Canadian Blacks are Catholic, one quarter of Black Canadians claim "other" (non Christian, non-Jewish, non-Muslim) religious affiliations. A very small number with historic ties to India via the Caribbean and Eastern African nations such as Uganda and Tanzania hold "Eastern" religious beliefs.

[10] Ironically, in this novel set in Maycomb, Alabama, in the 1930s, a Black man by the name Tom Robinson was sent to prison for a rape he did not commit. He was shot to death by a prison guard on an alleged attempt by him to escape. Atticus, was a conscientious White lawyer, the father of Scout and Jem, who defended Tom Robinson at the trail made up of an all-White jury.

Chapter 4

The African Diaspora: Historical and Contemporary Immigration and Employment Practices in Toronto

JOE T. DARDEN

INTRODUCTION

Toronto, Canada's most ethnically and racially diverse CMA, has served as a magnet for people of African descent. Statistics Canada (2006) recorded 310,500 Blacks living in the Toronto CMA in 2001, 7 percent of the total population, and the highest proportion among Canada's CMAs.[1] As of 2001, 178,250 (57 percent) of Toronto's Blacks were immigrants, and 73 percent of these foreign-born Blacks were from the Caribbean. The highest proportion came from Jamaica, with others from Guyana, Trinidad and Tobago, Barbados, and Granada (Milan and Tran 2004).

Statistics Canada provides data on the ethnic origin population by CMA. In the Toronto CMA, Jamaicans constituted 150,840 of the total number of people of African descent. Other West Indians totaled 40,600, with 38,215 considering themselves Guyanese. Although Black immigrants from Africa constitute the smallest percentage, their numbers are increasing.

Before 1967, it was very difficult or near impossible for Black immigrants to enter and settle in Toronto. Table 4.1 shows a 13 percent increase in people of African descent in Toronto from 1996 to 2001. The African population increased from 68,256 to 84,020, (23 percent), the highest increase among people of African descent. The smallest increase was among the Caribbean Blacks, who increased by 9.6 percent. Caution is advised in interpreting these changes due to changes in definitions of groups by Statistics Canada.

BARRIER TO ENTRY: CANADA'S RACIST IMMIGRATION POLICY

To understand the African Diaspora and its association with Toronto, one must understand various barriers people of African descent have faced from the pre-1967 period to the present. Canada's pre-1967 immigration was motivated by White supremacy, and dictated decisions on which groups of immigrants could become permanent residents of Canada. People of color in general, and Black people in particular, were viewed as mentally, physically, and socially inferior — a permanent "social problem" if admitted to Canada. This view, which motivated immigration policy, was based on the myth that Black people were biologically incapable of adjusting to the Canadian climate and culturally incapable of assimilating into Canadian society (Calliste 1991; Satzewich 1989; Winks 1971). With respect to assimilation, Canadian officials feared that an influx of Black immigrants would cause race problems similar to those experienced in the United States and Britain (Satzewich 1991).

Consistent with the ideology of White supremacy, immigration officials viewed Blacks as inherently suited for domestic work or other low level, "degrading" jobs at the bottom of the labor market. Canadian immigration officials justified restricting the entry of professional and skilled Black workers on the grounds that White Canadians were not accustomed to seeing Black people in positions that would place them on the same economic and social levels as Whites (Smith 1957). Therefore, Canadian immigration officials gave preference to Northern Europeans specifically, and other White Europeans generally and virtually excluded people of color, specifically Asians and Blacks (Palmer 1976).

Thus, except for a few West Indian and African Americans who were allowed to enroll as students in Canadian universities (Hill 1960), most Black immigrants in Toronto before 1967 came from the Caribbean under special contractual arrangements to satisfy the labor needs of Canada. Most Blacks came to Toronto as domestics or nurses (Darden 2004). Those who came as domestics arrived via the Caribbean Domestic Scheme.

Table 4.1.
People of African Descent in the Toronto CMA, 1996 and 2001.

Group	1996	2001	Percent Change
Total Blacks (Based on visible minority* category)	274,425	310,500	13.2
African**	68,256	84,020	23.0
Caribbean**	168,948	185,092	9.6

Source: Statistics Canada. 2001. Public Use Samples (PUMF). Ottawa: Minister of Industry.
* According to the definition provided by the employment equity act and used by Statistics Canada, visible minorities are persons (other than Aboriginal persons), who are non-Caucasian in race or non-White in color (Statistics Canada 1997).
** Based on ethnic origin, which refers to the ethnic or cultural origins of the person's ancestors. Ancestry is not the language the group speaks and it should not be confused with citizenship or nationality (Statistics Canada 2001).

The Caribbean Domestic Scheme

What was this domestic scheme and what was the Canadian policy regulating it? First, it was a domestic work program. The Caribbean Domestic Scheme was a worker program to import domestic women workers from the Caribbean region. Under this program, single women of good health between 18 and 40 years of age with no dependents and at least a grade eight education were accepted into Canada as landed immigrants on the condition that they would spend at least one year as domestic workers before being free to choose other types of work (Arnopoulos 1979).

Before 1955, Canada's domestic work program recruited primarily White women. Women of color were conspicuously absent, reflecting Canada's broader racially exclusive immigration policies at that time (Daenzer 1993). The pre-1955 era, characterized by the exclusion of women of color (especially from the West Indies) in the immigrant domestic work program, changed after the Second World War. Following the War, fewer women from Britain (Canada's preferred choice) immigrated to Canada to work as domestics. This created a labor shortage which forced Canada to find a new source of domestic labor. It thus became difficult for Canada to continue to deny women of color entry into the program.

Many Canadian White women were pleased because they viewed Caribbean women as a "cheap" source of servant labor. However, Canadian immigration officials realized that to admit Caribbean women would be contrary to Canada's racially exclusive immigration policies. Nevertheless, the policy decision was made May 10, 1955 (Dawson 1955). In June of 1955, 100 Black women from the British West Indies were approved for admission to Canada as domestics. Between 1955 and 1960, an average of 300 Black women domestics was admitted to Canada annually. Between 1960 and 1965 the number had increased to 1,000 Black domestics per year (Bolaria and Li 1985).

The advent of the Caribbean Domestic Scheme marked the gradual shift from a predominantly White European labor pool in domestic service to one in which the majority consisted of women of color. Although Canada did not have the widespread tradition of Black enslavement, the ideology of White supremacy was just as ingrained in Canadian society as it was in America. As Stouffer (1984) reveals in his assessment of the views of Ontario journalists in the 19th century, "Blacks, it seemed, were fit merely to become the 'good servants' of Whites who were their natural leaders and guides." The degraded status of domestic work and people of color was mutually reinforcing as women of color became identified with the occupation in Canada (Macklin 1994).

The domestic scheme was virtually the only way Black women could enter Canada during the mid-fifties, since Black Caribbean women were barred from entering Canada through normal channels. At this time, Canada still actively discouraged people of color as immigrants (Daenzer 1993).

Although the formal scheme was abolished in 1966, certain components continued in revised form in all subsequent immigration policies. It is important to note that the *single women only* aspect (i.e., without family commitments) of the policy remained a key future throughout its existence (Daenzer 1993), thus ensuring that their loyalty was thus to the White master. Canadian officials discouraged the sponsorship by Black domestics of any of their family members (Calliste 1991).

The only right granted to the Black women domestics from the Caribbean upon their arrival in Canada was the right of full landed status, however, this was a right in principle only. Unlike the policy of *inclusion* for White domestics from Germany, Italy, and Greece, the Canadian government issued a carefully worded policy which set the Black women apart in social status and privilege and thus redefined their citizenship (Daenzer 1993, p. 53). The Canadian government carried out a policy agreement with the Caribbean nations which treated Caribbean women differently, rendering them to the lowest status within the occupational hierarchy where the potential for exploitation was greatest.

Domestic work was different from other occupations because of its depressive dead end nature. It included long hours, few opportunities for training and advancement regardless of years of service, little economic security for periods of illness and old age, and had a social stigma attached to the work (Canada Employment Immigration 1981).

The nuclear patriarchal family was regarded as the norm in Canada. Men, not women, were expected to be the primary wage earners. However, Caribbean Black women were to be single and not sponsor any mates or relatives. Canadian immigration policies regarding Blacks from the Caribbean resulted in rejection of applicants with spouses and/or children. Thus, Canadian immigration policy forced Black families to evolve in a way that ran counter to the established norm (Petrykanyn 1989).

In addition to the single and childless policy requirement, the age requirement was important to ensure "physical suitability" to perform the "backbreaking" nature of domestic work (Darden 2004, p. 52). The Caribbean Domestic Scheme was replaced by the Foreign Domestic Workers program in 1981 and later the Live-in Caregiver Program (a revised version of the Foreign Domestic Workers program) in 1992.

From 1982 to 1990, the total number of women admitted as domestic workers increased to almost 11,000 (Canada Employment and Immigration 1991). By 1996 the total number of domestic workers had declined, but Caribbean women still constituted 9.6 percent of the total (Statistics Canada 1998).

Toronto was the final destination for many of these women. Prior to 1961, of the Black women from the Caribbean and Bermuda who settled in Canada, 43 percent settled in Toronto. From 1961 through 1996, the majority, i.e., more than 50 percent of all immigrant women from the Caribbean, chose Toronto as their destination (Statistics Canada 1998). Today, the Philippines, which comprises 68 percent of Program participants, surpasses all other regions as the predominant country of origin for domestic workers in Canada.

In sum, Canadian immigration policy regulating Caribbean entry to Canada has excluded Black men and families, and has been biased in favor of Black women. This biased nature has disproportionately restricted Black men and created a gender imbalance, with Black women far exceeding Black men. Moreover, Black women were required to be single. Such policy restrictions have had a serious impact on the Black family structure unlike that of any other immigrant group. The outcome has been a disproportionate number of Black female-headed households (Ornstein 2000; Galabuzi 2005).

Thus, the present Black family structure, with its high proportion of lone female Black parents, is directly linked to Canadian immigration policy regulating Caribbean Black entry to Canada, in general, and Toronto, in particular (Darden 2006). It was this policy that required Black women to disconnect from their roles as mothers, partners, and caregivers in their own families, and become resources that nurtured White Canadian families (Shingadia 1975; Stasiulis 1987).

CANADA'S POST-1967 IMMIGRATION POLICY AND THE CHARACTERISTICS OF BLACK IMMIGRANTS

After Canada removed its racially-restrictive barrier to immigration, it replaced it with a class-based policy. Using a point system, Canada gives priority to immigrants who are highly educated and skilled and speak English or French. Under Canada's system, 67 points on a 100 point test is generally a passing score for entry (Mason and Preston 2007).

As more Black immigrants have arrived in Toronto since the 1980s, the Black population has remained gender-imbalanced (females outnumber males), fragmented, more diverse, and more educated. What these Black immigrants brought with them (social capital, e.g., education and skills), are theoretically important in enhancing their ability to secure employment and increase their earnings. Data from Statistics Canada (2006) revealed that in 2001, foreign-born Blacks of prime working age (25–54) were more likely to have a college degree than the total foreign-born population. However, the total foreign-born population was more likely than the Black foreign-born population to have a university degree (Milan and Tran 2004). However, Canadian-born Blacks are as educated (college and university degrees) as other Canadian-born groups. Despite equal education (i.e., social capital), such an asset for Blacks, whether foreign-born or Canadian-born, does not translate into equal employment or income. Foreign-born Blacks had an age-standardized unemployment rate that was higher than the age standardized unemployment rate for the total foreign population. Moreover, the age standardized unemployment rate for Canadian-born Blacks was also higher than the age standardized unemployment rate for the total Canadian-born population.

Although Canadian-born Blacks, ages 25–54, were just as likely to be university educated as the total Canadian population in the same age group, Canadian-born Blacks' average employment rate was lower. Although there is little difference between the educational attainment of foreign-born Blacks and the total foreign born, the former earned less in employment income (Milan and Tran 2004). Past studies suggest that the gap in unemployment rates and earnings may be due to racial discrimination.

Full-time women workers in Toronto, regardless of racial/ethnic group, have a lower median income than men ($27,000 compared to $31,000). In addition, female-alone parents, regardless of racial/ethnic group, have a lower median income, a higher incidence of poverty, and a lower homeownership rate than either couples or male-alone parents (Ornstein 2000). Black, African and Caribbean full-time women workers have a lower median employment income compared to other women full-time workers. Black women's income from full-time employment is $18,000 compared to $27,000 for all women workers, making it 66 percent of the median income of all women workers, i.e., the lowest median income of any racial/ethnic group in Toronto (Ornstein 2000). Also, Black, African and Caribbean female-alone parents with children under 19 (with the exception of Middle Easterners, West Asians, and Latin Americans) have the highest incidence of poverty. Finally, Black, African, and Caribbean families have the lowest homeownership rate compared to other families (Darden and Kamel 2000).

According to Henry (1994), as a group Caribbean people in Toronto do less well on a number of economic indicators than do other groups. They earn lower incomes and have a lower homeownership rate and higher poverty rates, due, in part, to a higher proportion of families headed by single females (Henry 1994).

BARRIERS TO BLACK EMPLOYMENT: THE TYPES OF RACIAL DISCRIMINATION

Unlike the United States, racial discrimination in employment in Canada is difficult to detect. Canada has a tradition of denying that racial workplace discrimination occurs, thus any discrimination that does occur is more likely to be subtle than overt. Canadians are likely to state, "There is no discrimination here. We are just one big happy family" (Billingsly and Muszynski 1985).

Evidence of Racial Discrimination in Employment: Past Studies

Compared with other multi-racial, White-dominated societies such as Britain and the United States, studies of Canadian racial discrimination in employment are limited. Some of the most relevant studies, reviewed here, used the following methods to detect racial discrimination: (1) complaints from those persons who feel or perceive that they have been discriminated against; (2) audits or tests to assess the direct behavior of employers to determine whether they treat employees differently; and (3) regression analysis to determine how much racial differences in occupation can be explained by such factors as education and experience among Blacks and Whites.

Perception of Discrimination in Employment by Blacks

In 1974, Wilson Head conducted surveys of 210 Black adults in Metropolitan Toronto, sampling populations from all socioeconomic levels. In response to the major question "To what extent do you feel that discrimination exists against Blacks in Metropolitan Toronto?" 76.3 percent felt that there was discrimination against Blacks in the area of employment. Of this percentage, 36 percent felt that there was a great amount of discrimination, the highest percentage of all areas. A larger percentage of West Indian Black respondents (39.5 percent) than Canadian-born Blacks (14 percent) felt there was a great amount of discrimination in employment (Head 1975).

Breton (1981) examined the perceptions and experiences of several ethnic groups in Toronto. West Indian Blacks and Chinese had the highest percentages of respondents who perceived discrimination in employment as a very serious or somewhat serious problem. Indeed, a large majority of the West Indians surveyed (72 percent) perceived discrimination in employment to be a serious problem. Among the Chinese, 24 percent perceived discrimination in employment as a serious problem. For the non-visible minority groups in the study, 22 percent of Italians and 17 percent of Jews and Portuguese perceived it as a serious problem.

When asked about personal experience with discrimination, the responses from West Indians and Chinese were about equal. Twenty-eight percent of West Indian respondents and 29 percent of Chinese respondents said they had personally experienced discrimination. A smaller percentage of non-visible minority groups said they had personally experienced it.

In 1989, Kasozi conducted a survey of a representative sample of 250 Black African immigrants who had been surveyed in 1986 to define their employment and adjustment needs in the Toronto CMA. Of those surveyed, 23 percent said they were discriminated against because of race or color when searching for a job (Kasozi 1989).

One of the weaknesses of perceived discrimination studies, especially perceptions of discrimination by Blacks from Africa, the Caribbean, or Canada, is the subjective definition of discrimination. Some respondents may not interpret an action as discriminatory, while another may interpret the same action very differently and perceive the full burden of discrimination. Thus, each person has a different threshold or tolerance for discrimination (Young 1992).

Another category of study examines the actual behavior of employers. Such studies are much more effective in detecting discrimination.

Audits or Paired Tests of Discrimination

Racial discrimination in employment is best documented using tests or audits resembling "natural" experiments. The first major study to use this approach to assess employment discrimination was Henry and Ginzberg's (1985) *Who Gets the Work*. The authors defined discrimination as those practices or attitudes, willful or unintentional, which have the effect of limiting the rights of an individual or group to economic opportunities because of irrelevant traits such as skin color. In this study, employment discrimination as it occurs at the point of selection was tested by actually sending job seekers into the employment arena. Two forms of field testing were employed. First, teams of job applicants, matched with respect to age, sex, educational, and employment histories, were sent to answer advertisements for jobs as listed in the classified section of a major Toronto newspaper. Each applicant carried resumés which had been carefully constructed to meet the requirements of the jobs being tested. The job applicants were as similar to each other as possible and the majority of them were professional actors who assumed the various roles required for the different jobs tested. The only major difference between the testers was that of race.

This study of racial discrimination in employment was guided by two questions: (1) is there a difference in the number of jobs offered to White and Black applicants of similar backgrounds when they applied for the same job; and (2) are there any differences in the ways in which White and Black applicants are treated during the contact or interview situation with the employer? Both questions were tested by means of direct person-to-person job applications and by telephone inquiries by persons using foreign accents and names asking if an advertised job were still available. Racial discrimination was said to occur when the White applicants received a greater proportion of job offers and were called back for a second interview in greater proportions than the Black applicants, and when the White applicants were treated fairly and courteously, and the Black applicants were accorded rude or blatantly hostile treatment.

The authors' sample consisted of 201 cases using the direct in-person method and 237 cases using the phone method. The results for the in-person method revealed testers received 46 job offers. There were 10 cases in which both Black and White testers received offers. However, of the remainder of cases in which offers were made, 27 went to Whites compared to only nine offers to Blacks. Using a chi-square test, the authors concluded that this difference could not have occurred by chance and that racial discrimination was a factor in the results. These findings clearly indicate that Whites and Blacks do not have equal access to employment in Toronto. Racial discrimination in employment, in the form of clearly favoring White applicants over Black ones with equivalent resumés, took place in almost 25 percent of all job contacts tested in this study.

When the results of the telephone testing were examined, the pattern of discrimination was revealed again. Over half of the employers contacted practiced some form of discrimination against one or more of the callers. Blacks from the West Indies were told that jobs were closed or no longer available in 36 percent of the cases. The White immigrant Canadians were told that jobs were not available 31 percent of the time, whereas White non-immigrant Canadians were told that jobs were closed in only 13 percent of the cases tested. The authors concluded that there is a considerable amount of racial discrimination in employment in Toronto (Henry and Ginzberg 1985).

In sum, in 1985 a large majority of Toronto employers had no policies to prevent discrimination or promote employment equity. Moreover, they did not want such policies and claimed that they were not needed (Billingsly and Muszynski 1985).

Testing Black Employment Discrimination using Regression Analysis

Unlike the United States, prior research on racial discrimination against Blacks and other (visible) minorities in the occupational structure in Canada is limited (Darden 2005). Research in this area has its origin in the rigid ethnic stratification revealed by Porter (1965) with its domination by Canadians of British origin within a vertical mosaic. Although some researchers are convinced that ethnicity is no longer a barrier to social and occupational mobility in Canada (Isajiw, Sev'er and Dreidger 1993), other researchers have provided evidence that Canada has indeed retained a vertical mosaic based on color (Agocs and Boyd 1993; Geschwender and Guppy 1995). These authors suggest that whereas ethnic stratification has lessened among White European groups, differences between racial minority groups have persisted and that Canada's modern day mosaic is, in effect, one based principally on skin color.

This position is reinforced by Lian and Matthews (1998), who examined 1991 census data on ethnicity and income differences within educational categories and came to the following conclusion. By 1991, for the majority of ethnic groups in Canada from all parts of Europe, there was very little evidence of inequality due to discrimination against any one group. On the other hand, there is clear evidence that visible minorities have not fared well in Canada. When education and a range of other social variables were controlled for, visible minorities continued to have below average earnings, while those of European origin had above average earnings. Further, Ogmundson and McLaughlin (1992), who argue strongly that ethnic stratification is now minimal, suggest that such equality may not extend to Blacks due to racial discrimination.

In 1990, Reitz examined occupational status inequalities among selected White ethnic groups and West Indians in Toronto. Employing regression analysis, the author found that West Indians had a different experience in the labor market than the selected White ethnic groups (Germans, Ukrainians, Italians, Jews, and Portuguese). For the White groups, job qualifications explained their occupational status. For West Indians, however, job qualifications did not explain their low occupational status. Reitz concluded that there was "status" discrimination against West Indians who have high levels of education but low occupational status. For West Indian men, there was a status disadvantage of between 4 and 5 points after adjustments for qualifications. For West Indian women, the status disadvantage after adjustments was 10 points (Reitz 1990). The author concluded, therefore, that there was evidence of discrimination against West Indians.

OCCUPATIONAL INEQUALITY BETWEEN BLACKS AND WHITES IN THE TORONTO CMA

The key question "To what extent is race a factor in the denial of employment to Blacks?" was examined in previous research employing ordered probit regression (Darden 2005). The analysis controlled for demographic characteristics and qualifications of Blacks and Whites to determine the effect of race on occupational achievement. The results revealed that, other things being equal, the predicted probability of occupational achievement for *Black males* is 0.3 percent less than the CMA average, 0.9 percent more for *Black females*, and 5.7 percent more for *White females*. In other words, *Black males* tend to be in lower-level jobs, while *Black females* and *White females* are more likely to be in higher level jobs. Unlike the case of *Black males*, being a *Black female* or *White female* increases the probability of occupational achievement (Darden 2005).

While acknowledging that gender is also important in explaining occupational achievement in the Toronto CMA, the results of the research support the hypothesis that race has a significant effect on the level of occupational achievement of Black males and females, even when they have the same characteristics as Whites (i.e., education, experience, immigration status). Under the assumption that Black people, like White people, are rational and seek higher-level jobs to maximize their utility, the results indicate that racial discrimination does exist. Discrimination by employers places White males at an advantage in the job market (qualifications notwithstanding). On the other hand, Black females, followed by White females, were preferred by employers for higher-level jobs over Black males. Discrimination by employers negatively influenced Black males' chances of occupational achievement more than other groups, and is responsible for the lack of occupational achievement, rather than differences in education, experience, and immigration status. Generalization of the results, however, is limited to the Black and White population of the Toronto CMA. However, overall, the pattern observed in the Canadian context is somewhat similar to a pattern of racial differential treatment observed for decades in the United States' labor market by other researchers (Schmidt and Strauss 1975a, 1975b, Schmitz, Williams, and Gabriel 1994).

Past research using probit regression has revealed evidence of discrimination and differential treatment in the Toronto CMA's labor market, especially against Black males. Discrimination occurs despite the existence within the federal government of what Canada calls employment equity, i.e., the legal requirement for diversity in the Canadian workplace which has existed since 1986 and which corresponds (albeit only very loosely) to affirmative action programs in the United States (Agocs, Burr, Somerset, and Balkin 1993).

Employment Equity vs. Affirmative Action

Research in the United States provides sound evidence that affirmative action does work if done properly, i.e., targeted to address specific under-representation levels where White and minority or women applicants have similar qualifications. Several examples exist. Thomas (2000) conducted a study of Los Angeles based on interviews of hiring officials, half of whom were subject to affirmative action regulations. The study found that employers subject to affirmative action regulations modified the way they advertised job openings, and screened applicants from a pool of candidates, such that the underrepresented group (Blacks) was more likely to obtain employment. Importantly, these modifications resulted in hiring qualified Blacks over qualified Whites. The study concluded by suggesting that affirmative action regulations can represent an effective public policy for mitigating racial inequality in the labor market (Thomas 2000).

In an issue of the *Journal of Economic Literature*, Holzer and Neumark (2000) reviewed more than 200 scientific studies of affirmative action. The authors concluded that affirmative action produces tangible benefits for women and minority workers and for the overall economy. Employers who adopted an affirmative action policy increased the relative number of women and minority employees by an average of 10–15 percent.

Moreover, the authors found little credible evidence that affirmative action appointees performed badly or diminished the overall performance of the economy. Thus, the argument against affirmative action based on inefficiency is weak. Women hired under affirmative action, according to the authors, largely matched their male counterparts on credentials and performance. Blacks and Hispanics hired under affirmative action generally lagged behind on credentials, such as education, but usually performed about as well as White employees. Nevertheless, some critics argue that affirmative action creates a divisive workplace.

Dovidio and Gaertner (1996) described ways to reduce inter-group conflict and tension surrounding affirmative action. The authors examined unintentional bias, which can produce barriers to the employment and advancement of well-qualified members of historically disadvantaged groups. The researchers argued that affirmative action policies address contemporary, subtle racial biases more effectively than passive equal opportunity policies because the former emphasize outcomes, the latter emphasize intentions (i.e., good faith). The affirmative action policies also provide unambiguous standards of behavior, and establish monitoring systems that ensure accountability.

However, Canada preferred not to use the American concept of affirmative action, opting instead for the softer term "employment equity." Under the original Employment Equity Act of 1986, employers under federal jurisdiction were required to consult with employee representatives and implement employment equity by identifying and eliminating practices not authorized by law that resulted in employment barriers against persons in designated groups. Employers were also required to institute positive practices and policies and to make reasonable accommodation to ensure that designated group members would achieve a degree of representation in the various positions of employment that was at least proportionate to their respective representation in the workforce or those segments of the workforce identifiable by qualifications, eligibility, or geography from which the employer might be expected to draw or promote employees.

Despite the fact that the act covered only 5 percent of Canadian employees (hardly enough to make much impact), the act met with great resistence (MacAulay 1998). Following resistance and criticism of the 1986 Act (Redway 1992), a new employment equity act was implemented in 1996. The new legislation introduced measures specifying what actions employers are not required to take to achieve employment equity. For example, employers are not obligated to take measures that would: (1) result in undue hardship on the part of the employer; (2) obligate the employer to hire or promote unqualified persons; (3) require the employer to hire or promote without regard to merit; (4) obligate the employer to create new positions in their workforce; or (5) require the employer to hire or promote according to quotas (Tremblay 1996). It appears from data on occupational achievement that employment equity has been working to some extent on behalf of White women (Darden 2005). There is little to no evidence, however, that the Federal Employment Equity Act has been effective for Black men in Toronto.

To be sure, affirmative action or employment equity should be easier to implement in Canada, given its restrictive immigration policy which selects the educated and the experienced. Given this pool, the government must identify those employers who continue to discriminate in hiring and promoting Blacks, especially Black males, to professional and managerial positions and enforce stronger anti-discrimination measures. Only when employees are hired and promoted based on merit, and not discriminated against based on race and gender, will the full incorporation and utilization of Blacks into the Toronto CMA labor market occur. However, Black immigrants from Africa and the Caribbean also face a more hidden barrier to employment. Their educational credentials are often not recognized by their potential employers.

SOPHISTICATED INSTITUTIONALIZED DISCRIMINATION: THE NON-RECOGNITION OF FOREIGN CREDENTIALS

A long-standing discriminatory issue that continues to negatively affect Black immigrants and refugees in Toronto, and Canada, in general, relates to having Provincial bodies recognize the immigrants' professional and educational credentials. Some Black immigrants include health professionals, skilled trades workers, and teachers. Although trained and experienced, due to Canada's credentialing barrier, they are prevented from putting their knowledge and experience to use in Toronto. Thus, many of these new Black immigrants and refugees are underemployed for long periods (Canadian Human Rights Commission 1998).

The issue of foreign credentials as a barrier to the employment of immigrants has been recognized by immigrants of color for many years, but the Provincial governments of Canada have not taken significant action to remove them. Twenty years after Canada changed its racially discriminatory immigration policy, credentials barriers to employment were still noted by Blacks and other people of color in Toronto. During the early 1980s, Blacks and others continued to request a comprehensive investigation of the issue of non-recognition of foreign credentials. The Ontario government eventually agreed to conduct a review.

The government hired Abt Associates of Canada, a research consulting firm, to conduct the study in 1987. The specific purpose of the investigation was to identify entry requirements for trades and professions which appear as barriers for those trained outside of Canada and which have a disproportionately negative impact on members of minority or ethnic groups (Abt Associates of Canada 1987).

Respondents identified a large number of professions that pose barriers. Medicine and teaching were identified as problems by the majority of those interviewed, followed by engineering, nursing, law, dentistry, and architecture. Fewer respondents mentioned entry barriers in the trades. Those trades mentioned as having barriers were auto mechanics, electricians, millwrights, hairdressers, welders, and watch makers. Discrimination was the major barrier for immigrants. The general perception was that those who were granted credentials equivalent to Canada were from White-dominated countries, particularly England, the United States, and Australia (Darden 2004).

The study concluded that: (1) entry requirements have a disproportionate impact on minority and ethnic groups, and (2) systemic, administrative, economic, and cultural or racial barriers exist.

The granting of equivalencies favors White-dominated countries, and a perception exists that unless one is trained in a White-dominated country, Canadian-trained professionals and trades people are automatically superior to the foreign trained. This is demonstrated by the use of the term "upgrading" when evaluating the foreign trained from non-White dominated countries (Abt Associates 1987).

In 1988, McDade issued a report entitled *Barriers to Recognition of the Credentials of Immigrants in Canada* that assessed the processes by which immigrants seek recognition of their credentials in Canada. Immigrants who wish to work in Canada must establish the value or equivalence of their qualifications in terms of Canadian standards, and must seek academic equivalency. Second, they must seek credit for relevant work experience in their country of origin. For skilled workers, this involves the additional step of achieving recognition of certification in a trade or profession. Finally, the responsibility for assessing the qualification of immigrants rests with each Province's educational system and employment regulations.

A variety of evaluative procedures have been established in the professions to assess the competence of candidates who have not received their training and work experience in the province of Ontario. After a review of entry requirements, McDade (1988) concluded that in Ontario, weaknesses in the processes could have a disproportionately negative impact on members of minority and ethnic groups who were trained outside Canada. These weaknesses were in most cases attributable to subjective methods of evaluation. The use of objective means of evaluating candidates would remove many of the potential barriers by eliminating the opportunity for bias in the consideration of visible minorities for employment.

In 1989, Peter Cumming chaired the Task Force on Access to Professions and Trades in Ontario. The Task Force was charged with reviewing all rules and practices affecting entry to professions and trades to determine whether they have an actual or potential discriminatory effect on persons with training or experience from outside of Canada. The Task Force found widespread and generalized evidence of discriminatory practices (Cumming, Enid, and Dimitrios 1989). Despite the recommendations of the Task Force in 1989, by 1994 the issue still had not been resolved. Also in 1994, Mata issued a detailed report declaring that Canada's distinction between accredited and non-accredited universities (i.e., place of education) may be indicative of discriminatory practices that contradict the equal rights code in the Charter of Rights and Freedoms. He noted that the economic integration of immigrants is crucial not only to their survival, but is a considerable if not controlling factor to integration in other spheres of life. Mata (1994) further concluded that the issue of non-accreditation affects not only the individual applicant, but also society as a whole. It has an impact on the economy, race and ethnic relations, and human rights. More importantly, according to Mata (1994), non-accreditation imposes macroeconomic costs on Canadian society in terms of income, taxes, and unemployment payments, not to mention the colossal waste of human resources due to labor market inefficiency.

Seven years after Cumming's PLAN recommendation, Maraj's (1996) thesis on foreign educated, immigrant professionals found that professionals from non-White countries continue to have more barriers and to face more discrimination than simply their education and training per se. In 2005, Jeff Reitz prepared a report for the Institute for Research on Public Policy. The objectives of the report were to examine the significance of immigrant skills underutilization and the repercussions of declining employment prospects for new immigrants, and finally to identify any institutional obstacles and constraints that must be addressed to forge an effective immigrant skill utilization policy (Reitz 2005). Reitz determined the economic impact of skills underutilization. Foreign-educated immigrants earn $2.4 billion less than native born Canadians in Canada as a whole. Overall earnings disadvantages and the extent of skill underutilization are greater for immigrants who are Black, or who belong to a racial minority group, than they are for those who are White or of European origin. Thus, qualified and skilled Black immigrants appear to have difficulty gaining access to work in knowledge occupations, and end up working in less-skilled occupations than do comparably qualified Canadian-born groups (Reitz 2005). Racial minorities encounter even greater barriers to managerial occupations than the professional occupations. Black immigrants who gain access to professional fields are often barred from further promotion to the more lucrative senior management roles (Reitz 2005). Reitz (2005) concluded that these barriers to managerial jobs lead to earnings disadvantages and disproportionate poverty. It may also lead to higher unemployment (Galabuzi 2006), segregated labor market participation, and differential access to housing and segregated neighborhoods (Darden and Kamel 2000; Galabuzi 2005).

CONCLUSIONS

This chapter has examined equality in the workforce over time, and discrimination barriers to equality of employment and occupational integration for Canadians of African descent in the Toronto CMA. Based on data from Statistics Canada and a review of previous research, we conclude that people of African descent have faced racially restrictive immigration policies that reduced their access to Toronto and shaped their family structure. Once allowed to settle in Toronto, the two major barriers to integration in the workplace were racial discrimination and the non-recognition of their educational credentials. Although educated and trained (the requirements to enter Canada), many immigrants from Africa and the Caribbean have continued to have difficulty connecting their education and training into a job that is comparable to their level of education and skills. These barriers have resulted in lower wages, higher poverty, and unemployment for African and Caribbean immigrants, while racial discrimination against Blacks, including those born in Canada, has led to a lower quality of life for Blacks in Toronto compared to many other groups.

Implications for Public Policies

These results suggest that the Federal Employment Equity Act passed in 1986 to eliminate barriers for women and minorities and promote access to all levels of jobs has not succeeded. The representation of people of African descent has continued to be below the benchmarks set by the federal government. Moreover, not a single government department or agency received a "notable" rating on employment equity according to a recent government-wide performance report on employment equity (Doyle 2007) despite the government of Canada's *A Canada for All: Canada's Action Plan Against Racism*, which is designed to assist victims and groups vulnerable to racism and other forms of discrimination (Government of Canada 2005). In a recent survey, 32 percent of Black Canadians reported that they had been discriminated against or treated unfairly by others because of their ethnocultural characteristics. This percentage was higher than that of any other group (Government of Canada 2003; Winnemore and Bills 2006).

After continued criticism, the Ontario government took one small step that may pacify the critics. In December of 2006, the Ontario government passed Bill 124 of the Fair Access to Regulated Professions Act of 2006. The intent of the Act is to ensure a fair, open and transparent process for obtaining registration and licensing in regulated professions for internationally trained individuals (Ontario Ministry of Citizenship and Immigration 2007). The province also created a Global Experience Ontario as an access and resource center for the internationally trained professional to "break down barriers" to licensing and accreditation in Ontario.

The federal government of Canada established the Foreign Credentials Referral Office in May 2007. This office offers internationally trained and educated individuals authoritative and accurate information on the Canadian labor market and Canada's assessment processes (Government of Canada 2007). The Canadian government plans to provide prospective immigrants to Canada with information before they arrive in Canada under its Federal Skilled Workers Program, which is part of the Canadian Immigration Integration project. These policy initiatives by both the Ontario and the federal government are the first steps to addressing the long delayed equity issue of the non-recognition of foreign credentials. More time is needed to assess their effectiveness.

By 2010, measurable results should be revealed as to whether educated and trained African and Caribbean immigrants no longer have to overcome the barrier related to non-recognition of their credentials. If provincial and federal governments are serious about removing all barriers to professions, sufficient time will have occurred by 2010 for an evaluation of the results of public policies.

NOTE

[1] Canada's CMA differs slightly from the metropolitan area in the United States, although the delineation methodologies are similar. For example, the critical population threshold of 50,000 is lower in the United States. In Canada, a CMA is formed by one or more adjacent municipalities centered on a large urban area known as the urban core. The census

population threshold of the urban core is at least 10,000 to form a census agglomeration and at least 100,000 to form a CMA. To be included in the CMA, adjacent municipalities must have a high degree of integration with the central urban area, measured by commuter flows derived from census place of work data (Statistics Canada 2002).

Chapter 5

Housing Experiences of New African Immigrants and Refugees in Toronto

CARLOS TEIXEIRA

INTRODUCTION

One of the defining characteristics of recent immigration to Canada has been its cultural and racial heterogeneity. Not only have the source countries of immigrants to Canada and its largest city, Toronto, changed from predominantly West European to a greater proportion of immigrants from Asia, Africa, the Caribbean, and South America, but also recent immigrants tend to come from a wider spectrum of socio-economic backgrounds (Bourne and Rose 2001; Murdie and Teixeira 2003). The Black community of Toronto reflects the immigrant heterogeneity of Canada. While the mass media routinely portrays the Black community as a singular group, it is actually a very diverse population and includes Black Canadians, Black Americans, Black South Americans, Black Africans, and Blacks from the Caribbean (Opoku-Dapaah 2006). Immigration has contributed to the growth of this population in recent years, with about half of Canada's Black population (52 percent) consisting of immigrants, most of whom have arrived since the early 1980s (Mensah 2005). Statistics Canada records Canada's 2001 Black population at 622,210, making it the third-largest visible minority group in the country, after Chinese and South Asians. Most of Canada's Black population have settled in one of the two largest urban centers, with 46.8 percent living in Toronto and 21 percent in Montreal.

Black immigration from Africa to Canada is a relatively recent phenomenon. Canadian immigration policies historically have been prejudicial and discriminatory based on race, and have not encouraged the resettlement of African refugees in Canada. Today, despite immigration policy liberalization and adoption of more objective criteria for immigrant selection, immigration from Africa tends to be very low relative to other so-called "non-traditional" sources of Canadian immigration. For example, Africa currently contributes just 5 to 7.5 percent of all immigrants to Canada, although this number has been increasing over the last 10 to 15 years. (Danso and Grant 2000; Mensah 2005). African immigrants to Canada encounter longer delays and reduced prospects in comparison with immigrants from Europe or East Asia. As a result of these blocked immigration channels, most Africans in Canada come as refugee claimants and most settle in Toronto (Opoku-Dapaah 2006).

Toronto is Canada's traditional "port of entry" for all new immigrants, and is the country's largest and most culturally diverse city. It is also one of the most expensive housing markets in Canada. New immigrants to Canada are likely to face the greatest affordability problems in this housing market (Hulchanski 2001; Murdie 2003). As a consequence, the settlement of immigrants in Toronto, and the corresponding transformation of the city's ethnocultural mosaic, has been marked by increased segregation and poverty levels in sections of the city, and by high levels of residential mobility (sometimes "forced" relocation) and suburbanization. The settlement patterns (choices made by groups of people/immigrants regarding type of residence, neighborhood and city in which to live) of new immigrants have become increasingly diverse. For example, Asian business immigrants settle in relatively high-priced, single-family, detached suburban dwellings, while refugees are forced into lower-rent, private-sector apartments, many of which have poor maintenance standards. Recent evidence suggests that new immigrant groups and visible minorities, including Black Africans, are more likely than non-immigrants to live in poor-quality housing and in neighborhoods with high rates of poverty (Kazemipur and Halli 2000; Opoku-Dapaah 2006), and extreme poverty among some immigrant groups. "Immigrants and refugees are increasingly falling under the category of absolute homelessness," and these groups are "now part of the new face of homelessness" in Toronto (Ballay and Bulthuis 2004, p. 119).

Many factors limit access to housing for recent immigrants. For example, the lack of federal commitment to affordable housing in the 1990s, and reductions in the commitments of many Provincial governments during this same period (with notable exceptions, such as Quebec which remained active in supporting non-profit housing), resulted in Canada having the smallest non-market housing sector of any major Western nation, except the U.S. Additionally, relatively few rental units have been built in Toronto since the mid-1990s, and rents have increased at approximately twice the rate of inflation. For many new immigrants and visible minorities, these economic factors are aggravated by barriers such as discriminatory practices in the private rental market (Dion 2001; Novac et al. 2004). Thus, race remains an important barrier to equal treatment in Canada's housing market (Danso and Grant 2000; Murdie 2003, 2002; Darden 2004; Hulchanski and Shapcott 2004), and because of economic and discriminatory barriers, new immigrants and visible minorities may be directed into low-cost housing that, when clustered, can become urban or suburban "ghettoes" (Pruegger, Cook, and Hawskworth 2004).

Many aspects of the complex housing experiences of immigrants and visible minorities — including the processes involved in gathering information about housing and vacancies — still remain unclear and unstudied, even though "access to housing" is one of the primary routes for immigrants to achieve social and economic integration into the host society (Rose and Ray 2000; Murdie and Teixeira 2003). This integration is based on the successful attainment of several basic needs, however, a number of factors obstruct this process for many new immigrants and visible minorities, including economic disadvantage and housing costs, a lack of knowledge of the housing market, lack of fluency in English or French, and racism and discrimination by landlords, private and non-private housing agencies, and real estate agents. Indeed, even the housing information available to newcomers is subject to biases and constraints (Newburger 1995; Teixeira and Murdie 1997). Although discrimination and prejudice are recognized as barriers to equal access in the housing market (Darden 2004; Novac et al. 2004), discrimination in Canada's housing market remains largely unstudied. In particular, little is known about ethnic and racial differences in accessibility to Canada's urban rental housing markets. Similarly, the Black African housing experience in large urban areas has been largely ignored (Danso and Grant 2000; Mensah 2005; Owusu 2006). What is known from recent research is that new immigrants, refugees, and visible minorities seem to cluster spatially, and generally live in poor-quality housing, usually in low-income neighborhoods, where they rent rather than own residences. These groups also tend to be marginalized economically and socially (Ballay and Bulthuis 2004; Preston and Murnaghan 2005; Opoku-Dapaah 2006).

Greater understanding of the housing experiences of new immigrants and visible minorities, such as Black immigrants in Toronto, is necessary as the housing search strategies and adaptations to barriers adopted by these immigrants in Toronto's housing market have great significance for the future social well-being and economic growth of the city (Murdie 2003). Moreover, as the constraints noted above may contribute to the creation and maintenance of racial and ethnic segregation in urban housing (Qadeer 2004; Preston and Murnaghan 2005), the study of these constraints, and the outcomes for these groups, has direct policy implications for government, business, and community leaders.

FROM POSTCOLONIAL AFRICA TO MULTICULTURAL TORONTO

Black Africans from Angola, Mozambique and Cape Verde Islands — three former Portuguese colonies in Africa — comprise three largely unknown and unstudied immigrant groups in Canada. According to the 2001 Census, about 2,500 members of these communities are living in the country, of which the Angolan group comprises 60.8 percent, the Mozambican group 33.2 percent, and the Cape Verde Islands group 6.0 percent. The province of Ontario is home to the largest concentrations of Angolans (904), Mozambicans (535) and Cape Verdeans (114); the majority of whom live in the Toronto Census Metropolitan Area.[1]

This exploratory study examines the housing experiences of three relatively recent African immigrant groups from former Portuguese African colonies — Angolans, Mozambicans, and Cape Verdeans — in Toronto's rental market by focusing on their settlement experiences, housing search processes, and ultimate outcomes. The focus is a preliminary understanding of the housing experiences, rather than generalizing to the entire population of each study group. The key questions addressed were: What barriers do the groups face in the private rental housing market? Does race or skin color matter in seeking/locating rental housing in Toronto? Sixty questionnaires per group were collected from respondents from Angola and Mozambique (the two largest groups in Toronto), and 30 questionnaires from the Cape Verde Islander group, for a total of 150 questionnaires (Figure 5.1).

Figure 5.1.
Angolan, Mozambicans and Cape Verdeans in the City of Toronto, 2006.

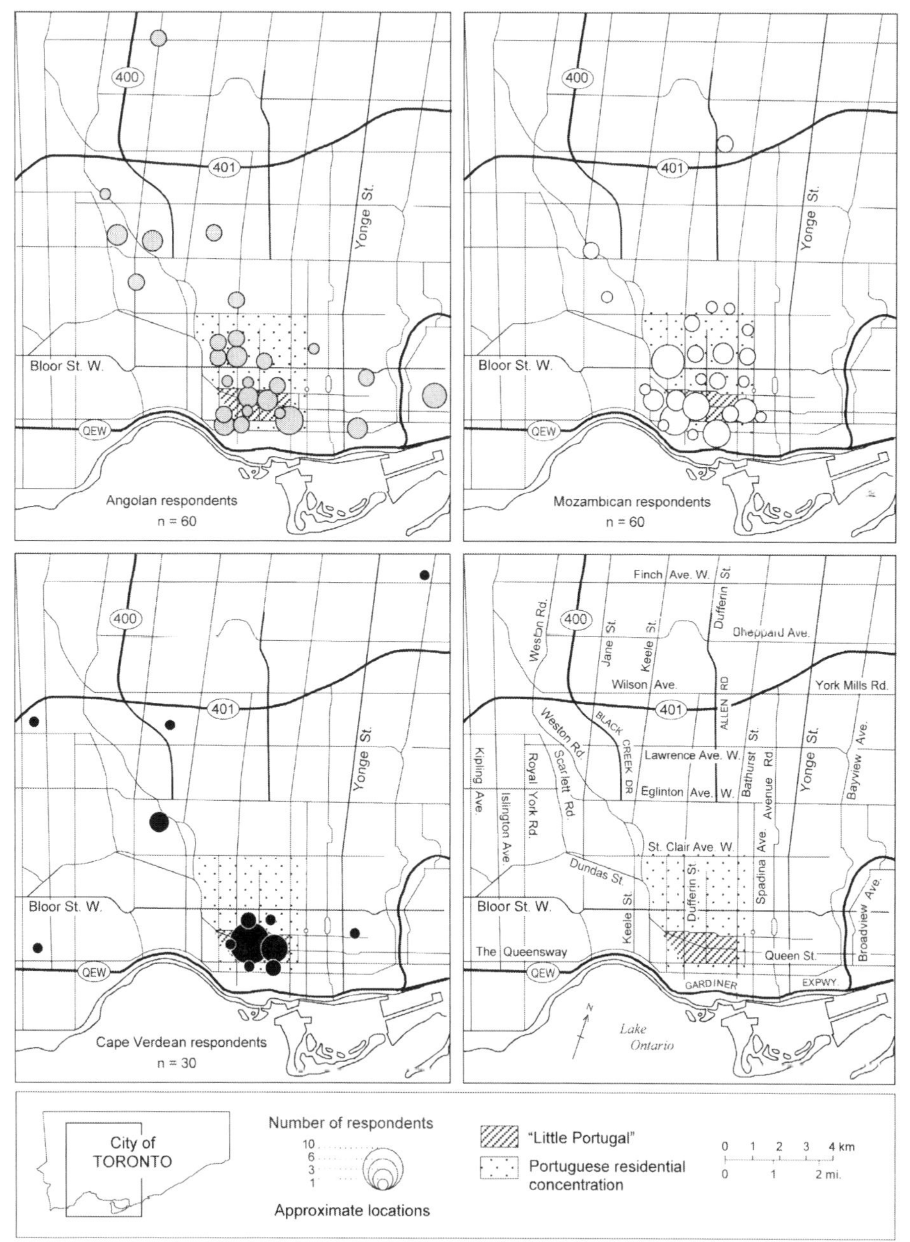

RESEARCH DESIGN

Data for this study were generated via a questionnaire administered in Toronto in Summer, 2006 to native, Portuguese-speaking Angolans, Mozambicans, and Cape Verde Islanders who arrived in Canada between 1990 and 2006. The respondents also had to reside in rental accommodations in the City of Toronto, and to have moved at least twice since arriving in the City. Respondents' selection occurred in several steps. On a few occasions, and when requested, the research assistants visited potential respondents at their homes or at a place of their choice to explain the questionnaire as well as the goals of the study. The survey, with a letter explaining the objectives of the study, was mailed to potential respondents asking for their participation. Additionally, as requested, research assistants conducted face-to-face interviews with potential respondents and explained the questionnaire, and importance of the study. Each respondent received a $25.00 gift certificate for participating in the study.[2]

Survey responses indicate that most of the Cape Verdeans (76.7 percent) and Mozambicans (65 percent) arrived in Toronto in the early 1990s (1990–1995), while most Angolans (60.0 percent) arrived in the late 1990s (1995–2000). More than two-thirds (88.3 percent of the Angolans and 78.3 percent of the Mozambicans) came from urban areas ("big cities") compared to only 16.7 percent for the Cape Verde Islanders, and emigrated to Canada in search of a "better living environment/economic opportunities" (80.0 percent for Cape Verde Islanders, 50.0 percent for Angolans and 75.0 percent for Mozambicans), or "physical safety or political freedom" (68.3 percent for Angolans, 43.3 percent for Mozambicans, but only 1.8 percent for Cape Verdean immigrants). In contrast to Cape Verdeans, for both Angolans and Mozambicans the political instability in their countries following independence from Portugal (which both countries achieved in 1975) was a major "push" factor for their migration to Canada.

The respondents differ in immigration status and average age upon arrival in Canada. Most Angolans (85 percent) arrived in Canada as refugee claimants, while most Cape Verde Islanders (70 percent) and Mozambicans (65 percent) arrived as temporary visa holders. The average Angolan respondent was 27 years old, and the average Mozambican and Cape Verde Islander 31 and 30 years old, respectively. Based upon this, we can speculate that Angolans (most of whom arrived as refugees and at a younger age) might take longer than Mozambicans and Cape Verde Islanders to adjust to the new environment and might face more barriers in the housing search for adequate and affordable housing. Differences in immigration status and average age may have negative implications for housing experiences in Toronto's rental market (Murdie et al. 1996; Murdie 2003).

In general, Angolan, Mozambican and Cape Verde Islander migration to Canada is characterized by household fragmentation, with family left behind in Africa — or in Portugal where important Black African communities from the former Portuguese colonies migrated and continue to reside — waiting for an opportunity to join their families in Canada. Almost half of the respondents from the three groups arrived in Canada alone (46.7 percent for Cape Verdeans, 45.0 percent for Angolans, 41.7 percent for Mozambicans). For the study groups, immigration status upon arrival, the absence of the household and extended family, and the lack of an existing community in Toronto, influenced where they looked first for help in finding housing. Most of the Angolans arrived in Canada as refugee claimants, and showed a greater reliance on non-ethnic organizations and government programs (60.0 percent), compared to Mozambicans (26.7 percent) and Cape Verde Islanders (23.3 percent).

Prior acquaintance with people already established in the host country or city — especially people from the same ethnic background — is of particular importance in the initial search for housing (see Murdie et al. 1996). More Cape Verdeans (76.7 percent) and Mozambicans (70.0 percent) knew someone in the Toronto area before arriving in the city than Angolans (31.7 percent). The Angolans (mostly refugees) lacked social networks and ethnic sources of housing information, had fewer housing choices, and may have faced more barriers in securing housing. Not surprisingly, 47 out of 60 of Angolan respondents (78.3 percent percent temporarily resided in shelters upon arrival in Toronto. Only nine Mozambicans (15 percent) and two Cape Verdeans (6.7 percent) stayed in shelters. Pre-existing social networks among Cape Verde Islander and Mozambican immigrants seem to have helped the initial settlement of respondents from these groups.

Most respondents from the three study groups experienced some disappointment/"culture shock" on arrival in Toronto, with respect to finding affordable and high quality rental housing. The fact that a majority of the three groups of respondents — Angolan (66.7 percent), Mozambican (85 percent) and Cape Verde Islander (70 percent) — had owned an apartment/townhouse or single family dwelling in their home countries may explain their frustration during the initial settlement period. When respondents were asked about their housing expectations before coming to Canada, most respondents described a wide gap between their expectations and the reality they found. Many Angolans (40.7 percent) and Cape Verdeans (50 percent) thought it would be relatively easy to find affordable housing in Canada's largest and most multicultural city. Similarly, half of Mozambicans (50 percent) were expecting better housing conditions/quality. Moreover, the three groups seem to have expected that Canada, as one of the richest countries in the world, would have better quality housing stock/supply as well as better government programs to accommodate new immigrants' and refugees' housing needs/preferences.

TORONTO'S "LITTLE PORTUGAL": RECEPTION AND SETTLEMENT AREA

While none of the three groups had a well-established co-ethnic community within which to settle upon arrival in Toronto, all three had close links with the Portuguese. All respondents were fluent in Portuguese (native speakers) and had cultural connections with Portugal. In the last five decades, the Portuguese have constructed a thriving and institutionally complete community in Toronto — "Little Portugal" — setting up civic organizations, businesses, religious organizations and services in their own language. The Portuguese group is also known for its high levels of homeownership in Toronto's housing market. Many of these homes possess rooms/flats and sometimes a finished basement (quite common in a Portuguese house) used for "informal renting" (illegal/renting without papers).

The respondents were asked about the role and impact of the Portuguese community on their housing search and settlement. Fewer than half of the Angolans (43.3 percent), and Mozambicans (16.7 percent) settled in the Portuguese community on first arrival. In contrast, the majority of the Cape Verdeans (70 percent) settled on arrival in/around the Portuguese community. Those respondents who initially settled in the Portuguese community received help on arrival from different sources, including Portuguese civic organizations, social agencies and churches.

Angolans relied particularly heavily on the Portuguese Catholic Churches in Toronto. Some of the Portuguese priests serving in these Churches had served as priests during the colonial wars in Africa, and thus were highly sensitive to the needs of these Black Africans. Several respondents from the Angolan community highly praised the work of Portuguese priests and the Church in helping them get adjusted to their new environment (e.g., providing food, some money, and space in the Church Hall to meet and socialize, etc.). Since the independence of the former Portuguese colonies, the Portuguese Church in Toronto has been highly active in fundraising to support causes in Africa. In these appeals, Toronto's Portuguese community has always participated generously in terms of donations.

All three groups, particularly the Angolans and Cape Verdeans, relied extensively on Portuguese organizations/social agencies, but complained about the lack of Black Africans working for them. Mozambicans, and to a lesser degree Cape Verdeans, shared the view that Portuguese social agencies/organizations in Toronto should have more members of their backgrounds working for them in order to provide a better settlement services and to cope with the issue of "mistrust" that exists between Black African groups and the Portuguese (White) workers.

When asked how they would rate the importance of the Portuguese community in helping them adjust to their new environment, only 41.7 percent of respondents from Angola and 11.7 percent from Mozambique said the Portuguese community was "very important" or "important." Cape Verde Islanders had a different opinion, and praised the importance of the Portuguese community (60 percent) in helping them adjust to a new milieu. Thus, for Cape Verdeans, it seems that the Portuguese community in Toronto had a stronger and a more positive impact on settlement in/adjustment to Toronto. Some of the Cape Verdean responses indicated that there was a much easier integration/adjustment due to the cultural connection to the Portuguese community at the early stages of settlement in Toronto. As one Cape Verdean respondent explained:

> Culturally speaking we are the closest group from Africa to Portugal and the Portuguese culture. . . . They [Portuguese landlord] were helpful to my family . . . but in my case I think he rented me a place in 'Little Portugal' simply because he didn't want a renter more Black than me.

It may be that the absence of a divisive colonial war in the Cape Verde Islands — in contrast to the situation in Mozambique and Angola — as well as more exposure to Portuguese culture and ultimately more socialization with individual Portuguese, explains this closer "cultural proximity" between the Cape Verdeans and the Portuguese community in Toronto. It should be noted that in Portugal, the oldest and most important immigrant group from its former African colonies is the Cape Verdeans (Fonseca 2005). Thus, it is not surprising that in Toronto, according to "key" informants, between 65 to 75 percent of all Cape Verdeans living in the city reside in "Little Portugal" and/or in neighborhoods close to it. Among the three study groups, the Cape Verdeans "social/cultural" proximity to the Portuguese community seems to be the strongest.

The existence of a strong network of contacts (e.g., friends — Portuguese and non-Portuguese — and relatives already established in Toronto) that characterizes the Cape Verdean group in Toronto may also explain their settlement experiences and social proximity to the Portuguese community. The "ethnic" networks were cited as being very important for this group, providing them with accommodation on arrival, sometimes on a temporary basis, as well as in helping them find jobs. In contrast, Angolans and to a large degree Mozambicans, see their relationship with the Portuguese community differently than the Cape Verdeans. As some Mozambican respondents explained:

> Our contact with the Portuguese community is minimal . . . culturally we don't have too much in common other than the language. . . . Also the colonial war didn't help . . .
>
> Look where Mozambique is in an African map . . . we are far . . . far away from Portugal . . . I never felt I belonged there [Portuguese community] . . . moreover I came to Canada not to "Little Portugal." I am more interested in my integration into Canadian society . . . and I wanted to improve my English.

Beyond the relationships of the Angolans, Mozambicans and Cape Verde Islanders with the Portuguese community, a number of other factors may explain the particular search behavior and housing choices of the three study groups on their arrival in Toronto. For example, the generally high education levels of Angolans and Mozambicans before emigration to Canada,[3] as well as their ability to speak and read English upon their arrival (70 percent of the Angolans and 80 percent of the Mozambicans could speak English "a little" or "very well") may help explain their autonomy in their initial housing search and choice. In contrast, most Cape Verdeans attained only primary/high school (70 percent), and thus had a lower knowledge of the English language (speak/read 30 percent). The closer geographical proximity of the Cape Verde Island Archipelago to Portugal may also explain this closer "social/cultural proximity" between the Cape Verdeans and the Portuguese community of Toronto. In this context, one question that deserves further research is: Does "social/cultural" proximity between groups translate into greater acceptance by Portuguese landlords in terms of facilitating access to rental housing in "Little Portugal?" Given the differences between the three groups, this question requires more study.

With regard to other characteristics, most respondents were working full time (68.3 percent for Angolans, 86.7 percent for Mozambicans and 93.3 percent for Cape Verde Islanders) at the time of the interviews. While none of the Cape Verdean respondents declared receiving an income from social assistance, a few Angolans (23.3 percent) and Mozambicans (13.3 percent) were receiving an income from social assistance. Also, the majority of the respondents had already attained landed immigrant status or Canadian citizenship (78.3 percent for Angolans, 90 percent for Mozambicans and 96.7 percent for Cape Verde Islanders). Both Angolans and Mozambicans have plans of retiring in Africa (50.0 percent and 88.3 percent, respectively). In contrast, Cape Verdeans came to stay in Canada, with only 30.0 percent of the respondents showing an interest in returning one day. Thus, these findings indicate that members of these groups wanted to integrate into mainstream Canadian society, rather than establishing their own institutionally complete immigrant communities. Ultimately, the individual and household characteristics highlighted here have implications for their settlement location choices, housing experiences in Toronto's housing market, and their adaptation/integration to Canadian society.

RESIDENTIAL MOBILITY AND THE HOUSING SEARCH PROCESS IN TORONTO'S RENTAL MARKET

The questionnaire asked respondents about their housing searches for both their first permanent residence, as well as their current residence in Toronto's rental market. Results are presented separately for the following interrelated aspects of the relocation process:

a) the most important reasons for moving,
b) information sources used in the search process,
c) difficulties experienced in the housing search and reasons for the difficulties,
d) searching for housing in the Portuguese community, and
e) the housing outcome and levels of satisfaction with present dwelling-neighborhood.

Reasons for Changing Residence: "Push-Pull" Factors

Respondents were asked for the main "push" and "pull" factors influencing their decision to move (1) from their first permanent residence in Toronto, and (2) from their last residence to their current residence. For the Angolan group, "rents too expensive" (50.0 percent) and "overcrowding" (40.0 percent) were by far the most important reasons for moving from their first permanent residence in Toronto. For the Mozambican group, "housing conditions/facilities" (40.0 percent) and "size/number-rooms" (30.0 percent) were the most important factors in their decision to relocate. In contrast, for the Cape Verdean group "overcrowding" (sharing with relatives) (63.3 percent) and the wish to live in their own place ("privacy") were by far the most important reason for moving from their first permanent residence. Thus, for all three groups "overcrowding," or "size/number of rooms" was a major factor influencing relocation.

With regard to the most important reasons for moving from their last residence to their current residence (at the time of the interview) — Angolans again cited the high rents (41.7 percent) and "problems with landlords" (increases in rents and/or landowners sold the house/apartment) (16.7 percent) as the primary reasons for moving. For the Mozambican respondents "better housing conditions" (45 percent) and "proximity to the workplace" (41.7 percent) were the two most important reasons, while Cape Verdeans moved mainly in search of "better housing conditions/quality" (53.3) in a "better/safe neighborhood" (20 percent) which was "close to the work place" (20 percent). Thus, in general the respondents' reasons for moving reflect the reality of Toronto's rental housing market: lack of affordable rental housing/high rents, low vacancy rates, and poor-quality housing in certain areas of the City of Toronto.

The Issue of Housing Conditions and Overcrowding

Recent immigrants and refugees in Toronto have high residential mobility, caused partly by the need for more affordable and higher quality housing in Toronto's expensive private rental market. The study results indicate that both Angolans and Mozambicans sought better housing conditions after a short time (less than three months) living on a temporary basis in a shelter (78.3 percent versus 15 percent) or sharing space with friends or relatives (13.3 percent for Angolans and 68.3 percent for Mozambicans). In contrast to the other two groups, Cape Verdeans' initial housing experiences (temporary) were mainly with relatives and/or friends (93.3 percent), with very few of them looking for shelters upon arrival. For all groups, the primary goal was to rent their own accommodation in the private sector.

In contrast to Mozambicans and Cape Verdeans, who after their first move considerably improved their housing conditions by renting their own place, most Angolans — even after a few moves — continued to share apartments with other members of the group. Thus, overcrowding (four or five people living in the same apartment) was much more common among the Angolans than among the Mozambicans and Cape Verdeans. For Angolans, group housing seems to have become a common practice; a survival strategy in Toronto's expensive rental market. In part, the Angolans' refugee status, as well as their youth (median age 27 years) may explain this reliance on sharing the rent. In "Little Portugal" and surrounding neighborhoods some apartment complexes have become "magnets" for young Angolans. Overcrowded conditions have become the norm for many Angolans, with low housing quality being a frequent source of complaint. In addition, several rental housing complexes located along the "immigrant corridor" have become major "meeting points" in which African newcomers settle. Sharing living quarters is often not a positive experience. One Angolan commented:

> The rents [have] increased considerably in "Little Portugal." Ten years ago [1996] housing rents were between $275 and $350 . . . today [Summer 2006] one room costs around $450 to $500. Yes one room . . . the kitchen, bathroom has to be shared with others . . . sometimes 5, 6, 7 . . . up to 10 people there . . . if you want the basement with bathroom you pay $700 to $900. . . . In the last few years we Angolans started looking elsewhere [outside "Little Portugal"] where housing is cheaper. I know an Angolan who started first by renting a house and after that he started renting rooms to other Angolans to make money and help pay the rent and the bills . . . thus, overcrowding becomes part of our lives in Toronto.

At the same time, the frequency of overcrowding among Black Africans in Toronto, and particularly among the Angolan group, seems to have become a source of friction with their landlords. For example, fourteen Angolan respondents (23.3 percent) said that they were forced to move at least once from an apartment because of "problems with the landlords," who wanted to raise the rents because of "overcrowding." In contrast, only six Mozambicans (10.0 percent) and one Cape Verdean (3.3 percent) moved for the same reasons. These results echo earlier research in Canada about how overcrowding is common among some new immigrant groups, especially refugees, in expensive urban rental markets. In the case of the Angolan group, overcrowding is related more to the high rents than to a preference for group living as an extended family (see Mendez, Hiebert and Wyly 2006).

The Housing Search Process: Search Effort and Information Sources Used

Gathering information about vacancies in Canada's largest and most diverse housing market can be very stressful, costly, and time-consuming for new immigrants and refugees, most of whom have little money and/or time to spare when they first arrive. Members of the Angolan, Mozambican and Cape Verdean groups are no exception to this rule .

How time-consuming was the search for rental housing? In this study, the housing search effort of our respondents was measured by time spent searching and the number of dwellings inspected. The first measure of search effort is the duration of the renter's active search. Respondents were asked to indicate the approximate amount of time they spent looking for housing (for both first permanent residence and current residence) in Toronto's rental housing market. Results from Table 5.1 shows that almost two thirds (65.0 percent) of Angolans spent more than one month looking for their first permanent residence in Toronto, compared to 40.0 percent for Mozambicans and only 13.3 percent for Cape Verdeans. The data reveal that Angolans by far invested much more time searching for first permanent residence than the other two groups. The minimal time invested in searching and inspecting dwellings by the Cape Verdeans is not surprising given the high reliance of this group on their own "ethnic" (community) networks of contact once they arrived in Canada. However, with regard to the amount of time searching for the current residence (the one they lived in at the time of the interviews), results show only slight differences between the three groups (Table 5.1).

Another important element in the renter's search effort is the total number of dwelling units inspected. Table 5.1 clearly shows that Angolans differ from Mozambicans and Cape Verdeans with respect to the number of dwellings inspected when looking for their first permanent residence. While half (51.7 percent) of Angolans inspected more than ten dwellings in their search, only 20.0 percent of Cape Verdeans and 16.7 percent of Mozambicans limited themselves to this range. The average number of dwellings inspected by Angolans (8.1), compared to Mozambicans (4.3) and Cape Verdeans (1.3), illustrates marked differences (Table 5.1). Differences between the three groups persisted with time. When looking for current residence, Angolans inspected more dwelling units than either of the other two groups (Table 5.1). These noticeable differences in search effort/behavior by our respondents may be explained, at least in part, by different "forces" at play in the rental housing market: the discriminatory behavior by some landlords/housing agencies and/or on the availability of information sources (ethnic/community networks) used in their housing search process. The role of information sources in the search process is the focus of our next questions, "Which sources did you use?" "How helpful were they?"

Information Sources Used

Respondents from the three groups used a variety of information sources when locating their first permanent residence, as well as the residence in which they now live. Table 5.1 reveals that Angolan respondents relied more extensively on Portuguese newspapers/bulletins (50.0 percent), Canadian newspapers/magazines (18.3 percent), and friends and relatives (15 percent) when locating their first permanent residence in Toronto. For these Angolans, reliance on Portuguese newspapers remained important in locating their current residence as well (35 percent). In contrast, very few Mozambicans relied on Portuguese newspapers as a source of housing information. Instead, respondents from Mozambique relied on friends and relatives (50 percent), followed by "Canadian newspapers/magazines" (30 percent). These same sources were used by Mozambican respondents in looking for and locating their *current* dwelling (30 percent and 38.3 percent, respectively) (Table 5.1).

Cape Verdeans relied more extensively on their own "ethnic" network of contacts, particularly relatives and friends from the same ethnic background when looking for and locating both the first permanent residence (56.7 percent) as well as their present residence (43.3 percent). In addition, "driving/looking around" for rent signs was also a popular method for locating their current residence (36.7 percent) (Table 5.1). Reliance on this "informal" source may be an indication of greater mobility/car ownership reflected in their housing search process. In sum, for both Mozambicans and Cape Verdeans friends and relatives were important cultural intermediaries — "bridges" — facilitating their housing search process. These "ethnic" (community) sources provided valuable housing information to both groups of respondents regarding price, type and quality of housing, and where to live (location/neighborhood). These "ethnic" sources were familiar with the cultural needs and housing preferences of these groups and thus they helped ease newcomers' housing search process in complex and expensive Toronto's rental housing market.

In general, a defining characteristic of these study groups is their reliance on informal and inexpensive access to housing information. Few Angolan, Mozambican or Cape Verdean respondents used mainstream private or non-private market organizations or institutions, including the numerous Portuguese social agencies or organizations available in Toronto, which could have provided these groups with assistance on housing-related issues. The importance of ethnic networks for the Cape Verdeans, and to a lesser degree to Mozambicans and Angolans, parallels other findings for recent immigrant groups in Toronto's rental market (Murdie 2003; Owusu 1999). Clearly, more research is needed on the role and impact of ethnic networks of friends and relatives (social networks) in facilitating the settlement and housing search experiences by newcomers to Canada. The quantity and quality of housing information provided to newcomers by these ethnic sources, as well as the extent to which reliance on these sources increases or decreases with subsequent searches, needs to be studied in more depth.

Difficulties and Barriers in the Housing Search Process

The barriers encountered in the housing search can limit new immigrants' ability to access housing and their choice of neighborhood. Canada, in contrast with other industrialized countries such as the U.S. or U.K., appears to offer a more "open" and less constrained housing market (Murdie 2003; Hulchanski and Shapcott 2004). The extent to which Canada's housing market remains more open to minorities is a question demanding further study, as evidence exists that in Toronto's rental housing market, prejudice and discrimination by landlords is a common practice (Dion 2001; Darden 2004; Opoku-Dapaah 2006).

Table 5.1.
The Housing Search Process.

	Angolans (N=60)		**Mozambicans (N=60)**		**Cape V. Isl. (N=30)**	
	First Perm. Residence %	**Current Residence %**	**First Perm. Residence %**	**Current Residence %**	**First Perm. Residence %**	**Current Residence %**
Number of Dwellings Inspected						
Less than 10 dwellings	#29	#34	#50	#54	#24	#22
More than 10 dwellings	31	26	10	6	6	8
Average Number of Dwellings Inspected	8.1	6.0	4	4.3	1.3	2.1
Length of Search						
One month or less	35.0%	48.3%	60.0%	40.0%	86.7%	43.3%
More than one month	65.0	51.7	40.0	60.0	13.3	56.7
Most Important Information Sources						
Friends/relatives	15.0	28.3	50.0	30.0	56.7	43.3
Portuguese newspapers/bulletins	50.0	35.0	8.3	10.0	30.0	13.3
Canadian newspapers/magazines	18.3	18.3	30.0	38.3	3.3	3.3
Driving/looking around/signs for rent	11.7	16.7	10.0	20.0	10.0	36.7
Other	5.0	1.7	1.7	1.7	—	3.3
Housing Search Difficulty						
Very difficult	66.7	50.0	8.3	5.0	6.7	3.3
Somewhat difficult	18.3	25.0	40.0	30.0	23.3	13.3
Somewhat easy/Very easy	13.3	21.7	48.3	60.0	66.7	80.0
D.K.	1.7	3.3	3.3	5.0	3.3	3.3
Search for Permanent Housing in the Portuguese Community	55.0		40.0		63.3	
Participation in the "life" of the Portuguese Community of Toronto	48.3		28.3		56.7	

Source: The Survey.

Table 5.1 indicates that for two of the three study groups — particularly Angolans, most of whom arrived as refugees, and to a lesser degree Mozambicans — the search for housing in Toronto's tight rental market was not easy. The majority of the Angolan (85 percent) and almost half (48.3 percent) of the Mozambican respondents found the search for the first permanent residence "very difficult" or "somewhat difficult." Over time the housing situation improved for the Mozambican group, while the Angolans continued to face difficulty. For example, with regard to the current residence, only 35 percent of Mozambicans compared to 75 percent of Angolans found their search "very difficult," or "somewhat difficult." In contrast, the Cape Verdean group showed overall less difficulty in searching for housing in Toronto's rental housing market. The extensive use of social networks that characterizes the Cape Verdean group may, in part, explain their generally lower level of difficulty in their housing search (30 percent for the first permanent residence versus 26.6 percent for the current residence) (Table 5.1).

Reasons for the Search Difficulty

Respondents were asked: If your housing search for your "first permanent residence" and/or your "current residence" was "very difficult" or "somewhat difficult," please identify the major reasons for your search difficulty? The majority of Angolans and Mozambicans identified the reasons for their search difficulties as: (i) race (being a Black person) and (ii) source of income/income level versus housing costs. In contrast, the Cape Verdean more often cited one reason only — their "income level" (Table 5.2).

As highlighted in Table 5.2, there were numerous "forces" affecting (negatively) the housing search process and outcomes. Among Angolans and Mozambicans in particular, there is agreement that the use of "race" by some landlords (Portuguese and "non-Portuguese"/White) ultimately determined what they found in terms of quality of housing, price and location/neighborhood. Most of these respondents also believed that landlords in Toronto's rental market do not provide full information about the vacancies, utilities and/or prices. Others simply refuse to rent to Blacks by asking for extra money for first/last months' rent to raise the financial bar, or untruthfully state that the accommodation was already rented. These are not legal, but are difficult to prove, and largely contribute to the housing search barriers in Toronto's rental housing market.

Personal and Group Discrimination

Given the number and complexity of the barriers encountered by the study groups, respondents were also asked a more general question as to whether they experienced discrimination against them and against their group in Toronto's rental housing market. The results suggest that Angolans experience more personal and group discrimination than Mozambicans. In general, Angolans reported "quite a bit" and "very much" personal and group discrimination, especially on the basis of "race" (being a Black person), "refugee status," and "source of income." Most Mozambicans reported "quite a bit" and "very much" of personal and group discrimination, especially on the basis of "source of income," "race" and "family size." In contrast, most Cape Verdeans indicated "quite a bit" on the basis of "ethnic/cultural/national background," "language accent" and "race."

These findings indicate that "race" (color of your skin) greatly affects the housing searches, particularly of Black immigrants from Angola and Mozambique. While it should be noted that the racism cited by respondents may be more "perceived" than "real" in some cases — an interpretation bolstered by the distinct Cape Verdean experiences — nonetheless, numerous studies have shown racism to be a major barrier in Canada's urban housing market (Darden 2004; Hulchanski and Shapcott 2004). Thus, there is the possibility that this type of discrimination will shape urban space by promoting social exclusion and the direction of certain visible minorities to low-quality housing in poorer neighborhoods, thereby reinforcing even more segregation than already characterizes some areas/neighborhoods of Toronto.

Table 5.2.
Major Reasons for Housing Search Difficult.

ANGOLANS
Race: "Because of my skin color — dark — I was being treated like a thug or criminal of some kind and I would be asked to pay more rent than originally asked." "People would tell me the apartment is no longer vacant, but in reality the landlords didn't want people of my background ... Blacks ... renting their apartments. This situation was really frustrating and very difficult to bear." ***Source of income/income level versus housing costs:*** "Finding a guarantor due to the fact that we were receiving social assistance at that time [first permanent residence] and most landlords were reluctant to offer us an apartment." "My big problem was my income. It was not enough for renting a decent basement much less an apartment or a house."
MOZAMBICANS
Race: "Some landlords are not comfortable renting to a Black person ... he asked for two months rent paid in advance ..." "The first encounter with the landlord and people would judge me because I am Black: whether I had money to pay the rent; whether I would be able to keep the apartment clean; if I had children — how well behaved they were; what kind of food I will be cooking, etc.... I gave up looking for housing ... finally I found one building with people from my background [visible minorities] living there." ***Source of income/income level versus housing costs:*** "I didn't have financial stability, therefore I had to spend more time searching for cheaper housing...." "Being a female and single mother with few money ... not easy."
CAPE VERDEANS
Income: "I consider my situation very lucky because I know people from other countries ... they have big problems, especially if they are Blacks ... easy for me I had references from my uncle." "My income was the major issue ... I went through many housing searches before I found the apartment I could afford ... I could see ... some [landlords] refuse right away because they were not comfortable ... they would ask the question if I had enough money to pay the rent...." "My income was not enough but I found housing in the Portuguese community.... The landlord was a good Portuguese person. Helped me a lot."
Source: The Survey.

The Portuguese Community and Black Immigrants' Housing Search Process

Given that immigrants from Angola, Mozambique and Cape Verde Islands speak Portuguese fluently, it would be logical to expect them to gravitate to Toronto's "Little Portugal" upon arrival in the city. This leads to the question: To what extent does the Portuguese community facilitate the housing search process of Angolans, Mozambicans and Cape Verdeans in Toronto?

When respondents were asked whether they had looked for permanent housing in Toronto's Portuguese community, 55 percent of Angolans, 40 percent of Mozambicans and 63.3 percent of Cape Verdeans stated that they had searched for permanent housing in Little Portugal (Table 5.1). When invited to comment upon their housing search experiences in the Portuguese community, the responses from Angolans and Mozambicans were a mixture of positive and negative. Some respondents felt the Portuguese community was welcoming and helpful in their housing search, while others were not happy at all and referred to discrimination by some Portuguese landlords based mainly on their race (being a Black person) and/or on the source of their income/income level.

Other respondents, particularly Angolan and Mozambican also severely criticized the way some Portuguese landlords (particularly the ones that live in the same house alongside their tenants) for their "*amadorismo*" (amateurishness) regarding the way they do "business" (informal housing renting) in Toronto. On this issue one respondent complained:

> Very easy to find . . . the houses are in a good state of repair, pleasant but with it came unexpected "policies" I have never heard in my whole life. . . . The landlord seem to like to know too much about my life and control who comes to see me . . . too controlling, violated my privacy several times . . .

In contrast, Cape Verdeans had fewer (negative) reasons to complain about the Portuguese community and Portuguese landlords. In fact, with a few exceptions, the majority of respondents from this group felt they had a good relationship with the Portuguese community by residing in "Little Portugal" or in its vicinity and renting from Portuguese landlords. Quite often we find Cape Verdeans working for Portuguese entrepreneurs (e.g., in construction, restaurants). As some respondents noted: "They helped me . . . I work for a Portuguese boss and live in close proximity to the Portuguese community"; "I had no problems finding housing"; "I always felt at home in the Portuguese community. My wife is Portuguese . . . we have a lot of friends there and I shop there." The fact that some of them found work in the Portuguese community and participate more actively than Angolans and Mozambicans in the "life" of the Portuguese community of Toronto (Table 5.1) may explain the differences in the Cape Verdean responses from those of the other two groups.

Thus, results seem to indicate that a shared language (fluency in Portuguese) did not help Angolans and Mozambicans as much as it did Cape Verdeans, who had an easier housing search experience and felt more at "home" in the Portuguese community. In the case of the Angolans and Mozambicans, the advantage of a shared language is offset by some prejudice and discrimination on the basis of color of skin by some Portuguese landlords. Even if this racism is more "perceived" than "real," the perception, especially among Angolans and Mozambicans, becomes "real" to the extent that it shapes the housing-search process.

A shared language — which should have been an important bridge between Portuguese landlords and the respondents — seems to have worked only for the Cape Verdean group. In contrast to most Angolans and Mozambican respondents, who felt "lost" in their housing search experiences in the Portuguese community, Cape Verdean respondents benefited from the "cultural comfort" and support they needed in the Portuguese community. Thus, being members of a former Portuguese colony and speaking the same language did not serve as cultural tools, to the same degree, for the three study groups. Within this context, it seems that the "race" factor —Angolans and Mozambican being more Black (darker color of skin) than Cape Verdeans — seems to make a difference. Thus, the latest group seems to be more favored than the previous two when looking for housing and getting rental housing from Portuguese landlords.

Involvement and Participation in the Life of the Portuguese Community

To better understand the complex relationship between the Portuguese community in Toronto and Portuguese-speaking Black Africans, the Angolan, Mozambican and Cape Verdean respondents were asked about their involvement and participation in the life of the Portuguese community. Results indicate that Cape Verdeans (56.7 percent) more often than Angolans (48.3 percent) and Mozambicans (28.3 percent) participate in the "life" of the Portuguese community in terms of living within the community, or by working or shopping in Portuguese stores (Table 5.1). However, in terms of participating in the life of the Portuguese community in cultural and social ways, the levels of participation of all three study groups are much lower (20.0 percent for Angolans, 18.7 percent for Mozambicans and 36.7 percent for Cape Verdeans). "Cultural" barriers — partly as a legacy of Portugal's turbulent colonial history in Africa — seem to separate the Portuguese from the Black Africans, and particularly from Angolans and Mozambicans.

For those members of the groups who cited their participation in the Portuguese community, the Angolans and Mozambicans saw their participation mainly in terms of shopping and some social interaction, while the Cape Verdeans were more actively engaged in social and cultural events. Note the different explanations members of each group have for their participation in the following representative responses:

> *Angolans:* Because of my skin color I am not welcome there . . .
> *Mozambicans:* I don't have Portuguese friends . . . difficult to relate to them.
> *Cape Verdeans:* I am looking for other cultures . . .

These responses reflect not only the distinct experiences of the Portuguese community by each group of Black Africans, but also highlight the issue of discrimination in the views of a number of the respondents.

To further learn about the role of the Portuguese community, all respondents were asked: In your opinion how are immigrants and refugees from Angola, Mozambique, and the Cape Verde Islands being received by the established Portuguese community? No consensus exists among the three study groups, suggesting this is a sensitive and controversial issue for all groups, with opinions differing greatly. For example, approximately two thirds of Cape Verdeans said that Black Africans from the former Portuguese colonies have, in general, been well received by the Portuguese community of Toronto. Some respondents noted:

> I think these immigrants and refugees are well received since they speak the same language [Portuguese]. I think a lot of people find work and get a lot of support from the Portuguese community . . .

> The Cape Verdean people here are not considered refugees [like Angolans or Mozambicans] and they get along with the Portuguese very well . . .

However, some Cape Verdean respondents also recognized that some groups from the former Portuguese colonies (e.g., Angolans, Mozambicans, Guinea-Bissau . . .) are less welcomed than others (e.g., Brazilians) by the Portuguese community. They recognize that Cape Verdeans receive a different (more positive) treatment from Portuguese. One respondent noted:

> Everyone that I know from some of these communities [Angola, Mozambique, Guinea-Bissau] are not the favorites of the Portuguese community. . . . Look at the way Brazilians are integrated in the Portuguese community . . .

In contrast to Cape Verdeans, Angolans and Mozambicans were more critical vis-à-vis the reception they have had in the past by the Portuguese community. Approximately half (46.7 percent) of the Angolans and 25.0 percent of the Mozambican respondents noted that the Portuguese community could have been more helpful to them. Some respondents complained:

> In my view there is no friendship among these communities [Black Africans and the Portuguese community]. Based on what I have seen only the Brazilians fit there [in "Little Portugal"]. . . . The Portuguese community seems far away from Angola . . . Africa . . . years of distance. The distance among all these communities is noticed on the streets, workplace and more and more where they live . . .

> I normally feel that no matter where you are from the former Portuguese colonies there is resentment from some Portuguese immigrants, particularly the ones that once lived in the colonies . . . the "retornados" [Portuguese living in Africa forced to return back to Portugal after the independence of the Portuguese colonies] . . . they from one form or another . . . some of them were forced to leave the colonies and they strongly resent that. . . . They ["retornados"] tend not to like us . . . the relationship between us and them is almost non-existent.

Based on the above responses it seems that much more work needs to be done by the established (first generation) Portuguese community of Toronto. More "dialogue" is needed in order to eliminate the "social/cultural" distance that seems to separate the Portuguese White community (the former colonizer) from the emergent Black African communities of Toronto (formerly the colonized). There is a feeling among respondents that Portuguese and the Black African immigrants and refugees presently live in "two worlds." However, there are signs that new generations of Portuguese Canadians (born in Canada) have a different attitude than first generation immigrants born in Portugal in accepting Black African newcomers, and appreciating their distinct social/cultural contributions to the Portuguese community. Marriages between Portuguese and Black Africans may indicate a new relationship between these groups (Oliveira and Teixeira 2003).

In sum, findings suggest that more research is needed on the role and impact of well-established ethnic communities in the social inclusion of new immigrants and visible minorities. In particular, given differences in the perceived social distance between groups of Portuguese-speaking Black Africans — Cape Verdeans, Mozambicans and Angolans — and Toronto's Portuguese community, further research is needed to understand the complexities of culture, language, and prejudice in shaping the settlement of immigrant communities in urban Canada.

Outcomes of the Housing Search Process

As noted in the previous section, some respondents faced major barriers/obstacles in Toronto's tight rental housing market. Whether some respondents had a "choice" in their last move, or were "involuntarily" moved (forced) from their last residence was the focus of our attention here. Respondents were asked: When you decided to move to your current place, did you want to move or were you forced to move — that is, did you choose to move, or did you have to move? Results show that Angolans (21.7 percent) more often than Mozambicans (8.3 percent) and Cape Verdeans (3.3 percent) were "forced" to leave their last residence (Table 5.3). Some of the respondents who experienced these "involuntary" moves blamed the landlords, noting a range of deceptive practices:

> "The landlord had to sell the house and I was left without any choice. . . . Later on I realized that he didn't sell it . . . he wanted me and my friends out of the apartment."

Other respondents asserted that racism was behind their involuntary move:

> "The landlord was [White] and was a racist . . . and I argued with him."

Most respondents from the study groups are currently renting an apartment or flat in the private sector (53.3 percent of the Angolans, 81.7 percent of the Mozambicans and 70 percent of the Cape Verdeans) (Table 5.3). Very few (4 Angolans, 1 Mozambican and 1 Cape Verdean) lived in public housing, most likely due to the shortage of public housing in Toronto, and the long waiting lists for affordable housing.

For almost all respondents, the ultimate goal is to own a home of their own, with 93.3 percent of Angolans, 96.7 percent of Mozambicans and all (100 percent) Cape Verdeans expressing a strong desire to own property. Respondents from the three study groups are unanimous that owning property on Canadian soil would give them more privacy, equity/credit in the new society and some form of control of their own destiny. However, owning a home also has a range of different meanings for these respondents (Table 5.4).

Many respondents expressed a desire to live in neighborhoods with people from a variety of ethnic backgrounds (Table 5.3). For some of those respondents it is very important to avoid living in areas with high concentrations of people of the same ethnic background/color, and/or areas where the language used by most residents is not English (e.g., Portuguese). Some respondents noted:

> Avoid areas in the City with people of the same ethnic background . . . color . . . so that it is easier to fit in the Canadian community.

> Avoid Portuguese areas . . . College/Dundas [West] . . . because you will never be able to communicate in English.

Table 5.3.
The Housing Search Outcome:
Neighborhood, Housing Situation and Levels of Satisfaction with Present Dwelling/Neighborhood.

	Angolans (N=60)	**Mozambicans (N=60)**	**Cape V. Isl. (N=30)**
	%	%	%
Voluntary vs. Involuntary Move			
Voluntary move/Wanted to move	70.0	90.0	83.3
Involuntary/Had to move (a "forced" move)	21.7	8.3	6.7
Don't Know	8.3	1.7	10.0
Tenure			
Renter in private sector	53.3	81.7	70.0
Renter in public housing	6.7	1.7	3.3
Renter in non-profit or Co-operative	11.7	13.3	6.7
D.K./No answer	28.3	3.3	20.0
Satisfaction With Current Dwelling			
Very dissatisfied	11.7	6.7	3.3
Dissatisfied	18.3	6.7	6.7
Satisfied	55.0	78.3	66.7
Very satisfied	10.0	3.3	20.0
D.K.	5.0	5.0	3.3
Satisfaction With Neighborhood			
Very dissatisfied	11.7	1.7	—
Dissatisfied	8.3	8.3	3.3
Satisfied	63.3	66.7	60.0
Very satisfied	11.7	6.7	33.3
D.K.	5.0	16.7	3.3
House as "Home"			
Not at all a "home" (Very dissatisfied)	8.3	1.7	3.3
Not much of a "home" (Dissatisfied)	23.3	11.7	18.3
A "home" to some extent (Satisfied)	40.0	66.7	45.0
Very much a "home" (Very satisfied)	26.7	18.3	33.3
D.K.	1.7	1.7	—
Neighborhood as "Community"			
Not a "community" at all (Very dissatisfied)	10.0	20.0	—
Not much a "community" (Dissatisfied)	20.0	30.0	6.7
A "community" to some extent (Satisfied)	48.3	41.7	70.0
Very much a "community" (Very Satisfied)	16.7	5.0	20.0
D.K.	5.0	3.3	3.3
Neighborhood Preference/Ethnic Composition			
To live near members of the same ethnic group	15.0	6.7	20.0
To live in neighborhood with people from a variety of ethnic backgrounds	43.3	23.3	50.0
No preference/Don't mind	35.0	53.3	30.0
D.K.	6.7	16.7	—

Source: The Survey.

Table 5.4.
The Meaning of Homeownership.

a) Happiness/privacy: “To feel happy . . . it’s a human dream”; “something for me and my kids . . .” “When I left the islands [Cape Verde] I had this big dream [homeownership] . . . to own . . . nobody can take it away from me. It makes me feel more stable here as an immigrant. It represents success and a stake in a new land.”
b) Owning something they can call “home”/control: “To own my place . . . it belongs to you. Don’t have to pay rents . . . I can do whatever I want with my house” “Renting is never yours. . .” “One way to have control on my life . . . destiny in a new land. . .”
c) Some form of recognition/credit by the new society: “It gives me more credit [acceptance/respect] to society and in particular to the credit institutions” “Owning bring great rewards in the future” “Means you have accomplished something here and your life is in the right path”
d) Avoid stereotypes: “I [Angolan] am tired to live around poor people [Black renters] around me . . . it always made me feel I was born wrong and because of my color I was less than everyone’s else” “The day I buy . . . I will be free at my own house. . .”)
e) Tradition [back home] in the family to own property: “In Africa [Mozambique] in my family everyone owns a home . . . well . . . is always safe emotionally” “We lived in poor a country [Cape Verde Islands] . . . Owning back home means you achieved something in your life, that you are proud off . . . the same here [Canada].”
Source: The Survey.

Level of Satisfaction with Present Dwelling and Neighborhood

With regard to their levels of satisfaction with their present residence and neighborhood, most Angolans, Mozambican and Cape Verdean renters were either “satisfied” or “very satisfied” with what they have now (Table 5.3). However, when questioned about their “house as home” and their “neighborhood as a community” respondents were less positive (Table 5.4). With regard to “house as home” almost one third of Angolans (31.6 percent), 13.4 percent of Mozambicans and 21.6 percent of Cape Verdeans answered that in their present residence they do not feel at home, citing poor quality of the dwelling, size/overcrowding or tensions with landlords. Some respondents noted:

> I have to share the kitchen and washrooms . . . sometimes that makes me feel uncomfortable.
>
> Its dirty . . . too much insects, stink . . . it’s awful.
>
> My house has many things to fix and the landlord always postponed . . .

On the question of the “neighborhood as a community,” the respondents in general — and Angolans and Mozambicans in particular — were less positive (Table 5.3). Half (50 percent) of Mozambicans and almost one third (30 percent) of Angolans answered that they do not think the neighborhood they now live is an area with a “sense of community” — citing as major reasons for this dissatisfaction (“feeling”) issues such as safety, crime, drugs, cleanliness, noise, lack of services and bad neighbors. They noted:

> They brought a pitbull to scare me . . . because the color of my skin.
> I don't talk with my neighbors and they don't talk with me. . . . Also increased violence, ongoing robbery in the apartments [Eglinton/Don Mills], vandalism/sabotage of cars in parking lots. . .

In contrast, Cape Verdeans show higher levels of satisfaction than their counterparts — Angolans and Mozambicans — with both "house as home" and their neighborhood as "community" (see Table 5.3).

Housing Recommendations

With regard to recommendations for the future, respondents were asked for their advice on improving housing for newcomers. Specifically, we asked questions about what changes need to be made to improve the housing options and housing conditions to newcomers: a) What do you think should be done to improve housing opportunities for immigrants and refugees? b) What housing types or options should be more available? c) What aspects of landlord procedures or policies should be changed? d) What would improve your neighborhood? and e) If you lived in public housing (government housing, such as the Metro Toronto Housing Authority [MTHA]), how can the housing authority and staff better serve newcomers to Canada?

With regard to the question — What do you think should be done to improve housing opportunities for immigrants and refugees? — respondents suggest that more funding be available for affordable housing, which would ease their dependence upon sub-standard housing in Toronto. Also, some respondents cited regulatory changes to enforce the law in such areas as discrimination in rental housing. Respondents observed:

> The Federal government in partnership with the Provincial government should put more money for building affordable housing especially for new immigrants. They will be allowed to stay for at least two years and after that immigrants are required to vacate the place.

> Creation of open policy about housing. Many of us know very little about procedures and policies and this is a hurdle for many of us to overcome discrimination. Social workers, community organizations, churches should be able to help us learn about our own rights [as tenants].

> I think the government should crackdown on landlords that discriminate against new immigrants for the simple reason because of them being people of color and poor.

> Tougher laws against all kinds of discrimination . . . create better mechanism to mix more the areas . . . not only people from one group.

With regard to the question of — What housing types or options should be more available? — respondents noted that affordability was a key issue, as was public governance (including both subsidized government housing as well as non-profit/co-operative housing) to avoid discrimination, as respondents feel the private sector will not resolve this problem on its own. In the respondents' words:

> I do believe Toronto Metro Houses should be more available to those in need. This way private landlords will not abuse so much to those who don't know much about their rights . . . in this case refugees and newcomers.

> Any type of housing is necessary as long they are livable and affordable for families or singles.

> Good housing, with park, gardens, townhouses, low rise buildings, houses like the ones made by Habitat.

> Subsidized government housing . . .

When asked "What aspects of landlord procedures or policies should be changed?" respondents focused on preventing discrimination in Toronto's rental market. Respondents suggest some regulatory body or means of oversight to prevent this from occurring. In their words:

> Being accepted as of people from around the world . . . not judged by color, race or ethnicity.

> The curfew policy must be changed. Some landlords ... love to play Mom and Dad.... The aspect of utilities should be changed too. Most landlords like to add the utilities so as to rip us off.... Many basements are rented in Toronto, but by law they're not supposed to be rented. They are not high enough to live a person ... just like my shack...
>
> Landlords should replace or repair old stuff immediately in the absence of the tenant. Landlords should not go inside of the house without the renter's permission ... particularly the Portuguese have this bad habit, as well as Italians.
>
> Increasing the rent without any advance **notice**, visiting the tenant when they want.

In response to the question — What would improve your neighborhood? — respondents focused again on the question of discrimination as well as on the need for more policing to reduce crime. In respondents' words:

> Stop discrimination no matter your color, status or accent.
>
> Policing to protect the kids and build parking for recreation so the parents can play with their kids...
>
> Respect each other ... no discrimination ... everybody is the same whether is the color or language accent.
>
> No racial discrimination ... no violence.

With regard to the question — If you lived in public housing (government housing, such as MTHA), how can the housing authority and staff better serve newcomers to Canada? — respondents emphasized not only respect but also professionalism. They observed:

> Give them dignity ... there is no end to the harassment and abuse...
>
> Zero tolerance ... I believe that lack of serious policies that govern the public housing are ruining this noble concept.
>
> Do the necessary service to newcomers ... don't undermine newcomers ... respect our claims.
>
> I live in public housing [Spadina/Dundas] and it seems like no one **cares** about the place. Housing authority and staff should get closer and interact with residents. If they take this approach together we will be able to clean up the community. Interaction makes communication easier.
>
> Equal treatment ... be more helpful.
>
> Do the repairs sooner than later.

In general, recommendations from respondents point to a need for greater public governance in the housing sector. This is seen as yielding multiple benefits, not only in terms of provision of more affordable quality housing, but in particular in how this would contribute significantly to reducing discrimination against people of color in both profit- and non-profit housing.

CONCLUSION

This study investigated the housing experiences of three relatively recent African immigrant groups — the Angolans, Mozambicans and the Cape Verdeans — in Toronto's rental market, by examining their settlement experiences, housing search processes, and ultimate outcomes. As these Portuguese-speaking African groups lacked well-established co-ethnic communities in the city to assist them, the role of Toronto's Portuguese community in these immigrants' settlement was a particular focus of this study. There were differences between the groups in this regard, for in contrast to the experiences of the Cape Verdeans, the Angolans and Mozambicans felt that the Portuguese community did not facilitate their reception or social inclusion, and attributed this to discrimination. Indeed, with regard to the barriers encountered by the respondents when looking for housing, results echo earlier research in Canada in suggesting that discrimination by landlords is common in Toronto's rental market.

However, it is clear that more research is needed on landlords' behaviour in the rental market, and on the role of race and discrimination in the allocation of housing in Canada. The different experiences of the Cape Verdeans — of Toronto's housing market and of "Little Portugal" — from that of the other two Black African groups suggest that this issue of discrimination has complexities requiring more detailed study. Findings suggest complex interactions among race/group characteristics, including: immigration status on arrival, age, the housing search process, landlords' discriminatory practices, and the housing strategies adopted by immigrants. In order to better understand the complex housing experiences of immigrants and visible minorities in Toronto, more comparative studies are needed — of visible and non-visible minorities, including newcomers from Francophone, Anglophone, Spanish and Portuguese-speaking Africa — to determine why certain groups are more successful than others in finding affordable housing in a neighborhood of their choice. In this regard, further research is also needed into housing discrimination by the diverse urban social gatekeepers involved in the production and allocation of housing, which seems to negatively impact access by new immigrants and visible minorities to affordable housing in Toronto.

Acknowledgements

Financial support for this study was provided by CMHC (Canada Mortgage and Housing Corporation). The author would like to express his appreciation to all members of the Cape Verdean, Angolan and Mozambican communities for sharing with us their housing experiences in Toronto. The author also wishes to thank Julia Sanca, Esperanca Panzo and Inacio de Natividade from these study communities for their advice and for helping in the data collection.

NOTES

[1] These numbers may be inaccurate due to undercounting the substantial number of illegal immigrants/refugees from these communities residing in Toronto. Conversations with key members of these groups suggest that a more accurate estimate of the total population of the three groups would be 4,000 to 5,000 people.

[2] The author's familiarity and previous contacts (via research) in these communities (the summers of 2004 and 2005) proved very helpful in identifying potential respondents for the research conducted in the summer of 2006. Also, the author relied upon the help of two research assistants (one Angolan and one Mozambican) and a community leader (Cape Verdean) in the distribution (by mail or by hand) of the questionnaire to potential respondents. In order to get as much exposure as possible for the study, the Portuguese media, including newspapers (e.g., Sol Portugues/Portuguese Sun and Correio Canadiano-Nove Ilhas/Nine Islands) and one of the local TV stations (Program — "Angolanidade TV-Rodgers Television-Channel 10") announced the study and encouraged the participation of community members. The study was also announced in one of the Sunday masses of a Portuguese Catholic church in Toronto.

[3] Half of Angolans (50 percent) and three-quarters of Mozambicans (75 percent) attended/completed college/university.

## Chapter 6

Race, Place, and Social Mobility of Jamaicans in Toronto

TERRY-ANN JONES

INTRODUCTION

Multiculturalism reflects a range of racial, ethnic, and national groups. The city of Toronto, known for multiculturalism, houses a Jamaican population that has made a significant mark on the city's cultural landscape. Large scale Jamaican migration to Toronto began in the mid-20th century, primarily with Jamaican women migrating as domestic workers. Changes in Canadian immigration policies in 1962 that lifted the restrictions on immigrants from non-European countries facilitated Jamaican immigration to Toronto, peaking in the 1970s, and continuing even as labor demands changed. In 2001 there were 122,340 Jamaicans in Canada, accounting for 0.2 percent of the Canadian population. Of this number, 93,315 reside in the Toronto Census Metropolitan Area (Statistics Canada 2001), accounting for approximately 75 percent of the total Jamaican population and 2 percent of the Toronto population. These figures do not include undocumented Jamaican immigrants. This chapter examines Jamaican migration to Canada, focusing on the Greater Toronto Area where the majority of Canada's Jamaican population is concentrated.

The chapter discusses the socioeconomic status of Jamaican immigrants in Toronto vis-à-vis their education, occupation, and income. Patterns of residential concentration are also discussed. In addition, the chapter examines the racial and ethnic composition, labor markets, and other characteristics of metropolitan Toronto that affect the Jamaican immigrant population.

RACIAL AND ETHNIC COMPOSITION

Although Jamaicans in Toronto have the advantage of a large network, this migration is fairly recent. Jamaicans account for a significant portion of Toronto's Black population. Toronto does not have a large population of native-born Blacks. In fact, Blacks comprise only 7 percent of Toronto's population, and only 2 percent of Canada's population. Of Canada's Black population, 47 percent reside in Toronto. Furthermore, 57 percent of Toronto's Black population is foreign-born, and among them 73 percent were born in the Caribbean or in South or Central America, primarily Jamaica, Trinidad and Tobago, and Guyana (Milan and Tran 2004).

Blacks have lived in Canada in small numbers since the beginning of the 17th century, mostly concentrated in Ontario and Nova Scotia. The Black population in Canada did not become numerically significant until the latter half of the 20th century, when profound changes in immigration policies resulted in a shift from the emphasis on racial and national preferences, which favored European immigration, to the current system, which emphasizes employability. The Black population in Canada grew from 32,100 in 1961 to 239,500 in 1981 and 662,200 in 2001 (Milan and Tran 2004).

The vast majority of Canada's Black population is foreign-born, although the number of second-generation Black Canadians is rapidly growing. Most of the native-born Blacks live in the Maritime Provinces, particularly in the province of Nova Scotia. In 2001, 10 percent of Blacks in Canada were third generation Canadians, meaning that their parents were also born in Canada. By contrast, 84 percent of Blacks in Nova Scotia were at least third generation Canadians. Toronto and Montreal attract the largest numbers of contemporary Black immigrants (Milan and Tran 2004).

WHY DO JAMAICANS CHOOSE TORONTO?

Clearly, push-pull factors influence Jamaican migration to Canada. Toronto, which is notorious for its harsh winters, abbreviated summers, and often non-existent falls and springs, attracts migrants because better opportunities exist in Toronto and the benefits of leaving outweigh the costs of remaining. Toronto has become a magnet for some Jamaicans (similar to New York or Miami, for example) because previous Jamaican migrants have developed a support network of family, friends, a place to stay, and employment opportunities (Jones 2008).

Social and familial networks are central to immigrant decision-making processes. The importance of networks is underscored by the fact that the overwhelming majority — more than three-quarters — of Jamaicans in Canada reside in the Greater Toronto Area, as Figure 6.1 shows. Because Toronto was a primary destination for earlier flows of Jamaican migration to Canada, other family members, friends, and members of the same communities and networks later followed. Canada has additional attractions such as universal health care and a reputation for ethnic diversity (Abu-Laban and Gabriel 2002). A 2001 Statistics Canada study showed that, following family and social networks, the second most important reason that migrants chose Toronto is because of its job prospects (Chui 2003). As a large and economically vibrant city, Toronto holds much appeal for immigrants.

Some prospective immigrants choose Canada over the United States because of differences between the immigration policies of the two countries. Canada's immigration policies favor immigrants who have the education and skills that would enhance employability, while the U.S. policies prioritize family reunification. Consequently, Canada is the preferred option for individuals who do not have family in the United States, but whose education, work experience, or other qualities enable them to qualify for entry under the Canadian system. Canada's immigration policy is based on a points system that allots points based on characteristics of prospective immigrants such as level of education, years of experience in their field of employment, and proficiency in either English or French. The points system is discussed in further detail below. While U.S. immigration policies also accommodate employability, the primary means by which immigrants arrive legally in the U.S. is through family reunification. Through this policy, family members of U.S. citizens and permanent residents are able to sponsor close relatives living abroad, with priority given to the immediate relatives of U.S. citizens. For prospective immigrants who do not have relatives living abroad, Canada presents a more viable option, especially for those who have the education and skills needed to earn the 67 out of 100 points that are required for admission (Jones 2008).

CHARACTERISTICS OF THE JAMAICAN POPULATION

Gender and Age

There is a slight majority of women in both the Jamaican and Canadian populations. Among the Jamaican population residing on the island, 50.7 percent are female and 49.3 percent are male, while the Canadian population is 51 percent female and 49 percent male. The age and gender distribution of Jamaican immigrants in Toronto reflect the patterns of migration to Canada. The majority of Jamaican immigrants in Toronto are women. Of the Jamaican population in Canada, 58 percent are female and 42 percent are male. In Toronto, 59 percent of the Jamaican immigrant population are female and 41 percent are male (Statistics Canada, Census of

Population 2001). This majority is amplified among Jamaican immigrants in Toronto, and is primarily the result of the labor market, which demanded female workers during the mid-20th century when significant female Jamaican migration began. As increasing numbers of Canadian women began working outside of the home, more foreign women, including Jamaicans, were needed for domestic jobs. Although both women and men migrated from Jamaica to Toronto to engage in other forms of labor, domestic labor was certainly influential during this period. Many of the early Jamaican immigrants in Toronto arrived during the 1950s as domestic workers under a scheme that enabled them to gain permanent-resident status. Today, Jamaican immigrants are overrepresented in health care occupations such as nursing because Black women nurses were permitted to immigrate as "women of exceptional merit" from 1950–1962 (Calliste 1993; Darden 2004, pp. 54–55). Although it is no longer uncommon to find men in these occupations, women remain the majority.

Figure 6.1.
Jamaican Immigrants in Canadian Urban Centers.

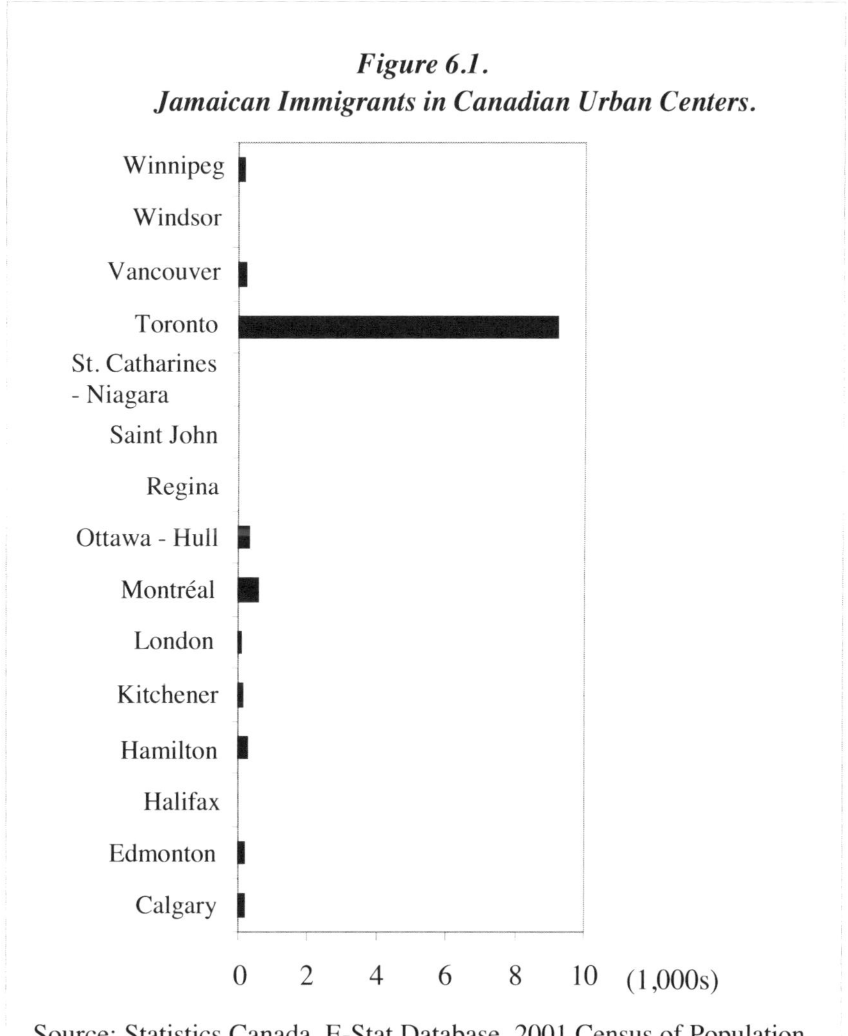

Source: Statistics Canada, E-Stat Database, 2001 Census of Population, Citizenship, Immigration, Birthplace, Generation Status, Ethnic Origin, Visible Minorities and Aboriginal Peoples, 2001 – Large Urban Centers in Canada.

Similar to gender, the age distribution of the Jamaican population in Toronto is also determined by migration patterns. Migrants most often make the transition from their origin to destination country when they are of working age, when they are most employable and most apt to attain upward socioeconomic mobility. Fifty-eight percent of Toronto's Jamaican population migrated when they were over the age of twenty, while 36 percent migrated between the ages of 5 and 19 years. The volume of Jamaican migration to Toronto peaked in the 1970s, as is reflected in the age distribution depicted in Figure 6.2. Toronto received 34 percent of its Jamaican population between 1971 and 1980, 24 percent between 1981 and 1990, and 27 percent between 1991 and 1995 (Statistics Canada 2001).

Figure 6.2.
Jamaicans in Toronto by Age.

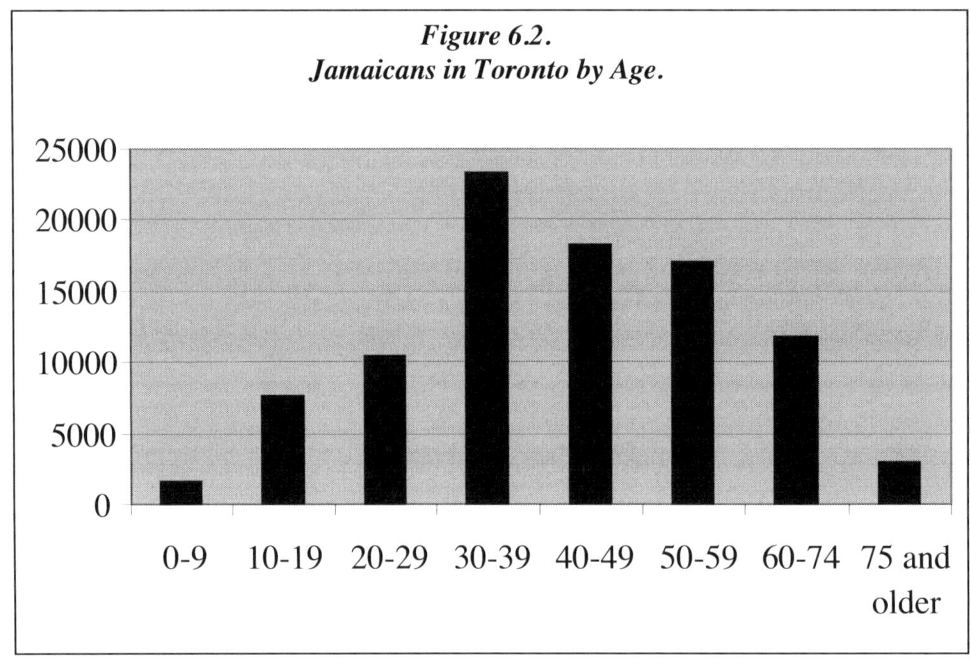

Education

Levels of education among Jamaican immigrants in Toronto are somewhat similar to those of both native-born Canadians and Canadian immigrants. Twenty-eight percent of Jamaicans in Toronto and 27 percent in Canada did not graduate from secondary school. Sixty-four percent of Jamaicans in both Toronto and Canada have at least a secondary school diploma. Eight percent of Jamaicans in Toronto and 9 percent in Canada have a Bachelors degree or higher. The percentages of native-born Canadians and Canadian immigrants are comparable among those who did not attain a secondary school diploma. However, there are a significantly greater number of Jamaican immigrants who completed secondary school but did not obtain a Bachelors degree than there are among the other populations. Approximately 64 percent of Jamaican immigrants in Toronto completed high school, but did not receive a Bachelor's degree. The figure is comparable for the Jamaican immigrants across Canada. For the native-born Canadians, and other immigrant groups, comparatively few complete high school, but many fail to receive a Bachelor's degree. For Canadian immigrants in general, 21 percent receive a Bachelor's degree. For Jamaican immigrants only 9 percent do so.

Accordingly, there are fewer individuals within the Jamaican population with a Bachelors degree or higher than there are among the other populations. As a whole, the Canadian immigrant population has a larger number of individuals with a Bachelors degree or higher, than the Canadian-born population. Table 6.1 summarizes the levels of education for Jamaican, immigrant, and non-immigrant populations in Canada.

Although only 8 percent of Jamaican immigrants in Toronto have a Bachelors degree, numerous nurses and other professionals attained certification at the college level, but did not complete a Bachelors degree. Many professions, e.g., early childhood education and nursing, require certification at the college level, but do not require a Bachelors degree. A disproportionately large number of other health care professionals, such as health care aides and registered practical nurses, are Jamaican. As with residential patterns, networks affect occupational choices. Recent immigrants trying to find employment and seeking to further their education are influenced by the occupational choices of their family and friends. Health care professions such as nursing are appealing to Jamaican immigrants for several reasons. Positions have for the past few decades been in high demand, and remain occupations for which there is fairly consistent job availability. The educational requirements for nurses or health care aides in Toronto are such that Jamaican immigrants can take courses on a flexible, part-time basis while maintaining other forms of employment. Because many nursing programs do not require a Bachelors degree, it is a relatively quick process, which is essential to a recently-arrived immigrant.

Table 6.1.
Canadians 15 and Older by Level of Education
(Percentages)

Level of Education	Jamaicans in Toronto	Jamaicans in Canada	Canadian Immigrants	Canadian Non-immigrants	Canadian Population
No Secondary School Diploma	28	27	30	31	31
Secondary School — no Bachelors Degree	64	64	49	55	53
Bachelors Degree or Higher	8	9	21	14	16

Source: Statistics Canada, Census of Population, CO-0851, Target Group Profile – Population born in Jamaica, Montreal, 2001.

Although Antecol et al. (2003) assert that Canadian immigration policies have little impact on the skill levels of immigrants, Milan and Tran (2004) found that recent Black Canadian immigrants have higher levels of education than Canadian-born Blacks, mainly because the immigration policies emphasize education and skills. In their comparison of the language fluency, education, and income of immigrants in the United States, Canada, and Australia, Antecol et al., found that there were higher levels of education and language fluency among Canadian and Australian immigrants than among U.S. immigrants. However, they attribute this discrepancy to the countries and regions from which U.S., Canadian, and Australian immigrants arrive. They contend that the significantly higher number of immigrants from Latin America, in general, and Mexico, in particular, lowers English fluency, education, and income in the U.S., in comparison with Canada and Australia. However, Milan and Tran (2004), as well as Borjas (1993), suggest that the points system plays a role in the higher educational attainment of immigrants in Canada.

The points system was established in 1967 with the objective of increasing the number of skilled immigrants to Canada by determining the employability of prospective immigrants and admitting them on this basis. Barring any serious health concerns or criminal offences (determined by medical/criminal-background checks), immigration candidates may be approved if they gain 67 of 100 possible points from six categories: education, language ability in English or French, work experience, age, arranged employment, and adaptability. Furthermore, applicants must have either an offer of employment or the financial means to support themselves in an amount of C$10,168 for an individual, plus C$3,000 increments for each additional family member. This class of admission accounted for 54 percent of Canada's immigrants in 2002, illustrating that many immigrants arrive expressly for employment and because of their employability. Among immigrants to Canada, those who migrate under the economic class have the highest employment rates.

Occupation

Census occupational categories can be somewhat vague, and identifying specific occupations based on these categories may be difficult. However, based on the 2001 Canadian census, 32 percent of Jamaican immigrants in Toronto have occupations that fit the *management and professional* category. *Production, transportation, and material moving* follows, accounting for 24 percent of the Jamaican labor force in Toronto. Twenty-two percent of Jamaicans in Toronto are employed in services, and 18 percent are in sales and office occupations. The categories *farming, fishing, and forestry*; *construction, extraction, and maintenance*; and *military* have only a negligible number of the Jamaican workers in Toronto, accounting for a total of 4 percent of this labor force. Although these categories are ambiguous, they provide some indication of the general employment trend among Jamaicans in Toronto. For example, at least 32 percent of the Jamaicans in Toronto may be considered professionals (Statistics Canada 2001), with possibly others from categories such as services and sales. Definitive classification is difficult due to ambiguity of the census category.

Employment status among Jamaicans is based on factors such as their education, language skills, and the length of time they have been in Canada. A 2003 Statistics Canada study found that immigrants who were admitted based on their employment skills have the highest employment rates, as expected (Chui 2003). However, even those who were able to migrate because of their education, skills, and work experience sometimes face challenges in transferring their foreign credentials to Toronto. The host society in many cases places limitations on immigrants' employment potential by rejecting their foreign education or work experience. While highly educated and skilled professionals are encouraged to migrate to Canada, upon arrival they often must seek employment below their skill level or return to school, in many cases repeating courses and levels of education that they had already attained. This is a challenge that many immigrants from developing countries face on arrival in Canada (See chapter 5).

Jamaicans in Toronto have a relatively low unemployment rate in comparison to other Black immigrants, yet it is higher than the average for the population as a whole. In 2001 Jamaicans had an unemployment rate of 8 percent, while Ontario had a 6 percent unemployment rate (Milan and Tran 2004). Nationally, the Canadian-born Black population had an unemployment rate of 7.9 percent, and foreign-born Blacks had 9.6 percent unemployment. One possible explanation for this discrepancy is that much of the recent Black immigration to Canada is from Africa. Although African immigrants have levels of education and rates of employment that are comparable with those of Jamaicans, in many cases African immigrants arrive in Canada as refugees. Consequently, gaining employment may be delayed.

Employment prospects are also related to the three broad categories under which Canada accepts immigrants, not including refugees. Within the family category, Canadian citizens and permanent residents are able to sponsor close relatives. They must agree to support them as needed for a period of three to ten years, depending on the circumstances. Investors, entrepreneurs, and self-employed persons are able to migrate under the business category. Business migrants are required to have the experience and finances to contribute to the Canadian economy according to the specific stipulations of Citizenship and Immigration Canada. Finally, many skilled workers migrate to Canada through the points system, which is central to Canada's immigration policy (Jones 2008).

Income

Income levels in Toronto are higher than the Canadian average by a margin of almost C$6000 (U.S.$4000). However, Jamaicans earn slightly less in Toronto than they do in Canada as a whole. There are several plausible explanations for this discrepancy, one being that Jamaicans outside of Toronto earn disproportionately more. Consequently, there are a greater variety of occupations and income levels among the Jamaican population in this city, thereby raising the mean income for Jamaican immigrants in Canada as a whole. For example, highly educated professionals have access to employment opportunities that enable independence from the social networks on which most immigrants rely. Their choice of residence is shaped more by occupation and employment than by familial or social networks. Those whose employment bring them to locations with fewer Jamaicans, Blacks, or immigrants are likely to balance that decision with higher wages and/or lower costs of living (Portes and Rumbaut 1996).

The average income of Jamaican immigrants throughout Canada (C$29,722/U.S.$19,170) and Jamaican immigrants living in Toronto (C$29,722/U.S.$19,170) is comparable with the general Canadian population (C$29,769/U.S.$19,200), and slightly lower than Toronto's average income (C$35,618/U.S.$23,009) (Jones 2008). There is also a disparity in income between Canadian-born Blacks and the rest of the Canadian population. Milan and Tran (2004) suggest that this gap in both income and rate of employment is a possible indication of discrimination against Blacks in Canada. In 2000, the income of the overall Canadian population was 25 percent higher than that of Black Canadians (Milan and Tran 2004).

RESIDENTIAL PATTERNS

Toronto is renowned as a multicultural city, where immigrants are welcome and different races, ethnicities, nationalities, and cultures coexist harmoniously. While there is some truth to this utopian image of Toronto, divisions do exist, and are articulated through geographic space. There are identifiable Black and Jamaican commercial and residential areas in Toronto. As in many U.S. and Canadian cities, residential location is closely related to socioeconomic status. In Toronto, immigrant residential location is largely based on affordability and networks of national or ethnic groups. Immigrants, particularly recent arrivals, tend to live in areas of affordable housing that are close to family or friends, ethnic grocery stores and restaurants, employment opportunities, and the community or social networks that facilitate their transition into the destination society.

Because Jamaicans only account for two percent of Toronto's population, they are not easily identifiable among Blacks in terms of residential distribution. There is considerable overlap among ethnic neighborhoods in Toronto. Guyanese or Barbadian communities, for example, can be found alongside Jamaican communities. Of more relevance in immigrant residential patterns in Toronto are socioeconomic status and period of migration. Pockets of Jamaicans are identifiable in neighborhoods of varying income brackets. For example, the area commonly known as Jane and Finch, surrounding the intersection of Jane Street and Finch Avenue in the city's northwest area, has a sizeable immigrant population. The community has gained a reputation for a variety of criminal activities and gang violence, yet the undeniably strong sense of community is evident in the ways that members of the community organize and rally against the problems that promote such a reputation. In this area, among others, many of the lower-income, working class, and some recent immigrants from Jamaica are able to find affordable housing.

As Jamaican immigrants settle and acculturate in Toronto and are able to become upwardly mobile through further education, career advances, or simply the saving potential that time in the destination country affords, they tend to move into the more suburban areas to the north (Markham), west (Brampton) and east (Pickering and Ajax) of the city (Jones 2008). Figure 6.3 highlights the areas of concentration of the Jamaican population in Toronto, according to the 2001 census. Within the city, Scarborough in the east and Etobicoke and Rexdale in the west have the highest concentrations of Jamaicans. In the suburbs (periphery of the city), Jamaicans tend to reside in Brampton to the west and Pickering and neighboring Ajax to the east. While there is a sizeable Jamaican population in Markham, they are far outnumbered by East Asian communities there. Seven percent of Toronto's population is Black, which is the highest proportion of all Census Metropolitan Areas in Canada. The proportions of Blacks in Brampton, Pickering, and Ajax are even higher, partly due to the concentration of Jamaicans and other West Indian immigrants — 10 percent, 9 percent, and 10 percent respectively. Figure 6.4 depicts the overlap between the areas of residential concentration of Jamaicans and Blacks in Toronto.

Figure 6.3.
Number of Jamaican Immigrants Living in Metropolitan Toronto by Census Tracts, 2001.

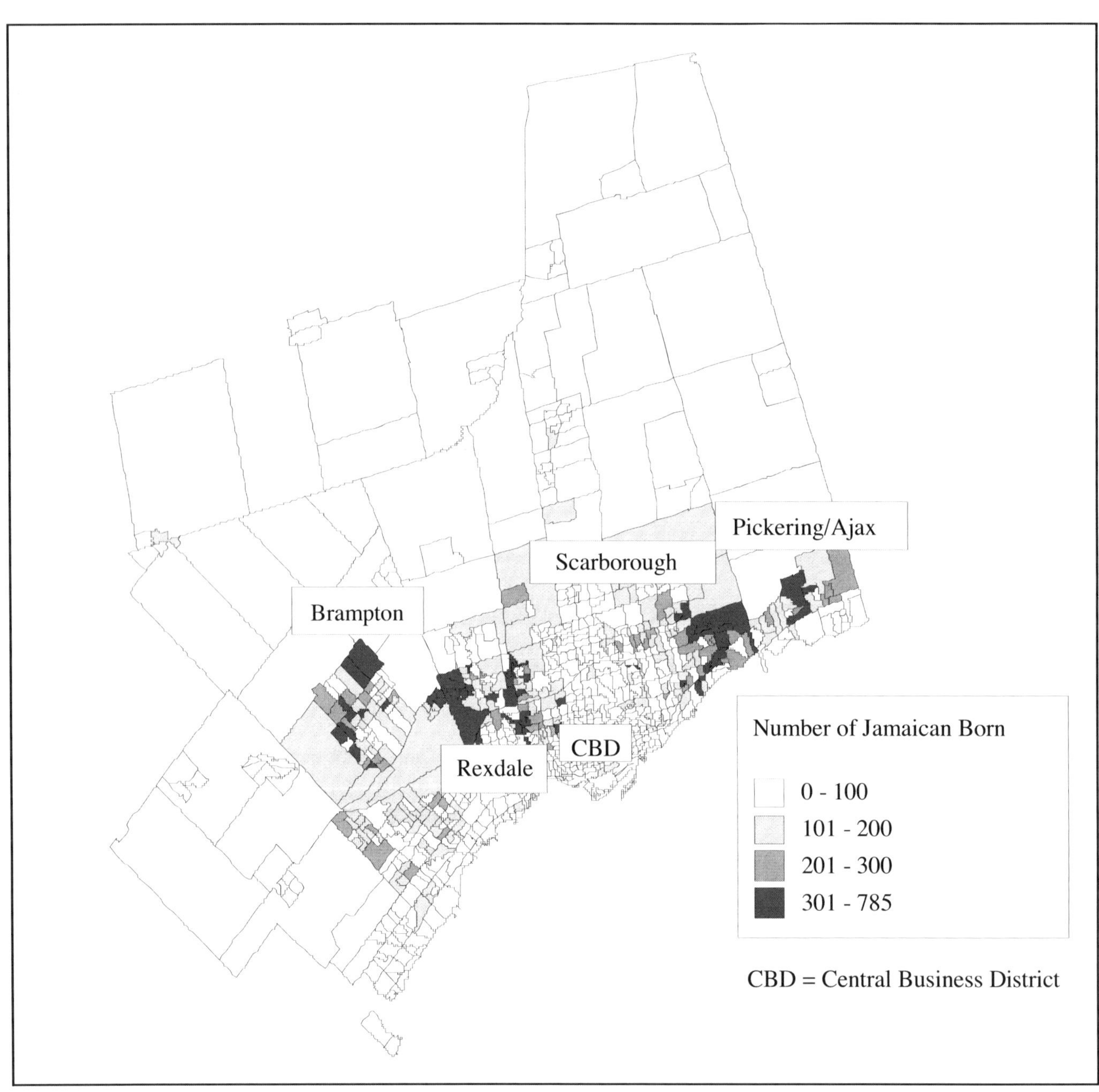

Source: Author.

Figure 6.4.
Number of Blacks Living in Metropolitan Toronto by Census Tracts, 2001.

Source: Author.

JAMAICAN IMMIGRANT INCORPORATION INTO TORONTO

Jamaicans in Toronto face a variety of impediments to their incorporation and acculturation into the city. Although Canada is often touted as being a place of racial and cultural acceptance, there are racial tensions in education, employment, and housing (Henry 1994). Many Jamaican Canadians recognize racism as an obstacle to their incorporation into Toronto, yet the subtle racism is neither easy to identify nor to address (Jones 2008). Direct hostility toward Jamaicans is particularly salient in police harassment, especially of Jamaican youth. Other systemic forms of discrimination that Jamaicans encounter impede their incorporation into the Toronto society, and their upward socioeconomic mobility.

One example of this type of impediment that Toronto's Jamaican immigrants contend with is employers' refusals to recognize Jamaican education and work experience. This is a problem that immigrants from many developing countries face. While Canadian businesses and government offices in many cases accept qualifications from U.S. and some European institutions, Jamaican credentials are often delegitimized. Many professionals find that they need to return to school upon arrival in Canada in order to secure jobs for which they already qualified. Similarly, some employers do not recognize work experience that was not gained in Canada, which creates a significant employment barrier for recent migrants. The irony is that many Jamaicans arrived in Canada by means of the points system, which emphasizes employability and admits them based on the education and work experience that they gained in Jamaica.

SUMMARY

One-third of the Blacks who migrated to Canada before 1961 are Jamaican-born. In the 1960s, 1970s, and 1980s Jamaicans continued to be the leading source of Black immigrants to Canada, followed by Haitians (Milan and Tran 2004). While there is certainly a history of a native-born Black presence in Canada, this population has been relatively small in Toronto. Besides recent African immigrants, Jamaicans and other Caribbean nationals and their descendants now comprise the majority of the Black Torontonian population. Jamaicans are particularly dominant, because of their numbers and their visibility. This community is a visible, vocal component of Toronto.

Despite obstacles that Jamaican immigrants may face in Toronto, migration continues from the island to the city, suggesting that the results have been positive for Jamaicans, or at the very least that the opportunities that Toronto offers continues to make migration a better option. Although unemployment rates among Jamaicans in Toronto are higher than the city's average and incomes are lower, the spatial movement of Jamaicans from working class communities within the city to middle class neighborhoods in the suburbs suggests that Jamaicans are attaining upward socioeconomic mobility.

Section 3: Perspectives on the U.S. African Diaspora

Chapter 7

A Perspective of the African Diaspora in the United States

NEMATA BLYDEN AND FENDA A. AKIWUMI

INTRODUCTION

The dispersion of population resulting from international migration frequently occurs unheeded. African migrations are an example. However, when the Schomburg Center launched a website on African-American migration,[1] several newspaper articles commented on recent African migration. For example, a February 21st *New York Times* article had a headline reading: "More Africans enter U.S. than in days of slavery," and noting that "for the first time, more Blacks are coming to the United States from Africa [emphasis in original] than during the slave trade" altering the concept of African-American (*New York Times*, February 21, 2005). An earlier article revealed "twice as many sub-Saharan Africans — about one million — have migrated to the United States in the last 30 years as during the entire era of the trans-Atlantic slave trade" (*New York Times*, Feb. 2, 2005). The interest in African immigration to the United States provided "... a new interpretation of African-American history.... We're seeing the centrality of migration in the African-American experience. [The late 20th and early 21st century Black migration] from Haiti, the Caribbean and Africa [reveals] a new diversity, people coming with their languages, their cultures, their food" (from Felicia Lee article), enabling a redefining or broadening of the concept of the African Diaspora (Sylvaine Diouf, quoted in Felicia Lee article, *New York Times* 2/2/05). Although "diaspora" provides multiple conceptualizations, a broad interpretation of the term permits greater understanding of various diasporic groups because the timing and conditions of migration vary.

Traditionally, African Diaspora studies have focused on people of African descent outside Africa, or within Africa but far from their birthplace. With emphasis usually on large movements and relocations resulting in the global dispersal of Africans and their descendants, and the transatlantic slave trade of the 15th to 19th centuries, scholars disagree on what constitutes the African Diaspora. Some scholars focus on the dispersion of Africans through the slave trade; others define the African Diaspora as the connections of people of African descent around the world, who are linked by their common experiences and their genetic makeup (Gomez 1998). Forced migration and racialization are key components of an earlier African Diaspora in the United States, but African Diaspora history is not always rooted in slavery. During voluntary migration in the late 19th and early 20th centuries, people of African descent continued to immigrate to the United States, making racialization important, but not a key component of this African Diaspora. Thus, the role of African and West Indian migrants to the United States in the post-slavery era is blurred. Are they part of the African Diaspora or merely immigrants? The term diaspora (and its definition) is similarly blurred. Some argue that it is too broad and has the potential for encompassing every movement of Africans over long periods of time. Its application to more recent groups of Africans is inaccurate. Those who employ the term need to clarify the distinction between diaspora and other forms of movement, such as migration. All movement and migration do not result in diaspora, and it is important to distinguish diaspora correctly from other population movements (immigrant, nomadic, refugee, exiled communities) (Butler 2001).

A different view sees diasporic identities as fluid and historically and socially contextualized, rather than fixed. Diaspora is both a process that is remade through migration and movement, and a condition. This definition includes more recent African and Caribbean migration into the United States; however, limitations to the term diaspora exist and misuse is possible (Kelley and Patterson 2000).

One of the earliest historians of the African Diaspora conceptualizes it as the global dispersion (voluntary/involuntary) of Africans throughout history, "the emergence of a cultural identity abroad based on origin and social condition, and the psychological or physical return to the homeland."[2] Thus, Africans who have left the continent to settle in the United States in the last thirty years become part of the "new" African Diaspora, distinguishable from those Africans brought to the Americas forcibly during the era of the Atlantic slave trade. The broad definition contributes to recognizing multiple identities in this Diaspora.

Diaspora provides a framework for analysis rather than an ethnic label, and has no fixed definition. Diaspora scholars must search for a consensus on the definition of diaspora ... [that will] "transcend specific diasporan histories" (Butler 2001, p. 190). Employing diaspora as theory — for understanding the formation of communities, we are able to understand issues that are unique to diasporas. Butler focuses on five approaches to research on diasporas that examine the recent African Diaspora: 1) reasons for and conditions of dispersal; 2) relationship with homeland; 3) relationship with host land; 4) interrelationship with other diaspora communities; and 5) comparative studies of different diaspora communities (Butler 2001). These five approaches allow similarities and differences in the experiences of various African Diaspora groups, as well as similarities and differences between earlier and more recent diasporas to emerge. These five approaches reveal important characteristics of older African Diaspora communities in the United States, and the more recent African immigrant populations, many of whom have been in the United States for long enough to be considered diasporas. Comparisons of historic and recent African Diasporas of the United States reveals both similarities and differences.

THE EARLY DIASPORA IN THE UNITED STATES

Despite evidence for an African presence in the United States as early as 1526 (Gomez 1998), the first known Africans to settle British North America were the twenty brought to Jamestown in 1619 as indentured servants. Africans continued to be brought to the United States over the course of the 17th century as slavery spread. By 1649 in Virginia's total colonial population of about 18,500, there were 300 Blacks who comprised a distinct minority, referred to as Negroes. By the end of the 17th century, there were 6000 Blacks in Virginia, and they continued to arrive at the rate of 1000 a year. By 1750 the Black population in the United States numbered 750,000 (Gomez 1998), and had grown to 4.5 million in 1860 (Gomez 1998).

In the pre-Civil War era Blacks were excluded from citizenship and had few rights and privileges.[3] The economic condition of most Blacks declined as immigration from Europe increased and Blacks began to lose their jobs to White immigrants. In the late 18th and early 19th century, states and the federal government passed discriminatory legislation. Most states prevented African Americans from voting (Wright 1993, p. 144). A clause in a 1788 Massachusetts law excluded Blacks who could not prove citizenship in the states. Immigration and naturalization laws limited citizenship to Whites. The 1790 Naturalization effectively excluded Blacks from citizenship, stipulating "That any alien, being a free White person, who shall have resided within the limits and under the jurisdiction of the United States for the term of two years, may be admitted to become a citizen thereof" (Historical Documents in United States History, http://www.historicaldocuments.com/ImmigrationAct of1790.htm).

In the early 19th century it seemed the expansion of democratic rights for Whites led to a decrease in Black rights. Faced with this growing segregation and discrimination, African Americans struggled to fit into American society. Illinois' 1819 Black Laws made it impossible for Blacks to enter and reenter the state, requiring African Americans to register and obtain certification. Blacks in many states were prevented from voting, serving on juries, and testifying, among other things (Wright 1993, pp. 133–134). In 1857 the Dred Scott decision settled the question of Black citizenship when it declared that African Amerians were not citizens of the

United States.[4] Slowly the few rights that free African Americans had achieved in the colonial period were eroded.

The Civil War era was a time of hope for African Americans. The war ended slavery, and expanded the rights of Blacks, at least on paper. The 14th Amendment gave Blacks citizenship (1868), and in 1870 African Americans got the right to vote. African Americans with great enthusiasm participated in the political process, taking advantage of their new rights. Despite these changes, Blacks faced many challenges from discriminatory laws that impeded their progress. Whites, especially in the South, unhappy with the status quo, launched attacks on Black rights. Intimidation and outright violence by Whites kept African Americans from exercising their new rights. Additionally, legislation during the period of Reconstruction and after eroded the rights Blacks had gained in the post Civil War period. Beginning in the 1870s some states began to implement segregation (Jim Crow) laws. Poll taxes and literacy tests prevented Blacks from voting. In 1896 in *Plessy vs. Ferguson*, the United States Supreme Court upheld segregation laws as constitutional, with its "separate but equal" doctrine (Hine and Harrold 2000). As the new century dawned African Americans continued to fight for equality. In recent years, African Americans have witnessed new immigrant populations who benefit from the institutional and societal changes that Blacks struggled to achieve. Black immigrants, in particular, have been a group that African Americans have viewed with great wariness. This chapter focuses on African populations, including a brief discussion of Afro-Caribbean people entering the U.S.

Caribbean Immigrants

African populations from the Caribbean were a large component of the Black population in the United States as early as the 18th century. A significant number among the enslaved population in North America had been born in, or lived in the Caribbean, where they had been "seasoned" to slave life. Most Africans brought to British American Colonies before 1720 were brought from the West Indies, as forced migrants (Hine and Harrold 2000). It was not until the beginning of the 20th century that we can see a significant migration of Caribbean Blacks to the United States. According to the 2000 census, 60 percent of foreign-born Blacks were from the Caribbean (McKinnon and Bennett 2005).

Early 20th century restrictive legislation such as The Immigration Act of 1924, which limited the number of non-European immigrants served to restrict non-White populations and resulted in a decline in Caribbean immigration. The number of immigrants dropped from 10,630 in 1924 to 321 in 1925 (*In Motion* 2005). After World War II, Caribbean immigration increased and continued to rise (*In Motion* 2005). More liberalized immigration laws made it possible for non-White immigrants to enter the United States and immigration from the Caribbean islands continued. Although the Immigration and Nationality Act of 1952 (McCarran-Walter Act), placed quotas on immigration, it did allow non-European immigrants to enter the United States. Likewise, the 1965 Immigration Act allowed immigration from all countries into America, though it imposed ceilings (Historical Documents in United States History, http://www.historicaldocuments.com/ImmigrationActof1790.htm). Economic and political conditions in the various Caribbean islands, along with expanding economic opportunities for Blacks in the United States, prompted increased migration. Figure 7.1 provides the migration trends of Afro-Caribbeans to the United States between 1989 and 2002. Jamaica provided the largest number of Caribbean immigrants during this seven-year period.

Largely skilled and professional workers, Afro-Caribbean people settled in states with large urban populations, including Florida and New York, gradually dispersing to suburban areas. New York, for example, saw a steady flow of Caribbean immigrants over the course of the twentieth century. Figure 7.2 shows the dispersion of Caribbean immigrants in selected metropolitan areas of the United States in 2000.

Caribbean immigrants established a variety of social, cultural, and religious institutions, and, especially at the beginning of the twentieth century, were active in political movements. Perceived as Black by the larger society, Caribbean immigrants often found common cause with native-born Blacks, rallying around social and political causes. They share food, music, and other cultural elements with their new homeland. By 2000, the U.S. Census reported that Caribbean immigrants constituted 10 percent of the foreign-born population in the

United States. Today there are an estimated 3 million Caribbean-born immigrants in the United States. The now several generations of American-born children of Caribbean immigrants increasingly identify themselves as African Americans. In recent decades, Africans from various nations have joined Caribbean immigrants in the United States (McKinnon, Bennett, and Bennett 2005).

Figure 7.1.
Migration Trends of Afro-Caribbeans to the United States, 1989 to 2002.

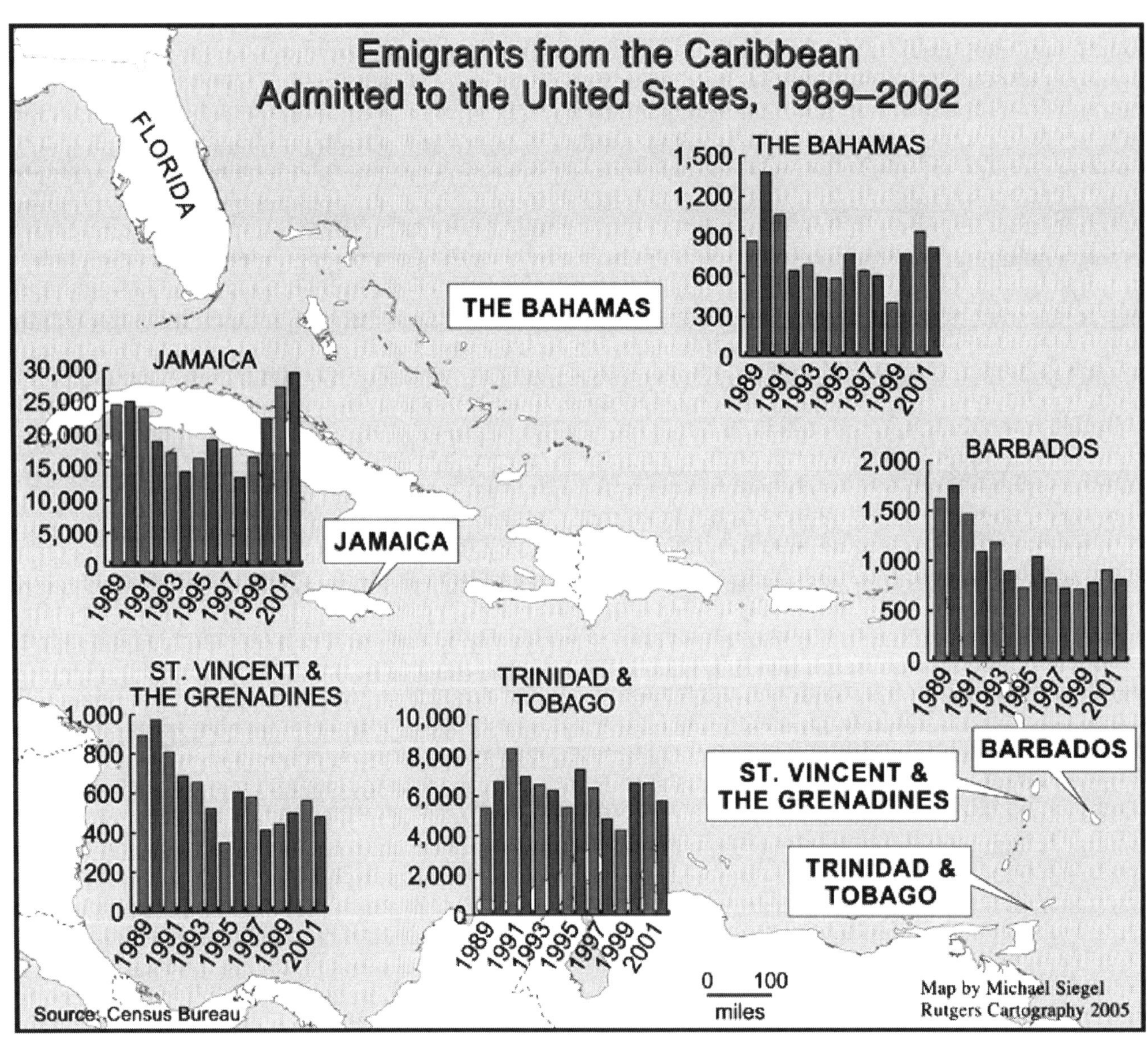

Figure 7.2.
Dispersion Trends of Afro-Caribbean Immigrants in Selected Metropolitan Areas of the United States.

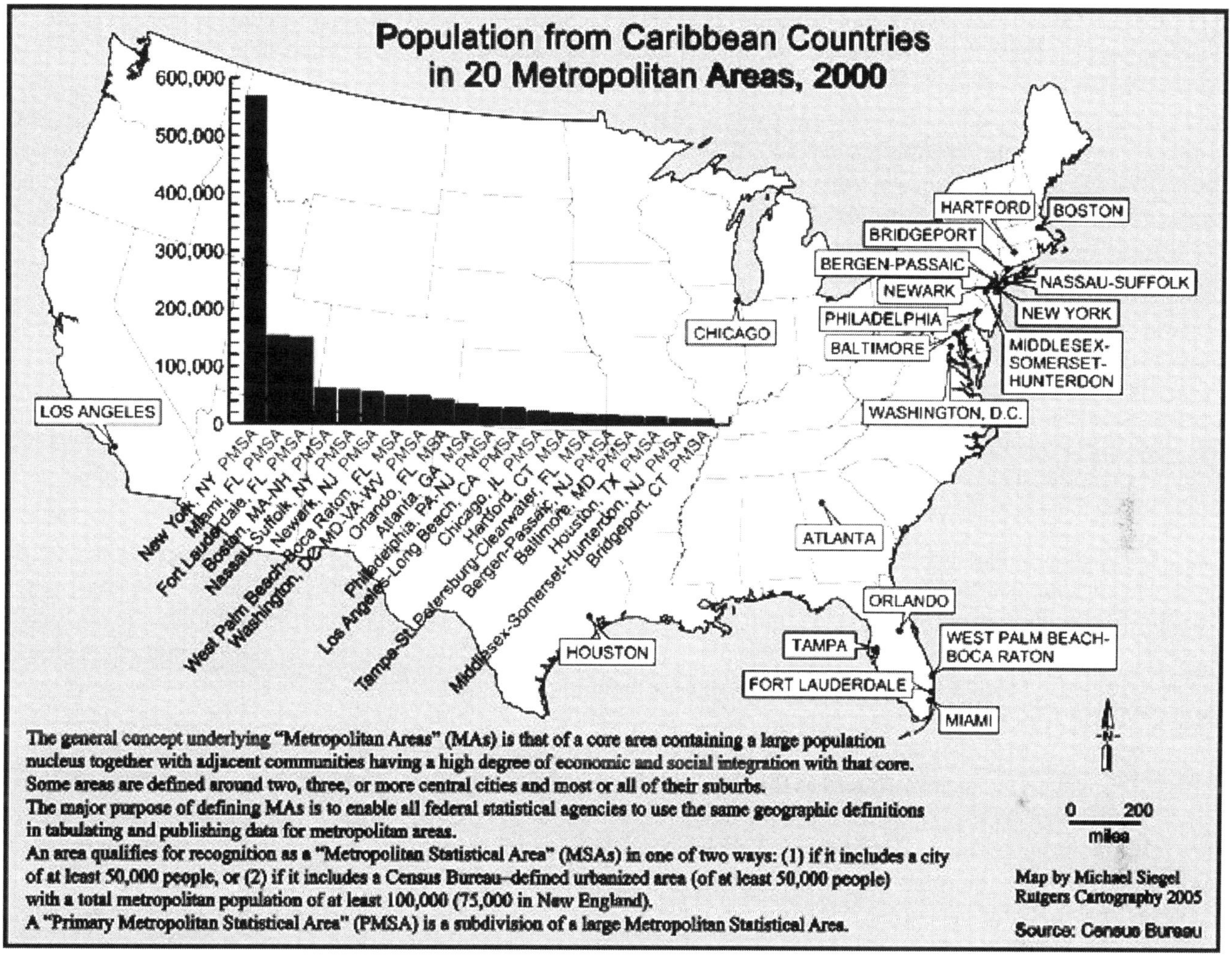

African Immigrants

Large-scale migration of Africans from the continent is relatively recent and has occurred over a short time span. Data show about 350 African migrants coming to the United Sates between 1891–1900 (Gordon 1998). In the 19th century Africans from the small island of Cape Verde, off the West coast of Africa, settled in the United States. The peak of their migration was in the first two decades of the 20th century. Settling mostly in the Northeast in places like New Bedford, Massachusetts, they worked in seafaring occupations and as agricultural labor in the cranberry industry. The Cape Verdeans created their own community enclaves, disassociating themselves from African Americans despite their own classification as Black by the larger White community, and maintaining their ethnicity as Portuguese colonials and stressing their cultural distinctiveness (Halter 1993).

The late 19th and early 20th century also saw a small number of Africans coming to the United States. Between 1900 and 1950 an estimated 31,000 Africans immigrated to the United States (Gordon 1998). Many Africans also came to the United States as students, with some sponsored by American missionaries who hoped they would return to Africa to become missionaries (Williams 1980). In the 1950s and 1960s a small number of Africans continued to attend colleges and universities in the United States, coming during a period of great change.[5] The first four decades of the twentieth century saw major social, cultural and economic changes for most U.S. Blacks.[6] However, by the Second World War a color barrier remained. Blacks responded by challenging the status quo. Groups such as the National Association for the Advancement of Colored People (NAACP) were founded and by the mid 1950s an all-out challenge to racial segregation in public schools was mounted.[7] It was into this milieu that African and Afro-Caribbean immigrants came and many identified with African Americans and their plight. The common bond of race and discrimination at that time often led to solidarity between African and Caribbean immigrants. Many Africans were influenced by the civil rights movement in the United States, returning to their homeland championing ideas of independence and autonomy. Immigrants of African descent also helped each other on a more personal level. In his autobiography Kwame Nkrumah tells the story of how he was helped by a fellow student from the Caribbean. Out of work, and with no place to stay during a break from college:

> I was wandering down Seventh Avenue in Harlem wondering where I could turn next when I suddenly ran into a fellow student from Lincoln who came from Demerara in British Guiana. I told him of my difficulties; no money, no job and nowhere to go. "Don't worry old chap," he said encouragingly, "I think I can solve the accommodation problem as a start." He explained that he knew a West Indian family who were extremely kind and sympathetic and that if he went along and put my case before them, he felt they might help me out. Sure enough, by the time I had told my story tears were in the eyes of the womenfolk who offered me their small spare room, and added that I was not to worry about payment until I managed to find a job. (Nkrumah in Tolbert)

Nkrumah's story illustrates bonds that often develop between populations in diasporas as a result of the racism experienced upon coming to the United States. Despite coming from a colonial background, the number of Africans in the Gold Coast relative to the United States would have made his U.S. experience in the United States more harsh. Harlem, at the time a largely Black community, served as a safe haven for Black immigrants. Housing discrimination meant Black immigrants could not find housing in non-Black neighborhoods and were forced to live among African Americans. Africans seeking education in the United States came with the goal of returning home to help their nations, through the 1960s. Some became active in the growing nationalist movements in Africa, influenced by African Americans in the civil rights movement.

However, by the 1970s inhospitable reception of returning Africans by their former colonial administrators resulted in increased migration to the United States that continues to grow. Figure 7.3 shows the number of African immigrants admitted to the United States between 1989 and 2002. African-born migrants numbered 2538 in 1900, and had increased 363,819 in 1990. By 2005 African-born U.S. residents numbered a little over a million, (Crary 2007). The U.S. Immigration and Naturalization Service recorded approximately 110,000 African immigrants in the twenty years between 1961 and 1980, and nearly five times that number (>530,000) between 1981 and 2000 (Takougang 2002). For example, in 1993 more than 21,000 of practicing physicians in the United States were Nigerian (United Nations Human Development Report, cited in Sako 2002). In recent years African immigration has been facilitated by the Immigration Reform and Control Act of 1986 and the Diversity Visa Program ("the lottery") of the Immigration Act of 1990 (Djamba 1999) and by Refugee Resettlement Policies. This has resulted in the arrival of both skilled professionals and unskilled workers. The diversity lottery visa program and refugee schemes have eroded the quality of African immigrants, which is reducing the high position originally held by Africans in terms of educational attainment. In 2001 of the 69,000 refugees who arrived in the United States, 28 percent were from Africa, a little under 20,000. Most of these refugees were from Sudan and Somalia; however, Liberia and Sierra Leone provided 18 and 11 percent, respectively (Grieco 2004). Increasingly, Africans residing in the United States are seeking to make their status legal. The Department of Homeland Security Office of Immigration statistics show that in 2002, 60,269 immigrants from Africa acquired permanent residence status legally (Grieco 2004). Table 7.1 shows the number of refugee admissions to the United States from Africa from 1980–2006 and Table 7.2 shows refugee arrivals to the United States from selected African countries between 1997 and 2006.[8]

Figure 7.3.
African Immigrants Admitted to the United States, 1989 to 2002.

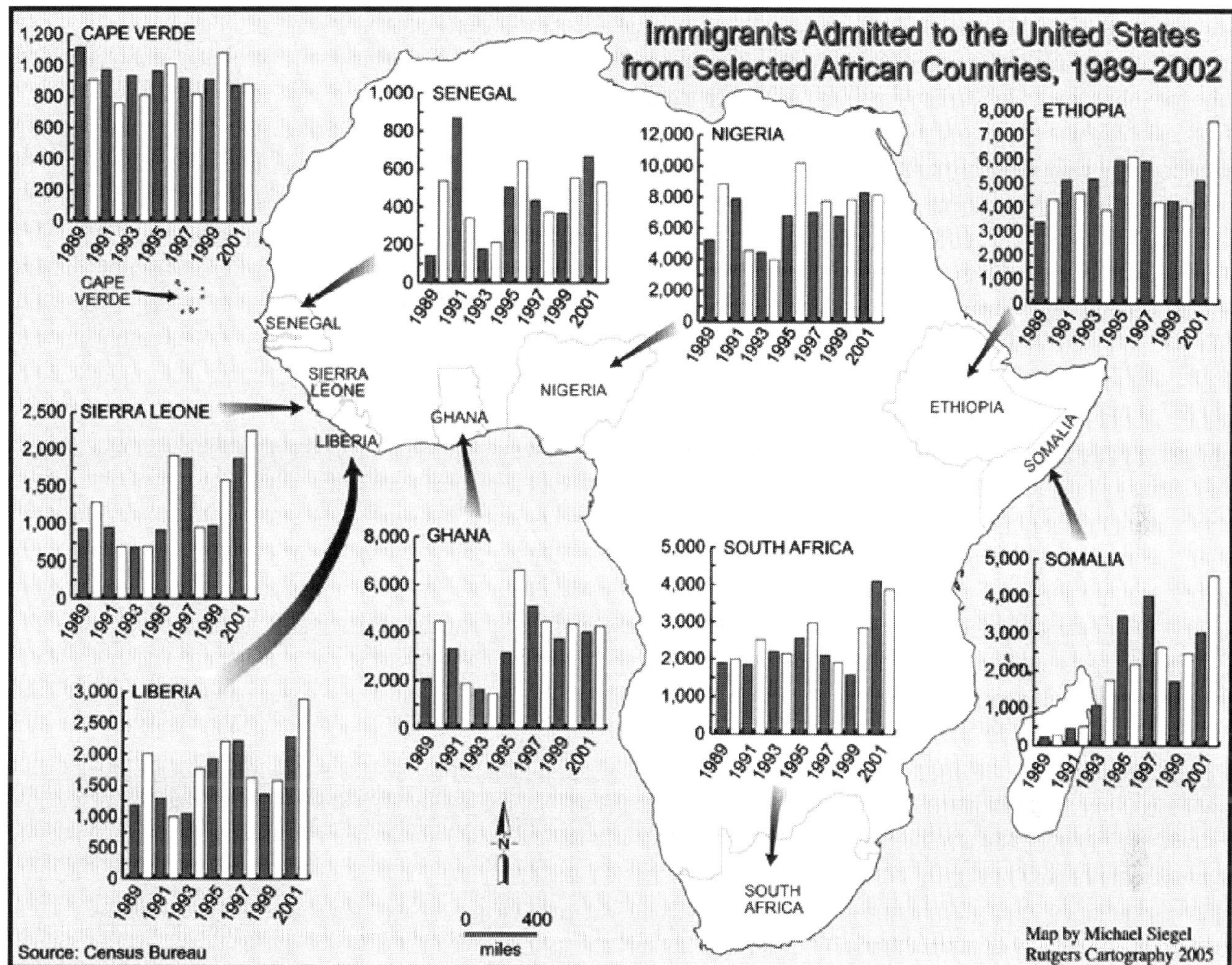

SETTLEMENT PATTERNS OF AFRICAN IMMIGRANTS

Similar to non-African migrants, large metropolitan areas attract the largest number of African immigrants.[9] Figure 7.4 illustrates the state-level settlement patterns of African-born populations for the year 2000. Washington, DC, New York, Chicago, Los Angeles, Houston, Dallas, Atlanta, and Boston are the primary immigrant metropolitan settlement areas. For example, the Washington, DC area attracts the largest number of African immigrants of major U.S. metropolitan areas due to the presence of friends and relatives, a sense of community, and initial assistance until new arrivals become established. Other factors include employment opportunities, and racial climate (Springer, Freidman, Cheung and Price 2001). The economic opportunities available in large metropolitan areas enable highly educated Africans to accept low paying jobs initially, while they seek something more desirable. In recent years, Africans have gravitated toward states in the Midwest such as Ohio and Minnesota that have not traditionally been attractive destinations. Either as first destinations or secondary migrations, these migrants have been aided by resettlement agencies and programs that place African refugees near support resources, which has led to a changed demographic landscape (Mott 2006).

Table 7.1.
Refugee Admissions to United States from Africa, 1980–2006.

Fiscal Year	No. of Refugees admitted
1980	955
1981	2,119
1982	3,412
1983	2,645
1984	2,749
1985	1,951
1986	1,322
1987	1,990
1988	1,593
1989	1,902
1990	3,453
1991	4,420
1992	5,470
1993	6,967
1994	5,860
1995	4,827
1996	7,604
1997	6,065
1998	6,887
1999	13,043
2000	17,561
2001	19,021
2002	2,548
2003	10,717
2004	29,125
2005	20,749
2006	18,182
Total	203,137

Source: U.S. Department of State, 2006
www.state.gov/g/prm/refadm/rls/85970.htm.

Table 7.2.
Refugee Arrivals to the United States from Selected African Countries, 1997–2006.

African Country	Year 1997	1998	1999	2000	2001	2002	2003	2004	2005	2006
Algeria	—	—	12	57	31	—	4	D	D	D
Angola	—	—	—	D	34	16	21	20	21	13
Burundi	33	24	223	165	109	62	16	276	214	466
Cameroon	19	15	9	7	5	6	6	D	6	29
CAR	—	—	D	—	D	—	D	24	—	23
Chad	45	41	22	D	D	D	D	4	—	4
DRC	45	52	42	1,354	260	107	251	569	424	405
Rep. of Congo	—	—	27	11	6	5	41	73	43	66
Cote d'Ivoire	—	D	5	—	D	3	4	—	5	23
Djibouti	16	15	8	—	12	D	D	6	—	—
Equatorial Guinea	—	—	—	12	—	—	D	—	25	11
Eritrea	7	9	32	94	109	13	23	128	327	538
Ethiopia	197	152	1,873	1,347	1,429	330	1,702	2,689	1,663	1,271
Gambia	16	50	13	13	5	—	9	3	—	6
Kenya	—	13	D	11	13	24	3	—	D	5
Liberia	231	1,494	2,495	2,620	3,429	559	2,957	7,140	4,289	2,402
Mauritania	—	—	D	—	202	6	—	—	3	88
Nigeria	7	312	625	50	85	28	57	34	11	15
Rwanda	100	86	153	345	94	47	47	176	183	112
Sierra Leone	57	176	675	1,128	2,004	176	1,378	1,086	829	439
Somalia	4,974	2,951	4,320	6,026	4,951	237	1,994	13,331	10,405	10,357
Sudan	277	1,252	2,393	3,833	5,959	897	2,139	3,500	2,205	1,848
Togo	30	15	93	511	280	16	47	35	72	18
Uganda	9	D	12	18	12	D	D	8	10	20
Zimbabwe	—	—	—	—	6	—	—	D	D	13

D = Data withheld to limit disclosure

Source: Homeland Security, 2007. Yearbook of Immigration Statistics: 2006 www.dhs.gov/ximgtn/statistics/publications/YrBk06RA.shtm.

Figure 7.4.
Settlement Patterns of African-Born Populations by State for the Year 2000.

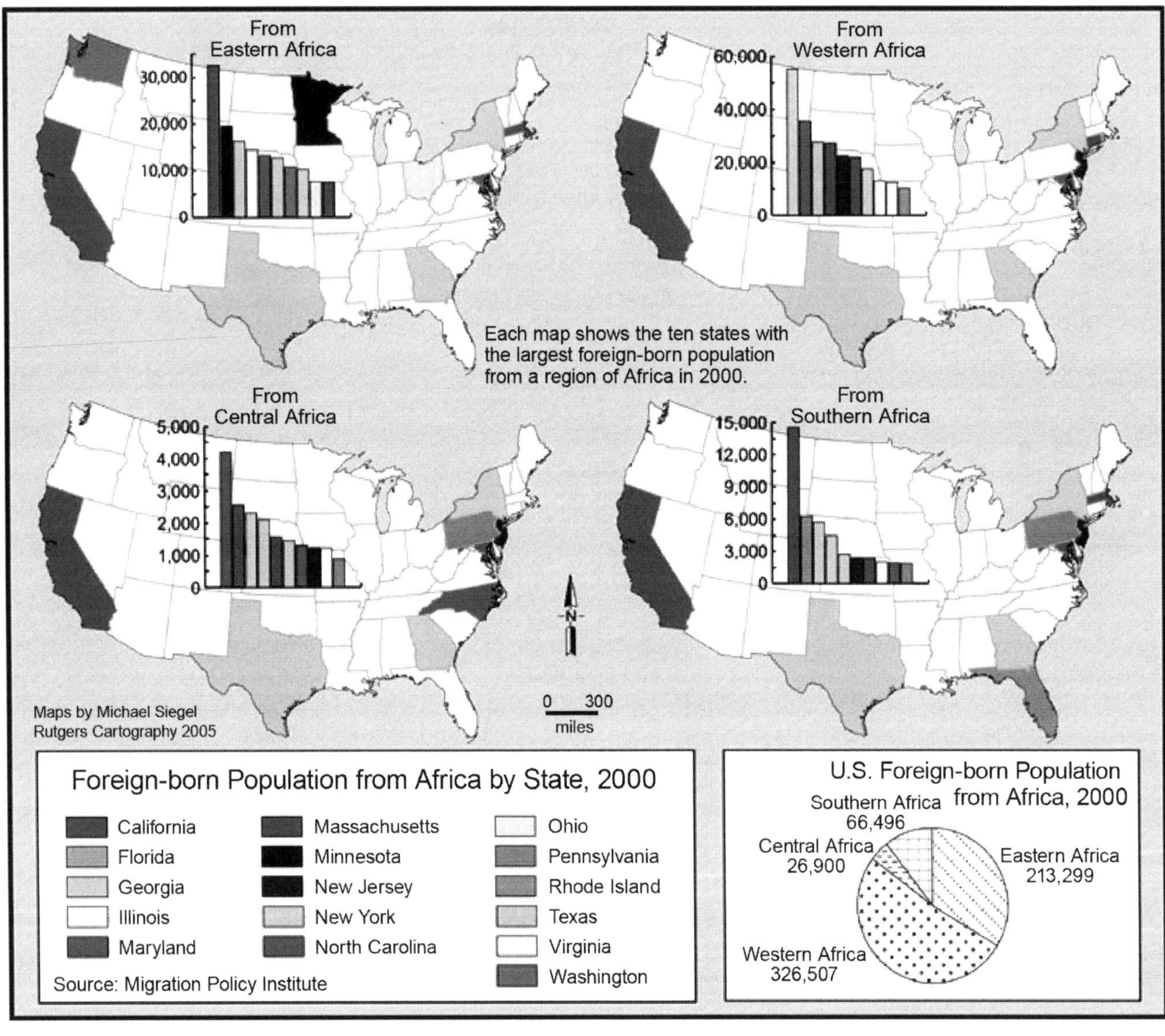

Blacks no longer settle exclusively in large urban centers, but increasingly seek suburban and rural areas or mostly White smaller urban areas (e.g., the Somalis in Maine). Nonetheless, urban areas remain important destinations for Black populations, both native and immigrant. Urban places become not only where African immigrants choose to settle, but also a means of creating communities and of establishing distance between themselves and other groups. Black immigrants recognize their minority status and the consequences of race and ethnicity in the United States, and choose to settle either in areas with significant Black populations, or in largely non-Black neighborhoods and communities. In the former, they are assuming a racial identity within the context of race relations in the United States; in the latter they are removing themselves from that identity. In order to acculturate, Black migrants "face an entirely different set of issues [and] . . . must reconstruct and redefine their identity in terms of the American society's system of race relations and hierarchies" (Benson 2006, p. 221). Despite the lack of acceptance and the racial stereotypes of Whites, some Black immigrants prefer settling among mixed or largely White populations (Obiakor and Grant 2002). African immigrants are unlikely to spatially assimilate in African-American neighborhoods because it would hinder socio-economic advancement, accelerate the loss of ethnic identity and they are less likely to identify deeply with post-slavery issues than native-born American Blacks (Freeman 2002).[10]

The growing number of immigrants from Africa and the Caribbean has led to debates and discussion about who can be classified as African American. After a few years in the United States many African immigrants often refer to themselves as African Americans much like Irish or Italian Americans might. American-born children of African and Caribbean migrants are more likely to identify themselves as African American while acknowledging that their parents may hail from a country in Africa or the West Indies. Settlement into Black neighborhoods tends to increase the identity as African American. However, Black immigrants who settle in areas with few African Americans are more likely to identify themselves ethnically rather than in racial terms. Thus, "Blackness among Black immigrants in the African Diaspora is lived in many different ways. These include assimilation into African-American culture, adherence to an ethnic culture or choosing an 'immigrant identity'" (Pierre 2002). The deliberate creation by Black immigrants of a distinct identity from traditional African Americans permits the hope of protecting their children from racialization in American society. The success of immigrants and their U.S.-born children depends in part upon place. The residential location of immigrants can enhance or limit success.

An important factor that hurts one's chances of success is residence in a somewhat isolated, large, and poor residential concentration of one's ethnic group (Frazier, Margai, and Tettey-Fio 2003). Such places seem to be the contexts in which many teens form oppositional identities, usually either Black or Mexican or Puerto Rican or Latino . . . [because these areas breed feelings of being marginalized] (Allen 2006, p. 25).

While retaining some aspects of their cultural heritage, some Africans make a concerted effort to assimilate into American society, involving themselves in local politics, business, and professional sports (e.g., basketball and football — especially Nigerians). Because most immigrants from the Caribbean and Africa choose to settle in urban areas, they are more likely to be in close proximity with African Americans, resulting in some friction, but also affording an opportunity for the groups to learn about each other, and in some instances, to work together in both social and political causes, and also on an individual level. Cultural clashes and misunderstanding between Africans and African Americans occur because native-born Blacks often perceive the Black immigrant population as a threat or competition for jobs and other resources, and as reaping the benefits of their hard won struggles. The two groups have little cultural connection. African immigrants believe that charges of discrimination leveled at the dominant society by African Americans are exaggerated and claim they do not experience racism (Apraku 1991). However, as the Black immigrants experience racial discrimination they develop a common interest with African Americans. More recently efforts are being made on both sides to recognize their commonalities, and to come together for mutual benefit and advancement. In June 2005, for instance, the African Catholic Ministry of the Roman Catholic Archdiocese in Indianapolis sponsored an event that brought together African Americans and Africans. "A Celebration of the African Family Tree" allowed both groups to learn about elements of each other's cultures and to recognize their common ancestry (Perry 2005).

African immigrants have the highest level of education of all immigrants to the United States (Logan 2007), but oftentimes face downward mobility upon arrival.[11] In spite of structural limitations like race, however, African immigrants possess cultural values that can facilitate integration and upward mobility in American society. The socio-economic status of African immigrants, although higher than native Blacks, is nineteen percent lower than Whites (Dodoo 1997) due to racial discrimination (Dodoo and Takyi 2002).

Political integration of African immigrants into American political institutions is similarly limited (Shobo 2005). Until recently there have been low rates of naturalization among Africans as they often expressed hopes of returning to their homeland, articulating the idea that their stay in the United States was temporary. Africans did not seek to challenge the status quo and were not necessarily politically active. In recent years this has changed as African immigrants have championed political causes. In 1999 when Amadou Diallo, a Guinean immigrant was shot to death by New York City police officers, African immigrants joined African American groups in rallying and protesting the injustice. Likewise, African immigrants are engaged in various ways in educating the African community as to their rights in the United States. In 1999 The Africa Legal, Human and Civil Rights Center was established in Washington, DC to educate and represent African immigrants. The center provides legal services to immigrants, aids Africans who might find themselves homeless, and works with Africans seeking asylum in the United States (Iwarere 2004).

Cities across the United States are also reaching out to African immigrants. In 2006, the Mayor of Washington, DC and its City Council established the Office of African Affairs in response to the calls of African activists. The purpose of the Office on African Affairs is to provide "constituent services and information to African communities through programmatic activities and outreach materials; serves as a liaison between the African communities, District government agencies, and the Mayor; and provides briefings to the Mayor and District government agencies about the particular needs or interests of the African residents of the District of Columbia" (oaa.dc.gov). Citing the fast-growing population of African immigrants in the region, supporters cited the need for a service that would address issues of cultural isolation, inadequate resources, and lack of employment opportunities for Africans (Woodlee 2005). In September 2007 the Office, co-sponsored with African businesses and other organizations, celebrated the contributions of African immigrants to the city by an event bringing together native Africans living in the Washington, DC metropolitan area. Despite greater integration into American society, generally African immigrants continue to maintain strong ties with their homelands, sending large-scale remittances back to the Continent because they have a vested interest in their homelands.

The large sums of money that immigrants send home has a tremendous impact, and is an important source of development. Research shows that as the earning power of the Diasporic Africans grows, the remittances increase. Africa's development efforts can be enhanced by increased cooperation between its Diaspora and continental Africans (Erhagbe 2007). Although they might be critical of the economic and political policies of their homeland, Africans continue to maintain pride in their countries, and cultural, family, and political ties with their homeland. In recent years Diasporic Africans, while assimilating to life in the United States, have found ways to remain engaged with political developments in their countries, monitoring elections, campaigning for their candidates of choice, and even donating money to political causes.

SUMMARY AND CONCLUSIONS

As more and more migrants from Africa and the Caribbean come to the United States, the definition of "Who an African American is" has surely broadened. The children of migrants from Africa and the Caribbean often don't think of themselves as Nigerian, Jamaican, African, or West Indian, but as African Americans. It is clear that these immigrants have had a significant impact on the United States, whether in terms of numbers or cultural influences. As their numbers continue to grow, African and Caribbean immigrants are influencing the landscape of many cities and towns in the country. More stringent immigration laws notwithstanding, it seems likely that these immigrants will continue to come to the United States. Debates are likely to continue about how to define African Americans, and who can qualify as African American. There will be a need for people of African descent, whether from Africa, the Caribbean, or those who consider themselves the true African Americans, to create a shared identity (Copeland-Carson 2004).

NOTES

[1] The Schomburg Center for Research in Black Culture launched a new digital website in February 2005.

[2] "The African Diaspora concept subsumes the following: the global dispersion of Africans throughout history; the emergence of a cultural identity abroad based on origin and social condition; and the psychological or physical return to the homeland, Africa. Thus viewed, the African Diaspora assumes the character of a dynamic, continuous, and complex phenomenon stretching across time, geography, class and gender" (Harris 1982).

[3] Blacks born in the U.S. gained citizenship through the Fourteenth Amendment to the Constitution July 28, 1868; and the right to vote with the Fifteenth Amendment February 3, 1870. www.nps.gov/archive/malu/documents/amend14.htm

[4] The judge in the case noted: "For if they were so received, and entitled to the privileges and immunities of citizens, it would exempt them from the operation of the special laws and from the police regulations which they considered to be necessary for their own safety. It would give to persons of the negro race, who were recognized as citizens in any one State of the Union, the right to enter every other State whenever they pleased, singly or in companies, without pass or passport, and without obstruction, to sojourn there as long as they pleased, to go where they pleased at every hour of the day or night without molestation, unless they committed some violation of law for which a White man would be punished; and it would give them the full liberty of speech in public and in private upon all subjects upon which its own citizens might speak; to hold public meetings upon political affairs, and to keep and carry arms wherever they went. And all of this would be done in the face of the subject race of the same color, both free and slaves, and inevitably producing discontent and insubordination among them, and endangering the peace and safety of the State." Extract from the Dred Scott Case: The Supreme court decision (http://www.pus.org/wgbh/aia/part4/4h2933t.html).

[5] Lincoln University, founded by White missionaries in 1854, was host to many African students during the 19th and into the 20th century and that tradition continues today. The first African students came to Lincoln in 1873. Other universities like Fisk and Oberlin also admitted African students in this period. Most of these students returned to Africa, either to serve as missionaries or teachers. Lincoln University continued to recruit African students. Perhaps its most famous African alumni were Kwame Nkrumah and Nnamdi Azikwe, who were to become the first post independence leaders of Ghana and Nigeria respectively. Black migration continued in the early 20th century as African Americans moved from rural to urban areas and from South to North and across the country. But Blacks had difficulty finding jobs, faced housing problems and were mostly segregated.

[6] The National Association for the Advancement of Colored People was founded February 12, 1909.

[7] Professionals are generally students who remained in the U.S. or educated, new immigrants from Africa. A 1972 study found that one-third of African immigrants were professionals, a higher percentage than those from Asia, Europe and South America (Fortney 1972). In spite of this, Shobo (2005) reports that Asians and Europeans have higher socio-economic outcomes.

Refugees may not be skilled for the American environment. For example, Rural Somali Bantu are unskilled, but many Liberian and Sierra Leonean refugees fleeing war are highly educated. The 1980 Refugee Act allowed eligible refugees to attain permanent residency after one year in the United States. Subsequent legislation allowed larger numbers of refugees to settle in the United States. The largest number of refugees has been from the Horn of Africa from the countries of Somalia, Sudan and Ethiopia. Following conflict in Liberia, Sierra Leone and Democratic Republic of Congo, significant numbers were granted asylum from those countries. The proposed ceiling for African refugees for 2007 is 22,000. This is a higher number of refugees than allowed from other regions — Europe, Asia, Latin America and Caribbean (www.state.gov/documents/organization/74762.pdf).

[8] Maps reprinted by permission of Schomburg.

[9] Crary cites the case of a professional couple from Ethiopia who having left a comfortable life and professional jobs in their homeland, now struggle to begin a new life. The husband, once a bank manager, now works as a bank teller.

[10] Typically, African immigrants have a high level of human capital, but due to the structural constraints imposed by race in the United States this does not equate to a parallel level of socio-economic achievement.

[11] Jacqueline Copeland Carson has done a case study on a non-profit group on Minneapolis which works with populations of African descent in an attempt to create a sense of community and identity. There are other groups throughout the United States that are working towards the same goal.

Theme 1:
Persistence of Inequalities

## Chapter 8

Austin: A City Divided

EMILY SKOP

Segregation means "to set apart from others or from the main mass or group; to isolate" (Webster 1983). Because segregation frequently stems from callousness, it may be a difficult subject to discuss. To acknowledge it today is an admission that despite over 150 years of laws and court decisions, behaviors and attitudes have not changed universally. Austin, Texas provides a case study of modern segregation. Social privilege and the processes of minoritization and racialization create the circumstances whereby Blacks in Austin are repeatedly marginalized and dislocated.

This chapter interjects a counter narrative to Austin as an economically booming, idea city, home to young, restless, and White members of the creative class, instead describing an Austin characterized by racial and spatial division, particularly between Blacks and the White majority. Based on detailed analysis of newspapers, government, corporate, and non-governmental organization documents, this chapter charts past and present institutional and political forces that have produced a racially and spatially divided Austin. The results indicate that four public policies have been, and continue to be, especially important in creating and maintaining segregation in Austin: the 1928 City Plan, the 1956 Federal Highway Act, the 1972–1975 Urban Revitalization Program, and the 1998 Smart Growth Initiative. Each of these public policies played an active role in imposing both symbolic and ecological constraints on people's movement, and thus effectively isolated Blacks from the rest of the community.

MINORITIZATION AND RACIALIZATION

Regarding social conditions that lead to the formation of segregated neighborhoods, Hayden, an urban historian, argues "one of the consistent ways to limit the economic and political rights of groups has been . . . by limiting access to space" (Hayden 1995). Indeed, numerous scholars have pointed out the key role of space in the negotiation of social identities, and in creating both spaces of inclusion and spaces of exclusion (Anderson, 1987; Jackson 1987; Dear and Wolch 1990; Duncan and Ley 1993; Bonnett 1997; Frazier and Tettey-Fio 2006). Space, they argue, serves to reify disempowerment, disadvantage, and exploitation, at the same time that it also reinforces power, privilege, and prestige.

Laguerre's concept of minoritization figures into this discussion of the identity politics of American cities (Laguerre 1999). Laguerre points out a kind of conflation between metaphorical and geographic space, noting that to be "minority" is not necessarily to belong to a numerical minority, but rather refers to a minor share of social power, which results in and reinforces a concomitant spatial marginalization (Chappell 2006). At the same time, he argues that certain spaces in the social landscape take on a "minoritized" character when they are designated as the proper place for minoritized populations. A landscape of exclusion emerges, and space serves to reinforce racial categories.

Geographers have gone further to articulate how race is not only socially constructed, but spatially constituted (Dwyer and Jones 2000; Kobayashi and Peake 2000; Pulido 2000; Hoelscher 2003; Skop 2006). They provide a framework for understanding the ways in which race and ethnicity intersect with other social differences in shaping unequal geographies of mobility, belonging, exclusion, and displacement. These scholars contend that in order to fully understand identities in contemporary cities it is necessary to examine how different subject positions of residents shape their socio-spatial experiences. Particularly important are the socio-spatial relations and struggles between racial minorities and the White majority.

Thus, research focuses on the ways in which minorities are "racialized" both socially and spatially to conceptualize their inclusion/exclusion. Both subtle and overt ways in which racial boundaries have been maintained and transformed through time are identified as key in the racialization process. Subtle methods are mostly symbolic constraints, like an invisible "unwelcome mat" laid out in certain areas and neighborhoods of the city, and/or discrimination and racism by outsiders that is difficult to document. Overt actions are more obvious, including physical punishment and violence against individuals when they enter particular areas of the city, various forms of mobility control that restrict access, zoning ordinances and fire and safety regulations that facilitate the production of different kinds of spaces, and highway construction projects that divide neighborhoods through concrete and material barriers.

Thus, the particular social and spatial practices of racialization are connected to the wider social structure in which those practices are embedded and from which their meanings and values are derived. These new geographies outline the hierarchies, institutions, and changing ideologies of race and racialization as they relate to and reproduce existing social, economic, and political structures. Racial and ethnic identities do not emerge in a vacuum untouched by the spaces and places within which they exist. As Mitchell contends, "The relationship between material form and ideological representation must be the center of our examinations" (Mitchell 1996). Certainly, the buildings and neighborhoods that mark particular racial and ethnic groups cannot be underestimated in their reinforcing roles in the process of racialization and minoritization. Urban spaces, then, are more than a passive backdrop for the negotiation of racial and ethnic identities.

RESEARCH QUESTIONS, DATA AND METHODS

Locating space and place in contemporary racial and ethnic processes enriches our understandings of majority/minority experiences in U.S. society. Thus, in this chapter, I utilize the concepts of minoritization and racialization to theorize how members of both minority and majority groups construct their respective "other," and thereby themselves. The key idea guiding this research is that identity politics are often articulated spatially; thus, conflicts often become manifest as struggles and claims for control of territory and place.

This chapter is part of a larger project that draws upon a variety of data sources and methods to explore the process of racialization in Austin (Skop 2007). The project has three phases; the first phase involved a detailed analysis of the 1990 and 2000 U.S. Census Public Use Microdata Sample (PUMS), five percent sample files, as well as the 2005 U.S. Census American Community Survey, one percent sample files. These data were obtained through the Minnesota Population Center's Integrated Public Use Microdata Series (IPUMS) website (usa.ipums.org) for each of the three time periods (Ruggles et al. 2004). IPUMS is a particularly useful resource as it provides detailed information about sample households and their component individuals; data that other secondary sources do not incorporate. These data include a housing unit record, which provides details on a variety of housing characteristics, and a person record, which specifies social, economic, and demographic attributes.

The second phase required the collection and analysis of more than one hundred archival and "fugitive" documents (those items that are likely to disappear since they are unlikely to be archived, like event flyers and Internet website calendars) (Skop 2008). These documents, which came from a variety of government, corporate, and non-governmental organizations, along with assorted media materials, were essential in uncovering the practices and discourses of urban planning politics in Austin. Documents were coded and analyzed following the "grounded theory" framework and the use of computer-assisted qualitative data analysis software, NUD*IST, to allow for automated coding, text search and retrieval, and pattern discernment (Strauss and Corbin 1998).

The third phase is ongoing and involves primary data collection, relying on both semi-structured interviews with key informants (city council members, city planners, members of the business community, reporters, members of various non-governmental organizations, and neighborhood activists) and direct observation of planning meetings associated with the "Smart Growth Initiative" beginning in 2002. This method permits first-hand observation of how interest group positions are articulated and contested.

In the inductive tradition, this research has proven to be a dynamic process — those questions that I started out with have shifted and transformed as I come into contact with more individuals, institutions, and documents. Thus, in this chapter, I specifically focus on public policy to outline the nature of belonging and membership and the way in which processes of inclusion and exclusion are institutionalized. Public policy is viewed by many scholars as a discursive form that scripts the racialization of groups. In other words, public policy is often seen as a way for elites to construct borders and maintain privilege, power and prestige. Ultimately, public policies construct and maintain borders of exclusivity and barriers to mobility, thus reinforcing the racialization process. Public policy can also take on a spatial component, and territorial claims reflect the nature of power relations and the ability of one group to determine, superimpose, and perpetuate lines of separation, or to remove them.

I highlight four policies that have a particular socio-spatial component that have continually reinforced difference in Austin: the 1928 City Plan; the 1956 Federal Highway Act, the 1972–1975 Urban Revitalization Program, and the 1998 Smart Growth Initiative. While much of what created segregation came about informally, without the sanction of the law, I argue that public policy was critical in constructing racial divides in Austin. I contend that though some of these policies may at first appear to be benevolent and benign, all of them have ultimately proven to be exclusionary to minorities, thus reinforcing the racialization process.

WHY AUSTIN?

Unfortunately, when we look at Austin's landscape, there are a variety of indicators that suggest a racially divided city: socially, economically, and spatially. This observation runs contrary to the more popular and familiar imagined geographies of Austin. After all, Austin has become a well-known icon: it's the Live Music Capital, the home of the South X Southwest music and film festival and Austin City Limits, and the "most livable" city in the South. The city is even reputed for keeping things "weird" in a campaign to protect local businesses from the encroachment of franchise chains. In the past twenty-five years, Austin has become internationally renowned for its accelerated creative-based economic development.

Austin's high-tech development began with the rise of Dell Computers, and was followed by companies like Motorola, IBM, Advanced Micro Devices, and Sematech. All of this high-tech growth has led to the area becoming known as "Silicon Hills." From 1985 to 2006, based on extensive academic-business-government collaboration from the local to the global scale, the metropolis has managed to consistently outperform national growth levels (Badenhausen 2003). As a result, Austin continuously ranks at the top of a well-known index of creative cities (Florida 2002).

According to this powerful narrative, Austin has the three "T's" that are the main prerequisites of creative cities: Talent (have a highly talented/educated/skilled population), Technology (have the technological infrastructure necessary to fuel an entrepreneurial culture) and Tolerance (have a diverse community, which has a "live and let live" ethos) (Florida 2003). City boosters have done extraordinarily well in cultivating this image of Austin as a creative center — and newly established and relocated high-tech and creative industry firms, along with the young, college-educated, and mostly White Americans who arrive in Austin every day to take advantage of strong job markets, continuously reinforce this representation. They see Austin as the ideal, multimedia playground for those with social privilege who are seeking not only adventure, but also for those looking for a liberal and open-minded environment (especially considering Austin's geographic location as the most moderate hub in an otherwise conservative region).

The major problem with this geographical imagining is that it has been created and reinforced by those with social privilege, in an (often well-meaning) effort to capitalize on what has obviously become a highly successful model of urban development. While some privately recognize that all this creative growth cannot come without a price, few are willing to jump off the bandwagon and say so.

Even a brief analysis of 2000 U.S. Census data, however, dramatically reveals great socioeconomic divides between the largest population groups in Austin. These disparities are most apparent along racial and ethnic lines; as Table 8.1 illustrates, most minority groups in Austin are disadvantaged when compared to the White majority in terms of education, household income, poverty, and other measures. Blacks, especially, stand out in terms of low levels of education (18.3 percent of Blacks aged 25 and older have not graduated from high school), high levels of poverty (14.5 percent of individuals live below the poverty level), and median incomes far below Austin's average (Black households average $37,700 vs. the overall metropolitan area average $49,800). It is important to point out that Blacks fair even worse than most recently arrived immigrant groups in Austin, the majority of whom (74 percent) arrived after 1990 (Skop and Buentello 2008).

Table 8.1.
Socioeconomic Indicators for the Austin Metropolitan Area, 2000.

	Native-born White	Native-born Hispanic	Native-born Black	Native-born Asian	Native-born Other Race	Foreign-born Mexican	Foreign-born Indian	Foreign-born Vietnamese	Foreign-born Chinese	Foreign-born Canadian	Total Population
Educational Attainment*											
% without a HS Diploma	5.3	27.6	18.3	6.3	11.2	87.2	8.1	21.6	6.0	1.8	14.3
% with a BA or higher	46.4	19.6	23.0	53.9	34.5	6.8	83.0	31.9	78.1	58.7	38.8
English Ability**											
Speaks English only	95.5	37.1	95.9	51.8	90.1	4.9	13.0	6.7	4.1	76.9	74.1
Speaks English Well or Very Well	3.7	57.9	3.9	45.3	9.4	41.0	79.2	69.3	78.3	21.5	19.9
Speaks Not Well or Not at All	0.4	5.0	0.2	2.9	0.5	54.0	7.6	24.0	17.7	1.5	6.0
Socioeconomic Status											
Median Household Income ($) in 1999	55,000	40,800	37,700	30,000	45,000	34,400	65,100	60,400	46,000	65,600	49,800
Mean Household Size (persons per household)	2.3	2.9	2.7	2.0	2.3	4.4	2.7	3.3	2.4	2.3	2.6
% of Individuals Living in Poverty	6.8	15.0	14.5	18.4^	7.7	23.0	13.0^	7.0	7.7	5.5	10.4

**for the population aged 25+*
***for the population aged 5+*
^When the population enrolled in universities is excluded, the native-born Asian poverty rate drops to 6.8 percent and the foreign-born Indian poverty rate drops to 8.9 percent
Source: Authors' calculations of 2000 5% PUMS data obtained from www.ipums.org
Note: group quarters population removed from analysis; METAREA variable used to delineate Austin metro (Travis, Hayes, and Williamson counties only)

These socioeconomic disparities also become manifest in the residential geographies of population groups in Austin. Social privilege sustains landscapes of exclusion in the most desirable areas of the metropolis. Meanwhile, non-Whites in the community are repeatedly marginalized, dislocated, and relegated to the least desirable environments. A clear east-west divide marks the city. Interstate 35 concretizes racial divisions between east and west Austin and serves as a symbolic and physical barrier between racialized minorities and the White majority. Figure 8.1, especially, illustrates the clear east-west divide between Blacks and other population groups in Austin.

The East Austin enclave is a site where Blacks have found their homes largely as a result of factors imposed from the outside by those with more power upon those with less. Indeed, East Austin, whose greater area covers about 20 square miles just east of Interstate 35, is a border that has traditionally separated the area both physically and symbolically from both the bustling downtown and the rapidly growing suburbs of Austin.

For many years, this minoritized space has reinforced and maintained racial/ethnic categories in place. But in recent years, as more and more White residents (especially those newly arriving, young "creative" professionals that are not aware of the symbolic divide between east and west Austin) have discovered, the highway could be regarded as a mere physical divide that is easily crossed. It is the proximity of this area to the city's heart, coupled with the fact that real estate is about half of what it costs downtown, that suddenly makes East Austin a hot market for new residential and commercial businesses. Thus, another story has also begun to emerge in this place, one where Blacks are once again being displaced as a result of the actions and inactions of the White majority.

In the end, the evolution of the East Austin landscape tells a tale that has been largely overlooked in accounts of Austin's history. Patterns of spatial exclusion and marginalization of the impoverished have existed throughout Austin's history, and thus should be considered a constant in this urban landscape. Contemporary segregated cultural landscapes of Austin are a legacy of the city's racial divide. Today's limited mobility is based in historical racial dynamics between Whites and minorities in Austin. By outlining some of this history, we can at least begin to reconcile some of the harsh realities of Austin's past, which can then be considered as we construct Austin's future. As Cloud argues, "East Austin is an area steeped in heritage. It is not the same heritage that is reflected in the monuments that reside on the lawn of the State Capitol, but it is a history that is important nonetheless" (Cloud 2006).

Figure 8.1.
Pre-1928: The Emergence of Freedom Towns.

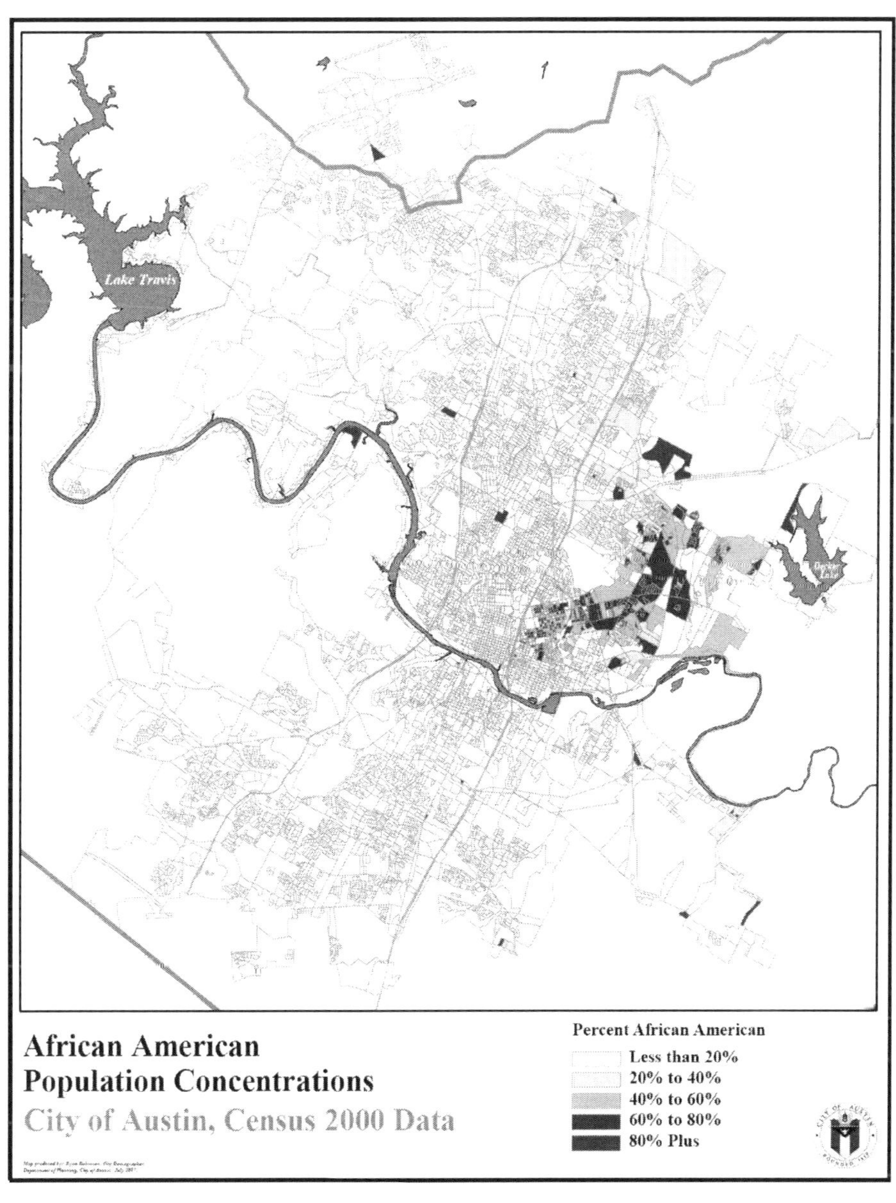

The initial plan of Austin emerged in 1838, when a man named Edwin Waller led a group of surveyors to plan and construct a new city in the hill country of central Texas. Waller narrowed the site to 640-acres that fronted the Colorado River and was nestled between Waller Creek on the east and Shoal Creek on the west. From these east-west divides, he created a fourteen-block grid that was bisected by Congress Avenue, and extended northward from the Colorado River to "Capitol Square."[1] That original grid still exists in the central city today, and continues to define the core of the central business district.

Shortly after proclaiming the territory that would become Austin, mostly White European settlers began to move to the area. They were largely attracted to Austin's natural beauty, healthfulness, abundant natural resources, central location in the Texas Territory, and promise as an economic hub. Many also brought slaves to the area; indeed, in 1860, 35 percent of Austin's families owned slaves (Lack 1981).

After the civil war ended, Austin's Black population increased dramatically. At this time, Austin became a federally protected sanctuary from the violence that was a gruesome reality for freed Blacks living in many parts of Texas. The image of the city as a tolerant place thus emerged in this early history.[2] As a result, hundreds of freed men and women came to Austin seeking "education and economic opportunities as well as the protection of federal troops" (Hardy et al. 2000). By 1870 Austin's 1,615 Black residents comprised 36 percent of the city's 4,428 inhabitants.

But as the capital city grew, and the Black population increased as a percentage of the population, White residents became less tolerant of their newly emancipated Black neighbors. A system of segregation emerged, with Blacks separated from Whites in distinct areas of the city and its outskirts (Hardy et al. 2000). Throughout the 1860s and 1870s, the city's Black populace established many residential communities, including Masontown, Kincheonville, Wheatville, Pleasant Hill, and Clarksville, among others. These "freedom towns," as they came to be called, could be found interspersed throughout the city; some families lived in housing near the Capitol, others clustered in dwelling units on the west side of town, and through time, many others created separate enclaves along the eastern edge of Waller Creek, on the easternmost border of the city limits (Orum 2002).

Wheatville, for example, was an area of several acres on the northern end of town (which today houses the fraternity and sorority houses of the University of Texas) that was named for James Wheat, a Black freedman. He purchased the first plot of land in the area just after Emancipation. Several Black families quickly followed in his footsteps and established households in the community. Wheatville was a very lively place, with a commercial strip that housed a number of Black-owned businesses. It was a self-contained community for many years, until actions by the ever-growing state university, backed by city policy, began to push Blacks out of the area.

Most displaced residents, along with newly arriving Black migrants, began to take up residence just on the other side of what was then known as East Avenue (and which today is known as Interstate 35). Though there is some mystery about how Blacks came to be concentrated in the East Austin sector of the city before the 1920s, a variety of subtle and overt measures were known to be effective in manipulating the residential and social mobility of Black residents. The result was a sea change in the distribution of Black settlements in the City of Austin; by 1931, approximately 70 percent of Austin's Black residents would be concentrated in two census tracts located in the area that would eventually come to be known as East Austin (Blunt, Frye, and Walker 2006).

1928: Austin's City Plan

By the late 1920s the methods by which the minority section of town developed became quite clear and to-the-point. Instead of subtle measures to "encourage" Black residents to abandon their homes scattered throughout Austin, an overt plan was crafted by city planners to remove and dismantle all Black enclaves not located in East Austin, and to design a deliberately segregated city.

Thus, the codified racial segregation of Austin began with the city's first Master Plan of Development of 1928, as illustrated in Figure 8.2. In just a few sentences, the city relegated an entire population of "colored" people to one area of the city.

> In our studies in Austin we have found that the Negroes are present in small numbers, in practically all sections of the city, excepting the area just east of East Avenue and south of the City Cemetery. This area seems to be an all Negro population. It is our recommendation of this district as a Negro district; and that all the facilities and conveniences be provided the Negroes in this district, as an incentive to draw the Negro population to this area. (Hardy et al. 2000)

Figure 8.2.

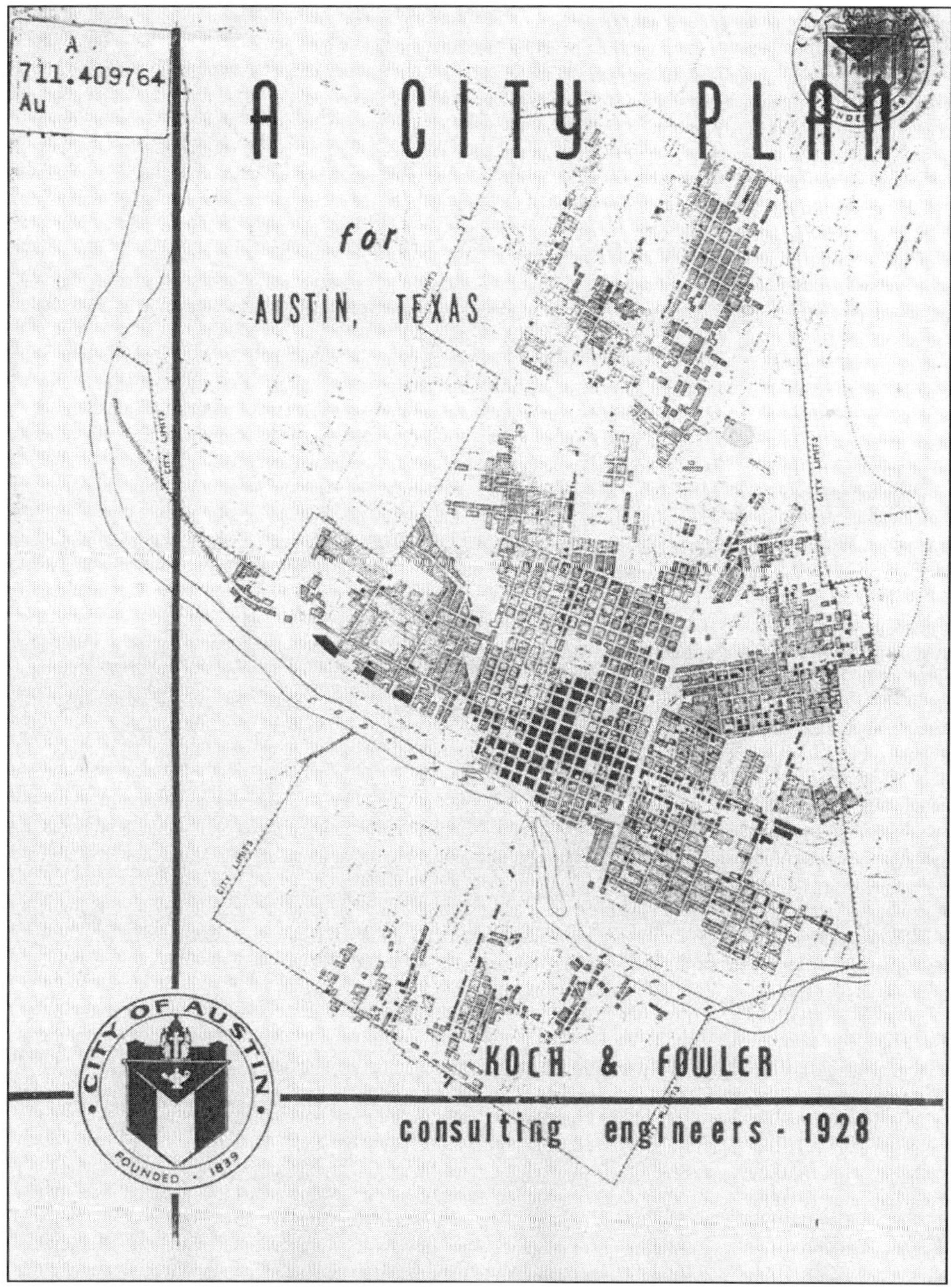

Under the 1928 City Master Plan, minority-accessible municipal services were relocated to the Eastside and city services were withheld from minority enclaves outside of East Austin to induce their relocation. All facilities and conveniences were to be provided in East Austin; chief amongst these were to be new schools for all Black children in the area, since Blacks were not allowed to attend the same schools as Whites. "This will eliminate the necessity of duplication of White and Black schools" in the same neighborhoods, and will act "as an incentive to draw the Negro population to this area" (Orum 2002). So, if a Black family wished its children to attend school, the plan indicated, the trek across town from places like Wheatville would take so long the family would be forced to move to be nearer the school.

By city policy, then, the minority Black population of Austin was pushed into the East Austin district and the social fabric of an early Austin was thus woven. Indeed, East Austin became East Austin as a result of this master plan, in a time when "the problem of segregation" mentioned in the plan referred to how segregation could be properly administered, not defeated.

Of course, city boosters argued that the plan was required to develop Austin's strengths as a residential, cultural, and educational center. They viewed the plan as a comprehensive cure-all for the ills that pervaded the city (poorly paved streets, lack of sufficient pure water, inadequate sewage disposal, poor health conditions, and not enough hotel rooms) (Blunt, Frye and Walker 2006). The city plan marked a turning point for urban design and framed Austin's future. A $4.25 million bond issue, Austin's largest to date, provided funds for streets, sewers, parks, the city hospital, the first permanent public library building, and the first municipal airport.[3] A recreation department was also established, and within a decade offered most Austin residents a profusion of recreational programs, parks and pools.

But the plan also reinforced White privilege and encouraged the minoritization of others. Much like Jim Crow laws present throughout the South during this period, the result ended with each race in its own place and little mixing in between. The 1940 census, for example, shows that of the 14,861 Blacks tallied, fully seventy-five percent lived in the two major census tracts of East Austin (Orum 2002). And by the mid-1940s, minority-accessible facilities had been almost completely consolidated and schools, parks, and health clinics began to anchor the Black community to East Austin.

1956: The Federal Highway Act

The Eastside, despite being on "the wrong side" of town, or more likely because of this, developed into a thriving community in the 1940s and 1950s. East Austin offered many Blacks in the post-World War II generation a chance to buy a home, and over the years, institutions such as Ebenezer Baptist Church, NAACP, and the Austin Area Urban League, made East Austin home. Despite the racial discrimination and municipal neglect that characterized the times, East Austin also became an "educational haven for Black families," having its own neighborhood elementary schools, a public high school and two colleges (Hardy et al. 2000). The area also developed a successful central business district, with many Black-owned franchises. As Dr. Urdy, former professor at Huston-Tillotson University as well as former Austin City Council member remembers, "East 11th and East 12th Street were the heart and soul of East Austin. Practically everything we needed or wanted was either on those streets or near to those streets. It was sort of the business hub for East Austin. And it is where most people spent most of their time outside of work. Most people only left East Austin to go to work."[4]

As some scholars have rightly pointed out, the production of marginalized spaces is ambivalent: while minoritization is and has been historically a strategy of confinement and exclusion, the creation of these racialized landscapes also provides a space that affords certain spatial and social resources for the production of local knowledge. Villa terms this knowledge "barriology" to refer to the consciousness shift whereby the marginalized begin to view their neighborhoods as a kind of valued cultural and social space (Villa 2000). As Chappell argues, "While barriology is by no means compensation for the social violence that is required to construct and maintain borders of exclusivity and barriers to mobility in the modern city, it does give minoritized people a resource through which they can lay a claim to authority and agency in a situation that would tend to restrict both" (Chappell 2006). In other words, creating community is a way to create respect in situations of little or no respect.

Unfortunately, the construction of Interstate 35 eviscerated the heart of East Austin, as illustrated in Figure 8.3. City officials, with the idea of improving traffic flows within and through Austin, passed a proposal to build a portion of federal highway through the central city. They argued that highway construction would create jobs, stimulate economic growth, and revive the central business district. They also suggested that the interstate would cause little disruption to the community, since the majority of the construction would occur along the blighted areas surrounding East Avenue.

Figure 8.3.

But in reality, the highway split the city in two and concretized racial divisions between east and west Austin. Even before Interstate 35 was constructed in the 1950s, some Austin residents sensed the substantial social disruption the freeway would bring to the city. "Opponents [of the new highway] suspected a plot to isolate and destroy the Black and Hispanic neighborhoods in East Austin," according to historian Humphrey (Humphrey and Crawford 1985). Some Black activists even suggested that the highway represented "the White man's road through the Black man's bedroom" (Rose 1989).

East Austin felt the effects of the highway before, during and after construction. Land was seized for building the freeway and what was once primary living space for Blacks was now being turned into a concrete jungle. The cultural landscape became one of distress, since the freeway destroyed the sense of place felt by many residents of the community. Interstate 35 also endangered the quality of life in this Black neighborhood, since this new structure became a barrier to mobility across space.

It is true that these visible walls were erected by those with power, to not only confine those who have little or no power, but to also perpetuate their powerlessness (whether consciously or unconsciously). Through spatial control (in schools, housing, public facilities, transportation, etc.) "first class" citizens are often separated from "lesser" groups (Sibley 1995). Highways, in particular, are seen as powerful symbolic and physical divides. Thus, even as Black residents attempted to collectively reinvigorate the place consciousness of East Austin, to Whites, the highway reinforced the image of East Austin as an undifferentiated slum, which was a drain on resources, a threat to social peace, and generally, a useless place.

1972–1975: The Urban Revitalization Program

The construction of the federal highway, along with a series of local, state and federal laws enacted in the 1950s and 1960s to help ban segregation and discrimination, made the once thriving, close-knit ethnic enclave of East Austin an ill-fitting, blighted area by the early 1970s. As integration became the law of the land, opportunities for living and working in other neighborhoods led many Blacks beyond the traditional boundaries of East Austin. In the old community, signs of deterioration emerged everywhere: commerce declined, crime increased, and schools became worse (in fact, Anderson High School, a point of pride in old East Austin, was closed by the Austin ISD in 1972).

East Austin saw its residents leave in a steady trickle as greater earning potential and changing residential opportunities gave Blacks a way out of the Eastside; the once well-established Black community seemed powerless to respond to the forces of urban decay and municipal neglect. The culmination of these factors was that the neighborhoods began to empty and deteriorate. Because East Austin homes lacked commercial value sufficient to justify home improvement loans (according to the practices of banks who red-lined the area throughout this period), houses were condemned or left to fall over (Hayden 1995). Meanwhile, as upwardly mobile Black residents moved out, land speculators bought the properties and became slumlords. Central East Austin became a place where, according to reporter and community activist Monsho, "mostly poor Black folk lived" (Monsho 2004).

Because the area was perceived as a derelict landscape with any number of social ills (even though a derelict landscape can also be read as the physical expression of a community striving to make do with scant resources), the area became marked for urban renewal in the 1970s. City officials claimed that the living conditions of Black residents in East Austin were so poor as to be publicly inappropriate for a "progressive" community (Orum 2002).

The idea behind urban renewal was for local authorities to use federal funds to acquire slum properties, assemble them into large parcels, clear them of existing structures, and prepare them for "redevelopment" (Massey and Denton 1993). In Austin, local planning agencies worked with private developers to demarcate aging and decaying areas of the city in need of revitalization and rehabilitation. Using the power of eminent domain, the city seized hundreds of properties for the new "public purpose" of slum clearance and/or prevention, mostly in the areas of downtown and East Austin.

Satirically referred to as the Urban Removal Program by local residents, the city destroyed many homes in East Austin through the condemnation process. Under the federal grant program, the city bulldozed housing it deemed to be derelict. While promising newly constructed housing for residents (primarily because local redevelopment authorities had to guarantee that a certain supply of replacement housing would be made available to displaced families in order to receive federal funding), few replacement houses were ever built. Instead some public housing projects were constructed on the cleared land, though not nearly enough units were available at rents within the means of the dislocated. As many scholars have argued, the urban renewal program was partially to blame for the decimation of Black neighborhoods throughout the U.S., since urban renewal almost always destroyed more housing than it replaced and since public housing only temporarily solved the problems of blight, crime, and instability (Bauman 1987).

Because East Austin was in many ways decimated by the processes of urban renewal, many residents had no option but to leave the community. Ray Robertson, now 77, said many of his friends were pushed out of their homes because of urban renewal, "You had to get up and move out, or they moved you out. A lot of people left here — they relocated or moved out of Austin" (Norton 2006). Indeed, Austin's Black share of the total population began a steady slide beginning in the 1970s, even as the absolute number of African Americans continued to increase. While Blacks made up around 15 percent of Austin's population in 1960, according to the 2005 American Community Survey, Blacks represented just 6.4 percent of the total population (Skop 2007).

Many of those remaining in the community blame this population decline on the urban renewal program, which they argue left a once-thriving community a near ghost town, with few opportunities for those who stayed.

Indeed, by the end of the 1970s, there were many vacant lots in East Austin. While some was to be held in perpetuity by the city, much of that property was conveyed to private developers at greatly reduced values. New ordinances allowed a significant proportion of that vacant land to be rezoned for industrial use, and many noxious industrial users — recycling yards, chemical storage facilities, sheet metal shops, welding yards, and the like — began infilling the spaces between and around the East Austin community. Ironically, then, during this period of urban renewal, the Eastside was once again reinforced as a racialized and minoritized space within the larger social landscapes of Austin.

1998: The Smart Growth Initiative

Through more than 150 years of actions and inactions, Blacks in Austin, and the spaces in which they reside, have been subjugated, castigated, and excluded. But in the present day, East Austin (and the residents that live there) has become *the* site of an important political struggle over the future of the city's space economy and society. This is largely the result of the Smart Growth Initiative, passed by city council in 1998.

Using concepts that seem to have come straight from "new urbanist" planning textbooks, Austin City Council and the city planning commission have, since the mid-1990s, steeped themselves in terms such as "smart growth," "livable city," and "urban infill" in their attempts to mitigate the effects of an ever-growing population (Clark-Madison 2006). After hundreds of hours of debate within the council and amongst various neighborhood organizations, along with thousands of dollars spent with a private consulting firm, the council crafted and passed the first new master plan for the city since the infamous 1928 City Plan. Much like that plan, along with the other public policies discussed thus far, in the guise of stimulating urban renewal and economic development, the plan in fact serves to undermine local residents and reinforce their racialization.

The Smart Growth Initiative focuses on the sustainable development concept: the idea is to build a livable city by reducing urban sprawl and maximizing environmental protection. The focus is on transit-oriented and pedestrian-friendly development that will strengthen the economic vitality of the urban core and its property tax base. Words like cleanliness, desirability, and high-quality, along with such celebratory terms like revitalization, blight elimination, and redevelopment, are interspersed throughout most discussions and documents regarding the initiative, and the rhetoric used makes it appear that everyone will be a winner.

In the current iteration of the master plan, the city is divided into two basic growth zones, as illustrated in Figure 8.4. There's the Drinking Water Protection Zone (DWPZ), comprising the west-of-town watersheds, like the Edwards Aquifer and Barton Creek, which supply water directly or feed into the river upstream of the first water treatment plant (Clark-Madison 2006). Then there is the catch-all Desired Development Zone (DDZ), which comprises the rest of the city.

Given Austin's geographical development and physical environment, the city determined that the central and eastern portions of Austin would be the easiest (and most environmentally conscious) to build on as the population grows; thus, the "Desired Development Zone" label. But the city went even further in their plan when they designated the central business district, and parts of East Austin, the "Urban Desired Development Zone (UDDZ)."

This UDDZ nomenclature has become incredibly significant in the years since the initiative passed. Indeed, it means that all eyes (and many dollars) have suddenly focused on East Austin. No longer, then, is this part of town seen as "out of place." Crossing the border now serves the fiscal interests of Austin's elites, since the area has the key ingredients needed for growth — low land values, proximity to downtown, some sturdy housing stock, much vacant land, and little clout with city hall.

Faced with a growing population and an exploding sprawl line, city planners now look to urban infill as both "sustainable" and "smart." They argue that urban infill will make better use of existing urban space by rezoning and redeveloping the derelict spaces of the Eastside. After all, much of the land in this area is vacant, and much of it is owned by the city (thanks to the urban "revitalization" efforts of the 1970s). Infill, they argue, will stimulate urban renewal and economic development in a neighborhood that has been suffering for many years.

Figure 8.4.

Smart Growth Mixed-Use Corridors
Proposed Rail Corridors
Smart Growth Transit Nodes
Park and Ride Facilities
Destination Park/TND
Barton Creek Buffer Zone
BCCP
0 10000 20000 Feet
Austin
Smart Growth Zones
Desired Development Zone
Central Business District
University Area, CURE
Urban Core
Inside Full Purpose Jurisdiction
Outside Full Purpose Jurisdiction
Drinking Water Protection Zone
Inside Full Purpose Jurisdiction
Outside Full Purpose Jurisdiction
DRAFT
http://www.ci.austin.tx.us/smartgrowth
Produced by PECSD, Planning Division
June 2000 Disclaimers Apply

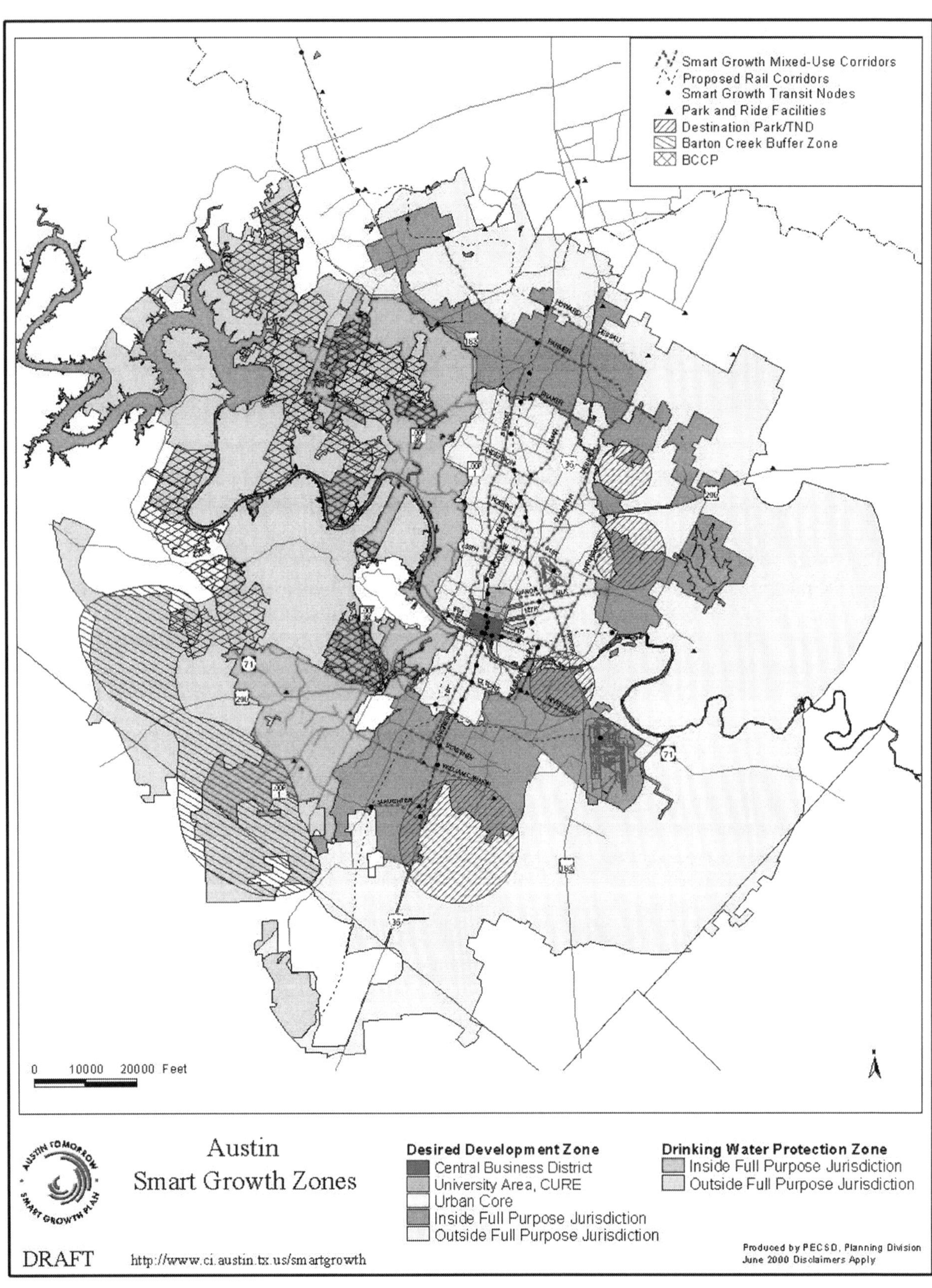

But as many scholars and community activists have argued, the ever-present problem with this ideology is that the subjective definition of a "derelict" landscape can turn a blind eye to the inscription of meanings in place by local residents. As Cloud argues, "Infill suggests pre-existing emptiness simply awaiting improvement"; however, in the case of the East Austin neighborhood, this infill means the erasure of local knowledge and history (Cloud 2006).

Indeed, no one really cared about this "dilapidated" neighborhood until the city announced its interest in the area through the UDDZ designation. Despite claims that the planning process has been consensus-building, collaborative, and inclusionary (primarily because of the incorporation of the Austin Revitalization Authority, a non-profit group whose chief interest is to determine how best to approach redevelopment in East Austin, into planning discussions), there has, in fact, been little help and many unfulfilled promises for local residents. But for developers and investors, the Smart Growth Initiative has been a boon. The plan has spurred a frenzy of real estate sales and a glut of houses built for quick turnover. East Austin now contains some of the most sought-after real estate in the city, and was even featured in a recent issue of the *New York Times* real estate section (Graham 2006). Property taxes in the neighborhoods have been rising at an unprecedented rate. According to city tax records, property values in Central East Austin rose 137 percent between 1995 and 2002, compared with 132 percent for the entire city (Almanza 2006). As a result, several longtime residents have been forced to sell their homes because they can't afford the increased property taxes (Matthews and Adams 2007). For the remaining original residents, the rising costs of taxes as well as the changing nature of the neighborhoods provide additional reasons to leave. Additionally, for those who have resolved to stay, they are assaulted daily by offers to buy their homes, assume their mortgage, and refinance their homes.

Increasingly, then, the residential areas of East Austin are earmarked for gentrification, especially as the existing housing stock is deemed to have "character" (which by the way, is the same "bungalow-style" housing that once was viewed as rundown and ramshackle). New, young, wealthy and highly educated "transplants" are also attracted by the romance of urban culture and diverse cultural icons to be found interspersed throughout the East Austin landscape, which the city is doing its best to promote through its "Keep Austin Weird" and "Iconic Preservation" ordinances. Obviously, too, the geographical nearness to downtown, the simple economics of still-affordable property and a retreating social stigma about East Austin have led new residents to the area.

East Austin has been a neglected corner of the Austin community for many years. From the mid-1800s onward, the Eastside (and the residents that live there) was as much perceived in mental maps and images as it was a visibly separate space of concrete highways and barbed-wire fences. But now, decades after its creation, East Austin's proximity to downtown means that empty lots are being bought up and built upon, and entire city blocks of old housing and old businesses are receiving new paint, new siding, and new fences (Norton 2006). While these terms bring to mind an efficient and bustling, environmentally sensitive city of the future, policy shifts to this end do not come without consequence or conflict. The East Austin improvements are overdue but local leaders, and many residents, believe these new plans carry a cost. Indeed, despite all the changes going on in East Austin, evidence from the U.S. Census suggests that the class position of Black residents has not necessarily risen, despite the increases in property values in the neighborhood.

CONCLUSION

In the case of East Austin, due to a largely minority population and their low socio-economic status, residents have historically held little sway with city officials. The racism of city policy towards East Austin was overt and obvious in the 1928 City Plan, but became much more subtle and unclear in the 1956 Federal Highway Act, the 1972–1975 Urban Revitalization Program, and the 1998 Smart Growth Initiative. With each of these public policies, however, the "derelict" nature of East Austin was reaffirmed. That is, until now, when the city is reinventing this space to suit its own needs. But much like in the past, it appears that the city is once again going to deny self-determination to an existing Black community, since most of the decision-making lies outside residents' control (Chusid 2006).

East Austin's African-American population has dropped by over 25 percent since 1980, while the White population increased by 30 percent in the same time period (Skop 2007). These trends are not just at the neighborhood level, however, and the decline cannot only be explained by the powerful forces of suburbanization drawing Black residents away from the central city. In fact, the city demographer predicts that by 2020, Blacks could represent less than 5 percent of Austin's population and constitute the smallest minority group in the metropolitan area (Robertson 2007).

Why are Blacks leaving Austin? Is it by choice, because opportunity calls elsewhere? Or is it because this city that promotes itself as being "T" for Tolerant is not actually all that open-minded? In the end, Austin is a segregated city; here, poverty exists in the midst of increasing plenty, scarcity in the center of abundance. In glaring contrast to the rest of Austin, the Black community in East Austin has been racialized and minoritized. Clearly, the different subject positions of residents shape their socio-spatial experiences.

NOTES

[1] See http://www.klru.org/austinhistory/history.html. Notice that this "brief history" of Austin glosses over the racial dimensions of the city's past. The 1928 city plan makes no mention of the displacement of minorities, same is true of the 1950s Highway, the 1970s urban revitalization, and the 1990s Smart Growth Plan.

[2] Interestingly, Austin would again reinstate its "sanctuary" status in 1997, when a city council resolution forbade city agencies and the police from asking people's immigration status. This policy is now being threatened by a growing backlash against immigrants in Austin (see Emily Skop, *Austin City Limited*, for more details).

[3] See http://www.klru.org/austinhistory/history.html.

[4] See http://www.klru.org/austinnow/archives/gentrification/index.asp.

## Chapter 9

The African Diaspora in a Changing Metropolitan Region: The Case of Atlanta, Georgia

ROBERT D. BULLARD

INTRODUCTION

Metropolitan Atlanta has experienced constant growth through the 1900s. With population growing at an annual rate of 2.9 percent since 1950, in the 1960s Atlanta established its regional dominance. During the 1970s and 1980s the city of Atlanta proper, became increasingly Black, and experienced a steady decrease in its share of the metropolitan population. *Metropolitan Atlanta* continued to experience breakneck growth from the 1990s through 2004 (Frey 2006), with African American in-migrants comprising much of the new resident group.

Approximately 85,000 people moved into the Atlanta metropolitan area annually since the 1990s (Atlanta Regional Commission 2006a), compared to an annual average of 62,000 in the 1980s. The region has gained more than 77,000 new residents each year since 2000 and nearly 112,000 in 2006 alone, the most recent year for which data are available (Atlanta Regional Commission 2006a, 9). The ten-county Metropolitan Area (Cherokee, Cobb, Douglas, Clayton, Fayette, Fulton, Henry, Gwinnett, DeKalb, and Rockdale) had a population of over 3.7 million people in 2004 (Atlanta Regional Commission 2003), 3.8 million people in 2005, and almost 4 million in 2006 (Atlanta Regional Commission 2006a). The twenty-eight county Metropolitan Statistical Area of Atlanta grew from 4.2 million in 2000 to 4.7 million in 2004 — making it the eleventh largest metropolitan area in the United States (King 2006). Planning officials' estimates indicate that the region will receive another 2.3 million people by 2030, increasing the region's total population to more than 6 million people (Atlanta Regional Commission 2006b, p. 4).

Between 1990–2005, the Atlanta region added 1.25 million persons. Population growth was slow in the city of Atlanta, increasing by only 26,900 or less than three percent of the total population gain. On the other hand, the northern portion of the region gained 616,000 residents or almost 50 percent of the region's population growth; the southern part of the region gained 289,900 persons or 23.1 percent of the population gains during 1990–2005. Fulton County continues to be the region's largest county with 874,100 residents in 2005. Gwinnett County led the region in net population increase, adding more than 21,000 persons each year since 2000 (Atlanta Regional Commission 2006b, p. 3).

RACIAL DIVERSITY

Between 2000 and 2004, African Americans, Hispanics, and other racial minorities accounted for more than 80 percent of the population growth in the 28-county metropolitan Atlanta area, in reducing the region's White population from 71 percent in 2000 to 57 percent of the 4.7 million people in metro Atlanta by 2006 (Atlanta Regional Commission 2006a). Each year, the region adds about 100,000 people to the suburban and exurban counties, with four of five newcomers being racial or ethnic minorities (King 2006).

Unable to annex surrounding unincorporated areas as Houston, Phoenix, and San Diego have, Atlanta proper is only the forty-first largest city in the nation, largely because its growth has been primarily suburban sprawl development. According to the Atlanta Regional Commission (Atlanta Regional Commission), the city's 2006 population estimate of 451,600 is higher than it has been in at least twenty-five years. During 2000–2005 the Atlanta metropolitan area added 245,982 African Americans, bringing the regional total to 1.4 million — or roughly 35 percent of the region's population (Bullard 2007). The number of new African Americans to the region was nearly twice the number of African Americans who moved into the next-fastest-growing metro area for African Americans in the United States (Miami-Fort Lauderdale). Atlanta moved from having the seventh-largest African American in-migrant population in 1990 to having the third-largest in 2004 (Frey 2006).

For much of its history Whites and Blacks constituted the vast majority of Atlanta's resident population. In 1940 only 1.4 percent of Atlanta's population was foreign-born, with little change a decade later. In the early 1980s, however, the ethno-racial landscape of both the city and the metropolitan area began to change, as private relief agencies resettled refugees from Southeast Asia, Afghanistan, Ethiopia, Eritrea, Somalia, and Eastern Europe in the area, and Atlanta's booming economy drew large numbers of immigrants from Mexico and other countries in Central and South America, the Caribbean, the Middle East, and West Africa.[1]

For example, Atlanta has seen a 285 percent growth in its African-born population since 2000 (Thompson 2005). In addition, metro Atlanta's Jamaican population nearly doubled from roughly 13,500 in 2000 to 24,000 in 2005 (ARC 2004). Jamaicans are now the region's fourth-largest immigrant group[2] behind Mexicans, Indians and Koreans (Feagans 2007, D1). Today, White school-age children in the region are in the minority — making up just 49.8 percent of that age group. The city of Atlanta added nearly 10,000 people in 2005. Atlanta's population stood at 416,474 in 2000, 415,200 in 1990, 424,922 in 1980, and 495,039 in 1970 (Pendered 2006).

The in-migration of mostly well-heeled middle-income and upper-income newcomers is bringing new sources of revenue for the city to support roads, sewers, parks, schools, and other city services. The city's budget has risen 31 percent since 2000 — from $448 million to $589 million in 2006. Not everyone sees these changes as a good thing, especially if gentrification causes loss of home or neighborhood due to increased property taxes.[3]

Conflicts abound between older residents who are struggling to stay in their in-town neighborhoods and newcomers who are intent on pushing them out to make way for their upscale "McMansions," large new houses that are far beyond the size of the older neighbors.

The face of the city of Atlanta is rapidly changing. For the first time since the 1920s, the African American share of the City's population is declining[4] and the White percentage is rising (Dewan 2006). Changing demographics have introduced uncertainty into local politics, which African Americans have dominated since 1973. Some African American community leaders warn of the dilution and possible demise of Black power, suggesting that second-term Mayor Shirley Franklin, who cannot run again because of term limits, may be the last African-American mayor for some time.

Even the Old Fourth Ward neighborhood of Dr. Martin Luther King is less than 75 percent African American, down from 94 percent in 1990. Here housing prices and property taxes have skyrocketed, while low-rent apartments have been demolished and replaced with new developments and new residents. *Black Commentator* Editor Bruce Dixon (2006, p. 1) describes the last thirty years of the "Black Mecca" as a "failure of the Black leadership class" to deliver significant benefits to the poor and working-class African Americans who have assisted and supported them in governing Atlanta. Dickson (2006) writes:

> Maynard Jackson's former chief of staff Shirley Franklin today presides over 475,000 Atlantans in the hollowed out core of a metro area ten times that size. For a generation, Georgia's White business and political elite have relentlessly punished Atlanta for the sin of being ruled by Black faces, confining most public and private investment to the sprawling suburban donut that surrounds the city. Hence metro Atlanta is the least densely populated of the nation's large cities. The airport, freeways and a small number of subway lines are already built. The only remaining goodies left to hand out in Shirley Franklin's Atlanta are the few remaining public services that can be privatized, the future tax revenue which can be diverted to favored bankers and middlemen via bond issues, and the land under the city itself, which can be eased into the hands of well-connected developers by a number of means. (p. 3)

The legacy of past residential segregation, as well as the more recent urban sprawl, work against inner city Blacks. This is the "Atlanta Paradox" (Sjoquist 2000). The "Black-Mecca" leads the nation in numbers of African-American millionaires, and simultaneously leads the nation in the percentage of children in poverty. Mayor Maynard Jackson is heralded for making from 33 to 35 Black millionaires during his administration. Andrew Young and Shirley Franklin kept the momentum going. On the other hand, in 2004, nearly half (48.1 percent) of Atlanta's Black children lived in poverty (U.S. Census Bureau 2004).

UNEVEN GROWTH AND UNEQUAL HOUSING

Suburbanization usually means out-migration of Whites. However, the 1990s saw a sizable number of middle-income and poor Black Atlantans move to the suburbs for home ownership opportunities, or suburban apartment rental units in the post-1996 Olympic glut. Nevertheless, suburban residence has not improved the economic situation for poor Blacks who are "stuck in the burbs," distant from jobs, public transit, and their informal community network. A geographic divide[5] encircles the city of Atlanta, separating the mostly Black city center from the predominantly White suburbs.

New housing subdivisions mushroomed in metro Atlanta's suburbs, forests, and rural farmland. Eight of every ten new units built during the 1990–2000 period were single family (ARC 2005, p. 21). The ten-county Atlanta metropolitan region added 180,425 housing units during the 2000–2004 period, a 13.6 percent increase, with the bulk of the housing concentrated in the northern suburbs, north of I-285. One of every four housing units built in the region during the period was in Gwinnett County. Together, Gwinnett, Fulton, and Cobb counties accounted for nearly two-thirds of the region's net increase in housing during the period (ARC 2005, p. 21). The housing inventory in North Fulton County more than doubled between 1990 and 2004.

Much of the housing boom passed over the city of Atlanta, which added only 14,732 new housing units between 2000–2004 period (7.9 percent increase), compared to 41,983 units in Gwinnett (20.0 percent increase), 31,593 units in Fulton (9.1 percent increase) and 22,332 units in Cobb (9.4 percent increase). These growth trends point to clear disparities between the mostly Black city of Atlanta and its mostly White suburbs (ARC 2005, p. 21).

Black expansion into Atlanta's suburbs reveals the segregated housing pattern typical of central-city neighborhoods. Segregated middle-income Black suburban "enclaves" have become a common residential pattern. For example, South DeKalb rivals Prince George County, Maryland as one of the most affluent African American communities in the nation. Nevertheless, many obstacles keep many affluent and poor Blacks out of the newer suburban developments, including low income, housing discrimination, restrictive zoning practices, inadequate public transportation, and fear.

Race matters in urban credit and insurance markets (Dymski 1995, pp. 37–74; Squires 1996a, pp. 63, 70). The insurance industry, like its housing industry counterpart, "has long used race as a factor in appraising and underwriting property" (Squires 1996b, pp. 45–50). Many inner-city neighborhoods are left with check-cashing stations, pawn shops, storefront grocery stores, liquor stores, and fast-food operations — all well buttoned-up with wire mesh and bullet-proof glass (Bullard, Grisby and Lee 1994, p. 3). A 1996 *Atlanta Journal-Constitution* survey discovered stark disparities in property insurance rates between Black and White Atlanta neighborhoods (Emling 1996a). The redlining issue prompted newspaper reporter Shelly Emling to title her story: "Insurance: Is It Still a White Man's Game?" (1996b) Emling answered her question as follows: "Insurance companies create pricing zones that are mostly White or mostly Black, and homeowners in the Black zones are paying top dollar" (Emling 1996a).

Insurance redlining is not isolated to an individual insurance agent. The practice is widespread among big and small companies. The largest insurance companies in Georgia (i.e., State Farm, Allstate, Cotton States, Cincinnati Insurance, and USAA) routinely charge consumers 40 to 90 percent more to insure homes in Atlanta's predominantly Black neighborhoods than for similar or identical houses in mostly White suburbs (Emling 1996a). The premium disparity holds true whether Blacks live in the low-income Vine City neighborhood or the wealthy Cascade neighborhood that houses Atlanta's Black elite. As the racial composition of a neighborhood becomes mostly Black, the price of homeowner insurance rises dramatically (Emling 1996a).

Using the state rates for a hypothetical $125,000 brick house (with $250 deductible), the *Atlanta Journal-Constitution* study concluded that "State Farm and Allstate, Georgia's largest insurers, tend to charge their highest rates in zip codes that also contain the highest proportion of Black residents" (Emling 1996a). The premium differentials become apparent when one compares the hypothetical $125,000 brick house in different locations in metropolitan Atlanta. Shelley Emling writes: "To insure that house with State Farm in Black sections of the city of Atlanta would cost about $612 a year; in Buckhead, the rate falls to $459. In Cobb, Gwinnett and North Fulton, all more than 80 percent White, the price falls to $363 a year" (Emling 1996a).

The premium differentials between Black and White neighborhoods cannot be explained solely by loss data, i.e., theft, vandalism, fire, and larceny crimes. In reality, the highest loss ratios are not in Black areas. A loss ratio is the sum an insurance company pays in claims vs. the amount it collects in premiums. For example, a ratio of 68 percent means that a company paid out 68 cents for each $1 it collected. In general, a company that has a loss ratio of 65 percent turns a healthy profit.

The loss ratio in mostly Black Allstate Zone 2 (Central Atlanta) is 79 percent, yet they pay a whopping $705 in annual premiums. On the other hand, the loss ratio in mostly White Atlanta Zone 18 (North Fulton, Northwest DeKalb) is 92 percent, and the homeowners pay $349 — less than half what is paid by residents in Zone 2. There is little doubt that the mostly White suburban communities with the highest loss ratios are not paying their fair share. These premium disparities further illustrate the benefits suburban Whites derive from discrimination.

Predatory lending also creates separate and unequal housing opportunities (Association of Community Organizations for Reform Now 2004, p. 5), and disproportionately hurts Black Atlantans. Predatory practices by some subprime lenders have resulted in extremely high foreclosures in once-stable neighborhoods. There were 1,313 foreclosures in the five largest counties in Georgia in August 2001, approaching the record of 1,578 in April 1991 (Bennett 2001). Fulton County had 568 foreclosures in March 2002 compared to 340 in March 2001 (Torpy 2002), while Dekalb had 619 foreclosures in March 2002 (Adams 2002). Over 41 percent of advertised foreclosures in DeKalb County were actually on loans that were less than two years old (Bennett 2001).

Using HUD's list of subprime lenders for the Atlanta MSA, the Home Mortgage Disclosure Act (HMDA) data show dramatic growth in subprime lending in the Atlanta MSA, over 500 percent from 1993 to 1998 — from 1,864 to 11,408 (Eagan 2002). The volume of foreclosures grew 232 percent from 1996 to 1998, while the number of mortgages only grew 7 percent. Forty-four percent of subprime loans had high interest rates (defined as 4 percent above the Treasury bill rate). Subprime lending was three times more significant in low income neighborhoods than in the overall market; and seventy-four of the 101 census tracts with high subprime activity (25 percent or more of mortgages) were predominantly Black.

The overall share of foreclosures for subprime went from 5 percent in 1996 to 16 percent in 1998; median age of subprime foreclosures was two years compared with four years for prime loans. In the end, predatory lending has a devastating impact on Black homeowners in the Atlanta area by denying them a basic form of wealth. It also destabilizes entire neighborhoods.

In some metro counties, foreclosure rates have nearly doubled since 2004, and the rate for the 10-county core of metro Atlanta is twice the national rate (Atlanta Neighborhood Development Partnership 2007). African-Americans in Atlanta were 3.4 times more likely than Whites to be put into a high-cost loan.[6]

REGIONAL SPRAWL AND THE IMPACT ON ATLANTA AREA BLACKS AND THE POOR

The boundaries of the Atlanta metropolitan region doubled in the 1990s. The region measured 65 miles from north to south in 1990. Today, Atlanta's economic dominance reaches well beyond 110 miles from north to south (Leinberger 1998, pp. 28–33). Much of the region's growth in the 1990s was characterized by suburban sprawl and economic disinvestment in Atlanta's central city (Goldberg 1997a). The Sierra Club rated Atlanta as the "most sprawled threatened" large city (over one million people) in the nation (Sierra Club 1998, p. 3). Among large metropolitan areas, Atlanta led all others in its Black population gains during both the 1990s and in 2000–2004 (Frey 2006). Atlanta's diversified and growing economy, large Black middle class and Black businesses, and concentration of historically Black colleges and universities (Atlanta University Center), all serve as a draw for African Americans from across the United States.

Atlanta is also a magnet for commuters with daytime Atlanta very different from resident nighttime Atlanta. For medium-size cities (250,000 to 500,000), Atlanta had the greatest daytime population gain with a 62.4 percent increase.[7] The Atlanta regional economy has boomed since 1990, undergoing one of the largest expansions of any urban area in history, and causing traffic congestion that affects the regional economy. The total workers in the region increased 33.6 percent during the 1990s, the sixth largest percentage increase among all the metropolitan areas in the U.S. (the national average was 11.5 percent). The region had two million jobs in 2001, a 42 percent increase over 1990, or nearly 600,000 new jobs (U.S. Census Bureau 2006b, p. 10).

Newcomers flocked to the region for economic opportunity. Unemployment remained low and job growth remained strong. Between 1990 and 2003, over 508,000 new jobs were added to the region, most outside the city, which lagged far behind the jobs-rich suburbs. The city captured about 40 percent of the region's jobs in 1980. By 1990, Atlanta's share had slipped to 28.3 percent and 22.0 percent in 2000 (ARC 1998a) (ARC 2006b).

Atlanta's northern suburbs reaped the lion's share of new jobs, adding over 267,000 jobs from 1990–2003, or 52.6 percent of all jobs added to the region. Almost 97,000 jobs (19.1 percent) were added in the southern part of the region, while fewer than 14,000 were added in the central core of Atlanta, representing only 2.8 percent of all jobs created during the economic boom (ARC 1998a; ARC 2006b).

Fulton County, where Atlanta is located, continued to be the largest employment center in the region, with more than 738,200 jobs in 2001, or 36.5 percent of the region's total employment. Fulton, DeKalb, Cobb, and Gwinnett together accounted for 76 percent of jobs, 67 percent of the workers, and 65 percent of the population in the region (Center for Neighborhood Technology 2004, p. 32). Economic opportunity exists in the largely White zones, and most poor Black Atlantans are not near jobs. The economic isolation of Black Atlantans is complicated by inadequate public transit (limited, unaffordable, or inaccessible service and routes, and security and safety), lack of personal transportation (34.6 percent of Black Atlantans do not own a car), spatial mismatch (location of suitable jobs in areas that are inaccessible by public transportation), and concentrated poverty. For the minority population located within the city proper, residential location becomes synonymous with lack of employment opportunity.

The majority of entry-level jobs in metro Atlanta are not within a quarter mile of public transportation. Only 11.3 percent of the Metro Atlanta's jobs are located within a 3-mile radius of the CBD; 38.1 percent are located within a 10-mile radius, and 61.9 percent are located outside the 10-mile ring (Glaeser, Kahn and Chu 2001, p. 5). Getting to job sites is next to impossible if you are carless in Atlanta, since the Metropolitan Atlanta Regional Transit Authority or MARTA is limited to only two counties — Fulton and DeKalb Counties.

MARTA – MOVING AFRICANS RAPIDLY THROUGH ATLANTA

In the 1960s, Metropolitan Atlanta Rapid Transit Authority (MARTA) was hailed as the solution to the region's growing traffic and pollution problems. The first referendum to create a five-county rapid rail system failed in 1968. However, in 1971, the City of Atlanta, Fulton County and DeKalb County approved a referendum for a one percent sales tax to support a rapid rail and feeder bus system. Cobb County and Gwinnett County voters rejected the MARTA system. The vote ran strictly along racial lines. Yet, Clayton and Gwinnett were allowed to sit on the MARTA board and determine its fate — including raising fares and cutting service. The MARTA Board is also made up of State officials — even though the State does not fund MARTA. In the end, Gwinnett, Clayton, and state officials make decisions about MARTA, but are not accountable to the political jurisdictions whose residents pay for the system — the city of Atlanta, Fulton and DeKalb counties. This form of "representation without taxation" lies at the heart of the growing transportation equity movement in metro Atlanta.[8]

The percentage of Atlanta commuters using public transit to get to work, 4.7 percent, is lower than the national average, but African American commuters are more likely to use public transit than are Whites. In Atlanta, 28.2 percent of Black males and 35.0 percent of Black females take public transit to work. On the other hand, 4.4 percent of White male and 6.7 percent of White female Atlantans ride public transit to work (Davis 1994, p. 79).

MARTA has grown from 13 rail stations in 1979 to its current 38 rail stations (Figure 9.1), making it the ninth largest transit system in the U.S. operating 556 buses (441 compressed natural gas and 145 clean diesel) with 120 bus routes (MARTA 2005, p. 5). The agency also operates 110 lift-vans for paratransit services, and 338 rail cars on 47.6 miles of rail. Over thirty miles of rail are located in Fulton County, nearly 15 miles in DeKalb County, and 7 miles (to Hartsfield-Jackson Atlanta Airport) are located in Clayton County. The system handles more than 461,600 passengers on an average weekday, carrying 259,000 passengers on rail lines, and the rest on 121 bus and van routes. Where MARTA builds the next lines is hotly debated among diverse neighborhood constituents in Atlanta, Fulton County and DeKalb County.[9]

Figure 9.1.
Atlanta Transportation Networks.

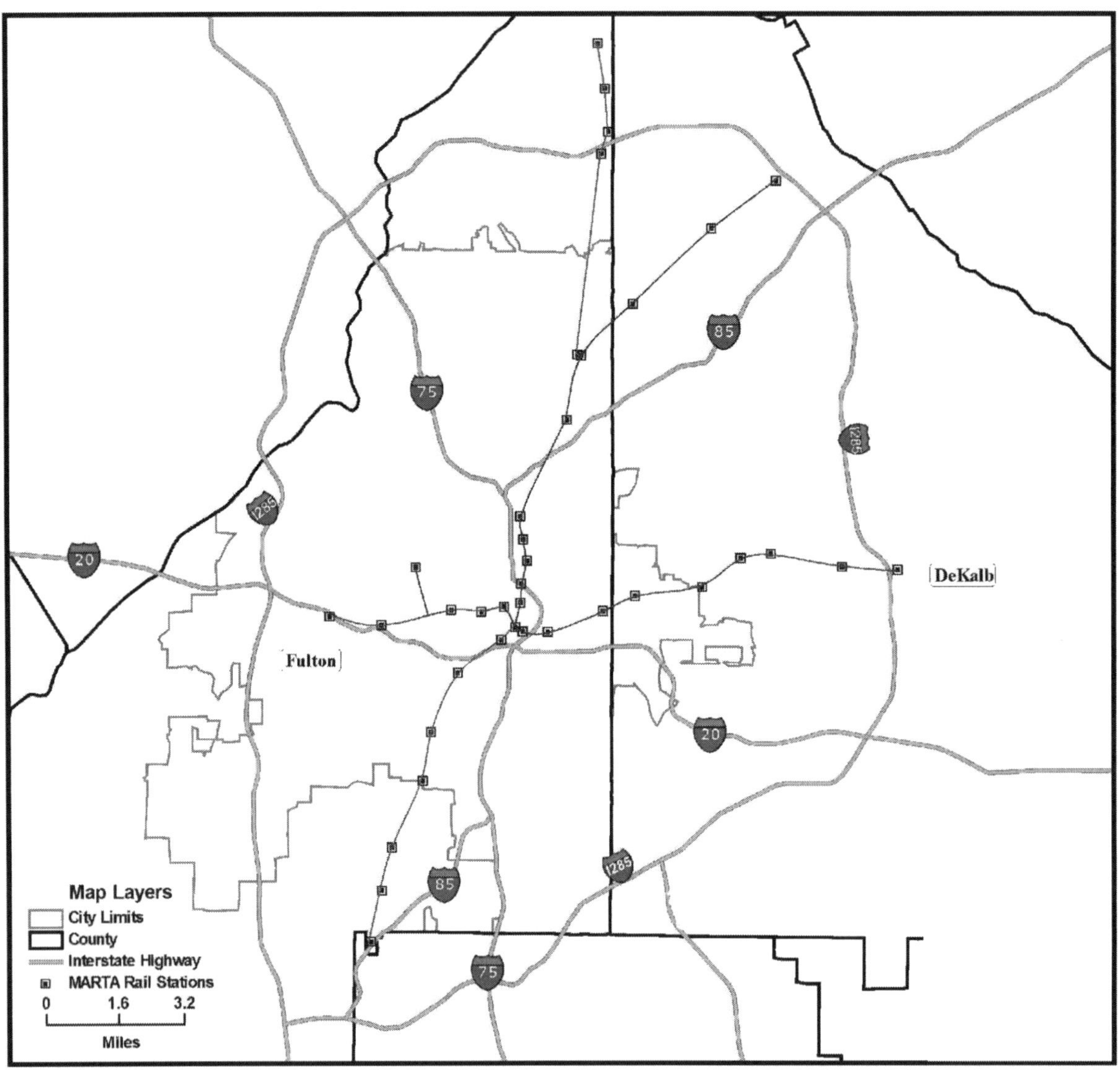

Most Metro Atlanta counties decades ago opted not to join MARTA, a decision tinged with racial overtones. Today, Fulton and DeKalb taxpayers are still questioning MARTA routes, with politics likely playing a determining role in where the next MARTA lines go (Laccetti-Meyer 1998). Only Fulton and DeKalb County residents pay for the upkeep and expansion of the system with a one-cent MARTA sales tax. Revenues from bus fares generated $5 million more revenue than taken in by rail in 1997 (MARTA 1996). The regular one-way fare on MARTA was $1.00 in 1992. MARTA's one-way fare is currently $1.75 compared with $1.50 in Chicago, $1.35 in Los Angeles, $1.25 in San Francisco, $1.20 in Washington, DC, $1.10 in Newark, and $1.00 in Boston (APTA 2003).

MARTA offers over 28,000 parking spaces at its rail stations. Parking at MARTA lots is free. Overnight parking at some MARTA lots is $3. Parking at most of the secure overnight parking decks is $6. A 1999 license tag survey, "Who Parks-and-Rides," covering the period 1988–1997, revealed that 44 percent of the cars parked at MARTA lots were from outside the Fulton/DeKalb County service area. Fulton and DeKalb County tax payers are subsidizing people who live in outlying suburban counties, who park their cars at the park-and-ride lots, and ride on MARTA trains into the city and to the airport.

On November 28, 2000, the Metropolitan Atlanta Transportation Coalition (MATEC), a coalition of eleven Black Atlanta organizations, filed an administrative complaint with the U.S. Department of Transportation on behalf of their minority and disabled members. The MATEC organizations charged MARTA with racial discrimination under Title VI of the Civil Rights Act of 1964. The coalition pointed out overcrowded bus lines, lack of clean compressed natural gas (CNG) buses and bus shelters, and fewer amenities provided in people of color communities compared to White communities. The group also charged MARTA with failure to comply with the federally mandated Americans with Disabilities Act (ADA) (Suggs 2000).

Race has always played a pivotal role in MARTA's creation and governance. Over nearly four decades, all five MARTA general managers had been White males, until December 2000, when after growing community pressure, MARTA selected its first African American general manager (Shelton 2000). A Black general manager reinforced the transit agency as a Black-run system, presenting an uphill battle to secure earmarked regional and State funding.

The Atlanta region needs a strong MARTA, and raising fares while providing substandard transit services to the poor and people of color runs counter to smart growth. The MARTA user base is typically non-White lower-income, carless (or own fewer automobiles), children or elderly people from larger households, who live near transit stations. African Americans make up 73 percent of its customers (MARTA 1999).[10] The non-White population is the most dependent on MARTA and the most likely group from whom new riders will be drawn. Improving service quality and fares for this group is more likely to result in increased ridership than expanding service in currently underused White areas.[11]

Fledgling moves at improved service for non-White Atlantans are occurring. For example, in December 2002, MARTA received 50 new "Clean Diesel" buses to replace old (some more than 12 years old and with more than 600,000 miles) buses at the Hamilton Garage — that serves the mostly Black South Fulton County. While this concession does not get clean CNG buses in the mostly Black service area, this is the first time in over 10 years that this facility received new buses since the previous practice was to move the old buses to this facility and place the new buses at the other two garages.

Also several train stations in Black areas have received upgrades and maintenance such as Hamilton Holmes (new roof), West End (power scrubbings), and Ashby Street (elevator and escalator repairs). MARTA has begun a program to install 600 shelters and 300 benches, giving minority, low income, and transit-dependent areas priority placements. It established the SMART Team program that uses a number of the agency's employees to identify, assess, and recommend solutions to maintenance problems in and around MARTA's train stations.

There is no regional transit system that can work in metropolitan Atlanta without having the mature MARTA system at the core. MARTA is the most comprehensive transit system in the region, operating both buses and rail. This mature transit system has taken four decades to develop, with only two of the counties in the region paying for the system.[12]

Transportation is critical to economic opportunity, and requires capital for upkeep and expansion. MARTA's operating budget comes from sales tax (46 percent), fares (34 percent), the Federal Transit Administration and other sources (20 percent). In addition, only Fulton and DeKalb County residents pay for the upkeep and expansion of the system with a one-cent MARTA sales tax. Of the ten largest transit systems in the nation today, MARTA is the only one that does not receive a regular allocation from the State. MARTA has been operating at a deficit for seven years, paying the shortfall out of reserves, a situation that will require service reductions.

Cobb County created an independent transit system, Cobb Community Transit (CCT), in 1991 that operates 41 buses over 345 miles, carrying an average of 9,300 passengers per weekday. CCT has limited links to MARTA, but the two systems do not share funds when riders transfer. Express commuter buses also provide transit service to the Atlanta area.

GRTA's express commuter buses from Clayton and Rockdale Counties drop passengers off in downtown Atlanta. These are the first two of 12 routes that GRTA is planning to operate from suburban sites to employment centers in the metropolitan area to provide suburban drivers an option for dealing with traffic gridlock. Funding problems are likely to hit the Gwinnett, Clayton, and other start-up circulator bus systems in Atlanta's suburbs as they, like MARTA, do not have long-term funding beyond the U.S. Department of Transportation's three-year transit system start-up funds. The ARC is commissioning an in-depth future study of transit funding and solutions.

Many Black Atlanta neighborhoods have waited decades for the economic benefits associated with MARTA stations, particularly central city neighborhoods. In recent years, MARTA has begun to take a more active role in encouraging transit-oriented development (TOD) around its rail stations. MARTA and the Atlanta Development Authority (ADA) have identified nine sites for mixed-use developments (Pendered 1998; 1999). TOD got a shot in the arm in 1999 when BellSouth (one of the area's largest employers) announced that it would move 13,000 of its employees to new offices to be built near the MARTA Lindbergh station (Ledford 1999). MARTA's TOD projects are in various stages at Lenox, North Avenue, Medical Center, Chamblee, Sandy Springs, Avondale, King Memorial and Lakewood/Ft. McPherson stations. Despite efforts at improving the residential-employment location mismatches by constructing development projects near transit opportunities, in the case of Atlanta, many new immigrants and low-income residents will be displaced as a result of MARTA projects.[13]

Housing and commerce have been rising along MARTA's rail lines, and the system's bus routes have been rethought for the first time in two decades. For example, the Metro Atlanta Chamber of Commerce spent months pushing the "flex-trolleys" for the busiest metro corridors. Other transit talks in the city have focused on the Proposed Beltline — a 22-mile transit loop. The proposed Beltline would connect 49 Atlanta neighborhoods with a new transit line and linear park; bicycle and pedestrian pathways will follow along the loop. It will connect with existing MARTA stations at five locations and; it will utilize the Old "Belt Line" Railroads developed after the Civil War.

Highway Sprawl

Large population concentrations provide the labor pool necessary for economic development, but also create negative environmental consequences. To address the burgeoning population growth, the Atlanta-area government built highways to the suburbs and subsidized the construction of suburban homes (Conservation Law Foundation 1998, p. 18). However, many transportation activities had unintended negative consequences of dividing, isolating, disrupting, and imposing different economic, environmental, and health burdens on some communities. In Atlanta, this impact was most acute for Blacks. Writing in the Foreword to *Just Transportation*, longtime civil rights activist and Georgia Congressman John Lewis (1997) states:

> Even in a city like Atlanta, Georgia — a vibrant city with a modern rail and public transit system — thousands of people have been left out and left behind because of discrimination. Like most other major American cities, Atlanta's urban center is worlds apart from its suburbs. The gulf between rich and poor, minorities and Whites, the "haves" and "have-nots" continues to widen. (pp. xi–xii)

Metropolitan Atlanta has been shortchanged in the state allocation of transportation funding for years, largely based on the State's rules that motor fuel taxes can only be used for roads and bridges — and not a dime can go toward transit. Still, metro Atlantans do not get a fair return on the money they pay in gas taxes. For example, between 1992 and 1997, the 10-county region received back only 55 cents on every dollar paid out in gas taxes — resulting in a $518 million shortfall (Saporta 2003). Metro Atlanta has 42 percent of the state's population, but only 17 percent of the state's gas-tax revenue actually comes back to the region — a classic case of transportation injustice (Bullard, Johnson and Torres 2004).

Metro Atlanta is expected to add another two million people by 2030 and requires spending $50 billion over the next 25 years on transportation (*Atlanta Regional Commission Mobility 2030*). Yet, this massive expenditure is expected to do little in terms of relieving congestion mainly because it again shortchanges transit — and practically leaves MARTA off the funding table. Public transit in Metro Atlanta is in a "Catch-22" predicament — by state law it is easier to spend money for roads and not transit, so the region gets more roads and gridlock (Saporta 2004a). The decision by the 39-member ARC board to spend $50 billion mostly on roads makes more political sense than economic sense.

Atlanta's regional transportation policies are implicated in land-use patterns, unhealthy air, and sprawl. Traffic and air pollution resulting from sprawl have caused the region's ranking as a favored corporate location to be downgraded. The region's economy depends heavily on keeping traffic moving along the three interstate highways (I-20, I-75, and I-85). Atlanta sits at the hub of this sprawling auto-dependent region. The Tom Moreland Interchange or "Spaghetti Junction" (the interchange where I-85 and I-285 comes together) typifies the traffic and pollution that poor planning has brought to greater Atlanta. Traffic gridlock and polluted air help make Atlanta one of the "most sprawl-threatened large cities" in the United States (Sierra Club 1998, p. 5). The Atlanta region had more than 2.9 million registered vehicles in 2003, up from 1.5 million registered vehicles in 1980. Vehicle emissions produce ozone in large enough quantities that the Atlanta metropolitan area has been in violation of the Federal Clean Air Act for some time. The region is a non-attainment area for ground level ozone, with cars, trucks, and buses as the largest source of this pollution (Schmidt 1998, p. 276). Transportation and land-use plans have also contributed to and exacerbated social and economic inequities, with the greatest negative impact on poor and Black Atlantans. Sprawl forces Atlanta residents with automobiles to drive long distances to work, shop, play, and school. Atlantans are expected to travel an average of 15,000 miles per year through the year 2020. On average, people in the region drive 34 miles per day — more than anyone else on the the planet (50 percent farther than Los Angeles area residents). Atlantans lead the nation in miles driven per day (over 100 million miles per day).

Assisting those without cars is complicated by use and amount of the state's motor fuel tax. The State tax structure has no incentives to support mass transportation, and the Georgia motor fuel tax currently can only be used for roads and bridges. Generating interest in a public transportation system to assist the poor and the Black in Atlanta would reduce the amount of funding to other regions of the State, and decrease the amount devoted to highway development. However, in the late 1990s, the ARC was required to develop a Transportation Improvement Plan (TIP) that would conform to federal standards (ARC 1998). Because of the severe ozone non-attainment, the federal government criticized the ARC's plan because it concentrated too heavily on roads and did not show how the region's poor air quality would be improved. As a part of the TIP, the ARC "grandfathered" the funding of sixty-one new road projects. Environmental organizations and a coalition of mainly Black environmental justice, neighborhood and civic groups filed suit because the highway-dominated plans would disproportionately and adversely affect the health and safety of African Americans and other people of color.

The lawsuit resulted in elimination of 44 of the 61 grandfathered road projects (Goldberg 1999), and permitted 17 projects because Georgia DOT had already awarded construction contracts. The settlement freed millions of dollars for transportation alternatives that will improve air quality and mobility in the region (SELC 1999, p. 1), and among other impacts, requires the U.S. DOT to study the social equity impacts of transportation investments in the region (Southern Environmental Law Center 1999, p. 1).

Equity concerns revolve around three broad areas: how environmental justice issues are addressed in the planning process; how the benefits are distributed across various populations; and how the burdens of transportation investments are distributed across various populations. All three concerns are of interest to Black Atlantans (U.S. Department of Transportation 1999, p. 1).

Getting metro Atlantans out of their cars and into some form of coordinated and linked public transit may well be the key to solving a major part of the region's traffic and air quality problems, as well as some economic issues facing poor and minority Atlantans. A June 1998 *Atlanta Journal/Constitution* poll showed that seven of every ten suburban residents supported some form of a unified rail and bus system (Goldberg 1998a). One of the first acts the newly-elected Democrat Governor Barnes pushed for was the creation of the Georgia Regional Transportation Agency (GRTA) (Goldberg 1998b), which received final approval from the Georgia General Assembly on March 1999 (Pruitt 1999a). When a 15-member GRTA board was appointed by Governor Barnes in June 1999 (Goldberg and Pruitt 1999), he cautioned Atlantans not to expect GRTA to be a "miracle cure." "This is not the end of problems. . . . It's not even the beginning of the end. But it does give us the tools to begin with" (Pruitt 1999b).

The GRTA mission is to improve Georgia's mobility, air quality, and land use practices. GRTA is still an unproven quantity, despite the support of Republican Governor Sonny Perdue. The Atlanta metropolitan area growth rate, the region's housing starts, job growth, and low unemployment rate, as well as the health of the majority African American city are all important to the overall metropolitan region's vitality. New challenges are being raised to address imbalances resulting from sprawl. What happens outside the city affects all Atlantans. The future of the region is intricately bound to how government, business, and community leaders address Atlanta's quality of life and equity issues.

Will the Atlanta region take a bold stance and address central city reinvestment and redevelopment, fair housing, public schools, public transit, and public health needs? Or will it pander to the forces of racial segregation, discrimination, and blocked economic opportunity? Clearly, the "Black Mecca" continues to attract large numbers of African Americans seeking opportunity and a better life. Atlanta is no "Mecca" for a large slice of the African American community — families stuck in concentrated poverty with little hope of escape. Lack of a comprehensive regional transit plan and closed opportunity block thousands of Black Atlantans from accessing job centers and "opportunity-rich" suburbs. Dismantling this "invisible" wall will benefit the entire region.

NOTES

[1] Immigrants were both legal and illegal during this time.

[2] If current trends continue, Atlanta will soon overtake Chicago in total Black population. The Miami metropolitan area was second, adding nearly 97,000 Blacks during the five year period. Miami rose from having the eighth largest Black population in 2000 to sixth in 2004.

[3] Property taxes have skyrocketed — making Atlanta unaffordable for many long-time African American residents (Dewan 2006). Older neighborhoods are being taken over by mostly White childless couples, singles, and middle-age "empty nesters" who have grown weary of the gear-grinding commutes — the longest in the country.

[4] African Americans comprised 67 pecent of Atlanta's population in 1990, 61 percent in 2000, and 54 percent in 2004.

[5] Atlanta is encircled by the "Perimeter" Highway, Interstate 285, which delineates the majority Black interior of the city from the mostly White — though rapidly diversifying — suburbs. Many locals refer to the term ITP (Inside The Perimeter) and OTP (Outside The Perimeter) to describe neighborhoods, residents, and businesses. Thus, the Perimeter often serves as a geographic, social, and racial "code" similar to that of the Capital Beltway around Washington, DC.

[6] Other U.S. cities with similar foreclosure rates are Minneapolis, where the figure was 3.9 times; San Francisco, 4.5 times; New York, 4.6 times, and St. Louis, 3.1 times (Trivedi-St. Clair 2007).

[7] Other cities with large daytime gains include: Tampa, 47.5 percent; Pittsburgh, 41.3 percent; St. Louis, 35.1 percent; Cincinnati, 31.0 percent; Minneapolis, 25.0 percent; Cleveland, 24.0 percent, and Buffalo, 16.3 percent.

[8] The ten-county Atlanta metropolitan area has a regional public transit system only in name. Race was a major driver in shaping public transit in the Atlanta region. The Metropolitan Atlanta Rapid Transit Authority (MARTA) serves just two counties, Fulton and DeKalb. For many White suburbanites, "MARTA" stood for "Moving Africans Rapidly through Atlanta" (Bullard, Johnson and Torres 2000, pp. 39–68). "Many Whites see MARTA as a black, transit-dependent system." In 2001, the financially strapped MARTA system budgeted $700,000 to hire a marketing firm to study and implement a program to polish its image (McCosh 2001).

[9] Competition between MARTA's service area "haves" and "have-nots" will likely intensify in the future. Just how far MARTA lines extend has proved to be a thorny issue. In July 2002, the MARTA Board of Directors asked staff to initiate the Alternatives Analysis for the North Line Corridor from the North Springs Station to Windward Parkway. Locally Preferred Alternative, prefers a heavy rail extension to the interchange of Martin Luther King, Jr. Drive and I-285 and a Bus Rapid Transit (BRT) segment along I-20 to Fulton Industrial Boulevard.

In October 2002, MARTA initiated the West Line Alternatives Analysis/Draft Environmental Impact Statement (AA/DEIS) for Fulton Industrial Boulevard. The DEIS was submitted to the Federal Transit Administration for review in March 2005. And in the Spring of 2003, MARTA initiated a study identifying strategies to implement BRT-type service in the Memorial Drive corridor from the former Avondale Mall location to the park and ride lot at Stone Mountain. The timeline for implementation of the Memorial Drive BRT is early 2008 (MARTA 2005, p. 11).

[10] MARTA is a necessity for the individuals who do not own cars. Only 6.3 percent of Whites compared to 26.5 percent of Blacks who live in the MARTA service area are without cars. More than 34.6 percent of Atlantans are carless.

[11] In September of 2002, the FTA advised the MATEC groups of its plan to mediate their complaint with MARTA representatives. Mediation was completed in mid-October 2002. Some changes at MARTA were cosmetic and mere window dressing. Others were more substantive. Today, MARTA provides sign language at all of its public meetings. It has taken steps to remedy the disparity in service toward Latino riders. Currently, MARTA provides Spanish-English literature and flyers at train stations and public meetings. A Spanish-English interpreter is now available at all Board meetings and public hearings. Also, MARTA's Costumer Service Hot Line is now able to provide assistance to Spanish speaking customers. Beginning in 2003, all emergency information was published in Spanish.

[12] Race still matters in planning transit in metropolitan Atlanta. Until racism is reigned in, the Atlanta region will continue to have a patchwork of unlinked, uncoordinated, and "separate but unequal" transit (bus) systems "feeding into" and "feeding off" MARTA.

[13] In Fiscal Year 2005 (FY05), construction started on Uptown Square, a 362 multifamily apartment development, as well as 208,893 feet of retail space at Lindbergh City Center. Combined, the two projects are projected to eventually generate over $200 million in lease revenue for the MARTA. At Lakewood/Ft. McPherson station, nearly 6 acres of land was sold for $982,000 to the Urban Residential Finance Authority to build 192 apartments (MARTA 2005, p. 13).

Chapter 10

Geographic Racial Equality in America's Most Segregated Metropolitan Area—Detroit

JOE T. DARDEN

GEOGRAPHIC RACIAL EQUALITY

Although racial inequality is the predominant pattern in metropolitan Detroit, geographic racial *equality* also exists, though it is often ignored. Geographic racial equality is defined as those places (i.e., municipalities) that have been incorporated and have low levels of racial residential segregation (below 50 percent) and where Blacks have reached *parity* with Whites in education, income, and occupational status. This chapter examines such places in the Detroit metropolitan area, America's most racially segregated area, and compares their socioeconomic characteristics with the metropolitan area as a whole. The results challenge traditional views of Black suburbanization and place stratification.

BLACK SUBURBANIZATION: THE TRADITIONAL VIEW

Black suburbanization and its relationship to socioeconomic status has been the focus of study by several social scientists since the 1960s (Taeuber and Taeuber 1965; Farley 1977; Frey 1984; Darden 1987a; Stahura 1988; Massey and Denton 1993; Schneider and Phelan 1993; Farley 1995; Frazier and Tettey-Fio 2006). Research conducted prior to the 2000 census showed that most Blacks faced barriers when they attempted to move to the suburbs, regardless of their level of socioeconomic status. In other words, the Black overrepresentation in central cities is primarily because of racial discrimination in suburban housing. Researchers have also found that the patterns of segregation in central cities are being repeated in the suburbs, with Blacks who move to the suburbs confined to a few deteriorating inner suburbs (Alba and Logan 1993). Also, Blacks with a high socioeconomic status were found to be much less likely than Whites with the same status to move to the suburbs (Fielding 1990). This lack of spatial mobility occurs in spite of the fact that Blacks are dissatisfied with public services in central cities (Darden 1987b; Welch, Combs, Sigelman and Bledsoe 1997).

> The traditional view of Black suburbanization is that when Blacks do manage to move to the suburbs, the municipalities open to them are more likely to include those with a poor tax base, low service expenditures, and a high population density. Black suburbanization has been traditionally viewed within the context of ecological theory, a theory that posits a group's social and economic status strongly influences its ability to obtain access to housing within the suburbs of metropolitan areas. (Darden 1990)

Some researchers found weaknesses in ecological theory when applied to Blacks, which has led to the introduction of the *place stratification concept* (Alba and Logan 1991). According to this concept, movement to the suburbs does not necessarily lead to residential integration, equal access to resources, or racial equality. This is because the more powerful, White-majority group maintains its advantaged position by keeping less advantaged minority groups out of the most desired municipalities. This behavior results in racial and ethnic groups being sorted by each group's relative standing in society. The outcome is a hierarchy of places within metropolitan areas, including places within the suburbs. Disadvantaged groups such as Blacks may remain segregated in undesirable places even within the suburbs.

This structural inequality in residential locations occurs through public and private discrimination in the housing market (Fong and Shibuya 2000). Thus, Blacks may attain income, education, and occupational status equal to that attained by the White majority group and still face difficulties in purchasing a suburban home in certain places. The place stratification concept implies that some groups, especially Blacks, may not be able to convert socioeconomic gains into the quality of suburban neighborhoods occupied by Whites who have comparable socioeconomic status (Alba and Logan 1993). In other words, regardless of their socioeconomic status, Blacks may be steered away from certain suburban places or face discrimination in obtaining mortgages from financial institutions (Turner et al. 2002). Therefore, because of racial steering and limited mortgage financing, Blacks in the suburbs may experience as much residential segregation as Blacks in the city (Darden and Kamel 2000a, 2000b). Moreover, greater Black movement to the suburbs may not necessarily reduce racial residential segregation within the metropolitan areas.

THE RACIAL DIVIDE AND SOCIOECONOMIC AND DEMOGRAPHIC CHANGES IN METROPOLITAN DETROIT: 1990–2000

The Detroit Metropolitan Area experienced slow growth over the last decade. In 2000, the Detroit Metropolitan Area (Wayne, Oakland, and Macomb counties) consisted of 4,043,467 people. Of this total, 2,720,689 were White (67.2 percent), while 1,000,853 were Black (25 percent). Of these, 96 percent of all Whites lived in the suburbs and only 4.3 percent resided in the city, as Whites continued to move out of the city of Detroit to the suburbs over the decade. On the other hand, 77 percent of Blacks reside in the city of Detroit, and only 23 percent live in the suburbs. Thus, the city-suburb dissimilarity index in 2000 was 72.7. This was the second highest city-suburb dissimilarity index among metropolitan areas of 500,000 or more people. Only metropolitan Gary, Indiana, had a higher index at 76 (Frey and Myers 2001). The index indicates that 72.7 percent of all Blacks in the Detroit metropolitan area would have to relocate to the suburbs to be spatially distributed the same as Whites.

By 2000, the city of Detroit had declined in population from one million people in 1990 to 951,270. It had also become 81.3 percent Black, up from 75 percent in 1990 (U.S. Bureau of the Census 2002). Indeed, over the decade, Detroit lost 44.5 percent of its White population. On the other hand, the decline of the Black population was less than 1 percent. The Detroit metropolitan area's socioeconomic condition improved sharply between 1990 and 2000. Indeed, improvements in per capita income, median household incomes, and a reduction in poverty improved Detroit's position from 36th to 21st among the 50 largest metropolitan areas (Logan et al. 2002). Much of the improvement in Detroit's socioeconomic condition may be related to the decline of high poverty neighborhoods, where the poverty rate is 40 percent or higher. Most are disproportionately Black. Metropolitan Detroit's decline in high poverty neighborhoods was substantially larger than that of any other metropolitan area (Jargowsky 2003). As a result, the concentrated poverty rate among Blacks in metropolitan Detroit declined from 53.9 percent in 1990 to 16.4 percent in 2000, a drop of 37.5 percentage points. According to Jargowsky (2003), this reduction in the concentrated poverty rate between 1990 and 2000 changed metropolitan Detroit's ranking from the number one metropolitan area in 1990 for Blacks in concentrated poverty to a rank lower than that of Chicago, St. Louis, Baltimore, Tampa, Houston, New York, Philadelphia, Atlanta, and Los Angeles.

Despite these socioeconomic changes, Detroit was among the top 10 metropolitan areas with the largest increases in family-income inequality between 1970–2000 (Watson 2007). Income inequality is measured by the ratio of the income of a typical high income (80th percentile of family income) to that of a typical low income

(20th percentile of family income). The ratio for metropolitan Detroit in 1970 was 2.48 which increased to 3.58 in 2000 (Watson 2007, p.9).

In addition to income inequality, Blacks and Whites in metropolitan Detroit continued to live in separate neighborhoods, resulting in an index of dissimilarity for the metropolitan area of 85 percent. The index for Blacks and Whites was higher than the index for any other group in America's large metropolitan areas. A major factor in the high level of metropolitan segregation is that so few Blacks reside in the suburbs compared to the percentage residing in the central city.

Some researchers have argued that the few Blacks who do manage to enter suburban municipalities are restricted to places with characteristics similar to central cities. They argue that Blacks are largely restricted to inner suburbs that are located near the central city and have significantly lower median household incomes than other suburban municipalities; such suburbs are often declining in population while other suburbs are growing (Schneider and Phelan 1993).

The key objective of this chapter is to examine those places where Blacks have achieved parity with Whites in income, education, and occupation and where they share residential space. First, I discuss the extent of racial inequality and metropolitan fragmentation in the metropolitan area as a whole.

RACIAL INEQUALITY AND POLITICAL FRAGMENTATION IN METROPOLITAN DETROIT

One distinguishing feature of metropolitan Detroit is the visible racial change between the city and the suburbs. Since segregation in the region occurs most rigidly along racial lines, there is an increasing tendency for political boundaries to become racial boundaries (Orfield 1976; Orfield 2002).

Suburbs also vary by socioeconomic status in ways that are important for differences in attitudes, policies, and levels of cooperation in the delivery of services (Squires and Kubrin 2006). Suburban jurisdictions also differ by lifestyle, with such differences crucial to understanding the fragmentation of metropolitan government itself. For example, some local governments may be willing to surrender autonomy over routine system-maintenance functions, but zealously guard their autonomy over policies governing housing and education that impinge upon the lifestyle values of the community (Squires and Kubrin 2006).

The differential movement of demographic groups and resources has caused the system of governments and political boundaries in metropolitan Detroit to become a stratification system as well (Hill 1974). Many suburban residents want to live in municipalities that are occupied by households that are similar in race, in come, education, and occupation. They also want to live near people with similar values and lifestyles. The poor and racial minorities have often been excluded, resulting in "place" as a status symbol. Local governments have acted through land use controls to keep out some affordable housing. The politics of exclusion have been the norm in metropolitan Detroit. Exclusionary practices have been the primary reason for segregation by class and race (Darden, Hill, Thomas and Thomas 1987). Some relatively homogeneous communities have used political boundaries as defenses against low-income and minority residents (Darden 1990, 86).

Realtors clearly have been involved in the politics of exclusion by virtue of steering minority group members and persons of low socioeconomic status away from White, middle-class neighborhoods. When Blacks have succeeded in moving from Detroit to the suburbs, many have become resegregated in suburban enclaves (Darden and Kamel 2000a).

The practice of steering Blacks to certain neighborhoods has implications for segregation by neighborhood socioeconomic characteristics across the Detroit metropolitan area. Thus, Blacks and Whites within Wayne, Oakland and Macomb counties (i.e., the Detroit Metro Area) reside in neighborhoods (census tracts) with different levels of poverty and other socioeconomic characteristics. For example, 56.3 percent of all Blacks in the tri-county area reside in neighborhoods (census tracts) where poverty levels range from 19.9 percent to 61.2 percent. On the other hand, only 2.5 percent of all Whites in the tri-county area reside in such poverty-stricken neighborhoods. A little over a quarter of Whites (27.6 percent) live in neighborhoods where the level of poverty is less than 2 percent, yet only 2 percent of all Blacks in the tri-county area reside in such neighborhoods, which illustrates extreme race and class inequality (Wilson 1992). The key question, however, is whether any geographic racial equality can be found in a metropolitan area with such extreme inequality. Given such extreme inequality by race and class, if places of geographic *racial equality* are to be found, the places to look are in the suburbs where the Black middle-class has been growing.

BLACK DIVERSITY, THE BLACK MIDDLE-CLASS, AND METROPOLITAN DETROIT

As far back as the 1980s, researchers observed a growing educated and prosperous Black middle class (Landry 1987). For those Black middle-class residents in the suburbs, little research has been conducted on their condition compared to the amount of research on Blacks left behind in the central cities. Moreover, virtually no research has been done to determine the characteristics of places where Blacks have reached *parity* with Whites. Some research on Black immigration to the United States in the 21st century suggests that the growing Black middle-class may be due in large part to the influx of immigrants from Africa and the Caribbean (Logan and Deane 2003).

Many metropolitan areas in the United States have indeed been experiencing an increasing foreign-born population from Africa and the Caribbean. However, metropolitan Detroit's Black middle-class is overwhelmingly native-born because Afro-Caribbeans and Africans have avoided metropolitan Detroit and settled in other metropolitan areas. Logan and Deane's (2003) analysis of large metropolitan areas revealed that Detroit was not among the metro areas with the largest representations of either the Afro-Caribbean population or the African-born population in 2000. Instead of Detroit, Afro-Caribbeans are heavily concentrated in metro areas on the East Coast. Six out of ten live in New York, Miami, and Fort Lauderdale (Logan and Deane 2003). Africans have concentrated primarily in Washington, DC, New York, and Los Angeles (Darden 2007). The only Midwestern metropolitan areas with high concentrations of Africans are Minneapolis-St. Paul and Chicago (Logan and Deane 2003). In 2006, Africans and West Indians, combined, constituted less than 1 percent of metropolitan Detroit's total population (U.S. Bureau of the Census 2007). Thus, while foreign-born Blacks are more represented among the Black middle-class (i.e., have higher education levels and incomes) and live in neighborhoods with a higher socioeconomic status than American-born Blacks in the nation as a whole, foreign-born Blacks have not been a significant factor in the Black middle-class in metro Detroit. Despite the level of segregation illustrated for Detroit that makes it America's most racially segregated metropolitan area, evidence of geographic racial equality also exists, identifiable at a different geographic scale.

THE SIGNIFICANCE OF SCALE

Although most studies of racial equality have used the metropolitan area as the spatial unit for analysis (Albelda 1986; Semyonov et al. 2000; Ovadia 2003), this unit is not appropriate to assess racial equality, as it is too large in size. Moreover, metropolitan areas are complex, socioeconomic entities not governed by a single governmental unit. Instead, they are fragmented spatial units comprised of numerous villages, townships, and cities, each with its own independent government. The strongest governmental entity consists of incorporated places or cities, therefore, the municipal level, not the metropolitan area, is the most appropriate unit for measuring geographic racial equality. At the metropolitan level, racial equality is seldom found (Ovadia 2003). Within metropolitan areas, racial equality is most prevalent in suburban municipalities and is most likely *not* found in central cities because Blacks in the suburbs are more likely than Blacks in central cities to be middle- or upper-class. Finally, racial equality is best examined at the municipal scale because land use policies are established, zoning regulations are implemented and local tax and fiscal policies are created at that level. Public service delivery (crime and safety, garbage collection, school quality, and other amenities) is among the most important factors that influence household choice of residence. In the post civil rights era, race and class inequality is most often maintained by exclusion of Blacks from certain small, suburban municipal units (Feagin 1999).

MAINTAINING RACIAL SEGREGATION AND RACIAL INEQUALITY IN THE POST CIVIL RIGHTS ERA

After the Fair Housing Act of 1968, racial and class inequality within metropolitan areas was maintained primarily because of the residential segregation of Whites in certain suburban municipalities and their various means of excluding Blacks and the poor. The Tiebout model (1956) emphasizes a sorting process with special emphasis on "pull factors" in determining residential location by municipality. The absence of Blacks and/or other racial minorities may serve as one pull factor.

INCORPORATED PLACES OF RACIAL EQUALITY IN METROPOLITAN DETROIT

Metropolitan Detroit is very fragmented with the tri-county area of Wayne, Oakland, and Macomb counties comprised of 325 cities, villages, and townships and 71 incorporated places in the tri-county area in 2000. Because incorporated places have the greatest power to tax and to exclude via zoning and housing policies, they form the focus of this study. Among the 71 incorporated suburban places in metropolitan Detroit (Wayne, Oakland, and Macomb counties), four municipalities were places where Blacks and Whites had equal incomes, education, and occupations. The incorporated suburban places and the percentage of Blacks and Whites residing there are listed in Figure 10.1 and Table 10.1. Eastpointe (once named East Detroit) is the only incorporated place of racial equality in Macomb County. There were 1,578 Blacks living there in 2000, constituting 4.6 percent of the population. Eastpointe was 91.8 percent White. Three places of geographic racial equality were located in Oakland County (namely Farmington Hills, Rochester Hills, and Southfield). The percentage of Blacks in these places ranged from 2.1 percent in Rochester Hills to 53.3 percent in Southfield. No places of racial geographic equality were found in Wayne County (the county with the highest percentage of Blacks). Together, these suburban places constituted 50,501 Blacks and 190,892 Whites.

While no data exist on Eastpointe due to its smaller population, recent data have been provided by the U.S. Bureau of the Census (2007) on the foreign-born population in Farmington Hills, Rochester Hills, and Southfield. In 2006, 21.3 percent of the total population of Farmington Hills was foreign born. However, only 1 percent of the total population was of sub-Saharan African or West Indian descent. In Rochester Hills, 18.5 percent of the total population was foreign born, but similar to Farmington Hills, only 1 percent of the total population had come from sub-Saharan Africa and the West Indies. The composition of the population of African descent was somewhat larger in Southfield. In 2006, 10.3 percent of the total population was foreign-born and 4.5 percent of the total population was of sub-Saharan African and West Indian ancestry (U.S. Bureau of the Census 2007). In comparing the places of geographic racial equality to the metropolitan area as a whole, metro Detroit was 8.5 percent foreign born. However, less than 1 percent of the total foreign-born population was from sub-Saharan Africa and the West Indies (U.S. Bureau of the Census 2007). Only Southfield, a majority Black suburb had a significantly higher Black population (4.5 percent) from sub-Saharan Africa and the West Indies than the metropolitan area (less than 1 percent). In sum, places of geographic racial equality in metropolitan Detroit are occupied overwhelmingly by the American-born Black population.

The mean percentage by race was 16.8 percent Black and 75.8 percent White. The percentage of Blacks in the metropolitan area as a whole was 25 percent compared to 67 percent for Whites. The mean percentage of Blacks and Whites in the suburbs as a whole was 6.2 percent and 86.9 percent respectively. Macomb County was 2.7 percent Black, and 7.3 percent of all Blacks in Macomb County lived in a municipality where Blacks had reached parity in income, education, and occupation with Whites. Oakland County had 120,720 Blacks, constituting 10.1 percent of the population in 2000. Moreover, 40.5 percent of all Blacks in the county resided in places of geographic racial equality.

Figure 10.1.
Location of Incorporated Places of Geographic Racial Equality in Metropolitan Detroit, 2000.

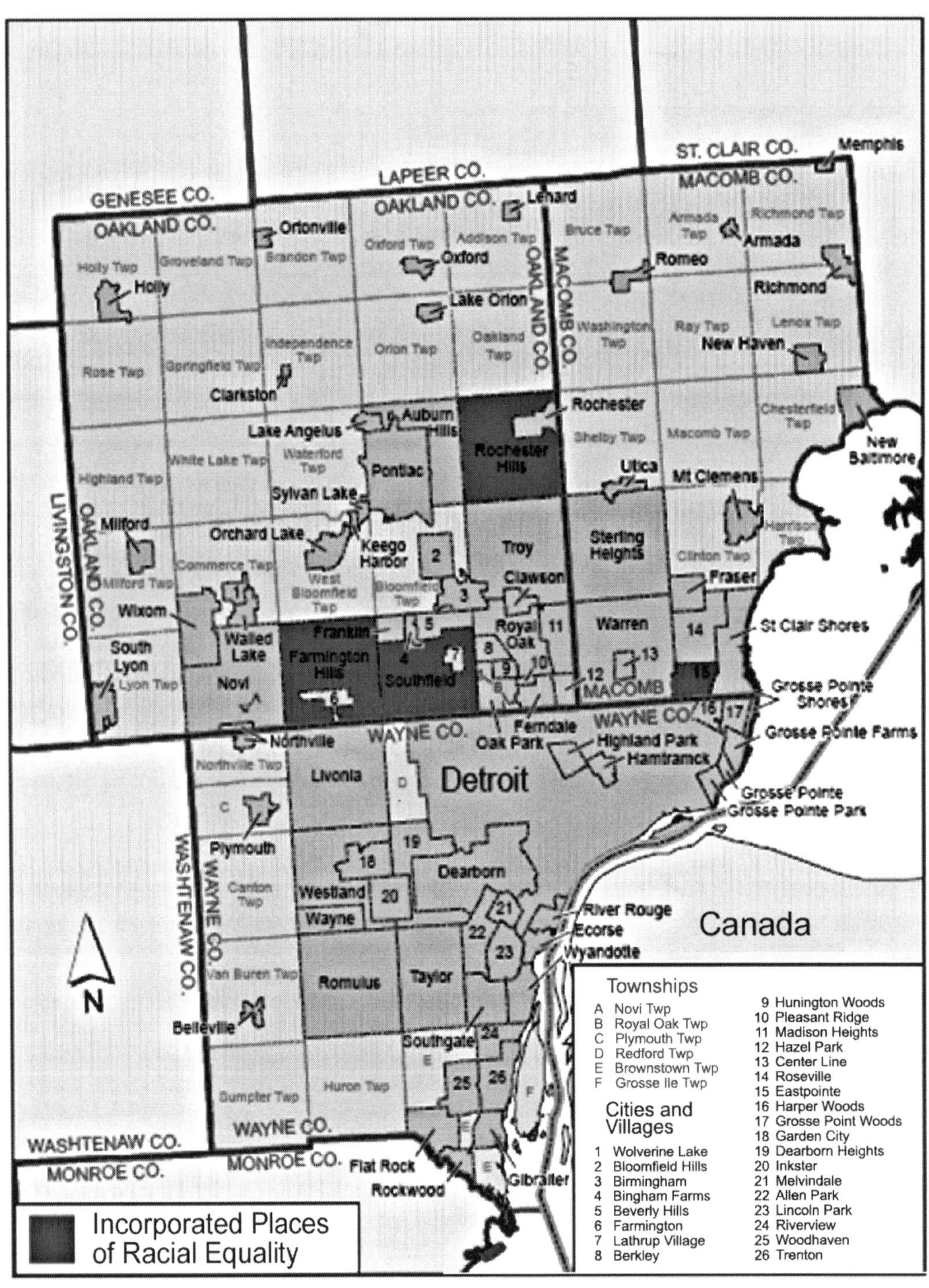

Table 10.1.
Racial Composition of the Population in Places of Racial Equality* in Metropolitan Detroit.

Suburban Municipality	Total Blacks	%	Total Whites	%
Macomb County	21,326	2.7	730,270	92.7
Eastpointe City	1,578	4.7	31,275	91.8
Oakland County	120,720	10.1	988,194	82.8
Farmington Hills City	5,743	7.0	68,125	83.0
Rochester Hills City	1,437	2.1	60,973	88.6
Southfield City	41,743	53.3	30,519	39.8
Total	50,501		190,892	
Mean		16.8		75.8

* Racial equality here compares Blacks and Whites.
Source: U.S. Bureau of the Census (2002). Summary File 3. State of Michigan.

Table 10.2.1 presents the median household incomes for Blacks and Whites. In each of the four municipalities, Blacks not only equaled Whites in income, but exceeded them. In Eastpointe, Blacks exceeded Whites in median income by $19,868. The Black median income was $65,536 compared to $45,668 for Whites. The smallest gap between Black and White median incomes was in Rochester Hills, where the Black median income was $75,706 compared to $74,215 for Whites, a difference of $1,491. The median income of Whites and Blacks in the metropolitan area was $55,106 and $40,595, respectively, a difference of $14,511 in favor of Whites.

Table 10.2.1.
Median Household Incomes of Blacks and Whites, 2000.

Suburban Municipality	Blacks	Whites	Difference
Macomb County			
Eastpointe City	$65,536	$45,668	+$19,868
Oakland County			
Farmington Hills City	$75,999	$66,484	+$9,515
Rochester Hills City	$75,706	$74,215	+$1,491
Southfield City	$57,526	$43,967	+$13,559

Source: U.S. Bureau of the Census, 2002. Summary File 3. State of Michigan.

Table 10.2.2 presents the extent of racial equality in educational status. Educational status was defined as the percent of the population with a bachelor's degree or higher. In Rochester Hills, 52 percent of all Blacks had a bachelor's degree or higher education compared to 45 percent of all Whites, a difference of 7 percentage points. Blacks in Southfield, a majority Black suburb, exceeded Whites in the percentage with a bachelor's degree by 2 percentage points, i.e., 37 percent of Blacks in Southfield had a bachelor's degree, compared to 35 percent of Whites. On the other hand, in the metropolitan area as a whole, among Blacks only 18.5 percent of its total population 25 years and older had received a bachelor's degree or higher, compared to 29.1 percent of the White population in this age category, a difference of 10.6 percentage points in favor of Whites.

Table 10.2.2.
Educational Status of Blacks and Whites, 2000.

Suburban Municipality	Percent Blacks	Percent Whites	Difference
Macomb County			
Eastpointe City	15	11	+4
Oakland County			
Farmington Hills City	48	45	+3
Rochester Hills City	52	45	+7
Southfield City	38	34	+4
Mean	38	34	+4

Educational status was assessed based on the percent of the population with a bachelor's degree or higher.
Source: Computed by the author from data obtained from summary file 3 (SF3), State of Michigan.

Table 10.2.3 shows the extent of racial equality in occupational status. Occupational status was defined as the percentage of the population who held managerial and professional positions. In Rochester Hills 27.9 percent of Blacks held managerial or professional positions compared to 22.6 percent of Whites, a difference of 5.3 percentage points. While 11 percent of Blacks in Eastpointe held managerial and professional positions, this was still higher than the 9.5 percent held by Whites. In the metropolitan area as a whole, 35.7 percent of Whites held management, professional and related high status positions compared to 27.6 percent of Blacks, a difference of 8.1 percentage points in favor of Whites.

Table 10.2.3.
Occupational Status of Blacks and Whites, 2000.

Suburban Municipality	Percent Blacks	Percent Whites	Difference
Macomb County			
Eastpointe City	11.0	9.5	+1.5
Oakland County			
Farmington Hills City	27.9	22.6	+5.3
Rochester Hills City	28.0	23.8	+4.2
Southfield City	20.6	18.0	+2.6
Mean	21.8	18.5	+3.3

Occupational status was assessed based on the percentage of the population who held managerial and professional positions.

Source: U.S. Bureau of the Census, 2002. Summary File 3. State of Michigan.

RESIDENTIAL SEGREGATION IN PLACES OF GEOGRAPHIC RACIAL EQUALITY

What is the importance of such racial equality based on socioeconomic status compared to the level of racial residential segregation? Geographic racial equality is not complete unless Blacks and Whites also share residential space, thus reflecting low levels of residential segregation. If low levels of residential segregation are found, it would lend support to the spatial assimilation model described by Massey and Mullen (1984) and Massey and Denton (1985). It would mean that for Blacks residing in those places of geographic racial equality, socioeconomic status did in fact lead to a higher-status suburban place and paved the way for residential desegregation (Massey and Mullen 1984). It would also mean that, contrary to spatial stratification theory, Blacks in those places were able to convert socioeconomic gains into quality suburban neighborhoods occupied by Whites who have socioeconomic status equal to or less than Blacks (Alba and Logan 1993). Finally, it would mean that, contrary to the traditional view of Black suburbanization, Black movement to the suburbs can result in reducing residential segregation substantially below the level in the central city (Darden and Kamel 2000a).

Table 10.3 shows the level of Black-White residential segregation in places of geographic racial equality. The level of segregation ranges from 47.2 in Eastpointe to 26.5 in Farmington Hills. The mean level of segregation for the four places was 35.7. The mean index of dissimilarity is very low when compared to the level of Black-White residential segregation for the Detroit metropolitan area (85).

OTHER CHARACTERISTICS OF PLACES OF GEOGRAPHIC RACIAL EQUALITY

Past researchers have suggested that Blacks in the suburbs are restricted to places that (1) are close to the central city, (2) have significantly lower median household incomes, and (3) have declining populations (Alba and Logan 1993; Schneider and Phelan 1993). I assess each of these factors here to see if they apply to places of geographic racial equality.

Table 10.3.
Racial Residential Segregation in Places of Racial Equality (Black vs. White)* in 2000.

Municipality	Index of Dissimilarity**
Eastpointe	47.2
Farmington Hills	26.5
Rochester Hills	32.6
Southfield	36.5
Mean	35.7

Source: Frey, W. H. and D. Myers. Analysis of Census 2000; The Social Science Data Analysis Network. http://www.censusscope.org.
*Non-Hispanic only
**Based on census tracts. The index ranges from "0" (no residential segregation) to "100" (complete residential segregation). The higher the index, the greater the amount of residential segregation.

Distance to Central City

Table 10.4 shows the distance of each place from the city of Detroit. While Eastpointe and Southfield border Detroit, Farmington Hills is 16 miles away and Rochester Hills is 23 miles from the city. The mean distance of the places of geographic racial equality is 9.8 miles. Thus, only Eastpointe and Southfield would qualify as close to the central city.

Table 10.4.
Mean Distance from City of Detroit of Places of Racial Equality.

Municipality	Distance (in miles)
Eastpointe	0
Farmington Hills	16
Rochester Hills	23
Southfield	0
Mean	9.8

Source: Computed by the author.

Median Household Income

Eastpointe, which is located in Macomb County, had a Black median household income of $65,536, which was $13,434 higher than the median household income for the county as a whole. Similarly, both Farmington Hills and Rochester Hills had a Black median household income that exceeded Oakland County's median of $61,907. Only in Southfield was the Black median household income below the median for Oakland County. The gap, however, was not very large ($57,526 for Blacks compared to $61,907 for the county, or a total difference of $4,381) (see Table 10.2.1).

Population Change, 1990–2000

Table 10.5 shows the patterns of population change from 1990–2000 in places of geographic racial equality. Contrary to traditional ideas and past research on Black suburbanization, all municipalities except Eastpointe increased in population (Schneider and Phelan 1993). The increase in population in Farmington Hills and Rochester Hills was 10.1 percent and 11.2 percent, respectively. This growth in population was similar to the 10.1 percent growth for Oakland County as a whole.

Table 10.5.
Population Change 1990–2000 in places of Racial Equality.

Municipality	Percent Increase
Macomb County	9.9
Eastpointe City	-3.4
Oakland County	10.2
Farmington Hills City	10.1
Rochester Hills City	11.2
Southfield City	3.4

Source: http://www.fedstats.gov/qf/states/26000.html.

CONCLUSIONS

This chapter focused on metropolitan Detroit and examined the extent of geographic racial equality in the most racially segregated metropolitan area in the United States. It defined geographic racial equality as those incorporated places where Blacks have achieved *parity* with Whites in income, education, and occupational status. Four places were found. After comparing the characteristics of places of geographic racial equality with the metropolitan area as a whole, the results revealed that the places of geographic racial equality constituted a sizeable percentage of Blacks in the two suburban counties (Oakland and Macomb). Moreover, Blacks residing in places of geographic racial equality experienced substantially lower levels of residential segregation, higher median household incomes, and growing populations. Such places presented a mixed pattern demographically, ranging from 2.1 percent Black in Rochester Hills to 53.3 percent Black in Southfield. Not all places were bordering the city of Detroit. The distance from the city ranged from 0 to 23 miles from Detroit's border. The mean distance from the city of Detroit was 9.8 miles.

These characteristics of suburban places of geographic racial equality challenge the traditional view of the characteristics of Blacks in the suburbs. Blacks in places of geographic racial equality were able to convert socioeconomic gains into quality suburban places reflecting their equal status with Whites.

AREAS FOR FURTHER STUDY

While much has been revealed about places of geographic racial equality that challenges the traditional view of Black suburbanization, further study surrounding the issue of geographic racial equality is needed. Among the unanswered questions are: Are Blacks in places of geographic racial equality able to gain access to the highest quality public schools compared to Blacks in other suburbs and in the central city? Are Blacks in places of geographic equality able to experience the lowest crime rates compared to Blacks in other suburbs and the central city? (Emerson, Yancey, and Chai 2001). Are Blacks residing in places of geographic racial equality able to experience less interpersonal racism and discrimination than Blacks in other suburbs, the central city and the metropolitan area as a whole? (Cashin 2007; Pattillo-McCoy 1999; Feagin 1999). Answers to these questions will provide a better understanding of the Black quality of life on a place basis.

Chapter 11

Place, Race and Displacement Following Hurricane Katrina in New Orleans

LISA R. RAWLINGS

INTRODUCTION

Derived from the Latin *platea* (street) and Greek *plateia/platys* (broad), place refers to "a particular area or locality; region ... the part of space occupied by a person or thing; situation." (Webster's Unabridged Dictionary 1370). Geographically, place is the site where life is rooted and sustained. Place retains meaningful organization to the people who reside there and provides links to other places. Place is an appropriated space (Easthope 2004). Contemporary concepts of space include broader conceptual frameworks, including social and psychological structures. For example, psychological concepts of space portray the individual and his/her adjustment to space. Coping with change of milieu generates stress reactions for many people. Understanding the meaning of place and the sense of "loss of place" becomes important for understanding personal responses to disasters and displacement. Experiences by Gulf Coast residents following Hurricane Katrina included this sense of loss. This chapter focuses on the impact of Katrina on the unique place of New Orleans and the implications of the widespread displacement it spawned.

SPACE, LOSS, AND THE PSYCHOLOGY OF PLACE

Perhaps the single most dramatic economic, social and demographic shift in recent American history occurred in the aftermath of Hurricane Katrina in 2005. The impact, the scope of the dislocation, and breadth of the displacement spawned a "Katrina Diaspora" that included an estimated one-million-plus people nationwide. The poor, the Black and the vulnerable were disproportionately affected, and bore the greatest long-term burden of the failed response.

Comprehending the impact of Hurricane Katrina on Gulf Coast residents, especially lower income, minority, and special populations requires an understanding of the historical consequences of slavery, previous experience with disasters, race relations, government mistrust, and contemporary concepts of place taken from several disciplines, that underscore place as a central component of individual's lives.

Fullilove's (1996; 2004) discussion of the psychology of place rests on the assumption that people strive for a "... sense of belonging, which is necessary for psychosocial well-being, [and] depends on strong, well-developed relationships with nurturing places" (1996, p. 1517). In a relational context, place is the "psychosocial milieu" that consists of the social influence, interactions and transactions, particularly as they relate to inclusion and/or isolation. Massey (1995) suggests that social relatedness is inherent in place. Sacks (2001) describes place as "the primary means by which we are able to use space and turn it into a humanized landscape," (p. 233) which reinforces the human interactions concept. Place develops special meaning through social processes (Low and Altman 1992).

Paasi, suggests that place is the setting for the life story (1991), suggesting that place has individualized meaning. Thus, this "personal 'sense of place' is shaped by the person's past, as well as by the person's attitudes, beliefs and actions in the present" (Fullilove 1518). Culture often plays a role in shaping how individuals appropriate the environment. Additionally, Mock (1993) suggests that place should aid people in finding existential meaning in life, a symbolic role, that becomes critical when examining the emotional impact of displacement.

In sum, Fullilove (1996) contends that *place* "provides the physical structures within which human relations unfurl" (p. 1518) or the "emotional ecosystem that attaches us to the environment" (Fullilove 2004, p. 17). Place creates the backdrop for life; it influences the individual or community associated with it. Place is also shaped by physical, economic and social factors. It establishes continuity and a sense of equilibrium while defining normality for each individual or community within it. *Place* provides the "external realities within which people shape their existence" (Fullilove 1996, p. 1518). These conceptualizations of place suggest a mutuality of the person-in-environment construct sustained through key psychological processes: familiarity, attachment and identity. These processes are overlapping and mutually inclusive, as are the consequences of their disruption.

FAMILIARITY AND DISORIENTATION

Place provides people with a cognitive map or gestalt of their surroundings, shaping how they move through space (Wallace 1957). Landmarks, landscapes and community icons are markers of *place,* each with their respective and collective histories. They lend a sense of continuity and equilibrium in the lives of residents and shape how people secure food, where people find shelter, where they seek comfort and refuge and whom they can trust. Freeman (1984) speaks to people's need for a stable place: "Stability allows for people to develop intimate knowledge of their settings and to develop trusting relationships with place and with each other" (Freeman in Fullilove 1996, p. 1521).

Without this familiar map, navigation of the environment may be affected, resulting in a period of paralysis, disorientation and confusion. Fullilove explains that this disorientation jars the emotional, sensory and muscular memory. "The sudden loss of the exterior world that conditioned those motions is perceived as a loss of the self" (Fullilove 1996, p. 1518).

PLACE ATTACHMENT AND NOSTALGIA

Bowlby, father of attachment theory, argues that everyone's personal environment or outer ring shapes their world. The homeostasis of this *place*, supports and influences the homeostasis of the individual (1973). Fullilove conceptualizes place attachment as "a series of emotions and behaviors that modulate distance from, and hence maintain contact with, the object of attachment, which is a source of protection and satisfaction" (Fullilove 1996, p. 1519). The expressions of these bonds may be shaped by individual and cultural differences (Tuan 1980; 2001).

Low and Altman explain in *Place Attachments* (1992) that attachment to home is at the center of these place attachments. Home, as the individualized place, signifies a place of refuge, safety, security, and nourishment. Saunders and Williams (1988) describe home as the "fusion" of the "physical unit of the house" and the "social unit of the household" (Saunders and Williams, p. 83). Home is a critical place since it is where "basic" social relations and institutions are developed. Easthope argues that home is a "socio-spatial entity, a psycho-spatial entity and an emotional warehouse" (Easthope 2004, p. 134). It provides ontological security by maintaining a sense of constancy, providing the location within which daily routines are formed, promoting a sense of autonomy and freedom and serving as a secure base (Dupuis and Thorns 1996).

Though home is the central developmental place for most, it is not the only place to which people become attached. Low and Altman argue that place attachments expand concentrically out from the home to include neighborhood, region and country (1992). These attachments are illustrated by neighborhood and local community affiliation as well as larger movements of nationalism.

Because disruptions in attachments to place and persons often occur simultaneously, Fried (1963) suggests they "may well have synergistic effects, producing outcomes for physical and mental health far more disruptive than those resulting from an injury to one alone" (Fried in Fullilove 1996, p. 1519). As with other losses, the grief that accompanies loss of a home or a place has psychological implications, including depression. Additionally, those who have experienced extended or habitual displacement, may have their ability to attach to any place impaired.

PLACE IDENTITY AND ALIENATION

Fried explores the influence of *place* on individual identity, ". . . a sense of spatial identity is fundamental to human functioning. It represents a phenomenal or ideational integration of important experiences concerning environmental arrangements and contacts in relation to the individual's conception of his own body in space. It is based on spatial memory, spatial imagery, the spatial network of current activities and the implicit spatial components of ideals and aspirations" (Fried 1963, p. 156).

"Place is incorporated into the sense of self as a core element in identity formation. . . . One's place must be understood according to its symbolic construction by those within the place and by the larger society" (Fullilove 1996, p. 1520). Further, *place* may designate the social location or status of an individual or community of people in a society. This conceptualization may have geographic boundaries as well as social, ideological, economic and political dimensions and consequences.

The security of an individual's place identity is rooted in having a place to call your own and having that place valued by others. People may experience feelings of alienation where they feel that their sense of place is not esteemed by others. Psychiatrist Julie Eilenberg (1995) in her exploration of alienation among the displaced concluded that the "loss of visibility has led to a profound collapse in self-pride" (Eilenberg in Fullilove 1996, p. 1520).

DISPLACEMENT

Conceptualizing Displacement

It should be noted that displacement is a process with events and experiences unfolding over time. Ross-Sheriff and English (2000) have outlined five phases of this process: pre-uprooting, uprooting, transition, settlement and adaptation. Each stage includes common events and associated psychosocial experiences.

During the pre-uprooting phase, individuals have an established "sense of place," which is often characterized by familiarity, attachment and/or identification with the place. Depending on the suddenness and nature of their uprooting, there may also be some uncertainty, anxiety or fear about the impending uprooting.

In the uprooting phase, which entails separation from one's place of origin or habitual residence, either voluntarily or involuntarily, several events may be experienced. These include physical departure, difficult life circumstances and multiple losses, including loss of family, friends, health, community and culture. These events may be accompanied by persistent uncertainty, anxiety, fear, trauma, stress or relief depending on the nature of the uprooting.

During the transitional phase, there may be mounting losses and institutional living. This phase may produce additional stressful or traumatic events. Conflict with the host community, depressive or anxious symptoms as well as unrelenting feelings of uncertainty, fear and anxiety are common. Conversely, feelings of elations and relief may also be experienced.

Settlement occurs when a permanency plan has been developed by or for the uprooted. Continued institutional living or more permanent arrangements are potential outcomes which may require rebuilding family and community. During this phase, some social and health services may become available; there may be some acceptance of and by the host community and the beginnings of a more routine existence.

The final stage, adaptation/integration may continue with rebuilding family and community and establishing and maintaining routines. Acceptance of and by the host society may also be experienced.

The Berry model acknowledges that multiple losses, separation, stress and trauma are potential byproducts of displacement (Berry 2001). It recognizes the importance of social supports and coping on behavioral outcomes and conceives of this process as an evolution of overlapping events and experiences. The model can be applied broadly to displacement that may result from a variety of sources including immigration, homelessness, persecution, war and disasters.

While similarities in the displacement process exist regardless of source, it must be noted that the nature and source of the uprooting agent has tremendous implications for these subsequent events and the psychosocial experience. Differential psychological responses to displacement may be based on the human agency in displacement. Forced, as opposed to voluntary uprooting is often colored by the experience of disempowerment and loss of autonomy. Likewise, the cause, or perceived cause, of the uprooting may also shape individual responses. As it relates to disasters, the cause (or perceived cause) of the disaster may impact how people respond and recover. Displacement perceived to be caused by malicious human intent or neglect often bodes ill for individual's subsequent psychological functioning.

Root Shock: Psychological Impact of Displacement

> "*At the heart of the experience of displacement is the sense that one is without a place to be.*"
>
> (Fullilove 1996, p. 1521)

In addition to the external challenges faced at the various stages, displacement may produce serious psychological implications, which are understood to be linked to the disruption of the key processes of familiarity, attachment and identity with potential consequences of loss, sadness and depression, disorientation, and alienation (Fullilove 1996).

In *Root Shock*, Fullilove elaborates on the psychological consequences of displacement, describing a traumatic stress reaction resulting from the disruption in "all or part of one's emotional ecosystem" (Fullilove 2004, p. 11). She contends that individuals naturally develop an external protection mechanism to relate to their outer worlds or "mazeway." When this "mazeway" is damaged, the person experiences *root shock*. On an individual level, it causes "profound emotional upheaval that destroys the working model of the world that has existed in the individual's head" (Fullilove 2004). The loss of this working model handicaps the individual in responding effectively in the immediate or even long-term aftermath of displacement. A new "mazeway" must be created to restore functional capacity. An individual's ability to do so may be shaped by both individual and social resources as well as the character of the displacement experience.

On a community level, *root shock* "ruptures bonds, dispersing people to all directions of the compass" (Fullilove 2004). This was dramatically illustrated in the aftermath of Hurricane Katrina. This loss of community and social support contributes to the resource deficit of the displaced, making recovery more challenging. Fullilove suggests that the *root shock* experience is not only acute, but has lifelong, even generational implications.

The concepts of *psychology of place, displacement* and *root shock* provide useful frameworks to conceptualize the importance of place to well-being and conversely the traumatic impact of the disruption. These concepts are particularly salient to the experience of those displaced by Hurricane Katrina. Because people vulnerable to disasters are highly vulnerable to displacement, a discussion of the factors associated with this increased risk will follow.

Disasters and Vulnerability

Vulnerability, defined here as potential harm from the impact of the disaster agent (Miller and Nigg 1993), offers a useful perspective in explaining relative risk of being displaced by disaster. This discussion will aid in understanding how race and other social variables may potentiate the individual's vulnerability to disaster-induced displacement. Although no community is immune to the risks associated with disasters, research demonstrates that disaster effects are not random and that inequality shapes vulnerability to harm and damage (Cochrane 1975).

Vulnerability is often studied in the context of socio-economic status, with poor people being more vulnerable to disasters than those with more resources. Although most vulnerability arises from the quality and location of housing, this examination of the concept of vulnerability to disasters holds that there are conceptually distinct types of vulnerability that can be considered independently as they relate to disasters: consequence and event vulnerability (Miller and Nigg 1993). Miller and Nigg define *event vulnerability* as household vulnerability associated with the direct impact from a disaster agent; in other words, the susceptibility of the home to the devastation from the disaster. *Consequence vulnerability* is defined as household vulnerability associated with the social and political processes of recovery from the disaster event, or the susceptibility of the household to an ineffective recovery experience (1993).

Other scholars conceptualize vulnerability as a spatial and contextual phenomenon. Curtis, Mills and Leitner (2007) suggest that vulnerability is related to the proximity of the disaster agent, as well as the context of the community — or *site* and *situation vulnerability*. This conceptualization complements the previous one in that site vulnerability has implications for both the event and its consequences. Additionally, the context, or social factors, associated with a particular group shape event and consequence vulnerability.

These differentiations help us to better understand the complexity of disasters. Because "disasters tend to intensify pre-existing status differences and inequalities" (Miller and Nigg 1993, p. 4), some demographic characteristics, including income, gender and age may have heightened vulnerability. Interestingly, their findings suggest that race and income have separate effects and that "there is something particular about the recovery process itself that makes people of differing race/ethnic groups more vulnerable" (Miller and Nigg 1993, p. 10).

Though these studies make no inferences about this "something particular" that increases the vulnerability of ethnic groups, this author posits that it is the legacy of racism, marginalization, mistrust and discrimination experienced by people of color that is responsible for their heightened vulnerability. The case of Hurricane Katrina in New Orleans will be examined in this light in the second part of this chapter.

Event, consequence, site and situation vulnerability provide useful perspectives to understand the displacement experience of poor people of color affected by disasters. It informs this work by sensitizing it to the more subtle influences that social and racial dynamics play in the impact and aftermath of disasters. Although these conceptualizations of vulnerability encompass only the physical damage to locations and/or structures, the vulnerability to the loss of place has implications for emotional security and well-being as discussed in the previous section.

This section has provided the conceptual underpinnings of the significance of place, the potential implications of and the differential vulnerabilities to its loss. The next section builds on this foundation in the discussion of the case of Hurricane Katrina in New Orleans.

PRE-HURRICANE KATRINA NEW ORLEANS

The Meaning of New Orleans

"But we cannot understand the losses unless we first appreciate what was there."

(Fullilove 2005, p. 20)

To grasp the full impact of root shock in New Orleans, one needs a context for the place and its culture. A brief glimpse of the pre-Katrina "Crescent City" as described by residents, scholars and promoters helps provide some context. Morris explains: "It's always been an exciting and depressing place at the same time. Maybe exciting and tragic" (Morris in Slevin and Whoriskey 2005).

New Orleans culture is often described as embodying a spirit of sensuality, individuality, and *joie de vivre*. It is a city that revels in the pleasures of food, drink, music and art. Piazza, longtime New Orleans resident and author, examines the rich culture, the complex history, the social interconnectedness and the symbolic and psychic meaning of New Orleans in his book *Why New Orleans Matters* (2005). He aptly captures the unique sense of place that was New Orleans.

Piazza discusses *rootedness* as experienced by the people of New Orleans: "New Orleanians are attached to tradition; which is fused to a sense of place, to the ground itself" (Piazza 2005, p. 104). This description sums up the pre-Katrina psychology of place as it relates to New Orleans — the deep familiarity, strong attachment and suffused identity. This attachment of peoples to their neighborhoods is evident. "In parts of New Orleans, there are still people — or there were, until Katrina — who have rarely been out of their neighborhoods in their lives" (Piazza 2005, p. 84). Louisianans tend to stay rooted in their place of origin. In fact, of the fifty states, Louisiana, has the highest percentage (79 percent) of residents who were born in the state (U.S. Census 2003). Because they are less likely than other Americans to be mobile, being uprooted is a much less anticipated and a more devastating experience.

This connection of people to their environment has shaped the culture and spirit of the city. This slow pace of change has maintained much of the character and cultural integrity — its "unique flavor that comes from hundreds of years of slowly mutating culture" (Piazza 2005, p. 156).

Its uniqueness can be attributed to a parallel yet quite distinct evolution from the rest of the United States. Native Americans were the first inhabitants of the region. The French and Spanish wrestled for control of the region, firmly implanting the Roman Catholic tradition. The strong, early presence of Blacks — both free and enslaved gave rise to religious syncretism, or the melding of African based and Native American spiritual traditions with Roman Catholicism.

The first groups of immigrants came from France, Switzerland and Germany. Post-Haitian Revolution, refugee planters, free Blacks and enslaved Africans from Haiti and later from other Francophone Caribbean islands such as Martinique followed. Additionally, large groups of French Canadian, Italians, Irish and Croatians made New Orleans their home. Each immigrant wave deposited unique cultural artifacts and traditions, the sediment of which has melded into the culture of the Big Easy. This ability to integrate many cultures into one is perhaps the defining feature of New Orleans.

Race Relations: The Historical Context

During the pre-Civil War era, unlike most other parts of the South, Blacks (whether free, enslaved or mixed) were not only able to interact, but they were also allowed to practice their many varied indigenous cultural traditions — particularly those of a musical and spiritual nature — as well as invent new ones. These unique social arrangements speak to the duplicity and flexibility of the people of New Orleans and underscores the complex fabric of race relations in New Orleans.

Post Civil War race relations in New Orleans continued to be a rather contentious and complicated interplay. On one hand, the physical proximity of Blacks and Whites (especially with the degree of intermixing) might suggest a level of egalitarianism that was not evident in other facets of New Orleans society. On the other hand, the system of White supremacy was brutally enforced. During Reconstruction, the Mechanics Hall riot left many dead or wounded, contributing to the presence of federal troops in the South to enforce Reconstruction policies. Violence erupted as Black and White delegates attempted to draft a new state Constitution that extended political franchise to Black men. Overall, 87 Black men were elected to the state legislature and one to the House of Representatives (but denied this seat) during Reconstruction in Louisiana. With the abrupt end to

Reconstruction in 1877, Blacks in New Orleans, and throughout the South experienced a vicious backlash in the form of the Ku Klux Klan's reign of terror (Blassingame 1973).

With the 1954 Supreme Court decision that mandated de-segregation, New Orleans experienced massive White flight. Losing much of its tax base, New Orleans experienced marked economic decline. The city has also been under assault environmentally, earning the moniker "Cancer Alley" for its myriad environmental threats that were disproportionately concentrated in poor communities of color (McQuaid 2000). Further, reports of discrimination and especially the long and very brutal history of police brutality in New Orleans highlights the complexity of these relationships (Human Rights Watch 1990).

Mistrust and Corruption

This climate of antagonistic race relations sustains and exacerbates an environment of mistrust. "Blacks mistrust Whites, and vice versa. People in the state distrust the city" (Morris in Slevin and Whoriskey 2005, A01). This mistrust is fueled by pervasive corruption. According to Piazza "For some reason or complex set of reasons, Louisiana politicians in general, and New Orleans politicians in particular, have turned the official corruption and patronage that always come with government to an art form . . . it is difficult at this point for Louisianians to fully trust any politician who **isn't** trying to bilk them" (emphasis added by author; Piazza 2005, p. 88). In 2004 alone, 44 public officials, including judges, police, teachers, administrators and traffic court workers, were indicted on charges of skimming, bribery and shakedowns (Slevin and Whoriskey 2005).

This lack of faith in public officials, is perhaps most dramatic in the police department. Piazza explains that although

> ". . . most New Orleans cops are hardworking decent men and women, Black and White, who take their jobs and responsibilities seriously, amid many difficulties, not the least of which is a culture of bad behavior among some of their brother and sister officers. A significant percentage of these brother and sister officers participate in a kind of cowboy culture; they act as entrepreneurs, independent franchises, freelance badasses whose antisocial impulses rival those of the thugs they are suppose to be controlling." (Piazza 2005, p. 83)

Unfortunately, those who often have felt the brunt of this police misbehavior have been the poor and Black residents of New Orleans.

Perhaps even more defining than the pervasive corruption and discrimination in New Orleans is the astounding poverty. In fact, pre-Katrina, New Orleans had the second highest rate of concentrated poverty of any city in the U.S., with over 38 percent of its residents living in high poverty neighborhoods (Freeman 2004; Katz 2006).

It is within this unique backdrop — a landscape of cultural amalgamation and racial antagonism, of communal solidarity and class hegemony, of Southern hospitality and deep-seated mistrust and corruption, of rich cultural traditions and profoundly entrenched concentrated poverty — that the drama of Hurricane Katrina unfolded.

Hurricane Katrina in New Orleans

> *"The situation, over the week, went from frightening, to desperate, to indescribably brutal and sad and finally to incomprehensible."*
>
> (Piazza 2005, p. xiii)

The "Katrina experience" will be considered the period in New Orleans from Sunday, August 29 through Saturday, September 5, 2005 that included the impact of Hurricane Katrina, levee breeches, subsequent flooding, and the response paralysis. Piazza provides a vivid, heart-rending description.

> "Women who were raped in the chaos that the government was so slow to recognize and take steps to stop, people whose lives ended on a sidewalk where their bodies lay uncovered for days rotting in the hot sun, or trapped and drowned by rising flood waters in their own attics, and the people who saw all that, who smelled all that, even as they were sustaining their own traumas, people who walked through streets crying, holding on to small children, or who swam through oil-slicked, sewage-filled water, unsophisticated people with no one to call and no idea where to go. And the lucky ones who were rescued, brought to the Superdome, where the roof blew off and the toilets overflowed and the food ran out and so did the medicine. Or were set down by the side of an interstate somewhere on the fringes of a city, or at the Convention Center next to rotting corpses, and eventually airlifted or bussed out to Red Cross camps in Iowa and Michigan and Missouri and Oklahoma." (Piazza 2005, pp. 140–1)

The Impacts of Hurricane Katrina

Hurricane Katrina exacted a devastating toll on many areas of New Orleans. Property damage and loss were extensive. The scope of the physical damage alone exceeded that of all other disasters of recent history. Hurricane Katrina wreaked havoc on an area that spanned 22 miles from east to west and 15 miles from the north to south. In total, 41 of Louisiana's 64 parishes experienced serious damage. Almost all of St. Bernard Parish and over 77 percent of Orleans Parish were affected. At peak flooding, 80 percent of the city was under water, with some places experiencing flooding 20 feet deep.

The official Hurricane Katrina death toll stands at 1695 in total, with 1464 of the deaths in Louisiana. There are 135 people officially listed as missing. The Department of Homeland Security claimed that the post-Katrina displacement was the largest internal migration in the United States since the Dust Bowl migrations of the 1920s and '30s (Chertoff 2006). Over a million people were displaced throughout the country. Four hundred thousand people were displaced from the city of New Orleans alone. Over 5,200 children were separated from their families, the last of whom were finally reunited with family members six months post-impact (National Center for Missing and Exploited Children 2006).

According to the National Hurricane Center, "it was the costliest and one of the five deadliest hurricanes to ever strike the United States" (Mayfield 2005). Many sectors of society were severely impacted. Over 18,700 businesses were severely damaged or destroyed. About 220,000 jobs are estimated to have been lost due to the hurricane. In Louisiana, forty public K–12 schools were destroyed by the hurricane and 835 schools received some damage. Over 12,000 teachers and 175,809 public school students were displaced. Thirty hospitals were initially closed due to hurricane damage. Twenty of these hospitals remained closed six months later.

As the literature would have predicted, those who were poor and Black were disproportionately affected by Hurricane Katrina. Over a fifth (21 percent) of the population affected by Hurricane Katrina was poor, as compared with 15 percent in undamaged areas (Gabe, Falk, McCarty and Mason 2005; Logan 2006). It is also estimated that 73 percent (272,000) of the population displaced from Orleans Parish were Black (Gabe et al. 2009). Less than half (49 percent) of bus routes have reopened. Further, only 21 percent of the pre-storm child care capacity is available, limiting the options for many working families, especially mothers who are already at an increased risk. Two and a half years post Hurricane Katrina the U.S. Census estimated that approximately half of the evacuees had returned (McCulley 2008).

The Response to Hurricane Katrina

Although hurricanes are typically classified as natural disasters, the level of human culpability in exacerbating the Hurricane Katrina experience renders it a compound disaster — one that is due both to human agency and nature. The lack of preventive measures, inadequate preparedness plans and a generally deficient response, were responsible for additional lives lost and untold human suffering. Human causation, because of its perceived level of preventability and predictability and the question of intentionality, has profound consequences for its victims.

In addition to the extensive physical damage and devastating human impact, Hurricane Katrina was unprecedented in several other ways that can be attributed to failures of individuals, government and society. First, preventive measures to repair an inadequately built and poorly maintained levee system were abandoned. This occurred, despite the well-established threat to the city posed by a large hurricane. In fact, a 2001 FEMA report recognized New Orleans' vulnerability to a devastating disaster. Then in 2004, FEMA ran a simulated exercise (named Hurricane Pam) of the impact of a Category 4 Hurricane on New Orleans. The damage of "Hurricane Pam" was ominously similar to that wrought by Hurricane Katrina.

Second, given the many warnings and frighteningly accurate predictions in the days leading up to Katrina, the lack of preparedness was alarming. Max Mayfield, Director of the National Hurricane Center reported making personal appeals to New Orleans Mayor Nagin and Louisiana Governor Blanco telling them that even while Katrina was not yet a Category 4 storm, that it was building up to be "... the worst hurricane that he had ever seen and that officials should do all they could to get folks out of danger" (Dyson 2006, p. 58). Nevertheless, Mayor Nagin hesitated in calling for a mandatory evacuation, ignoring the explicit knowledge that there were an estimated 130,000 New Orleans residents who would require evacuation assistance (Dyson 2006).

Third, a week elapsed before relief reached those most severely affected, needlessly extending the emergency phase. This lack of an immediate response by the local, state and federal governments contributed to additional lives lost, horrors endured and trauma suffered.

This response inadequacy was detailed in a bi-partisan Congressional report that concluded that the response effort suffered from "a failure of initiative," which they entitled their final report. This inability to prepare for anticipated post-landfall conditions, given the level of information and warning that had been shared at all levels, was a major human failing. Further, it explains that "the incomplete evacuation led to deaths, thousands of dangerous rescues, and horrible conditions for those who remained ... failure to anticipate post-landfall conditions delayed post-landfall evacuation and support" (U.S. House of Representatives 2006, p. 2).

Further, when a response was finally initiated, it was a hostile as opposed to a humanitarian one. Because of sensational media reports, "... the seeds were planted that the victims of Katrina should be kept away, or at least handled with extreme caution" (Pierre and Gerhart 2005, A8). As a result, responders and would be helpers "steeled themselves for battle" (Pierre and Gerhart 2005, A8). At a time when thousands were stranded, starving, sick and dehydrated, martial law was declared and troops were authorized by Governor Blanco to "Shoot to kill" (Reuters 2005). Blockades were erected that prevented desperate people from fleeing the flooded city to Gretna, St. Bernard Parish and other neighboring vicinities. Some report that they were fired on as they attempted to approach the blockades. Others report that their meager water and food supplies were confiscated as they waited on the bridge to Gretna for relief (Dyson 2006; Lee 2006). These hostilities in the face of suffering more profoundly impact the psychological reactions of survivors than the physical damage caused by the disaster.

The bipartisan report posits that "passivity did the most damage. The failure of initiative cost lives, prolonged suffering, and left all Americans justifiably concerned that our government is no better prepared to protect its people than it was before 9/11" (U.S. House of Representatives 2006, p. 359). It concludes that "The failure of initiative was also a failure of empathy, a myopia to the need to reach more people on their own terms" (U.S. House of Representatives 2006, p. 362).

The report does not speculate as to the origin of this myopia. Given the context of a racially divided city steeped in mistrust of politicians and authority, it is not surprising that the response would come under such serious scrutiny. Devoid of satisfactory justification and accountability, many have concluded that this empathy deficit results from a racial disconnect — the failure, inability or unwillingness of the privileged to recognize the dignity and humanity inherent in others, especially those who are poor and Black.

RACE, CLASS AND MISTRUST

It may never be definitively determined if racism played a role in the response and if so, to what extent. However, given the history of racial mistrust and political corruption in New Orleans, it is understandable how the legacy might have influenced (actually or theoretically) the failed response to Hurricane Katrina. The feeble response also has implications for the deepening of historical feelings of mistrust. These feelings were further compounded by comments of prominent Americans and influential officials that were considered insensitive. Richard Baker, Republican Congressman from Baton Rouge, was quoted telling lobbyists "We finally cleaned up public housing in New Orleans. We couldn't do it, but God did" (Baker in Babington 2005, A04). Barbara Bush, former first lady, in a visit to a Houston emergency shelter commented that "... so many of the people in the arena here, you know, were underprivileged anyway, so this — this is working very well for them" (Bush in Dyson 2006, p. 131). These comments support the belief that those in power are disconnected or unconcerned about the well-being of most affected.

Several aspects of the experience generated considerable fuel for the claim of racism and classism. Feelings of abandonment and neglect were bolstered by the experience of being stranded for days on rooftops and bridges and in the Convention Center and Superdome by rising flood waters and watched helplessly while friends, neighbors and loved ones perished. The fact that these people were overwhelmingly Black contributed to the perception that they were abandoned because of their race. Sixty-one percent of those interviewed in a shelter within two weeks of the disaster indicated that they believed that based on the response, the government does not care about people like them (Pew Center for People and the Press 2005).

Some believe that the levees in the lower Ninth Ward were intentionally blasted to relieve the surging waters; in effect, sacrificing the lower Ninth Ward for more affluent communities (Lee 2006). This belief is perhaps rooted in an earlier era in New Orleans, when the levees were intentionally breached, decimating a poor community and sparing a more affluent community. Many of those who survived Hurricane Katrina carry this in their personal or generational memory.[1]

These events contribute to the perception that there existed an underlying disposition of indifference to the suffering of so many. It is this perception, regardless of the intent of official actions that may increase the risk of poor psychological outcomes for those affected. Disaster survivors who believed that they are "unloved and alone" fared worse than those who believed that they are cared for by others (Norris et al. 2002).

There are widespread beliefs of preferential treatment based on race among people of color. These beliefs fuel mistrust in those who may be most vulnerable and find themselves in most need. They also have implications for how future communications campaigns and relief operations can be conducted. The *Failure of Initiative* explains that "If people don't hear a message from someone they trust, they will be skeptical" (U.S. House of Representatives 2006, p. 361). The longstanding communal mistrust of authorities erects a barrier to receiving services and renders people less likely to seek help because they do not feel that they will receive it, further serving as an impediment to an individual's ability to recover.

The undercurrents of mistrust and insensitivity have fomented pervasive beliefs, particularly among Blacks, that racism created and exacerbated the catastrophe by ignoring the precursors, miserably mishandling the response and crippling the recovery. Several post-Katrina studies and polls have found that the perception by the vast majority of Blacks surveyed (between 60 percent–68 percent) was that the response to Hurricane Katrina was related to race (Pew Center for People and the Press, 9/08/05; CNN/USA/Gallup Poll, 9/13/05; *Washington Post*/Kaiser/Harvard, 9/13/05).

Place and Root Shock

Displacement is a common post-disaster occurrence. Many of the displaced evacuated prior to Hurricane Katrina making landfall. For many others, Katrina resulted in a calamitous, though well-intentioned, process of uprooting. In some cases, women were separated from men, infants from their mothers, children and the infirm from caregivers, and then dispersed without consultation, to various locations near and far. For some, it conjured up the historical memory of the *maafa*, that centuries old trauma of forced uprooting from familiar African communities to endure a harrowing and uncertain journey to an undisclosed and unfamiliar destination.

Piazza describes the responses of a convoy of buses of Black evacuees from New Orleans who eventually found refuge in Missouri after being turned away from locations in Texas and Arkansas for four days. Gratitude at being someplace stable and supervised; paranoia about who lives in the surrounding area and whether they wear white hoods at night; anxiety about how to contact distant relatives in distant cities; questions about family members from whom they had been separated; pure confusion and fear at being pulled out of a place where they more or less understood the rules and set down in a place where anything might be true" (Piazza 2005, p. 147).

Though temporarily relieved from the suffering on bridges, rooftops, and deplorable conditions in the Superdome and Convention Center, many endured additional harm in the evacuation, a by-product of the unintended (yet clearly foreseeable) consequences — of hundreds of thousands of uprooted and disconnected people cast in all directions of the compass with neither basic information nor communication capabilities and without a systematic plan. "Those are the people who have been uprooted from the only house, neighborhoods, customs, landscapes and friendships they have ever known, and they will be experiencing the terrible practical deprivation and spiritual pain of the memories they carry, the age-old pain of exile and homelessness" (Piazza 2005, pp. 142–2).

The haphazard "human distribution" operation caused undue and preventable distress. The uprooted found themselves in unfamiliar locations far removed from home, separated from their families, without social support, job prospects, or a relocation plan. It is also estimated that on average, evacuees moved 3.5 times adding further disruption to their lives (Appleseed 2006; Abramson and Garfield 2006).

The Census Bureau reports that initially the entire New Orleans area lost over 378,000 residents (2006). Ten months after the storm, there were still about 150,000 evacuees in Houston, 50,000 in Baton Rouge and 5,000 in Birmingham with the "impossibility of prompt return," a source of tremendous stress (Appleseed 2006).

The *Katrina Advisory Group* found that the most serious post-hurricane problems were financial (61 percent), housing (50 percent), services (40 percent), employment (37 percent) and insurance (34 percent) (Kessler, et al. 2006). The *Continuing Storm* report also underscored the ongoing need for housing, long-term healthcare needs, mental health services, education, employment and legal assistance (Appleseed 2006). The Conservations of Resources theory would contend that not only the loss of these important resources, but also the energy invested in attempting to resolve these issues without adequate resource recovery, place these individuals at risk for increased levels of distress (Hobfoll et al. 1995).

Additionally, the pace and progress of the recovery process has been raised as an exacerbating factor. The rate of return of Black and White residents is disproportionate. Those who remained were more likely to be White, older and with higher incomes and education (Frey, Singer and Park 2007). One year post storm, the percentage of non-Hispanic Whites increased by 57 percent, while the Black population declined 36 percent (Frey, Singer and Park 2007).

Fulillove's (1996; 2005) discussion of the psychological consequences of displacement, including the undermined sense of identity, compromised attachment, and disrupted sense of familiarity are illustrated by this ordeal. "Displaced people go through extreme mental and emotional stress, especially when they have been taken out of one set of understood social conventions and class assumptions and placed in a context completely foreign to their conventions and assumptions" (Piazza 2005, p. 146).

The initial uprooting was a stressor, layered, for too many, on top of the stress of surviving the Hurricane, of being exposed to the surging floodwaters, and of enduring the hellish chaos during the post-breach and pre-evacuation days. The long-term consequences for the displaced are perhaps an even greater concern. It is within the context of their present lives that they must adjust and integrate these horrific experiences, while forging a new set of assumptions about their lives.

THE DISPLACED

"We in Storage. We just in storage."
(Ann Picard, Katrina evacuee in FEMA trailer housing community in Dewan 2007: A01)

The holding pattern of uncertainty, instability and insecurity is the reality of many Katrina evacuees. Even two years post impact, many remain in a state of suspended animation. They are in storage — feeling as if they are moveable objects, held in conditions not meant for long-term habitation.

Root shock explains that the losses they sustain are not only physical, but intangible. It recognizes the importance of loss of community. A study of women in disasters found that "neighborhood social structure is often viewed as being more important than losing personal possessions, including one's home" (Fordham in Curtis, Mills and Leitner 2007, 323). This phenomenon may be even more prevalent in the close-knit Black communities of New Orleans. "Of particular importance to low income African-American women in New Orleans, is the loss of neighborhood support structure, which often extends beyond females in the household (mothers and grandmothers) to include immediate neighbors and community elders. Louisiana and especially New Orleans is renowned for its culture and communities with many neighborhoods having distinct character. Within these neighborhoods, community ties, often based around churches are especially strong" (Curtis, Mills and Leitner 2007, p. 323).

Further, because of the interdependence inherent in neighborhood recovery, many must consider the futility of rebuilding their homes when a recovery plan has not been officially approved and there is uncertainty about whether neighbors will rebuild. Because of this dependence on neighbors, return and recovery favors those who come from communities with higher incomes and more resources.

The displaced have lost income, security and stability and have experienced a decline in their mental health. Mental health needs have exceeded the capacity of the mental health system in New Orleans (Saulny 2006). The consequences of this excess need are tremendous. The New Orleans City Council reports (estimates of) nearly doubled depression rates (Saulny 2006). The homeless population is estimated to have doubled pre-Katrina levels (Gonzalez 2007). The Deputy Coroner estimates that suicide rates have nearly tripled (Columbus 2006; Saulny 2006), and these were only for those deaths that could be verified as suicides. According to the American Medical Association, mortality rates in New Orleans have increased by almost 50 percent (AMA, medicalnewstoday.com 2007). Additionally, in New Orleans, reports of homicide and violent crime have skyrocketed, with some reports as high as a 69 percent increase in the murder rate (Levin 2006).

Those who continue to live in FEMA housing or supported communities often face additional challenges. Post displacement, living in institutional accommodation is associated with poorer mental health outcomes (Porter and Haslam 2005). Almost two years post impact, there are over 30,000 people living in FEMA housing (Dewan 2007). Additionally, those living in temporary FEMA housing communities not only face the stress of being in a strange place, navigating it without their support structure, but also face increased risk from crime and fear for safety (Abramson 2006; Curtis, Mills and Leitner 2007).

A study of Hurricanes Katrina and Rita displacees living in temporary FEMA housing found that "mental health is a significant issue for both parents and children" (Abramson and Garfield 2006, p. 2). Over half of the female caregivers in the 656 households surveyed met the clinical criteria for depression or anxiety disorders. Compared to a pre-Katrina sample, female caregivers were six times more likely to report difficulty coping and problems meeting parental demands. Almost half of the parents reported that "at least one child has emotional or behavioral difficulties that he or she didn't have before the hurricane, such as feeling depressed, being nervous or afraid or having problems sleeping or getting along with others" (Abramson and Garfield 2006, p. 2).

On the other hand, a study of those affected in Mississippi, Louisiana and Alabama presented more encouraging findings. In examining post-traumatic growth, i.e., indications of growth or positively modified beliefs resulting in their coping with a trauma, over eighty-eight percent of respondents in a post-hurricane survey reported positive outcomes. These "respondents [88.5 percent] said that their experiences with the hurricane helped them develop a deeper sense of meaning or purpose in life; 83.8 percent said that the hurricane led them to realize that they had inner strengths that they did not previously know they had; and 83.4 percent reported that they had a lot of faith in their own abilities to rebuild their lives" (Kessler 2006, iv).

SUMMARY AND CONCLUSION

The psychological implications of Katrina-induced displacement are expected to be extensive, profound, and enduring. Because of the importance of a secure and stable place in mental well being, the loss of place — particularly in deeply rooted New Orleans — is potentially devastating. The nature of this forced displacement, coupled with this rootedness, may have significant implications for the disruption of familiarity, attachment and identity, and may lead to disillusionment, alienation and depression. The heightened vulnerability of Blacks and the poor was clearly evident in the aftermath of Hurricane Katrina.

Using the lens of Hurricane Katrina in New Orleans, the aims of this discussion were threefold: 1) to foster an appreciation for the role that communal and cultural places play in the underpinnings of emotional security and psychological well-being, 2) to explain the potential psychological consequences of a sudden and involuntary uprooting, and 3) to recognize the complicating roles race and poverty inject into the disaster and displacement predicaments. Although some consideration was given to these issues, several other questions remain that perhaps can be explored in subsequent discussions.

Are the displaced finding a new sense of place in other spaces? What are the mechanisms by which the displaced are able to establish a new sense of place? Do the beliefs about how and why the response in New Orleans failed affect attachment to New Orleans and/or new places? Has the identification with New Orleans hindered the ability of people to adapt to their host communities? Are there racial differences in the responses to these questions?

By considering these psycho-social components, we may be able to mitigate the impact of root shock for the tens of thousands displaced from New Orleans and the tens of millions displaced throughout the world, especially those who are most vulnerable.

NOTE

[1] This refers to the 1927 floods, where large parts of an upriver levee were blasted by engineers in an effect to save New Orleans. This displaced 10,000 people.

Chapter 12

Black New York City Out-Migrants, 1995–2000: Opportunity and Destination Choice

JOHN W. FRAZIER AND MILTON E. HARVEY

INTRODUCTION

As noted in chapter 1, immigration and race policies and practices play considerable roles in the locations and characteristics of domestic and immigrant groups. Black movements have changed American landscapes, but native-born Blacks and foreign born migrants may have different destination choices, because they have different experiences.

African Americans have a long history of changing settlement patterns explained by changing U.S. labor needs and institutional actions in response to racial struggles. The 19th Century amendments to the Constitution provided emancipation, citizenship and the same rights extended to all native-born and naturalized citizens. Nearly a century later, de facto and de jure limitations on these rights prompted the U.S. Supreme Court to review prior decisions (*Plessey v. Ferguson*; *Brown v. Board of Education*) and to consider the rights and treatment of those accused of crimes (*Miranda v. Arizona*; *Escobedo v. Illinois*). In addition, more recent legislation began to provide improved access to housing and employment for African-Americans (for example, the Civil Rights Act of 1964, Fair Housing Act 1968, and The Voting Rights Act of 1968). These actions influenced the mobility and settlement choices of African Americans.

At first the attraction of the Northern factory system, and later the slow pace of social and legal changes, encouraged the African-American Great Migration that relocated millions of Blacks from the American South to states in the North and West. Between 1910 and 1970, African-American migration transformed American Blacks from a predominantly southern, rural group to a northern, urban one (Frazier, Margai, and Tettey-Fio 2003). This movement and the changes it wrought lasted until its slow reversal in the 1970s, when the attraction of northern cities largely disappeared and Black migrants chose southern destinations as their "new" homes (Frey 2001).

At approximately the same time that Black migration reversed, the Black movement to suburbia was underway, prompted by the real economic gains by Blacks (Clark 1979; Frazier and Anderson 2006). Black suburbanization and the reversal of the Great Migration constitute significant structural changes in American society and in Black settlement patterns.

As for Black immigration, changes in U.S. immigration policies influenced Black diversity, migration, and settlement patterns. Beginning with the provisions of the 1965 INA (amended Hart-Celler Act), and legislation such as the 1990 INA that has provided access through the "Diversity Visa," the Black foreign-born population (predominantly African and Caribbean origins) increased from approximately one-quarter of a million people in 1970 to nearly 2.5 million in 2000. The U.S. also increased access for refugee groups, including both Africans and Caribbeans. Together, these are changing the definition of being Black in America and are contributing to new Black migration and settlement patterns that are still emerging. Spatially, foreign-born Blacks have tended to concentrate in gateway cities, those cities that accept a disproportionate number of immigrants, such as

New York, Chicago, Miami, Los Angeles, San Francisco, and San Diego (Frey 2002; Singer 2006). From these initial landing points many foreign born are making secondary migrations (Hempstead 2007).

Together, the native-born and the foreign-born Black populations have contributed to a net Black migration loss in all U.S. regions except the South; however, destination choices and settlement patterns vary between and within major U.S. regions (Frey 1996; Frazier and Anderson 2006). For example, the flows of Black New York City migrants to Atlanta and Miami differed significantly by nativity between 1995 and 2000. A greater proportion of native-born Blacks moved to Atlanta, while a greater proportion of foreign-born Blacks moved to Miami (Frazier and Anderson 2006). In 1999, Djamba noted that native Blacks were more widely distributed than foreign-born Blacks, who appeared to be highly concentrated in fewer states (Djamba 1999). More specifically, gateway cities have become important settlement locations for immigrants, who are largely urban dwellers in the U.S. In fact, more than 90 percent of all immigrants reside in metropolitan areas of the U.S.

Despite the importance of gateways for Black immigrants, many have joined native Blacks in secondary migrations, including to the South. This leads to a series of questions. What factors guide Black destination choice? Do native-born and foreign-born destinations vary? If yes, how are they different? Are some factors more important than others in explaining these patterns of destination choice? Perhaps one obvious answer is the long associations of African Americans with older cities such as Atlanta, while new global cities, such as Miami, have attracted significant numbers of Latinos and Caribbean-based Blacks, making Miami's ethnic attraction stronger for these groups than for African Americans. A complex set of factors explains Black migration patterns. Although Black migrations from New York City likely adhere to general distance decay theory (less frequent moves occur with increasing distance from the origin), unique destination-choice differences may arise between native-born and foreign-born Black migrants because place utility, or the value placed on a destination according to what it may provide a potential migrant, reflects differences in economic and cultural "pull factors."

The purpose of this chapter is two-fold. First, we examine the preferred destination choices of Black New York City out-migrants, 1995–2000. Second, we construct a general theoretical model of Black migrants' destination choices, including native and foreign born, and test parts of that model using the most recent available data on Black migration out of New York City to other U.S. counties.

MIGRATION THEORY: SOME GUIDING PRINCIPLES

Migration occurs most frequently in rapidly expanding economies where technological advances spur innovation and economic progress. The earliest migration studies suggested that people are "pushed" out of their origins, and are "pulled" by attracting forces to new destinations (Ravenstein 1889). This "push-pull" hypothesis elaborated by many social scientists of the 20th century classified influences on a migrant's decision as dissatisfaction with the origin, attraction to a destination, intervening obstacles between the origin and destination, and personal factors, including educational attainment (Lee 1966). The gravity model posited that movement resulted from the difference in magnitude between the origin and destination populations, and were inversely related to distance.[1]

The "push-pull hypothesis" (Pandit and Withers 1999) also incorporated economic factors to understand migration, which included labor mobility theory. This argument suggested that migration occurs rationally because society adjusts to regional changes (differences) in the demand and supply of labor as reflected in regional wage differentials. Places with higher wages and lower unemployment attract migrants from lower-wage regions. Thus, employment opportunity influences migration (Fischer and Nijkamp 1987). A single economic concept is insufficient to explain complex behavior; therefore, others employed non-economic factors to understand migration. Human capital, for example, as measured by educational attainment and special skills, reformulates the economic perspective to include "social capital" as a marketable commodity that increases opportunities. Managers, highly skilled technical workers, and those with special skills secure greater economic benefits through migration than low-skilled workers. Differential opportunity explains greater mobility and migration rates for those with social capital (Sjaastad 1962; Massey 1994).

More recent economically based global explanations of migration incorporate the same factors, but offer a different philosophical perspective. Global migration results from dependency relationships, with wage differentials, resulting from the uneven economic development of capitalism, as the causal factors. Global corporate capital is manipulated to result in uneven wealth and control by a few nations that seek to minimize their labor costs and maximize profits, creating social distinctions (social capital and class standing) that foster mobility. Uneven economic growth and wealth also generate a low-paid, service-class of workers (the hour-glass economy). Thus, the poor and unemployed seek survival wages through migration to regions offering potential service employment, occasionally through formalized institutions such as employment agencies that structure destination choice (Goss and Lindquist 1995). Migrants with strong social capital select destinations where their skills are valued and rewarded (Gurak and Kritz 2000). Both factors explain why the U.S. receives large numbers of high-skill and low-skill immigrants (including Africans and Caribbeans), but do not explain secondary migrations within advanced economies.

Wolpert's multi-faceted "place utility" explains a migrant's decision process, beyond purely economic motivations, by a subjective perception of present location based on characteristics internal and external to the individual household, including the changing attributes of the household (education level, income, life cycle) and characteristics of the external world (the dwelling unit, neighborhood, etc.). These characteristics are dynamic and influence the individual's (or household's) decision to stay or move. Once a decision to seek a new residence has been made, benefits (utility) of the present place are weighed against those of potential destinations, and information is vital to the decision so that comparative assessment of place utilities may be made. Assessments of economic, social, and environmental attributes of potential destination choices are often optimistic, and made without first-hand experience. Information (economic, cultural, social, and environmental) shapes imagery of place:

> "This is precisely why . . . information is so important in long-distance migration . . . (compensating) for the absence of personal information." (Wolpert 1965, p. 162)

Information is important to migration decisions at all scales as not all migrants are exposed to the same information. Social network externalities provide benefits to potential migrants. Beyond positive information about a destination, such networks offer the potential for assistance with housing and other needs. Networks also may provide negative feedback to potential migrants. When migrants relocate to a destination despite receiving negative signals, this is termed "herd behavior," which suggests selecting a destination because other co-ethnics and/or families selected the destination (Epstein 2008).

Characteristics of potential movers are important predictors, as seen in migrant selectivity theory which states that the "pushes" and "pulls" of place are experienced selectively, based on household or individual characteristics, and include perceived distance, education, and age, among others (Tobler 1995; Long 1988; Schacter 2001; Reisinger 2003). Generally, a migrant tends to select destinations near her/his origin, however, one with highly developed job skills or social capital may migrate a greater distance. Age also is a selective characteristic, with an increased propensity of retired people and for people between late teens to age 40 to migrate than those in the 40-to-retirement age group (Reisinger 2003). The subjective attractiveness of any destination involves numerous dimensions and has led to a migration theory termed "destination choice modeling," which conceptually and empirically measures the features of potential destinations.

EXPLANATIONS OF NON-WHITE MIGRATION: PAST STUDIES

Unemployment differentials, per capita wages, and distance predicted interregional migrant flows in California. While wages and distance were important determinants of interregional migration flows, younger White adults were found to be more responsive to economic opportunity than those who were older (Rogers

1967 and 1968). However, these factors were weak predictors of non-White migration, and led to the conclusion that non-White migration decisions "are probably largely non-economic in character." More recent qualitative research findings on the African-American reverse migration to North Carolina offers some support to early findings, illustrating that Blacks were returning to some of the state's poorest counties for non-economic reasons (Cromartie and Stack 1989; Stack 1996).

The expanding literature on destination choice modeling supports Ravenstein's (1889) early claim that pull factors are more important to the migration decision than push factors at the origin. Destinations associated with two phases of the Great Migration support this contention and illustrate how particular forces change the attraction of place over time. For example, by 1940 and at the end of the first wave of the Great Migration, Blacks were "pushed" out of their Southern origins due to poor conditions, while being drawn to a particular set of Northern destinations. The model theorized that Southern Blacks were drawn to the strong wage differentials between Northern cities and their Southern origins. This relationship was expected to be strongest among those in the youngest and most educated African-American age-cohorts, who would be drawn to destinations where education levels, average wages, and Black populations were comparatively higher than those at their origins. Distance was believed to reduce this attraction, indicating the preference for the shortest move possible for these 1940 Black migrants. The findings revealed that Blacks of all levels of education migrated, but those with the most education were the most likely to migrate from their Southern origins. In 1940, Northern destinations with high proximal earnings certainly pulled Black migrants, but the expectation that skilled Black migrants would be drawn by greater wage differentials did not materialize. Distance emerged as a strong predictor of Northern destination choices (Vigdor 2001, 2006).

By 1970, the destination choices of native-born Blacks had reversed; Northern cities had lost appeal for the majority of African-American migrants. At the same time, the factors driving Black migration also had changed. The overall importance of wages fell dramatically and ceased to influence the African-American migration pattern of 1970, the end of the second phase of the Great Migration. Black regional migration flows were reversed for the first time in five decades (Frey 2004). The magnetism of the Northern and Western cities had evaporated. While modernization and improved racial tolerance supported by long-term Black topophilia (emotional attachment to place, Tuan 1974) toward the South pulled African Americans "home," Northern "disamenities" pushed many Northern and Western Blacks to Southern destinations (Frey 2004). By 1970, African-American migrants, irrespective of education level, were more likely to select Southern destinations, especially those containing large Black populations, than other locations. Although Blacks of all educational levels migrated, high levels of education and shorter distances were statistically significant predictors of movement in the 1970 analysis (Vigdor 2001, 2006).

Other state-level migration analyses have emphasized the importance of structural and social changes in the U.S. (Massey 2008). State-level studies of Black migration, 1965–70 and 1975–80, argue that the restructuring of the American economy to create new employment opportunities and the improving social conditions in the American South, channeled Black movements. Employment prospects were passed to potential Black migrants through "word of mouth" social networks, including family, friends and associates, and by the mass media. Together, structural change and socio-behavioral forces reshaped the Black migration process (Mc Hugh 1987).

In exploring the foundations for Black migration after 1970, "stock" factors (the number of previous Black migrants, total Black population) were attractions for migrating Blacks, based on "word of mouth" information from Black social networks (McHugh 1987), as were distance, income, welfare, and Blacks employed in the military.[2] For 1965–70, welfare was not a statistically significant factor. For the next migration period, 1975–80, welfare, as well as the other previously mentioned variables, became important in explaining Black migration flows.

Other general theories relevant to the Black migration process include "life history," which emphasizes the importance of human attachments to place (topophilia) that influence the migrant's destination (for example, McHugh 1984). A life history that includes visits to friends and relatives, vacations, former residential locations, and other encounters, results in relatively few place experiences for potential Black migrants, which limits potential destination choices based on life experience. Knowing few special places limits the destination choice set and reduces the psychological and economic costs associated with securing information about unknown locations. "Prominent ties" with friends and relatives and experiences with specific places are influential factors, followed by employment opportunity, at inducing migration (McHugh 1987; Cromartie and Stack 1989; Stack 1996).

Both native- and foreign-born migrants seek destinations that promise potential employment and an improved quality of life, security, and a relatively low cost of living (Frey 2000; Liaw and Frey 1998 and 2003; Frey and Liaw 2005), however, foreign-born and native-born destination choices vary considerably. Foreign-born migrants tend to settle in metropolitan areas of coastal regions, while native-born Blacks are more likely to migrate to more dispersed destinations, including small and large metropolitan regions (Frey 1996).

CONCEPTUALIZING DESTINATION CHOICES FOR BLACK MIGRATION

The literature illustrates that the relocation decision involves destination choices, selection criteria, personal priorities, and evaluations for each decision maker, with economic, social, and environmental characteristics influencing destination choice in similar ways for Black people and non-Blacks. However, the potential differences and nuances of Black destination choices are important and deserve examination separate from an overall American view to discover how the subpopulation makes its choices. By understanding subpopulations, we can also assess between-group differences. First, however, the major concepts of general migration theory are discussed because they provide the leading principles for our research. Bollen defines a concept as "an idea that unites phenomena" (Bollen 1989, p. 190). Constructs are less abstract than concepts, which cause their formation (Abler, Adams, and Gould 1971). These are important elements in our conceptualization of the Black migration system.

The Place Attractiveness Concept (Place Attraction)

The Tiebout (1956, p. 418) hypothesis suggests that migration decisions are cost-benefit considerations with the prospective migrant selecting among alternatives (e.g., deciding to remain in situ, to migrate to an urban area, to migrate to a rural area) (Haapanen 2000). A major factor in these types of cost-benefit studies is earning potential in that region, which has been applied in a number of contexts (Haapanen 2000), including for U.S. White and Black migration (Cebula 1974), reflecting comparative place attractiveness, or place attraction. Niedomysl noted that "the extent to which a place may fulfill the needs, demands and preferences of a migrant, . . . the greater the attractiveness of such a place" (Niedomysl 2006, p. 13).

In this study we explain Black migration in terms of two major (higher-order) place attraction concepts — Opportunity and Socio-Economic Well Being. Opportunity includes economic potential and cultural niche, which reflect employment opportunities and ancestry/social institutions, respectively. Socio-economic well being reflects the local incentives and disincentives. Finally, while independent of a higher-order concept, a local geography construct is an important cause of the migration destination. These causal relationships appear in Figure 12.1. We explore some of these causal relationships between place attractiveness concepts and constructs and the destination choices of Black New York City migrants from 1995 to 2000.

1. Opportunity

Opportunity presents a chance for personal progress or advancement, through economic opportunity (potential) and cultural niche (Figure 12.1). Our model suggests that the general concept, opportunity, causes the two constructs, economic and cultural niche.

a. *The economic opportunity construct* is the potential to improve economic well-being. Bernanke asserted that economic opportunity exists when every person has a realistic chance to improve his or her economic condition (Bernanke 2005). Many early migration studies measured this construct by a surrogate of income or earnings (Greenwood 1985; Cebula and Vedder 1973). Our conceptualization illustrates that *economic opportunity* includes four highly inter-correlated employment indicators.

Figure 12.1.
A Conceptualization of the Factors that Explain U.S. Black Migration.

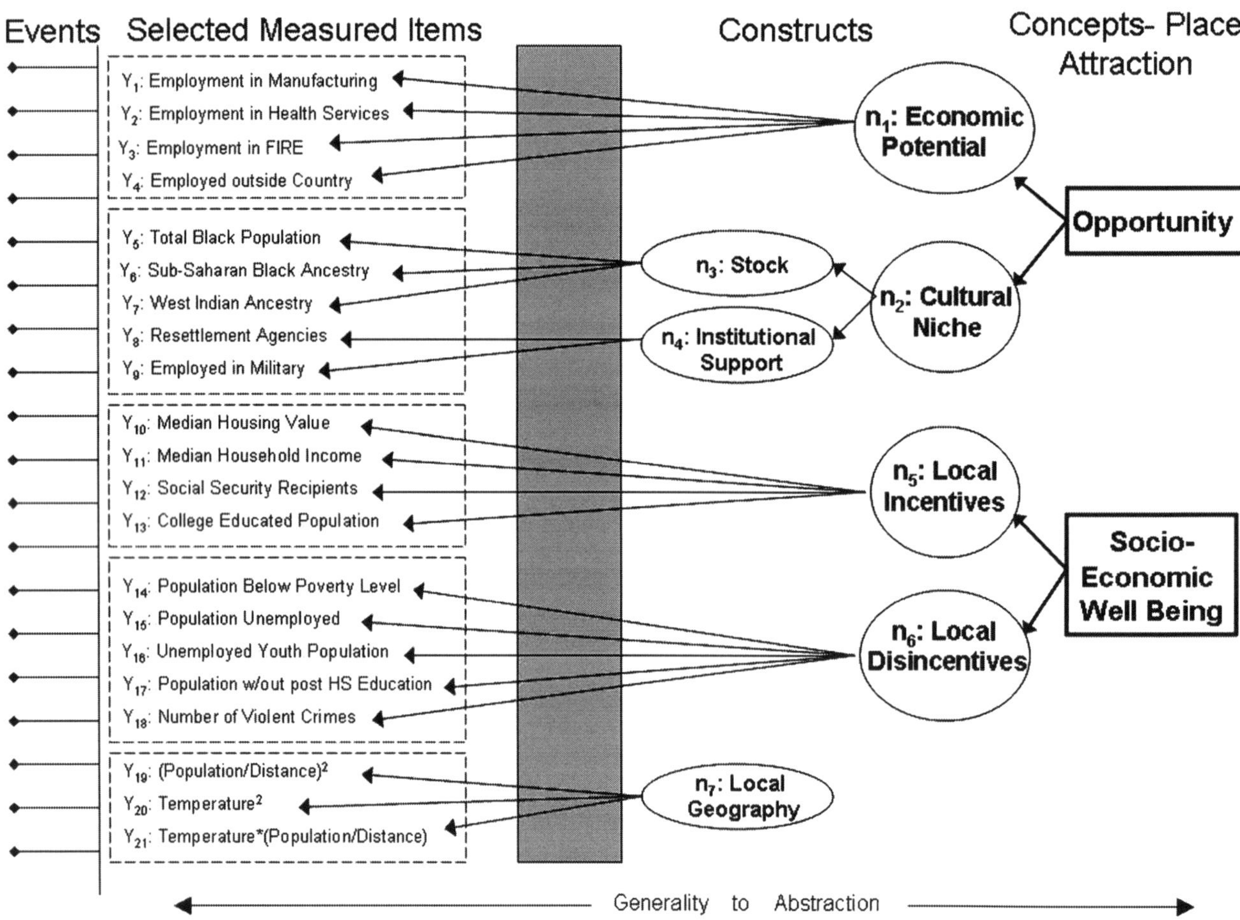

b. *The niche construct* describes a geographic area supportive of a particular group, similar to the biological context of a habitat zone. The concept, applied in sociology and geography to describe land use zones, and socio-economic niches, social fluidity, and social and spatial assimilation, has been employed to understand organizational behavior (Debrev, Kim, and Hannan 2001). In the migration context, the niche is an area (state, county, or zip code) that contains co-ethnic groups and/or institutions that can facilitate a migrant's adjustment process and, therefore, influence the migration decision.

Our niche construct is expressed by two types of culture-ethnic support sub-constructs, *stock* and *institutional support*, which represent supportive activities important to Black migration decisions. The cultural stock construct (Dorkoosh 1982; McHugh 1987) recognizes ethnic and cultural affinity and serves as an attraction for migrants. In contrast, the institutional support construct converges on types of specific occupational and cultural groups that complement the migrant ethnic group. This suggests that social institutions are important forces in the migration process. As noted by others (McHugh 1987), a disproportionate number of Black Americans are employed by the military. Upon leaving military service, many stay in the localities of their final duty station, or later in life, return to these places. These migrants serve as another form of "word of mouth" attraction for friends and relatives that are considering migration.

Resettlement programs that have proliferated in the U.S since 1965 also have had impacts on the settlement choices of various groups from Europe, Asia, Africa, and the Caribbean. The resettlement of the "Liberians of War" (Scott 2006) is one example that illustrates the power of these agencies to direct Black migration and settlement to non-traditional destination "choices." The importance of these social institutions on future migration patterns has been noted as:

> ". . . when a particular refugee group is preceded by earlier migrants of the same or similar group, migration chain mechanisms operate, providing information flows, needed sponsorship, and the like." (Also,) ". . . as time passes, secondary migration occurs, especially among refugees not represented by earlier migrants, not in culturally comfortable communities, or not near other family or community members." (Brown, Mott, and Malecki 2007, p. 58)

In addition to institutions, total number in an ethnic group and ethnic identity are important to ethnic affinity and are dimensions of cultural stock because they affect the diffusion of information via social networks and encourage resettlement in particular places. Figure 12.1 illustrates that stock is measured by three items and supported by two indicators. The institutional support construct recognizes the importance of particular institutions in fostering Black migration to particular places, i.e., the military and resettlement agencies, which has been demonstrated for a variety of immigrant groups (Kraly and Van Valkenburg 2003; Hardwick and Meacham 2005; Hardwick 2006; Brown, Mott, and Malecki 2007), and for Black refugees in particular (Scott 2006).

The cultural niche recognizes the importance of cultural stock and institutional support that encourages Black migration to particular places. In this study the construct causes the two sub-constructs that are measured by five variables. For Black stock, these are the total Black population, the total number claiming Sub-Saharan ancestry, and the total population of West Indian ancestry. In statistical terms, we say that this construct converges on (causes) the two sub-constructs as represented by a statistic termed Cronbach's alpha ($\alpha = 0.848$). The number of resettlement agencies and the total number of Blacks in the military are measures of institutional support of Black culture that serve as an attraction for some potential Black migrants ($\alpha = 0.154$). For the niche construct (stock and support), $\alpha = 0.823$. Because the support niche is measured by only two items and the α-value is very low, the niche construct is evaluated by all five indicators.

2. Quality of Life (Socio-Economic Well Being)

The quality of life concept (QOL) is closely related to the way place utility is used in geography. The critical attributes that make a place attractive as a destination choice are the same critical elements of the QOL concept. Liu's quality of life definition remains appropriate:

> For any individual, QOL expresses that set of "wants" which after being supplied, when taken together, makes the individual happy or satisfied. However, human wants rarely reach a state of complete satisfaction, except possibly for a very short time: as one want is satisfied, another pops up to take its place. As a result, the concept of quality of life varies not only from person to person, but also from place to place and from time to time. (Liu 1975, p. 1)

Later Liu, Mulvey and Hsieh (1986) elaborate on the concept:

> Quality Of Life (QOL) is a fashion name for an old notion; it is a perceived conditional expression of the physical and psychological well-being of people under the same natural and institutional environment in which they live. For any individual, QOL expresses that set of "wants" or "desires" which after being supplied, when taken together, makes the individual happy or satisfied. . . . QOL indicators are static

measures reflecting the physiological and institutional conditions at a particular point in time. (Liu, Mulvey and Hsieh 1986)

Social well-being (QOL) influences life decisions. Most voluntary migrants believe that the end result of the move is a better quality of life (Reisinger, Frazier, and Tettey-Fio 2006). The reasons for migration and the corresponding destination can have an immense impact on migration experience and the quality of life after the move (Michalos 1997; Liebkind 1996). Many migration studies have been associated with the QOL (Michalos 1997). Directly pertinent to our conceptualization of Black migration are studies that assess the influence of quality of life, including income, unemployment, education, crime, Medicare, and climate as predictors of QOL (Rebhun and Raveh 2001). A recent study compared health and the quality of life of older people in British Columbia (Michalos et al. 2007). For our model of Black migration, the potential migrant assesses the socio-economic well being (QOL) of potential destinations on two antithetical dimensions: local incentives and local disincentives.

Local incentives pull Black migrants to particular destinations. This construct converges on four indicators: median housing value, median household income, number of social security recipients and the number of college educated. The first two are indicators of stable local environments that may be attractive to potential Black migrants. The other two are social indicators of the presence of elderly and an attractive educated public. The associated α value is 0.633. It is likely that local incentives influence all migrants, regardless of ethnicity.

Just as positive features of a place may improve the quality of life, *local disincentives* may repel potential Black migrants. These include poverty, unemployment, unemployed youth, educational attainment of high school or less, and violent crime ($\alpha = 0.956$). The Social Well being (QOL) concept, its two associated constructs, and their indicators (Figure 12.1).

In addition, models of interregional migration include measures of locational preference such as climate. An example of the use of these types of location-specific preferences in modeling destination choices is the inclusion of the average number of heating degree days, the average number of cooling degree days, proximity to the coast, and proximity to a mountain location (Cushing 2004). Many climatic variables have been studied in an inter-SMSA migration context, including temperature variability, annual wind velocity, annual average humidity, average annual cooling degree days, and the normal annual amount of heating degree days (Gravest 1980), but are not available at our micro-scale. Consequently, our locational preference construct is a combination of distance (D) from New York City, population of the destination node (P), and average annual temperature of that place (T). Migration deceases with distance from the origin, but (migration) increases with attraction potential (population). Zones of moderate temperatures (average, winter, for example) are attractive to certain population groups. The associated Cronbach's α value is 0.705.

We limit our tests in this chapter to the opportunity concept for three Black populations: total, native born and foreign-born. We also describe the spatial distribution of these concepts and constructs. Our disaggregated analysis differs from Rogers and Henning (1999) and similar studies by using a micro-approach, U.S. counties as the spatial unit, and by focusing on Blacks, America's second largest minority, subdivided into foreign-born and native-born.

THE DATA, HYPOTHESIS, AND STUDY AREA

There are a number of sources of data for this study. The Migration Data (CMD), 1995–2000, which are the most recent data available from the U.S. government, report county-to-county migration numbers for total, foreign-born, and native-born Blacks. These data, summed for the five boroughs of New York City (NYC), are treated as a single origin, and represent the Black migration system.

Our hypothesis predicts three dimensions of Black migration (total, native-, and foreign-born) at the micro-scale (Figure 12.1). The conditions measured and reported by the 1990 U.S. Census generally represent the motivating factors for Black destination choice between 1995 and 2000. Thus, the socioeconomic factors tested in our model were derived from the *1990 U.S. Census of Population and Housing* at the county-level. Additional variables include: 1) county-level violent crimes, which were tabulated in 1992 (The 1994 County Files, Geospatial and Statistical Data Center, University of Virginia Library) by the federal government and reported in *U.S. Crime Statistic,* and 2) mean annual temperature, provided by the NOAA website, 3) the resettlement data used in the analysis was provided by the Office of Refugee Resettlement, U.S. Department of Health and Human Services in 2006, and 4) distance, measured as a straight line from the centroid of the five boroughs of New York City to the centroid of each U.S. County.

New York City, a single origin that holds the "push factors" constant while focusing on the pull factors of destination counties, has a strong historical basis as a continuous U.S. immigrant gateway (Singer 2004 and 2006). *The Newest New Yorkers, 2000: Immigrant New York in the New Millennium* (2004) reported that 2.9 million foreign-born residents lived in the New York City region in the year 2000, a near doubling of the number reported in 1970. New York City is highly diverse and remains an immigrant city. Between 1970 and 2000, the total foreign-born population doubled. The African foreign-born increased from approximately 13,000 to 92,000 and the West Indian foreign-born rose from about 114, 000 to nearly 592,000. The Black foreign-born population of the City expanded at a much higher rate than the total foreign-born population. In the case of West Indians, approximately 39 percent of their U.S. total population resided in New York State, the majority of which were in New York City (Boswell 2006). In addition to being a gateway for foreign-born Blacks, New York City remains one of the major redistributors of the foreign-born (Frazier and Anderson 2006). In the period 1995–2000, more than one-hundred thousand Black migrants departed the five boroughs of New York City for other U.S. counties, making the City an important location for the study of U.S. Black migration.

THE METHODS OF ANALYSIS

The analysis, a Structural Equation Modeling (SEM) (Olmstead and Bentler 1992), is used to explain Black migrant destination choices for the period, 1995–2000. Specifically, SEM is used to calculate coefficients that reflect a) the effects of the constructs on the indicators and of the concepts on constructs, b) the strength of the causal effect of opportunity on destination choice, and c) scores of the constructs and concepts that are mapped.

PREFERRED DESTINATIONS: RELATING BLACK ANCESTRY TO PREVIOUS FINDINGS

The U.S. Census migration flow files do not differentiate Black migrants by specific ethnicity or ancestry, therefore, a culture-specific preference for particular destinations cannot be identified. However, previous studies suggest that native Blacks have a larger population in, and historical ties to particular southern communities, such as Atlanta, Mobile, and Birmingham. Similarly, foreign-born Blacks, such as Jamaicans, making a secondary migration from New York City, may prefer the Miami-Ft. Lauderdale region because of its proximity to Jamaica, the relatively high proportion of West Indians residing there, and the region's climate. The migration flow data, not in a form to test these suppositions, report total Black migration, native-born Black migration, and foreign-born migration. Data from the 1990 and the 2000 U.S. Censuses help to ascertain Black settlement patterns, and clarify the ethnic mix of the county-level destination-county preferences determined by the migration flow files data. Specifically, the 1990 and 2000 variables include foreign-born and native-born Blacks by county, as well as Black ancestry variables, differentiated by West Indian and Sub-Saharan African ancestry, both predominantly Black.

The Preferred Destinations of Native- and Foreign-born Blacks

The preferred destinations of native-born and foreign-born Blacks between 1995 and 2000 (Figure 12.2) illustrate the 100 most-preferred counties of both groups.

Northeastern counties, including the five New York boroughs serving as the gateway, are the preferred destination of both native- and foreign-born Blacks, reflecting distance decay. Most moves are either short distance, or intra-urban migration, explaining the shared preference for counties within Megalopolis (the highly urbanized East Coast between the Washington, DC metropolitan area on the south to just north of the Boston suburbs) by both groups, as well as those proximal Upstate counties containing the suburbs of New York City, and the larger Upstate cities of Albany, Binghamton, Syracuse, Rochester, and Buffalo. Native Blacks also preferred Albany's adjacent counties, as well as those in the Utica-Rome region (**green**), which were not included in the foreign-born Blacks' top 100 destinations (see Figure 12.2). The unique preferences of foreign-born Blacks (**blue**) during this five-year period were counties located west and south of Boston, of southern Connecticut, and of northern Megalopolis. In addition, southern and western sections of Megalopolis, Berks County, PA (also home to an increasing number of recent Latino migrants), and counties between Camden and Atlantic City, NJ were also among the unique destination choices of foreign-born Blacks, as were the metropolitan counties between Washington, DC and Baltimore, MD.

Figure 12.2.
The 100 Preferred Counties of NYC Black Migrants, 1995–2000.

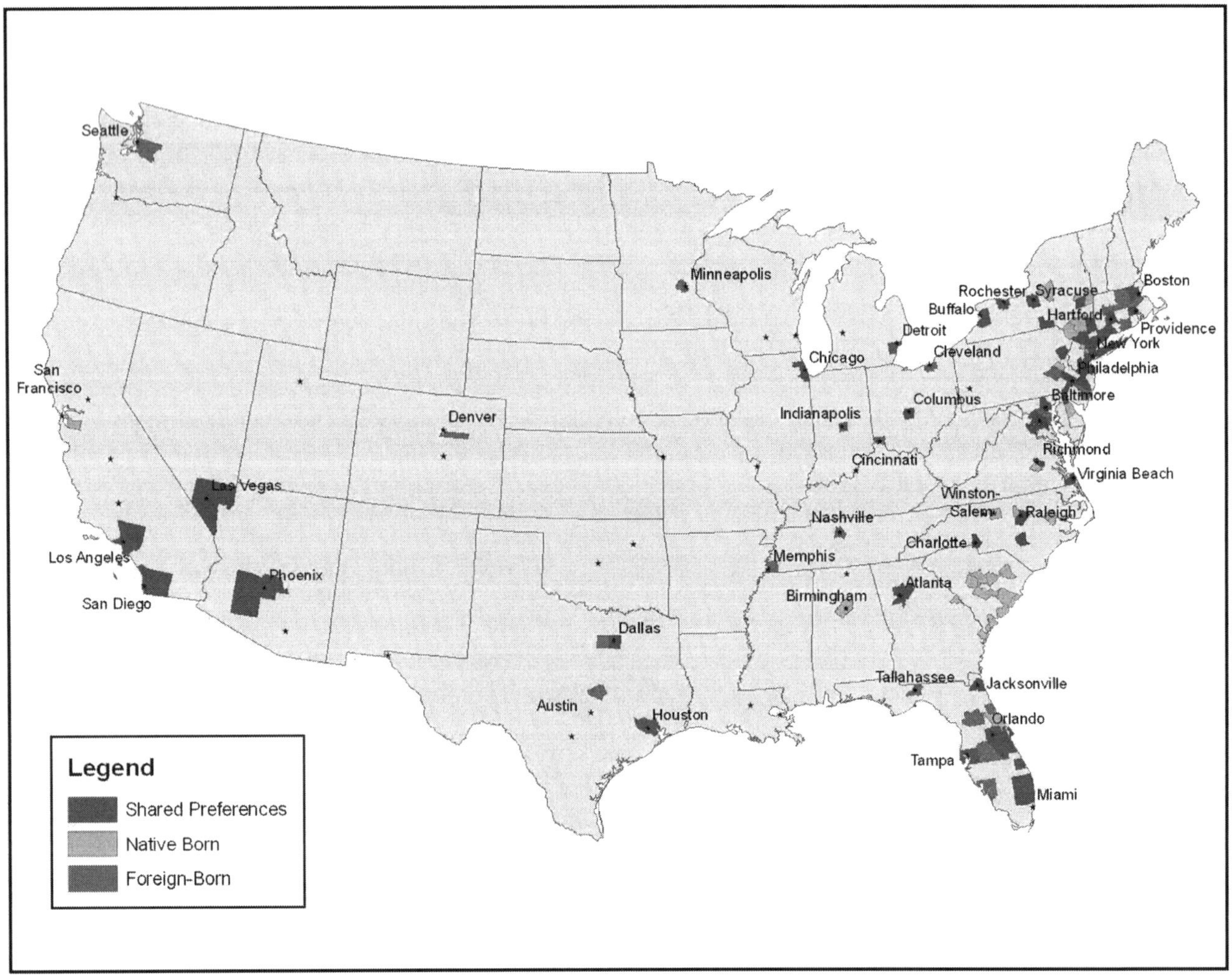

The native-born and foreign-born Black migrants shared a preference (top 100) for many counties with large urban populations, highly concentrated on the East Coast and in the Midwest, or very large western counties containing Dallas, Houston, Phoenix, Las Vegas, Los Angeles and San Diego. The native-born preferences pattern is concentrated in the East, including Megalopolis and nearby (distance decay effect), northern counties, a heavy concentration of Southern counties that have pulled reverse migrants from the North, and a single California county (Alameda) that has a very large African-American population.

Foreign-born Black New York City migrants deviate substantially in regional distribution when their unique top 100-preferred counties are mapped. They, too, locate in Megalopolis, but in suburban counties near Boston, southern Connecticut, near Philadelphia in both Pennsylvania and New Jersey, and in metropolitan Washington, DC and Maryland. They also have relocated to several Florida counties near Orlando and Daytona Beach in central Florida, the Tallahassee area in the Florida Panhandle, and on the southern Gulf Coast near Ft. Myers. In the northern section of the South, only two counties emerge in the top 100-preferred; both are in Tennessee.

The preferred 100 destination choices in Midwestern counties revealed a very different pattern for these Black New York City migrant groups. Counties with the two largest cities, Chicago and Detroit, and Columbus, Ohio were the only three places shared in the destination preferences of the two groups. Only the foreign-born Blacks identified counties in this region on their top 100-preferred destination choices. In the West, very large cities seem to be attractive to both groups and only one unique county for each group emerged.

Figure 12.3, which illustrates the distribution of foreign-born Blacks, indicates the impact of foreign-born Black immigrants and secondary migrants at the county level by 2000. This map will be useful for comparative purposes when we present the causal influence of our constructs on the spatial distribution of the Black migration system.

Figure 12.3. Foreign-born Blacks by U.S. County, 2000.

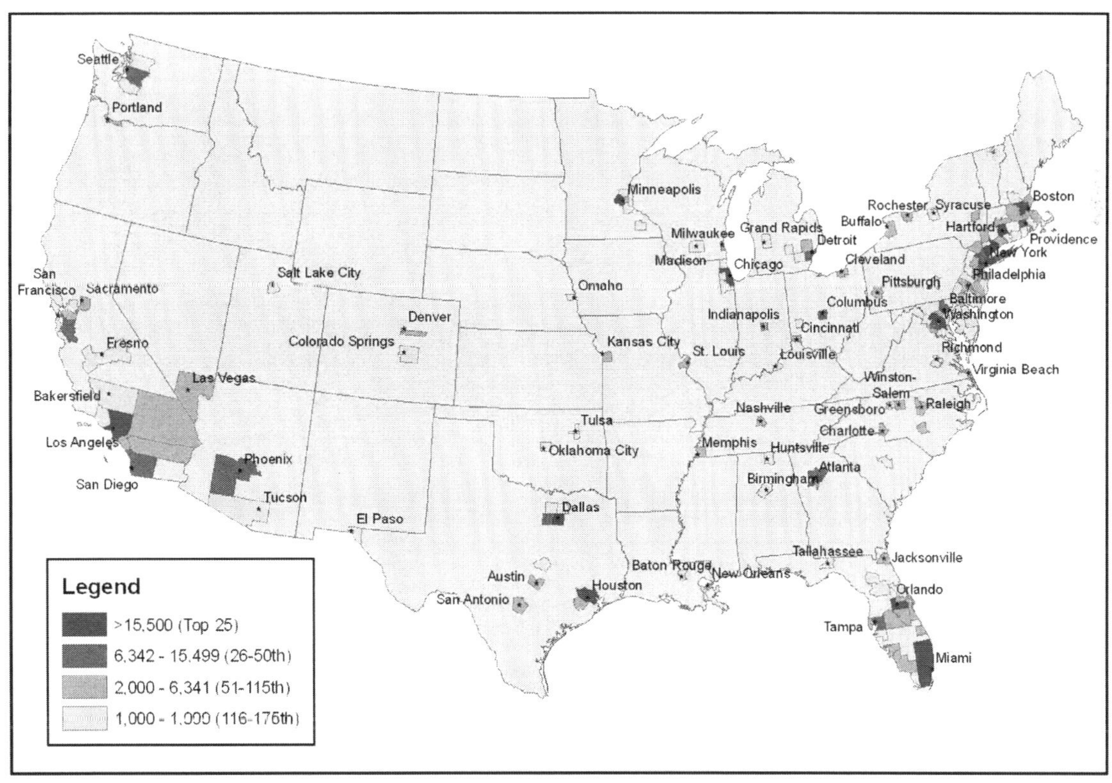

1990 Black Ancestry and the Preferred Destinations of Foreign-born Black Migrants, 1995–2000

To clarify the "pull" to specific regions and counties, we employed Black ancestry by country for 1990, as a surrogate for Black migrant ethnicity. These data illustrate the share of each Black ancestry group and, thus, may account for a county's attractiveness to foreign-born migrants.

Figure 12.4 is a complex map because it reports more than one activity. First, each circle represents one of the top-100 preferred counties of New York City Black migrants, 1995 to 2000. Second, each circle contains the share of West Indians and Africans from South of the Sahara (SOS) at that location. In other words, each circle illustrates the potential dominance of one Black ancestral group over the other.

The 1990 ancestry data indicate the importance of the New York City region and the core of Megalopolis as important intra-urban destinations for both Black migrant groups. They also illustrate the dominance of the West Indian population over Sub-Saharan African ancestry at these particular destinations. These counties, of course, had increased their African South of the Sahara (SOS) populations by 2000. Also, the ancestry pattern changes in the southern sector of Megalopolis, where the proportion of Africans (SOS) increases (suburbs of Washington, DC and Baltimore) and is larger than those indicating West Indian ancestry. This pattern of African ancestry dominance continues into the South. The green circles in the Carolinas and Georgia indicate that the relocated Blacks are of native ancestry. These African (SOS) ancestry patterns may indicate the importance of recent Black immigration, but they also most likely represent the reclaiming of Southern roots and place ties discussed earlier in this chapter. In short, these patterns reflect the impact of the contemporary Black "Reverse Migration."

Figure 12.4.
NYC Black Out-Migrant Preferences by Nativity (1995–2000) and Black Ancestry Categories.

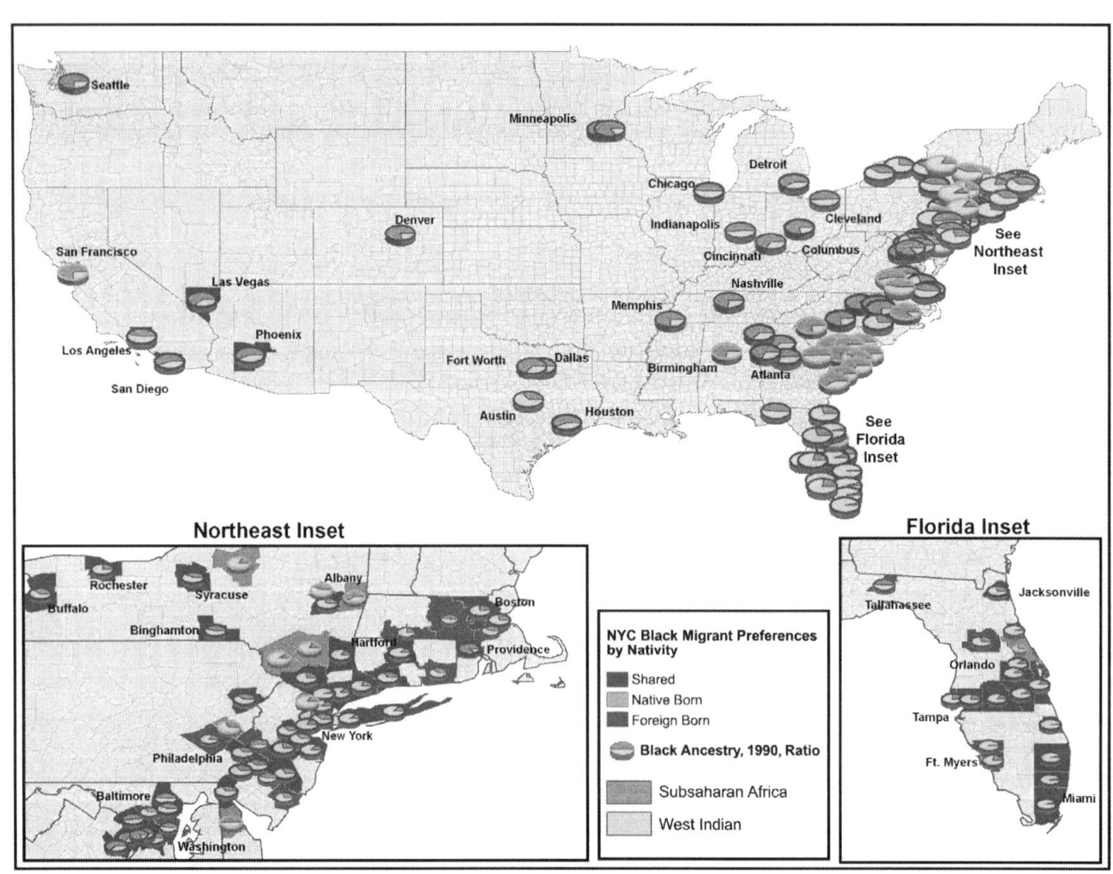

Florida provides a different set of patterns than other states in the Deep South. First, most counties are shared destinations for the two ancestral groups. There is a pattern of attraction for both groups in South Florida, stretching from Miami-Dade to Palm Beach, and across Central Florida, from Brevard County (Melbourne-Palm Bay) to Hillsborough (Tampa). The Jacksonville area (Duval) also exhibits this pattern. In all of these counties, however, the largest Black ancestral group is West Indians.

The Florida counties that were among the foreign-born unique 100 preferred destinations contained counties that included the cities of Orlando, Tallahassee, and Ft. Myers. Not surprisingly, these counties also had proportionately more Blacks of Sub-Saharan African ancestry than most other Florida counties.

The remainder of preferred destinations in Figure 12.4 spread across the nation. It is clear from the map that the counties containing the largest cities (Detroit, Chicago, Houston, Dallas, Los Angeles, etc.) tend to be shared-preference destinations for these 1995–2000 Black New York City migrants. However, it is also apparent that other counties with significant populations (Cleveland, Cincinnati, Columbus, Minneapolis, Denver, Austin) are important preferred destinations of foreign-born Blacks and have larger African SOS ancestral populations than West Indians. A few of these communities will be the subjects of subsequent chapters.

With these patterns in mind, we now turn to the results of the casual models.

MODEL RESULTS

The model results are reported in Table 12.1. The final column contains the proportion of variance (reliability) of each item (variable) that is explained by the appropriate construct. The results for each of the six concepts/constructs are briefly discussed below:

1. *Migration System*: Of the two ethnic migration subsystems, the native-born has a larger coefficient than the foreign-born, but the standardized coefficients suggest that the three subsystems are equally important to our understanding of the out-migration system from New York City. The reliability values indicate that this migration system and all three subsystems are valid.
2. *Economic Potential*: As shown in Table 12.1, this four-item construct is valid. While the economic potential construct is causally linked to all four variables, the two most important items are total employment in manufacturing and health services. Employment outside the county is the least important of the four measures.
3. *Cultural Niche*: This construct is measured by five items. It is causally linked to all five variables. The number of resettlement agencies has the lowest coefficient and the least explained variance. This may be because of the recent data, which were published after the actual migration period. The strongest causality for this construct is with the three variables that reflect the cultural importance of the concentration of different ethnic groups — total Black population, total African ancestry, and total West Indian ancestry.

Table 12.1.
Coefficients and Standardized Coefficients of Measurement Models.

Latent and Observed Variables	Coefficients		R^2 (Reliability)
	Reference Based (Unstandardized)	Completely Standardized	
1. Migration System			
X_1: Total migration from New York City	1.000	0.991	0.982
X_2: Foreign-born Black migration from N.Y. City	0.584	0.972	0.946
X_3: Native-born migration from New York City	0.766	0.986	0.974
2. Opportunity Concept—Economic Potential			
X_4: Total Employment in Manufacturing	1.000	0.973	0.947
X_5: Total Employment in Health Services	0.900	0.950	0.902
X_6: Total Employment in FIRE	0.844	0.935	0.873
X_7: Total Employed outside the County	0.954	0.918	0.844
3. Opportunity Concept—Social Niche			
X_8: Total Black Population	1.000	0.818	0.670
X_9: Total Black of Sub-Saharan Ancestry	0.728	0.887	0.787
X_{10}: Total Black of West Indian Ancestry	0.649	0.799	0.638
X_{11}: Number of Resettlement Agencies	0.036	0.442	0.196
X_{12}: Total Employed in the Military	0.490	0.770	0.593

Measurement Models — The Mapped Latent Variable Scores

The previous section confirmed our hypotheses regarding the effect of the concepts on the selected variables. In this section, we examine the spatial distribution of these constructs by generating and mapping the Structural Equation Modeling (SEM) scores. Unlike the coefficients used in the previous section, which were correlations, the SEM scores are z-scores, and are mapped for the migration system, the economic potential concept, and the cultural niche concept. These provide the spatial distribution derived from the measurement models.

Migration System (*Structural Equation Model Scores*): The scores for the migration system represent a linear combination of the variable loadings for combined three-migration subsystems. The distinctive patterns on the Atlantic and Pacific Coast are apparent in Figure 12.5. The largest concentration appears on the East Coast, especially in Megalopolis and extends northward into New York State counties, followed by the concentration in coastal Virginia and the Carolinas, parts of Georgia and then, into the state of Florida, which constitutes one of the most dominant migration states for this Black migration system. The pattern is less consistent on the West Coast, but counties in southern California (Los Angeles and San Diego areas) and counties near Seattle, Washington, illustrate the Black migration system operating from New York City to these distant counties.

Another set of counties, although small in number, appears on the Southwest border with Mexico, in the areas around Phoenix and Tucson. The same counties appeared on the 2000 foreign-born Black population map reported as Figure 12.3. A few scattered pockets of counties on or near the Gulf Coast, including those around Houston and Mobile, also appear in Figure 12.5. Specific counties within metropolitan areas of Texas also are parts of Black New York City migrants' pattern, including those in the Dallas-Ft. Worth area and Bexar (San Antonio). Finally, there is a scattered pattern of large- and medium-size metropolitan counties in the interior of the country, including the Detroit, Chicago, Minneapolis-St. Paul, the Denver-Colorado Springs region, as well as the Cincinnati-Columbus, Memphis, and Nashville areas.

Figure 12.5.
NYC Black Migration Scores, 1995–2000, by County.

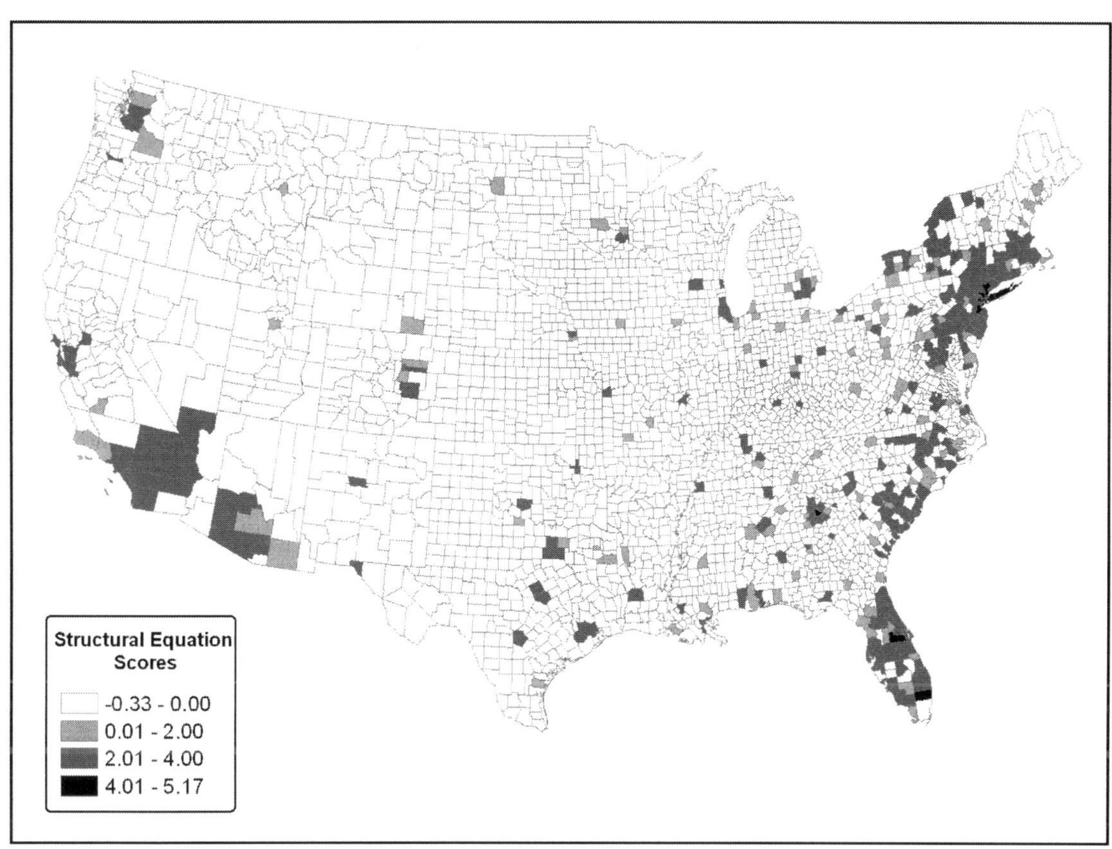

Economic Potential (*Structural Equation Model Scores*): The combined scores for the economic concept are mapped and presented in Figure 12.6. The geographic patterns, while similar to the migration system patterns, are more widely dispersed and, in addition to manufacturing employment, likely reflect the importance of the expanding tertiary service industry employment opportunities by 1990, including health services. They may also suggest the next potential destination choices of migrants.

The obvious geographic patterns include the same tri-coastal distributions observed earlier, the strength of the East in Megalopolis and Florida, sections of the Gulf Coast, and large sections of the West Coast. The same is true for the border counties of the Southwest and interior Texas. However, with these mapped scores, a linear pattern (perhaps following interstate highways) becomes obvious, especially on the I-35 corridor in central Texas through counties in Oklahoma. In the scattered metropolitan regions of the interior U.S., the economic attraction is visible around the same metropolitan regions and their counties mentioned previously.

Cultural Niche (*Structural Equation Model Scores*): The cultural niche scores are mapped by county for 1990 and appear in Figure 12.7. This map must be interpreted carefully. It combines the co-existence of distinctly different cultures, namely African Americans and the many ethnic groups of immigrant African and West Indian nations. Taken together, these are perceived as attracting the combined Black migrants of New York City. Thus, it is likely that where the SEM scores are highest, these groups co-located in 1990. While this is an important observation, it does not necessarily inform us of the places that are distinctive and preferred by one group or another.

Figure 12.6.
The Economic Construct, 1990, by County.

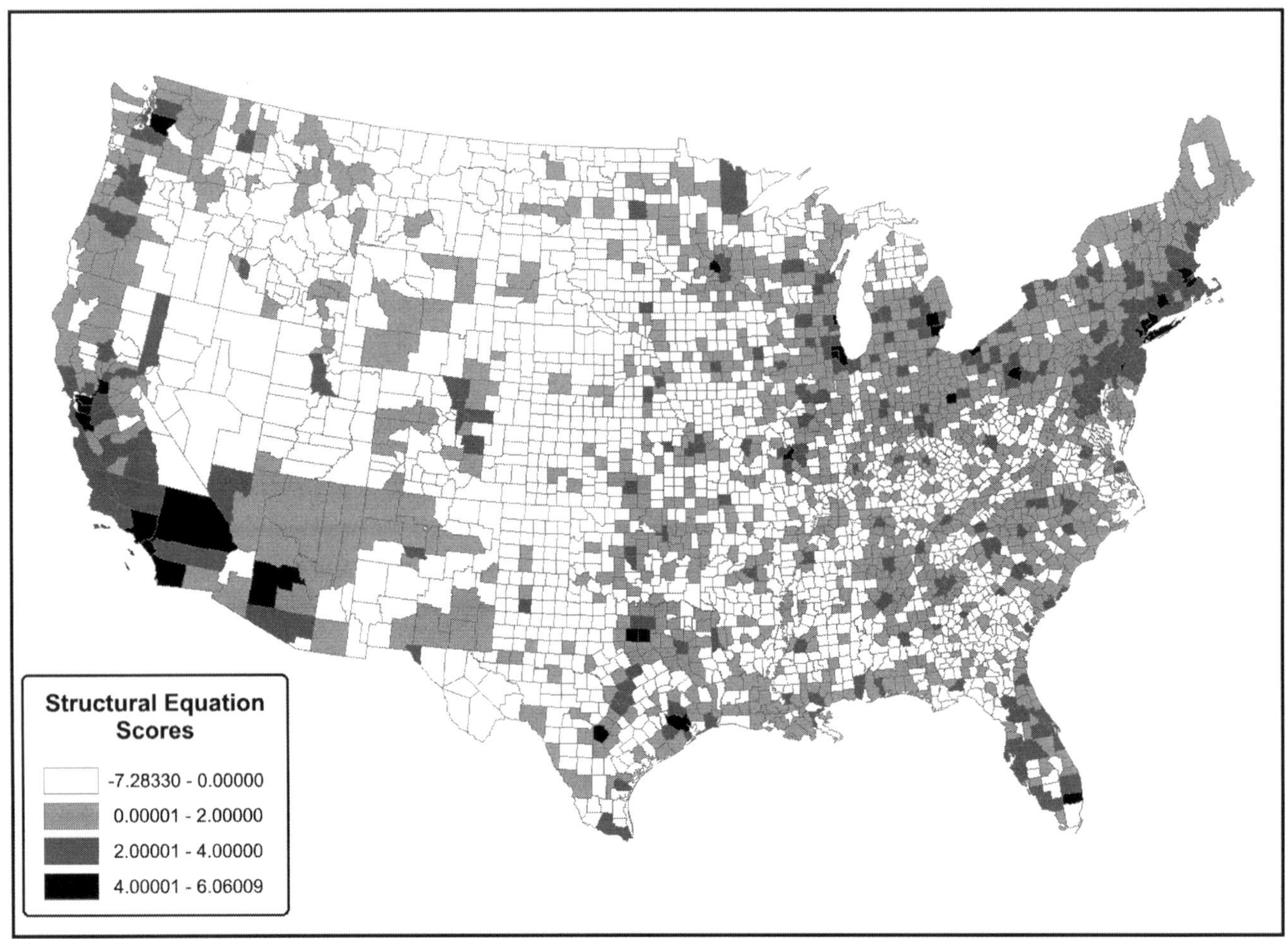

Figure 12.7 illustrates the cultural niche dominance of the American South. Although there are a few pockets of relatively high scores, it is the nearly complete coverage of the Southern counties that reminds us that this is the home of the majority of the U.S. Black population. There is an unbroken crescent pattern stretching from northern Megalopolis to Florida and, then swinging almost continuously along the Gulf Coast to southern Texas, and extending north and west into Oklahoma and northward into Tennessee. A similar pattern holds for the California Coast southward to borderland counties of Arizona and New Mexico, and to the north (with some breaks) into Oregon and Washington states.

These patterns are helpful to visualize concepts and constructs of our conceptualization of U.S. Black migration, which is the basis for the causal analysis that follows.

Figure 12.7.
The Cultural Niche, 1990, by County.

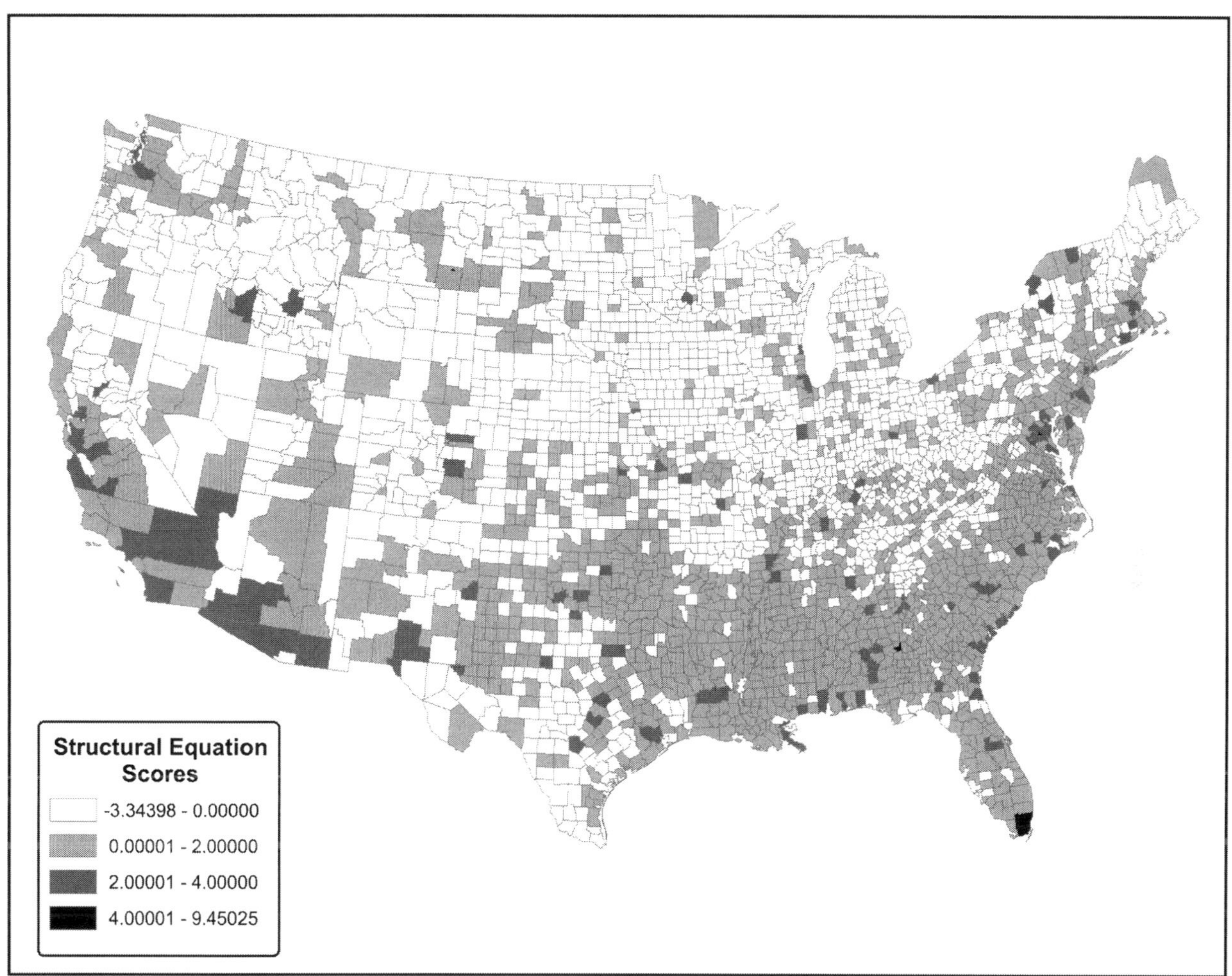

DISCUSSION OF CAUSALITY

When determining causal relationships, the factor that is the cause (independent) must precede the effect (the dependent factor). Thus, data establishing cause and effect must not be collected simultaneously. In this study, the data used to calibrate the migration system (M) are from the 1995–2000 period, and most of the items (variables) used for calibrating and testing the exogenous constructs are for the 1990–1992 period. The analysis is at two complimentary levels: the conceptual and the construct.

The Conceptual Level

At the conceptual level, the Migration System is a function of opportunity. We hypothesize that opportunity is a higher-order concept that explains the two lower-order constructs (the economic and cultural). The results (Table 12.2) confirm the importance of the mapped SEM scores. The results show that the opportunity concept is more associated with the cultural niche construct than the economic opportunity construct. However, the opportunity concept explains both constructs. The scores associated with both constructs are presented as Figure 12.8.

Table 12.2.
Convergent (Causal) Validity of the Opportunity Mega-construct on the Lower-order Constructs of Economic Opportunity and Cultural Niche.

Construct	Model 1: Original Model			Model 2: Military added to Economic Opportunity		
	Opportunity Loadings			Opportunity Loadings		
First-Order	Coeff.	Stand.	R^2.	Coeff.	Stand.	R^2
Economic Opportunity	0.661 (60.74)	0.941	0.885	0.601 (53.79)	0.867	0.752
Cultural Niche	1.100 (49.34)	0.980	0.960	1.116 (50.47)	0.981	0.961

The causal spatial impacts of the 1990 economic construct and the cultural niche construct on the opportunity concept are illustrated in Figure 12.8, revealing the relatively highest SEM scores for overall opportunity are on the two major coasts and scattered about the interior U.S. as previously noted. Interestingly, among the highest scores are those in southern California and Arizona, where few Blacks reside but where economic and potential and cultural niche suggest overall opportunity, despite Frey's observation that the Western region is losing Black population due to its net out-migration (Frey 2004). The same attraction exists in parts of the South, and other small pockets, such as the counties containing Chicago, Houston, and Dallas. Although scores are relatively lower and moderate along sections of the Atlantic Coast including parts of Megalopolis, Florida, and Deep South areas, overall these regions provide the opportunity perceived by members of the "Reverse" migration and newer Black immigrants. Other more scattered opportunities also exist in the interior counties of the nation.

Related to these findings of the SEM model, specifically the importance of the cultural niche concept and the stock variables in explaining the destination choices of Black New York City migrants, our earlier map analysis of foreign-born Blacks and Black ancestries revealed every county among the preferred destinations had at least one thousand foreign-born Blacks by the year 2000. The spatial analysis illustrates that the Black West Indian and South of the Sahara African ancestries varied, sometimes substantially, between the preferred destination counties of these 1995–2000 Black migrants. However, both were generally well represented in the preferred destination counties by 1990. It is likely that the ancestral patterns illustrated in the mapped distribution influenced the decisions of some migrants as illustrated by our SEM model results. Although data are not available at this time to test such a hypothesis, we believe that it is likely that foreign-born Africans (SOS) and West Indians were influenced by these broad ancestral patterns. For example, it is likely that Jamaican and other Caribbean migrants that are well represented in New York City were drawn to co-ethnics in particular counties in the core of Megalopolis and in Florida, among other destinations. Similarly, some native-born (second generation) Blacks of West Indian ancestries also were "pulled" to similar destinations (This topic is considered in chapter 14). Conversely, some foreign-born Africans (SOS) who decided to leave New York City have been attracted to the growing number of Africans residing in parts of northern Megalopolis or to the Washington, DC-Baltimore region of south-central Megalopolis, traditionally an area of significant numbers of African Americans, and an emerging area of foreign-born Blacks. The same may be true of the preferred destinations within the interior U.S. Some of these patterns are discussed in later chapters.

Figure 12.8.

The Opportunity Concept and its Economic and Cultural Niche Constructs, U.S. Counties, 1990.

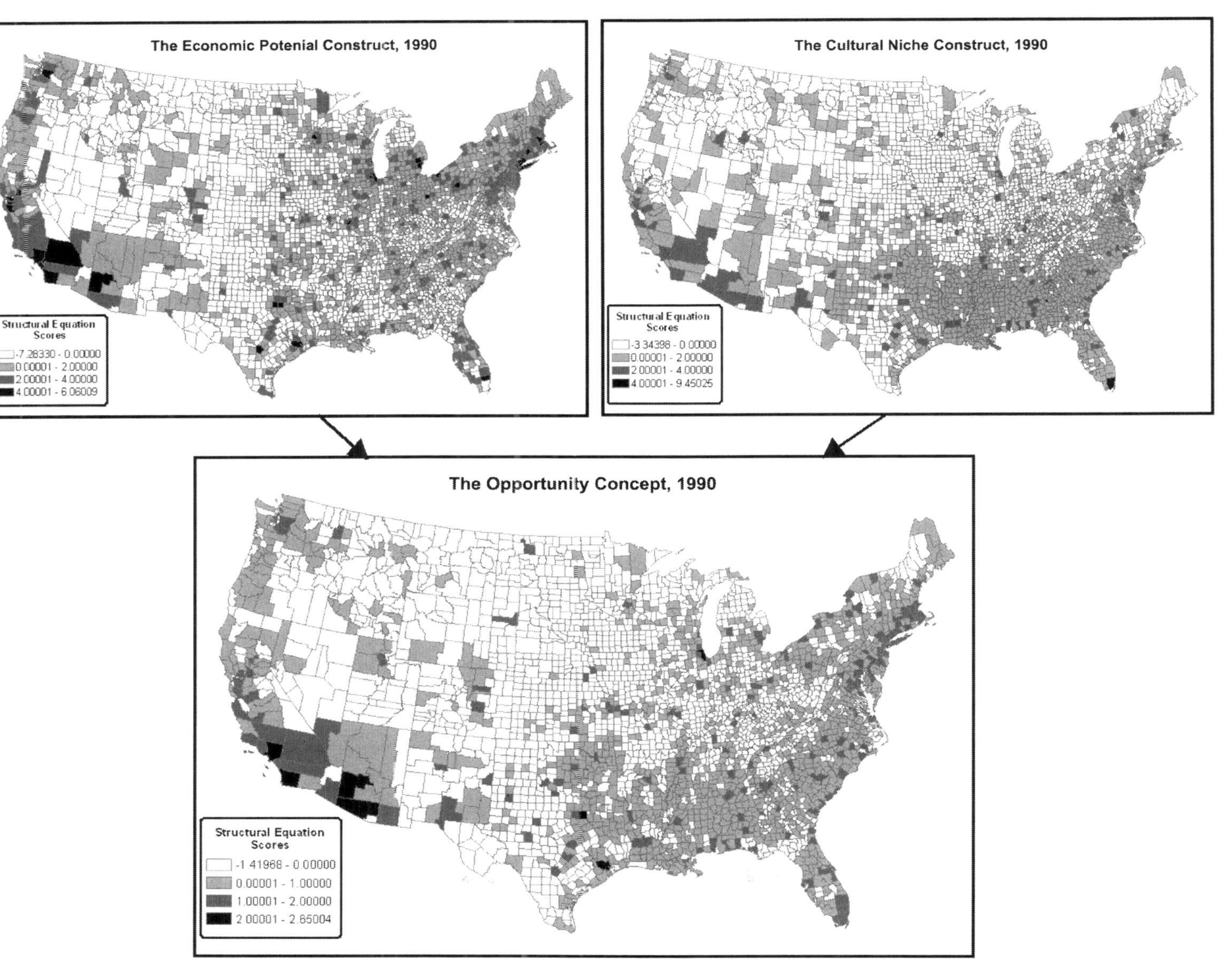

Results of Three Competing Causal Models: Destination Choice as a Function of Opportunity

At the construct level, three competing destination choice models are tested. Table 12.3 summarizes the causal effect of opportunity on migration. Overall, opportunity explains 43.6 percent of the variability in the migration system. Model A tests the hypothesis that Black destination choices are caused by the overall opportunities in a county. Opportunity explains at least 37 percent of both the foreign-born and native-born migrant systems. Model B adds the effect of military employment on the migration systems as a measure for both the cultural niche and economic potential constructs (see Figure 12.9). In contrast to Models A and B, Model C examines destination choice as a function of the two first-order constructs (economic and cultural). These three models and the estimated coefficients are reported in Figure 12.9. What is important is the relative strength of these three models in explaining the causal effects on the Black migration system. Models A and B examine the effect of the global construct of destination opportunity, and we examined whether it converged significantly (p-value less than 0.01) on the two first-order constructs. The results, summarized in Table 12.3, indicate that the global construct, opportunity, indeed caused the two lower-order constructs in both models A and B. In both of these models, the reliabilities of these first-order constructs are very high (the lowest R^2 is over 70 percent). In both models, the reliabilities are higher for cultural niche than for economic opportunity.

Of the three models, Model C is the weakest, with economic opportunity explaining 27.6 percent and cultural niche about 21.9 percent of the destination choices, respectively. In spite of these relatively low percentages, their effects on the total system and on the individual migration patterns (total, foreign-born and native-born) are all significantly different from zero. These effects are also significant for Models A and B. Moreover, Model B, which includes the military item in the economic opportunity construct, improved the explained variance of the destination choice model by 13.76 percent. Based on this, we conclude that Model B is the "best."

Table 12.3.
Standardized Effect of Second-Order (Opportunity) or First-Order (Economic, Niche) Constructs on New York Out-Migration Flows.

Migration Systems	**Model A:** Original Mega-Construct	**Model B:** Modified Mega-Construct	**Model C:** First Order Constructs	
	Opportunity	Opportunity	Economic	Niche
Total Migration	0.623	0.664	0.492	0.121
Foreign-born Blacks	0.371	0.388	0.287	0.070
Native-born Blacks	0.477	0.508	0.376	0.092
R^2	0.436	0.496	0.276	0.219

All coefficients are significant at alpha = .01.

Figure 12.9.
Results of the Three Destination Choice Models of Opportunity.

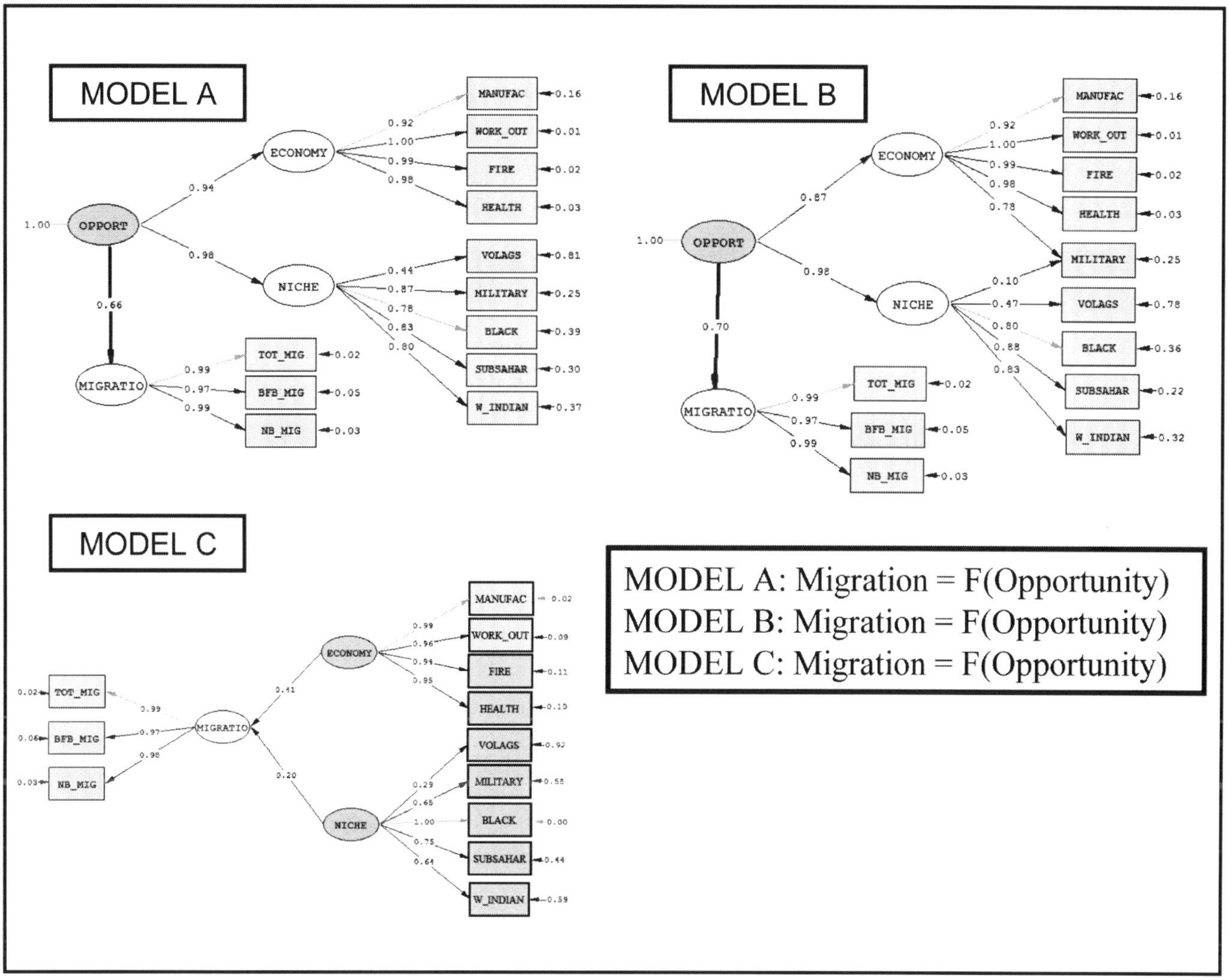

MODEL A: Migration = F(Opportunity)
MODEL B: Migration = F(Opportunity)
MODEL C: Migration = F(Opportunity)

SUMMARY

Theoretical concepts and constructs are central to social science progress. These must be measured by at least three carefully selected variables. The strength of the linkages between our items (variables) and the concepts and its constructs were tested by confirmatory factor analysis and associated maps were produced to illustrate their spatial distributions in the U.S. In all cases, the concept and the constructs were (statistically) significantly associated with the items (variables) chosen. We also tested three causal models to test the hypothesis that three Black migration systems from New York City, 1995–2000, to other U.S. counties were a function of opportunity. The second model, which included employment in the military, best explained the three migration systems. Overall, we demonstrated the relevance of opportunity in the Black migration system at the concept and construct levels. Unlike previous studies that aggregated migration data into broad regional structures and aggregated minority ethnic groups, we focused on the county-level and Black migrants from New York City between 1995 and 2000. Testing various models at this scale illustrated the greater relative importance of the cultural niche construct compared to the economic opportunity construct, although both were significant.

Our mapping analysis of the 100-preferred destination counties of Black New York City migrants provided valuable insights into the similar and different destination choices that native- and foreign-born Blacks made between 1995 and 2000. Black ancestry mapping, although not causal, contributed further potential explanations for the different destination choices of Black migrants. Mapping of the SEM scores generated by Structural Equation Modeling provided a visual and theoretical basis for understanding the spatial expression of forces that may guide future Black destination choices.

NOTES

[1] In the Gravity Model larger population size implies a greater range of opportunities and, therefore, attracts. However, the friction of movement increases with distance and decreases the desire to move long distances.

[2] Distance represented the "friction," or the negative psychological and economic costs of long-distance travel, while the other factors were expected to positively influence the pull of a Black migrant to a potential destination.

Theme 2:
Perspectives on Recent Black Immigrants

Chapter 13

Deconstructing the Black Populations of New York City and Miami-Dade County

THOMAS D. BOSWELL AND IRA M. SHESKIN

The Black populations of the United States as a whole, New York City (*NYC*) and Miami-Dade County (*Miami*) are particularly interesting groups to compare and contrast with one another because of intriguing similarities and differences. In some ways, New York City and Miami may be seen as harbingers for the changes likely to occur over the next decades in the composition of the Black population across the United States. This chapter focuses on the Black populations of New York City and Miami.

Although the population sizes, settlement patterns, and immigration histories of New York City and Miami differ significantly, both cities are large urban agglomerations. New York City's population is an order of magnitude larger than Miami's, 8.2 million vs. 2.4 million in 2006 (Table 13.1), and it developed in the pre-automobile era. Miami developed in the post-automobile era. New York City's population density is far higher than Miami's, which developed a much more dispersed, suburban population. New York City is a much older[1] Northeastern city, with a long and storied immigration history, while Miami is a relatively new Southern city, whose reputation as a major magnet for immigration traces only to the late 1950s and early 1960s, when large numbers of Cubans fled communism. Both cities have been vitally affected by immigration. About 51 percent of Miami's population is foreign-born, the highest percentage for any city *in the world* with a population of more than one million. About 37 percent of NYC's population is foreign-born, which also is among the world's highest percentages (U.S. Bureau of the Census 2006).

Both cities have large Black populations, with NYC's being much larger.[2] Table 13.2 shows that about 30 percent of both cities' Black populations are foreign-born, compared to only 7 percent of the United States' Black population as a whole. Because immigration has played such a significant role in the recent histories of these two cities, it is not valid to refer to the Black populations as relatively homogeneous. Thus, we deconstruct (disaggregate) the Black population into its West Indian and Sub-Saharan African-born components to discern how these immigrants alter the demographics of the Black population (Shaw-Taylor and Tuchs 2007). We briefly review changes occurring in the Black populations of both cities, followed by a discussion of the residential distributions of all Blacks and the degree to which foreign-born Blacks are segregated from other populations and from each other (West Indians, Haitians, Jamaicans, and Sub-Saharan African-born Blacks). Then we analyze the socioeconomic status (SES) of Blacks in both New York City and Miami, comparing various Black groups to Hispanics and Non-Hispanic Whites (NHWs).

In this chapter, "Blacks" refers to all persons who identify themselves as of black color in the United States. "West Indians" refers to Non-Hispanic (non-Cuban, non-Dominican, and non-Puerto Rican) immigrants and their progeny from the Caribbean Basin. "Sub-Saharan Africans" refers to Africans born south of Western Sahara, Algeria, Libya, and Egypt. Note as well that the term "Hispanic" is used rather than "Latino" because "Hispanic" is used almost exclusively in Miami to refer to this group.

Table 13.1.
Racial and Hispanic Composition
New York City, Miami, and the United States: 2000 and 2006.

Year	Total Population	Blacks *	Hispanics **	Non-Hispanic Whites ***	Blacks *	Hispanics **	Non-Hispanic Whites ***
New York City							
2000	8,008,278	2,274,049	2,160,554	2,801,267	28.4%	27.0%	35.0%
2006	8,214,426	2,152,001	2,267,827	2,854,519	26.2%	27.6%	34.8%
Miami							
2000	2,253,362	487,015	1,291,737	465,772	21.6%	57.3%	20.7%
2006	2,402,208	485,164	1,471,709	432,130	20.2%	61.3%	18.0%
United States							
2000	281,421,906	36,419,434	35,305,818	194,552,774	12.9%	12.5%	69.1%
2006	299,398,485	39,151,870	44,252,278	198,176,991	13.1%	14.8%	66.2%

* Blacks alone or in combination with other races.
** Hispanics may be of any race. In 2000, there were 223,285 Black Hispanics in New York City, 38,842 in Miami, and 1,035,683 in the U.S.
*** Non-Hispanic Whites alone.
Note: Percentages do not total 100 because of overlap between Blacks and Hispanics and because other racial groups (Asians, American Indians, etc.) are not shown.
Sources: U.S. Bureau of the Census, *2000 Census of Population and Housing*, Summary File 1, Tables P7, P8, P9, and P10 and U.S. Bureau of the Census, *2006 American Community Survey*, Tables B02009 and C03002.

THE GROWTH AND CHANGE OF THE BLACK POPULATIONS OF NEW YORK CITY AND MIAMI

The number of foreign-born Blacks in the United States more than tripled from 1980 to 2005, with about two-thirds from the Caribbean and Latin America and about one-third from Africa. Approximately 40 percent of the African Blacks arrived between 2000 and 2005 (Kent 2007).

Immigrants have always been an important component of both the New York City and Miami populations. The first settlers in New York City (then New Amsterdam) were Dutch immigrants. The first settlers in Miami included in-migrants from the northeastern United States, Black immigrants from the Bahamas, and U.S.-born Blacks. The Black population of Miami always has hovered between 13 and 22 percent, while NYC's Blacks have been a more variable percentage of that city's population.

Blacks first appeared as a significant percentage of NYC's population in the late 1890s and early 1900s. The growth in the Black population was fueled by immigration from the West Indies, in-migration from the American South, and natural increase. By 1920, about 20 percent of NYC's population were immigrants. However, World War I, the change in immigration laws during the early 1920s, the Great Depression, and World

War II all had dampening effects on Black immigration. While the Black population continued to increase due to continued heavy in-migration from the South and natural increase, the immigrant percentage of NYC's Blacks decreased to a low of about 8 percent in 1970. This trend was changed by the Immigration Amendments Act of 1965, which discontinued the favoritism granted to immigrants from Europe, replacing geographical preferences with priorities given for family reunification and employment skills. This increased the flow of immigrants from the Caribbean, especially from Jamaica, Haiti, Trinidad and Tobago, and Guyana. By 1990, the immigrant component of NYC's Black population surged to 24 percent[3] and by 2000, to 30 percent.

The change in America's immigration policy in 1965 also resulted in an increase in the Non-Black immigrant population, especially from Latin America and Asia. The foreign born comprised almost 36 percent of NYC's population in 2000 and 37 percent by 2006, which was far higher than the 20 percent in 1920 following the great immigrations from eastern and southern Europe via Ellis Island. Of course, the immigrant population of the nation as a whole had also increased from about 4 percent in 1970 to 13 percent by 2006, with New York City and Miami as extreme cases.

The ethnic changes in Miami are even more pronounced than in NYC. In 1960, about 5 percent of Miami's population was Hispanic. By 2006, 61 percent of Miami's population was Hispanic and the percentage of immigrants increased to slightly more than 50 percent (U.S. Census 2006). The large-scale immigration of Hispanics has affected change in other population components. Since the 1970s, considerable "White flight" has occurred, as Non-Hispanic Whites (NHWs) have migrated out of Miami in droves due to increasing competition from low-cost Hispanic immigrant laborers, increasing friction over the use of Spanish, and the need to be bilingual in the workplace. The number of NHWs decreased by 55 percent, from 782,000 (62 percent of the total population) in 1970 to only 432,000 (18 percent of the total population) in 2006 (Boswell 2007), despite a positive natural increase and a net immigration from international sources during this time period.[4]

More recently, the Black population has decreased in both New York City and Miami, as U.S.-born Blacks have suffered competition from low-wage immigrants. Between 2000 and 2006, the number of Blacks decreased by 122,000 in New York City and by 1,850 in Miami (Table 13.1). A recent study in Miami determined that the out-migration of Blacks is disproportionately middle-class because they can afford moving and job search costs (Metropolitan Center, Florida International University 2007). This has left lower-income Blacks in Miami, creating a "brain-drain" among Miami's Blacks, and reducing their socioeconomic status (SES).[5] When compared to NHWs and Hispanics, Blacks have fallen further behind. Meanwhile, the SES of NHWs has increased because most NHW out-migration has been by persons employed in blue collar occupations, which are most likely to suffer from competition with low-paid immigrants. The average SES of Hispanics also has increased, as the pervasiveness of Spanish has assisted Hispanic immigrants in their adjustment to Miami's economic environment. In addition, Hispanic immigrants to Miami, when compared to Hispanic immigrants to the Northeast and Southwest, are disproportionately selected from middle-class backgrounds in Latin America and they migrate to Miami with considerable human capital (e.g., better education levels, some monetary resources, and job experiences).

Similar data are not available for NYC's Black population, but it is possible that a similar dynamic occurs in that city. The continued heavy immigration to New York City of Blacks from the Caribbean, along with Hispanic and Asian immigrants, also has increased competition, especially for low-skilled and low-paying jobs.

Table 13.2 shows data on nativity and place of birth for Blacks, Hispanics, and NHWs in NYC, Miami, and the United States as a whole. Blacks occupy an intermediate position between Hispanics and NHWs on these measures. In NYC, Miami, and the United States as a whole, Hispanics have, by far, the largest percentage of foreign-born and NHWs have the lowest. Most Blacks were born in the state in which they currently reside, with a significantly smaller number born in other states, and a very small number of U.S.-born Blacks born outside of the United States.[6]

A larger percentage of foreign-born Blacks than Hispanics have become naturalized United States citizens in New York City and the United States as a whole, but not in Miami. The lower naturalization rate of Hispanics than Blacks in New York City and the United States as a whole is related to the higher percentage of Hispanics who are recent immigrants (entered the United States between 1990 and 2000).

While in New York City NHW immigrants have naturalization rates that are only slightly higher than Blacks, the NHW naturalization rates in Miami and the United States as a whole are considerably higher than the rate for Blacks. Citizenship acquisition is important because it allows for greater federal government benefits eligibility as well as facilitates access to jobs that are restricted to citizens.

Table 13.3 shows a significant difference between the region of birth of Blacks and NHWs, but relatively little difference between Blacks and Hispanics. The vast majority of both Black and Hispanic immigrants come from Latin America, whereas Europe is the largest source of NHW immigrants. Although Africa serves as a relatively minor source of Black immigration to New York City and Miami, it is the source for 24 percent of Black immigrants to the United States.

Why do the vast majority of both Black and Hispanic immigrants come from Latin America? For Hispanics, the answer is obvious, as Spain is the only Hispanic country outside Latin America. Table 13.4 shows the countries from which Black Latin American immigrants derive. Most come from Caribbean islands with former plantation economies that had imported African slaves to perform hard labor. Almost ten times as many Africans had been transported to the Caribbean (about five million) than to the United States (less than half a million), mostly because of the hazardous nature of harvesting sugar cane in the Caribbean. The hot tropical sun, humidity, and the use of machetes to cut sugar cane all contributed to a higher mortality rate among Caribbean slaves than those sent to the United States (although their lives also were not easy). After the elimination of slavery, as the plantation economy in the Caribbean waned, population pressures mounted and employment opportunities dwindled. The United States, as the nearest developed country to the Caribbean, became an attractive alternative residential location.

The largest numbers of Black immigrants to NYC, Miami, and the United States as a whole came from Haiti and Jamaica, with smaller but significant numbers from Trinidad and Tobago, Cuba, and the Dominican Republic. Most Hispanics who immigrated to New York City and Miami from Cuba and the Dominican Republic were White, because both islands had largely White populations. The plantation economy had predominated for a longer period of time in the British, French, and Dutch colonies than in the Spanish colonies of Cuba, the Dominican Republic, and Puerto Rico. As a result, British, French, and Dutch colonies were more dominated by Blacks who had been transported to work on the plantations and in other jobs (West and Augelli 1989).

RESIDENTIAL DISTRIBUTION AND SEGREGATION OF BLACKS IN NEW YORK CITY AND MIAMI[7]

This section compares the residential patterns of Blacks in New York City and Miami with Hispanics and NHWs. Because of the significant foreign-born component in the Black population, several selected Black subgroups (West Indians, Haitians, Jamaicans, and Sub-Saharan African-born) are also examined. Residential location is affected by a number of factors, including race, ethnicity, socioeconomic status (SES), housing availability and price, and discrimination. Seventeen maps are used in this analysis, 16 of which are paired to facilitate comparisons between New York City and Miami.[8]

The index of dissimilarity (ID), used as a measure of segregation, is expressed as a percentage of either of two given populations that would need to move so that the two populations are geographically distributed among a set of geographic units in the same manner.[9] Census tracts are used as the geographic units in both New York City and Miami because the U.S. Bureau of the Census specifically delineates census tracts to capture the concept of neighborhoods.

As an example, an ID of 50 percent between Blacks and Whites means that 50 percent of either Blacks or Whites (or some combination of the two) would need to move to another census tract for the distributions of these two populations to be identical. IDs greater than 60 percent are considered in the *high range*; 40 percent to 60 percent, in the *moderate range*; and below 40 percent, in the *low* range.[10] Table 13.5 shows the 50 IDs used to analyze differences in residential patterns between various population subgroups in New York City and Miami.

Table 13.2.
Nativity and Place of Birth
Blacks, Hispanics, and Non-Hispanic Whites
New York City, Miami, and the United States: 2000.

Variable	New York City	Miami	United States
Blacks * (*Percentages*)			
Native-Born	69.7	69.3	93.3
In state of residence	53.7	51.9	67.1
In another state	13.9	16.0	25.3
Outside U.S.	2.2	1.5	0.9
Foreign-Born (FB)	30.3	30.7	6.7
Naturalized U.S. Citizen (% of FB)	50.8	42.7	43.3
Entered U.S. 1990–2000 (% of FB)	34.0	38.4	41.8
Hispanics ** (*Percentages*)			
Native- Born	58.8	28.6	59.8
In state of residence	42.3	17.9	44.9
In another state	2.1	6.2	10.2
Outside U.S.	14.4	4.4	4.7
Foreign-Born (FB)	41.3	71.4	40.2
Naturalized U.S. Citizen (% of FB)	33.7	46.8	27.9
Entered U.S. 1990–2000 (% of FB)	44.2	35.4	45.8
Non-Hispanic Whites (NHWs) *** (*Percentages*)			
Native-Born	76.8	85.2	96.5
In state of residence	61.2	38.7	63.3
In another state	14.6	45.1	32.5
Outside U.S.	1.0	1.4	0.7
Foreign-Born (FB)	23.2	14.8	3.5
Naturalized U.S. Citizen (% of FB)	53.9	49.3	54.3
Entered U.S. 1990–2000 (% of FB)	43.1	39.3	34.3

* Blacks alone or in combination with other races.
** Hispanics may be of any race.
*** Non-Hispanic Whites alone.
Source: U.S. Bureau of the Census, *2000 Census of Population and Housing*, Summary File 4, Table DP-2.

Table 13.3.
Region of Birth
Foreign-Born Blacks, Hispanics, and Non-Hispanic Whites.
New York City, Miami, and the United States: 2000.

Place of Birth	New York City	Miami	United States
Blacks * (*Percentages*)			
Europe	1.4	0.8	2.7
Asia	0.5	0.3	1.3
Africa	9.5	1.3	23.6
Oceania	0.0	0.0	0.1
Latin America	88.2	97.3	71.6
North America	0.4	0.3	0.8
Hispanics ** (*Percentages*)			
Europe	1.0	1.0	0.7
Asia	0.2	0.1	0.2
Africa	0.1	0.0	0.0
Oceania	0.0	0.0	0.0
Latin America	98.6	98.9	99.0
North America	0.0	0.0	0.0
Non-Hispanic Whites (NHWs) *** (*Percentages*)			
Europe	79.2	47.0	66.5
Asia	12.0	9.2	13.2
Africa	2.9	3.2	3.0
Oceania	0.7	0.4	1.1
Latin America	3.3	33.7	5.0
North America	2.0	6.3	11.1

* Blacks alone or in combination with other races.
** Hispanics may be of any race.
*** Non-Hispanic Whites alone.
Source: See Table 2.

Table 13.4.
Place of Birth of Blacks*
New York City, Miami, and the United States: 2000 (Percentages).

Place of Birth	New York City	Miami	United States
Born in U.S. or Its Possessions	69.2	68.3	93.0
Born Outside U.S. and Its Possessions **	30.8	31.7	7.0
The Caribbean Basin	21.9	28.7	3.9
Bahamas	0.1	1.5	0.1
Barbados	1.1	0.1	0.1
Cuba	0.2	2.2	0.1
Dominican Republic	2.0	1.3	0.2
Guyana	2.9	0.2	0.3
Haiti	4.2	14.8	1.1
Jamaica	7.7	6.7	1.4
Trinidad & Tobago	3.7	0.8	0.4
Africa	2.9	0.4	1.6
Sub-Saharan Africa	2.8	0.4	1.5
Rest of the World	6.0	2.6	1.5

Note: Table only includes countries that contribute 1% or more to the population in at least one of the three columns.
*Blacks alone or in combination with other races.
** Percentages for *Born Outside U.S.* are slightly higher than the percentages of *Foreign-Born* in Table 2. See text for an explanation.
Sources: U.S. Bureau of the Census, *2000 Census of Population*, Public Use Microdata Sample (PUMS), 1% sample for U.S. and 5% samples for New York City and Miami.

Table 13.5 shows IDs comparing 25 different population subgroups for New York City and Miami.[11] The third column shows the absolute difference between the IDs in New York City and Miami. As an arbitrary and general rule, if an absolute difference is within 10 percentage points, the IDs are termed *similar* (these cells are lightly shaded). If an absolute difference is between 10 and 20 percentage points, the IDs are termed *moderately different*. If an absolute difference is more than 20 percentage points, the IDs are termed *very different* (these cells are darkly shaded).

Table 13.5.
Indexes of Dissimilarity for Racial and Ethnic Groups
New York City and Miami: 2000.

Groups Being Compared	Indexes of Dissimilarity (ID)		
	New York City	Miami	Absolute Differences *
1) All Blacks vs. All Whites	72.8	71.1	1.7
2) Non-Hispanic Blacks vs. Non-Hispanic Whites	83.9	72.9	11.0
3) Non-Hispanic Blacks vs. Hispanics	58.2	73.4	15.2
4) Non-Hispanic Whites vs. Hispanics	67.1	43.9	23.2
5) Hispanic Blacks vs. Non-Hispanic Blacks	37.1	50.4	13.3
6) Hispanic Blacks vs. Hispanic Non-Blacks	33.1	37.8	4.7
7) Hispanic Blacks vs. Non-Hispanic Whites	78.9	55.4	23.5
8) **West Indians** vs. Non-Hispanic Blacks (*excluding West Indians*)	40.7	51.0	10.3
9) West Indians vs. Non-Hispanic Whites	83.7	67.3	16.4
10) West Indians vs. Hispanics	67.5	71.1	3.6
11) **Haitians** vs. Non-Hispanic Blacks (*excluding Haitians*)	56.4	57.9	1.5
12) Haitians vs. West Indians (*excluding Haitians*)	44.7	52.8	8.1
13) Haitians vs. Non-Hispanic Whites	86.4	74.2	12.2
14) Haitians vs. Hispanics	78.7	78.5	0.2
15) **Jamaicans** vs. Non-Hispanic Blacks (*excluding Jamaicans*)	37.8	44.2	6.4
16) Jamaicans vs. West Indians (*excluding Jamaicans*)	34.4	48.8	14.4
17) Jamaicans vs. Non-Hispanic Whites	86.5	63.1	23.4
18) Jamaicans vs. Hispanics	70.7	67.6	3.1
19) **Sub-Saharan African-Born** vs. Non-Hispanic Blacks (*excluding African Born*)	49.5	64.7	15.2
20) Sub-Saharan African-Born vs. West Indians	57.7	58.7	1.0
21) Sub-Saharan African-Born vs. Non-Hispanic Whites	80.0	59.3	20.7
22) Sub-Saharan African-Born vs. Hispanics	59.7	70.2	10.5
23) Blacks in Poverty vs. Blacks Not in Poverty	31.1	28.8	2.3
24) Hispanics in Poverty vs. Hispanics Not in Poverty	27.4	26.8	0.6
25) Non-Hispanic Whites in Poverty vs. Non-Hispanic Whites Not in Poverty	35.3	30.2	5.1

* Lightly shaded cells contain ID differences of less than 10 percentage points. Darkly shaded cells contain ID differences of more than 20 percentage points.
Source: U.S. Bureau of the Census, *2000 Census of Population*, Summary Files 1, 3, and 4.

Blacks, Whites, and Hispanics

Row 1 in Table 13.5 compares All Blacks and All Whites, where both racial groups include some Hispanics. The IDs for both New York City (72.8) and Miami (71.1) are high and are similar. When Non-Hispanic Blacks are compared to NHWs (Row 2), the ID increases by more than 11 percentage points (from 72.8 to 83.9) in NYC, but remains about the same for Miami (from 71.1 to 72.9). In addition, Non-Hispanic Blacks and NHWs are more strongly segregated from each other in New York City than they are in Miami (83.9 vs. 72.9).

Figure 13.1 provides selected place names for New York City neighborhoods. Figure 13.2 (a and b) shows the residential patterns of Non-Hispanic Blacks in New York City and Miami. In NYC, Blacks are concentrated in three major areas: 1) northern Manhattan, from Central Park through Harlem and extending into the Bronx; 2) Central Brooklyn, including such neighborhoods as Bedford Stuyvesant, Brownsville, Canarsie, Crown Heights, East Flatbush, Flatbush, and Prospect; and 3) southeastern Queens (north of JFK Airport), including Brookville, Cambria Heights, Jamaica Center, Jamaica Estates, Richmond Hill, South Jamaica, Rosedale, Springfield Gardens, St. Albans, and Queens Village. In Miami, most Blacks live in two major areas: 1) a northern wedge that extends just north of the central business district (which is just south of Overtown) through Liberty City, Opa-Locka, and Carol City; and 2) the southern part of Miami, including Richmond Heights, Cutler Ridge, Perrine, Homestead, and Florida City.[12]

Figure 13.3 (a and b) shows the residential patterns for NHWs in New York City and Miami. In both cities, these maps show a pattern very much the reverse of the patterns shown on Figure 13.2 (a and b), graphically illustrating why the IDs in Row 2 of Table 13.5 are so high. This is especially apparent in NYC, where the major areas of Black residence (Figure 13.2) are the opposites of the areas of high concentrations of NHWs. In Miami, NHWs are concentrated in two major areas: 1) a northern area from Miami Beach through North Miami Beach, and into Aventura; and 2) the coastal area from Coconut Grove to Pinecrest. These findings of significant segregation are consistent with the findings of numerous studies of other cities in the United States.

Figure 13.4 (a and b) shows the residential patterns for Hispanics in New York City and Miami. In NYC, Hispanics are concentrated in the south Bronx and northern Manhattan, south of La Guardia Airport, and in several other areas of western Queens and Brooklyn. In Miami (which was 57 percent Hispanic in 2000), Hispanics are concentrated in the northwestern sector, including Hialeah and the central sections of the city, including Little Havana, Sweetwater, and Westchester.[13]

Unlike the significant segregation between Blacks and Whites in all American cities, there is no general agreement in the literature about whether Hispanics are more segregated from NHWs than they are from Non-Hispanic Blacks, although most studies show moderate to high levels of segregation between Non-Hispanic Blacks and Hispanics.

NYC and Miami differ in their levels of segregation of Non-Hispanic Blacks (Rows 2 and 3 in Table 13.5). In Miami, levels of segregation between Non-Hispanic Blacks and NHWs (72.9) and Non-Hispanic Blacks and Hispanics (73.4) are about equal. In NYC, on the other hand, Non-Hispanic Blacks are less segregated from Hispanics (58.2) than they are from NHWs (83.9), probably due, in part, to the fact that 10 percent of Hispanics in New York City are also Black, compared to only 3 percent in Miami (Table 13.1). Thus, in Miami, the Hispanic population is much "whiter" than in NYC.[14] In NYC, the two largest components of the Hispanic population are Puerto Ricans and Dominicans. Both these groups tend to have a larger share of Blacks, particularly the Dominicans. In Miami, nearly 95 percent of Cubans classify themselves as White. Thus, the color lines are more sharply drawn in Miami between Hispanics and Non-Hispanic Blacks than in NYC. One of the things many visitors to Miami comment on is how much whiter the Miami Hispanics appear when compared to Hispanics in the Southwest or in NYC. Visibly, Hispanics in Miami tend to be less recognizable and distinguishable from NHWs.[15]

Figure 13.1.
Place Names: New York City.

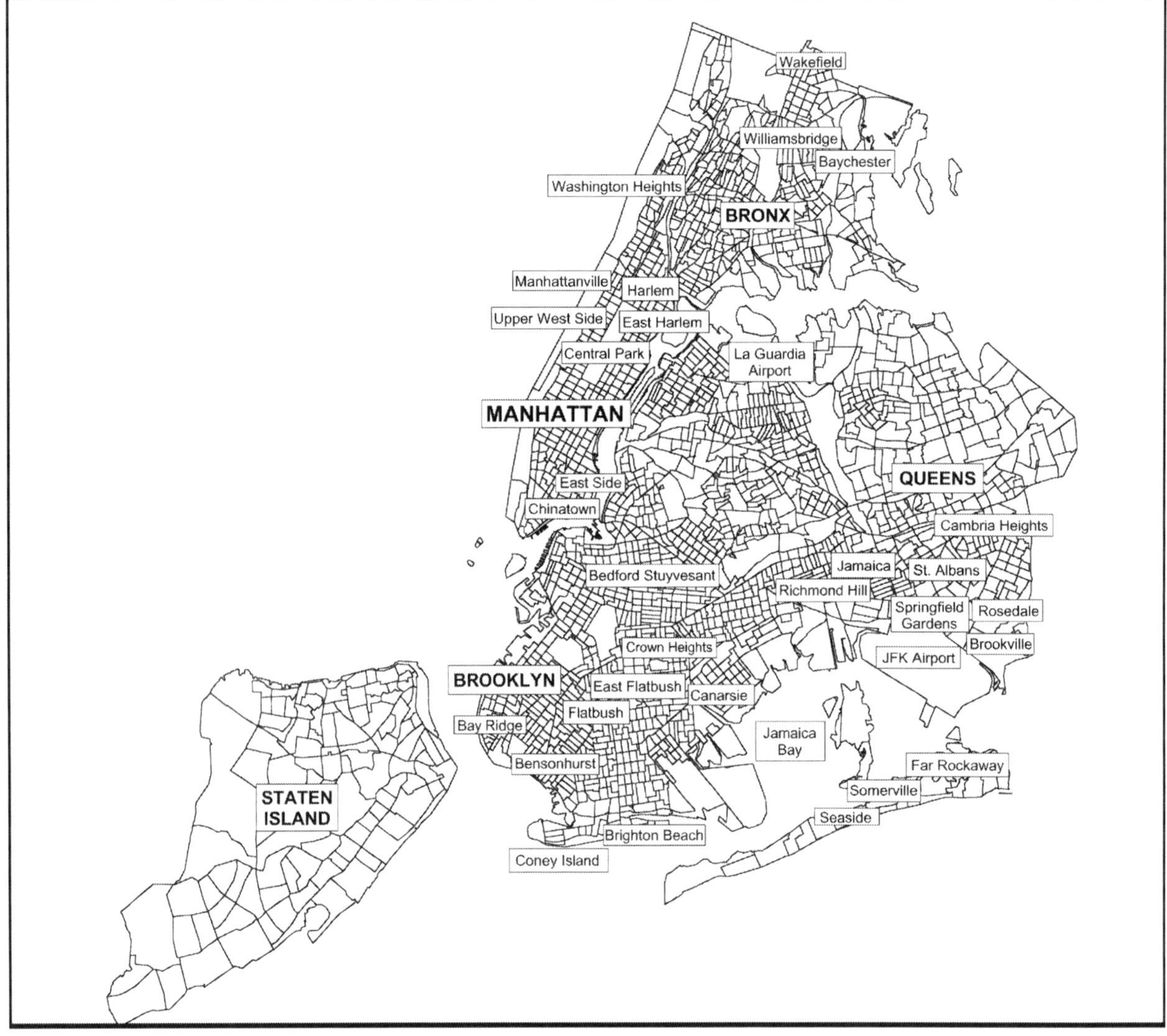

Row 4 of Table 13.5 shows that NHWs are much more segregated from Hispanics in New York City (67.1) than in Miami (43.9). This is in part related to the whiteness of Miami Hispanics and to the fact that Hispanics, being 57 percent of the population in 2000 and very often being of middle and upper income, are simply found in almost all areas of Miami. The two IDs are very different (23.2) (Row 4 in Table 13.5).

What about Hispanic Blacks? Where do they fit into the social equations of New York City and Miami? Are Hispanic Blacks more likely to live in Black neighborhoods or are they more likely to live in Hispanic neighborhoods? That is, does race trump ethnicity or does ethnicity trump race? We can answer this question by comparing the residential locations of Hispanic Blacks with both Non-Hispanic Blacks and Hispanic Non-Blacks. If race trumps ethnicity, the ID for Hispanic Blacks compared to Non-Hispanic Blacks (Row 5 of Table 13.5) should be lower than the ID for Hispanic Blacks compared to Hispanic Non-Blacks (Row 6 of Table 13.5). That is, if race trumps ethnicity, Black Hispanics would exhibit a greater tendency to live in Black neighborhoods than Hispanic neighborhoods. The results in Table 13.5 suggest the opposite. Black Hispanics in both New York City and Miami are more likely to live in Hispanic neighborhoods than in Black neighborhoods. This difference is slight in New York City (37.1 vs. 33.1), but is more significant in Miami (50.4 vs. 37.8). So, for Black Hispanics, ethnicity seems to be more important than race, especially in Miami.

We believe that language plays a major factor in ethnicity trumping race. Most Black Hispanics (especially immigrants) may feel more comfortable speaking Spanish than speaking English and that may be why they show a preference for Hispanic neighborhoods. The reason this preference is stronger in Miami is that a larger segment (61 percent) of the population in Miami is Hispanic than in New York City (28 percent). In other words, Spanish is more widely "usable" in Miami than in NYC.

Hispanic Blacks are more segregated from NHWs (Row 7 of Table 13.5) than they are from either Non-Hispanic Blacks (Row 5) or Hispanic Non-Blacks (Row 6), in both New York City and Miami, but this difference is especially strong in NYC. The two IDs are very different (23.5) (Row 7 in Table 3.5). This may be because NHWs in Miami represent a smaller percentage (18 percent) of the total population than they do in New York City (35 percent), so less possibility exists of living in a neighborhood with significant numbers of NHWs in Miami.

Figure 13.2.
Percent of Total Population That is Non-Hispanic Black: 2000.

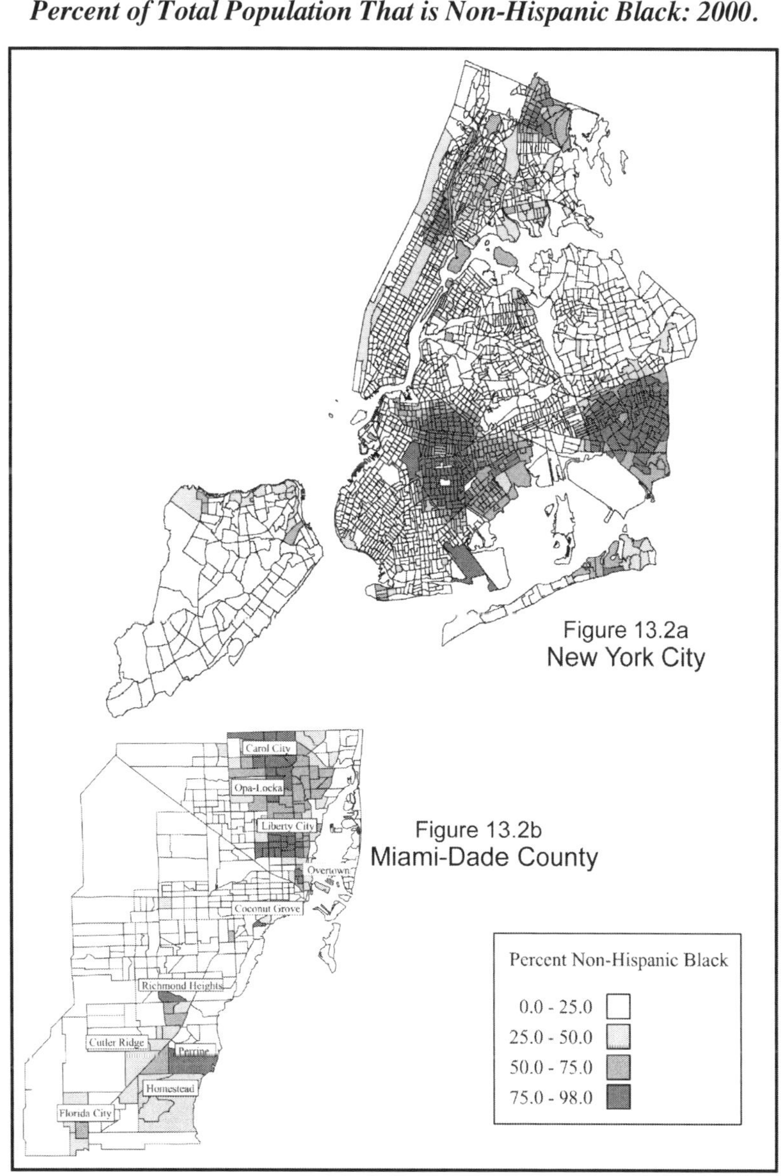

Figure 13.3.
Percent of Total Population That is Non-Hispanic White: 2000.

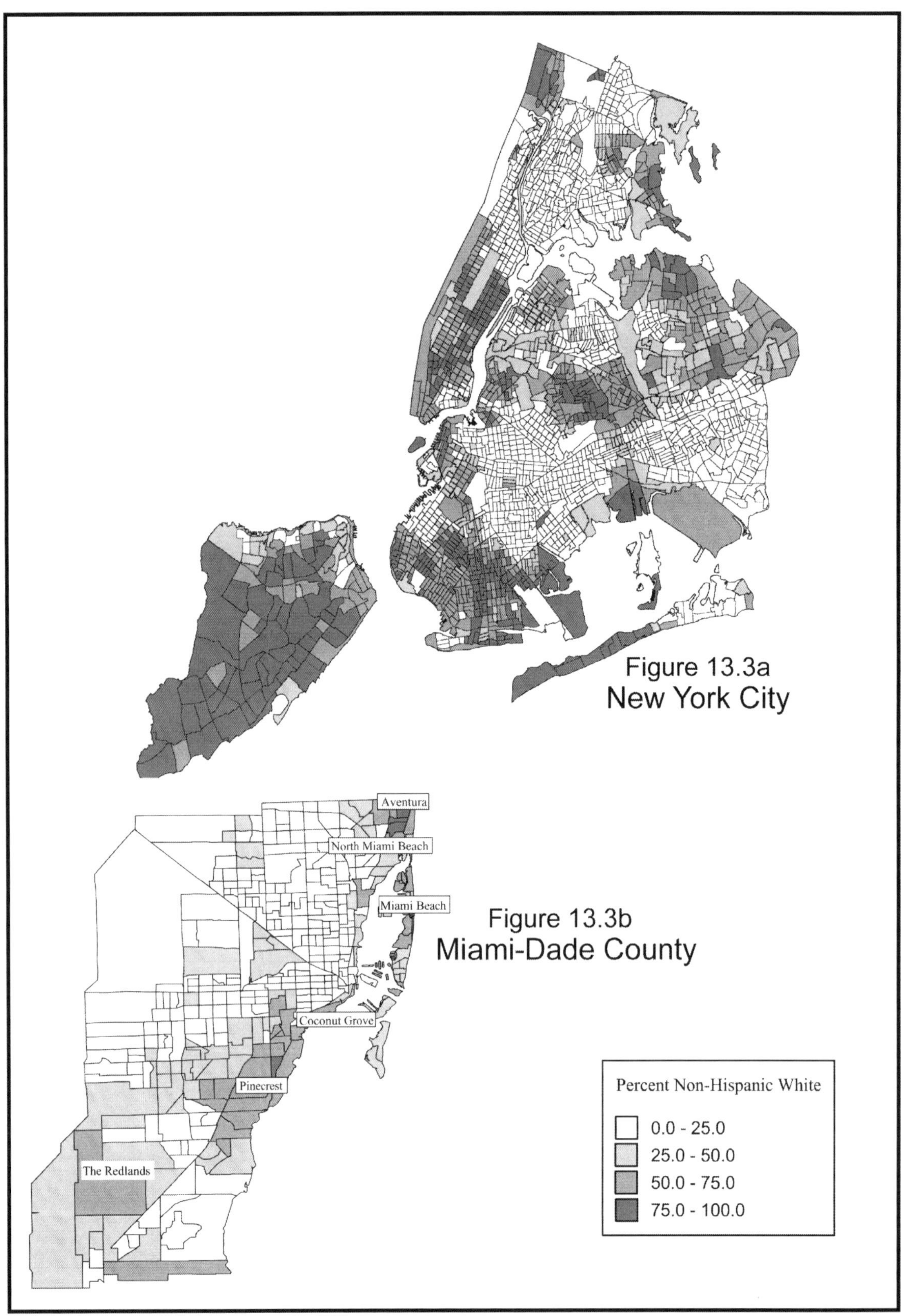

Figure 13.4.
Percent of Total Population That is Hispanic*: 2000.

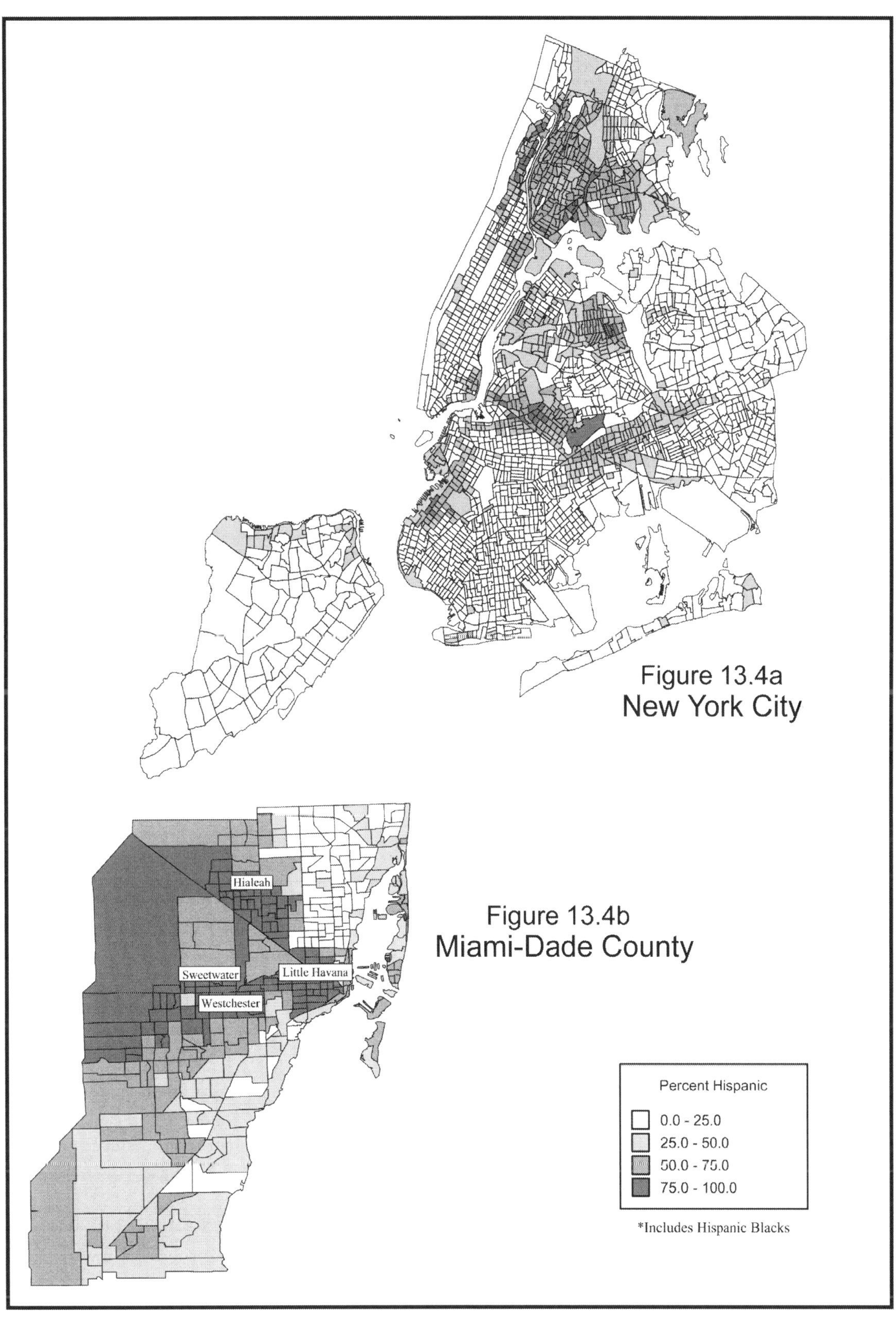

West Indians and Haitians

Rows 8–18 in Table 13.5 compare West Indians as a whole and their two largest national components, Jamaicans and Haitians, with one another and with Non-Hispanic Blacks, Non-Hispanic Whites, and Hispanics. "West Indians" refers only to Non-Hispanic (non-Cuban, non-Dominican, and non-Puerto Rican) immigrants and their progeny from the Caribbean Basin.[16] While some researchers include Haitians as being West Indian, others do not (Foner 2001). Thus, we will first analyze West Indians including Haitians and then analyze West Indians excluding Haitians.

West Indians are, in a sense, a double minority, as most are Black[17] and most are either immigrants or children of immigrants and are thus members of both a racial group and an ethnic group. Do most West Indians choose to live in Black neighborhoods or are they more widely dispersed among the general populations of New York City and Miami? Previous research suggests that West Indians are concentrated in Black neighborhoods, in both New York City and Miami (Foner 2001; Boswell and Jones 2006).[18] Still, West Indians are moderately segregated from Non-Hispanic Blacks, in both New York City and Miami (Row 8 in Table 13.5). They are not evenly distributed throughout Black communities, but tend to concentrate in selected neighborhoods. Because West Indians are concentrated in Black neighborhoods, the data show they are strongly segregated from NHWs (Row 9). Row 10 shows that West Indians are also strongly segregated from Hispanics.

A strong argument for excluding Haitians from West Indians can be made. Haitians are culturally distinct and can be shown to be at least moderately segregated from the Non-Hispanic Black populations in New York City and Miami (Row 11 in Table 13.5). Haitians speak a type of Creole and some also speak French because Haiti was originally a French colony. The vast majority of other West Indians speak English because their islands of origin were former British colonies.[19] What happens when we extract Haitians from West Indians? The IDs in Table 13.5 indicate a moderate degree of segregation between Haitians and West Indians when excluding Haitians (Row 12 in Table 13.5). Table 13.5 also shows that Haitians are heavily segregated from both NHWs (Row 13) and Hispanics (Row 14) in both New York City and Miami.

Figure 13.5 (a and b) for West Indians (excluding Haitians) can be compared to Figure 13.6 (a and b) for Haitians and Figure 13.2 (a and b) for Blacks as a whole, to help understand the varying residential patterns for West Indians (excluding Haitians) and Haitians in both New York City and Miami. It is clear that the vast majority of both West Indians and Haitians live in Black neighborhoods in each city. However, it is also clear that they are not evenly dispersed throughout the Black areas, as noted earlier in this chapter. There is some overlap between where Haitians and West Indians live, as their residential segregation is only moderate. Figure 13.5 (a and b) shows West Indians also are located mainly within Black neighborhoods, which corroborates the findings of other studies mentioned earlier.

In NYC, West Indians are concentrated in three major areas: 1) the northern Bronx, including such neighborhoods as Baychester, Wakefield, and Williamsbridge; 2) central Brooklyn, including such neighborhoods as Brownsville, Crown Heights, East Flatbush, and Flatbush; and 3) southeastern Queens, including such neighborhoods as Brookville, Rochdale, Rosedale, and St. Albans. Haitians live in some of these same neighborhoods, but are not concentrated in the northern Bronx, and tend to be clustered on the western edge of the concentration of West Indians in central Brooklyn and on the southeastern edge of the West Indians in southeastern Queens, especially in Brookville and Rosedale.

In Miami, West Indians are concentrated in two major areas: 1) the northern half of the northern Black wedge of Miami discussed earlier, including such upper lower and middle-class neighborhoods as Coral City, Norland, and North Miami; and 2) the upper lower- and middle-class neighborhoods of southern Miami, including such neighborhoods as Cutler Ridge, Perrine, and Richmond Heights. Because Haitians are only moderately segregated from West Indians in Miami (Row 12 in Table 13.5), there is some overlap in residential location, but the Haitians are more noticeable in the southernmost neighborhoods of Miami's northern Black wedge, especially in the poorer areas of Liberty City and Little Haiti. In southern Miami, the Haitians are more concentrated in the poorer neighborhoods, including those surrounding Florida City. The distributions of Haitians and West Indians in Miami suggests the possibilities of a class distinction. The West Indians are more concentrated in middle-class Black neighborhoods, whereas the Haitians are more concentrated in poorer areas, although this distinction is by no means absolute. Because Haitians and West Indians live mainly in Black neighborhoods, it is not surprising that the IDs shown in Table 13.5 reflect their strong segregation from both NHWs (Row 13) and Hispanics (Row 14).

Figure 13.5.
Number of West Indians Excluding Haitians: 2000.

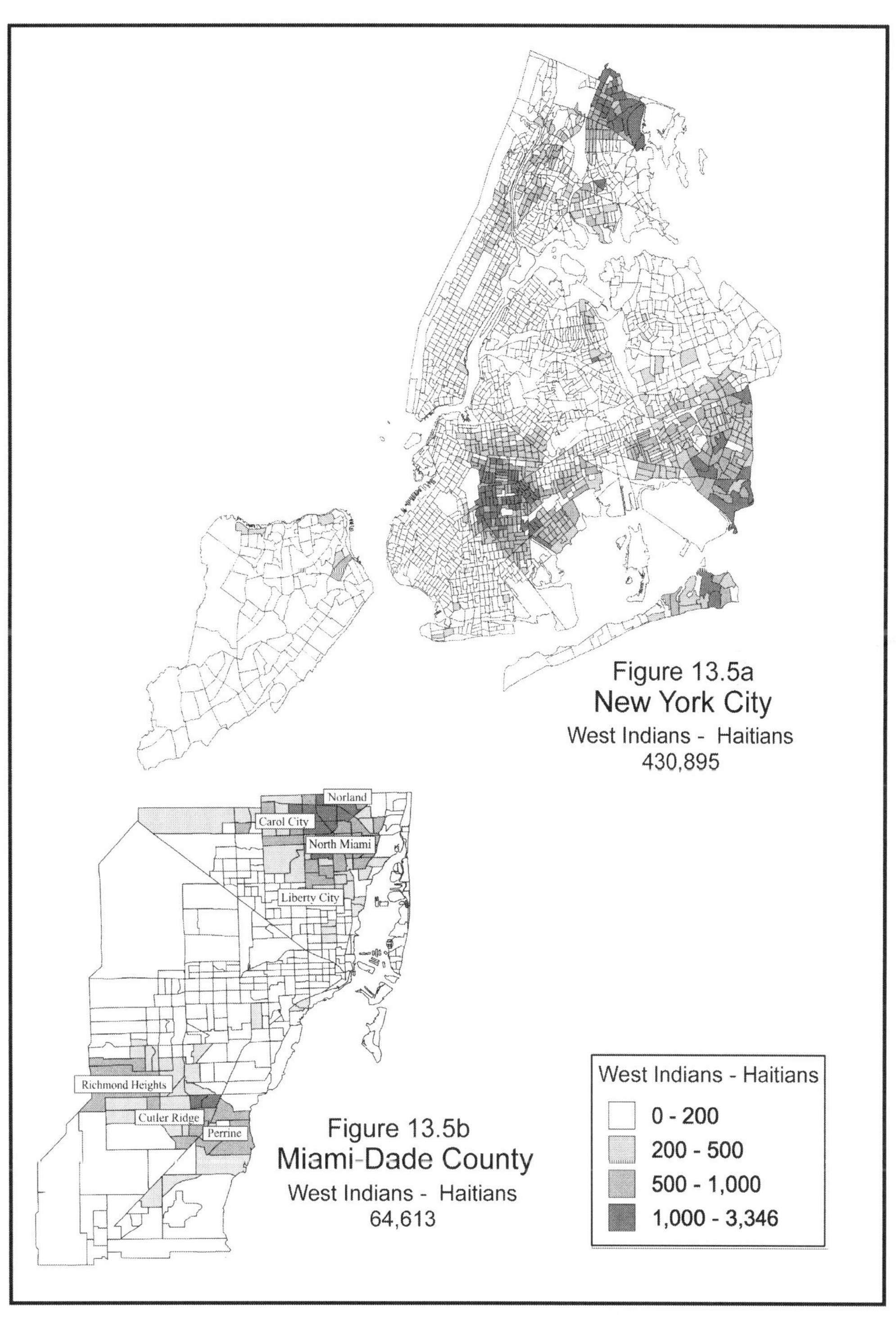

Figure 13.6.
Number of Haitians: 2000.

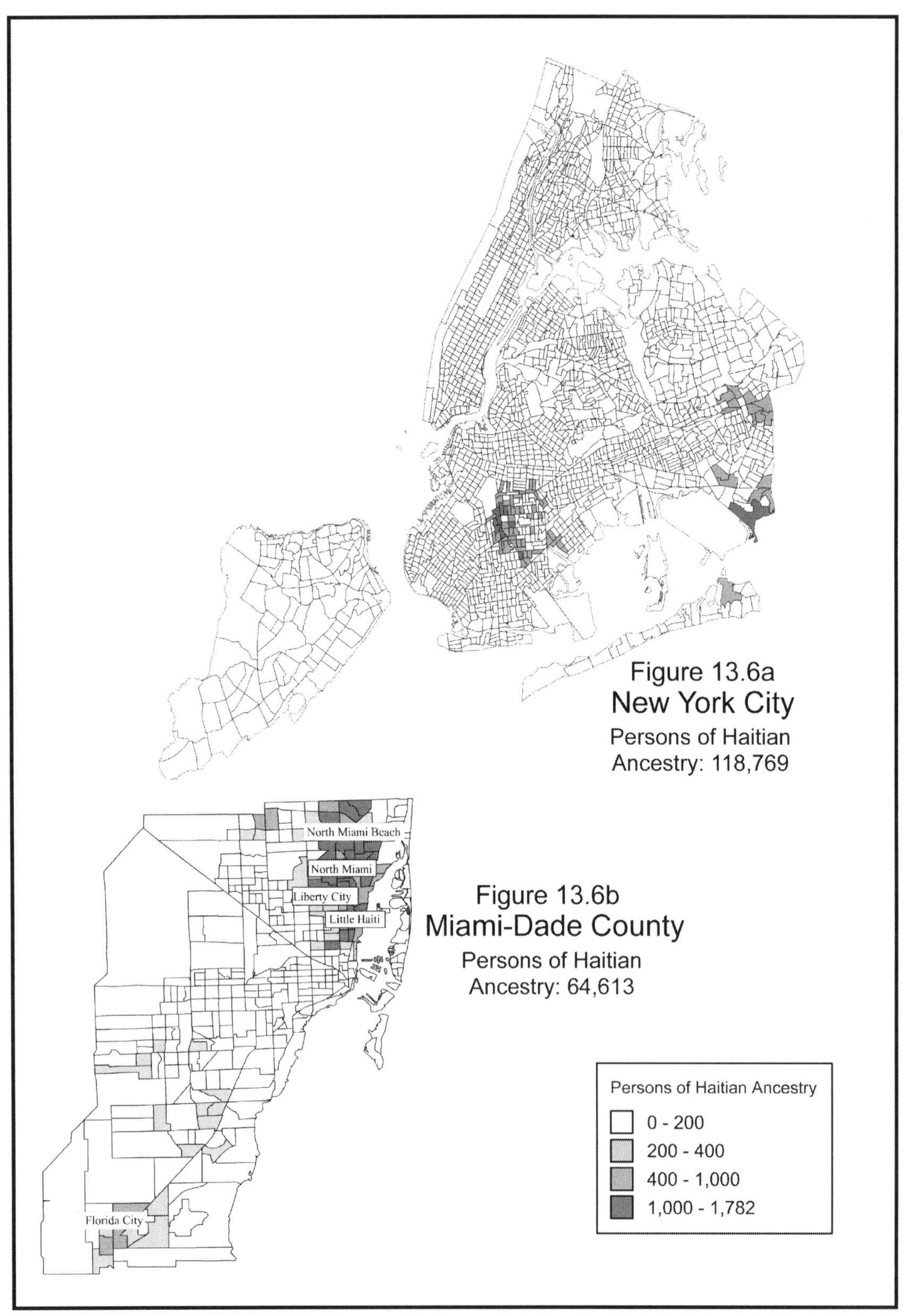

WEST INDIANS AND JAMAICANS

Rows 15–18 in Table 13.5 compare Jamaicans with West Indians as a whole and with Non-Hispanic Blacks, Non-Hispanic Whites, and Hispanics. Figure 13.7 (a and b) shows that Jamaicans are especially concentrated in the West Indian neighborhoods of the Black areas in both New York City and Miami. The first preference of Jamaicans is to live among other Jamaicans. Their second preference is to live in neighborhoods containing other West Indians. Their final preference is to live in Black neighborhoods. Jamaicans are less segregated from West Indians (excluding Jamaicans) (Row 16 of Table 13.5) than are Haitians (Row 12) in both New York City and Miami. In fact, the IDs for comparing Jamaicans with West Indians (excluding Jamaicans) (Row 16) and Non-Hispanic Blacks (Row 15) in New York City are low. In Miami, these IDs are just barely above the low range. Conway and Bigby (1992), using 1980 Census data, found this **same triple layering effect** for West Indians in New York City and Crowder and Tedrow (2001), using 1990 Census data, noted the same tendency. Thus, this spatial process of triple layering has been extant in New York City for at least three decades.

The same triple layering process seems to be occurring in Miami, although large-scale West Indian immigration to Miami is a more recent phenomenon (mainly since the 1970s) than in New York City (where West Indian immigration is more than a century old). In Miami, there are no West Indian (excluding Haitian) dominated neighborhoods (where West Indians constitute as much as 50 percent of a census tract's population) and there are only two census tracts (one in Little Haiti and one in North Miami) where Haitians comprise half or more of the total population. Conversely, in NYC, there are a number of neighborhoods where West Indians, Haitians, and Jamaicans dominate their neighborhoods.

Why do West Indians in both New York City and Miami exhibit a preference for Black neighborhoods? Foner suggests four possible answers (Foner 2001). First, there is a fear of racial prejudice. Most West Indians think they can escape most racial prejudice by living in predominantly Black areas. Second, because West Indians have higher average socioeconomic status (SES) than U.S.-born Blacks (see below), they can more successfully compete with local Blacks for business and better jobs in Black neighborhoods than in NHW neighborhoods. Third, the large Black population serves as a ripe market for goods and services produced by West Indians. Fourth, migration is a network-driven process, in which information flows through immigrant networks that tend to perpetuate ethnic neighborhoods. West Indians already residing in Black neighborhoods attract additional West Indian and Jamaican immigrants to their neighborhoods. The established residents provide information to prospective immigrants about job opportunities, housing, health care, education, and possibly provide a place to live until newer residents can support themselves economically (the process of "chain migration").

Sub-Saharan African-born

Rows 19–22 in Table 13.5 compare the Sub-Saharan African-born (SSA) with Non-Hispanic Blacks, West Indians, NHWs, and Hispanics.[20] In 2000, almost 69,000 Sub-Saharan Africans lived in NYC, while only 2,922 lived in Miami (U.S. Census 2000, PCTIA). Studies report that African immigrants have higher socioeconomic status (SES) than U.S.-born Blacks (Logan 2007). This contention will be tested later in this chapter for New York City and Miami.

Sub-Saharan Africans are moderately and highly segregated from Non-Hispanic Blacks (Row 19 of Table 13.5) in New York City and Miami, respectively. Sub-Saharan Africans also are moderately segregated from West Indians (Row 20), and they are moderately to highly segregated from NHWs and Hispanics (Rows 21 and 22). Thus, Sub-Saharan Africans are notably segregated from all the major racial and ethnic groups in both New York City and Miami.[21]

Figure 13.8 (a and b) shows the residential patterns for Sub-Saharan Africans in both New York City and Miami. In NYC, Sub-Saharan Africans are weakly concentrated in areas surrounding the three main areas of Black population, but also are located in non-traditional Black areas, including the Manhattan neighborhoods of the Lower East Side, Manhattan Valley, and the Upper West Side, and areas next to Chinatown. Sub-Saharan Africans also are found in the Brooklyn neighborhoods of Coney Island, Fort Hamilton, and Sea Gate.

A similar pattern is seen for Miami, where Sub-Saharan Africans live in some of the more affluent northern Black neighborhoods, including Carol City, Norland, North Miami, and North Miami Beach and in the southern neighborhoods of Cutler Ridge and Richmond Heights. In addition, Pinecrest, a traditionally White, upper-class area next to Biscayne Bay, also shows a Sub-Saharan Africans presence. The higher SES of Sub-Saharan Africans may cause them to eschew the poorer Black neighborhoods.

Figure 13.7.
Number of Jamaicans: 2000.

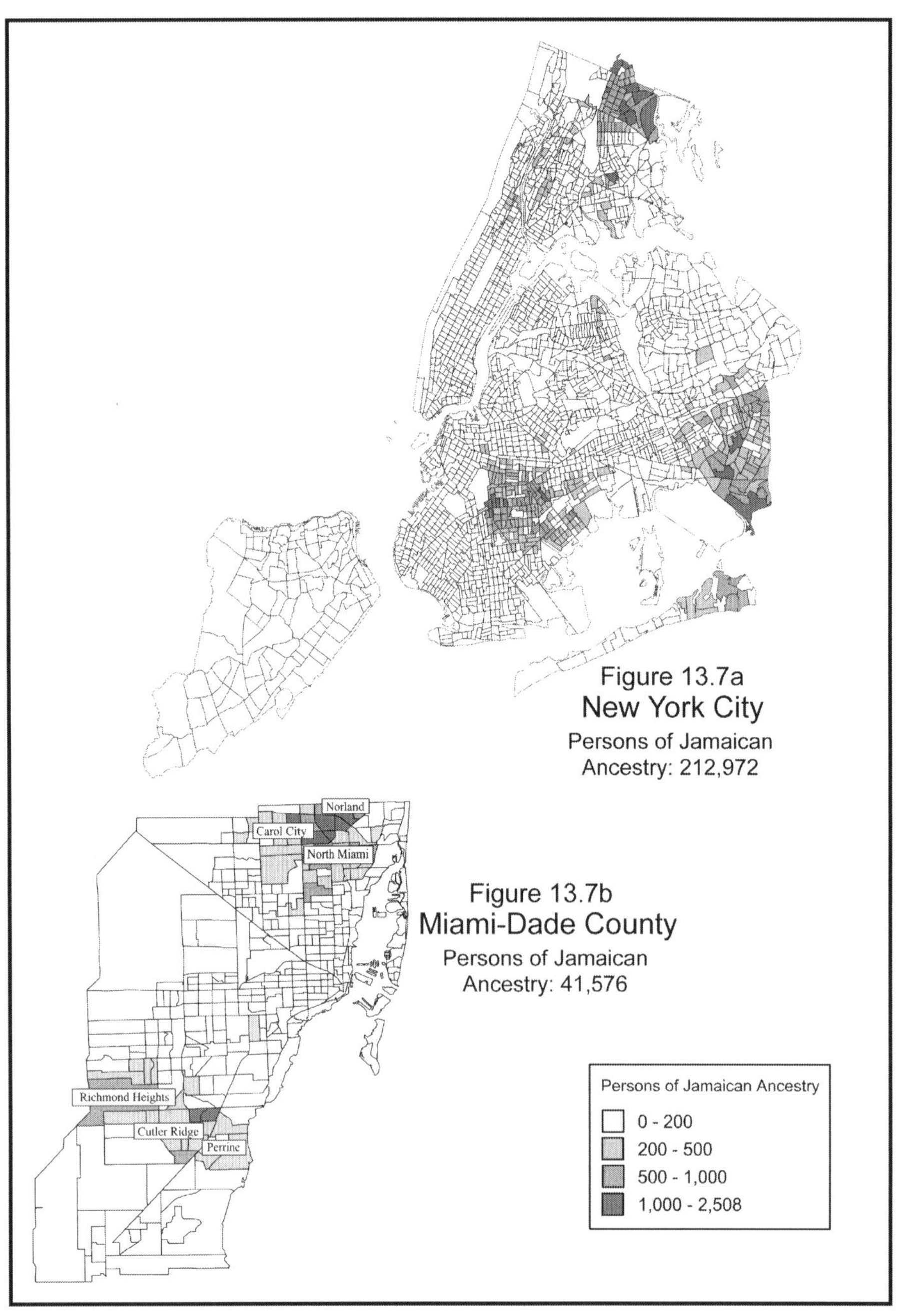

Figure 13.8.
Number of Persons Born in Sub-Saharan Africa: 2000.

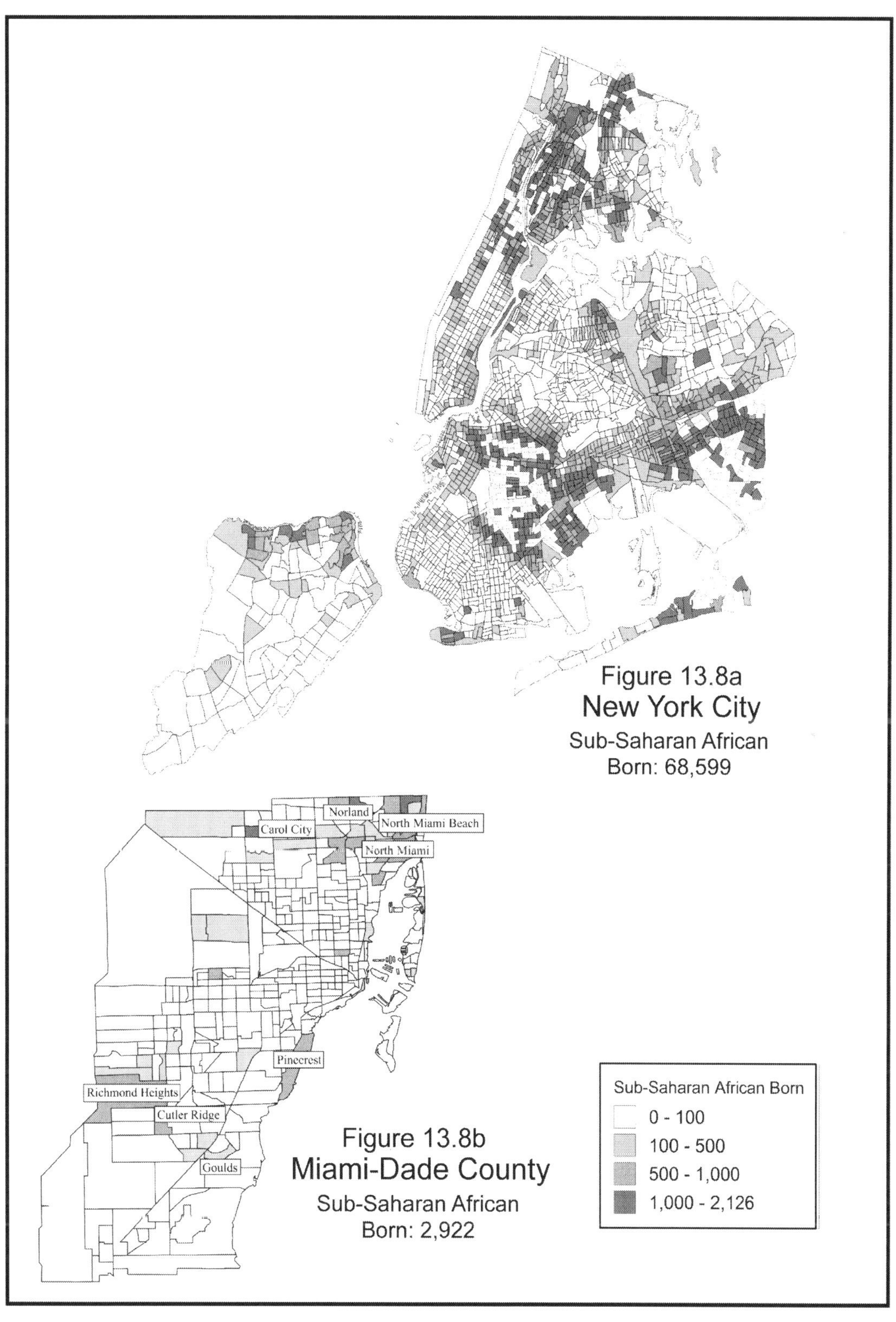

INCOME AND RESIDENTIAL LOCATION

Income may be an important factor affecting the residential location of Blacks and may be one reason Blacks are highly segregated from Whites, given the much lower average incomes of Blacks (see below). Rows 23–25 in Table 13.5 compare income levels ("in poverty" vs. "not in poverty") for the three major groups (Blacks, Hispanics, and NHWs) to examine if, for each group, middle and upper income households live in neighborhoods with lower income households. Surprisingly, the ID figures in Table 13.5 suggest that income is not much of a factor affecting where Blacks live. For New York City and Miami, the IDs are 31.1 and 28.8 (Row 23), respectively, both well within the low range. Similar low IDs are shown for Hispanic (27.4 and 26.8 in Row 24) and NHWs (35.3 and 30.2 in Row 25). Thus, for all three groups, income does not appear to segregate the population nearly as much as one might think. We are reluctant to extend these results to suggest that income is not a factor in residential location, as this seems counterintuitive.[22] All we can say definitively is that, at the census tract scale, whether people live below or above poverty does not appear to make a significant difference in residential location in either New York City or Miami.

THE SOCIOECONOMIC STATUS OF BLACKS IN NEW YORK CITY AND MIAMI

Socioeconomic status (SES) is a multivariate concept that usually includes measures of education, occupation, and income. For this analysis, SES includes two measures of education (percent of persons age 25 years and over who have not graduated high school and percent of persons with a four-year college degree), two occupation variables (percentage employed in high-paying management and professional jobs and the percentage in lower-paying construction, extraction, maintenance, production, and transportation jobs),[23] and two income variables (mean per capita income and percent of persons in families below the poverty level). In this section, the SES of Blacks in NYC, Miami, and the United States as a whole is investigated by comparing Blacks to Hispanics and NHWs in Table 13.6 and by comparing Black Haitians, Black Jamaicans, Other Blacks of West Indian Ancestry, and Sub-Saharan African-born Blacks in Table 13.7. The results comparing NYC and Miami should be interpreted in light of the differences in cost of living between the two cities. Table 13.6 shows that:

- Blacks in New York City generally have higher SES than Blacks in Miami, with better jobs, higher incomes, and lower poverty levels.
- Blacks in New York City also have generally higher SES than Hispanics in New York City and Hispanics in the United States.
- Blacks in Miami generally have lower SES than Hispanics in Miami, due to job competition from immigrant Hispanics. Miami is now a majority Hispanic city and, many times, Hispanics favor hiring other Hispanics (who speak Spanish), especially when they are in competition with Blacks (most of whom do not speak Spanish).
- Blacks in NYC, Miami, and the United States as a whole have lower SES than NHWs.

Table 13.7 shows that:

- In Miami, Black Haitians, Black Jamaicans, and (to a lesser extent) Other Blacks of West Indian Ancestry tend to have lower SES than Blacks in New York City and the United States as a whole. In general, Miami's West Indian groups have lower education levels, less favorable occupation structures, lower incomes, and higher poverty rates.
- The SES of Black Jamaicans and the Blacks of Other West Indian Ancestry in New York City and in the United States tend to be similar.

Table 13.6.
Socioeconomic Status
Blacks, Hispanics, and Non-Hispanic Whites
New York City, Miami, and the United States: 2000.

Socioeconomic Status Categories	New York City	Miami	United States
Blacks * (*Percentages*)			
No High School Degree	29.8	26.9	27.6
BA Degree or Higher	15.9	11.7	14.5
Management, Professional, and Related	28.2	22.9	25.3
Construction, Extraction, Maintenance, Production, and Transportation	16.3	22.3	24.9
Per Capita Income	$15,219	$12,022	$14,222
% Below Poverty	25.6	28.3	24.7
Hispanics ** (*Percentages*)			
No High School Degree	46.6	38.8	47.6
BA Degree or Higher	10.6	18.1	10.5
Management, Professional, and Related	19.6	25.4	18.1
Construction, Extraction, Maintenance, Production, and Transportation	26.4	25.4	34.3
Per Capita Income	$12,206	$16,194	$12,111
% Below Poverty	30.8	17.5	22.6
Non-Hispanic Whites (NHWs) *** (*Percentages*)			
No High School Degree	15.3	11.2	14.6
BA Degree or Higher	41.9	37.9	27.0
Management, Professional, and Related	51.2	47.0	36.6
Construction, Extraction, Maintenance, Production, and Transportation	11.6	11.4	22.8
Per Capita Income	$36,800	$31,059	$24,819
% Below Poverty	11.5%	5.1%	8.1%

* Blacks alone or in combination with other races.
** Hispanics may be of any race.
*** Non-Hispanic Whites alone.
Note: Educational levels are for persons age 25 and over; occupational data, for persons age 16 and over.
Source: U.S. Bureau of the Census, *2000 Census of Population and Housing*, Summary File 4, Tables DP-2 and DP-3.

Table 13.7.
Socioeconomic Status
Black Haitians, Black Jamaicans, Other Blacks of West Indian Ancestry, and Blacks Born in Sub-Saharan Africa
New York City, Miami, and the United States: 2000.

Socioeconomic Status Categories	New York City	Miami	United States
Black Haitians (*Percentages*)			
No High School Degree	29.2	47.2	35.1
BA Degree or Higher	18.3	9.2	15.9
Management, Professional, and Related	24.3	14.7	21.0
Construction, Extraction, Maintenance, Production, and Transportation	18.9	25.8	21.2
Per Capita Income	$18,221	$13,255	$18,109
% Below Poverty	20.2	29.6	20.2
Black Jamaicans (*Percentages*)			
No High School Degree	28.6	29.9	26.2
BA Degree or Higher	18.3	14.2	19.3
Management, Professional, and Related	25.8	23.5	26.1
Construction, Extraction, Maintenance, Production, and Transportation	17.5	19.7	19.0
Per Capita Income	$23,273	$20,292	$23,970
% Below Poverty	15.0	15.2	16.1
Other Blacks of West Indian Ancestry (*Percentages*)			
No High School Degree	25.3	22.3	19.8
BA Degree or Higher	17.2	18.3	21.4
Management, Professional, and Related	26.1	29.8	30.4
Construction, Extraction, Maintenance, Production, and Transportation	18.9	15.3	17.8
Per Capita Income	$23,235	$18,009	$24,424
% Below Poverty	15.4	23.5	16.4
Blacks Born in Sub-Saharan Africa * (*Percentages*)			
No High School Degree	20.7	10.8	13.8
BA Degree or Higher	30.3	47.6	37.9
Management, Professional, and Related	28.4	49.1	31.9
Construction, Extraction, Maintenance, Production, and Transportation	19.6	10.3	21.1
Per Capita Income	$21,006	$25,972	$22,026
% Below Poverty	21.4	30.9	21.6

Note: Educational levels are for persons age 25 and over; occupational data, for persons age 16 and over.
Sources: U.S. Bureau of the Census, *2000 Census of Population*, Public Use Microdata Sample (PUMS), 1% sample for U.S. and 5% samples for New York City and Miami.

- Haitians tend to be poorer than Jamaicans and Other West Indians in NYC, Miami, and the United States as a whole. Jamaicans and Other West Indians tend to be similar to each other. This is another argument (in addition to culture differences) for analyzing Haitians separately from West Indians.
- The Sub-Saharan African-born Blacks (SSA) in New York City have higher SES than both Blacks and Hispanics in New York City and the United States as a whole. SSA in Miami also appear to have higher SES than Blacks and Hispanics.[24]
- Sub-Saharan Africans have higher SES than Haitians in NYC, Miami, and in the United States, but a somewhat lower SES than Jamaicans and Other West Indians. Miami may be an exception to this latter statement.[25]
- Sub-Saharan Africans have higher SES than U.S.-born Blacks, Hispanics, and Haitians in New York City and in the United States. This also may be true for Miami. On the other hand, Sub-Saharan Africans have lower SES than NHWs, Jamaicans, and the Other West Indians. Portes and Rumbaut also have noted the relatively high SES of SSA and suggest that this may be because Sub-Saharan Africans have immigrated in large numbers only since passage of the *Amendments to the National Immigration Act of 1965* (Portes and Rumbaut 2006). Since few Sub-Saharan Africans had relatives in the United States, most qualified for entry because they possessed job skills needed in the U.S. Thus, Sub-Saharan Africans were more positively selected than were immigrants who arrived because of the family preference system. In recent years, more than 60 percent of legal United States immigrants have been admitted due to family ties,[26] rather than because of their job skills or their potential to contribute to the United States' economy.

SUMMARY AND CONCLUSIONS

The purpose of this chapter has been to illustrate some of the differences between the Black populations of New York City and Miami. It also has shown the salience of recognizing that the Black population is not a homogeneous group and that proper understanding behooves us to deconstruct this population into its significant components: U.S.-born Blacks, West Indians as a whole, Haitians, Jamaicans, and Sub-Saharan African-born Blacks.

The significant immigrations to New York City and to Miami have transformed the composition of their Black populations far in excess of most other United States cities: close to one-third of Blacks in both cities are immigrants, compared to only 7 percent of the Black population of the United States as a whole. Black immigrants are both a racial group and an ethnic group. Their race almost always influences the immigrants' and their children's decision to assimilate into the African American subculture instead of the White American mainstream (Waters 1999; 2001). On the other hand, their ethnicity results in cultural, social, and economic differences from U.S.-born Blacks.

Black immigrants to New York City and Miami have derived overwhelmingly from the Non-Hispanic islands of the Caribbean (the West Indies). Although the U.S. Bureau of the Census considers Haitians to be West Indians, our analysis provides good reason to separate Haitians from other West Indian groups. Haitians speak either Creole or French, while most other West Indians speak English as a first language. Haitians come from an island with a very different history than other Caribbean islands. Economically, Haitians tend to have much lower socioeconomic status than other West Indians. Haitians also have a moderately different residential pattern than other West Indians.

The Black populations of both New York City and Miami have been decreasing through domestic net out-migration, despite continued immigration and a positive natural increase. The domestic net out-migration is related to the immigration of large numbers of Blacks, and even larger numbers of Hispanics, which has created a low-cost labor force that competes with U.S.-born Blacks for lower-paying jobs. In Miami, NHWs have been migrating out of Miami since the late 1970s. Between 2000 and 2006, the NHW population decreased by more than 33,000 persons, despite a positive net international immigration and a positive natural increase for NHWs. Probably close to 20,000 NHWs have been leaving Miami each year for the past six years.[27]

This chapter also has explored Black segregation in both New York City and Miami. Blacks have been heavily segregated from Whites in both New York City and Miami. Blacks also have been significantly segregated from Hispanics. However, Non-Hispanic Blacks are less segregated from Hispanics in New York City than in Miami, probably because of their country of origin. More Hispanics in New York City are Black, since a significant number of them derive from the Dominican Republic and Puerto Rico, both of which have sizable Black and mulatto populations. In Miami, Hispanics have tended to come from the middle- and upper-classes of Cuba and Latin America and tend to be White. Thus, the color lines between Hispanics and Blacks in Miami has been more sharply drawn, whereas in New York City there has been more overlap between Blacks and Hispanics.

West Indians have tended to live in Black neighborhoods and have been therefore moderately segregated from Non-Hispanic Blacks, but heavily segregated from NHWs. However, West Indians are not evenly distributed throughout Black neighborhoods. Rather, they have tended to concentrate in West Indian enclaves located within Black areas. Furthermore, a tendency exists for Jamaicans and Haitians to concentrate in selected neighborhoods within West Indian enclaves. This residential pattern is termed a triple layering effect.

In Miami, Sub-Saharan African-born Blacks (SSA) have been most heavily segregated from Hispanics and less segregated from West Indians and NHWs. In NYC, Sub-Saharan Africans have been most strongly segregated from NHWs and least segregated from Non-Hispanic Blacks. However, these are complicated patterns that are difficult to explain. The Sub-Saharan African population is a varied group, some of whom have lived in Black neighborhoods, while others have lived in middle-class and upper-class neighborhoods, regardless of their ethnic or racial character.

Interestingly, we have found that on a census tract scale, only slight segregation levels exist between Blacks in poverty and Blacks not in poverty in both New York City and Miami. The same has been true for the Hispanics and NHWs populations in these two cities.

The last section of this chapter has investigated the SES of Blacks and their subpopulations in comparison with other demographic groups. In NYC, Blacks have had higher SES than Hispanics, but much lower SES than NHWs. In Miami, Blacks have had lower SES than Hispanics and NHWs. Hispanics have been economically and politically more successful in Miami than in NYC. In many respects, Hispanics control much of the economy of Miami. The greater success of Hispanics in Miami than in New York City has probably been related to their whiteness (resulting in less discrimination), the fact that many were middle- to upper-class in their country of origin, their overwhelming numerical domination of Miami's population, and their adroit political organization.

Haitians have been shown to have lower SES than both Jamaicans and Other West Indians. Furthermore, Jamaicans and Other West Indians also have had higher SES than U.S.-born Blacks and Hispanics in NYC, Miami, and in the United States, but not NHWs. Although Haitians have had the lowest SES among the West Indians, they still have had higher SES than Blacks in New York City and the United States as a whole, but not in Miami.

Haitians in Miami have tended to be poorer than Haitians in New York City and the rest of the United States. Haitians have been immigrating for a longer period of time to New York City than to Miami.[28] Also, Haitian migrants to New York City were more positively selected in terms of their SES because the cost of moving to New York City is higher (Boswell 1983). In Miami, many Haitians arrived illegally aboard small boats and with fewer resources.

Sub-Saharan African-born Black (SSA) immigrants have achieved an SES level comparable to Jamaicans and Other West Indians in NYC, Miami, and the United States as a whole. Virtually all have arrived since the 1970s, mostly during the 1990s. One reason Sub-Saharan Africans have done comparatively well is that most were admitted to the United States because of their high skill levels and educational achievements.

This chapter has made it clear that the Black populations of New York City and Miami are much more diverse than is usually recognized. Unless the immigration policy of the United States changes, there is every reason to believe that continued Black immigration to New York City and Miami will continue to increase and so will the diversity of those cities' Black populations. Moreover, what has been occurring in New York City and Miami may be a harbinger of things to come for the United States as a whole. A recent report from the Population Reference Bureau (Kent 2007) indicates that immigration contributed at least one-fifth of the growth in the U.S. Black population from 2001–2006. In some ways, this chapter has understated the current diversity of this population, because the 2000 U.S. Census data, which provided most of the information for this investigation, does not include this recent surge of foreign-born Blacks. An important implication of the changing nature of the Black population is the recognition that traditional economic and social policies to help this population may need revision as its diversity increases. Blacks are not one homogeneous group.

NOTES

[1] Although settlement in New York City by Europeans began in 1614 with the establishment of a Dutch fur trading post, the city was not incorporated in its present form (by consolidating its five boroughs), until 1898 with a population of about 3.4 million. Although Miami was first settled by Europeans in 1567 with the establishment of a Spanish mission, when the city was incorporated in 1896, the total population was only about 300.

[2] New York City had approximately 2.2 million Blacks vs. Miami's 0.5 million in 2006. About 26 percent of the population of New York City is Black, compared to 20 percent in Miami.

[3] This historical description is drawn primarily from Lobo and Salvo (2000).

[4] According to Boswell, *Profile of Black Population in Miami-Dade County*, p. 27, from 1990 to 2000, 166,800 NHWs migrated out of Miami to other parts of the United States, and there was a positive net immigration from other countries of about 39,000 NHWs and a natural increase of almost 19,000 NHWs. Therefore, the total decrease in the Non-Hispanic White population during the decade of the 1990s was reduced to about 109,000. From 1990 to 2000, 28,000 Blacks migrated out of Miami to other parts of the United States, but this was more than compensated for by the net immigration of 78,000 Blacks, primarily from the Caribbean, and a natural increase of 66,000 Blacks. According to the 2006 American Community Survey (ACS), the Black population decreased in Miami by almost 2,000 between 2000 and 2006, so the number of domestic out-migrants must have increased enough to offset the positive natural increase and the continued heavy immigration of Blacks that occurred during this six-year period. Note, however, that this decrease is within the margin of error of the ACS, which is a sample survey.

[5] These trends have continued from earlier years. Data available for 1980–1990 show that while the number of Blacks in Miami increased by 133,000, a natural increase of 70,000 and a positive foreign net migration of 85,000 was offset by a negative domestic net migration of 22,000. About 50,000 Blacks migrated into Miami and 72,000 migrated out from 1980 to 1990. See Sheskin (1992).

[6] *Foreign-born* are defined by the United States government according to the citizenship of their parents. Thus, *Native-born Blacks* born outside of the United States were born to at least one parent who was a United States citizen. Thus, not all persons born outside of the United States are *foreign-born*.

[7] For additional maps and data on race and ancestry in South Florida (Miami-Dade, Broward, and Palm Beach counties) see Winsberg (2006).

[8] A total of 27 maps were created, but space considerations obviate publishing them all. We only include those maps that seemed most interesting. Figure 13.1 shows place names for selected neighborhoods in NYC. New York City has more than 2,200 census tracts (compared to Miami's 348) and, to avoid clutter, a separate map is used to show New York City place names. Place names for Miami are shown on each Miami map. All data for the maps were derived from Summary Files 1, 2, and 4 from the *2000 Census of Population and Housing*.

[9] The index of dissimilarity (ID)= $\Sigma \mid X_i - Y_i \mid / 2$

where:

X_i = the percent of the first population in the ith census tract
Y_i = the percent of the second population in the ith census tract

[10] No universal agreement exists in the segregation literature on the values of these percentages, but most authors employ percentages close to these figures. (Massey and Denton 1993; Lobo and Salvo 2000; Crowder and Tedrow 2001).

[11] The data are derived from both a complete count and a 17 percent sample from the *2000 Census of Population and Housing*. The data on race and Hispanics (White Hispanics, Black Hispanics, NHWs, Non-Hispanic Blacks, and All Hispanics) are from the complete count in Summary File 1. The data for West Indians, Haitians, Jamaicans, and Sub-Saharan African-born are from Summary File 3. The data for Blacks, Hispanics, and NHWs in poverty are from Summary File 4. Because the data derived from Summary Files 3 and 4 are based on a 17 percent sample, some sampling error exists.

[12] The residential distribution of Blacks in 2000 is strikingly similar to the residential distribution in 1970. See David B. Longbrake and Woodrow W. Nichols, Jr., *Sunshine and Shadows in Metropolitan Miami* (Cambridge, MA: Ballinger Publishing Company 1976), p. 19. This illustrates the significant "permanence" of Black areas.

[13] Unlike the situation for Blacks noted in the previous footnote, because the percentage Hispanic in Miami increased from 24 percent in 1970 to 57 percent in 2000, the residential distribution of Hispanics is far more geographically dispersed in 2000 than it was in 1970 (Longbrake and Nichols 1976).

[14] In Miami, 89 percent of Hispanics classified themselves as White and 11 percent, as some other race in the 2000 Census, whereas in New York City the comparable figures were 41 percent and 59 percent. U.S. Bureau of the Census, *2000 Census of Population and Housing*, Summary File 1, Tables P8 and P10.

[15] Although Cuba has a large Black population, most (but not all) Cubans who immigrated to the United States (particularly in the late 1950s and early 1960s) were from the White, upper- and middle-class population who fled the communist Castro revolution. The middle- and upper-classes were more likely to lose their houses, property, and businesses and therefore had the greatest incentive to emigrate to the United States. Furthermore, most Latin Americans who have moved to Miami also come from the middle- and upper-classes of countries like Argentina, Colombia, Peru, and Venezuela and they are also more likely to be White.

[16] When presenting ancestry data, the U.S. Bureau of the Census includes Haitians under "West Indians." See, for example U.S. Bureau of the Census, *2000 Census of Population and Housing*, Summary File 3, Table PCT18, "Ancestry (Total Categories Tallied) for People with One or More Ancestry Categories Reported."

[17] In the 2000 Census, about 90 percent of persons of West Indian ancestry classified themselves as Black, as did about 96 percent of persons of Jamaican ancestry, and 98 percent of persons of Haitian ancestry. U.S. Bureau of the Census, *2000 Census of Population and Housing*, 1 percent Public Use Microdata Sample (PUMS).

[18] For instance, see Lobo and Salvo (2000); Crowder and Tedrow (2001); and Boswell and Jones (2006).

[19] While there are some West Indians in New York City and Miami from French and Dutch-speaking Caribbean Islands, they are so few in number that the U.S. Bureau of the Census does not list them separately. U.S. Bureau of the Census, *2000 Census of Population and Housing,* Summary File 3, Table PCT19.

[20] Only persons *born in Sub-Saharan Africa* were used for this analysis, rather than persons of *African Ancestry*, because the African Ancestry data include many U.S.-born Blacks whose African ancestry traces back many generations.

[21] The fact that the absolute number of Sub-Saharan Africans is so small, particularly in Miami, complicates the interpretation of the Indexes of Dissimilarity. Because their numbers are so few, Sub-Saharan Africans simply can not be found everywhere.

[22] Census tracts may be too large to capture an income effect. If the analysis were completed at the block group level, the findings might be different. Also, dividing the population into only two income groups (above and below poverty) may be too coarse a metric.

[23] These lower-paying jobs are sometimes called 3-D jobs (dirty, or dangerous, or demanding in some other way).

[24] The analysis of Sub-Saharan African-born Blacks in Miami is subject to significant sampling error because the sample is only 90. With this sample size, the margin of error around percentages of about 10 percent is plus or minus 6.2 percent; around 30 percent, plus or minus 9.5 percent; and around 50 percent, plus or minus 10.3 percent.

[25] Again, the small sample for Miami demands caution in interpreting these results. See previous footnote.

[26] During the 2003–2005 period, almost 64 percent of the legal immigrants entering the United States did so through family preferences. About 17 percent entered under employment-base preferences. Philip Martin and Elizabeth Midgley, "Immigration: Shaping and Reshaping America," *Population Bulletin*, Vol. 61, No. 4, p. 5.

[27] The average annual loss of NHWs (33,000 divided by 6 years equals 5,500 persons per year) was less than 20,000 because some of this loss was compensated for by immigration and natural increase.

[28] Haitian migration to New York City began during the late 1950s and 1960s, whereas large-scale Haitian migration to Miami did not commence until the mid-1970s.

Chapter 14

Jamaicans in Broward County, Florida

JOHN W. FRAZIER

INTRODUCTION

The last half century has witnessed nearly three million arrivals from nations around the world into New York City, making it a continuous immigrant gateway. Immigration law (Kraly and Miyares 2001; Foner 2001) and powerful ethnic networks (Massey 1999) have been credited for the recent and continuing surge. Caribbean flows have been particularly strong to New York City. Foner noted the relatively strong pre-1965 West Indian population as a cultural attraction and support network that pulled West Indians to the City (Foner 2001, 2000, 1987). Economic opportunity in the City supported this movement of "two great waves" of immigration, the latter containing greater ethnic diversity and more substantial social capital related to professional skills and education (Foner 2000).

Foner, in *New Immigrants in New York* (Foner 2001) explores the various impacts of immigrants on the City, and the City on Black immigrants, stressing the need to compare other places with large numbers of West Indians to the patterns and experiences of those cultures in New York. Boswell and Sheskin (chapter 13) provide a useful comparison of the West Indian populations in New York City and Miami-Dade. They note that Jamaicans are the largest West Indian population in both locations. South Florida, where proximity to homeland, economic opportunity, and easy access to co-ethnics encouraged their influx, contains two important Black immigrant gateways, Miami and Ft. Lauderdale. Within South Florida another migration process has occurred. As Miami-Dade County has continued to grow and change, Jamaicans, among others, have chosen to migrate northward to Broward, Palm Beach, and other locations.

This chapter focuses on Broward County's Jamaicans as they emerge as a dominant minority ethnic group and establish a new cultural center for themselves and other West Indian groups. The purpose of this chapter is to examine West Indian and particularly Jamaican migration, socioeconomic status (SES), and settlement patterns and to compare them to patterns established in New York City.

Before examining Jamaican experiences in Broward County, a brief review of literature dealing with West Indian, and in particular Jamaican culture, ethnicity, and experiences in New York City, is provided as a basis for comparison with Broward County.

WEST INDIAN AND JAMAICAN EXPERIENCES AND PATTERNS IN NEW YORK CITY

West Indians have been New York City's largest immigrant group since the 1965 Hart-Celler Act revolutionized U.S. immigration. Their population exceeded a half million and accounted for approximately one-third of the City's Black population by the year 2000 (Foner 2001). Among West Indians, Jamaicans are the largest ethnic group in the U.S. and in New York City. Although their attraction to the City has diminished, New York remains their largest center and provides the basis for comparison with other locales of increasing importance to this group. Given place differences and the variety of place experiences in the U.S., it is important to examine ethnicity on a place-by-place basis prior to formulating general theory.

In New York City, West Indians have tended to cluster in and around native-Black neighborhoods. They also share some cultural traits and interests. These commonalities have contributed to White perceptions of a monolithic Black culture. This perceived lack of cultural distinctiveness among African Americans and Black immigrant groups (Foner 2001; Vickerman 2001), or ethnic "invisibility," may change due to the increasing numbers, changing status, and strong ethnic expressions of West Indian groups, including Jamaicans (Kasinitz 2001). However, change does not come easily and their increasing group identity and visibility is an evolving process challenged by White racism (Waters 1999; Neckerman, Carter and Lee 1999; Vickerman 2001). Wishing to be ethnically distinct, Jamaicans emphasize their cultural differences from African Americans, such as cultural history and different values.

Jamaican Culture and Ethnicity

Jamaican culture is, in part, distinguished by its history, beliefs and institutions. Despite their experience under British imperialism and a plantation-type economy, Jamaicans maintained basic cultural features associated with their native food, music, poetry and other cultural expressions. For example, traditional food staples and preparation involving baked goods, rice, spices and meats, including curried goat and chicken, and oxtail, remain distinctly Jamaican today. Indeed, Foner noted that foods (plantain and curried goat), as well as family, religion and women's roles were important elements of Jamaican ethnicity in New York (Foner 2001, p. 11). Regarding Jamaican-American ethnicity, Foner observes that within and beyond their neighborhoods, recent Jamaican immigrants have added their sounds and spices to the City's cultural and culinary life (p. 17). Transnational ties between Jamaican Americans and their homeland reinforce these cultural elements and Jamaican ethnicity. According to Vickerman (2001), Jamaican culture is particularly distinctive from their American counterparts in terms of racial constructions. He argues that the color line differs between the U.S. and Jamaica because distinction by skin color is less important in Jamaica. While the color line defines American racial differences, Jamaican racial construction emphasizes class distinction, particularly education and occupational differences. The corollary is that education and achievement are imbedded in Jamaican culture, despite its colonial imperialism experience. As a result, in New York City and other places, Jamaican ethnicity is largely shaped by an identity of achievement and Jamaican Americans are defined and distinctive from African Americans because they are "hardworking, goal-oriented, success-driven individuals" (Vickerman 2001, p. 207). One way this is expressed geographically in New York City is through Jamaican home ownership rates that are relatively higher than those of other groups.

Conservative attitudes and strong family values are other elements of Jamaican culture that shape Jamaican-American ethnicity. Conservatism is expressed in a number of ways, including "avoidance of conflict (that) seems engrained in the culture" (Vickerman 2001, p. 209). It also materializes as strong respect for law and order, especially among the Jamaican professional class, as well as for senior family members, the position of children in the household and their discipline, and respect for the traditional roles of women, such as in food preparation (despite their participation in the workforce) (Vickerman 2001). Woven into the Jamaican cultural fabric, and carried into their ethnicity, are British influences such as the English language, and recreational activities of soccer and cricket. The rich ancestry and culture developed in Jamaica structures Jamaican ethnicity abroad and has expression in New York City and, likely, in other American places where they reside in large numbers.

West Indian Occupational Structure and Socioeconomic Status in New York City

West Indians have been described as being "in the middle of the immigrant pack" in terms of education and job skills (Foner 2001). Wright and Ellis, in referring to a remaking of the labor market in New York City along ethnic lines, report recent gains for West Indians in several categories, including high and low paying "personal service jobs, professional services, and public employment" (Wright and Ellis 2001, p. 99). They also indicated the continuation of persistent occupational niches in healthcare. West Indian employment niches are not all gender-based in NYC and reveal "old and new opportunities" in the city's economy (Model 2001). Although transportation (trucking and taxis) is a male niche, hospital jobs and public administration are shared niches of West Indian men and women (Model 2001). Personal service, a traditional niche for women, is still important but has declined recently, while healthcare, especially nursing, has grown in importance. While the income provided by these employment opportunities varies dramatically, the recent influx of more highly educated and skilled West Indians (selective migration), particularly many Jamaicans, has improved their overall socioeconomic status in the City over time.

Earlier in this volume, Boswell and Sheskin reported that West Indians and Jamaicans in the U.S., especially NYC and Miami, enjoyed higher socioeconomic status than native Blacks and Hispanics, due in part, to their emphasis on education, achievement, and upward mobility. Residential clustering also contributes to strong West Indian and Jamaican ethnic identities. Some New York City neighborhood enclaves express aspects of this ethnicity, through high rates of home ownership, and links with native Black-American neighborhoods.

Black Residential Patterns and Ethnic Landscapes in New York City

New York City neighborhoods have been reshaped along racial, ethnic, and class lines. Following earlier studies (Waldinger 1987; Conway and Bigby 1992; Crowder 1999; Foner 1992 and 1998), Crowder and Tedrow (2001) stressed the importance of race, ethnicity, and class relationships in the creation and maintenance of Black residential patterns termed by some as "triple layering." Race was "a primary determinant of the residential incorporation of West Indian Blacks" (p. 110) into particular Black neighborhoods. They suggest that lack of access to White neighborhoods is comparable to that experienced by African Americans and "relegated" immigrant Blacks to African-American neighborhoods. In addition to racial geography, an apparent ethnic geography operates as well, whereby West Indian neighborhoods were imbedded within the better sections of racialized African-American residential space. The ethnic enclaves experienced relatively higher home ownership rates and contained households with higher social capital than neighboring predominantly African-American areas. The third level of this triple layering process involved the clustering of specific West Indian cultures, such as Jamaicans, in their own neighborhoods within the West Indian enclaves. Crowder and Tedrow (2001) saw the class and ethnic based patterns as channeling "ethnic resources" into these areas and serving as an "important tool" to preserve ethnicity and provide "social protection." Boswell confirmed the continuation of triple layer though an analysis of 2000 census data for New York City (Boswell and Jones 2006). Also, Boswell and Sheskin use Foner's observations in chapter 13 to argue that there are four reasons for West Indians' "preference" for Black neighborhoods in New York City and Miami: racial discrimination, SES that provides competitive advantage in African-American neighborhoods, the market opportunity provided by all-Black neighborhoods, and the influences of social-ethnic networks (chapter 13). This concept of a triple-layered settlement also will be examined for Broward County Jamaicans.

Due to ethnic strength and the magnitude of New York City's West Indian settlements (Kasinitz 2001), visible cultural patterns, or cultural landscapes, are apparent:

> "West Indian beauty parlors, restaurants, record stores, groceries and bakeries dot the landscape. . . ."
> (Foner 2001, p. 16)

Residential concentrations also have led to West Indian and Jamaican political influences in New York City. This influence can be in voting districts where they operate at times as voting blocks, or when they sometimes vote on a racial basis, supporting common issues with African Americans (Foner 2001). However, as others have noted, the type and quality of ethnic relations between West Indians and African Americans varies substantially by time and place.

Race and African-American Relations

The color-based American racial construction presents a bitter experience for many West Indians, including Jamaicans, who are frustrated, puzzled, and repulsed by the American racial environment that blocks upward mobility and material achievements that education and skills would permit without prejudice (Vickerman 2001). Foner argues that "being Black is the master status" (p. 10) for West Indians, having many negative impacts, from residential steering and white flight that changes mixed-race to all-Black neighborhoods, to lower quality schools and diminished services (Foner 2001). Thus, while many West Indians have sought Black neighborhoods as safety nets, their ethnic neighborhoods become the victims of white flight and the well-known consequences of racial segregation. These experiences have led to a shared bond with African Americans based on perceived victimization by Whites. At the same time, some West Indians have benefited from the upward mobility associated with New York City's large and growing Black middle class (Neckerman, Carter and Lee 1999). Thus, other types of bonds with African Americans are possible.

These experiences with African Americans and America's unique racial climate have resulted in Jamaicans experiencing "contradictory pressures" of race and ethnicity. They seem to carry an indelible racial stamp that classifies them as "American Blacks" and they often suffer from the same stereotypes — lacking family values and "low achievers" — that especially influence the workplace (Vickerman 2001). This, of course, is a bitter pill for Jamaicans, who self-identify as a hardworking, driven, educated people. One result of these "contradictory pressures" involves a compulsion for "distancing" themselves from African Americans on an ethnic basis (Waters 1999). Sometimes this action results in negative perceptions of African Americans, who sometimes reciprocate with a nativist perspective and accuse West Indian immigrants of usurping their rightful socioeconomic gains. These ethnic conflicts can escalate. Jamaicans use their ethnic identity, stressing positive cultural traits, to contrast Jamaican qualities with those of African Americans. Such comparisons suggest that African American professionals lack the aspirations and work ethic essential for success and that, more broadly, African Americans lack strong family values and fail to discipline and guide their children on a path to educational success. Jamaicans see their culture as superior based on opposite values: valued education, strong family, child discipline, respect for law and order, and a strong work ethic (Vickerman 2001).

Thus, these "contradictory pressures" result in both strained and positive relationships between Jamaicans (and other West Indians) and African Americans. Solidarity results when circumstances and cultural characteristics provide the glue. This can be as simple as shared musical tastes to more complex political coalitions on particular issues. Distancing occurs when issues separate the groups. Stimuli range from competitive economic opportunities to racial stereotyping that is perceived as unfair racial association. It is doubtful that America's color line and concomitant racial prejudice will soon escape its deep historical roots. As a result, West Indians likely will continue to have mixed experiences in America, and conflicts between racial and ethnic identities likely will persist. Waters has argued that American racism has and will continue to push West Indians down a path of Black-American assimilation (Waters 1999). Kasinitz noted that West Indians in New York City are becoming a more visible population due to their size and ethnic strength (Kasinitz 2001). As a result, their similarities and associations with African Americans and their ethnic uniqueness will become more apparent both there and in other places where they congregate.

With this knowledge of West Indians, generally, and Jamaicans in particular, our attention turns to South Florida, where Jamaicans have grown in number and created an increasingly important cultural center in Broward County.

BROWARD COUNTY, FLORIDA: POPULATION, DIVERSITY, TRENDS, AND EXPRESSIONS OF JAMAICAN ETHNICITY

The Study Area

Broward County is one of three counties in the Southeast Florida Metropolitan Statistical Area (also, Miami-Dade, Broward, and Palm Beach counties, see chapter 12). This SMA is the sixth largest U.S. Metropolitan region, which added approximately one million people between 1990 and 2000 and contains a total population in excess of five million. Broward County had slightly more than 1.6 million people in 2000 and it had the largest population gain during the period 1990–2000. The fastest-growing populations within Broward County, in the same period, occurred in municipalities in the western sections of the County. Thirty municipalities occupy only one-third of Broward County's land area and nearly two-thirds of the County lies in a conservation area containing the Everglades. The rapid increase in Broward's population includes an increase of 58 percent in the school-age population, which also resulted in rapid residential expansion, particularly in communities such as Coral Springs, Margate, Tamarac, Sunrise, Plantation, Miramar, Davie, and Weston.

Broward's Socioeconomic Characteristics and Economy[1]

In 2000 the U.S. Census Bureau reported labor participation by industrial category and showed a participation rate of 63 percent. Slightly more than one-third of Broward's labor force was employed outside the County. Approximately 83 percent were employed by the private sector. Women are an important component of the Broward labor force, including nearly the two-thirds of women having pre-school children. Two large industrial employment categories account for about one-third of the Broward labor force: educational-health services and retail trade. Another three categories, professional and business services, leisure services, and financial services, employ an additional 30 percent of Broward's labor force. Thus, five employment categories provide the majority of employment (62 percent). The only other categories that employ more than 50,000 Broward workers are construction and manufacturing, which account for an additional 14 percent of the jobs occupied by Broward residents.

Overall, Broward is an affluent county. Incomes increased by more than one-third between 1990 and 2000; median family incomes rose to $50,531, an increase of 37 percent, and median household income increased by 36 percent to $41,691. Additionally, higher-income families, those earning 200 percent plus of the County's median family income, increased by nearly 24,000, from approximately 44,000 to 68,000. Not surprisingly, many of those higher income households are located in the western communities of Broward that experienced population growth associated with suburban development. The proportion of residents with a college or professional degree also increased between 1990 and 2000. Educational attainment patterns, particularly an earned college degree, correlate highly with the income patterns of Western Broward communities developed above.

While the proportion of low- and very-low income persons residing in Broward County remained virtually unchanged (39 percent) between 1990 and 2000, the actual number increased by nearly 30,000 residents, totaling about 160,000. The largest number of these residents is concentrated in central Broward County, in Ft. Lauderdale and adjacent neighborhoods. Conversely, the number of low-income persons residing in the Western Communities of Broward is practically negligible.

Racial and Ethnic Diversity

America's increasing national racial/ethnic diversity and its impact on numerous places since Hart-Celler is well established (Frazier 2006). As the U.S. continued to diversify between 1990 and 2000, Broward County experienced a dramatic transformation. In 1990, Miami-Dade County was the state's most diverse county (as represented by Simpson's Reciprocal Index, Planning Services Division of Broward County 2004) and Broward was more diverse than the national average, but less diverse than Florida as a whole. However, 1990s migration dramatically changed these patterns. By 2000, Broward's diversity surpassed Miami-Dade, and most other Florida counties. Broward was Florida's third most diverse county, and ranked eleventh in diversity among the nation's most populous counties. During the same period, Broward's White non-Hispanic population increased slightly but its share of the total County population decreased dramatically, from 75 percent to 58 percent. Latinos experienced the County's largest percentage increase (9 percent to 17 percent), followed by the Black population (15 percent to 20 percent). The Asian population (16,395) more than doubled (38,165) between 1990 and 2000, but constituted the smallest minority group. Black population (325,205) continued to be the largest minority population in Broward County.

In 2006, the *Sun Sentinel* reported that Broward County continued to receive more migrants than it lost to migration (Soflo.org/media 2006). Led by Latinos and Blacks, the minority population of the County, including Asians, reached a majority status for the first time. This minority-majority likely will be 63 percent of Broward County's 2030 population. Among this growing minority population, the Black population grew by nearly 65,000 between 2000 and 2005 and is being fueled mostly by "immigrants from the Black Caribbean" (Soflo.org/media 2006). They also noted that Black Caribbeans and Northeastern American transplants are coming with economic assets.

Broward's Immigration and Ethnic Settlement Patterns

As in most U.S places, Broward County has a strong European-based pattern of ancestry that persisted until recent decades. Until 1990, Broward's immigrant origins were largely Western European. By 1990, this had changed dramatically due mostly to the entry of Latin American immigrants. The number of immigrants increased more than eightfold between 1970 and 2000, to 410,379 in 2000, about one quarter of the county's population. Most immigrants hailed from the Caribbean, Central, and South America. Doubling of Latino populations from some origins was common (Mexico, Cuba, Puerto Rico), but of particular importance to this chapter is the dramatic increase in the West Indian population during this period, which led all other groups. Those of West Indian ancestry ranked first among ancestral groups by 2000 and the numbers had grown to 156,343, from 56,893 in 1990. The County's Planning Division reported from The Immigration and Naturalization Service (INS) (2000) that Haitians and Jamaicans were the two largest immigrant groups entering the county. Together, they accounted for one-third of all annual immigrants in almost equal shares. The Planning Division report made two important points about Broward's racial and ethnic diversity. First, they noted that "in 2000, no single ancestry group exceeded a tenth of the County's population" and that the "number of naturalized citizens also exhibited considerable growth" (Planning Division, No. 1 July 2002, p. 2). The number of Broward's naturalized citizens increased more than five-fold between 1970 and 2000.

Broward's minority populations, with the exception of Blacks, are widely distributed throughout the County. Mexicans, Puerto Ricans, and Colombians are examples. All three groups constitute less than 3.5 percent of the County's total population, yet only Mexicans reside in census tracts (neighborhoods) representing more than 20 percent of (21.9 percent) of its ancestral group. In fact, beyond this tract, it is rare for more than 10 percent of any ancestral group to occur in a neighborhood.

Cubans also are fairly widely distributed. However, although only eleven tracts (neighborhoods) have Cuban ancestry in excess of 10 percent of their total population, most of those neighborhoods are located in the southwestern section of the County (such as Plantation, Davie, and Pine Ridge). In fact, two neighborhoods had more than one-quarter of their population reporting Cuban ancestry (27 percent and 29 percent). Clearly, the majority of persons of Cuban ancestry reside in the relatively affluent southwest one-quarter of Broward County. In summary, Broward's Latino population is widely dispersed with one exception, Cubans. Smaller numbers of other Latinos with social capital also live in this area. Clearly, some Latinos with social capital have settled in southwestern Broward County, especially South of I-75 and west of the Florida Turnpike. This observation is important when discussing Jamaican distributions.

Broward's Black Population and Settlement Patterns

Unlike the widely distributed Latinos, Broward's Blacks tend to be more concentrated in its central and southern municipalities, especially Ft. Lauderdale, which contains the majority of tracts with 50 percent or more Blacks. Since low-income populations also occupy central Broward, especially in Ft. Lauderdale, there is a link between being Black and being low-income in Broward County, although the poor also include other ethnic groups. Almost one in four (24 percent) Black households was classified as "single parent with children." Most Blacks residing in the County in 2000 were native and Florida born. Some analysis of the SES differences between Broward's foreign-born and native-born population will appear later in this chapter.

Another important observation about Broward's Black population involves their dispersion in the County. Despite being more concentrated than other populations, including in low-income areas, Broward's Black populations also are dispersed, especially those living in west central and southwestern municipalities, where they range from less than 5 percent to 25 percent of many neighborhoods, including middle and higher socioeconomic areas. As noted earlier, these include some of the most recently developed residential developments and likely contain members of the Black middle class. A more detailed analysis of the Jamaican distribution follows. Before this analysis, a brief review of the data sources is provided.

DATA SOURCES

Understanding Jamaican migration, settlement, and socioeconomic status (SES) requires data from a variety of sources at a number of geographic scales. Several sources supported the analysis presented in this chapter.

The U.S. Census Migration Data (CMD) for Blacks, including a special tabulation purchased from the Bureau, provided detailed income, age, and other characteristics of Black migrants.[2] The U.S. Census 1990 and 2000 Population and Housing data (STF-3 Summary File) provided ethnic and socioeconomic data for mapping. The Geo-Lytics Corporation boundary files of standardized census boundaries for the two decades allowed for spatial consistency in the maps. The U.S. Census Bureau 2000 five percent Public Use Microdata Sample (PUMS) for Broward County was used to study the occupational, demographic, and socioeconomic characteristics of Jamaicans in that County. This database provides detailed information on individuals. Finally, although PUMS is quite detailed, it does not permit detailed responses on specific questions. Survey data were required for that purpose.[3]

Therefore, two focus groups were conducted in September, 2007 that provided detailed responses on a variety of questions, including Jamaican reasons for migrating and settling in South Florida, means of preserving their ethnic identity, perceptions of African-American culture, and local settlement choices. All were Black immigrants and all but two members of the groups were born in Jamaica (one was from Barbados and one was from Haiti). All were employed as professionals, and ranged in age from their thirties to their sixties. This target population was deliberately selected to ascertain the potential role of class in the strength of ethnicity and selection of residential locations.[4] Thus, focus group responses were used to supplement the aggregate data from the U.S. Census and to provide insights that permitted comparisons with the findings in the literature on New York City Jamaicans.

Jamaicans in Broward County: An Overview

The intraurban exchange of Black migrants, 1995–2000, between Dade and Broward Counties, and SES trends provide insight into the Broward Jamaican community. Comments from the focus groups regarding their relocations to South Florida and Broward County reveal the attractiveness of Broward as a relatively new Jamaican-culture center. The center of Jamaican activity, called "Jam Hill" by local Jamaicans, has proven to be a pull factor for some migrants and an ethnic/cultural center for others.

Economic opportunity has been a powerful pull factor. Together, culture, economics, and climate have contributed to the influx of many Black immigrants from the Caribbean and from American cities. Given the importance of the economy and the desire to compare occupational structures of Jamaicans in New York City and Broward County, a brief analysis of the occupational structure of employed Jamaicans is provided in the next section. The final part of this section examines the spatial distribution of Jamaicans in Broward County, including the "triple layering" and the role of class in neighborhood choice and distancing from African-American neighborhoods.

Jamaicans and Others: Comparative Socioeconomic Characteristics and Internal Migration Trends

Socioeconomic Status (SES) Comparisons

Employing the 2000 PUMS data, several socioeconomic characteristics of Jamaicans are compared with other groups. Table 14.1 reports the sample size and characteristics for Whites, Latinos, Native-Born Blacks, West Indians, and Jamaicans. Generally, these data show that Jamaicans earned a higher average income than native-born Blacks in 2000, somewhat lower incomes than Latinos and other West Indians, and substantially less income than Whites in Broward County. All of these groups earned higher average incomes than their co-ethnics at the national and state levels (Boswell 2006), which reinforces the earlier observation that Broward is an affluent county.

Table 14.1.
A Comparison of Jamaican and Other Groups' Socioeconomic Characteristics, 2000.
Source: U.S. Census PUMS Data for Broward County, Florida.

Sample Size and Characteristics	**GROUPS**				
	Jamaicans	**West Indians Born (minus Jamaicans)**	**White Non-Hispanic**	**Latinos**	**Native-Blacks**
Sample Size PUMS	3,687	6.876	11,269	15,059	16,159
Average Income	$52,881	$56,470	$69,694	$59, 739	$47,831
Average Housing Value	$115,530	$134,997	$152,548	$136,491	$110,382
Percent Renters	26%	35%	24%	33%	42%
Percent Owners	74%	65%	76%	67%	58%
Average Age	34	30	41	32	28

Overall, the native-born Black population has the least favorable SES, compared to all groups, while non-Hispanic Whites eclipse all groups in terms of high levels of SES. Latinos are second only to the latter group, and West Indians are not far behind in SES. Jamaicans as a group lie between the native Blacks and other West Indians. For example, Jamaican average annual income is about $5,000 higher than native Blacks, but approximately $3,000 lower than that of other West Indians. Jamaican average housing value is slightly higher than that of native Blacks but substantially lower than that of other West Indians. The Jamaican home ownership rate in Broward County, as in New York City, is very high. In fact, at 74 percent, it is nearly the same as the White rate and is higher than the rates of all other groups.

Other than for the White population, Jamaicans had proportionally more home owners (and thus, fewer renters) than all groups, although on average their median housing value ($115,530) was somewhat lower than those of Latinos and other West Indians. These findings are in keeping with Boswell's results for the Miami-Ft. Lauderdale CMSA (2006; also see previous chapter in this volume). They also mirror the findings for New York City that Jamaicans are disproportionately high home owners, relative to other groups. Regarding the average age of Jamaicans relative to other groups, they are younger in age than native Blacks and non-Hispanic Whites. They are closer in age to West Indians and Latinos, perhaps indicating migrant selectivity yields younger ages for immigrants.

Table 14.2 reports the categorical distributions for Jamaican income, age and education. These data better illustrate the range for all distributions. Regarding income, about 55 percent earned less than $50,000 per year, while 45 percent earned more than that amount, including 10 percent who earned more than $100,000 per year. More than one-quarter (29 percent) were very young, under 21 years of age, while about 11 percent were age 60, or older. About 70 percent of these Jamaicans were under the age of 45. Educationally, nearly one-third of Broward Jamaicans (32.6 percent) have less than a high school diploma, which is a larger proportion than exists for Jamaicans in New York City, or for the U.S. as a whole. Similarly, the proportion of Jamaicans with a Bachelor's degree (11 percent) is somewhat lower than the percentages for New York City and the total U.S. Jamaican populations (Boswell 2007).

Table 14.2.
Jamaican Income, Age and Education Distributions in Broward County, 2000.

Household Income Categories	**Number**	**Percent**
Under $20,000	527	14.6%
$ 20,000–50,000	1,453	40.3%
$ 50,000–75,000	927	25.7%
$ 75,000–100,000	342	9.4%
$ 100,000 +	356	10.0%
Age Categories		
Under 21 Years	1,054	29.0%
21–29	465	12.6%
30–44	1,070	29.2%
45–59	676	18.5%
60–64	112	3.1%
65 +	277	7.6%
Education Categories		
No High School Diploma	1,200	32.6%
High School Diploma or Some College	1,972	56.4%
Bachelor's Degree or Higher	404	11.0%

Source: U.S. Census, 2000.

In summary, Jamaican SES in Broward County is diverse, being spread across the continuum of income and education. Nearly one-third did not finish high school and 11 percent earned a college degree. The incomes support this dispersion in education. Nearly 55 percent earned less than the average income in 2000. Yet, almost one in five reported annual incomes of over $75,000. Finally, this population is bifurcated in terms of age. Nearly three in ten are under the age of 21, but nearly one-half is between the ages 30 and 60. These demographic and SES characteristics may well influence where Jamaicans reside within Broward County.

Intra-Urban Migrants

Chapter 12 noted that foreign-born Blacks are drawn disproportionately to the Miami-Ft. Lauderdale region for cultural, economic, and climatic reasons. It also argued that the largest number of migrants move short distances, especially within the same metropolitan region (intra-urban migration). The total Black populations of Miami-Dade and Broward Counties increased each decade, 1970 to 2000. Likewise, the Black percentages of the total population increased for both counties. However, before 2000 the Black population as a share of the total population of Miami-Dade was higher than the same ratio for Broward County. Between 1990 and 2000 Miami-Dade's Black proportion of its total population increased less than a single percentage point, from 20.67 percent to 21.5 percent. Further, Boswell reported that between 2000 and 2006 Miami-Dade's "Black population decreased by almost 2,000," an indication that "the number of domestic out-migrants must have increased enough to offset the positive natural increase and the continued heavy immigration of Blacks that occurred" (chapter 13).

The migration statistics reported by the U.S. Migration Data (CMD) support this observation. Table 14.3 reports the in-migration and out-migration characteristics for Broward and Miami-Dade counties, between 1995 and 2000. These data reveal at the national level (Black migrants in and out, from and to all U.S. counties) Miami-Dade County experienced a net loss of 32,624, while Broward County had a net gain of 24,852. Native-born Black in-migrants accounted for the majority of in-migrants for both counties, and Broward County attracted nearly three times as many foreign-born Blacks from other U.S. counties (primarily in Florida, New York, and New Jersey) as did Miami-Dade.

Migrant characteristics support some aspects of migrant selectivity theory (e.g., Long 1988; Tobler 1995; Schacter 2001) for both counties (migrants tend to be younger, for example). However, the data reveal that Broward County's Black in-migrants for this five-year period, generally, had a stronger SES than those entering Miami-Dade County. Specifically, Broward's Black in-migrants proportionately had less poverty, earned more income (especially the $75,000+ category), had higher levels of education and had younger ages than the Blacks entering Miami-Dade. Both counties' in-migrants tended to be families with children under 18 years of age in the household (not shown in the table).

Reasons for Selecting South Florida: Responses from the Focus Groups

The "opportunity concept" found in chapter 12 was expressed by all of the West Indian (predominantly Jamaican) focus group participants, who were asked why they had migrated to South Florida. A few explained the economic opportunity.

> "Personal finances were the main consideration." (Haitian male, 1)

Another expressed his family's motivation was economic and, after following family, the economic opportunities caused him to remain in South Florida:

> "I followed my mother and father here. I stayed for the economic opportunities." (Barbados male, 1)

Table 14.3.
Black In-Migrant and Out-Migrant Characteristics, 1995–2000, for Miami-Dade and Broward Counties.

Counties	Migrant Selectivity, Socioeconomic and Demographic Characteristics, In-Migrants and Out-Migrants		
Totals	**Migrant-In totals**	**Migrant-Out totals**	**Net**
Broward	51,705	26,583	24,852
Miami-Dade	28,270	61,000	–32,730
Nativity	**Native-Born In**	**Foreign-Born In**	**Total**
Broward	29,243 (59%)	20,261 (41%)	49,504
Miami-Dade	18,720 (73%)	6,763 (27%)	25,483
Poverty-In Migrants	**Not determined Level**	**Below Poverty Level**	**Above Poverty Level**
Broward	1,269 (3%)	6,997 (14%)	41,230 (83%)
Miami-Dade	2,575 (10%)	5,070 (20%)	25,377 (70%)

Household Income-In	**Under $25,000**	**$25–50K**	**$50–75K**	**>$75K**
Broward	12,680 (25%)	16,140 (32%)	11,170 (22%)	10,710 (21%)
Miami-Dade	8,530 (34%)	8,450 (33%)	5,080 (20%)	3,360 (13%)

Ages-In	**5–14**	**15–24**	**25–44**	**45–64**	**65–plus**
Broward	10,512 (20%)	7,767 (15%)	23,058 (45%)	7,850 (15%)	2,484 (5%)
Miami-Dade	2,277 (9%)	5,778 (23%)	12,004 (48%)	3,481 (14%)	1,620 (6%)

Education-In	**In- <H S Diploma**	**In-H S Diploma**	**In-College/Graduate**
Broward	5,709 (18%)	18,538 (58%)	7,630 (24%)
Miami-Dade	3,817 (25%)	8,543 (48%)	2,749 (18%)

Source: U.S. Bureau of the Census Migration Flow Files, 2000.

A Jamaican female indicated that education was the first and temporary attraction, but love and marriage kept her in New York. She later moved to Florida after a visit:

> "I needed to go to college and my parents gave me a choice. So, I came to the U.S. on a student visa. On vacation, I met a boy and he kept me here.... When I visited Florida, I loved it. I thought This is paradise because you have our culture — the music, the food, and without crime — and to go home you just hop on a plane." (Jamaican female, 1)

The attraction to culture and weather was echoed by the majority of participants. One Jamaican lady summarized the importance of culture this way:

> "People look like you, speak like you, and are in important positions." (Jamaican female, 2)

Ethnic Attraction: Culture Attraction/Opportunity in Broward County

Just as Foner noted, sights and smells that signal West Indian cultures in New York City, West Indian, and particularly Jamaican, cultures are visible on the Broward County landscape, particularly west of Ft. Lauderdale, centered on an area termed "Jamaica (or 'Jam') Hill" by local Jamaicans. One Jamaican explained its attraction:

> "I wanted to live in the cultural center of my people. I am living there." (Jamaican male, 1)

Many identifying places and symbols of West Indian and Jamaican presence in this area include beauty shops, markets, restaurants, including fast food operations, Jamaican flags, and night clubs. Perhaps the most tangible manifestation of West Indian influence in the area, the first cricket stadium in the United States, still under construction in Lauderhill (see Figure 14.1A–B), will seat 5,000. This $70 million dollar development is part of the County Park system. It also will provide an important social space for the interaction of West Indians living in Broward County and surrounding areas. Its cultural significance has been noted by the regional media, including the following report that addressed "Why in Lauderhill?"

> "Lauderhill's new immigrants brought with them a bit of their culture. In 1996, the Caribbean National Cultural Association launched an annual three-day celebration of Caribbean food and music known as Unite-A-Fest. And, there can be no Caribbean festival without cricket. That is when city officials heard the need for a decent cricket field. . . ." (www.dreamcricket.com, last accessed October 11, 2007; also see Miami Herald.com 12/31/06)

A trip by Mayor Kaplan and other officials to Trinidad soon after the Fest opened local political eyes to an economic opportunity that focused on Lauderhill becoming the "cricket capital of the U.S." Noting the large local West Indian population, especially Jamaicans, this media report noted Lauderhill's advantage over other areas with large immigrant populations was due to the fact it "claims the highest percentage of Jamaican-born elected officials anywhere outside of Jamaica" (www.dreamcricket.com, last accessed October 11, 2007). Thus, as in New York City, Broward's West Indians have exercised political influence.

Despite this major landscape imprint, the Jamaican Hill area cannot be described as a uniform landscape, such as a Chinatown. Rather, landscape cues are scattered but clearly visible along the major commercial networks. Food and music are two important elements that measure ethnic identities for all West Indians. The majority of focus group members emphasized the importance of these items in the presentation of their culture when living in the U.S. One Jamaican male described it this way:

> "The culture surrounds you, the music, and the food. It is important to use Caribbean restaurants, play cricket, soccer, etc. It is all here too." (Jamaican male, 2)

Figure 14.1.
West Indian Social Spaces I.

Photos by Author.

Most focus group participants mentioned food and its preparation as important to their ethnicity and the availability of numerous Caribbean-style restaurants.

> "Jamaican food is unique by its preparation and the traditions. Rice and peas is traditional food on Sundays. It is cooked in a different way, with coconut milk mixed with rice and other ingredients. We also prepare fish, goat, and chicken dishes. Rice is a staple in the Jamaican diet . . . curry also is an important ingredient." (Jamaican female, 3)

Others mentioned the importance of music and West Indian clubs:

> "What I really like here is the music, to just go to a club for three or four hours and enjoy yourself." (Jamaican male, 4)

Photographic evidence indicates the importance of these features on the local landscape. Ethnic businesses serve the desire for convenience and function as social spaces for West Indians. Figure 14.1 (C and D) illustrates West Indian and Jamaican restaurants, including those with walk-up windows. Figure 14.2 (A–D) are photographs of other West Indian/Jamaican social spaces that provide food, such as Jamaican breads and a variety of other West Indian goods. Figure 14.3 includes photographs of outdoor dining, a West Indian "club" located in a typical strip mall, and a Haitian restaurant. Caribbean music, food, and drink regularly attract West Indians, as do other specialty shops. These types of Jamaican and West Indian businesses are common sights in the Jam Hill area. Finally, the Jamaican and American flags are commonly displayed on this landscape, indicating both ethnic and national pride (Figure 14.3).

Jamaican Occupational Structure in Broward County

Earlier in this chapter discussion of West Indian occupations in New York City suggested employment success in personal services, professional services, and public employment. Personal services, a traditional Jamaican female niche, were less important in 2000 compared to previous periods. Transportation, specifically trucking and taxi driving, is an occupational niche for Jamaican men in New York. Shared male and female niches include medically-related employment, including hospital jobs and nursing, and public administration.

While niches are not studied here, Table 14.4 illustrates the breadth of occupations held by the Jamaicans in the Broward workforce. "Managerial, Professional, and Related Financial Occupations" constitute their largest proportion in Broward County, with the majority in management, health, and technical support occupations. Female registered nurses and female medical assistants constitute the largest two occupations within the health category.

The next two broad categories, "Service" and "Sales and Office" occupations, each accounted for about one-quarter of the Jamaican labor force reported. "Service" occupations involved health-related jobs, and the health-support occupations, largely held by females, dominated this subcategory (>90 percent). Among the other categories, "personal care" also was dominated by females (nearly 70 percent), although its importance in the broader category was small.

The other major occupational category, "Sales and Office," accounted for 26 percent of all PUMS-reported Jamaican occupations and involved only two subcategories. These were "Office and administrative support" and "sales." Thus, the first three major occupational categories (in bold in Table 14.4) account for nearly 80 percent of all Jamaican occupations in Broward County.

The remaining two major occupational categories were of substantially less importance but together accounted for about 21 percent of the occupations held by Jamaicans in Broward County. The "Construction-Maintenance" and "Production, Transportation, Material Handling" categories accounted for 11 percent and 10 percent, respectively. Males accounted for 60 percent of the occupations within the "Construction and Maintenance" category, but held more than 95 percent of all positions in the construction and installation/repair subcategory.

Figure 14.2.
West Indian Social Spaces II.

Photos by Author.

Figure 14.3.
West Indian Social Space and Flags.

Photos by Author.

Table 14.4.
Occupational Structure of Jamaicans in Broward County Labor Force, 2000.
Source: U.S. Census Bureau, 2000, PUMS.

Managerial, Professional, and Related Financial 116 employed in management 263 employed in health/technical support	692 (28%)
Service Occupations 299 in healthcare 91 in food prep/service 81 in personal care 77 in building/grounds maintenance	589 (24%)
Sales and Office 344 in office/administrative support 299 in sales	643 (26%)
Construction, Extraction, Maintenance 135 in construction 134 in installation/repair	269 (11%)
Production, Transportation, Material Handling 139 in transportation/Material 115 in production	254 (10%)
Total number of occupations reported = 2,484	Total 2,447

Males also dominated the final category shown in Table 14.4, "Production, Transportation, and Material Handling." The occupations in this category included operating automotive machines, and moving transit, such as bus drivers, and production-related activities.

These occupation data illustrate that both men and women play important roles in numerous occupations in the Broward County labor force that differ in some respects from niches held by their Jamaican counterparts in New York City. However, there are both similarities and differences between Broward and New York City. Among the striking similarities are the professional health and service occupations, and the disproportionate role Jamaican women play in these occupations in both places. Other similarities include male-dominated construction and transportation occupations.

Despite the similarities and the importance of specific occupations, and more broadly, the "Managerial-Professional-Financial" and "Service" categories, the "Sales and Office" sector provided the second largest proportion of occupations for Jamaicans in Broward Country. In fact, it provided only 2 percent fewer occupations to Jamaicans in 2000, than the "Management-Professional-Financial" category. This certainly contributes to and illustrates the diversity of occupations held by Jamaicans within Broward County. Finally, although the "Transportation" category provides important opportunities, unlike New York City, employment in Broward involved transportation and material handling jobs that were less important in New York. The importance of private transportation service, including taxi driver (and jitney) occupations is negligible for Broward County Jamaicans. This diversity of occupations among Broward's Jamaicans suggests a wide range of income and residential locations within the County.

Jamaican Residential and SES Patterns in Broward County

As noted previously, triple layering (the tendency of West Indians to "prefer" Black neighborhoods) provides security against discrimination, a built-in market for services, and the ability to compete with native-born Blacks. It also suggests that within Black urban areas, West Indians settle in the best, most upscale neighborhoods. Triple layering also recognizes the clustering of specific groups such as Jamaicans, within West Indian settlements. Similarly, "distancing" involves the desire to be seen as different from African Americans. To achieve this, West Indians distance themselves culturally from African Americans in New York City. As earlier noted, West Indians also have conflicting attitudes about African Americans, which range from strong support on some issues to criticism on others. For example, West Indians sometimes self-identify as being culturally distinct and superior to African Americans and create a "distance" between themselves and African-American culture. Neither of these concepts has been applied in Broward County, nor has the role of SES, or class, been explored in Jamaican settlement preferences. In this section, triple layering, distancing, SES, and class are explored in Broward County using 1970 through 2000 U.S. Census data, supplemented by focus group responses.

Changing Black neighborhoods are examined in Figure 14.4, which illustrates the growth of Broward's census tracts containing 25 percent + Blacks from 1970 to 2000 (standardized boundaries). The 1970 maps illustrate the distributions of a predominantly native-born Black population, when West Indian immigration was modest. Each county had multiple small Black enclaves that became the basis for expansion in future decades. By 1980, Miami-Dade's Black population had spread northward and continued to expand in subsequent decades until it formed a continuous settlement with southern Broward's Black population.

In Broward County, between 1970 and 2000, the Black population expanded northward in the Ft. Lauderdale, Oakland Park, and Deerfield Black areas. It also expanded west from Ft. Lauderdale and Oakland Park into the Lauder Lakes, Lauderhill, and Sunrise areas. Figure 14.5 includes two maps of West Indians as a percentage of total ancestry reported for Broward and Miami-Dade Counties' Census Tract, 1990 and 2000. The overlap of West Indian populations in Black neighborhoods is obvious when Figures 14.4 and 14.5 are considered. However, by 2000, the distribution of West Indians suggests more than the layering of different ethnic groups in the County. West Indian settlements in 2000 included areas in which they are only 10 percent to 25 percent of the total population and these areas are not Black enclaves of traditional African-American settlements. In fact, an earlier section of this chapter noted that some of these areas in western and southwestern Broward County were of relatively high annual incomes (e.g., parts of Miramar, Pembroke Pines, Davie, and Plantation).

Figure 14.6 illustrates the distribution of Jamaicans in Broward County in 2000. Not surprisingly, Jamaicans follow the same pattern as West Indians. Certainly triple layering occurs within West Indian areas and Black neighborhoods. However, like other West Indians, Jamaicans have moved into more middle class and more affluent neighborhoods that are majority white and not traditional African-American neighborhoods. In these cases, class, not preference for Black neighborhoods, is operational. Clearly, Broward County Jamaicans and West Indians have sought neighborhoods with housing values that exceed those in the traditionally Black neighborhoods. Their SES has permitted locational choice of neighborhoods.

Figure 14.4.
Black Population Percentage, 1970–2000: Broward and Dade County Census Tracts.

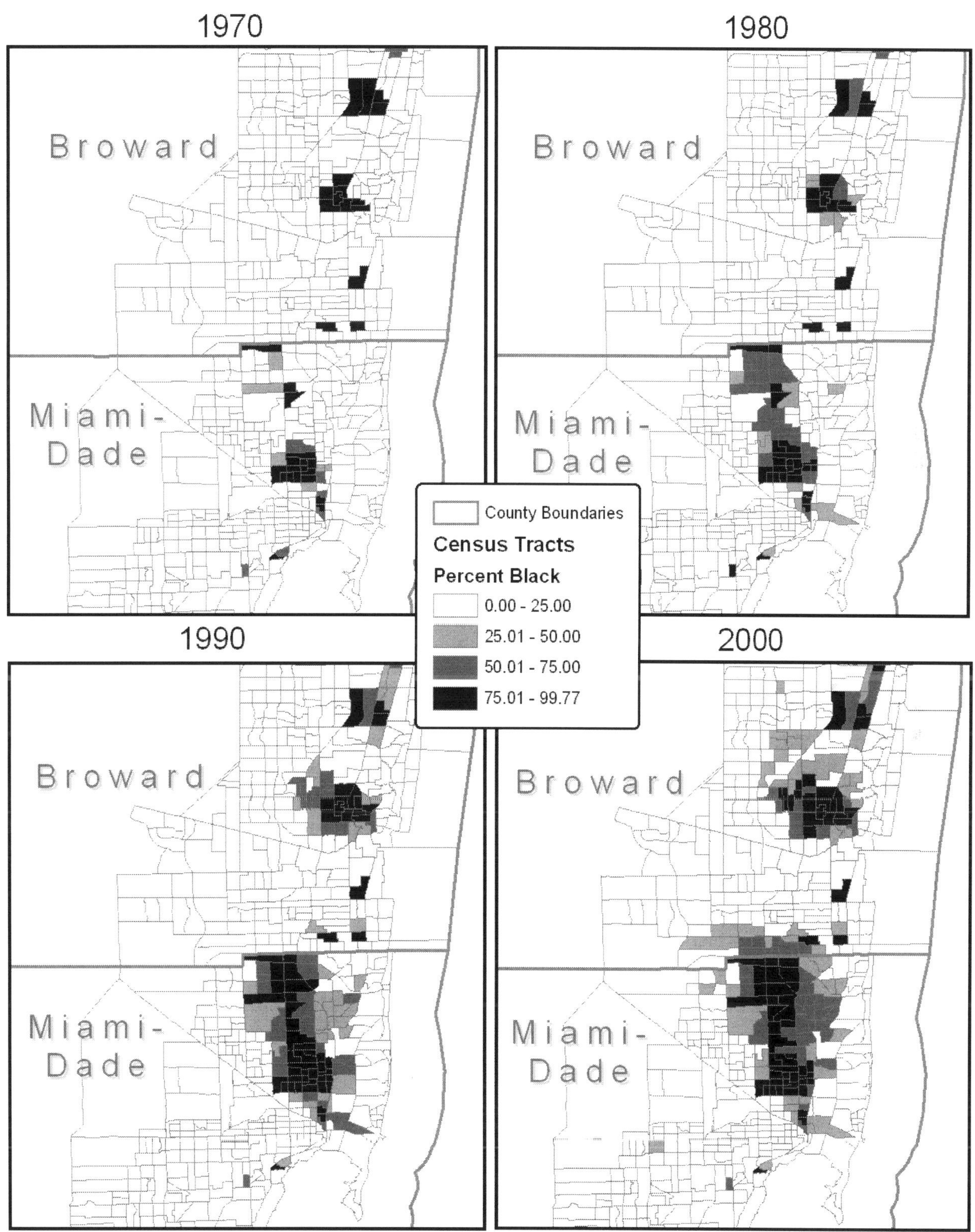

Source: GIS Core Facility, Binghamton University.

Figure 14.5.
West Indian Ancestry Percentage, 1990–2000: Broward and Dade County Census Tracts.

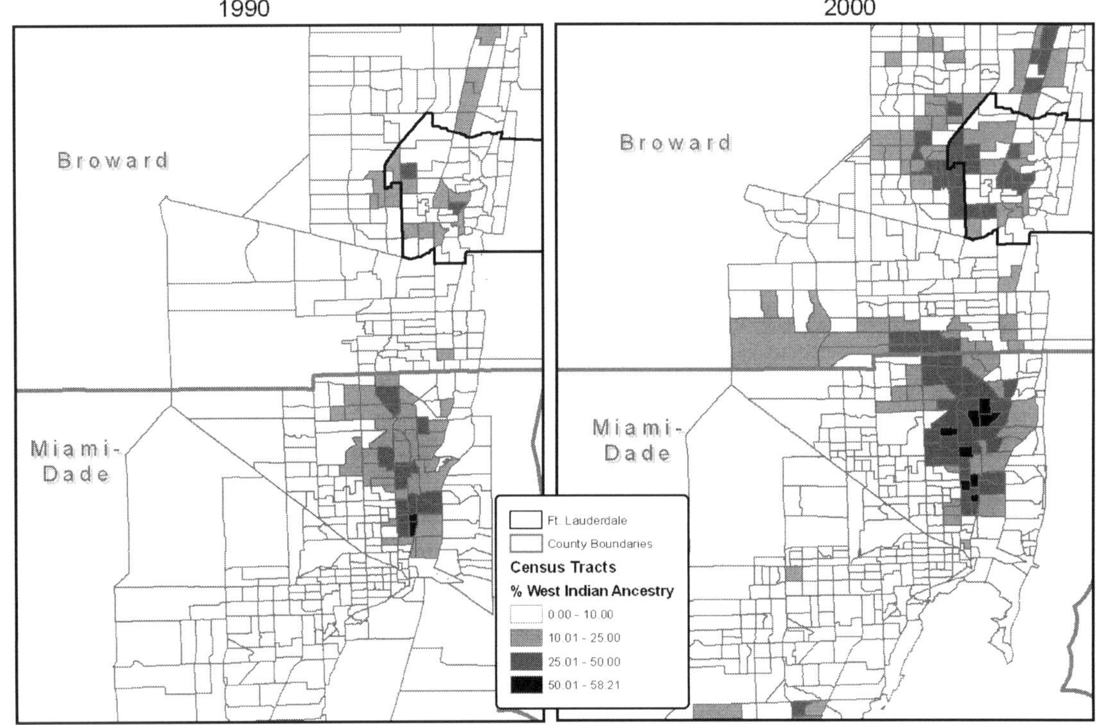

Figure 14.6.
Jamaican Ancestry Percentage, 2000: Broward Census Tracts.

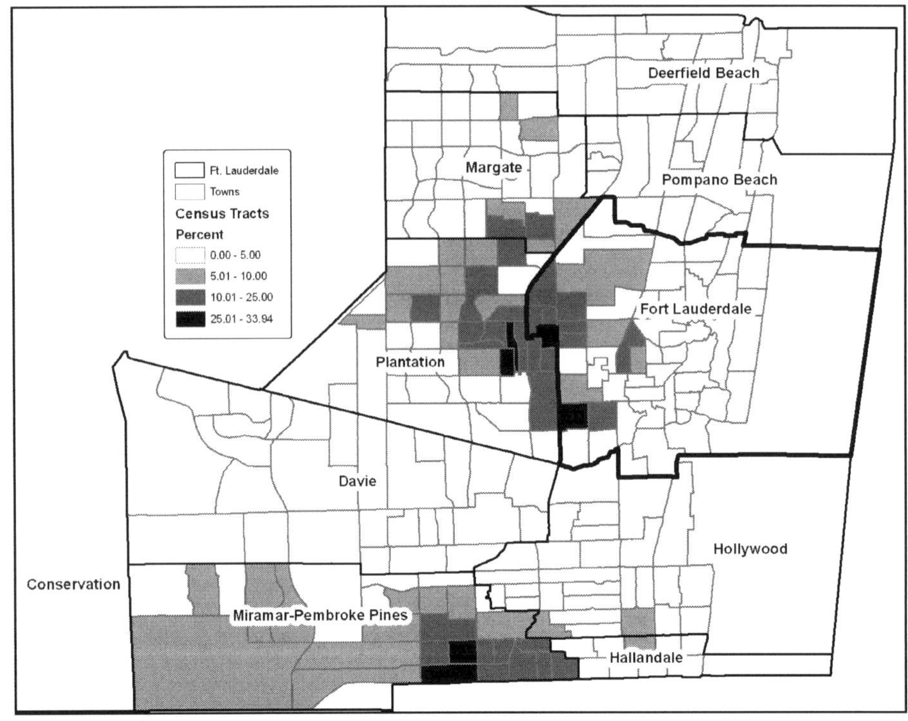

Source: GIS Core Facility, Binghamton University.

Figure 14.7 further supports this finding. Neighborhoods (year 2000 census tracts) with fifty or more Jamaicans residing in areas having annual median incomes above the County median (Map A) and areas exceeding a $75,000 median income (Map B) are shown. Clearly, thousands of Jamaicans resided in more affluent suburbs that are disproportionately West Indian or majority White, but also are located some distance from the traditional African-American enclaves of Broward County. In these cases, West Indian culture, SES, and quality of neighborhood are the likely forces behind West Indian and Jamaican settlement patterns in Broward. Table 14.5 reports data that support the triple layering in some Broward County municipalities. The neighborhoods reported in the table, compared to other neighborhoods in the County, show disproportionately high Black middle and lower-middle class residents in Ft. Lauderdale and its adjacent areas (Oakland Park, North Lauderdale, Lauder Lakes, Lauderhill, and Sunrise) to the north and west. Figure 14.8 (A–B) provides examples of housing in these types of lower-middle income Black neighborhoods. However, for many of Broward County's foreign-born population, including those with social and financial capital, the expansion has been to the western one-half of the County. As noted earlier, the municipalities within that part of the County have relatively higher incomes than Ft. Lauderdale and its adjacent communities. It is into these wealthier areas that West Indians and Jamaicans locate. As Table 14.6 illustrates, almost all of these neighborhoods (census tracts) have relatively low Black populations. In fact, all are majority White areas and, in some cases, contain Latinos such as Cubans. All of these neighborhoods are above the County's median household income in 2000, including those that are more than double that median income. Figure 14.9 is a map of the distribution of Jamaicans ancestry and income for Broward County. This map clearly indicates that thousands of Jamaicans reside in suburban Broward's middle and upper middle, White-majority neighborhoods. Figure 14.8 (C and D) shows housing in a few of these neighborhoods, which range from middle to upper-middle income neighborhoods and are located away from the triple layering that occurs largely in older areas of Ft. Lauderdale and vicinity. There is no doubt that native-born African Americans of the same socioeconomic status are also present in these more affluent western neighborhoods. They, like other residents, prefer to live in the security of the County's better neighborhoods, rather than in areas of predominantly Black settlement or in other areas that contain housing of less value. There is little doubt that class is at work in this county, regardless of ethnicity, and leads to a preference for housing, security, and other amenities located in the majority White and wealthy suburbs of Broward County.

What does this suggest about culture and ethnicity? Is this an attempt by Jamaicans and other West Indians to spatially and socially assimilate with Broward's White and other populations? Do ethnic feelings fade in such neighborhoods? What does it suggest about the role of class and attempts by West Indians to distance themselves from African-American neighborhoods? Focus group responses, drawn from local professionals, provide insights into answers to these questions.

Figure 14.7a.
Census Tracts with More Than 50 Jamaicans and a Median Household Income Higher Than Broward County's, 2000.

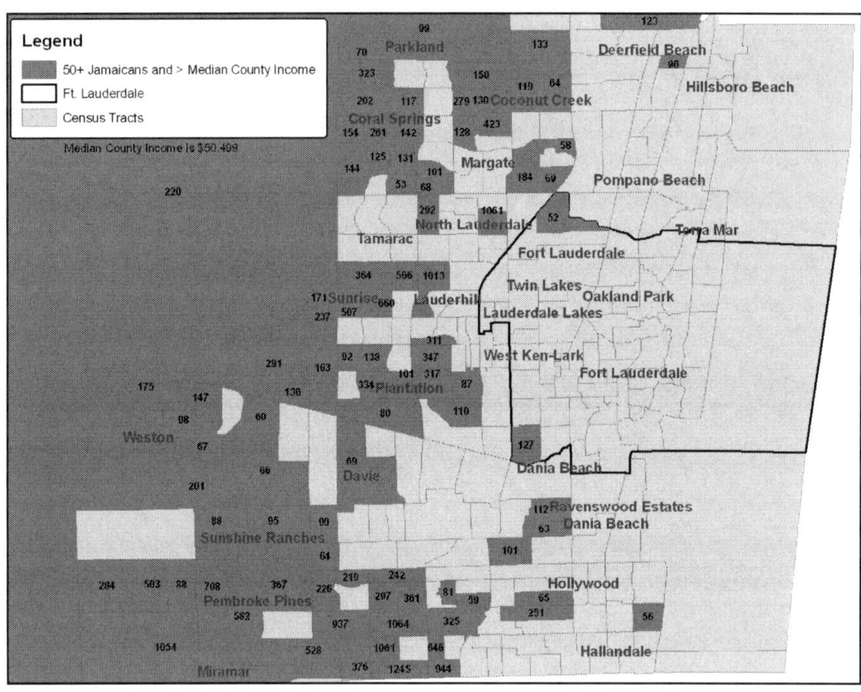

Figure 14.7b.
Census Tracts with more Than 50 Jamaicans and a Median Household Income Higher Than Broward County's, 2000.

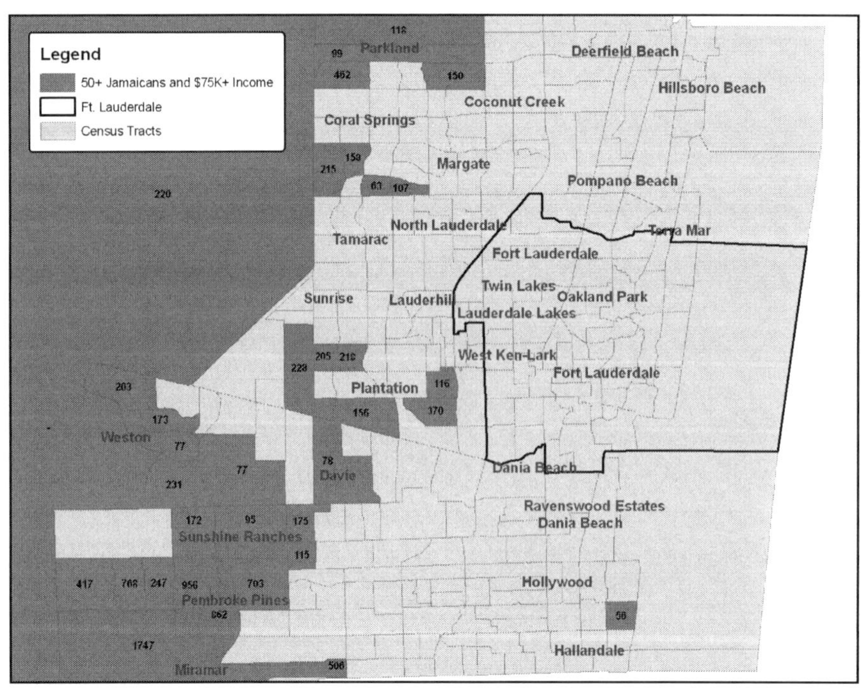

Source: GIS Core Facility, Binghamton University.

Table 14.5.
Evidence of Triple Layering in the Ft. Lauderdale-Lauderdale Lakes and Other Areas in Broward County, 2000.

	Tract #	% Black	Total Black Population	West Indians	Jamaicans	Median Income
Ft. Lauderdale	409.01	91.1	4,504	1,396	575	$31,322
	409.02	91.9	3,465	1,017	232	$38,150
	428	63.4	4,672	1,645	701	$38,432
	429	87.6	6,123	2,818	1,576	$48,860
	503.01	85.2	6,301	3,203	1,618	$48,526
	503.03	39.6	2,335	1,487	1,072	$29,767
	503.05	41.8	3,217	1,871	1,191	$41,231
	503.06	80.8	2,854	1,229	386	$30,482
	503.07	74.5	4,677	2,090	851	$34,523
	503.08	91.4	3,208	1,676	694	$35,962
	508	90.1	3,927	424	307	$36,627
Oakland Park	507.02	34.9	2,146	841	128	$34,547
	508	90.1	3,927	424	307	$36,697
Lauderdale Lakes	503.01	85.2	6,301	3,203	1,618	$48,526
	503.03	39.6	2,335	1,487	1,072	$29,767
	503.06	80.8	2,854	1,229	386	$30,482
	503.07	74.5	4,677	2,090	851	$34,523
	503.08	91.4	3,208	1,676	694	$35,962
North Lauderdale	204.04	41.8	2,881	1,956	1,061	$55,344
Hallandale	1003	70.3	1,347	564	123	$35,379
	1004	87.4	3,615	565	190	$28,131
Lauderhill	603.02	88.4	6,110	2,668	1,613	$32,718
	603.03	86.1	5,823	2,072	876	$32,563
	603.04	91.7	3,298	1,494	754	$29,820
	604.01	75.1	3,575	1,277	810	$40,821
	604.02	90.5	5,754	2,715	1,945	$35,177
	604.03	74.9	3,797	1,917	1,039	$62,576
Sunrise	602.03	68.1	3,754	2,021	1,315	$36,213
	602.08	60.3	3,446	1,756	976	$44,433

Source: U.S. Census STF3, 2000.

Figure 14.8.
Variable Housing Quality in Neighborhoods with West Indians.

Photos by Author.

Table 14.6.
West Indian and Jamaicans in Majority White, Upper Middle Class Neighborhoods in Broward County's Western Suburbs, 2000.

	Tract #	%Black	Total Black Population	W. Indians	Jamaicans	Median Income
Plantation	601.14	21.8	1,440	800	566	$ 57,537
	601.20	12.3	817	390	291	$ 68,708
	601.21	9.2	438	228	163	$ 11,547
	601.22	10.0	488	362	136	$ 66,009
	602.06	16.8	768	643	374	$ 68,511
	605.04	5.5	262	218	138	$ 95,657
	610.01	6.9	444	370	110	$ 86,169
Lauderhill	601.08	43.6	3,038	1,670	1,013	$ 67,896
	601.14	21.8	1,440	800	566	$ 57,537
Davie	703.08	4.7	503	203	175	$106,371
	703.13	6.2	601	231	201	$119,273
	703.15	5.7	296	172	88	$111,920
Miramar-Pembroke Pines	1103.02	14.8	1,234	768	503	$ 90,670
	1103.03	8.1	359	247	88	$109,644
	1103.04	14.1	1,606	956	708	$ 84,861
	1103.05	13.1	1,197	662	582	$ 92,293
	1103.17	18.1	3,338	1,747	1,054	$ 83,032
	1103.21	21.4	919	506	376	$110,609
Margate-Coral Springs	203.20	9.8	524	245	131	$ 70,639
	106.02	8.5	734	462	323	$100,889
	203.09	8.1	387	154	130	$ 68,424
	203.10	18.7	1,759	820	202	$ 53,478
	203.11	10.0	330	272	117	$ 69,363
	203.12	8.6	414	265	154	$ 68,138
	203.18	5.9	437	215	144	$115,786
	203.19	6.6	429	158	125	$ 91,701
	203.20	9.8	524	245	169	$ 70,639

*This table provides examples and is not intended to be exhaustive. Source: U.S. Census, STF3, 2000.

Figure 14.9.
Median Household Income and Jamaican Ancestry, 2000. Broward County Census Tracts.

Source: GIS Core Facility, Binghamton University.

Heterolocalism in Suburban Broward County

Heterolocalism occurs when an ethnic population is dispersed, yet retains its cultural ties through various ethnic interactions (Zelinsky and Lee 1998). Earlier in this chapter our focus group members, all residing in suburban locations, reported the importance of and various ways by which they preserve culture.

> "Our pastor . . . upgrades people every year through a Caribbean cultural festival of ethnic food, contests, and cricket . . . Cricket is played a great deal. Also, we have soccer teams, like Jamaicans vs. Haitians and other Ft. Lauderdale teams." (Haitian male, 1)

During one group conversation, the question of ethnic clustering with West Indians and African Americans was raised. One person noted that it is normal to cluster and to seek out others of your ethnic group and people with other similarities. She suggested that Black enclaves provide comfort and security, particularly for newly arriving immigrants. This response quickly generated an alternative and majority view. A typical response involved the desirability among professionals to live in a suburban area, as opposed to a Black enclave:

> "I beg to differ with what I am hearing about Caribbean people. Many feel that 'I don't want to be around problems that are happening a few miles away' so they look for newer places where people complement their views and where better schools exist. Those who are doing very well look to other places and they say: 'at least I can have the cultural experience and support but also be secure.' There is a class thing here." (Barbados male, 1)

Similar responses were provided in both focus groups. A Jamaican woman expressed the changing aspirations that come with improved status, which can lead to a desire to seek a different environment than an enclave:

> "There is a crutch living there but, in the long run, once people get to know the community, they move out to the suburbs to be with other professionals. There certainly is a class distinction here. I think so. The newcomers want to be in the older enclaves as a 'jumping-off' point. They also say to themselves 'These are my kinds of people that have been living here and they have been successful (moving to the better suburbs) so maybe I can come in and do the same thing — move out.'" (Jamaican Female, 4)

However, she noted that some newly arriving West Indians also move directly to the suburbs because they can afford to do so. Clearly, SES and class played a role for the majority of participants' decisions to live in a mixed race, majority-white suburban area, rather than in an African-American or West Indian neighborhood.

The discussion of suburban locations also led to a revealing discussion of "distancing" from African Americans among these professional Black immigrants. All indicated that they actually had avoided African-American neighborhoods.

Black Cultural Differences

The previous discussion about settlement patterns led to another about Black cultural differences and conflicts. A Jamaican lady expressed the role of aspirations that are tied to unique cultural histories.

> "African Americans were raised in the Black neighborhoods and always were deemed the lower culture. So, they are always looked down upon and when we came in we actually were almost on the same level. We came here and competed and because of that the communication between us suffered. . . . We will tell you straight away, we are not African Americans . . . truly, we are two cultures that have never communicated and have not been amicable to one another." (Jamaican female, 5)

Other Jamaicans noted the competition between the two cultures, including resentment due to job competition:

> "Simply put, we are Jamaicans and they are Black Americans. . . . I was an engineer at the Apollo Theatre. There were Black Americans there who said I should not have been given this opportunity because they were there before me. Their feelings were that someone had come into their community and taken something from them." (Jamaican male, 4)

Others explained African-American resentment.

> "If you are dating a Black-American girl, her family would treat you differently. One of the things I learned personally was from a Black-American young lady. I asked her directly: 'What is wrong with us Jamaicans?' . . . She said: 'Well, you guys weren't around when we had Jim Crow laws and we have done all these things and we still are not getting ahead.' I looked at it like 'You guys have to try harder as a group because no one helps you out in this community.' So I think there is animosity because of that." (Jamaican male, 5)

Even stronger perceptions, and emotions ranging from frustration and sympathy, were expressed by some Jamaicans.

> "You know, Black Americans write on bathroom walls, and we never do. The problem is you have to elevate yourself and some of them do not try. . . . Some pass it generation to generation, the bad things. When you do it and your kids do it, it is a problem. Some do rise above that. The main thing is we are Jamaicans and they are Black Americans." (Jamaican male, 6)

Another added:

> "My experience is that my generation before me came here to better themselves and moved up. People say of Jamaican immigrants 'Before you know it, they have a house and they are moving up,' while Black Americans are still stuck in poverty . . . they are not going to take jobs like cleaning toilets. So, they pass those jobs up. Meanwhile, other people have taken two of those jobs to get money and to move on out." (Jamaican male, 7)

A Jamaican woman actually indicated that African Americans were stripped of culture.

> "I have always sympathized with Black Americans. I used to get beat up (by African Americans) in school for being Jamaican. I was proud to be Jamaican and I sympathized with them because they could not understand what I was feeling. So, Black Americans have no culture." (Jamaican female, 6)

It is apparent from these discussions that most of these professional West Indian immigrants, largely Jamaicans, focused their differences with African Americans on perceptions associated with lower SES and social problems related to experiences in, or images of, poor inner-city neighborhoods that often are portrayed by the media. It is equally clear that some of their negative experiences with African Americans occurred during their formative years, an employment context, or some other limited exposure to African Americans. Whatever the case, there is a "distancing" by these professional class West Indians from African Americans in Broward County.

Although this study did not include interviews with African Americans, there is some evidence of local African-American resentment related to public spending on the construction of the cricket facility within the County Park system. This plan has brought complaints from the African-American community, including those presented to the Ft. Lauderdale City Council. Viewed from the perspective of a group who has the least positive SES gains, some African Americans have expressed dissatisfaction with government spending perceived as assisting immigrant Blacks at the expense of needy and deserving African Americans. The objection has included charges that local politicians are catering to the Black immigrants by using economic development funds and tax dollars for the stadium, rather than meeting the needs of the native Black population. African Americans accused government officials of "excluding non-Caribbean residents from the plan" and quoted African-American activist Alan Brown as stating:

> "They are abusing the processes of government. We just want to make sure our tax dollars are used for us. We don't want it tropical or Caribbean, just American." (www.narbosa.com July 17, 2007)

Jamaican officials answered the criticism by indicating that the project will create jobs for people of Broward County regardless of their ethnicity.

As was shown earlier in this chapter, there are major SES differences between native- and foreign-born Blacks in Broward County. There also are major differences in Ft. Lauderdale's poor neighborhoods, which are occupied predominantly by native Blacks, and the more affluent areas of Broward County, particularly in the western municipalities where the stadium is being built. It should be apparent that a substantial class difference is involved in this issue, as well as a native- vs. foreign-born element that becomes magnified when resources are at stake. This is not unique to Broward County. However, it underscores the ethnic tensions that sometimes occur when resources are at stake. This point was made for West Indians and African Americans in New York City. Apparently, a similar occurrence is present in Broward County, Florida.

SUMMARY

This chapter has answered a call to compare places of significant West Indian populations with New York City. The literature on the City's West Indians, especially Jamaicans, provides a basis of comparison in a variety of ways, including elements of their ethnicity and its expression as cultural landscape, their SES and occupational structure, neighborhood settlement patterns, and associations with African Americans. Broward County has become an emerging cultural center for West Indians, particularly Jamaicans, and provides a good comparison. Migration and immigration continue to fuel the growth of its Black population, which is led by Jamaicans. Broward County is now a stronger destination for foreign-born Blacks than Miami-Dade. Further, during the 1995–2000 years, Broward realized a net increase of Black foreign-born migrants, while Miami-Dade showed a net loss due to migration. Those Blacks entering Broward County had better SES than those departing the County for Miami-Dade. Since that period, Broward's Black population, fueled by Black Caribbean immigration, has continued to grow and it has become a minority-majority county.

This chapter demonstrates both similarities and differences between New York City's West Indians, especially Jamaicans, and those residing in Broward County, Florida. As in New York, ethnicity is strong among West Indians (and Jamaicans) in Broward County and is expressed in many ways, including as a unique cultural landscape. Regarding SES, West Indians, and Jamaicans alone, have better SES than native Blacks but are somewhat less well off than Latinos, and have lower SES than non-Hispanic Whites. However, as in New York City, Jamaicans stand apart from all but the White group in terms of having a high home ownership rate in Broward County. Regarding occupational structure, Jamaicans are relatively evenly distributed within three major categories, Managerial-Professional-Related Financial, Services, and Sales and Office. Another 21 percent of Jamaican occupations were in the two major categories of Construction-Maintenance and Transportation-Material Handling. This distribution illustrates a diverse Jamaican labor force, despite some concentrations in specific subcategories such as health professional and heath services. Further, women were more likely to be in nursing and men were more likely to be in other categories, such as maintenance and transportation subcategories. Thus, some similarities, such as health professionals and nursing, appear to be comparable to occupational structure of Jamaicans in New York City. Others do not, such as males in transportation in New York are highly represented in private transit (taxis, jitneys), whereas in Broward County they are employed in material handling and production occupations.

A triple layering settlement pattern has been reported for West Indian ethnic groups for decades. This concept has merit in Broward County but does not alone adequately describe the settlement pattern of Jamaicans, who have also settled in predominantly White, middle- and upper-middle income neighborhoods in Broward's western municipalities. Clearly, not all West Indians "prefer" to live in Black neighborhoods. Heterolocalism is the process of dispersed settlement while maintaining strong ethnicity. This, too, describes some professional Jamaican settlements in Broward County. Finally, the ideas of ethnic "distancing" and periodic ethnic conflict present in New York City between West Indians and African Americans also seems to apply at this time in Broward County. What remains unanswered is whether or not West Indian settlement in the majority-White suburbs will continue and reach a tipping point that will lead to White flight as it has in other communities, including New York. Or, will class (SES) overcome prejudice? Only time will tell.

NOTES

[1] The "Broward by the Numbers" publication series (2002–2006) produced by the Planning Services Division of Broward County was extremely helpful in the preparation of this section. Fieldwork supplemented that information.

[2] A grant from the Dean of Arts and Sciences and the Library at Binghamton University is gratefully acknowledged for this purpose.

[3] The author gratefully acknowledges a travel grant from the Dean of Arts and Sciences for this purpose.

[4] I am grateful to Roydale and Paulette Anderson for assistance in organizing these focus groups that were drawn from professional workplaces. Volunteers met in two separate groups and were provided dinner at a West Indian restaurant in return for their participation. A total of 16 West Indians, 14 of them Jamaicans, participated. All participants held professional employment and were immigrants. Some moved directly to Broward County from their homelands. Others migrated to Broward from New York City, Chicago, Atlanta, Miami, and other places. Professional employment included electronics, nursing, aircraft components technician, social services supervisor, aerospace, self-employed businessman, attorney, university academic advisor, documents image specialist, and a retired educator, among others. Thanks are also due to Roger Anderson and the Department of Planning, Broward County, for assistance in field work during this research.

Chapter 15

Africans in Washington, DC: Ethiopian Ethnic Institutions and Immigrant Adjustment

ELIZABETH CHACKO

Historically, for immigrants to the United States, ethnic institutions and organizations provided spaces where customs and traditions were practiced and preserved, and also provided support structures that aided in adjustment to a new setting with unfamiliar cultural mores. Religious ethnic institutions such as churches, mosques and synagogues, secular organizations such as ethnic clubs, professional associations, and ethnic media, as well as enterprises like ethnic stores and restaurants have traditionally played important roles in group coherence and survival in the host society. Ethnic institutions help ethnic groups stay connected and maintain traditions, but the value of ethnic organizations in promoting socio-cultural adaptation, greater political involvement and upward mobility is mixed. While ethnic communities, particularly through their collective assets and institutions, help in adjustment and integration (Bonacich 1973; Light and Gould 2000), critics argue that they may segregate the community from mainstream organizations and delay integration (Johnson 1988), and that adapting to the dominant group is the route to upward mobility (Sanders and Nee 1987).

In the 19th and early 20th centuries, ethnic institutions were almost entirely confined to ethnic enclaves, areas where distinct immigrant communities clustered due to segregation (forced or voluntarily). The United States shift from an industrial to a post-industrial economy in the late 20th century and a greater tendency for the post-1965 immigrants to be dispersed rather than clustered (Zelinsky and Lee 1998) diminished the traditional residential enclave. For example, Ethiopians represent a recent dispersed immigrant group to the Washington, DC metropolitan area. Religious and secular ethnic institutions and organizations assist in socializing this group, and have an impact on consolidating and advancing the community and preserving cultural heritage within the group. The roles played by Ethiopian ethnic institutions in keeping the immigrants connected to their traditions, while promoting integration and involvement in American society, provide insights into the many facets of the process of community building and the entrenchment of this group of African immigrants. Ethnic institutions metamorphose in response to greater diversity of new arrivals from the home country, but with longevity of the community in the host country, institutions also are established to fulfill the desires of more entrenched and integrated co-ethnics in the area of settlement. Although spatially concentrated ethnic institutions are no longer the norm, the institutions themselves remain important because they serve an increasingly diverse and scattered population of co-ethnics, and play a role in the adjustment process by changing their agenda as the longevity of the immigrant group in the host country increases.

A RECENT IMMIGRANT POPULATION, A NEW IMMIGRANT DESTINATION

The new African Diaspora to the United States emerged with the changes in the 1965 immigration law that allowed 170,000 admissions per year from the Eastern Hemisphere.[1] The Refugee Act of 1980 further eased the entry of Africans from war-torn and politically unstable countries.[2] While Somalis currently represent the largest group of refugees and asylees from Africa to be admitted to the United States, until 1990, the majority of African refugees were from Ethiopia (Figure 15.1).

Between 1971 and 2004, more than 43,000 Ethiopians who arrived as refugees/asylees were granted legal residence; 36,407 (over 80 percent) arrived between 1980 and 2000. The total annual number of African refugees to the United States rose from less than 1000 in 1980 to 29,124 in 2004 (Office of Refugee Resettlement 2006). The Diversity Visa Program of the Immigration Act of 1990 which permitted employment-based visas from countries with low rates of immigration to the United States provided an additional impetus for immigrants from Africa, because many desired to leave the continent due to economic and political problems in their home countries (Gordon 1998). As these immigrants became U.S. citizens, many sponsored parents and siblings for permanent residency. As a consequence, the annual number of Ethiopians who obtained legal residential status in the United States increased almost five-fold between 1990 and 2006, increasing from 2,694 to 13,395. By 2006 Ethiopians accounted for 12 percent of all Africans granted legal residence in the country (Department of Homeland Security 2006).

Figure 15.1.
Immigrants from Africa and Ethiopia to the United States, 1982–2004.

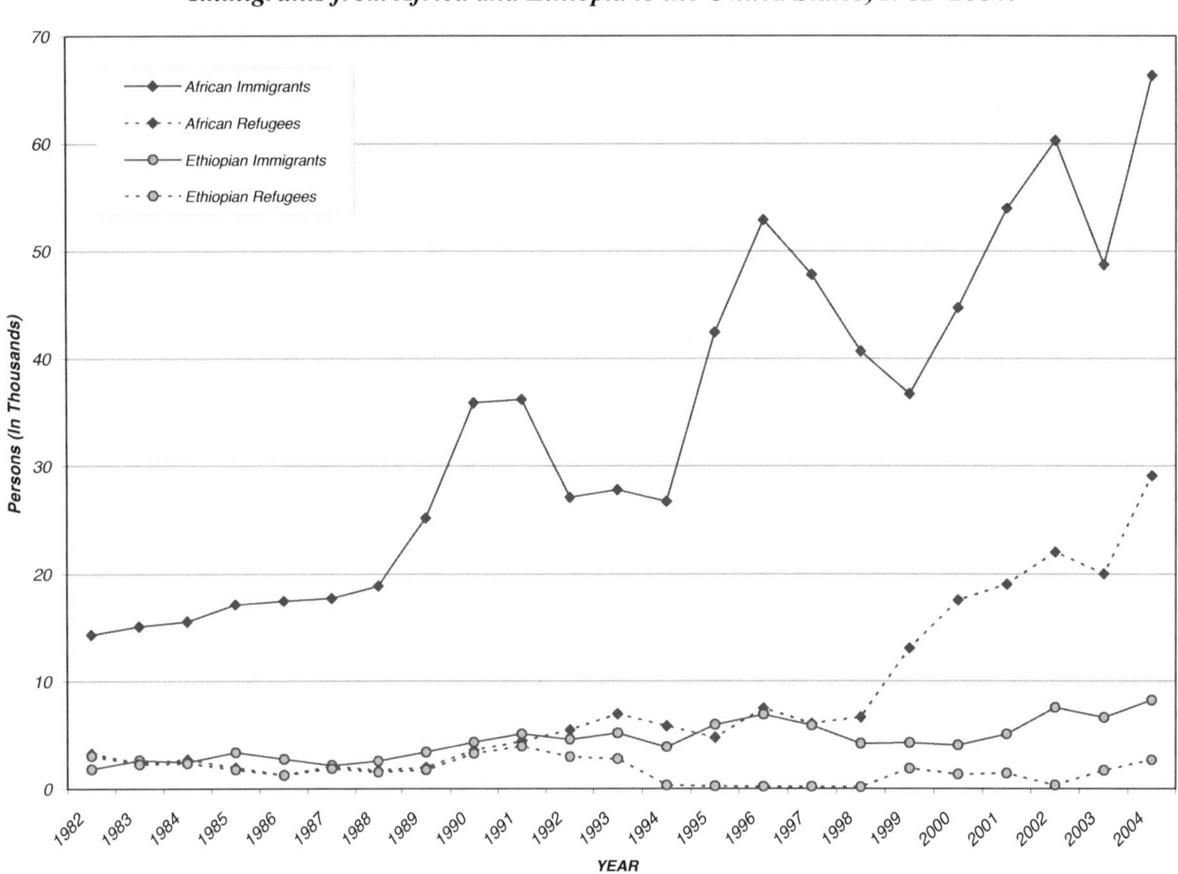

Source: Yearbooks of Immigration Statistics, Department of Homeland Security.

The Washington metropolitan region represents a relatively new immigrant destination, but one where the foreign-born population has grown exponentially (Singer 2004). Between 1980 and 2000, the Washington Primary Metropolitan Statistical Area's (PMSA's) foreign-born population increased by approximately 228 percent, while the share of the foreign-born in the metro area's total population more than doubled from 8 percent to 17 percent. Nearly half of the area's growth over this decade resulted from net international migration (U.S. Census 2000).[3] Due to the number and variety of immigrants present in the greater Washington, DC area, the region provides an ideal place to study immigrant behavior.

EXAMINING AN ETHIOPIAN IMMIGRANT POPULATION

Washington has attracted a disproportionate share of immigrants from Africa. African immigrants account for 13 percent of foreign-born in the metropolitan area, while they comprise less than 4 percent of all foreign-born in the United States (U.S. Census, ACS 2005). African immigrants tend to live in both ethnically diverse and Black-dominated neighborhoods in the metropolitan area (Friedman et al. 2005). Ethiopians, one of the oldest Black African immigrant communities in the Washington area, provide an important source of African immigrants to the metropolis (Bigman 1995). Comprising a fifth of the sub-Saharan foreign-born population living in the region, persons reporting Ethiopian ancestry were estimated at 28,583 by the American Community Survey, 2005. Community leaders place the number at over 100,000. Other significant African communities in the area (based on reported ancestry) include Nigerians (25,282), Ghanaians (11,209), Sierra Leonians (8,892), Somalis (3,642), Liberians (4,943) and Kenyans (2,873). Ethiopians living in the Washington area also account for a sizable proportion (~17 percent) of the entire reported population of Ethiopians living in the United States (U.S. Census, ACS 2005).

Washington, DC has been home to an increasing number of Ethiopians since the 1960s. Early members of the local diasporic community were educated and belonged to the middle and upper classes. Many Ethiopian diplomats and other professionals, including persons employed in the capital's many multi- and bi-lateral organizations, lived here. Ethiopian students, several on national scholarships, chose universities in the District of Columbia, particularly Howard University, to pursue higher education. Some members of this small core stayed on after completing their education, acquiring work visas and the status of permanent residents, augmenting the small Ethiopian population in the area (Selassie 1996).

The incipient community of Ethiopian immigrants in the Washington area grew from the 1980s onwards, stimulated by political and economic upheavals in the home country and aided by more lenient immigration legislation in the United States. The 1974–1975 civil war in Ethiopia and continued violence under dictator Mengistu Haile Mariam's communist government spurred outmigration; many of the country's elite and best educated moved to other countries (Woldemikael 1996). In the aftermath of the 1980 Refugee Act, the flow of refugees from Ethiopia increased tremendously. Many Ethiopians who arrived in the United States in the 1980s and 1990s were political immigrants (refugees and asylees), who sought to escape war and persecution.

To examine the behaviors and cultural ties of the Ethiopian immigrant population in the region, a survey was administered to persons who entered the country as refugees, asylees, family-sponsored immigrants and those with work visas and diversity visas. The political and personal contexts of persons belonging to each of these categories vary enormously, as do their legal and temporal access to resources that are wholly or partially provided by the state. It is believed that the 30 people surveyed represent a snapshot of the community in Washington.

Interviewees were identified with the help of the author's contacts in the Ethiopian community in Washington, and through snowballing. Additionally, data on the types of activities and services offered by religious and secular Ethiopian institutions in the Washington metropolitan area were obtained from key informant interviews with local Ethiopian leaders and heads/staff of Ethiopian institutions; websites, promotional literature and brochures.

Immigrants tend to concentrate in areas where there is an established community of compatriots. Ethiopian refugees, asylees and immigrants surveyed say they were drawn to the Washington area with its existing population of co-ethnics and its growing employment opportunities, particularly in the service sector. Between 1983–1990, Maryland and the District of Columbia respectively accounted for the third and fifth largest concentrations of Ethiopian/Eritrean refugees in the country (Levinson and Ember 1997). Legal immigrants from Ethiopia also included highly skilled professionals who entered under employment-based visas as well as permanent residents who had originally entered on student and tourist visas, eventually changing their status to that of immigrant.

Figure 15.2.
Map Showing Distribution of Ethiopian Foreign-born as a Percentage of Total Foreign-born in Washington Metropolitan Area, 2000.

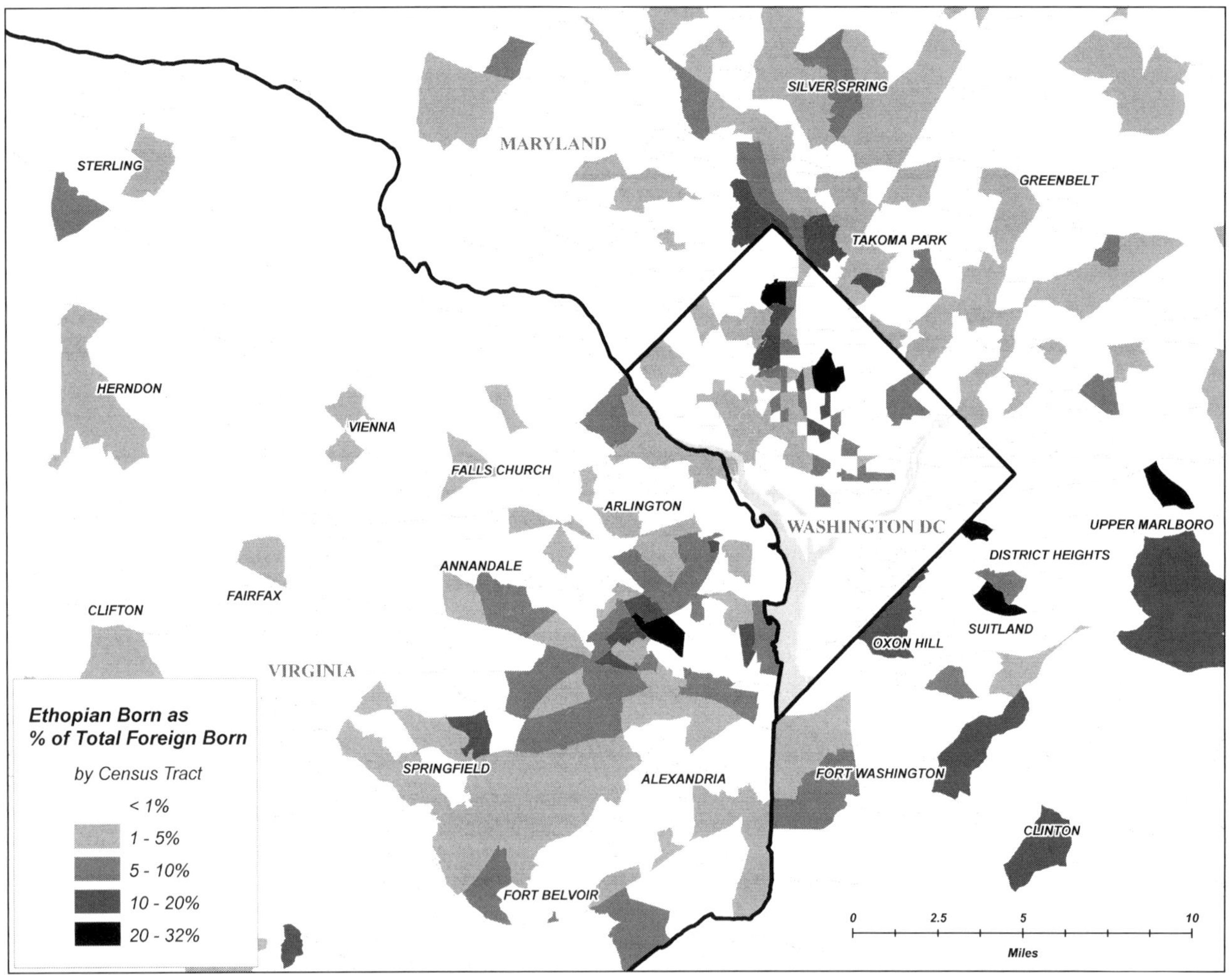

Source: United States Bureau of Census, 2000. Cartography by Nuala Cowan.

Ethiopians settled in the Adams Morgan, Columbia Heights, and Brightwood areas in the District of Columbia, and in the cities of Alexandria and Falls Church, and Arlington and Fairfax Counties, Virginia. Locales within Fairfax County include Annandale, Springfield, Vienna and Fairfax City. In neighboring Maryland, they lived in Takoma Park, Silver Spring, and Greenbelt in Montgomery County and in Upper Marlboro, District Heights, Oxon Hill, Fort Washington and Clinton in Prince George's county. As rents and real estate values in the Washington, DC vicinity continue to rise, Ethiopian immigrants are settling in areas in the more distant outer suburbs (Figure 15.2), such as Sterling in Loudoun County and Woodbridge in Prince William County in Virginia.

ETHNIC INSTITUTIONS AND IMMIGRANT ADAPTATION AND INTEGRATION

A greater openness to multiculturalism and diversity in the United States has led to a decreased emphasis on assimilation in which new immigrants were required to jettison their attachments, cultures and tastes in order to be accepted into American society. Immigrants selectively absorb elements of American culture as they integrate into the larger society. Traditionally, religious and secular ethnic institutions met the demand for services and sustenance required by new ethnic arrivals. They acted both as filter and a buffer against mainstream American culture. Robert Park asserted that immigrants formed ethnic organizations to help ease their adjustment to a new society and culture, but that the objectives of such organizations also reflected the emerging needs and aspirations of immigrant groups (Park 1920; 1967). Membership in an ethnic group also offered opportunities for employment in an ethnic economy, especially if the immigrants were spatially concentrated or had expertise in a particular trade. Self-employment was another avenue as immigrants set up businesses that served fellow country men and women and tapped into financial capital made available through ethnic group networks (Aldrich and Waldinger 1990; Portes and Stepick 1993).

As geographic clusters of immigrant groups in American cities shrank or disappeared, some of the ethnic institutions relocated with the community, while others vanished. However, the immediate concerns of newer immigrants when they entered the host country continued to be housing, employment and finances. Family, friends and acquaintances, if present in the area of settlement, were vital in helping the new arrivals find shelter and jobs. They also helped them adjust to life in an unfamiliar country and society. Paradoxically, as residential proximity decreased among co-ethnics, institutions and agencies that provided services to them took on greater importance as keepers of culture and for social, economic and political support for a scattered diasporic community.

Ethiopian Ethnic Institutions and Support Networks in Washington

The presence of a robust community of co-ethnics aids in the formation of ethnic institutions and organizations, which can vary considerably in their missions, objectives and functions. While ethnic institutions can be classified as religious or secular, the functions of most ethnic organizations defy easy categorization. Religious organizations often provide cultural, educational and social services, and some secular institutions collaborate with religious institutions and organize cultural celebrations with religious overtones. As Ethiopians tend to locate in ethnically diverse neighborhoods scattered across Washington, DC and its inner suburbs, group meeting places are critical for community consolidation (Chacko 2003a).

Religious Ethnic Institutions

Religious institutions have always been central in immigrant life (Ebaugh and Charfetz 2000; Foley and Hoge 2007) because religion is a significant component of cultural identity for many immigrant groups. By sharing sacred space, affirming a shared faith and participating in traditional rituals, immigrants re-create elements of "home" in ethnic churches, mosques, synagogues and temples in the host country. These religious institutions moor new arrivals by providing them with not only spiritual, but also cultural sanctuary, where a sense of belonging is fostered and promoted through the use of familiar traditions and rituals, often conducted in native languages (Kwakye-Nuako 2006). Ethnic religious institutions thus provide the spiritual support structures to maintain group identity while simultaneously reinforcing linguistic skills and cultural norms. They also help immigrants and refugees integrate into American society by serving as a link between the newcomers and the host society through church-based social, cultural and civic services.

Ethiopian immigrants to the United States are largely Christian, most being Amharic speakers who belong to the Orthodox Church. The country has a fairly large Muslim population, but there are proportionally few Muslim immigrants from Ethiopia (Levinson and Ember 1997). Not surprisingly, among religious institutions, Ethiopian churches play a significant role. The bedrock of religious life for most practicing Christian Ethiopian immigrants, churches provide a space to observe religious rituals and to meet far-flung fellow ethnics, while also offering services and activities for the benefit of the community (Broadway 1998). Fourteen ethnic Ethiopian churches are listed in the 2006 edition of the Washington Ethiopian Yellow Pages. These include Orthodox churches, and one evangelical church (Figure 15.3). In addition, there are two Catholic Churches as well as bible study and prayer groups that meet for worship in the Washington area. As the Ethiopian population of the region grew, the number of churches in the region and their membership multiplied, most churches reporting congregations in the hundreds. Meeting the needs of Ethiopian Muslims in the nation's capital is the First Hijrah Foundation, the oldest Ethiopian Muslim organization in the United States, which not only provides spiritual sustenance, but also promotes cultural traditions associated with this group that is believed to have emigrated from Mecca to Ethiopia.

Figure 15.3.
Ethiopian Evangelical Church in the District of Columbia.

Source: Author, 2007.

Keen to establish roots in Washington, some congregations rent space in other churches, while others have purchased buildings or land to construct churches. Shared religious beliefs, whether they are related to Ethiopian Orthodoxy, the Catholic Church, the evangelical movement, or adherence to Islam, give rise to solidarity within the Ethiopian religious communities. Cohesion that arose from a shared history in the home country and hardships in the United States, or strong feelings of unity and uniqueness as a religious ethnic community have helped generate and solidify linkages among Ethiopian immigrants.

The main function of Ethiopian churches is to provide a space for observing religious ceremonies and rituals. However, the church also is a venue for the interaction between members of a residentially dispersed community, thereby creating social networks and strengthening ties within a community of believers. Christian Ethiopian refugees and asylees interviewed for this study mentioned that attending church services was high on their list of priorities after arriving in the United States. All those who reported being affiliated with a church were regular attendees. Sunday church services that lasted from less than two hours to as much as four hours in the case of the Orthodox Church, were well attended. Ethiopian immigrants looked to the ethnic church and ethnic congregations to help keep religious traditions alive, while also partially fulfilling their social needs for interaction with compatriots, the support of a community with shared experiences and desires, and help in adjusting to an alien culture. In order to better reach the dispersed community, several churches advertise their religious services and special activities through native language newspapers, the Internet and also the Ethiopian Yellow Pages. Some such as the Ethiopian Evangelical Church in Washington, DC have broadcasts on weekends on the WUST 1120 AM station. Some church websites also provide audios of archived broadcasts and Sunday sermons.

Starting in the late 1980s, some Ethiopian churches also began expanding their services to include those in the secular realm, such as the provision of social services, citizenship training and Youth Programs. Many introduced English language classes for new immigrants, providing them with a necessary tool for social and economic advancement. A perceived need to keep young immigrants from losing their cultural moorings has led many churches to offer classes in the native language (mostly Amharic), tutoring, and group activities on weekends with a community of peers in a safe environment. Older members of congregations also assist youngsters with their studies and organize sports activities and outings for them.

Churches are also indirectly involved in helping parishioners find suitable employment. Established members direct fellow parishioners to local job fairs, connect co-ethnics seeking employment with potential employers both within and outside the ethnic community, pass along information related to job openings and even actively recruit new employees for their companies from among co-religionists. A quarter of the church-going interviewees mentioned that they had obtained leads and information related to employment from members of their church.

Concern for the physical as well as spiritual well being of their members has led some of the larger churches to conduct health information sessions for their congregations. One church had a health committee which took upon itself the task of providing members with information on local clinics and options for health insurance. The committee also organized free flu shots for members of the congregation as well as free mammograms.

Secular Ethnic Organizations

Secular organizations that assist refugees, asylees and immigrants run the gamut of federal agencies to local mutual assistance ethnic organizations. The Federal government of the United States, through its Office of Refugee Resettlement, provides the most comprehensive assistance to eligible political refugees, providing cash, medical care and social services to help them adapt to American society. Additionally, a select group of non-profit agencies, with the help of the government's State Matching Grant Program, assists refugees attain self-sufficiency in four months after arrival, by providing food, housing, case management and employment services. Refugees, asylees and immigrants also are helped by a host of ethnic mutual assistance organizations, built for and by the community.

A number of Ethiopian secular non-profit, non-political organizations such as the Ethiopian Community Development Council (ECDC) and the Ethiopian Community Center (ECC) were established in the 1980s in the Washington area to meet the needs of the flood of refugees and asylees who arrived during this period. Originally established to cater to an Ethiopian clientele, both the population and the mission diversified over time in response to the changing needs of the Ethiopians and the larger immigrant community.

The Ethiopian Community Development Council (ECDC), a non-profit community-based organization, was founded in 1983 with the primary task of resettling Ethiopian refugees and promoting cultural, educational and socioeconomic development in the refugee and immigrant community in the United States. The organization also conducts humanitarian and socio-economic development programs in the Horn of Africa. One of ten national resettlement agencies in 1990, the Virginia-based ECDC has assisted an increasingly diverse and dispersed refugee community through seven national affiliates that provide similar services in their communities. In the Washington area, ECDC serves an ethnically disparate community, while it continues to assist African refugees. Although the ECDC mandate is to serve both refugees and asylees, refugees make greatest use of the organization's assistance.

Ethiopian asylees tend to be more affluent than Ethiopian refugees, entering the country on tourist and student visas before applying for asylum, and they tend to receive settlement and employment assistance from non-government sources or ethnic organizations. The asylees in this study obtained information on housing, jobs and local services through their personal network of friends, family, and compatriots. Although asylees are eligible for the same cash and medical assistance as refugees, in the past these services were available only for eight months from the date of entry into the United States. Often, by the time asylum had been granted the assistance period had elapsed. Although asylees could receive help from social service agencies, many turned instead to acquaintances and friends. Asylees, along with those who entered on family reunification visas also tended to be more likely to work for Ethiopian enterprises in the early years. In fact, the first job of many Ethiopians without marketable skills or English proficiency was in an ethnic business (Ungar 1995).

The Ethiopian Community Center (ECC), established in 1980, has its office in the District of Columbia. Unlike ECDC, its geographical focus is limited to the Washington region and it continues to serve mostly Ethiopians, although the organization also currently assists rising numbers of Hispanic and Asian immigrants. The agency offers charitable assistance to needy members of the community and a broad range of social services that are critical to newly arrived immigrants and refugees. These services include information and referral services on education, employment, health care, housing, immigration and legal assistance to the community. Additional support provided includes English language classes and computer training, and translation and interpreter services. Asylees and immigrants who had entered on family-reunification and diversity visas made the most use of the services of ECC.

The Ethiopian Social Services in Silver Spring, Maryland, provides assistance to immigrant co-ethnics, offering advice on immigration-related issues, holding computer literacy classes, teaching traditions and languages to second generation Ethiopians, helping Ethiopian immigrants who have substance abuse problems, providing preventive health care information, and organizing conferences and seminars on issues related to Ethiopia. The Ethiopian Community Service and Development Council in DC provides a similar range of adjustment-related services primarily for new arrivals, including refugees, asylees and immigrants.

Ethnic Media Institutions

Ethnic media in the form of print, radio, television and interactive communications are important means of informing and educating immigrants, while maintaining community within the immigrant group. Ethnic media provide their clientele with local, national and international news, information and tools to help them navigate an alien environment and information on group-specific activities and programs in a culturally appropriate manner. For example, Ethiopian Community TV (ECTV), an independent organization, creates, produces and cablecasts Ethiopian programs in the Washington metropolitan area to "preserve, enhance, and share the Ethiopian diversity of thought and culture." In 2007, the range of television broadcasts from the Washington area was expanded with the establishment of Ethiopian Television Network (ETN) by immigrant journalists and entrepreneurs. ETN has 24-hour TV broadcasts that can be accessed in the United States, Canada and the Caribbean.

Many of the radio programs that cater to the community use the FCC licensed Washington, DC radio station WUST 1120 AM, which serves the city of Washington, DC, its suburbs in Virginia and Maryland, and the city of Baltimore. Individual radio programs such as EHN News, Radio Tewahedo and Hager Fikir Radio access the WUST 1120 AM frequency independently. Others, such as New World Radio (NWR) and DC Broadcast Radio, aspire to serve a larger community of immigrants. NWR dubs itself "the multi-cultural voice of the nation's capital" and broadcasts in over 17 languages, although many of its programs and advertisements appear to specifically target the Ethiopian community, broadcasting religious services from a number of churches and Christian denominations, and community-oriented programs in the Ethiopian languages Amharic, Oromo, and Tigrinya.

ETHNIC ORGANIZATIONS AND CULTURAL REPRESENTATION

Another set of ethnic institutions seeks to showcase Ethiopian civilization and cultures. Through ethnic assertion, or what has been referred to as the "politics of recognition" (Taylor 1994), Ethiopians strive for public affirmation of group identity. Such recognition is important for cultural survival. Ethnic organizations respond to the narrow depiction of Ethiopia by American media as an area of high poverty, recurring famine, and ethnic and state violence, and attempt to fend off discriminatory representations of their homeland by creating greater public awareness of Ethiopia's long history and rich cultures. Others look to enhance the local Ethiopian diasporic community's knowledge and appreciation of their heritage. For example, the Center for Ethiopian Arts and Culture (CEAC), located in Columbia Heights in DC, nurtures cultural identity and fosters the study, promotion and preservation of Ethiopian culture. The CEAC has collaborated with various mainstream cultural organizations in the United States and was instrumental in bringing Ethiopian dance, music and crafts to the city, especially through the Smithsonian Institution's yearly folk festivals.

There are non-religious organizations and groups that arrange regular activities or special cultural events that bring the community together. Each year, the CEAC organizes community celebrations of Inqutatash, the Ethiopian New Year, in spaces like hotels and parks. Meskal, an Ethiopian tradition of Coptic origin, is celebrated jointly in the Washington area by members of the Orthodox Church and other Ethiopian Christian denominations. The festival is held annually in the District's Malcolm X Park in late September. Ethiopian parents want their children to appreciate and understand Ethiopian cultures and languages as they adapt to American society. Both religious and secular organizations run weekend schools and organize camps for children that nurture cultural identity through formal and informal education. The second generation is taught to read and write native languages and become fluent in Ethiopia's cultural traditions.

The Ethiopian Sports Federation in North America, a pan-national organization, has organized and held the annual Ethiopian Sports and Cultural Festival multiple times in the Washington area. The Festival, which showcases traditional and popular Ethiopian culture through the performing and visual arts, and sports, is an important annual occasion for America's Ethiopian communities. The event attracts thousands of spectators and participants (Sun 1996). The organization also provides a limited number of scholarships to students of Ethiopian heritage and has plans to develop a network of academic mentors to prevent burnout among the group's high school and college students.

The Ethiopian Millennium, based on the Coptic calendar, occurred on September 12, 2007.[4] The community in Washington, DC was instrumental in persuading the mayor of the District of Columbia to declare September 12, 2007 as "Ethiopian Millennium Day." Institutions including churches and secular groups in Washington, DC celebrated the new millennium with pomp and circumstance over five days through a series of lectures, symposia, art and photography exhibitions and other events. A large cultural festival was organized on the National Mall near the Washington Monument on New Year's Eve (September 11), a locale that assured high visibility and provided sufficient space for the hundreds of Ethiopians and friends of the community who attended the festivities (Figure 15.4).

Figure 15.4.
Impromptu Dancing as Ethiopians Gather Near the Washington Monument to Celebrate the Ethiopian Millennium. September 11, 2007.

Source: Author, 2007.

The cultural festival included music, poetry, ethnic cuisines and appearances and speeches by local celebrities and political figures, and culminated in the burning of torches in the traditional *chibbo* ceremony. A "Demonstration for Democracy," took place on September 12, at the U.S. Capitol calling for peace, justice, and progress for the people of Ethiopia in the coming Millennium, bringing attention to human rights violations in the home country (Figure 15.5). However, for most, celebrating the new millennium was an opportunity to showcase Ethiopia's cultures and the contributions that Ethiopia has made to the world to the larger American community and to instill pride in their heritage among Ethiopian Americans who were born in the United States.

ETHNIC ORGANIZATIONS AND POLITICAL MOBILIZATION

As Ethiopians achieved critical mass and a significant presence within the Washington area and as a second generation of young Ethiopians who were born in the United States came of age, the needs of the immigrant community were transfigured. Longevity in the country was accompanied by a greater sense of being a part of U.S. society and the body politic, and in the case of the second generation, being Ethiopian-American rather than simply Ethiopian (Chacko 2003b).

Foreign-born Ethiopians, along with other fellow Africans, have traditionally demonstrated higher levels of educational achievement than either Native Americans or many other immigrant groups (Arthur 2000; Ashabranner 1999). While the lack of recognition of credentials acquired in the home country may have inhibited educated Ethiopians from getting jobs commensurate with their qualifications and skills, this store of human capital aided established immigrants in gaining a political voice in their adopted country (Chacko and Cheung 2006). Their incorporation into U.S. society and participation in political processes also was helped by proficiency in English even among first generation immigrants. Urban-educated Ethiopians are required to learn English in high school in their native country, a regulation that helped immigrants acquire the linguistic skills that would assist in a better understanding of the American political process and a speedier involvement in it. Especially during the 1970s and 1980s, many immigrants who fled Ethiopia had a history of political activism against the repression of the Mengistu regime. The political activism integral to this group also has helped motivate greater incorporation into neighborhood and city political processes (Chacko and Cheung 2006).

Despite residential dispersion in highly diverse neighborhoods, in recent years Ethiopian immigrants have made concerted efforts to maximize the group's political voice. The mission of organizations such as Ethiopian American Constituency Foundation (EACF) established in 2003 in Washington, DC is to facilitate the involvement of Ethiopian immigrants in U.S. political practice and acquire greater visibility and political influence for the group. First- and second-generation Ethiopian immigrants have joined forces to encourage the community to further the ethnic cause by increasing their political participation in U.S. society.

For example, the EACF was active in lobbying for the official designation of an "Ethiopian neighborhood" in the Shaw neighborhood of Washington, DC. The organization launched an online campaign, urging members of the Ethiopian community and others sympathetic to the cause to sign an Internet petition to the DC City Council asking for the creation of a city-recognized and designated ethnic neighborhood. Although the group decided to abandon the push for a designated Ethiopian neighborhood in the face of strong resistance from the local African American community (Chacko 2008), EACF is still very active in promoting the political involvement of Ethiopian immigrants in the city of Washington, DC. The Ethiopian community worked with other ethnic minority groups in the city to get the DC Language Access Act signed by the Mayor of Washington in 2004. This act assures those living in the District access to programs and services in five languages other than English, one of which is Amharic, the primary language spoken by Ethiopians in the city.

Another organization, Ethiocorps, was established in 2004 by young Ethiopian professionals and students who wished to create a corps of volunteers to work in Ethiopia for periods from six months up to a year. Targeting mainly second generation Ethiopians, the organization hopes to produce young leaders who will use their American education and acquired skills in conjunction with a sense of pride in their cultural heritage to serve as role models for Ethiopians and Ethiopian-Americans alike through transnational linkages.

Figure 15.5.
Demonstration for Democracy Outside the United States Capitol on September 12, 2007, the Ethiopian Millennium.

Source: Author, 2007.

The willingness and ability of Ethiopian immigrants and their ethnic institutions to utilize host country political processes to achieve their goals point to the increasing political assertiveness and activism of the group over time. Ethiopians in the Washington area also have effectively tapped into local and national political networks, engaging the interest and assistance of a former U.S. ambassador to Ethiopia, city council members of DC wards with a relatively high proportion of Ethiopians, the mayor of the District of Columbia and several congressmen affiliated with the Congressional Ethiopia and Ethiopian American Caucus in their quest for political recognition and economic development.

ETHNIC INSTITUTIONS AND BUSINESS OPPORTUNITIES

Foreign-born in the United States tend to have higher levels of self-employment than natives (Borjas 1986). Immigrants set up their own businesses because human capital in the form of foreign-earned degrees may not be recognized in the host country. Seeking upward socioeconomic mobility (Vesely 2005) many turn to ethnically-oriented businesses and labor markets, pooling ethnic labor power and family resources to keep the costs of running a new business low. Newly arrived immigrants often do not have sufficient capital or the collateral to qualify for credit from conventional banks. Besides, banks may be unwilling to lend to certain communities because of the high transaction costs involved in screening, monitoring and enforcing small loans. Ethnic communities overcome these problems by using rotating credit associations or mutual assistance groups in which each member of the lending group periodically contributes a given amount of money to a larger pool, the total amount of which was awarded to each member of the group on the basis of lottery, bid or need. In Ethiopia, such associations are called "ekub." Operating outside the formal economy, ekub depends on culturally enforced norms and trust among members so that individuals who have already received the pot of money will not default on payments before the end of a cycle of payment.

Strong within-group networks have resulted in the formation of organizations such as the Ethiopian Professionals Association Network (EPAN). Established in 1999, the goal of this association is to help Ethiopian professionals and students achieve competitive advantage in the workplace and institutions of higher learning by providing current information on job opportunities, possible careers and scholarships. The main objective of another organization, the Ethiopian Business Association (EBA), is to provide financial advice and help to co-ethnics who wish to start business ventures. The EBA also works to revitalize traditional norms, values, and civic unity within the community.

The Enterprise Development Group (EDG) is an affiliate of the ECDC that seeks to provide affordable financial services to immigrants and refugees. Using money obtained from the Federal Office of Refugee Resettlement, Small Business Administration, the Calvert Foundation and even some commercial banks, EDG offers loans of up to $50,000. The organization analyzes the business plans and credit histories of applicants before giving out loans, but also uses non-traditional collateral to secure a loan. Ethiopian immigrants and refugees who availed of EDG's microfinancing have used the money to buy taxicabs, set up stores and other small business ventures.

DISCUSSION AND CONCLUSION

This chapter considers the degree to which immigrants from Ethiopia draw on ethnic resources and ethnic institutions for assistance with adjustment and integration, and how much they benefited from the presence and availability of these organizations in the Washington metropolitan area. As this chapter indicates, Ethiopian ethnic institutions in Washington have multiple roles as they assist in socialization of immigrants from Ethiopia, consolidation of the community, and preservation of cultural heritage.

Secular ethnic institutions that cater to the needs of recently arrived immigrants, refugees and asylees focus their energies on helping this group settle in the United States and adjust to life in an unfamiliar city and culture. The institutions themselves and the close ethnic community and networks they are associated with try to provide a safety net for co-ethnics. Through outreach services and by providing practical assistance, organizations such as ECDC and ECC try to circumvent and solve problems experienced by immigrants while acting as buffers against culture shock.

However, among those surveyed for this study, most who had recently immigrated to the United States relied on family and informal ethnic networks for help in obtaining housing, employment and cash assistance. The strong ties associated with these did not always provide comprehensive or sufficient support. A few of those interviewed lamented the fact that they did not have the information needed to utilize the services that they were eligible for, and appeared to have been isolated from likely support systems due to the insularity of their ethnic connections.

Religious ethnic institutions such as churches draw members of the group from all over the metropolitan area. Cultural affinities and shared core values make churches important institutions where Ethiopian culture and community is maintained and promoted. While largely catering to the spiritual needs of the group, churches also are venues that support networking. The ties thus formed in churches often help members gain access to information about housing, schooling, employment, health care and financial assistance. Churches also work with secular organizations in keeping community together through shared festivities and celebrations of Ethiopian holidays. As per the survey, the groups that made the greatest use of the resources of the Church are 1st generation immigrants such as those who arrived on Diversity Visas, Family Reunification Visas and asylees.

On the other hand, middle-class educated Ethiopian immigrants who had studied in the United States were likely to establish/become involved in ethnic organizations that were organized around pluralism and identity formation/transformation, and assisting humanitarian and development efforts in the home country. These associations are of more recent vintage, most having been established in the 1990s onwards. Through the politics of recognition, these newer organizations sought to improve the image of Ethiopians in wider American society and articulate a viable ethnic identity within the American context. They used American channels and means to engage compatriots in the political process. These strategies included political mobilization and the use of the Internet and World Wide Web for making virtual connections to attain greater visibility as an ethnic community and exert greater political influence.

Modern systems of communications have facilitated the growth and maintenance of support networks through institutions that are not always rooted in physical space. Members of Ethiopian professional and business networking organizations meet physically on occasion, but are increasingly bypassing connections made in material space for those forged in cyberspace. Easy access to such virtual networks also has encouraged use of the Internet for political activism and the organization of social and cultural events. Institutions and organizations assist individuals and the community in their assertion and celebration of an Ethiopian or Ethiopian-American identity.

Traditionally, in the process of ethnic assertion, cultural organizations tend to emphasize intra-group cohesiveness and distinctiveness, implicitly indicating the existence of a boundary between the ethnic group and those who do not belong to it. Increasingly, however, politico-cultural ethnic institutions have made efforts to bridge the gap between insular identity politics and broader immigrant as well as American political and cultural realms. Without diminishing the specificity of ethnic concerns, Ethiopian groups are reaching out to other immigrant groups in the city, such as the Vietnamese, Salvadoran and Chinese communities and forming loose coalitions around common causes such as affordable housing in the District of Columbia, language translation services in local clinics and health care. They are attempting to forge stronger links with other African immigrant groups and with native Blacks, particularly in Washington, DC.

In conclusion, Ethiopians in the Washington metropolitan area use both ethnic and non-ethnic resources to help in adjusting to life in the United States and in integrating into American society while maintaining cultural distinction. Socioeconomic class and the circumstances of migration appear to play important roles in the likelihood of social and political integration of the community. Except for the refugees, much social support comes from within the ethnocultural community in the early years after arrival in the United States. Over time, individuals develop more wide-ranging networks that help them take advantage of mainstream institutions. Given a scant quarter century of immigration to the United States, Ethiopians have been extremely successful in signaling their presence as a growing visible minority in a multi-ethnic city through continued public expression and validation of their culture, an increasing number of ethnic institutions and through political assertiveness.

NOTES

[1] The 1965 Act also permitted 120,000 from the Western Hemisphere, with a ceiling of 20,000 annual visas per country. The bulk of the admissions (74 percent) were reserved for family reunification visas, 20 percent for occupational preference visas, and the remainder for refugees.

[2] The Act distinguished between refugees, who applied for sanctuary while still abroad, and asylees, who sought haven from within the borders of the United States.

[3] Figures from the American Community Survey indicate that the region houses over 1 million foreign-born residents (U.S. Census, ACS 2005).

[4] The Ethiopian Millennium occurred seven years after the year 2000 in the Gregorian calendar.

Chapter 16

Somalis in Maine

FENDA A. AKIWUMI AND LAWRENCE E. ESTAVILLE

INTRODUCTION AND PURPOSE

Somalis are a part of the recent African Diaspora to North America. Studying the migration of Somalis from the dry, tropical "Horn of Africa" to moist, cold Maine is an exceptional opportunity to elucidate an array of fundamental cultural geography concepts as they apply to significant contemporary events. The purpose of this chapter is to examine the cultural geography of Somali migration from Somalia to cities and towns in the United States and, then, secondary migrations, to the small Maine community of Lewiston. This chapter is based on both quantitative and qualitative data, and includes interviews of key informants, and fieldwork to observe first hand changes in the cultural landscape.

CHARACTERISTICS OF THE SOMALI POPULATION

Jutting out as the "Horn of Africa" to form a long eastern coast on the Indian Ocean and shorter coastline to the north on the Gulf of Aden, drought-prone Somalia borders Ethiopia (including its eastern Ogaden region) in the west, Djibouti on the northeast, and Kenya to the south (Figure 16.1). The U.S. Department of State (2007) estimated that almost all (99.9 percent) of the 8.5 million people in Somalia were Sunni Muslims in 2006. The main languages are Af Maay and Af Maxad. A complex system of major clans and sub-clans with subtle cultural and language differences permeates society. Major clans are the Hawiya (approximately 25 percent of the population), Darood (22 percent), Issaq (17 percent) and Rahanwein (17 percent), Dir (7 percent), and Digil (3 percent). The remainder of the population belongs to various minority ethnic groups. Such economic caste groups as the Yibir (hunters), Midgaan (leatherworkers), and Tumal/Tomal (blacksmiths) make the cultural mix even more complex (Cassanelli 1995; United Nations Development Program 2007; Laitin and Samatar 1987; European Commission 2002; Institute of Cultural Partnerships 1997).

The so-called "Somali Bantus" of the Lower Juba Valley in southern Somalia have been an historically marginalized minority that differs culturally from the majority of Somalis. The Bantus were originally from central Somalia and are descended from slaves taken from such present-day East African countries as Malawi, Tanzania, and Mozambique during the Indian Ocean slave trade in the 18th and 19th centuries. Unlike the predominantly nomadic Somali majority, the Somali Bantus are largely sedentary subsistence farmers who settled and cultivated their crops in the Juba River Valley, a savannah rich in wildlife that receives the greatest amount of rainfall in the country. Strictly speaking, Bantu is a linguistic term, and those referred to as Bantu actually comprise various groups of people with languages rooted in Bantu and socio-cultural similarities. Ancestral Somali Bantu languages include Mushunguli and Zigua (Afolayan 2003; Besteman 1999, 2007a, b; Menkhaus 2003).

Figure 16.1.
Somalia.

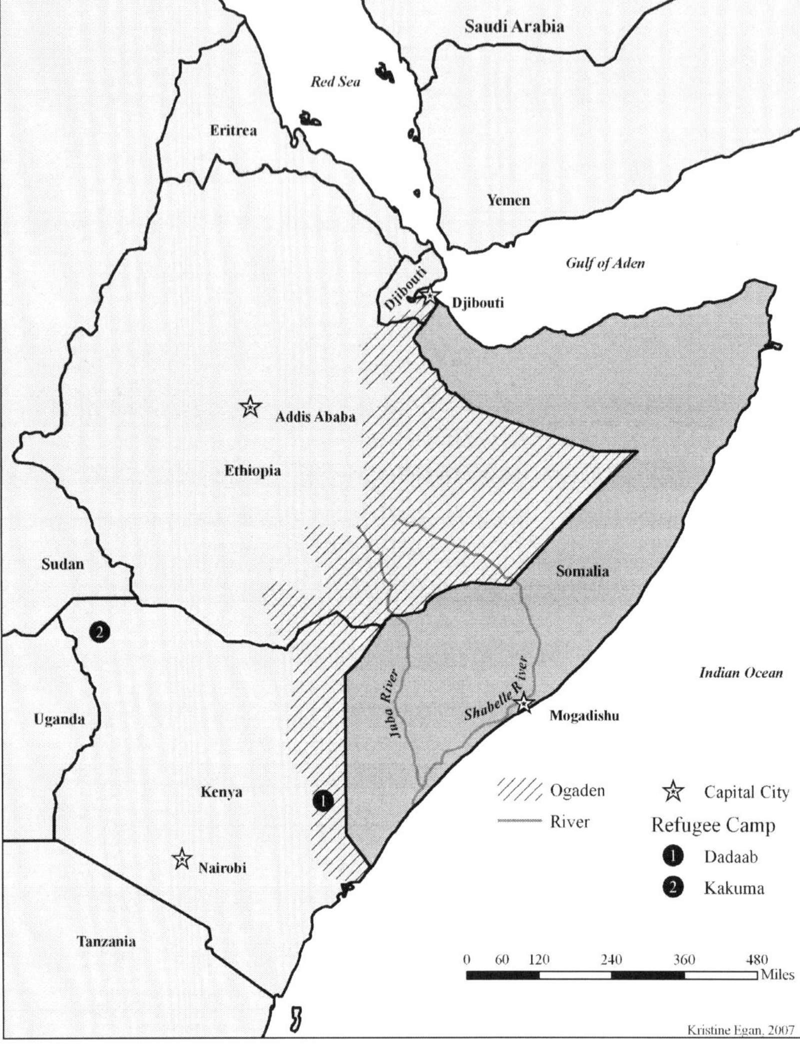

In 1960, after decades of European colonial rule, Somalia became a sovereign state. In an attempt to create a Pan-Somalia that included the Ogaden Region of eastern Ethiopia, with its large numbers of Somalis, President Siad Barre invaded Ethopia to annex the disputed territory. The ensuing war with Ethiopia and its Soviet Union and Cuban allies in 1977–78 led to a disastrous outcome for Somalia. Not only was the Somali army badly defeated, but clan based civil war erupted throughout the country in 1980 that led to a military coup overthrowing President Barre in 1991. Violence and anarchy have been pervasive ever since (U.S. Department of State 2007).

Decades of instability in Somalia displaced millions of people. The Ogaden War itself resulted in the forced resettlement of 1.5 million people into refugee camps throughout Somalia. As part of a 1980 agreement between Somalia and the United States, the U.S. acquired the Russian built naval base at Berbera and other facilities. In turn, the U.S. spent $132 million dollars in 1980–81 to help relieve the suffering of the 1.5 million internal Somali refugees (Gavshon 1981). Beginning in 1988, later waves of refugees moved into the Dadaab and Kakuma refugee camps across the border in Kenya (U.S. Department of State 2003a, b). Some refugees emigrated to the United States.

MIGRATION TO THE UNITED STATES

Somali refugees to the U.S. are from various clans, many of whom suffered persecution in clan warfare and anarchy dating back to the Barre era of the 1980s. Of the Somali refugees approved for resettlement in the U.S. in 1996, for example, approximately 4,500 were of the Tunni sub-clan from the Benadir Region along the southern Somali coast, and a small number of Ashraf, a group comprised of religious scholars and merchant families (Institute of Cultural Partnerships 1997). Somali clans committed atrocities against each other and on minority groups, with the Somali Bantus at home and in the Dadaab Refugee Camp in Kenya being frequent targets of discrimination and victimization (Besteman 2007a, b; Cassanelli 1995). In response, the United Nations High Commissioner for Refugees (UNHCR) in 1999 gave the Somali Bantus "special interest" status as a persecuted minority based on recommendations and verification by the UNHCR. In turn, however, resentment by the mainstream Somalis over the Somali Bantus preferred resettlement status simply exacerbated their suffering. The Somali Bantus were therefore moved 900 miles away to the specially constructed Kakuma Refugee Camp in northwestern Kenya to wait for processing and travel to the U.S. These Somali Bantus began arriving in the U.S. in 2003 as part of an overall resettlement program for approximately 12,000 Bantus. Like the earlier mainstream Somali resettlement, Somali Bantus were directed to selected locations throughout the U.S. (U.S. Department of State 2003a, 2006).

Somalis are thus a part of the recent African Diaspora to North America that has been estimated to include more than 100,000 Somali immigrants (Homeland Security 2006; Profile 2006). Of the African refugees admitted to the U.S., Somalis are the largest group with a total population of more than 65,000 (U.S. Department of State 2006). The decade between 1997 and 2006 saw a large Somali migration. In that time period 59,546 Somalis entered the U.S. (Homeland Security 2007). An additional 5,627 migrated to the U.S. by 2007 (Cultural Orientation Resource Center 2007). Roughly, a third of Somalis arrived in the U.S. under refugee-resettlement programs (U.S. Department of State 2006).

U.S. refugee policy is to establish clustered resettlement of in-migrants in selected locations to facilitate easy transition and integration, especially for rural and non-Western-educated refugees. Primary resettlement sites for Somali refugees were established in these metropolitan areas: Tucson and Phoenix, AZ, Salt Lake City, UT, Minneapolis-St. Paul, MN, Dallas and Houston, TX, St. Louis, MO, Nashville, TN, Clarkston, GA, Cayce, SC, Roanoke, VA, Erie, PA, Rochester and Utica, NY, Holyoke, MA, Concord, NH, and Portland, ME. Minneapolis-St. Paul has about 40,000 Somalis, the largest concentration in the U.S. (Swarns 2003). However, secondary migrations have underscored the Somali displacement chronicle in the U.S.

Voluntary agencies (Volags), working in cooperation with the U.S. Department of State, receive and place refugee groups in selected locations and assist them with basic amenities, English as a Second Language (ESL) classes, and job placement. In 2003, major Volags included the Church World Service, Episcopal Migration Ministries, Hebrew Immigrant Aid Society, Immigration and Refugee Services of America, International Rescue Committee, Lutheran Immigration and Refugee Services, United States Conference of Catholic Bishops, and World Relief Refugee Services. In addition, the U.S. Department of Health and Human Service's Office of Refugee Resettlement provides funding to the states and Volags for longer term refugee programs (U.S. Department of State 2006).

SOMALI REFUGEES IN THE UNITED STATES

Like earlier programs to resettle other refugees in the U.S. (e.g., the Vietnamese and Hmong of Laos after the Vietnam War), recent programs have placed the newly-arrived Somalis into cultural confusion and provoked clashes with the local populace and other migrant groups. The principal concern of the Somalis, particularly the poorly educated Somali Bantus, has been the maintenance of as many basic cultural traits as possible. The fears of the Somali community leaders have been well founded. After arriving in the U.S., their children quickly became mesmerized by American influences, both positive and negative. Such influences began to strain Somali family relationships and interactions with local residents and other refugee groups. Concomitantly, the local citizens in the American resettlement sites began to build up resentment about the government financial assistance given to Somalis and accused them of taking their jobs. As these cultural tensions heightened, especially in the larger metro areas like Clarkston, GA in the northeast Atlanta metro and the Dallas-Ft. Worth conurbation, the resettled Somali communities became culturally confused as their elders tried desperately to maintain as many African ways as possible, while their children were fast becoming a part of the American mainstream, learning English in schools, eating different foods, wearing different clothes, and hanging out with American friends, some of whom were gang members and drug users. Also pushing Somalis from their initial U.S. resettlement sites were high costs of living, loss of employment, and increasing crime (Bouchard 2002; Tilove 2002).

The disillusioned Somali elders responded by relying on the ancient nomadic practice of "sahan," literally meaning "to send out." Somali communities would send out scouts in search of better pastures for their livestock and good water supplies. Once these scouts returned with information about possible new sites, the communities selected the one they would move to next. Similarly, in the U.S., the Somalis put into practice the sahan to search for better places to live. Armed with information researched from the Internet and phone calls to government agencies and Volags about possible secondary migrations to particular states and cities, scouts were sent to a handful of new places to see first hand whether the quality of life, cost of living, government assistance, employment opportunities, educational systems, and crime rates would better fit the desired life styles of Somali families. The sahan included such places as San Diego, CA, Kansas City, MO, El Paso, TX, Nashville, TN, and Lewiston, ME. The Somalis liked Portland as an initial resettlement community, but the city could not accept any additional Somalis because of a lack of housing for them. In 2001, Somalis, mainly from Clarkston, GA, decided to move to Lewiston, a small town located 30 miles northwest of Portland (Yomoah 2007; Nadeau 2007).

SOMALI REFUGEES IN LEWISTON, MAINE

In 2001, Lewiston, the second largest city in Maine, had an exceptionally homogeneous population of about 36,000, 96 percent of whom were Caucasian (Figure 16.2). Yet, its citizens take pride in their city having been built by ethnic immigrants from its incorporation in 1863. The rise of textile mills and shoe manufacturing spurred economic growth in the 19th and 20th centuries. By the 1950s, Lewiston was the premier textile manufacturing center in Maine. Employment demands in the mills attracted Irish immigrants as early as the 1840s, and, from the mid-19th century to the Great Depression, thousands of French Canadians migrated to New England in search of jobs in the region's woolen and cotton mills. Many of these French Canadian families settled in Lewiston along the banks of the Androscoggin River. In fact, in 2000, 29 percent of Lewiston's residents, including the city's mayor, still identified themselves as French Canadian (Nadeau 2005, 2007; Gilbert 2007).

Lewiston's population began to decline in the 1960s as its economy weakened. With intense competition in the textile industries from other areas of the nation and the world, from the 1980s to the mid-1990s high unemployment forced hundreds of workers to leave. In response, community leaders began to diversify the local economy from manufacturing to service and light industry and to demand the state provide Lewiston's citizens more educational opportunities, particularly in higher education and job re-training programs. These economic restructuring efforts and the concomitant revitalization of the city's central business district have been successful in stabilizing unemployment (less than 4 percent in 2001) and in creating a new community spirit. A continuing challenge, however, is attracting employers that will be able to raise Lewiston's median family incomes that remain low in statewide municipal comparisons (Nadeau 2003, 2005).

Figure 16.2.
Lewiston, Maine.

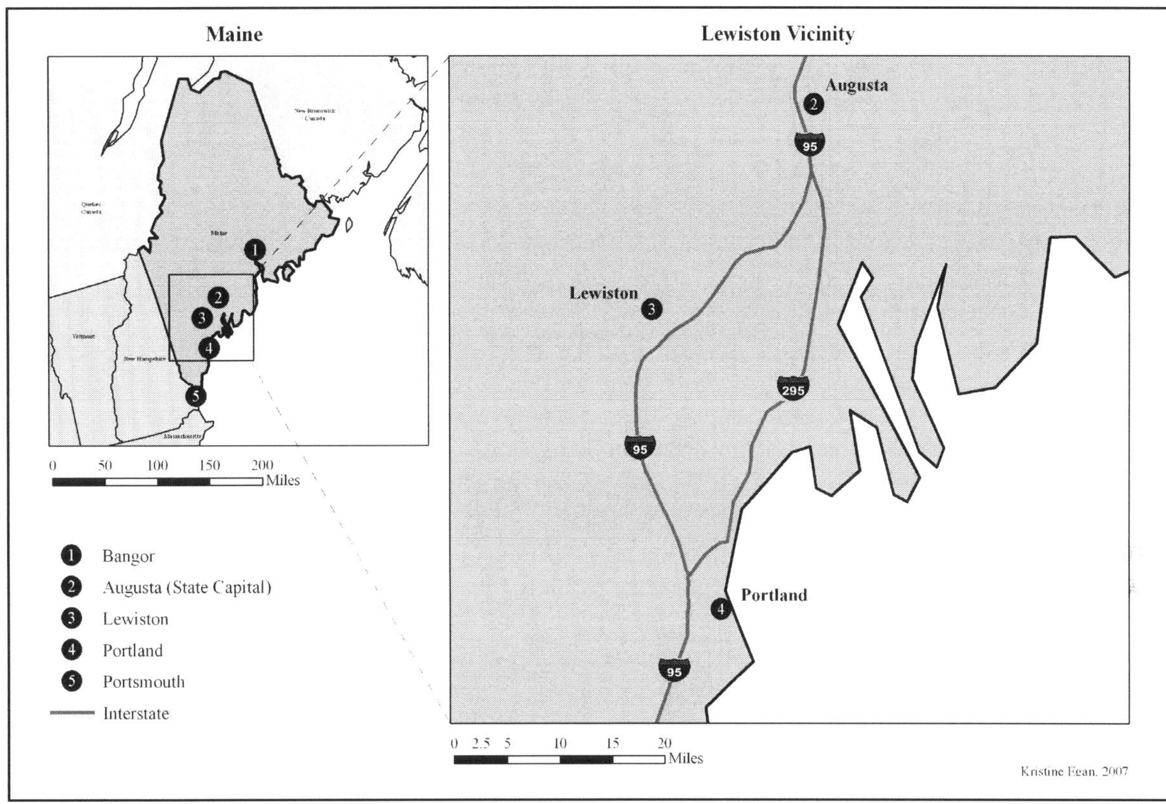

SOMALI CHAIN MIGRATION TO LEWISTON

Portland, Maine's largest city with about 60,000 people, was an initial settlement site for the Somalis and became a secondary migration site, especially for Somalis fleeing the Atlanta metro area. Portland's public housing, however, had reached its limits by 2001, and Somalis were being housed in municipal shelters and local hotels. The Portland Department of Housing and Human Services asked Lewiston leaders if they could help in reducing the Somali migrant pressures in Portland. In February 2001, the first Somali family arrived in Lewiston from Portland (Nadeau 2005; Taylor 2005). According to Lewiston's records, 260 Somalis relocated to the city by August 2001. But these Somalis were not all arriving from Portland. Although Portland seems to have been the initial magnet for family and friends that pulled Somalis from their primary settlement sites across the U.S. into Maine, migration chains quickly developed directly into Lewiston, drawing Somalis from Columbia, Kansas City, Memphis, Minneapolis-St. Paul, and New Orleans. Information via Internet websites, e-mail messaging, and phone communications, dramatically intensified and led to a completely unanticipated, "come on their own" arrivals of large numbers of Somalis directly into Lewiston. By July 2007, approximately 3,100 Somalis resided in Lewiston, increasing the city's population to nearly 37,500, with 8.5 percent being Somali (Nadeau 2003, 2005; maine.gov 2007).

The socioeconomic strains, however, of receiving 40–60 new Somali arrivals into Lewiston every month until 2002 produced both financial and cultural tensions in the community. The events that followed this initial Somali settlement became challenging and confounded at the local, state, and national levels and brought intense media scrutiny to a community that had few original African-American residents (only 361 Blacks in 2000) and little experience with immigrant resettlement programs. Thus, Lewiston's unique experience provides a worthwhile exemplar for other small communities across the U.S. to draw from as they enter the realm of the African Diaspora in North America.

In their secondary migration to Lewiston, Somalis were attracted by the same factors that Lewiston residents themselves find desirable: small town ambience and quality of life, improving employment opportunities, good schools, access to healthcare, and low crime rates. Some observers also suggest that a notable pull factor of Lewiston was the Somali perception of more efficient and accommodating social services compared to metropolitan places like Clarkston, GA, that have large and heterogeneous refugee populations competing for resources (Nadeau 2002, 2003, 2005, 2007; Gilbert 2007; Bouchard 2002; Tilove 2002). However, immigrants who undertake secondary migrations in the U.S., for whatever reasons, cannot bring along with them the direct federal funding that was provided in the original settlement sites. Moreover, in the Lewiston situation, the State of Maine was still in serious flux in trying to cope with its financial responsibilities from the new arrivals of Somalis and other African groups into the state, mainly in Portland. Lewiston was forced, therefore, to act quickly on its own to provide basic social services for these new, culturally different African people. Because of this anomalous external financial pressure to their community, concerns arose in the minds of Lewiston citizens, many of whom felt their taxes were already too high and who were just now beginning to enjoy the fruits of their years of economic redevelopment efforts (Nadeau 2002, 2003, 2005, 2007; Gilbert 2007).

In trying to cope with these fiscal challenges, Lewiston Mayor Raymond Laurier requested in an open letter published by the local *Sun Journal* (2002) newspaper to elders of the Somali community that they help to stem the increasingly large flow of Somalis into the city because of the socioeconomic stresses being placed on the community (mainetoday.com 2002). Although the Somali leaders in Lewiston understood the problem and did indeed help lower the subsequent number of arrivals, Laurier's letter created a firestorm of protest in which Lewiston's traditionally homogeneous White, Christian population was painted by the media in racist terms. These unfortunate perceptions led to a crescendo event on 11 January 2003, when nearly 4,500 people descended on Lewiston to protest and counter-protest their perceptions of the nature of race relations in Lewiston (Nadeau 2005, 2007; Gilbert 2007).

Perhaps, however, the most positive outcome of this emotional debate about race, culture, and religion in a post 9/11 context was that it demanded the rethinking of policy, funding resources, and organizational structures at the local, state, and federal levels that helped cause fundamental paradigm shifts to manage secondary migration into small American cities. The Lewiston experience thus led to innovative collaborations and initiatives within the city, with its Portland partners, and with statewide taskforces, committees, and networks, and several regional and national non-governmental organizations (NGOs), and propelled significant grant-writing efforts to obtain sustainable funding resources for the Somali immigrants. After undertaking these bootstrap efforts, some slow and painful, the marshaled resources provided an array of socioeconomic services for the Somalis, including Somali-language translators for 911 services, culturally sensitive city offices and police officers (including the creation of a comprehensive Limited English Language manual for city employees), and more understanding school environments, English as a Second Language (ESL) classes, healthcare access, and better job training and educational opportunities for their Somali neighbors. The successes in obtaining substantial funding transfers to Lewiston over the years has clearly improved the city's ability to sustain its Somali settlement programs and has opened new government positions and other local employment in various NGOs. In fact, the revitalization of the Lewiston CBD received an unexpected stimulus of both public and private monies to renovate dozens of nearby dilapidated mill-worker tenement buildings in a high-crime area into affordable and comfortable apartments where Somali families live adjacent to a new municipal park in a safe, congenial environment (Nadeau 2005, 2007; Gilbert 2007).

Over the years since the first Somalis arrived in 2001, Lewiston has matured in its understanding of the many manifestations of trying to do the right things in welcoming into their small town a group of Africans about whom they had little knowledge. Emblematic of these endeavors to be a place that is more culturally sensitive, Lewiston, with funds augmented by local philanthropists and Maine foundations, is creating in the city's public library the Marsden Hartley Cultural Center, which has as one of its fundamental goals the need "to support the acceptance and celebration of all cultures" (Lewiston Public Library 2007; Nadeau 2005, 2007).

SOMALI EXPERIENCE IN LEWISTON

Through the adaptation of their traditional sahan to discover better places to live, the Somalis were pushed geographically from their initial U.S. settlement sites and pulled into Lewiston to enjoy the ideals of American freedoms and to prosper with a good quality of life for their families, especially for their children. In meeting the challenges to create this optimistic new home, the Somalis certainly realized they had to enter into dynamic and innovative collaborations with the Lewiston community.

Demographics, Spaces, and Stratification

The dominant Somali clan in Lewiston is the Darood from southern Somalia. The Issaq clan is well represented as are the more recent arrivals of the Somali Bantus. Lewiston city administrators estimate the number of Somalis in the city at approximately 3,100, which roughly includes 80 percent mainstream Somalis and 20 percent Somali Bantus. An analysis of these 3,100 Somalis shows their population is youthful with 1,646 children under the age of 18 years old outnumbering 1,355 adults. Yet, 418 single males almost double the number of 216 single females. Interestingly, Somali households are overwhelmingly headed by 349 females; followed by 164 families with two-parent heads, and only 9 male-headed families (Yomoah 2007; Nadeau 2007).

Some observers think that the high number of households headed by females indicates that some Somalis engage in Islamic polygamy in which the female heads of households are actually wives of men at other residences. The Somalis deny the allegations by noting that some of these women have husbands who reside and work in other settlement sites in the U.S. or remain in refugee camps in Kenya, or the women are widows from the Somali warfare. Somalis know that polygamy is illegal in the U.S. and they may have separated their families into conjugal units, whereby females become the actual heads of household. Moreover, this female head-of-household dilemma has caused some federal resettlement officials concern about Somalis "working the welfare system" to the financial advantage of each separate household. The Somalis also know that welfare fraud will lead them to be deported and, along with refugee offices, carefully monitor their supportive governmental financial transactions (Bouchard 2002; Ludden 2005).

Although the Somalis are working hard to become integrated into the Lewiston community, they are spatially segregated in their residential locations. Approximately three-quarters of Somalis live northeast of the adjacent Lewiston CBD within a rectangle of about one-half mile on each side: Lisbon Street on the west border, Main and Sabattus streets on the north, Jefferson Street on the east, and Adams and Birch streets on the south (Figure 16.3). Many mainstream Somali families who are better educated and have attained some financial success have moved out of the central tenement area to two nearby apartment complexes, one a federal low-income housing unit in which 60 of its 90 apartments are now occupied by Somali families. These families either use the public bus network or have their own private vehicles for transportation (Nadeau 2007; SCM 2004).

Somalis living in the central Lewiston concentration are within easy 5–10-minute walks of the city, county, and state offices and nearby NGOs, particularly the activities that take place in the neighborhood at the Trinity Jubilee Center of Trinity Episcopal Church and the Catholic Charities (Wettlaufer and Ali 2007). Somali children attend nearby schools, and women in their colorful *hijabs* do their daily shopping only blocks away on Lisbon Street. The Somali cultural imprint is clearly evident in the heart of downtown Lewiston where spaces have been created to provide for their well being and the maintenance of their culture. A mosque, a halal market, and Somali shops, clothing stores, and a restaurant dot the central city landscape.

Communal gatherings of extended families on sidewalks outside the central tenement housing are reminiscent of typical African life (Figure 16.4). Extended families of six to nine people reside in sparsely furnished two or three bedroom apartments that evoke the artistic trappings of their Somali homelands through floor rugs and wall and window draping. With their shoes deposited at each doorway, children playfully interact from one family's space to the next (Figure 16.5). Somali families warmly welcome visitors with their traditional teas and sweets.

Figure 16.3.
Somalis in Lewiston.

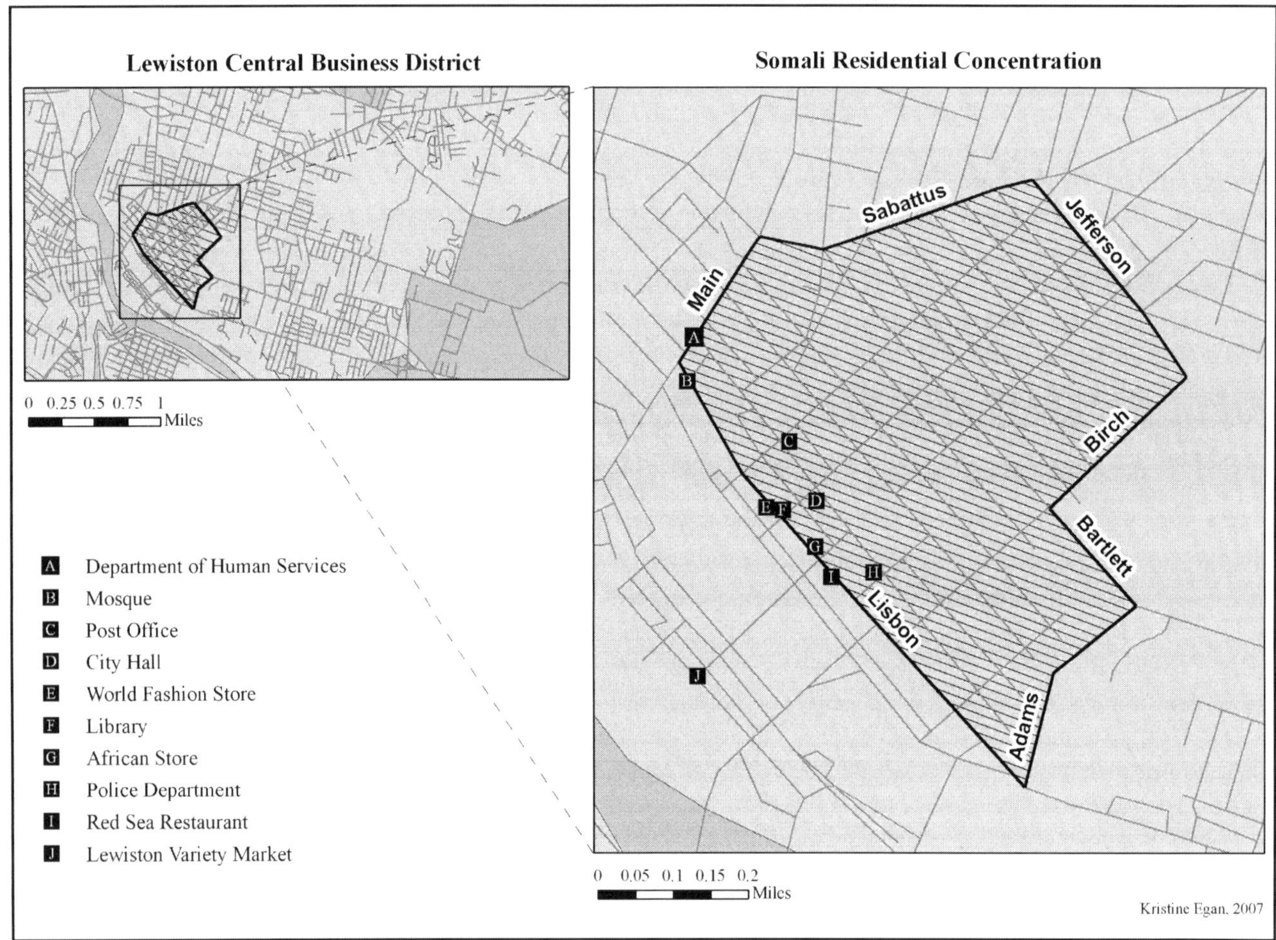

As it was in Somalia, in the Kenyan refugee camps, and in the initial U.S. resettlement sites, social stratification within the Somali community in Lewiston continues. Although some Somali elders deny that social stratification and prejudices exist among Somali clans in Lewiston, several Somalis and city and NGO administrators corroborate that these traditional African hierarchical relationships do operate in daily life in Lewiston. Tensions have occurred within sub-clans of both mainstream Somalis and Somali Bantus, but the most apparent discrimination is between the mainstream Somalis and the Somali Bantus, the persecuted former slaves in Somalia (SCM 2004; Finnegan 2006; National Somali Bantu Project 2007; Yomoah 2007; Nadeau 2007). These cultural lines are shown in the central tenement district where the households of the minority Somali Bantus, which are generally headed by females, are spatially segregated from the mainstream Somalis. This historic marginalization of the Somali Bantus, which typically excludes them from access to education, employment, and other resources, thus has been preserved through thousands of miles of migration from Somalia to Lewiston, Maine (Besteman 1999, 2007a, b).

Figure 16.4.
Somalis in Their Central Tenement District (by authors).

Figure 16.5.
Somali Family and Friends in a Tenement Apartment (by authors).

Education and Employment

Somali children are being educated in Lewiston's schools and have a variety of ESL and mentoring programs to try to bring them into the mainstream educational system and American society. With three-quarters of the adult population illiterate when they arrived in Lewiston, the Somali adult educational programs for ESL and job training face obstacles that include time-honored mores that women should not be educated. In fact, in the least educated Somali Bantus, men discourage their wives from attending ESL classes and job training programs. Lewiston city officials and local NGOs attempt to tie governmental financial support with adult educational achievements, a strategy that has legal constraints. The most important educational stimulus is that employers have standards of English usage for their employees to work in safe environments (*Washington Post* 2006; Nadeau 2007).

Jobs in services, construction, landscaping, housekeeping, and other unskilled labor are scarce in Lewiston and the surrounding communities. Some larger nearby employers, such as L. L. Bean, Home Depot, Fancy Stitchers, and Banknorth Group, have implemented programs to assist Somalis in job training, including translators and cultural sensitivity training, especially for daily Muslim prayers, for their local workers. The Somalis themselves recognize that the lack of formal western education is a major hindrance to sustainable employment and poses the risk of continued reliance on social services. Many Somalis, however, are seemingly eager to move toward self-sufficiency without dependence on government support (SBCMAA 2007; Chemlecki 2003; Nadeau 2007).

A few mainstream Somalis have established businesses, mostly in a four-block stretch on Lisbon Street in the Lewiston CBD, including A & R Halal Market, Somali shops, clothing stores, and a restaurant (Figure 16.6). Following the Islamic tenet that does not allow paying interest on money borrowed, these Somali entrepreneurs pool their funds to open their businesses (Yomoah 2007). Of course, these small start-up assets place the businesses in precarious positions at the outset, and several of the enterprises have failed or are only weakly sustainable. The symbolic importance, nevertheless, of Somalis working hard and investing their capital into the Lewiston community is not lost on the local residents (Nadeau 2007; Gilbert 2007).

Figure 16.6.
Somali Retail Shop on Lisbon Street (by authors).

Such NGOs as the Coastal Enterprises' New American Sustainable Agriculture Project (NASAP) have established farming cooperatives for Somalis to grow food for their families as well as to sell surplus produce at local farmers' markets and restaurants (Dannefer 2004; Burke and Yanga 2007; Ibrahim 2007). In cooperation with NASAP, the City of Lewiston set aside two parcels of land for these nearby farms that have proved to be a valuable transitional vehicle for the less educated, particularly Somali Bantu women (Nadeau 2005; Yomoah 2007). NASAP volunteers provide transportation and teach and work alongside Somali Bantu men and women to plant, harvest, and prepare the new vegetable crops in an attempt to replicate traditional African foods within the limitations of Maine's soils and climate. Somali Bantus, traditionally farmers, can thus use their agricultural skills, provide food for their families, generate income, and feel good about their accomplishments. Women with their colorful dress and babies carried on their backs in customary African fashion can be seen working gardens that seem as familiar and comfortable as those in Somalia (Figure 16.7) (Burke and Yanga 2007; Ibrahim 2007).

Figure 16.7.
Cooperative Garden Outside of Lewiston with an Aura of Traditional Africa (by authors).

Some Somalis travel from nearby states to purchase traditional Somali vegetables from the NASAP cooperative farms. NASAP also sponsors the establishment of goat farms in Maine to cater to the cultural diet of Somalis. The newly founded Lewiston Farmers' Market is set up to accept food stamps and provides a volunteer to work with the predominantly female farmers (Burke and Yanga 2007).

Islam, Cultural Maintenance, and Women

The overarching focus that guides the Somalis in Lewiston is their deep devotion to Islam. The first endeavor of pooling resources was for the purchase of a two-story building for a mosque in downtown Lewiston on Lisbon Street near the greatest concentration of Somalis (Figure 16.8). An Imam guides his people in the fundamentals of Islam, represents the foremost authority within the Somali community, and is a forthright proponent of the needs of his people in Lewiston. He and his advisors also interact with the Lewiston city officials to understand and to abide by governmental requirements regarding the maintenance and safety of those who observe their religious rituals at the mosque. The Imam provides transportation for worshippers to join in prayers and ceremonies at the mosque.

Figure 16.8.
Mosque in Downtown Lewiston (by authors).

Islam and its centrally located mosque in Lewiston stand at the heart of Somali religious and cultural practices. Cultural maintenance is also strongly reinforced by the elders in their neighborhoods and in the continuity of customs practiced by Somali women. The Internet and its easy e-mail communication with Somalis throughout the U.S. and around the world and a variety of educational Websites and "chat rooms" enable both Somali elders and children to stay connected with one another and with their cultural heritage. Indeed, news stories and online chat postings on several Somali websites about Lewiston are almost immediately read by refugees in camps in Kenya and Ethiopia (Bouchard 2002). Such real-time Internet connections likewise allow African Volags to disseminate more accurate information about cultural understanding and sensitivity of the immigrant Somali experiences. When the U.S. gave Somali Bantus special refugee immigrant status, as a case in point, substantial documentation about the issue was soon found on more than 150 websites (Lohrentz 2004). Somali groups, like the Somali Bantu Community Mutual Assistance Association, also use the Internet for advocacy and publicity of their goals (SBCMAA 2007).

More formally, organizations, local and national, have undertaken several initiatives to help Somalis maintain their cultural identity. To better inform Somalis of local issues, for example, Lewiston's website includes Somali events and concerns on its Office of Multicultural Affairs section (Nadeau 2007; Maine.gov). Faculty members at Bates College support the Juba Camp for Somali Bantu children. The University of Maine launched the interdisciplinary, community-based Somali Narrative Project in 2004 to help preserve Somali history and culture, and to record immigrant experiences through interviews with Somalis and community members in Lewiston and other places in Maine (Cohen 2006; University of Maine News 2007). And at the national level, Stanford University hosts a website titled "Somalia/Somaliland on the Internet" to reinforce larger issues of culture maintenance and support (SU LAIR 2007).

Somali women face their own unique set of challenges in the resettlement process. Somali women are of particular importance in the maintenance of Somali cultural heritage while they simultaneously assimilate into American society. Somali men seem determined to maintain the traditional gender hierarchy and relations in Lewiston. Women have few employment skills and weak English language usage, yet they head the majority of households and are responsible for caring for their children.

The historically marginalized Bantu women especially lack the skills and education to access resources within their rural worldview that has little understanding of "structured education." Somali women are then caught up in the middle between the men who want no change in gender relations and their children who are rapidly assimilating. NGOs have established mentoring and outreach programs to assist Somali women in their difficult transition. The United Somali Women of Maine, Lewiston-Auburn, for instance, was created to promote cross-cultural understanding and self sufficiency by assisting Somali women with services such as job assistance, skills development, and interpreting services. As they continue to unravel the complexities of their everyday lives, Somali women are cognizant that they must adapt to their new socioeconomic environment and the opportunities it affords (Taylor 2006; Yomoah 2007; Wettlaufer and Ali 2007; Nadeau 2007).

ASSIMILATION AND SOMALI FUTURE IN LEWISTON

In the end, many Somali children will become Americans in Lewiston. But many of them will not stay in the small Maine city. Somali children have access to all of the information on the Internet and are aware of opportunities across the nation, particularly in the fast-paced, exciting urban centers. Epitomizing this youthful outlook, one high school Somali girl freely expressed her desire to return to Dallas as soon as she can. Some adults are likewise continuing their search in a sahan manner, though more individually, and at least 15 families have moved away from Lewiston to other U.S. locales since 2002. A Somali male underscored this relocation trend from Lewiston by declaring, that after gaining an associate's degree, he would move his family to Phoenix where he had relatives and friends and would enjoy a more familiar climate.

The Somalis of Lewiston accomplished their goals for their secondary migration to Maine that slowed down their assimilation process, especially for their children, while taking advantage of a small town ambience and quality of life, accommodating social services, employment opportunities, good schools, access to healthcare, and low crime rates. Their unexpected arrival beginning in 2001 indelibly changed Lewiston as Africans from a very foreign part of the world imprinted their culture onto a homogeneous Maine community. Somali elders in a 2002 open letter to the Lewiston city administration expressed their sentiments to the residents of Lewiston:

> Finally, we would like to make it clear that the Somali community here have chosen and hope to become useful members of this community and its society. To that end, we ask the city to bear with us for a little longer until we are able to stand on our feet and be able to support our families with a minimal assistance. (Nadeau 2002)

After working diligently to understand the complexities and pitfalls of accommodating the unexpected arrival of Somalis that swelled to more than 3,000 migrants, the leaders of Lewiston and NGOs as well as the citizenry did a laudable job in welcoming their African neighbors into their new American home. Lewiston residents also benefited by being thrust quickly, sometimes chaotically, into a process of gaining, beyond their regional awareness, a more profound understanding concerning the diversity of peoples. And the city has institutionalized through governmental structures, programs, and positions these newly obtained perspectives of 21st century diversity (Nadeau 2005, 2007). Perhaps all of this work and commitment played a role in Lewiston being honored with the prestigious National Civic League's 2007 All American City Award (City of Lewiston, Maine 2007; Gilbert 2007).

CONCLUSIONS

Forced from their Somali homeland by warfare, ethnic cleansing, and discrimination, Somalis became swept up in the African Diaspora in North America. Having endured refugee camps in East Africa, they were scattered in a planned assimilation strategy to resettlement sites across the U.S. Unsatisfied with the socioeconomic environments of these primary settlement locations and to protect their children from the negative aspects of rapid assimilation and cultural clash, they were pushed into secondary migrations to places in which they could more comfortably transition into American society. Although a homogeneous community with little experience with immigrant resettlement, Lewiston pulled the Somalis into a place where they perceived they could be successful in becoming Americans and good neighbors.

The Somali secondary migrations were not dissimilar to the recent resettlement of the Hmong and Vietnamese in the 1970s and 1980s except for the enormous amount of information the Somalis quickly acquired from Internet connections. This continuous information stream allowed Somali leaders to make more timely decisions about prospective new places to prosper and to help maintain the core values of their traditional cultures, including preserving their own social structures and ethnic inequities brought from Africa. Time will tell if their secondary, or later tertiary, geographical decisions were correct.

ACKNOWLEDGEMENTS

We thank the many people we interviewed in our Lewiston fieldwork. Particular thanks go to Deputy City Administrator Phil Nadeau for his insights and for allowing us to draw extensively from his journal article, "The Somalis of Lewiston: Effects of Rapid Immigration to a Homogeneous Maine City." Providing essential understandings were Lewiston Mayor Laurent F. Gilbert; Maine State Refugee Coordinator Catherine S. Yomoah; Hawa Ibrahim, leader of Somali women farmers; Kim Wettlaufer, Executive Director, and Gure Ali, After School Director, of Trinity Jubilee Center; William Burke, Marketing and Production Coordinator, and John Yanga, Outreach and Training Coordinator, New American Sustainable Agricultural Project; Catherine Besteman, Professor, Colby College; Elizabeth Aimes, Professor, Bates College. We also thank Kristine Egan for constructing the maps.

Chapter 17

Liberians and African Americans: Settlement and Ethnic Separation in the Minneapolis-St. Paul Metropolitan Area

EARL P. SCOTT

INTRODUCTION

Nuanced landscapes and staple foods provide significant insight into the socio-cultural history of a people. In this chapter the focus is on how Liberians, as recent African immigrants, change established urban landscapes to reflect their cultural heritage, and how Liberians and other recent African immigrants convert existing residential communities in Minneapolis-St. Paul, MN to residences that are culturally comfortable and welcoming for them. In addition, we examine the historical and cultural attributes African Americans and Liberians share that have persisted nearly intact over time and space. The historic relationship between Liberians and African Americans is known, but few Americans are aware of the association between the Liberian deep culture and its relation to African American culture. This chapter begins by examining the settlement histories of African Americans and Liberians, how they retained significant aspects of their common heritage and culture, as expressed in strategies of minority populations, to forge and preserve a cultural identity. Specifically, the focus is on how residential patterns influence Liberians' transformation to African Americans. The third objective of this chapter is to explore the degree to which the African American and Liberian common heritage and culture has the potential for ethno-cultural solidarity and cultural convergence. This study draws attention to the spatial and socio-developmental consequences of residential patterns and the processes of cultural transformation as seen in nuanced landscapes, and outwardly similar, but substantially different attitudes and cultural practices. This chapter concludes with a discussion of the potential for Liberian-African American ethnic solidarity and cultural convergence, and the conscious or unconscious Liberian transformation to new African Americans.

THEORY OF VISUAL EXPLANATION

In cultural (human) geographical studies, the visible landscape is examined for insight into the society and the way of life of the people that built or altered it (Tuan 1979, 1991; Hart 1995). This humanistic approach to societal change is rooted in the belief that "geographers explore the earth less for its own sake than for what it can tell of its human residents and their character, which is revealed, above all, in the synergies of land and life" (Tuan 1991, p. 100). In order to explain society, Hart (1995, pp. 1–11) believes that "the inevitable starting point is the visible landscape . . . the form and appearance of human structures can tell us something about the "technical competence," the "cultural baggage" and the "socioeconomic status and gender" of the groups who built the landscapes. It is from the landscape that scholars extract data to construct scientific hypothesis. They look for what the landscape can tell, "in visible and unmistakable signs" (Tuan 1979, p. 101) of socio-economic, physical and cultural well-being of a people. This means that the total built landscape can be examined "subsidiarily," [that is], "how to see *from* the landscape *to* the values and pathos of a folk" (Tuan 1979, pp. 93).[1]

While landscape theorists agree that the landscape is their laboratory, they differ over whether the purpose of the built landscape is functional or aesthetic. Tuan's view (1979, p. 97) is that people everywhere seek to construct an "ideal and humane" or aesthetic living space, often integrating the functional and aesthetic into an "all-encompassing milieu." Hart, on the other hand, argues that "most people are motivated by functional, not aesthetic, consideration when they erect a structure, and most ordinary human structures must be understood in terms of their functions" (Hart 1995, p. 13). In urban America, the functional and aesthetic are usually combined in a single landscape. Structures are erected for specific purposes, but immigrants also embellish them to their aesthetic taste and occupy those that fit functionally and aesthetically with their perceived environment. Landscapes, then, are geographical expressions of a group's functional and aesthetic values as well as its symbolic culture.

The thesis advanced here is that the Liberian-nuanced landscape in Minnesota reveals a desire to reconstruct the totality of their traditional African landscape in a new space. In traditional West Africa, the compound is the fundamental social or family unit of the rural cultural landscape. Theoretically, the compound (James 1954, p. 45) is a "*compage*" or an assemblage of material structures, symbolic features, gender specific activity spaces, and locational qualities or advantages. Communities of recent Liberian immigrants, like compound dynamics, reflect the cultural retentions of an ethnic group and its acquisition of material possessions and symbolic attributes. These symbolic and material attributes of the community not only represent a socially constructed space with which people are comfortable, but also represent a space in which people engage in a way of life (Tuan 1991, p. 104) that includes their cherished values and norms combined with useful aspects of modernity to advance their overall well-being.[2] The African compage, though real in the life of Liberian and other West Africans, is employed here as a critical concept to examine the settlement experience of recent Liberian immigrants in Minnesota.

DATA COLLECTION

This study is based upon data derived from reconnaissance through Liberian business communities, family or group interviews, individual businessperson interviews and archives of local government and nongovernmental social service agencies. Because recent Liberian and other African immigrants do not substantially alter the physical structures of businesses and residencies, but instead embellish them with cultural symbols and styles, this study relied on reconnaissance to assess the degree and manner in which nuanced landscapes represent Liberian ownership and how they altered structures to make them feel comfortable in their new environment.

In addition to Liberian entrepreneurs, data were collected on Liberian families displaced by war as a unit or as individuals who were reunited in Minnesota.[3] Entrepreneurs and family interviews followed a structured questionnaire and the responses were recorded on tape. In both instances, the interviews were organized in a dialogue format, not question-and-answer, and all members of the family could contribute to the discussion. This open, group-interview method of data collection resulted in highly informative and rich answers. While several members of a family traveled together, seemingly experiencing the same horrors of war, deprivation, and fear, group interviews captured each member's feelings and expectations.

Liberians, unlike other recent African immigrants, have a unique historical and cultural relationship with America and African Americans that makes government and institution-based data collection especially difficult. As former free and enslaved Africans in America, many from Mississippi and Louisiana, Liberians and African Americans are physiologically and culturally very similar. From a histo-cultural perspective, Liberians embrace Western norms and values. That is, they speak English, practice Christianity, wear American attire, and eat American-based foods. In these and other ways, Liberians and African Americans are "look-alikes," a situation that is bittersweet. As recent immigrants, Liberians easily assimilate into American socio-culture and economy, but they are difficult to enumerate as a separate ethnic population. In contrast, Somali culture (i.e., religion, language, taste and dress) and heritage are very different from American culture and heritage, making assimilation much more problematic.

In general, the problem of enumerating Liberians is the same for other recent African immigrants. To address this problem at the local level, government agencies devised a method to generate a reasonable population estimate from the number of students that speak a foreign language in their home, plus their parents. Using this method, the districts identified at least eighty foreign languages spoken in the Minneapolis and St. Paul school districts. They included other Africans, but excluded Liberians as a separate population because Liberian students speak English in their home. Therefore, Liberian and government agencies' estimates of the Liberian population in the Twin Cities range from 10,000 to 30,000 plus. This guess-estimate means that what is clearly known about the Liberian population is that it is growing rapidly and that it is highly concentrated in the Twin Cities suburbs. The actual population size is unknown. The data examined here to show the change in residential patterns over time are derived from the number of Liberian births and community membership by zip code. The intent is to analyze the residential patterns of established (i.e., pre-1996 immigrants) and recent (i.e., post-1995) Liberian immigrants in the Twin Cities Metrpolitan Area.

THE FORMATION OF LIBERIAN COMMUNITIES IN MINNESOTA

The "Established" Liberian Immigrants: Pre-1996

Civil war brought global attention to Liberia and Liberian immigrant flows to the United States in the mid 1990s. However, a relatively small number of Liberians immigrated to America before 1996. Given its interior location, harsh winters, and predominantly northern European population, Minnesota appears to be an unlikely destination for Liberian immigrants. Still, a small number of African and Liberian immigrants immigrated to Minnesota. Two waves of Liberian immigrants are identified. The pre-1996 period is considered the first wave and the immigrants are termed the "established" Liberians. These immigrants, like others, sought better education, job opportunities, and generally, a better life that America could offer. While a small number of these original Liberians settled in small farm towns and university communities, the vast majority settled in the Minneapolis-St. Paul Metropolitan Area (Figure 17.1a). Similar to local African Americans, the established Liberian immigrants continue to reside near the inner cities of Minneapolis and St. Paul. However, Liberian immigrants of the second wave are mainly suburban residents. These are referred to as "recent Liberian immigrants," because they came after 1996 (Figure 17.1b). They also are mainly refugees of war and subsequent reprisals against selected citizens and families. A small number of the recent Liberians settled in small farm towns and university communities in rural Minnesota, but the vast majority settled in the Minneapolis-St. Paul Metropolitan Area.

Recent Immigration Process: Liberian Families of War

The recent Liberian immigrants comprise by far the larger of the two groups, and continue to arrive in Minnesota. In many instances individuals settled with existing families, but often entire families ultimately reassembled in Minnesota. Lutheran Social Service and other agencies assist refugees in their resettlement because Minnesota requires agency and family sponsorship. For most recent immigrants, especially Liberian families, the journey from war-torn Liberia to Minnesota was long, hard, and frightening. Most immigrants escaped the civil unrest and violence of the 1990s. Focused interviews with selected families provide a glimpse of what some immigrants endured to reach safety and freedom. Members of one family, who lived and worked in Monrovia, escaped arrest and possibly death moments before the soldiers arrived at their door. The family abandoned its home, valued possessions, and other properties, and with grandparents and children, it waded through mosquito-infested swamps, and hid with friends and acquaintances until the family reached its traditional vernacular region. After days of uncertainty, fear, and harassment by rogue elements, the family managed to cross the eastern border (Cavally River) where it found shelter and food in a refugee camp in northern Ivory Coast. The family stayed in the camp for over two years until the father, who had attended the University of Minnesota, reestablished himself with friends in Minnesota, and met the requirements of the Lutheran Social Services. Then, the entire family reassembled in Minnesota.

Figure 17.1.
Metropolitan Minneapolis – Saint Paul Region.

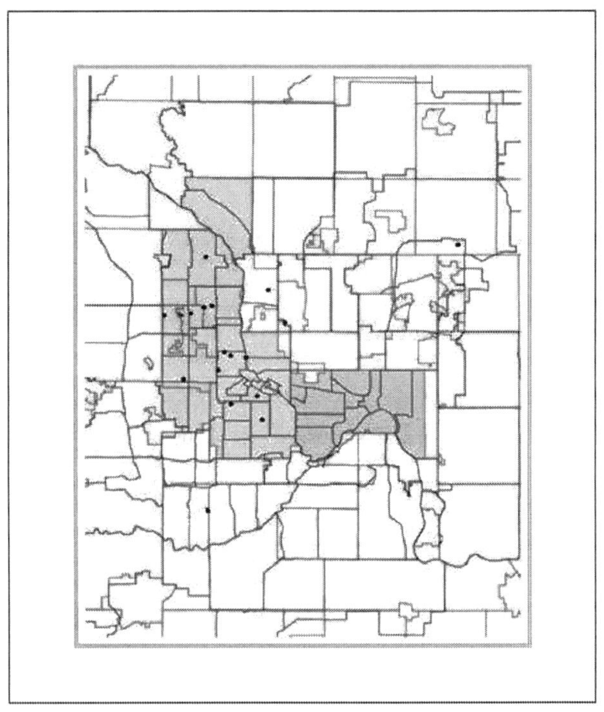

Figure 17.1a

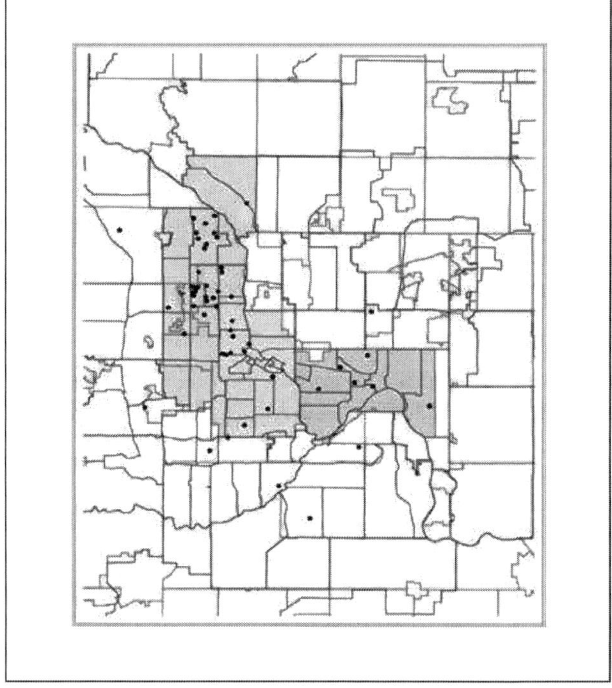

Figure 17.1b

Figures 17.1a and 17.1b show that from 1989 to 1996 a small number of Liberian immigrants settled in small farm towns and university communities, but the vast majority settled in the Minneapolis-St. Paul Metropolitan Area and in nearby suburbs north-east of Minneapolis. [Each dot represents an immigrant residential location by zip code.]

The Lutheran Social Services assists such individuals and families to settle into permanent homes, and obtain proper identification cards and employment. However, Liberian-organized agencies, such as the Pan-African Social Services and the Liberian Community of Minnesota Corporation, now have assumed the same responsibilities. These service organizations provide multiple functions. They not only support recent arrivals in their settlement, but also have become vehicles through which recent immigrants, via film documentaries and contemporary events, criticize American-Liberian policy, usually on immigration issues, and state their desire to return to Liberia to change their home nation.[4] Meanwhile, these immigrants of war make their homes in America, including the Minneapolis-St. Paul area, clustering in certain areas, reshaping the streetscapes, and expressing their ethno-national identity.

The number of Liberians residing in Minnesota and the Minneapolis-St. Paul Metropolitan Area is unknown. The U.S. Census undercounted Liberians in Minnesota due to the use of social constructs to classify non-White Americans, including African immigrants. The U.S. and State Censuses fail to distinguish Liberians as "Africans" and instead aggregate them into "Black" or "African Other" categories, obscuring their numbers. For example, according to the U.S. Census for 2000, the total number of African immigrants in Minnesota is over 43,000, with 3,126 Liberians, the third largest African immigrant population in the state. These figures are suspect because according to Federal statistics, fully 43 percent of immigrants in Minnesota in 2000 were classified as "African Other," meaning that Africans from small countries were lumped into one category.

THE SUBURBANIZATION OF POST-1996 LIBERIAN IMMIGRANTS

Liberian immigrants initially settled in the inner cities of Minneapolis and St. Paul, concentrated near existing African American neighborhoods. However, in recent years, a noticeable shift has occurred with the highly dispersed settlement of recent Liberian immigrants in suburbs throughout the Minneapolis-St. Paul Metropolitan Area. The Lutheran Social Service (LSS) operates one of the largest resettlement programs for Liberians in Minnesota. Between 1997 and 2002, the LSS assisted 816 Liberian immigrants, mostly families, to settle in several municipalities of the Minneapolis-St. Paul Metropolitan Area. Figure 17.2 reports the place names within the Minneapolis-St. Paul region. As Figures 17.3a and 3b show, most reside in familiar clusters of Brooklyn Center, Brooklyn Park, New Hope and Crystal (Walen 2002). Personal communication with an LSS representative confirmed this observation that current Liberian immigrants are now being placed with relatives in the suburbs, although the cities of Minneapolis and St. Paul continue to receive a few immigrant refugees (Walen 2002).

Figure 17.2.
Place Names of Liberian Residential Clusters: Twin Cities Metropolitan Area by City and Zip Code 2000.

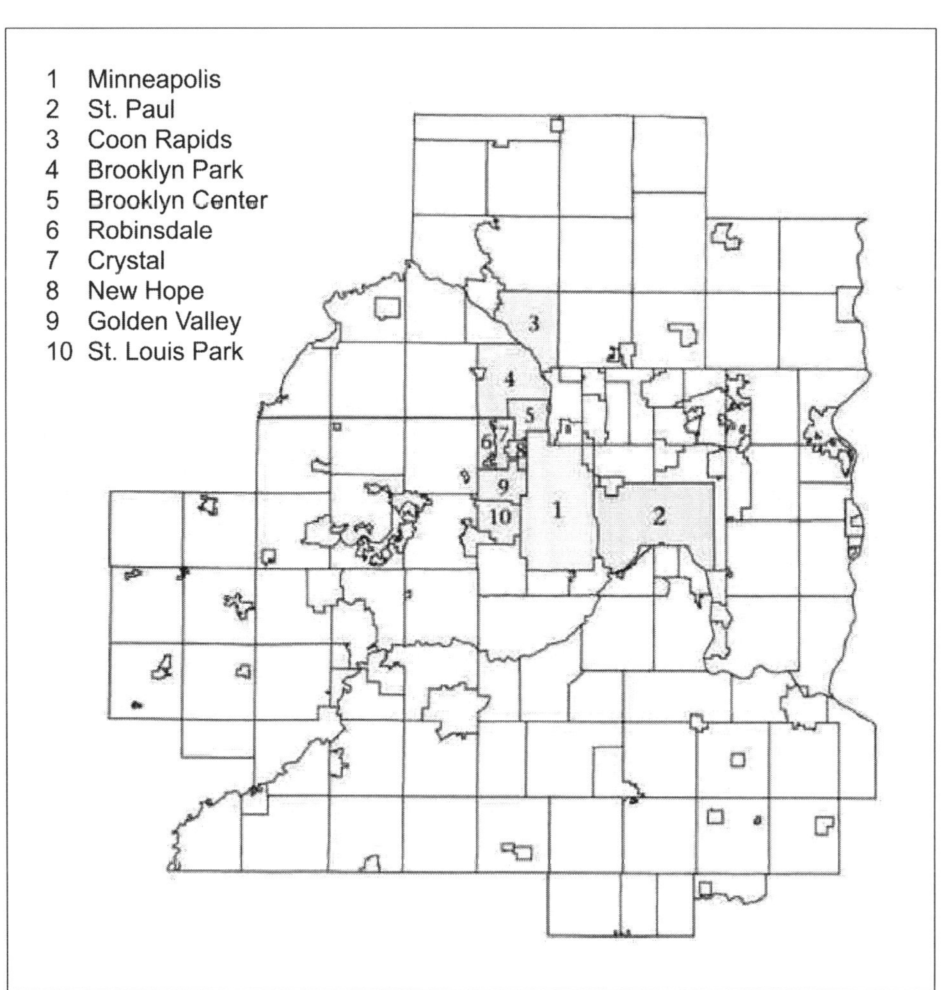

Figure 17.3.
Liberian Settlement Patterns in the Twin Cities, 1997 and 2000.

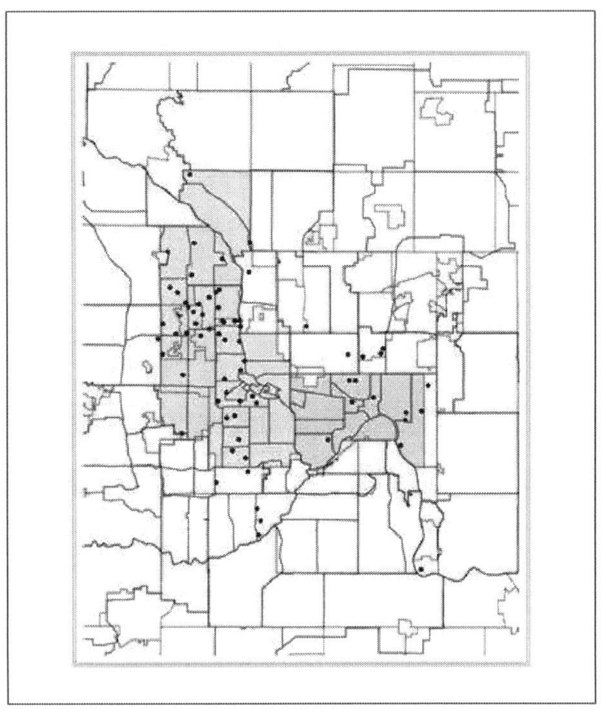

Figure 17.3a. 1997

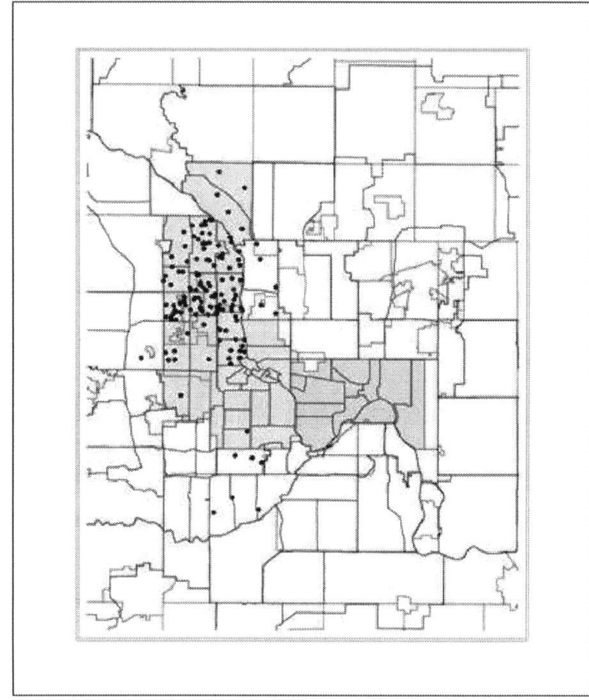

Figure 17.3b. 2000

Figure 17.3a shows that in 1997 Liberian immigrant settlers followed earlier residents, but in 2000, as Figure 17.3b shows the residential pattern was highly clustered in just a few communities north-east of Minneapolis with an increasing number in distant suburban areas. Each dot represents an immigrant residential location by zip code.

Vital statistics records for Minneapolis-St. Paul provide a larger and more comprehensive data source. Birth records supply location of births by ancestry and address of parents. These data are maintained by the Minnesota Department of Health's Center for Health Statistics (Sechler 2002), and contain the number of births by year. To show the residential pattern for both established and recent Liberian immigrants, the 1989–2000 births were mapped at the zip code level for the Minneapolis-St. Paul Metropolitan area (Figure 17.4a), which illustrates that the primary locations of Liberian immigrants are in particular suburbs of the Minneapolis-St. Paul metropolitan area. Figure 17.4b which shows the residential pattern of the Liberian Community Membership, represents a smaller data set, but it confirms the residential pattern derived from the analysis of total Liberian births. In addition, the map of Liberian Community Membership is representative of the established Liberian immigrant communities and show that established Liberian communities remain less dispersed than recent Liberian immigrants (The Liberian Community Membership Directory is published by the Organization of Liberians in Minnesota, founded in the early 1970s). This residential pattern of Liberian immigrant communities confirms that there is a spatial duality separating inner-city, established and suburban, recent Liberian immigrants.

One can infer from this distribution of births and from information provided by LSS and the Liberian Community Membership Directory that St. Paul and Minneapolis were the early cores of Liberian settlement and remain important centers of the established immigrant Liberians and their families. However, the data on births clearly indicate the increasing importance of the Minneapolis-St. Paul suburbs for recent Liberian immigrant settlement. Indeed, the largest concentration of recent Liberian births is in suburbia, where a wedge extends from the inner city core of Minneapolis out to the northwest in selected inner-ring suburbs of New Hope and Brooklyn Center, Brooklyn Park and Crystal, and the outer suburbs (Figure 17.2). The maps of Liberian residential distribution reflect a process of spatial inertia, with expansion occurring on the edges of the established Liberian communities toward the suburbs. This means that the relatively small "established" Liberian community lived mainly in the cities of St. Paul and Minneapolis, but the suburbanization of recent Liberian immigrants has shifted away from the African American inner city residential areas. The concentrations are expected, given the growth of the Liberian residential areas over time. However, the dispersed pockets of Liberians in the outer suburban areas are wholly unexpected. Recent Liberian immigrants and secondary immigrants are settling farther and farther away from the inner cities, creating greater spatial separation between themselves and the established Liberians, as well as the African American and other communities of African descent. This residential pattern confirms that there is a spatial duality separating established and recent Liberian immigrants. The suburbanization of recent Liberian immigrants is unusual for some African-born groups such as the Somalis (see previous chapter), but quite common for other recent ethnic immigrants in America (*Economist* 2004, pp. 31–2). The changing pattern of settlement of recent Liberian immigrants, who will be among the newest African Americans, have socioeconomic and cultural implications for possible ethnic solidarity and community development with the native-born African Americans and their communities.

Figure 17.4.
Total Births, 1989-2000 and Liberian Community Clusters.

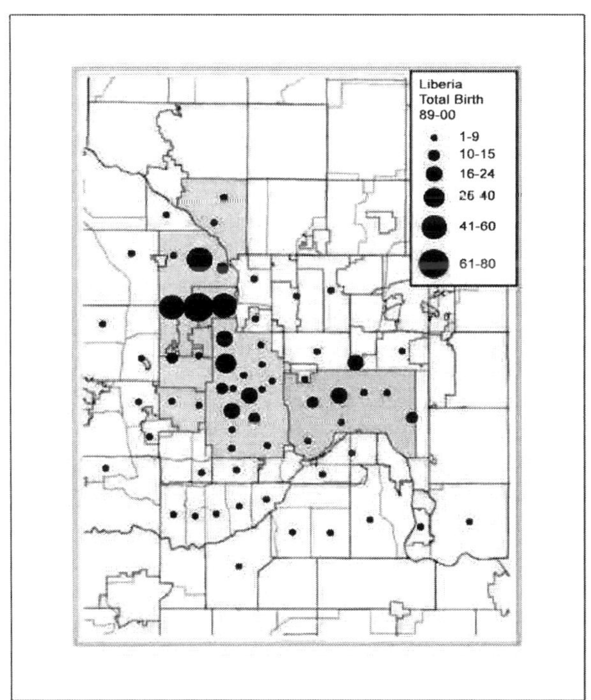

Figure 17.4a

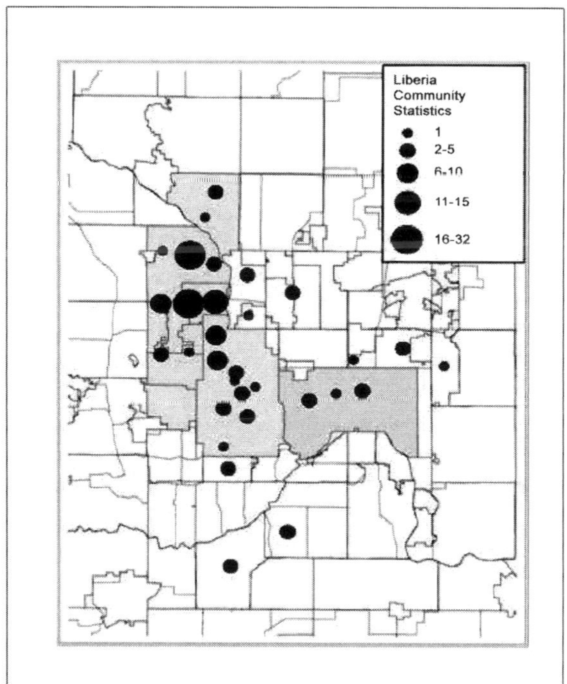

Figure 17.4b

Figure 17.4a shows the total births from 1989 to 2000 and Figure 17.4b shows the total membership of the Liberian Community Membership by Zip Code. These data, through unrepresentative of the actual Liberian population distributions, show the ongoing suburbanization of recent Liberian immigrants in the Twin Cities Metropolitan Area and the persistent residential clustering of "established" migrants in communities north west of Minneapolis, resulting in the spatial separation of the immigrant communities.

Besides spatial inertia stemming from social agencies' settlement policies, self-employment is also driving the suburbanization pattern. Like many recent immigrants, Liberian immigrants consist of entire families whose parents are usually educated, professionally trained entrepreneurs, bankers and government officials, but who are not qualified for similar jobs in America. In many instances, Liberians in Minnesota avoid years of retraining to acquire qualifications through self-employment, mainly by establishing small, ethnic-based businesses in suburban strip malls near their homes, but seldom in the inner city (Somali and Ethiopian businesses are inner-city based, occupying the old dilapidated neighborhoods, market centers, major thoroughfares and recently established shopping malls (Figures 17.5 and 17.6). Locational preference for suburbia is because businesses are ethnic based, following the spread of Liberian residents (Figure 17.7). They cater to Liberian food taste, service needs, and country ties, usually through relatives who live in Liberia. In addition, Liberian businesses are usually family owned and operated. New immigrant families often work as a unit and like to be close to their church and school, both of which are located in suburbia. The structures predate Liberian occupation and management, but they show modest or nuanced evidence of cultural transformation that reflect what Liberians are comfortable with, a phenomenon that characterizes efforts of all recent immigrants to construct a space with which they are comfortable. These changes include African names and cultural symbolism such as national colors. Less obvious is the social function the structures and businesses provide. Liberian barbers rely on Liberian customers who use the shop as a social space where young immigrants pass the time and reminisce about their country and home or vernacular regions (Figure 17.8).

Figure 17.5.
"Al Karama Mall" and other Somali businesses are located in refurbished commercial strips on thoroughfares near the central business district offering a wide range of retail opportunities.

Figure 17.6.
African restaurants like the "Kilimanjaro Café" are usually located near universities and use language, colors and other cultural symbols to attract familiar and adventurous patrons.

Figure 17.7.
"T & C Barber Shop" and other Liberian service enterprises serve as a social space for men from all over Liberia to reminisce about their vernacular or cultural regions, share ideas on achieving peace and prosperity and dream of returning home.

Figure 17.8.
Liberian Businesses, "Pepper Charm," are located in recently established suburban shopping centers that support the "Liberian Way" by offering imported foods, spices, and condiments required to prepare most Liberian dishes.

Ethnic-based business enterprises are small with limited potential for growth beyond the targeted ethnic community. In general, ethnic-based businesses are inward looking and culturally isolated, resulting in a high incidence of failure. Nevertheless, Liberian entrepreneurs are uniquely situated to rapidly expand their businesses, especially their food markets, restaurants, and bakeries. The potential market is African-American consumers whose tastes are similar to theirs, and when Liberians use local substitutes, the main dishes are virtually identical. However, Liberians and African Americans must improve communication for business expansion to occur. Both groups will have to create opportunities to teach the other about their cultural similarities that are based in their common heritage rather than their perceived differences. In order to target this "new" market, Liberian businesses must relocate to the inner city and educate African Americans about their products. Such purposeful efforts at socio-economic interactions could not only generate household prosperity, but they could also promote cultural convergence and ethnic solidarity between groups that have been separated by time and distance for too long.

LIBERIANS AND AFRICAN AMERICANS: SHARED HERITAGE AND CULTURE

As noted in the introduction, African Americans and Liberian immigrants share a common heritage and culture forged by their common history in America. Both are minority populations with a subculture that includes an acquired language and similar food traditions, such as preferred staple foods and preparation methods that have survived over time and space. Each component of that heritage and culture is described below.

Common Cultural Heritage

Initially, African slaves were concentrated in the Charleston area, the Chesapeake Bay region and the Carolinas, Georgia, and Florida coasts. Slaves from West Africa, who were familiar with paddy-rice production in river flood plains and reclaimed paddy areas, were brought to coastal river floodplains of the Carolinas, Georgia, and Florida and the Sea Islands to produce rice, sugar cane, tobacco, and other commercial crops. This clustering accounts for the development of an African-American culture in a society otherwise dominated by its White population (Gomez 1998). The African-based population lends support to the arguments favoring continuity and retention of culture. Close proximity ensured extensive interactions and fostered continuity and retention of an ethnic culture through shared ideas, beliefs, cooking methods, house building, and farm methods and techniques (Gomez 1998). This culture was further reinforced through mixed marriages between African ethnic groups and slave laborers, especially those who cultivated and harvested rice in the Carolinas and in the southern delta of Mississippi and Louisiana.

African slaves from several parts of Africa constructed their own socio-culture. They achieved a "self view" in opposition to the one prescribed by European power and authority (Gomez 1998). Gomez argues that the transformation of the African into the African American actually began on African soil. African captives quickly discovered that what they had in common was their "blackness." They were literally in the same boat, facing the same problems as intended slave laborers. The Middle Passage for the first time brought slaves together and provided an opportunity for them to experience their differences, especially in terms of language and staple foods. Being together for a long period during the Middle Passage and as plantation laborers, Africans then devised methods of speech and cooking that evolved into elements unique to African American colloquial language and cuisine, as we know them today.

Language as Cultural Identity

The American Colonization Society repatriated freed slaves to present day Liberia between 1821 and 1867. Many of the freed slaves were from the Mississippi Delta region, especially southern Mississippi and Louisiana. Similarities in the development of speech and the function of language of Liberian immigrants and African Americans evolved from the founding of Liberia and the settlement of freed slaves from America as a minority population called Americo-Liberians. Initially, Americo-Liberians from Louisiana, Mississippi, and elsewhere lived as American expatriates in the African colony, permanently away from home. Indeed, these expatriates carried their southern, and specifically, their African American cultural heritage with them. Once there, they recreated an American society and constructed a new "American" cultural landscape in a new place. Huffman (2004, p. 159) argued ". . . the history of the Mississippi colony and of Liberians, as a whole is both [a] transplanted African-American story and an African experiment with Western Culture." Liberians, like African Americans, valued their shared, American-informed culture. This common heritage is reflected in their beliefs, dress, taste, house types, and place names, including newly established residential communities. The long-term geographic and cultural isolation of these freed slaves, and limited cultural interactions and exchange or assimilation into the dominant culture, contributed to the preservation of their African American heritage and culture. Although a minority group in Liberia, Americo-Liberians assumed political and economic power and an aristocratic status in their new home.

Their geographic isolation also allowed Americo-Liberians to preserve other aspects of their transplanted culture. It fostered the preservation of their African American-based language, i.e., their cultural identity in a dominant culture, which is similar to the way African Americans use language in America. While English is the official and formal language in Liberia (i.e., the language of instruction and parliament and of professional speech), the common or everyday language is pidgin. Pidgin is "broken" or "shortened" English, which means that English words are literally shortened and speech is very rapid, making it unintelligible to the untrained ear. Liberians consciously use dual speech under certain circumstances to obscure or to clarify their meanings. This purposeful, functional use of language to preserve ethnic identity is steeped in traditional African American culture as well. In Minnesota, this dual language capability facilitates communication and understanding and ameliorates tension between Liberians from different vernacular regions in Liberia and between Liberians and Americans.

The best example of African American use of language to preserve cultural identity is on the Sea Islands (Gullah Islands). Among African slaves, English ultimately became the *lingua franca* or trade language in America with regional dialects and accents. On the more isolated Gullah Island, located off the Carolinas and Florida coasts, and on the coastal mainland, Africans developed a unique language called ***Gullah***, a language that is a combination of Caribbean and West African languages (e.g., Yoruba, Ibo, Sierra Leone, and Liberian, specifically the Vai). *Gullah*, sometimes derogatorily called ***Geechee***, "is an important reason why Sea Islanders have preserved a way of life that remains African in some of its essentials" (Blockson 1987, p. 735). Because *Gullah* is a combination of English, Caribbean and West African languages, it is virtually incomprehensible to non-speakers, including mainland African Americans. This means that the two communities, African American and Americo-Liberians, enjoy marked advantages in using both formal English and modified English in speaking. Just as in Liberia, English is the official and formal language that is used in instruction and professional speech on the Sea Islands. However, Sea Islanders also use dual speech to avoid stereotypes and embarrassment as country bumpkins. More importantly, *Gullah* (in America) and Pidgin (in Liberia) have functioned to define a small, mainly isolated group and had the effect of preserving a culture that is curiously similar in their food preferences and preparation.

Staple Foods as Cultural Identity

Like language, Americo-Liberians retained their American-based food ways and eventually reconstructed Liberia's cultural landscapes based on their preferred foods. African American expatriates introduced their staple crop, the long-grained, Carolina gold rice, into Liberia's existing food dishes, first on the coast and later into the interior. Carolina gold rice symbolizes the Liberian's curious Diaspora; wherever Liberians settle they maintain their preference for this specific rice.

> The circle of rice history in the Atlantic basin thus closes with the introduction of the Carolina rice of U.S. slavery to Sierra Leone and the West African rice region via freed men and Christian missionaries. Through another African Diaspora (i.e., the voluntary repatriation of the thirty-five surviving Amistads or the Mendi Mission), this one based on freedom and voluntary return to the continent by some of its descendants, Carolina rice reached into the heart of Africa all the way to the floodplains of the Niger river in Mali. . . . A cereal and a knowledge system that left West Africa on ships with slaves and became established in the Americas under bondage, returned once more to African shores in freedom through the agency of Black missionaries, freed slaves and recaptives. Known as Mereki, the rice drew its name from America, the continent of human bondage. But this time the history of those who brought it would not be forgotten. (Carney 2001, pp. 174–177)

Minnesota Liberians have brought the American-based Carolina gold rice nearly full circle, as one of many ethnic groups in the African Diaspora, by returning it to the United States.

Americo-Liberians' introduction of food preferences also transformed existing cultural landscapes. To do this, they combined local ingredients and Carolina gold rice into dishes using methods of food preparation developed in the American Southeast. Most Americo-Liberian dishes included the use of rice as the staple. Curiously, this aspect of the African American based cultural transformation is a distinctive cultural signature of the Liberian Diaspora. Liberian staple food dishes are explicitly of African American origin, evidence of the African American cultural influence in Liberia. More importantly, rice, like language, helped to preserve the African American based culture that recent Minnesota immigrants have brought with them. This curious but unique cultural phenomenon among recent Liberian immigrants in America not only informs our understanding of the common cultural heritage of Liberians and African Americans, but also demonstrates that these cultures have not diverged significantly over space or throughout generations of time.

It is useful to examine Liberian and African American food traditions in some detail because inspection reveals strong similarities. African American and Liberian staple dishes have diverged in terms of the ingredients used, but they remain similar in terms of the method of preparation and, in some cases, the actual name of the dish (Table 17.1). While these popular dishes link African Americans in America and Liberians in Liberia, the method of food preparation is greater evidence of their common origin. The interactions of the *Gullah* and the coastal groups developed a number of new staple foods based on leafy and fruity vegetables (mainly tomatoes), bean pods, nuts, sea foods, swine products (mainly sausage), chicken, corn and rice. As Table 17.1 shows, Gumbo, jambalaya, and various bean dishes are all prepared with rice and are common to both cultures. African-American desserts are also shared creations. Both employed local resources such as lemon, apple, pecan, sweet potato, and pumpkin. They also used corn and beans to make snacks such as hush puppies and bean cakes. In both cultures, foods are boiled or deep fat fried. For example, Greens, beans, and meats are all boiled and heavily seasoned, while chicken and fish are deep fat fried in a flour-based, seasoned butter. In America, these methods of food preparation are called "*Southern*" while in Liberia they are described as the *Liberian Way*.

In some instances, the cultures retained the actual name of selected staple dishes. For example, gumbo and lemon meringue pie are virtually the same in both cultures in preparation and name (Table 17.1). Smoked meats (i.e., sausage, ham, ham hocks, and fish) are important seasonings in "thick" soup-type dishes such as red beans and gumbo. Gumbo is sea food, okra or file base, but all gumbos are cooked with sausage, usually smoked pork, or chicken, and served over rice with corn bread. Carolina rice remains the staple crop in southeast America and gumbo is still prepared the same way by mainland African Americans and the *Gullah* on the Sea Islands. Food preference and preparation are part of a group's deep culture. They are what groups identify with and what identifies them (e.g., soul food in African American culture).

Food Display and Consumption as Cultural Identity

The final similarity between Liberian and African American cultures reflects the way foods are displayed for consumption. Liberians prepare and display several major dishes at one time for consumption at lunch and at dinner. Traditionally, an individual will take small portions of each dish, and, as in other parts of Africa, food is usually eaten with ones' hands. For example, rice is formed into a small ball, dipped into a meat, okra or other type of sauce, and eaten. The Liberian practice of eating with their hands is African in origin, but the practice of preparing and displaying several major dishes at one time is clearly an African American tradition. This combination of elements from two different cultures to create a new but unique Americo-Liberian way of dining is a good example of cultural syncretism.

Americo-Liberians structured a new society that was a blend of selected West African traditions and their southern African American culture. But geographic and sociocultural isolation facilitated their retention of certain elements of their African American based culture. These cultural similarities are the potential basis for cultural convergence and ethnic solidarity. However, for reunification to occur, Liberians and African Americans in Minnesota must acknowledge their common heritage and shared culture.

Table 17.1.
Liberian and African American Food Ways: Common Heritage and Cultural Reunification.

	Liberian[1]	**African American**
Snacks	Bean Cake	Hush Puppies
Breads	Corn Bread Short Bread	Same Same
Entrées	Rice Jallof Chicken Dumplings Seafood & Fish Fried Okra	Jambalaya Same Same Same
Vegetables	Collards	Same
Gumbos	Seafood Chicken Filé Okra	Same Same
Desserts	Lemon Meringue Pie Pumpkin Pie Butter Cake	Same Same Pound Cake
Drinks	 Lemonade	Sweet Tea Same

[1] Descriptions of selected Liberian dishes are based on discussions with Ms. Manzaler Toweh, a student in my course on West Africa and a member of one of the families interviewed for this study. Also see: *Liberia's Treasured Recipes from Out Kitchens*, Preference by Eric David, Chairman of Effort Baptist Church and Friends of Effort, USA. Descriptions of African American dishes are based on personal experience.

DISCUSSION AND CONCLUSION

There is little doubt that the suburbanization of Liberians in the Twin Cities region is placing a greater geographic and social distance between African-Americans and Liberians, making cultural convergence difficult. However, one must also recognize the strength of two different ethnic identities forged over a considerable period of time as a significant deterrent to cultural convergence of these two groups with a common heritage. Thus, geography and ethnic differences combine to present a serious barrier to the convergence of the two groups.

Ethnicity involves both shared traits and an affinity for place (home). African Americans, despite American racism, have only memories of American soil that likely splits their affinity between Africa and America, but positions their current cultural and African American ethnic identity more in the history of African-American struggle and in shared traits that coalesced in the rural American South, their "home." Those of Liberian descent also have a strong place affinity for home. Many intend to return there one day. In the meantime this affinity for home and the Liberian way of life is replicated in many ways in their current Minnesota home. Recent Liberian immigrant are reshaping the neighborhoods and streetscapes of their new home to reflect Liberian traits learned and associated with their homeland in Africa. They also continue in the beliefs and practices they value.

As the Liberian community has expanded and have become even more comfortable with their new home-space, interaction with other ethnic groups has been modest, resulting in little cultural exchange and transformation. Their Liberian self-identity and desire for ethnic distinction has strengthened. For example, when Liberians were asked how would they like to be identified in the U.S. Census, young Liberian males in particular said if they could not be called Liberian, they would rather be called "Black African" or Blacks from Africa, but not "African Americans." Liberians, like many other immigrant groups, wish to retain their ethnic identity. The Liberian Way is important to them as a people. This, along with their suburban settlement geography, has meant that the "new Liberian immigrants" (post-1996) are increasingly isolated and segregated from the African-American population and, perhaps, the "established" Liberian communities in the urban core as well. Consciously or unconsciously, the Liberian community of the Twin Cities region will not assimilate in the wider African-American subculture. Instead, they will be part of the pluralistic society that is growing in America, making Pan-ethnic solidarity harder to achieve. This does not mean that some cultural convergence is impossible. Rather, African Americans and Liberians must recognize their common heritage that provides a unique cultural association and, at the same time, they must realize that the two ethnic groups have also evolved different traditions and have unique attributes that provide different ethnic glue for each subculture.

Recent history indicates that the two groups can find their commonalities when interaction occurs. When Liberians and African Americans have had contact, positive outcomes follow. During the first wave of immigrants, Liberian ministries shared African-American churches until they were able to function on their own. During this period of adjustment, African-American and Liberian congregations participated in church dinners, funerals, marriages, and other shared ceremonies. These occasions provided opportunities for these groups to know each other, allowing for an acknowledgement of ethnic differences but also for greated appreciation of cultural similarities. African American and Liberian self-constructed identities and perceptions of each other ignore the reality of their common heritage. Cooperation can benefit both groups, while preserving the ethnic uniqueness cherished by both.

NOTES

[1] According to Tuan (1979: 89), "Landscape . . . is not to be defined by itemizing its parts. The parts of the landscape are subsidiary clues to an integrated image, which is a construct of the mind and of feeling." Landscape is a clue to rural Africa's dynamics and well-being. To see rural Africa as built landscape is to assemble its distinct parts into a single notion of human well-being. For us, landscape is a composite feature in which elements of material structures, symbolic retentions, aesthetic attributes, etc. are combined to reflect an environment or humane habitat that people are comfortable with.

[2] The author employed this theoretical analysis to examine rural landscapes in Zimbabwe, see: "Home-Based Enterprises, Landscape and Human Well-being in Rural Zimbabwe," *Contemporary Development Analysis* 2 (1) pp. 111–53.

[3] I would like to take this opportunity to thank Ms. Menzela Toweh, a student in my class on the Geography of West Africa and member of the central family interviewed for this study. Menzela also helped me to identify prospective interviewees, described a list of Liberian staple dishes and their associated ethnic group, and placed her family's experiences in Liberia's ongoing civil unrest.

[4] Recent film documentaries are critical of U.S. policies toward Liberia, accusing it of abandoning Liberia during its most severe humanitarian crisis (See Liberia: America's Stepchild and Liberian, An Uncivil War).

Chapter 18

Globalization and Ghanaian Immigrant Trajectories to Cincinnati: Who Benefits?

IAN E. A. YEBOAH

INTRODUCTION

Anyone following the immigration debate in the United States may get the impression that it is a Latino issue only (see Taylor 2005; Wilson 1999), yet over the past thirty years there has been a growing movement of Sub-Saharan Africans to the United States, mostly voluntarily but in some cases as forced immigrants (Takyi and Boate 2007). Sub-Saharan Africans constituted the major immigrant group during the era of slavery, and for the first three centuries after the discovery of the New World the principal immigrants to the United States were Sub-Saharan African slaves (Kennedy 1996). Roberts (2005) projects that twenty percent of America's five million population in 1880 were Black. Yet, from the 1880s to the 1980s, only a trickle of Sub-Saharan Africans immigrated to the United States. Since the 1980s, however, there has been a reversal of this trend.

The rather recent voluntary immigration of Sub-Saharan Africans is part of a globlized labor market (Sassen 1991; Dwyer 1999, Light 2004 and Yeboah 2008) that has been facilitated by changes in American immigration regulations (Lobo 2007 and Okome 2007), and deteriorating economic, social, and political conditions in Sub-Saharan African countries as a result of structural adjustment programs (Lobo 2007; Yeboah 2008). Currently, there are residential enclaves of Sub-Saharan African immigrants with well established communities in major immigrant receiving cities like New York City, Washington, DC, and Wooster, Massachusetts (see N'Diaye and N'Diaye 2007; Kwakye-Nuako 2007; and Abbott 2007). Increasingly, there is the emergence of Sub Saharan immigrant communities in smaller Midwestern cities such as Cincinnati and Columbus, Ohio (CQ Researcher 2003; Yeboah 2008).

Despite this trend, very limited research on the trajectories of Sub-Saharan African immigrants has been undertaken. Yet, how immigrants arrive in the United States influences life chances and their relationship with their origin. This chapter traces the trajectory of Ghanaian immigrants in the Greater Cincinnati area. The purpose is to learn of the experiences Ghanaian immigrants in Cincinnati and the potential economic growth impact these persons have on Ghana.

THEORETICAL AND CONCEPTUAL FRAMEWORK

This chapter is premised on two related theoretical underpinnings. First, Ghanaian immigration to the United States is part of a globalized labor market (Sassen 1991; Dwyer 1999; Light 2004 and Yeboah 2008), as part of the newest phase of capitalist expansion (Williams 1994; Rodney 1974; Wallerstein 2004; 2005). Capitalism, in its deliberate expansion historically and in contemporary times, has not only been exploitative (Rodeny 1974; Hoogvelt 2006; *Global Issues* 2007) but, also has looked to peripheral geographic regions like Sub-Saharan Africa for sources of labor. During the period of mercantile capitalism and the early part of industrial capitalism, between 6 and 30 million Sub-Saharan Africans were forcibly moved across the middle passage to the Americas. Today's immigration of Sub-Saharan Africans to the United States is a manifestation of capital taking labor out of the region in an era of globalization or what Hoogvelt (2006) has called post-modern imperialism.

For skeptics of globalization (Hirst and Thompson 1996), capitalist expansion in Africa began with the age of sea exploration or mercantile capitalism, followed by the age of land explorers and subsequent colonialism and imperialism. These eras were followed by independence and its associated neo-colonialism with it ideology of developmentalism. The current stage of today's globalization and its ideology of neoliberalism (see Wallerstein 2005; *Global Issues* 2007) complete this periodization of capitalist expansion. Specific mechanisms have been deliberately structured into each stage of capitalist expansion (Hoogvelt 2006) to assure that African labor has been at the beck and call of global capital.

Theoretically, therefore, this chapter is couched within world-system theory, especially its dependency strand (Frank 1967; Wallerstein 2004; Bosch 1997). What is presented in this chapter is the argument of skeptics like Hirst and Thompson, (1996) that globalization is not new but, simply a continuation of capital's expansion and that its effect on space is a transformational geography that reinforces the historical core-periphery relationship between places around the globe (Hoogvelt 2006). Today, structural adjustment programs have created push conditions in Sub-Saharan African countries (Konadu-Agyemang and Arthur 2007; Yeboah 2008) and individuals make conscious decisions to leave for greener pastures. In the same vein, the need for skilled and unskilled labor to meet capital's expansion has resulted in changes in American immigration policy to facilitate a selective flow of immigrants, including Sub-Saharan Africans, to the United States (Lobo 2007; Okome 2007). The questions that originate from this theoretical proposition are: Who immigrates to the United States from Ghana? What is their immigration trajectory?

Second, because of the globalized nature of immigration, immigrants no longer acculturate to the United States, but actively engage in transnational activities with one foot in America and the other in their source country (Owusu 2007; Yeboah 2008). Immigrants potentially have economic growth impacts on their source countries. Brain drain and remittances have been touted as both the costs and benefits of immigration for source regions in the global periphery (see Akokpari 2006; Ditta and Mbow 1999). These impacts of immigration on source regions reflect the economic growth impact of immigration to peripheral regions of the global periphery. Hass (2006), however, argues that the question is not whether emigration from source countries like Ghana is good or bad, but rather, whether these countries can institute policies to reap the benefits of emigration. A question that comes out of this theoretical proposition is: what is the economic growth impact of immigrants for countries like Ghana?

Theoretically and practically, globalization transforms places as is revealed by immigration to the United States. Fundamentally, decisions of emigration and immigration are geographic ones that reflect place differences between source and destination areas. These geographic decisions are structured by global capital in both historical and contemporary times. Immigrants actively assess their chances of bettering their lives by immigrating to other places, and in the process, act as agents of transformation within structures provided by capitalism. Geographic elements of emigration and immigration decisions imply that specific questions that emanate from the trajectories of immigrants in their destination countries, as well as from their source countries, need to be addressed.

Additional questions originating from these theoretical underpinnings are presented in Figure 18.1. These questions focus on the effects of emigration on source and destination places and the transnational relationship between these places. These questions guide the analysis that follows.

Figure 18.1.
A Conceptual Framework for Emigration and Immigration.

Questions of Source Places	Transnational Attributes	Questions of Destination Places
1. Who immigrates?		1. Why did they immigrate?
2. When do they immigrate?	1. How do source and destination landscapes change?	2. How does policy affect immigration?
3. How long have they been immigrants?	2. How do immigrants negotiate identity?	3. Where do they settle?
4. Who helps in immigration?	3. Is there a brain drain or gain?	
5. How do they immigrate?		

DATA SOURCE AND METHODS

Empirical data for this chapter are generated from a closed survey of thirty-seven Ghanaian immigrants resident in the Greater Cincinnati Area conducted during the Summer and Fall of 2006. Information including demographic background, length of time in the United States, reasons for immigration, trajectories of immigration, choice of settlement, role of networks, residential location in Cincinnati, gender and immigration, perceptions of Ghana, retirement plans, and transnational activities was solicited.

Surveys provide an opportunity to explore a population to identify key attributes that underlie the population (Kelley et al. 2003; Kitchenham and Pfleeger 2002), yet, their ability to capture intricate relationships is rather limited. Teasing out intricate relationships is often left to ethnographic approaches such as participation and focus group studies (Goss and Leinbach 1996). Personal insight reveals invaluable information as well.

The 1990 U.S. Census reports that only 13 of the 339 Africans residing in Cincinnati were of Ghanaian origin. Yet, by 2000, 1,500 of a total African population were Ghanaians (U.S. Bureau of the Census 1990 and 2000). These figures likely are underestimates due to undocumented immigrants not counted by the Census. This not withstanding, the inter-census growth of the immigrant Ghanaian population in the Cincinnati region has been remarkable. Although we cannot be certain of the total Ghanaian population, assuming that, for example, two adults (a couple) have an average of three children, then the estimated 300 Ghanaian families would contain 600 adults and 900 children. The thirty-seven adult interviews in this case would constitute slightly higher than a 6 percent sample of the adult Ghanaian population. If the population of Ghanaians in the region was large enough, the U.S. Census would have published data describing its demographic composition and various socioeconomic and occupational data as part of its 2000 PUMS data. Unfortunately, the Ghanaian population falls below the minimum requirement to do so. Thus, no detailed information of this population in Cincinnati exists.

The survey sample was drawn on a stratified basis, using the researcher's knowledge of the local Ghanaian community. Consideration was given to socioeconomic class, gender, age, length of stay in the area, and ethnicity. Overall, thirty-seven of the thirty-nine potential respondents replied with completed questionnaires. In most cases, the survey was hand-delivered to the respondent's home for completion, after a telephone conversation that resulted in agreement to participate. The form was returned via mail in a postage-paid envelope. There were a few exceptions to this method. If a potential respondent preferred to receive the form via mail, rather than being hand-delivered, this method was applied. Another exception involved deficient writing skills by a few respondents. In these cases, the questionnaire was administered in person by the author, who recorded answers. Similarly, if a respondent requested clarification on any survey item, these were handled via telephone or in person.

It is important to note that the researcher's visibility in the Ghanaian community contributed to the ability to stratify the sample and had a positive impact on the high response rate for the survey. Serving as an officer, secretary and president, of the regional Ghanaian Association (1996–2000), regularly attending the services of a variety of local churches, and serving as chairman and master of ceremonies for numerous public and private Ghanaian functions, such as holiday and other celebrations, parties, and funerals, contributed to substantial visibility and trust, which influenced the survey participation rate.

GHANAIAN IMMIGRANT TRAJECTORIES

Attributes of Ghanaian immigrant trajectories are presented in this section of this chapter. Trajectories refer to the paths followed within a dynamic system. In this case, they are the paths and progressions of immigrant Ghanaians as they influence several dimensions of their U.S. experience and have impacts in their homeland. These cut across questions of both source and destination and issues of their transnational activities. In this chapter Ghanaian immigrant trajectories examine immigrant and socioeconomic status, the processes involved in the Ghanaian Diaspora that brought them to Cincinnati, and consequences for their home nation. First are the demographic attributes of Ghanaian immigrants in Cincinnati. Second is the recency of Ghanaian immigrants to the United States. Third is the step-wise nature of Ghanaian immigration and the role of networks in the process.

Fourth is anecdotal evidence of regulation of their immigrant status. Fifth is the participation of Ghanaians in a globalized labor market. Sixth is the issue of brain drain or gain. Seventh is the transnational nature of Ghanaian immigrants in Cincinnati. These attributes provide input for answering the two questions posed at the beginning of this chapter.

Demography and the Decision to Migrate

Despite their slightly older aged profile, the overall demographic profile of these Ghanaian immigrants in Cincinnati suggests immigrant selectivity to the United States. The young and physically capable, and males participate in the market. The literature on who emigrates out of Africa is centered on three issues. First is the distinction between voluntary (see Dwyer 1999; Sassen 1991 for their assessments of immigration as part of globalized labor markets) and forced immigrants (see Segal and Mayadas 2005 and Binder and Tosic 2005 for examples of forced immigration) with the former arriving in destination countries mostly for economic and family reunification reasons and the latter because of reasons of politics, religions and social persecution. Despite the different motivations to emigrate out of Africa, both kinds of immigrants are tied to the increasing interconnectedness between places around the globe.

Second, with respect to voluntary immigrants a distinction is made between skilled and unskilled labor, and formally recruited versus those who arrive without recruitment (Rodriguez 2004; Raghuram 2004; Benson-Rea and Rawlinson 2003). In some cases, skilled migrants are not recruited to particular positions but are given entrance into destination countries based on their skills. Canada's immigration policy provides an example of this (see Dryburgh and Hamel 2004). Third, gender has increasingly become a central organizing theme of immigrant literature in terms of who immigrates (see Mahler 1999; Pessar 1999; King and O'Connor 1996). Demographically, young males dominate immigrant streams although female immigration is increasing (Dannecker 2005; Walton-Roberts and Pratt 2005; Silvey 2004; Dion and Dion 2001). Children are also becoming an important part of immigration (Portes, Fernandez-Kelly and Haller 2005; Portes and Rambaut 2001; Portes 1997) because immigrants generally desire to emigrate as a family (nuclear or extended).

According to the survey responses, Ghanaian immigrants in Cincinnati are similar to broader migrant characteristics, but show some differences as well. For example, Ghanaian males far outnumber Ghanaian females in immigration (see Table 18.1). Of the thirty-seven respondents interviewed, twenty-seven are male and only ten are female. However, most (thirty-three of the thirty-seven respondents) are married. Of the four who are not married, one is widowed. A large proportion of these married immigrants (twenty-seven of the thirty-three) are married to Ghanaians who live with them in the United States. Of the remaining married respondents, two are married to non-Ghanaians, and three are married to spouses who live in Ghana, but intend to emigrate to Cincinnati.

Table 18.1.
Demographic Aspects of Migrants.

Gender	**Male**	**Female**				
	27	10				
Marital Status	**Married**	**Not Married**				
	33	4				
Married to	**Ghanaian In USA**	**Non Ghanaian**	**Ghanaian In Ghana**	**Ghanaian Elsewhere**		
	27	2	3	1		
Age Cohort	**20–29**	**30–39**	**40–49**	**50–59**		
	2	15	14	6		
# of Children	**0**	**1**	**2**	**3**	**4**	**5**
# of Families	2	3	14	11	5	2

The majority of the survey respondents are in their thirties or forties, a slightly older age than the traditional twenty- or thirty-year-old migrants predicted by migrant selectivity theory. In addition, the majority of these immigrants have two or three children. Both age and family may account for a step-wise migration pattern seen for Ghanaian immigrants. According to the survey responses, immigration is a family decision involving women and children. Most Ghanaians are voluntary migrants who came to the United States without being recruited by an employer.

A combination of nuclear and extended family considerations affect the decision to emigrate. Often husbands emigrate ahead of their wives. Once they are settled, their wives and children join them. Because Ghanaians also value extended family connections, both husband and wife serve as conduits to bring extended family members to the United States. Thus, even though on the surface males dominate the early immigration pool, the decision is both a nuclear and an extended family one. Early male dominance in a new Ghanaian immigrant community is simply the leading edge of a family decision.

Recency of Immigration

Relative to other immigrant groups, African and Ghanaian voluntary immigration to the United States is a recent phenomenon (Takyi and Boate 2007). Ghanaian immigration trends are associated with changes in the global economy (Dwyer 1999; Lopez et al. 1995; Sassen 1991), and perceptions of Ghana *vis-à-vis* American immigration and foreign policies. Of particular note regarding changes in American immigration policy, is the Diversity Immigratino Lottery (DIL) that was a part of The 1990 Immigration Act.

The survey respondents' migrations clearly have been recent. As Table 18.2 shows the mean and modal length of stay in the United States is ten years, but emigration from Ghana occurred, on average, fifteen years ago. All but one respondent indicated that the United States is their final destination.

Very few respondents (eight of twenty-seven) have returned to live in Ghana since their initial departure. Returning to live in Ghana suggests that these migrants take different steps to arrive at their final destination. However, many have visited Ghana after they (twenty-three out of thirty-seven) regularized their stay in the United States. Generally, the number of visits was three or less.

Three categories of Ghanaian immigrants are discernable (see Table 18.2) as part of step-wise immigration, roughly similar to Lobo's (2007) categorization of the arrival periods of African immigrants to the United States. The first category consists of people who left Ghana before 1980, the time of increasing global interdependence (Lobo's first category is 1972–1977). Six of the 37 respondents left Ghana during this period, with one arriving in the United States. The remaining five went to other countries first and arrived in the United States later. The second category is 1980–1986, the era of intensification of globalization and the emergence of economic recovery and structural adjustment program in Ghana (Lobo's second category is 1978–1989). During this era, six of the thirty-seven respondents left Ghana, and two came directly to the United States. These immigrants were among the first to benefit from the Diversity Immigration Lottery after Ghana's status with the United States improved after J. J. Rawlings accepted economic development conditions of the World Bank and International Monetary Fund.

Table 18.2.
Length of Immigration.

# of Years out of Ghana	**Mean**		**Mode**		**Median**		**Range**
	15		15		7		3–32
# of Years in USA	**Mean**		**Mode**		**Median**		**Range**
	10.5		10		8		3–27
Categorization	**Pre 1980 Interdependence**		**1980–86 Intensification**		**Since 1987 Mature SAP**		
1st Left Ghana	6		6		25		
Arrived USA	1		2		34		
Back to Live in Ghana	**Yes**		**No**				
	8		29				
# of Times Back to Live in Ghana	**1**		**2**		**3**		
	5		2		1		
Visit Ghana from USA	**Yes**		**No**				
	23		14				
# of Visits	**1**	**2**	**3**	**4**	**6**	**11**	**15**
	4	3	4	2	2	1	1
Final Destination is USA	**Yes**		**No**				
	36		1				

The third and last category of immigrants that emphasizes the recent immigration from Ghana to the United States, in particular, is associated with both the mature phase of structural adjustment, as a part of globalization, and the favorable view of Ghana by United States immigration regulations (Lobo's third category is 1990 onwards). During this period, twenty-five of the respondents left Ghana for the first time and almost all of them came directly to the United States. The Immigration Act of 1990, instituted the Diversity Immigration Lottery and facilitated these persons coming to the United States. In addition, nine others who lived in other countries after leaving Ghana came to the United States during this third period. To an extent, the Diversity Immigration Lottery made it possible for Ghanaians to be rewarded by the United States for their country's improved image as a good student of neoliberal economic policies and in more recent times as a good example of democracy in Sub-Saharan Africa. Ghana has been one of the main source countries of the Diversity Immigration Lottery since the early 1990s (Tettey-Fio 2006; Takyi and Konadu-Agyemang 2007).

Step-wise Immigration and Role of Networks as Technologies of Globalization

Two important aspects of many migrations are a step-wise process and the role of social networks in that process. Step-wise immigration, a characteristic of internal migration in the global periphery (see Conway 1980), is a strategy adopted by many immigrants from Ghana. Konadu-Agyemang (1999) identifies this characteristic for Ghanaians in Toronto. His analysis shows that many Ghanaians in Toronto move from rural to urban areas in Ghana and then move from Ghana to Canada through a series of other countries. This is one way to get around unfavorable immigration regulations in Canada. Step-wise immigration is rather different from other forms of immigration. Step-wise immigration involves immigration through a process of spatial relocations or moves by stages designed to get to a final destination (Conway 1980). Often, intermediate moves are made when access to the final destination is either restricted or out of financial reach.

An inherent part of step-wise immigration is the role of networks at various stages. These networks have been facilitated by the technologies of globalization (Lopez et al. 1995). These include banking and money transfers, telecommunication and Internet use, ease of international travel and free trade in goods and services. Thus, the term "network" in the immigration literature seems to have been replaced by transnationalism and remittances but, as Abbott (2007) points out, it refers to family and community members who support immigrants in their move. Hermanu (2006) suggests that Salt and Stein's (1997) conceptualization of immigration as a "business" has focused attention on institutions, agents and individuals who serve for a fee. Yet, the encouragement received from friends, family and community members in both the decision to immigrate and the actual immigration process and settlement, which is often done free of charge, is an important part of the network.

Wong and Song (2006) indicate that with time, mainland Chinese immigrant women in Hong Kong changed their use of networks. In the early part of their settlement, these women utilized instrumental networks of family and kin whereas in later stages of resettlement, these initial sources declined and fellow women became more important sources of information and emotional and social companionship. Heering et al. (2004) show that networks are more important for female than male immigrants in emigration decisions of Moroccans who wish to travel to Western Europe. Their analysis show that networks are a manifestation of a family decision with women joining their husbands. Mohan (2006) provides an example of how complex global networks of Ghanaians in the United Kingdom operate over time.

The sample of Ghanaians in Cincinnati seems to follow step-wise immigration with one exception. In this case all respondents claimed to live in urban centers rather than rural places before they left Ghana. Seventeen of them lived in Accra, eleven lived in Kumasi and nine lived in other urban centers such as Sunyani, Cape Coast, Suhum, and Nkawkaw. Once these immigrants leave Ghana, many of them arrive in the United States by a step-wise process. To an extent, step-wise immigration is associated with changes in American immigration policy that has made it easier for Ghanaians to immigrate. Only seventeen of the sample came directly to the United States and most of these belong to the third category of migrants identified above who have benefited from Diversity Immigration Lottery and the favorable status of Ghana in immigration circles. Twenty of the sample belong to the first two categories and lived in as many as four countries before coming to the United

States. As Table 18.3 shows, they lived in a combination of core, semi-peripheral, and peripheral countries before arriving in the United States. Ten of the twenty lived entirely in core countries (such as Canada, the United Kingdom, Germany and Australia) and most of these tended to study in these countries whereas the other ten lived in a combination of peripheral, semi-peripheral and core countries (such as Nigeria, Cameroon, Libya, Israel, Germany and Italy).

Social networks played important roles at various scales of Ghanaian migration. Ghanaian immigrants in Cincinnati received instrumental assistance from family and friends in both their emigration out of Ghana and immigration into the United States. Twenty-four of the thirty-seven respondents received assistance to leave Ghana and twenty-seven of the thirty-seven enjoyed such network support to arrive in the United States. The importance of network assistance buttresses the argument that immigration is not just an individual decision, but rather it is an extended and nuclear family one (Heering et al. 2004).

The two most important forms of help offered by family and friends in emigrating from Ghana and immigrating into the United States are help with purchasing a ticket and offering the newly arrived immigrant a place to stay. In addition, assistance in obtaining a visa, obtaining employment, and introductions to people on arrival are important, whether the emigrant initially leaves Ghana for another country or for the United States. These network functions of intimacy and affection are the kinds of things that family members and close friends will normally do for each other. Yet, they have been facilitated by the technologies of globalization that make communication and travel around the globe easier than before.

Table 18.3.
Step-wise Immigration and the Role of Networks.

Residence In Ghana	**Accra**	**Kumasi**	**Other Urban**				
	17	11	9				
# of Countries Lived in Before USA		**0**	**1**	**2**	**3**	**4**	
	17	10	3	5	2		
Global Region	**1 Core**	**2 Core**	**3 Core**	**Core, SP**	**SP, Core**	**1 Peri**	
	7	1	1	1	1	3	
	2 Peri	**2 Peri, 2 Core**	**3 Peri, 1 Core**	**2 Peri, 1 SP**	**Peri, 2 Core**	**Peri/SP Core**	
	1	1	1	1	1	1	
Help leaving Ghana	**Yes**	**No**					
	24	13					
Type of Help	**Passport**	**Ticket**	**Place**	**People**	**Other**	**Visa**	**Employ**
	4	17	13	5	1	6	6
Help to USA	**Yes**	**No**					
	27	10					
Type of Help	**Ticket**	**Visa**	**Place**	**Passport**	**People**	**Employ**	
	13	8	18	3	7	10	

Immigration Regulations and Anecdotal Evidence of Regularization Paths

Immigration regulations in the United States and changes in these regulations have had a major impact on Africans, especially Ghanaians immigrating to, and regularizing their stay in the United States. Taylor (2005) argues that Western countries should change their immigration policies by cooperating with countries of origin and transit countries in an effort to manage rather than control immigration. In the context of such a paradigm shift, Lobo (2007) provides an account of recent immigration policy changes in the United States and how they affect African immigration. His view is that the 1965 Act placed all countries on an equal footing for their citizens to immigrate to the United States. Even though the Act emphasized family reunification, occupational skills, and refugees, because of the small base of Africans in the country at that time, it had a minor impact on African immigration.

The Immigration Act (1990) that introduced the Diversity Immigration Lottery, in conjunction with the H1-B program, have made it possible for many Ghanaians to join the globalized labor immigration pool to the United States. In addition, the status of Ghana (at least among United States immigration officials) seems to have improved after J. J. Rawlings finally succumbed to neoliberal ideas after embarking upon both an Economic Recovery Program and Structural Adjustment Program in 1983 and 1986, respectively (see Konadu-Agyemang 2000; Arthur 2000; Yeboah 2003, 2000; Grant and Yankson 2003).

Legal African immigration to the United States reflects changes in immigration policy in the U.S. Lobo (2007) provides statistics that show how the number of African immigrants increased from an annual average of 7,400 between 1972 and 1978 (a result of the 1965 Act), to an annual average of 15,466 between 1978 and 1989, and to 35,080 annually between 1990 and 2000 (the latter increase is to a large extent a result of the DIL). The bulk of Ghanaians in the survey arrived post-1986. A forgotten variable though is the use of H1-B visa to attract highly skilled and qualified Ghanaians to either move from other core countries such as Canada, or to stay in the United States after they complete their programs of study. Changes in immigration regulations and the H1-B visa are legitimate ways by which Ghanaians have arrived and stayed in the United States. Six of the respondents in the survey benefited from the H1-B program, and it is this group of professionals that was the seed to attract more immigrants to the area through their networks.

It is more difficult to determine the exact number of respondents who have benefited from the Diversity Immigration Lottery, but an interesting anecdotal observation is that before the introduction of photographs and biometrics for the DIL, Ghanaians used many strategies, as did people from other countries, to maximize their ability to win the lottery. One common strategy was for extended family members to attach themselves to people of the opposite sex who won the lottery. Another was for unrelated people to pay sums of money to attach themselves to winners of the Diversity Immigration Lottery to begin the interview process. With restrictions imposed on the administration of the DIL, these avenues have been closed.

A good number of Ghanaians also arrive in the United States either as students or visitors and overstay their visas. Despite the potential risks of overstaying visas, many people (not just Ghanaians) are able to survive in the United States because of the laxity of enforcement of immigration regulations once in the country, unlike in European countries like the United Kingdom, Germany and the Netherlands. A key issue is that there are substantial numbers of immigrants, from all over the world, who are out of status living in the United Sates. Anecdotal evidence indicates that to regularize their stay, Ghanaians, like people from other countries, have adopted well-tested strategies to formalize their stay.

The movie "Green Card" illustrates a key trend, marriages of foreigners to American citizens for green card purposes. Although it is difficult to research the extent to which this occurs, a recent *Washington Post* publication demonstrates the extent to which a network of contractors has established "green card" marriages for Ghanaians living in Virginia (see Arthur 2000; Markon 2006). Green card marriages may be real or fictitious in the minds of the non-Ghanaians involved. The insecurity of green card marriages has resulted in the preference for marriages to American citizens of Ghanaian ancestry, rather than to either African-Americans or other Americans. In some cases, fictitious marriages to extended family members (siblings, cousins, fathers, mothers, aunts and uncles) occur, supporting the view that family considerations are very important not just immigration decisions, but also in regularization decisions. Because of the sensitivity associated with regularization, the specifics of the sample from Cincinnati were not investigated. What is presented here is anecdotal evidence, acquired based on intimate knowledge of immigrant groups in the United States.

Ghanaians in a Globalized Labor Market

Dwyer (1999) and Sassen (1991) contend that recent trends of voluntary immigration reflect the emergence of a globalized labor market and this has resulted in a theory of immigration best summarized by Light (2004). Based on the original work of Sassen (1991), Light (2004) argues that the demand-driven theory of immigration (out of Massey et al.'s 1993 cumulative causation ideas) does not capture the supply-side of the immigration equation because the emergence of an informal sector in cities of the global core requires explanation. In this regard, Sassen (2000) acknowledges that there is a supply-side to global immigration. Light (2004) therefore, advocates that a two stage-model of immigration is a more compatible framework for assessing why people immigrate. In a recent analysis, Okome (2007) agrees that globalization has set into place an immigration of Africans to America, but this is more a reflection of the contradictions inherent in globalization itself. Africa's labor pool (both skilled and unskilled) has responded to demand consideration in the global core (through immigration regulation modifications) and a supply condition in Africa because of the adverse effects of globalization through structural adjustment programs and political instability (see Takyi and Konadu-Agyemang 2007). Thus, Africa and the United States seem to be in a near-equal action and reaction relationship in terms of population movements. Yet, considering that capitalism has not hesitated in the past to commodify and enslave humans (see Karenga 1993; Wallerstein 2005) for economic gain, one wonders whether there is a near-equal action and reaction between Africa and the global core. Perhaps, this is a rather deliberate manifestation of capitalism to acquire labor (both skilled and unskilled) in its recent phase of expansion known as globalization. At the root of the immigration decision is the differential between economies of the global core and periphery. This is what Okome (2007) terms a contradiction. What facilitates their ability to live and work in the United States, however, is the ease with which immigrants fit in because of the compatibility of educational systems and the use of English.

Reasons for immigration manifest these assertions and can be summarized as economic, social or political in both origin and destination places (Okome 2007). These reasons apply differently to both voluntary and forced immigrants. To a large extent, economic reasons trump why people in Ghana, Morocco, Senegal and Egypt intend to leave their country of birth (van Dalen, Groenewold and Schoorl 2005). Other social and political reasons (such as attending school, fear of persecution, and family reasons) account for less than 20% of intentions to emigrate from these countries. Thus, it is safe to conclude that economics, which reflects place-difference between global core and periphery, is at the heart of most voluntary African immigration to the United States. It should be borne in mind that these place-differences between America and Ghana were structured as part of capital's deliberate expansion (see Rodney 1974) and this is what Saravia and Miranda (2004) call opportunity differences. The compatibility between educational systems in former colonies and the global core attests to the deliberateness of capital structuring Sub-Saharan African societies during colonialism to benefit it at a later period (see Davidson 1994; Yeboah 2003).

The Ghanaian immigrant sample in Cincinnati reflects the economic reason for immigration to the United States, with one major modification. That is, even though the economic reason is important, their immigration is also about bettering life chances and making a living for these immigrants and their families. Place-differences and the well-being of family members come into the calculus of reasons to immigrate. Thus, the family (both nuclear and extended) is a major consideration in immigration decisions, but individuals in the family, especially men and women, do not have the same experience of immigration to the United States. Ghanaians in Cincinnati have been able to participate in this globalized labor market because of changes in immigration regulations, the compatibility between educational systems, the commonality of English as a medium of instruction and business, and the favorable position of American immigration policy towards Ghanaians. In fact, the move from a step-wise immigration towards a direct immigration to the United States reflects the emergence of globalized labor markets.

Table 18.4 shows that the majority of respondents believe that the economy of Ghana was either adequate or in bad shape when they left the country, a manifestation of the negative effects of globalization through Ghana's structural adjustment program (see Arthur 2000). In addition, a majority believe that the economy of the country has improved since they left Ghana. Yet, a further probing of reasons why Ghanaians left Ghana and why they arrived in the United States suggests that labeling their reasons for emigrating as simply economic does not capture their experience. To a large extent, the majority of Ghanaians immigrated as part of their strategy of "making a living and bettering themselves and the life chances of their families." Their concern is with family well-being differences between Ghana and the United States.

Table 18.4.
Reasons for Immigration.

Economy Left	**Good**	**Okay**	**Bad**				
	5	16	16				
Economy Today	**Improved**	**Same**	**Worse**				
	20	5	10				
Why Left Ghana	**Study**	**Work**	**Political**	**Family**	**Living**	**Citizen**	
	(11)	(7)	(1)	(3)	(1)	(1)	
	15	19	1	4	11	1	
Why USA	**Study**	**Work**	**Political**	**Family**	**Travel**	**Kids**	**Residency**
	(10)	(4)	(1)	(3)	(2)	(1)	(1)
	15	16	2	4	2	5	1

( ) number of times mentioned alone.

The fact that work features prominently in both leaving Ghana and arriving in the United States supports the importance of economic factors in a globalized labor market as reasons for immigration yet, the importance of education, joining family, and considerations for children indicate that perhaps it is not just about earning a good income, but also bettering one's self and one's family. The importance of children as a consideration in immigration needs to be explained. Some of these respondents are persons who immigrated to countries like Italy and were part of a guest-worker program. Economically, they did well to the extent that some even built houses in Ghana. Yet, they chose to leave Italy for the United States because their children were being educated in Italian and they perceived this as limiting their children's life chances. The overall concern with education for the entire family stresses betterment of self and family alongside making a living as the basis of immigration. It also buttresses the suggestion that immigration is a family decision.

BRAIN AND SKILL DRAIN OR GAIN

Global capital is after the best and brightest human resources to solve its problems. It is, therefore, selective of immigrants in this globalized labor market, be they skilled or unskilled. A concern of emigration from peripheral countries such as Ghana is the loss of professional, managerial, technical and skilled workers to countries of the global core. This is referred to as the brain drain (Logan 1999; El-Khawas 2004; Dodoo and Takyi 2007), especially of physicians, nurses, university lecturers, teachers, soccer players, and the like. Recent research on African brain drain has focused on the loss of health-sector professionals (Ahmad 2004; Akokpari 2006; Chikanda 2006; Clark, Stewart and Clark 2006;) to the exclusion of other sectors of African economies. It is estimated that in 2003 alone Sub-Saharan African countries lost over 8,500 physicians to the global core and semi-periphery. Ghana alone lost about 850 physicians in this exodus (Eastwood et al. 2005). Mullan (2007) quotes figures that suggest that five hundred and thirty-two (about twenty percent) of Ghanaian-trained physicians live in the United States alone, and another two hundred and fifty-nine (or ten percent) live in the United Kingdom and Canada.

Despite the overwhelming concentration on the health sector, the literature on brain drain has evolved around issues of whether brain drain is good or bad for sending countries (Akokpari 2006; Clark, Stewart and Clark 2006), how to manage brain drain (Eastwood et al. 2005; Morgan, Sives and Appleton 2005), the economic growth effects of remittances resulting from brain drain (Brown and Connell 2006; Hass 2006), the effects of brain drain on health care delivery (Chikanda 2006; Feeley 2006), the causes and consequences of brain drain (Ahmad 2004; El-Khawas 2004), and the reversal of brain drain (Logan 1999; Levy 2003; Eastwood et al. 2005; Kupfer et al. 2006; Pincook 2006; Zweig 2006). At the heart of brain drain, though, is a fundamental geographic issue of place-differences. Immigrant well-being is at stake and this affects their desire to find greener pastures in other parts of the world. This is more so in a globalized labor market with its relatively freer movement of people, goods and services. The concern here is the loss of human capital and its effects on economic growth in source countries of immigrants. One of the most important benefits of immigration from the global periphery has been remittances that are sent back home (Brown and Connell 2006; Hass 2006). India's experience, however, shows that the benefits of immigration of professionals can far exceed remittances, and includes return migrants contributing to growing the economy.

The experience of Ghanaians in Cincinnati suggests that there is not much of a brain drain. Rather, there is a skill drain and an inability of Ghana to capture potential brains that are developed in the United States but do not return home. Physicians and nurses were not well represented in the survey (there are only four Ghanaian physicians in the Cincinnati area). Of these only one received basic medical training in Ghana. The other three received their training in the United States. To the best of my knowledge, no nurse trained in Ghana works in a hospital in the Cincinnati area, despite a large number of Ghanaians embarking upon nursing training at all levels in the Cincinnati area.

Table 18.5 shows that the prevalent educational attainment for Ghanaians in the survey was either a polytechnic or teacher-training education. Seventeen had attained such education before leaving Ghana. Only eight had a college education. Twelve had either minimal education (middle school leaving certificate) or a vocational education, which is often a marginal step above the minimum. Thus, the view that Ghanaians in the United States are often highly educated is not accurate in this case. This is contrary to Lobo's (2007) view that the average African immigrant is better educated, yet worse paid, than their African-American counterpart (see Dodoo and Takyi 2007 for this argument as well).

While still in Ghana, the majority of respondents in the survey were employed (twenty-seven), with only six unemployed, and four still in their formative years as students. Sixteen of the employed were engaged in skilled work, so it is fair to say that there is a loss of skilled workers rather than a brain drain since only five were engaged in professional work. Irrespective of educational attainment of Ghanaians before they arrived in Cincinnati, they have invested in their human capital since arriving in the United States. Twenty of them have acquired an education in the United States (nineteen out of twenty have attained their terminal education in the United States. Three have attained Ph.D.s, five have attained master's degrees, seven have attained bachelor's degrees and five have attained associate degrees).

Immigration has offered these Ghanaians opportunities to become more educated by acquiring professional, managerial and technical skills, as part of their desire to make a living and better themselves and their families. Technically, they would be considered as part of the brain drain from Ghana, even though they did not have higher qualifications before arriving in the United States.

Table 18.5.
Brain Drain.

Job in Ghana	**Yes**	**No**	**Student**			
	27	6	4			
Type of Job	**Professional**	**Skilled**	**Non-Skilled**	**Business**	**Student**	**N/A**
	5	16	5	1	4	6
Education Level in Ghana	**MSLC**	**Vocational Secondary**	**Polytechnic Training Col**	**College**		
	5	7	17	8		
Acquired Education Since Ghana	**Yes**	**No**				
	20	17				
Level of Education Acquired	**Ph.D.**	**M.Sc.**	**Bachelors**	**Associate**	**N/A**	
	3	5	7	5	17	
Acquired Country of Education	**USA**	**Other**				
	19	1				

Transnational Activities Linking Ghana and the United States

Immigrants that assimilate discard the culture and values of their origin in favor of their destination country's. Transnationalism refers to the web of cultural, social, economic and political relationships, practices and identities built by immigrants across national borders (Guarnizo 1997; Owusu 2007). Transnationalism is facilitated by globalization's increasing interconnectedness and its technologies (Itzingsohn 2000). The question is whether immigrants lead new lives altogether or whether they engage in transnational activities with various aspects of their lives centered on various countries or places. Transnational activities of immigrants include flows of people between countries, money (both capital and remittances), goods, political relations and even political representation (Owusu 2007). Increasingly, family relations are becoming transnational with women at the forefront of these transnational families (Al-Sharmani 2006; Wong 2006; 2000). A distinction must be made between transnational lives and activities. The emphasis here is on transnational activities that connect immigrants across geographies of different countries, rather than whole lifestyles that are centered on more than one country. The difference here is selectivity or extent of transnationalism.

Two aspects of transnational activities for Ghanaians in Cincinnati are their relations to family and the extent to which they maintain connections in Ghana. To a large extent, transnational family structure and parenting are represented in the sample (see Al-Sharmani 2006; Wong 2000) and support the assertion that immigration for these Ghanaians is a family rather than a mere individual decision. The first aspect of transnational activity is that parents in America engage in transnational parenting through the fostering of their children by both their spouse and the children's grandparents (Wong 2000). As Table 18.6 shows, eighteen of the respondents left children behind in Ghana. Of these, eight have had some of their children join them in the short time they have been in the United States. Ten are yet to have their children join them, perhaps, a reflection of their inability to regularize their stay in America.

Table 18.6.
Transnational Families and Parenting.

Left Children in Ghana	**Yes**	**No**			
	18	15			
Children Joined You	**Yes**	**No**			
	8	10			
# of Children Joined Per Family	**0**	**1**	**2**	**3**	
	10	3	4	1	
# of Years for Children to Join	**1**	**4**	**5**	**6**	**19**
	(1) 2	(2) 3	(2)	(1)	(1)
# of Children Left in Ghana	**0**	**1**	**2**	**3**	**4**
	5	4	4	4	1
Had Children Outside Ghana	**Yes**	**No**			
	23	12			
# of Children Had Outside Ghana	**1**	**2**	**3**	**5**	**Total**
	5	8	9	1	53
# of Children Born in USA	**1**	**2**	**3**	**4**	**Total**
	10	8	4	1	

On average, two children have joined each family and it took between four and five years for these children to arrive. The majority of respondents still have between one and three children in Ghana and plan for them to emigrate to the United States. Many of these parents are involved in transnational parenting of their children left in Ghana (see Wong 2000). In Ghana, these children often live with the other parent, or if both parents have moved to the United States, with aunts, uncles, or grandparents. In some cases, children born in the United States are sent to live with grandparents to relieve the parents of some of the stresses of raising children in the United States.

Effectively, there is a fostering of grandchildren, as is the case where children are sent to live with grandparents in hometowns in Ghana. The parents, however, are intimately involved in the raising of their children, even from the remoteness of the United States. Not only do they remit money for tuition and day-to-day upkeep of their children, they also receive report cards, talk to the children by telephone and, in some cases, communicate with their children by e-mail. These are the specific ways transnational parenting, alongside fostering grandparents, occurs in Ghana.

Because immigration is seen as a family decision by these respondents, there is a continued growth of the family once both parents leave Ghana. Twenty-three of the respondents have had children since they left their home country. A total of fifty-three children have been born to these respondents, and of these, forty-two have been born in the United States. The average number of children that the respondents have had since leaving Ghana is between two and three children, with an average of two children per respondent born in the United States. Thus, the majority of children born since leaving Ghana have been born in the United States. As nucleated families were split at very young ages, once a couple meets in America, or elsewhere in the immigration chain, they continue to expand their family by having more children. Immigration's disruption and dislocation of family sometimes may have adverse effects because fathers are away during the developmental years of their children. Also, in cases where it takes long periods for husbands and wives to reunite, the potential number of new children is limited by the "biological clocks of women."

The second aspect of transnational activities of these migrants is that they do not sever ties with Ghana, but rather have strong geographic ties that go beyond keeping one foot in America and the other in Ghana. Their ties with other countries in which they have lived remain. However, they are not as strong as those with Ghana. Clearly, an emotional attachment to place exists, a topophilia towards Ghana (Tuan 1996). Table 18.7 shows that twenty of the respondents consider Ghana to be their exclusive home, whereas only four consider America to be their home. Another eleven claim that their homes are both Ghana and the United States. Generally, the latter group consists of immigrants who have lived in the United States longer and have children who are American-born. Their longevity in America and their connection to their American children makes them see both Ghana and the United States as home.

Table 18.7.
Transnational Activities.

Where is Home	**Ghana**		**USA**	**Ghana/USA**	**Other**	
	20		4	11	2	
	Yes	**No**			**Yes**	**No**
House in Ghana	19	18	**Business in Ghana**		3	34
House in USA	18	19	**Business in USA**		3	34
House in Other	1	36	**Business in Other**		1	36
Family in Ghana	37	0	**Visited Countries live in**		9	14
Family in USA	30	7	**Visit Ghana from USA**		23	14
Family in Other	33	4	**Send Money to Ghana**		37	0
			Call Ghana		37	0
Residence during Visits to Ghana	**Accra**	**Kumasi**	**Other Urban**	**Rural**		
	22	11	3	1		
Retire Where	**Ghana**	**USA**	**Don't Know**			
	28	6	3			
Why Retirement Preference	**Home**	**Close to Kids**	**Cost of Living**	**Medical**	**Don't Know**	
	28	1	1	3	1	
Visit USA After Retirement	**Yes**	**No**	**Don't Know**			
	33	1	3			
Children Visit Ghana after you've Retired	**Yes**	**No**	**Don't Know**			
	14	15	7			
Burial Country	**Ghana**	**USA**	**Anywhere**	**Don't Know**		
	21	4	7	5		

Just as many (about fifty percent) own houses in Ghana as they do in the United States. In a sense Owusu's (1998; 2007) assertion that Ghanaian immigrants in Toronto tend to build houses in Ghana even before they buy one in Canada is supported here. Only one owns a house in a different country where they had previously lived. In this case, the respondent intends to relocate to the United Kingdom, where his wife and children prefer to live.

All respondents have family in Ghana. They call and send remittances to these extended family members (see Wong 2006 for the role gender plays in remittance by Ghanaians). In this regard, these respondents engage in strong transnational activities with Ghana. The majority also have family in both the United States and other countries. A family network provides evidence that immigration decisions involve these extended family members. Anecdotal evidence shows that on occasions such as graduation of children, outdooring of new births, and funeral celebrations of parents who have died in Ghana, many of these extended family members (with legal documents) travel from all over the United States, Canada, and Europe to join them in Cincinnati on special occasions. Business ownership in Ghana and the United States is not strong, so it cannot be used as an index of transnational activities.

Since arriving in the United States, respondents have tended to visit countries in which they previously resided and Ghana at the same rate. This shows that transnational activities are not restricted to Ghana and the United States, but also operate with other places, especially in the core, such as the United Kingdom, Canada, Germany and Israel. To a large extent though, ability to leave the United States is a function of regularization of immigration status so it is difficult to determine the extent of transnational activities using this yardstick since some of the respondents have not regularized their stay in the United States. Most of the respondents originated from Accra, Kumasi, and other urban areas. Therefore, it is not surprising that these are the places they visit when they return to Ghana. The implication is that many benefits of return migration will perhaps be concentrated in urban rather than rural Ghana.

Asked to speculate on their future immigration plans, respondents reveal that their lives are characterized by transnational activities. As stated earlier, all but one view the United States as their final immigration destination. Yet, the majority of respondents expect to retire (twenty-five out of thirty-seven) to Ghana since they consider Ghana their home (twenty-eight out of thirty-seven). In a sense, they reflect not just a return to their roots, but a form of return immigration which may take much longer to manifest itself. Those who prefer to retire to places other than Ghana tend to be those who have been in the United States longest, are better educated, and have seen their children begin to become acculturated in the United States. For them, access to quality medical care also is a factor in their preference to retire in the United States.

Irrespective of their intended retirement destination, almost all respondents (thirty-three) will lead transnational lives after retirement, as they plan to visit the United States after retirement. Pragmatically, there seems to be an awareness that their children will not live permanently in Ghana, since only fourteen of the thirty-seven believe that their children would ever live in Ghana in the future. This has implications for second-generation immigrants. Finally, the majority of respondents wish to be buried in Ghana, but there is a strong sentiment that final resting place does not make much difference to them as individuals. Sixteen either wish to be buried in the United States, or wherever they die, or they really do not know. However, there seems to be an attitude of providing their children with access to their final resting place.

WHO BENEFITS OR LOSES FROM IMMIGRATION: POTENTIAL ECONOMIC GROWTH IMPACTS ON GHANA

Based on the preceding attribute of Ghanaian immigrant trajectories, it is germane to ask two questions: Who benefits or loses from immigration of Ghanaians? What are the economic growth impacts of this process on Ghana? Superficially, individual Ghanaians and their families who have immigrated to the United States benefit from emigration. They obviously better themselves economically and are able to lead transnational lives, but this often is at a social cost. They are included in American economy but are excluded from social life to a large extent. The paradox of their experience is that they commune and socialize mostly with other Ghanaians and Africans. African children also can be marginalized in school. Often, children with African names are ostracized by schoolmates. Thus, African immigrants tend to live on the margins of American society. In addition, over long periods of time they lose touch with friends, family, and colleagues in Ghana. In some cases, family dislocations are encountered with dire consequences for children and spouses. Thus, their economic benefits should be weighed against the social cost.

Capitalism benefits because it is able to attract both skilled and unskilled labor for both professional and menial jobs in America. Unlike the days of slavery when capital co-opted African human power without compensation (see Williams 1944; Karanga 1993; and Smedley 1999), today African labor is paid a decent wage because immigration regulations in the United States mandate such. As Graeber (2006) argues, the mode of production under industrial capitalism treated labor as slaves. This is not the case today for African immigrants, but capitalism is deliberate and will stop at nothing (if even it has to change immigration regulations) to meet its needs. In this case, the humane treatment of today's African immigrants compares in no way to the commodification of humans under slavery.

Immigration's economic growth effect on peripheral source countries like Ghana also has received attention in the literature. The two schools of thought on these effects are summarized as those who see the positive impacts of emigration on source regions (such as remittances, brain gain and technological and cultural transfers) and those who see it as negative (such as brain drain, loss of human capital, loss of economic growth capacity, and family disruption (Akokpari 2006). Hass (2006) believes that researchers and practitioners should not be asking whether emigration is good or bad for source countries, but rather why some countries have been able to benefit from the emigration of their citizens, while others have not. This implies that transnational migration should be the vein within which to assess the impacts of emigration.

Remittances have been hailed as the greatest positive impact of immigration. In Ghana, the 2007 National Budget statement estimates that remittances contribute over U.S. $4 billion, second in importance only to cocoa as a foreign exchange earner. Similarly, Diatta and Mbow (1999) argue that Senegal receives huge sums of money from remittances that rival the contribution of foreign direct investment to the country. Remittances also help alleviate poverty, especially in rural areas, since they go directly into the hands of the poor who most need them. Remittances, therefore, have great multiplier effects for source countries of emigrants since they increase the spending power of these countries (Hugo 2006). Despite the impact of remittances on economic growth, Akokpari (2006) points out that remittances typically result in a negative balance of payments for source countries of immigrants because recipients spend money on consumption (housing, education, health care, funerals), especially imported luxury goods. This is not to say that remittances are not invested in small businesses. The business development role of remittances has been understudied. Remittances used in consumption rather than production can result in inflationary pressures on countries of emigration by creating artificial increase in spending capacity. Because of the individual transfers of remittances, governments are not able to channel funds from remittances into productive investment. The double-edged nature of remittances lends support to Hass' (2006) belief that countries can benefit differently from emigration. For Ghana, the question should focus on how remittances from emigrants can best contribute to economic growth, rather than simply focusing on the size and value of remittances.

Brain drain has been touted as the biggest negative impact of emigration for source countries. Often the best and brightest (youthful, educated and productive) are the ones who emigrate from peripheral countries like Ghana (Dodoo and Takyi 2007). In terms of economic growth, this results in loss of human capital in critical sectors such as health, education, technology and manufacturing. For countries in southern Africa, facing high HIV/AIDS infection rates, the loss of physicians, nurses, and pharmacists, trained at very high costs, is remarkable (see Chikanda 2006 for the situation in Zimbabwe). This chapter noted the major loss of African physicians, especially in Ghana. The largest losses were to the U.S., United Kingdom, and Canada. Yet, the impact of brain drain is far beyond the health care sector. Akokpari (2006) notes that Zambia lost 200 university lecturers from the mid-1980s to the mid-1990s. This resulted in the closure of some departments and a lowering of standards of those hired to replace lost faculty. The impacts are felt in a variety of economic sectors.

Brain drain is often constructed as a negative for countries of the global periphery. However, when Hass' (2006) question of why some countries benefit from emigration is considered, the positive dimension comes into focus. Evidence from Ghanaians in Cincinnati shows that once Ghanaians arrive in the United States, they improve their educational and professional status (Yeboah 2008). The question, therefore, is not whether Ghana is losing its brains *per se* but, whether Ghana can capture this developed human capital in the future (see Groot and Gibbons 2007; Hart 2006). Logan (1999) speaks to this reverse transfer of technology as one of the benefits of brain drain. Zweig (2006) argues that brain gain or return immigration can only occur if sending countries offer globally competitive environments for their managerial, technical and professional emigrants. China seems to be taking steps in this direction. This is where the respondents' future immigration plans and their connectedness to Ghana through transnational activities is instructive.

The transnational nature of migration today (Owusu 2007) suggests that it is incumbent upon emigrant countries to tap into emigrant communities to aid in their economic growth. Most emigrants literally have one foot in source countries like Ghana and another in their destination country. Ghanaian physicians living abroad often volunteer their practice and teaching time to remote hospitals and teaching hospitals when they are on vacation in Ghana. University lecturers often spend their sabbatical leaves in Ghanaian universities contributing toward the training of Ghanaian students. These are informal ways of brain gain and technology transfer that have to be captured with the right kinds of policies by the state.

An often ignored component of emigration's contribution to economic growth is the technological and cultural transfer that visiting and return emigrants bring to a country. The economic growth divide between countries of the global core and periphery is not just an economic one but, also a cultural one. An understanding of how things are done and what capacities are needed to do things is vital. One key contribution of emigration is bridging the cultural and technological divide between the global core and periphery. Tapping into the transnational activities of emigrants should be a priority.

In a globalized labor market, immigration is a manifestation of place-differences around the globe. The key issue, therefore, is not whether emigration is good or bad for peripheral countries. What is important is the extent to which a country can capture the benefits of emigration by building capacity and implementing appropriate policies that recognize the transnational nature of migration. Providing national scale primary migration data for policy makers is a germane consideration.

CONCLUSION

Need for Policy on Emigration from Ghana

Emigration and immigration decisions are fundamentally geographic ones that rest upon place-differences. Today's immigration to the United States demonstrates how capital continues to use Sub-Saharan Africa as a source of labor as it did during preceding eras of capitalist expansion (Williams 1944; Rodney 1974). Trajectories of Ghanaian immigrants in Cincinnati demonstrate that capital changes immigration regulations in the core to achieve its labor needs through the creation of a globalized labor market (Sassen 1991; Light 2004). Individuals in peripheral countries who desire to better themselves and their families will emigrate from peripheral countries like Ghana to core countries like the United States. Even though Ghanaian immigrants are included in America's economy, they tend to be marginalized in American society, albeit in subtle ways. This is because they commune mostly with other Ghanaians and Africans (Yeboah 2008). This issue requires attention in the United States since it brings back the historical experience of African Americans, albeit on a smaller scale (see Smedely 1993; Karanga 1993).

Peripheral countries like Ghana should come to an understanding that their best and brightest are available to global capital in its expansion. Brain drain and remittances are likely features of their economies. These nations need to develop national multi-faceted emigration and immigration polices that will help them ensure that they get the best from the process. Among other things, these policies should consider the development of human capital for export, taxation arrangements with other countries for their emigrants to pay taxes in their home nation, incentives for return emigrants, transnational relations with their emigrants to invest at home, and cultural exchanges between emigrants and their home. As Hass (2006) argues, it is important to maximize and optimize the benefits of emigration, while minimizing the costs. This is the policy challenge that faces Ghana and other peripheral countries. Immigration is here to stay and it is better to strategize maximium returns than to bemoan the outflow of Ghanaians to the global core. After all, we are in a new imperialism (Hoogvelt 2006). The earlier this is understood by peripheral countries, the better their chances of benefiting from this era of capitalist expansion.

Chapter 19

Ethnic Small-Business Relocations: A Case Study in the Bronx, NY, 2007

Esther Ofori, John W. Frazier, and Eugene L. Tettey-Fio

INTRODUCTION

New York City, a continuous immigrant gateway since the 1700s, today has a significant and growing immigrant population of foreign-born Latinos, Asians, and people of the African Diaspora. Among New York City's boroughs, the Bronx represents a microcosm of the New York City migration system and provides an excellent source for case studies. The Bronx population, although majority-Latino in 2006, also contains foreign-born immigrants from many nations, which has created a demand for ethnic and specialty foods such as spices and meats. The Bronx Terminal Market, created in the 1920s, has provided a niche market for Latino customers since the 1960s, and more recently (1990s) has become home to African small businesses. Located along the Harlem River in the southeastern corner of the Bronx near Yankee Stadium, the Market contained wholesale suppliers of local restaurants and bodegas, and retailers that provided a shopping Mecca for the City's growing Latino, African, and Afro-Caribbean populations (Figure 19.1a).

Figure 19.1a.
BTM & Hunts Point Market Location.

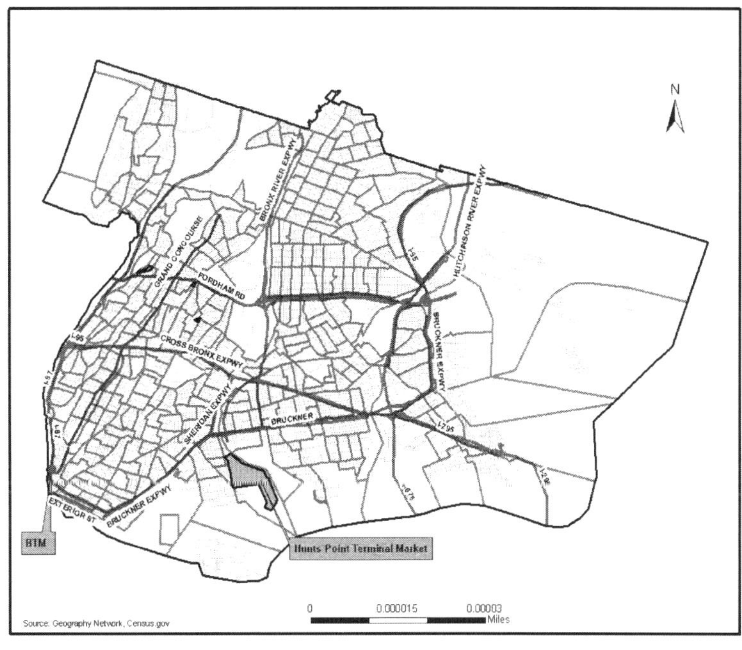

Despite serving these immigrant market niches, The Bronx Terminal Market, labeled an "eyesore" by City planners and the Mayor's office, became part of an area targeted for economic redevelopment. The designated economic development zone included a proposal for a new $300 million dollar mall to replace the Bronx Terminal Market. This gentrification plan also mandated the closing or relocation of the Market's businesses, with relocation assistance made available to the small ethnic businesses because of the decision to close the Market.

This mandated removal offered an unusual opportunity to chronicle and analyze the process by which a number of immigrant small business enterprises were affected by a city-supported gentrification program in the South Bronx. We examine the impacts of the mandated relocation and the behaviors of the small ethnic entrepreneurs. Despite being a small case study, this research may assist both other communities and their small ethnic businesses when gentrification is planned. In this study, we are interested in the impact on all of the small business entrepreneurs, but given the African focus of this text, we are particularly interested in those of African descent. Our research was driven by a number of questions, including: How did these small ethnic business entrepreneurs initially respond to the City government's plan? What was the impact of the mandated closings? What site selection procedures did the surviving small businesses employ? What is the resulting geographic pattern? How well are the relocated businesses performing one year after their relocations?

In the remainder of this chapter, we address these questions, after a brief review of site selection literature, business practices and the location of small ethnic businesses, observations of the study area, and a discussion of our methods.

SMALL BUSINESS AND ETHNIC BUSINESS PRACTICES AND SPATIAL DISTRIBUTION OF SMALL ETHNIC BUSINESS

U.S. and Canadian Small Ethnic Businesses: Characteristics and Practices

A minority business in the U.S. is "at least 51 percent directly and unconditionally owned by a minority group" (Sonfield 2005, p. 225). Women, Blacks, Hispanics, Native Americans, and Asian/Pacific Islanders are the specified minority groups eligible for this classification, which does not differentiate on the basis of foreign-born vs. native-born status because first-generation immigrant small business owners likely face many of the same barriers and limitations as native owners.

Some argue that ethnic designation is inadequate because it does not include community involvement (Chagnati and Greene, 2002), which should be a consideration because many ethnic entrepreneurs have a strong relationship with their communities that affects their success. Some research indicates that small ethnic businesses that are highly involved with their ethnic communities' activities have lower business performance (success) than those with lesser involvement (Chaganti and Greene 2002). The highly involved also tend to have fewer economic resources, less U.S.-based education, and more limited business experience. The performance of the highly involved small ethnic business entrepreneurs is less than their less involved counterparts, despite holding the same strong cultural values and an equal emphasis on business success. The less involved small ethnic businesses also place less emphasis on community needs and give more weight to price and cost issues related to business operations, than those who are more highly involved.

Ethnic small businesses are important to ethnic community members for socialization and for the maintenance of ethnicity in immigrant communities (Chacko and Chung 2006; Scott 2006). However, due to their more limited success, they require additional marketing efforts to sustain or increase their businesses (Wright, Martin and Stone 2003; Scott 2006). Lacking the advantages of large businesses (scale economies, computerized data bases, etc.), many of these family-owned businesses rely on ethnic social ties to maintain and grow clientele. This form of "relational marketing" helps explain some successful small enterprises, but also contributes to their classification as "high risk ventures" (Wright, Martin, and Stone 2003).

Limited theory exists on Black immigrant small businesses and their operations, and because Black cultures vary so strongly, it has been difficult to develop general theory about successful strategies for their growth.

However, some conceptual and empirical literature provides important insights into American minority businesses in a broader context. We briefly review some of this literature and focus, when possible, on research findings for Black businesses. Our focus is on Black immigrant entrepreneurs.

There is considerable literature on U.S. minority entrepreneurship using broad ethnic categories, which generally explores the formation and the self-employment and entrepreneurship success across broad ethnic categories (Light et al. 1984; Aldrich and Waldinger 1990; Bates 1997; Fischer and Massey 2000). Fischer and Massey (2000) organized this type of research into four primary theories. The first is "cultural theory," which suggests that certain cultural features influence the propensity to engage in and become successful in ethnic business. These take on different forms, including those rooted in the cultural fabric and involve family structure and family support that lead to entrepreneurship and success. One example of the applicability of cultural theory can be seen in Stoller's analysis of African traders in New York City (Stoller 2001). In this case, Senegalese immigrant men come to the U.S. and utilize a family tradition of trading rooted in their homeland's informal economy. This skill is passed not only from generation to generation but, in New York, from brother to brother. As one Senegalese family member returns home, he passes the business to another family member. Another form of cultural theory involves "alien status" that leads to group solidarity and community ties that enhance business success through access to resources such as loans (Light 1984; Fischer and Massey 2000).

The second theory is blocked-mobility theory (also termed structured and disadvantaged theory). This theory argues that certain minority groups experience structural barriers (racial) that block their labor market participation. In addition to racism, prejudice, and discrimination that create cultural barriers to employment, visible minorities may have "non-transferable skills" or lack English-speaking skills. Such factors result in entrepreneurship that involves a "survival strategy" (Fairlie 1996; Fischer and Massey 2000, p. 409).

A third theory combines elements of the structural and cultural perspectives and is termed the "middleman theory." This argument sees certain immigrants as initial sojourners that "predispose them toward middleman status" (p. 409), wherein they take goods from producers and distribute them to their co-ethnics. This type of entrepreneurship leads to their position in a narrow but successful niche and maintains a close relationship with their ethnic group.

An additional theoretical explanation of entrepreneurial, small business behaviors and successes is the "interactive model of business development," which also combines structural and cultural factors into an explanation. This fourth theory, also presented by Fischer and Massey, is termed "opportunity structures" (and/or enclave theory and also is based on the works of Aldrich and Waldinger 1990 and Light 1972). The theory stresses the importance of market and other structural conditions that constrain entrepreneurial success. This theory suggests that while an adjacent ethnic market (neighborhood or enclave) may be captive and result in easy entry and survival for an immigrant entrepreneur (Bates 1997), it also may limit the degree of success due to low socioeconomic status of neighborhood residents, discrimination, and other factors. Fischer and Massey summarize the four market types presented earlier by Aldrich and Waldinger (1990). The most relevant for our study is the market that has "demand for unusual or specialized goods" (p. 410). Such markets provide ethnic entrepreneurs success because they are "protected markets" for ethnic goods (p. 410). This may be, in part, an apt description of the Bronx Terminal Market due to its location in the South Bronx. However, as we will report later, the range of the Market's specialized goods reaches well beyond the local ethnic market to reach Connecticut ethnic consumers. Fischer and Massey noted that structural theory indicates that "some residential segregation" can support small business entrepreneurship (2000, p. 410). However, their analysis also indicates that relatively high segregation damages success. In fact, they argue that segregation is linked to poverty and, in combination with disadvantage theory, contributes to low entrepreneurship among Blacks in the U.S.

The theoretical perspectives reviewed indicate a number of generalizations. For example, a higher rate of entrepreneurship exists for immigrants compared to native-born minorities. In addition, educational attainment, family composition, English-language skill, experience, level of available capital, and other factors contribute to entrepreneurial success, independent of native status.

Beyond the special issues of ethnicity and small-business entrepreneurship, more spatial distribution questions permeate ethnic small business location.

Location, Location, Location: The Site-Selection Process

The substantial traditional literature regarding large corporate site selection decisions (e.g., Davies and Rogers 1984; Ghosh and McLafferty 1987; Jones and Simmons 1987) suggests the importance of analyses of trade area potential, site accessibility, growth potential, business interception, cumulative attraction, and competitive hazards in the selection of a retail business site. More recently, small-business models emphasize the relevance of more traditional factors, but include special needs and limitations faced by small businesses, who must consider their circumstances when making long-term decisions. Some decisions and factors do not vary between small and large businesses. For example, both small and large businesses should consider accessibility. However, the small-business model emphasizes the importance of small entrepreneurs that tend to have lower capital reserves and other financial constraints, including the cost of the site (rent), adequacy of parking, unfriendly competition, and the ability of the site to intercept traffic (Meir 2006).

Despite the importance of location to small ethnic business success, few studies have focused specifically on the site selection process and the spatial distribution of ethnic businesses. An exception is the work of Fong and his colleagues (Fong, Luk, and Ooka 2005) in Canada, who utilized three perspectives to examine ethnic business locations in suburban Toronto. These are highly correlated with the theoretical perspectives presented by Fisher and Massey (2000), but emphasize the distinctly spatial component of small ethnic business locations.

The first, the human ecological perspective, originated with the 20th century Chicago School and predicted a niche for ethnic businesses within ethnic neighborhoods. This theory suggested that the spatial distribution of ethnic businesses was related to three factor sets: characteristics of ethnic members, the size of the neighborhood, and neighborhood characteristics. Thus, "there is a strong association between ethnic spatial concentration and the number of ethnic businesses in a neighborhood with a new immigrants groups" (Meir 2006, p. 3). Fong and his colleagues indicate American evidence supports this theory in some cases, such as research on Korean ethnic business patterns associated with co-ethnic distributions in Los Angles (Lee 1995).

Ethnic characteristics also influence the spatial patterns of small ethnic businesses. For example, new immigrants with modest English skills tend to reside in close proximity to their ethnic community, which provides support and vital networks for housing and employment. Some work supports this contention, such as Jamaicans in New York and Florida (Boswell and Jones 2006). It also has been argued that locations in ethnic neighborhoods provide many advantages for ethnic businesses, including a potential captive or protected market, labor supply, financial support, and a shared identity (Lee 1995a, 1995b).

Ecological theory also reveals the importance of neighborhood characteristics. This factor argues that ethnic businesses are located in the less attractive "zones of transition." These areas "are characterized as destitute areas with high levels of poverty and social disorganization" (Fong, Luk, and Ooka, p. 218).

If these dimensions of ecological theory rooted in the Chicago School hold, then the number of ethnic business locations in an area would be associated with these three factor sets. Of course, the location of suburban ethnic businesses post-dates the theory and in this sense, the theory provides a "straw man" that easily is dismissed as inadequate.

The second theoretical perspective addresses the fact that ethnic business owners do not always reside in and rely upon the ethnic neighborhood containing their businesses. This perspective is drawn from economic ecology and distinguishes between "ethnic concentrated businesses" and "ethnic concentrated neighborhoods." Ethnic businesses become embedded in an ethnic commercial concentration and benefit from its social capital, labor, and opportunities that reduce operating costs associated with small business operations. Thus, the presence of other ethnic businesses attracts additional small ethnic businesses and influences the overall spatial distribution of the ethnic business pattern, including suburban ones. While the success is dependent upon the size of the ethnic market, it does not necessitate an ethnic enclave to survive and prosper.

The third theoretical perspective, organizational ecology, argues that the growth or decline of ethnic businesses in an area is a function of the total number and types of businesses that constitute an ethnic business niche. The smaller the number of same-type ethnic businesses, the more attractive the small business locational niche is to the new business of the same type, assuming that the niche is sufficiently large to be attractive in the first place. The opposite is also true. When the number of same-type small ethnic businesses exceeds a numeric threshold and creates disequilibrium between the ethnic population size and number of stores it can support, then the ethnic business niche is no longer attractive to new small ethnic businesses of the same type. Further, if the disequilibrium is excessive, the existing small businesses of the same type located within the niche likely will fail and the size of the small business enclave will decline (Fong, Luk, and Ooka 2005). Thus the business enclave, rather than the residential enclave, is a determinant of location and success.

Another recent Canadian study provides some insights into the business practices and site selection strategies of two immigrant groups in that country. The two immigrant ethnic groups, Portuguese and Black Africans/Afro-Caribbeans, are studied (Teixeira 2001) for their business practices and location decisions within the context of three of the above theories, blocked-mobility, cultural theory, and the opportunity structures theories. Comparisons include employee recruitment, use of social networks, location, community involvement, dependence on ethnic clientele, and success (performance). The underlying suspicion of racism and its outcomes in this study were based on observations that Canada's "visible" minority immigrants have higher unemployment, lower average incomes, and are more likely to live in poverty than their Portuguese immigrant counterparts. Another observation made was that those of the African Diaspora, although having higher educational attainment than the Portuguese immigrants, do not realize a concomitant benefit in income (Teixeira 2001).

The research findings indicated that some similarities between the two groups exist; both groups entered the business world because they desire independence and control of their lives. However, the "visible" minorities seemed to be "pushed" there by conditions, including the lack of employment opportunities, while Portuguese immigrants stressed the importance of family tradition in starting a business. The perceived barriers in establishing a business differed between the two groups. The Portuguese reported limited language skills and lack of information about business practices in Canada as obstacles. Black immigrant businesses, on the other hand, found a lack of access to financing and credit to be the most serious barrier to establishing a small business.

Regarding the business location decision, differences also were apparent. The Portuguese small businesses were located within ethnic enclaves, such as little Portugal, and thus were selected on the basis of proximity to co-ethnics. Unlike the Portuguese entrepreneurs, Black small businesses were less likely to be drawn to particular ethnic neighborhoods. Rather, they were more dispersed, or multinucleated in distribution, and reported that price and leasing costs were the strongest determinants in location choice. These findings differ from findings for the U.S. that report Black businesses are still primarily located in Black ethnic enclaves or Black ghettos (e.g., Boyd 1991). However, the American studies do not focus on Black *immigrant* entrepreneurs.

Despite their different spatial patterns, both Canadian groups had a high reliance on ethnic/racial customers. Located in Portuguese enclaves, the dependence of their entrepreneurs is spatially and culturally concentrated. In the case of the more culturally diverse Black entrepreneurs, their more dispersed locational pattern may be explained by their appeal to more than a single Black ethnic group, including West Indian and African people in the broader region. Despite their differences, the majority of responses from both Canadian groups indicate they enjoy business success and both groups attribute that success to reputation, strong ethnic markets, and their location choice.

Based on these and other findings, Teixeira concludes that this case study supports the "interactive model of business development" by combining the features of the structural and cultural theories, and contributes understanding of small ethnic business development (Teixeira 2001).

Overall, the American and Canadian perspectives and case studies presented in this brief review are thought provoking but suffer from inadequate empirical verification to be considered strong theories. Thus, the ideas and findings about operations and location decisions provide leading principles for additional research on ethnic small businesses. Further, our case is framed within the constraints of substantial pressure to make a quick decision about available sites, involving restricted choice by the small ethnic businesses. With this knowledge, we address our research questions for the small ethnic businesses forced to move or cease operations in the Bronx Terminal Market in 2006. Our purpose is not to generalize from our small case study, but rather to improve our understanding of and chronicle the impact and business decisions of a small group of ethnic entrepreneurs that included Black merchants. The experience of these entrepreneurs provides a valuable perspective for other cities planning gentrification projects, and for the small businesses that may be displaced or cease to function.

THE BRONX STUDY AREA: THE BRONX AND THE BRONX TERMINAL MARKET

The Bronx

Many factors have contributed to the changing ethnic structure of New York City, including the effects of globalization and U.S. immigration policy. The most significant contribution to the City's evolving ethnic structure is the decrease in the non-Hispanic White population and the increase in the Latino, Asian and the African Diasporas (Galligano and Frazier 2006; Lobo 2002; Alba 1995). The Bronx is one of New York City's five boroughs and the only one to be located on the mainland (others are islands). The U.S. Census in the year 2000 reported 48 percent of the Bronx was of Hispanic origin; nearly 39 percent was Black. Dominican enclaves had developed in the Southern Bronx by the year 2000 (Galligano and Frazier 2006). For the first time in 2005, the Bronx had a majority Latino population (52 percent) and the Black population (alone) was 32 percent. Those that claimed Dominican ancestry were 30 percent of the Borough's population in 2005. The increasing number of Latinos likely reinforced the ethnic concentrations observed in 2000. Of particular note were the concentrations of Dominicans as reported by the New York City Department of Planning (NYC Department of Planning 2004, pp. 51 and 54).

The same report referred to those of the African Diaspora as having "a nominal presence" (p. 54), which is true when considering the total population. The foreign-born populations, of course, were the most substantial market segment of the Bronx Terminal Market. In 2000, the Bronx foreign-born population totaled 385,827; it reached 418,643 by 2005. In 2000, those of the African Diaspora accounted for just over 30 percent of the total foreign-born; they remained near that population in 2005.

Also, when considering the total demand for specialty ethnic foods, the combined total of foreign-born Africans and West Indians is important. That total was nearly 115,000 in the year 2000. When considering those claiming the ancestry of both regions, the numbers are even higher. By 2005, the Census reported more than 100,000 West Indian ancestry and nearly 50,000 of Sub-Saharan ancestry. Clearly, there is a very significant Black ethnic population in the Bronx (ACS 2005). Many of these ethnic groups have clustered in the southwest Bronx, such as the Ghanaians in Morris Heights, Highbridge, and Tremont (NYC Planning Department 2004). These recent ethnic populations are important potential customers of small businesses in the Bronx Terminal Market that specialize in ethnic foods.

The Bronx Terminal Market

In the 1920s, NYC Mayor John F. Hylan presented the idea of a market place in the Bronx. His purpose was the relocation of vendors from Washington Market and the initiative met with little initial success. However, later fruit and vegetable vendors, many of them Italian, responded to Mayor LaGuardia's expansion of the Market along Exterior Street in 1935. The Bronx Market became a thriving market place of 100 merchants. When Hunts Point opened thirty years later, many vendors relocated and were replaced by Puerto Rican vendors. The Bronx Terminal Market quickly carved a niche as a tropical fruits and vegetable market catering to the growing number of Hispanic businesses, including bodegas. Figure 19.1a illustrates the locations of The Bronx Terminal and Hunts Point Markets in the southeast section of the Bronx. Figure 19.1b is a photograph showing the location of the Bronx Terminal Market on Exterior Street, just below the Major Deegan Expressway, with Yankee Stadium in the background.

Figure: 19.1b.
Yankee Stadium in the shadow of BTM.

Source: Joshua Norman.

In time, the Market established the reputation as the largest Hispanic wholesale foods market in the nation. As the African Diaspora began to expand in the City in the 1990s, the Market began selling products to serve them. Some stores, such as Latin 17, which once catered solely to Latino demands, refocused their product lines to include those of the African Diaspora. While wholesale merchants supplied wholesale goods to bodegas and restaurants during the week, weekends typically involved retail sales of goods to a variety of Black immigrant ethnic groups, including Nigerians, Ghanaians, West Indians, and others, who came to the Bronx Terminal Market by taxi, subway, bus, and private automobiles to purchase foods that were not obtainable in their immediate neighborhoods, nor from chain stores. These included a range of tropical foods and specialty meats as shown in Figures 19.1c and d. As a result, a number of African-owned small businesses opened in the Market to serve this growing clientele.

Finally, the market concept is a long-established concept in many African and Caribbean nations, and serves both social and retail functions. Some Bronx Terminal Market shops catered to Afro-Caribbeans and others catered to Africans. However, the number of African-oriented outlets was more prominent in the Bronx Terminal Market. This fact could influence the relocation strategy of African small businesses toward the less affluent, but relatively larger, African population in the southeastern Bronx.

It is important to note that while Africans and Afro-Caribbeans share tastes in certain foods, there are those specialty foods and their labels that are particularly and sometimes uniquely appealing to Africans. For example, Gari is a gritty, grated cassava root that is dried and baked and is African in origin. Similarly, Nido, a powder drink, and Milo, a well known cocoa drink, are both West African products. Similarly, specialized fish and meats appeal only to Africans. For example, tilapia is a tropical fish consumed in West Africa. It is available as a dried and smoked specialty at these African small businesses. Another example is a local mammal from Ghana, called a "Grasscutter," which also is available as a dried and smoked specialized meat.

Beyond the attraction to the local population, these specialty ethnic businesses can draw ethnics from substantial distances. One merchant captured the attraction of the Market to customers that traveled relatively long distances from adjacent states:

> "People come from as far as Connecticut to buy food from us. Sometimes they call us with a list of the things they want and then come down to pick them up later." (Small Business Owner #1, SBO1)

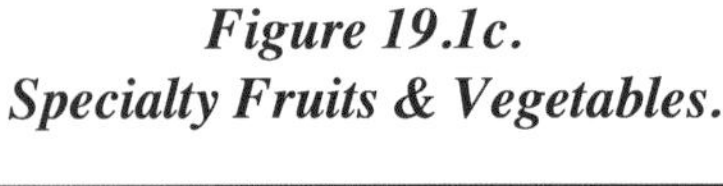

Figure 19.1c.
Specialty Fruits & Vegetables.

The market's produce is varied, colorful, and frequently not available anywhere else. Clockwise from top left; Nopales Cacti, which taste like green peppers. Red Onions. Ripe mangoes. Red peppers.

Source: Joshua Norman.

Figure 19.1d.
Specialty Meats.

Burnt cow foot is used by African immigrants in soups and stews. The meats on the right are particular to West African cuisine, especially snails and goat meat with the skin still attached.

Source: Joshua Norman.

Despite the importance of the Market to ethnic consumers for specialty products and low prices, it had become an "eyesore" and a contributor to area blight in the eyes of City Mayor Bloomberg and planning officials. Accordingly, as part of a redevelopment plan, the Bronx Terminal Market was targeted for removal. The proposed replacement was a $300 million mall with one million square feet of retail space, including specialty shops and department stores. The project is expected to create approximately 4,500 jobs. The Market simply had to close and be razed.

DATA AND METHODS

Both primary and secondary data were used in our analysis of the forced relocation of Bronx Terminal Market small businesses. The primary data were collected via a survey.

There were a total of twenty-three businesses operating at the Market at the time of its closing. A list of all 23 merchants operating in the Bronx Terminal Market was readily available to the public. The majority (nearly two-thirds) were owned by Hispanic/Latino small business entrepreneurs. We pursued all of those who relocated in the Bronx through the New York City Economic Development Corporation Planning assistance and fieldwork. Of the original 23, only 15 relocated. By the time of our survey, only 8 had relocated and remained in business in the Bronx. Thus, only 8 of the original small businesses were available for interviews and one refused to speak with us. Our sample reflects 50 percent of those who initially stayed in business and relocated, and 88 percent of those who remained in business by the time of the survey.

All 7 supplied detailed information on their experiences with the closing and the process of relocation. Although the sample is too small to make generalizations, it is important because it informs us of the consequences of this forced relocation under city-endorsed gentrification of the South Bronx. It also helps us to understand the experiences of the surviving small ethnic businesses, particularly the Black immigrant businesses that survived the mandated relocation.

We interviewed 7 merchants, using a pre-tested questionnaire. Given the small number of small business owners and the need for detailed information, the personal, face-to-face survey was the most appropriate method of data acquisition and these were conducted in June–July 2007. A standard set of questions was asked of each merchant. The survey instrument was designed to secure information about their initial reaction to the City's plan, the quality of government assistance they received, the factors considered when they selected their new site for their operations, and their experiences since opening, which occurred approximately one year prior to the interviews.

Secondary data were obtained from the U.S. Census 2000 and the ESRI website, and included census tract information for the Bronx, including total population, ancestry, and household income, geographic coordinates for Bronx County shapefiles, including roads and census tract boundaries. We transformed the small ethnic business information, including addresses into data points using ArcMap and ArcCatalog Geographic Information Systems (ArcGIS). Density and distance calculations performed for our analysis also were generated by ArcGIS, as were thematic maps of socioeconomic characteristics of the Bronx. U.S. Census data, small ethnic business locations, major transportation arteries, and subways were mapped to assist in the visualization and analysis of the relocated businesses. ArcGIS was used for mapping. We analyzed their spatial distribution relative to their ethnic markets and their ethnic competition.

THE IMPACT OF THE FORCED CLOSING OF THE MARKET ON ITS ETHNIC SMALL BUSINESSES

Our first two research questions dealt with the initial reaction of the small ethnic merchants and the impact of the mandated closing of the Market on the 23 small ethnic businesses operating there. As noted earlier, remaining at the Bronx Terminal Market was not an option for these small ethnic businesses. The City sent all of these ethnic merchants a letter in March 2006 informing them that they must vacate or face eviction. The initial intention of these small businesses was non-compliance with City Hall's directive. They grouped together to fight the relocation mandate, including a public protest carried by the national media. Despite the initial efforts to fight City Hall, it became clear that relocation was inevitable. A sentiment expressed by all of these small businesses can be summarized by the responses of two of the owners:

> "Initially, when we were informed to leave the Bronx Terminal Market, we fought. We formed a community market and faced the large cost for lawyers that came out of our pockets." Small Business Owner (SBO1)

> "We fought for one year, spending a lot of money. But, it was a big giant. The City wants to make big bucks. . . . We had no choice but to take the relocation money. Money is money. We would be better (off) to take some type of payment than nothing." (SBO2)

Thus, in the end, these small ethnic businesses could not afford a protracted legal battle and accepted the move, with reservation.

Perhaps most importantly, the immediate outcome of the mandated closing was the end of business for a large share of these small ethnic businesses. Of the 23 small businesses, 7 were owned by Black immigrants. Of the 23 operating at the time of the threatened eviction, only 15 relocated. Thus, 7 of the original 23, or nearly one-third, ceased their business operation immediately upon the closing of the Market. Of these 7, 3 were Black entrepreneurs. Two were African and one was an Afro-Caribbean. Thus, Black small business owners were negatively affected by the closing, as were other ethnic groups.

The impact of the Market closing continued, with 5 of the ethnic small businesses that relocated from the Market ceasing operation within a few months of their relocation. While none of these was a Black-owned business, the impact was severe for more than one-half (12) of the original ethnic small businesses that operated at the Bronx Terminal Market. This negative outcome may support the theory that small ethnic businesses are "high risk ventures" that are disadvantaged and often cannot access capital or credit when it is required (Wright, Martin, and Stone 2003). Unfortunately, no explanatory information is available to place the closure of these small businesses into an alternative context. Finally, two of these small operations (Hispanic/Latino) merged and became larger.

As noted earlier, 8 of the original Market ethnic businesses that relocated were potential interviewees but one, a man of Asian descent, refused to be interviewed. Of the remaining 7, the majority (4) had African (Ghanaians) owners. Thus, members of the African Diaspora were an essential segment of the relocation process and our small remaining sample. Of the 3 remaining, 2 are Hispanic/Latino, and one is an Asian.

CHARACTERISTICS OF THE SMALL ETHNIC BUSINESS RESPONDENTS

Our survey revealed that all of the small ethnic business owners were foreign-born, who range in age from 40 to 55 years. This group exhibited varied educational attainment, with 3 people holding college degrees and 3 with less than a high school education. All had substantial retail business experience, on average 16 years.

These small businesses were predominantly family-owned (6 of 7) with the majority of the owners living in the Bronx. Their average number of employees is small (5) and they are a mix of family and non-family members. Most had operated in the Bronx Terminal Market for a considerable period, averaging 16 years. The range was 8 years to 25 years.

FINDING A NEW LOCATION: A CASE STUDY OF RELOCATIONS

Another research question posed by our study involved the site selection procedures employed by these small businesses and the resulting geographic pattern. Before reviewing the responses of these small ethnic businesses to our survey questions, it is instructive to revisit the theory provided earlier in this chapter. We might expect, for example, that these small ethnic businesses would locate in close proximity to their ethnic clientele, particularly the Ghanaians in association with African immigrant populations. On the other hand, based on conventional site selection principles, we might expect the relocating Black small businesses to consider the location of relatively higher income Black neighborhoods that have disposable incomes that could benefit their enterprises. Another possibility is the location of other small ethnic businesses that provide advantages due to clustering and sharing of clientele. There also are other considerations. One might also hypothesize that rents would play a major role in the location of small businesses with limited capital. Other secondary factors could also help determine the site selected for the relocated business site, including easy access for customers via various forms of transportation.

As we noted earlier, there are competing and inadequately substantiated theoretical perspectives regarding site selection by small ethnic businesses. The disgruntled merchants protested and initially fought the City's mandate. The result was a narrow time frame that placed pressure on the merchants and City to find alternative locations for the operation of these small ethnic businesses.

Responses to the City's Initial Assistance

An important question in addressing the site selection procedures employed by these small businessmen involves the role of a consultant paid by the City to assist them. Initially, the City offered to work with affected merchants to develop a relocation plan. They proposed an $8 million assistance package that included grants and loans. In the end, a paid real estate consultant was made available to the small businesses and twenty-eight available but scattered properties in the Bronx were presented as options. According to the criticism reported by *The Village Voice*, none was sufficiently large enough to handle some displaced businesses and had other shortcomings, such as:

> "They didn't even have a loading platform."
> "The most important issue for us is the location."
>
> "We live off each other here. . .
> We share each others customers
> so we need to stay together." (*Village Voice*, March 22, 2006)

The first quote was by a wholesaler who had visited several properties offered by the City's real estate consultant and who had found these options inadequate. The second and third quotes refer to the importance of the well-known principle of retail affinity. Customers make multiple purpose shopping trips and do the comparative shopping. Having a range of small business retailers in a single location is appealing to shoppers and these small ethnic businesses recognized the importance of this concept.

Other complaints about the consultant's advice were related to the local Empowerment Zone (EZ) and its benefits. The EZ program is designed for distressed areas and is to serve as a revitalization tool. Empowerment Zone Areas are located in the South Bronx and were proposed by the consultant as worthwhile options. Among the EZ's tax incentives are wage credits and higher annual depreciation. Specifically, EZ employers can claim annually up to $3,000 per EZ resident employee as a tax credit. They also are permitted more than double the annual standard business deduction for depreciable property. Finally, EZ businesses are eligible for grants and low-interest loans. According to nearly all of the merchants interviewed, the consultant reported that small business relocations into the EZ would result in an outright grant. This is a serious misunderstanding or these small businesses were misled because very little of the EZ funds are "grant" money.[1] While the majority felt misled, the Ghanaian responses were the strongest:

> "Look at my place. It is just on the border (across the street) from the Empowerment Zone. I don't read geography. My business is to sell things. So, if it is a real estate plan, someone at the City is looking at this location and should have told us we weren't in the Empowerment Zone. We lost a lot of money." (SBO3)

> "We understand that it is a grant and, after five years, we must start repaying. Now, after moving in, we were informed to start paying now; we had no choice but to pay . . . about $450 a month . . . We spent all of our capital fixing this place." (SBO4)

It is clear from these responses, although they were not included as survey questions, that the majority felt deceived and that the EZ incentives were one consideration in their relocation decision.

The Black Ethnic Distribution of the Bronx

We learned from our survey that the two Hispanic/Latino businesses, which were significant wholesalers as well as retailers, chose to relocate in the southwest Bronx closer to the Hunts Point Market, one of the world's largest wholesale food and meat markets. This is a logical choice for small businesses focused on wholesaling. On the other hand, of the remaining five businesses, four are African-owned businesses. Thus, if ethnicity and income are factors in their relocation (site selection), then these four theoretically should have considered the Black ethnic and income distributions in the Bronx and selected a relocation site that maximized access by those with the desired characteristics.

In this section, we provide a visualization of the distribution of the Black ethnic populations thought to be a major part of the local trade area of the displaced small ethnic businesses. These distributions appear as Figure 19.2. Generally, the two Black groups are widely distributed in the Bronx. However, Afro-Caribbeans are more numerous and more concentrated in the central Bronx, especially in the north central area as shown in Figure 19.2. Africans are more numerous and appear more densely populated in the eastern Bronx, especially in the east central and southeastern Bronx areas as shown on the map in Figure 19.2. The map in Figure 19.3 identifies the areas with relatively higher median family incomes (middle class or higher). This map illustrates that the highest income groups in the Bronx live in the extreme northwest of the area. Of particular note for this study is the relatively high income area in north central Bronx, where the greatest density of Afro-Caribbeans reside.

Figure 19.4a combines the income and Black ancestry variables of the previous maps and portrays areas by income and ethnicity. The hatched area in Figure 19.4a combines those with relatively high proportions of their populations claiming African and West Indian ancestry and relatively higher incomes (>$33,000 annually). These areas are generally located in the northern Bronx, especially north of Fordham Road and between the Bronx River Expressway and the Hutchinson River Expressway. As noted, this is an area with far greater numbers and density of Afro-Caribbeans than Africans.

The areas of more modest incomes (<$33,000 annually) and a relatively lower number of Black ancestry in 2000 are largely in the south-central and southwestern Bronx, especially west of the Bronx River Expressway and south of Fordham Road. Recall, from Figure 19.2, that the African distribution is more scattered than the Afro-Caribbean and far more prevalent in the area east and south of the Bronx River Expressway and south of Fordham Road. The Afro-Caribbeans are highly clustered in the north-central section of the Bronx in a section with relatively higher median family incomes than the southern Bronx. It is when we combine both ancestries and see one market that the northern-central Bronx would be a highly attractive market for the small ethnic businesses forced to relocate, if ethnicity and income were the most important factors in relocation. Specifically we should expect that these African-owned small businesses would relocate generally north of Fordham Road to have access to higher income, ethnic Blacks.

Figure 19.2.
African and Afro-Caribbean Ancestry.

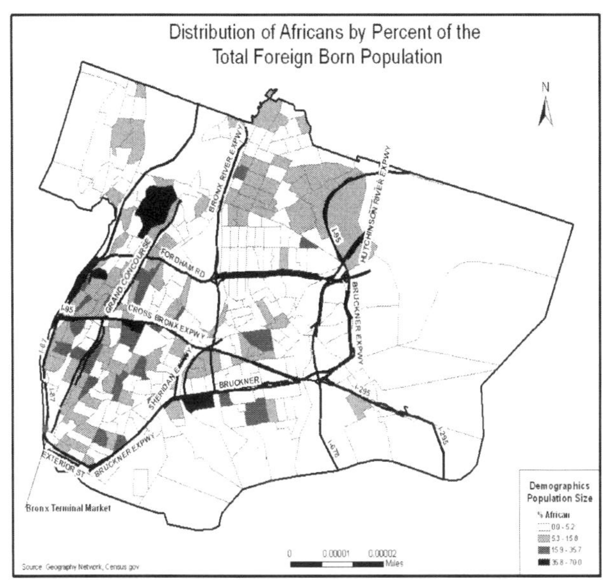

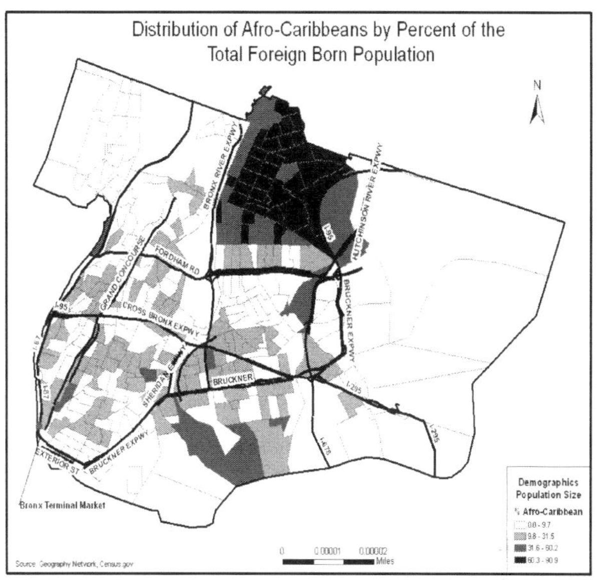

Figure 19.3.
Total Median Family Income by Census Tracts, Bronx, New York.

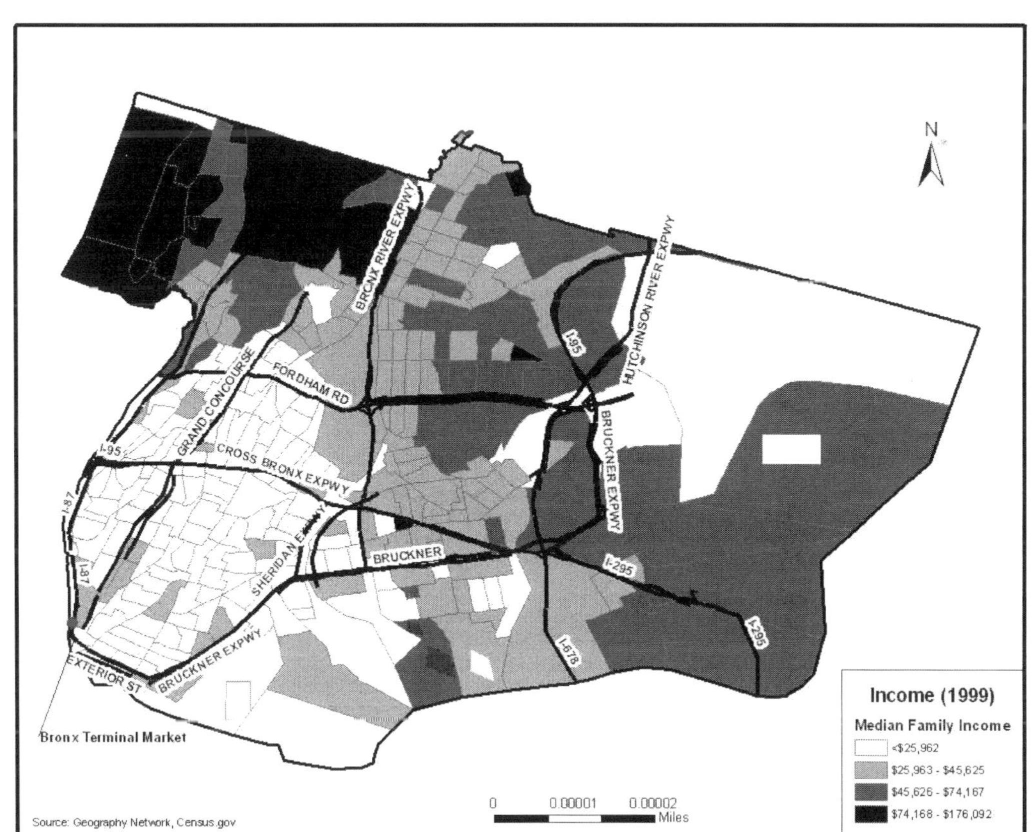

If on the other hand, because of the apparent emphasis on African goods, a desire for retail affinity, being close to business of similar types with easy highway or subway access, and easy access to their African ethnic market are the most important considerations, then the locations of existing ethnic businesses and access for customers of African ancestry to transit should be important to the site selection process. Figure 19.4b provides the locations of the relocated small business of this study. The map in Figure 19.5a portrays the distribution of other existing small ethnic business locations at the time the displaced ones were searching for new locations. These existing stores are all south of Fordham Road, with two exceptions. Seven stores are located between Fordham Road and the Cross Bronx Freeway, and an additional seventeen African and Caribbean retail businesses are in the Southwest Bronx, below the Cross Bronx Expressway and west of the Sheridan expressway. Only two of these existing ethnic stores are east of the Sheridan Expressway. These two have wholesale functions noted earlier and were attracted to the nearby large Hunts Point Market.

Figure 19.5b provides an overlay of the newly selected sites of the displaced businesses on the existing small ethnic businesses distribution. All of the new sites are in the Southwest Bronx. Figure 19.5b also provides an additional perspective of retail affinity by examining the number of co-existing small businesses, newly located or already in existence, within a 1/2 mile radius of each new site. In every case west of the Bruckher Expressway, the newly selected sites, all of which are located in the southwest Bronx, had one or more other small businesses within this radius. We believe this expresses retail affinity and the importance of access to a relatively large number of co-ethnics with moderate incomes, but tastes for their ethnic foods.

Regarding accessibility by the clientele, Table 19.1 reports the distance to the closest major artery or subway stop that provides easy access to these small businesses. The results indicate these small ethnic businesses are located on average seven (7) minutes walking distance from a major highway, ten (10) minutes from a subway stop, and eight (8) minutes from a bus stop. These are modest walking distances that most immigrants are willing to accept in order to secure the specialty foods that are desired.

The small business owner survey responses addressed the most important reasons for their locational choices. These are discussed next.

Figure 19.4a.
Ethnicity and Income Distributions.

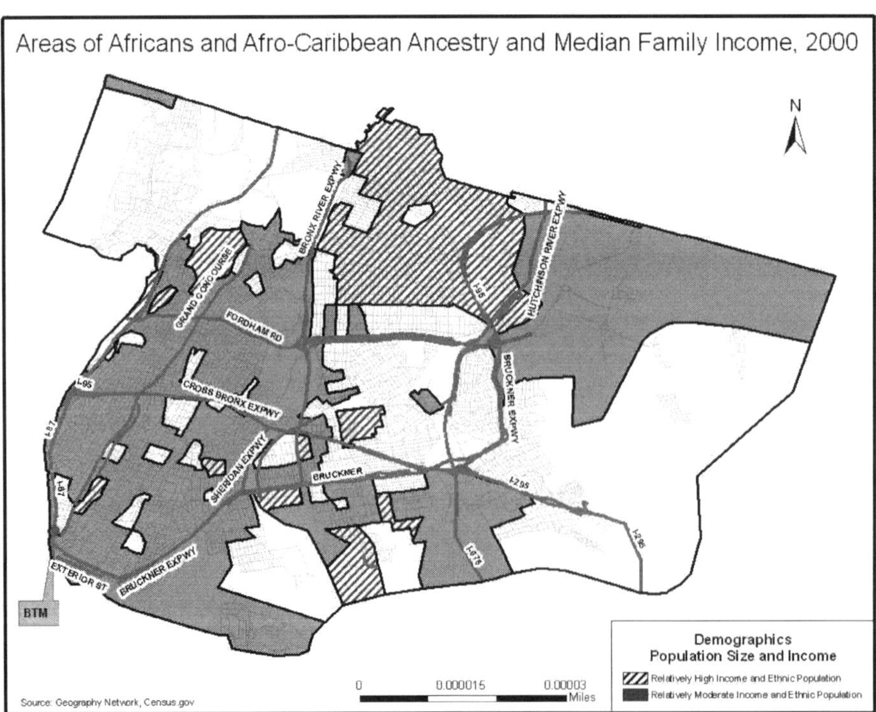

Figure 19.4b.
Relocated Ethnic Businesses, Ethnicity and Income.

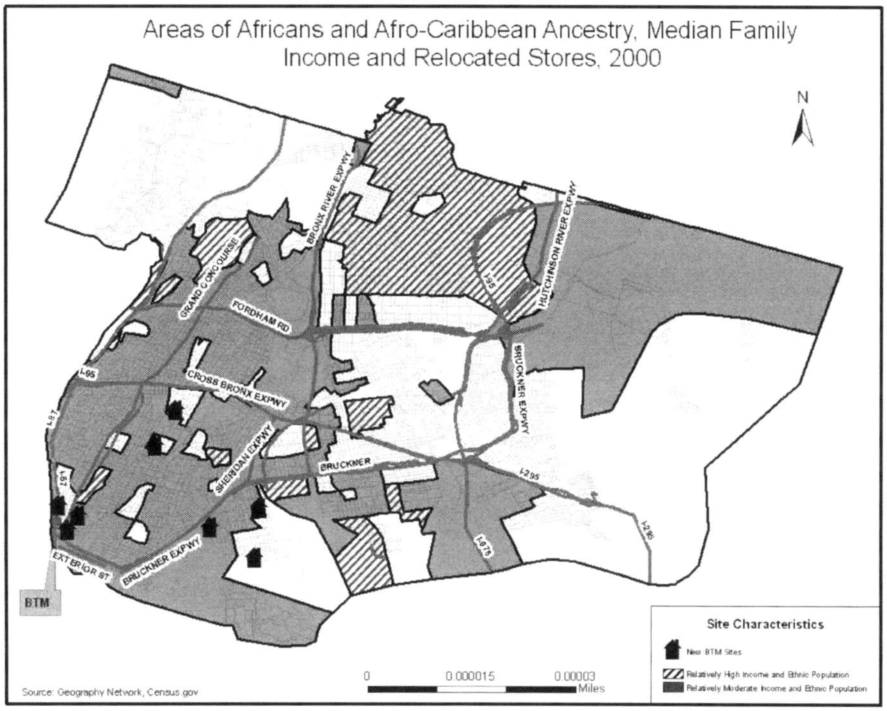

Figure 19.5a.
The Distribution of Ethnic Businesses in the Bronx.

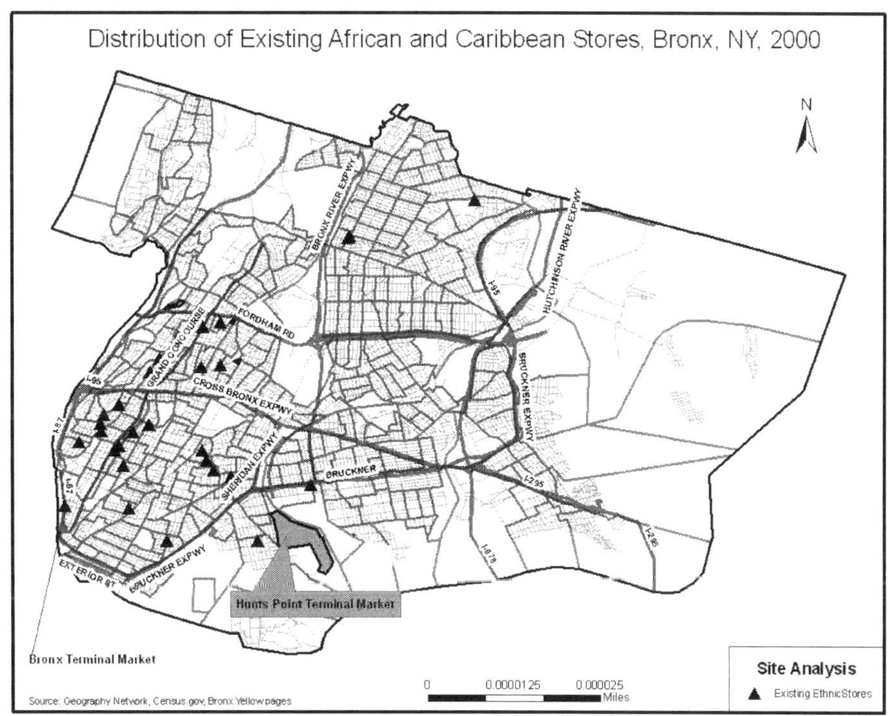

Figure 19.5b.
Relocated Ethnic Businesses and Retail Affinity.

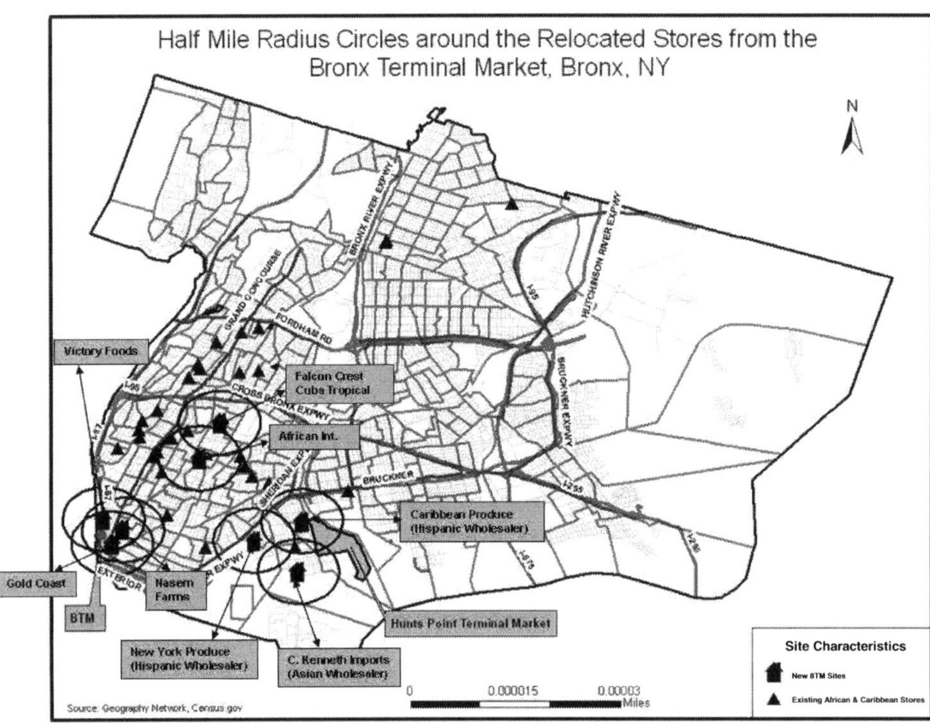

Table 19.1.
Relocated Ethnic Businesses and Distance (in minutes).

Business Name	Address	Distance in Minutes from Major Rd	Subway Stop	Buses
African International	3494 Park Avenue	10	10	5
Falcon Crest & Cuba Tropical	441 Claremont Pkwy	5	5	1
Nasem Farms	209 E 138th St	5	5	2
Gold Coast	381 Canal Pl	10	5	5
New York Produce	1111 Grinnell Pl	5	10	10
Caribbean Produce	1360 Lafayette Ave	10	15	20
C. Kenneth Imports	250 Coster Street	10	20	15
Victory Foods	441 Exterior Street	2	10	5

Source: authors.

Site Selection: The Small Business Owner's Responses

The responses of these small businesses clarify the circumstances under which their relocation decisions were made and the factors considered in their decision process. The two wholesale-oriented businesses indicated the importance of proximity to other wholesalers in the relocation decision. The remaining businesses had a retail-orientation and answered somewhat differently. It became apparent from discussions with them that they felt a sense of urgency to find their new business locations. One business person found the consultant helpful but emphasized how the time pressure influenced the location choice:

> "The real estate consultant actually helped us pick the location. We did not like the location but because we had to leave at the end of the month, we had one week, so we picked it." (SBO 5)

This response refers to notification from the City reportedly received by all of the Market's small businesses. It specified that failure to vacate the premises by the end of the month would result in eviction.

All of the other small business people reported the consultant was not helpful. Typical of these responses was:

> "I did everything on my own. The real estate guy, or the guy from the city, didn't have the merchants in mind. He just wanted us out of the place [BTM] as quickly as possible." (SBO 6)

We asked two questions of these merchants. The first offered a set of factors that potentially influenced their relocation decision. The second was an open-ended question that simply asked them to identify the most important factor involved in their relocation decision. This open-ended question in our survey clarified the importance of the time constraint of the decision related to threatened eviction. Without prompting, the majority indicated that *time* was the most important consideration. Clearly, for most, including the African owners, the relocation decision occurred under the perception of a severe time constraint. This is an important context for interpreting the remainder of their responses.

Regarding the list of factors that may have influenced their site selection decisions, none agreed that rent or competition were considerations in the selection of the new site. All of the merchants reported multiple factors involved in their site selection process, with the three most frequent answers being proximity to other businesses, proximity to ethnic customers, and accessibility for customers. Thus, retail affinity and accessibility far outweighed the fear of competition. We should recall the comment made by one of these merchants to the *Village Voice*:

> "We live off each other . . . We share each others customers. . . ."
> (*Village Voice*, March 22, 2006)

The responses by these small business merchants provide support of our mapping analysis; clearly, retail affinity, African ethnicity, and accessibility were important to their site selection. One African merchant was very explicit about the importance of accessibility for the customers:

> "We were supposed to move together to one place but we couldn't find any place that would hold us. If we did, then the Market would have stayed a Market. Proximity to the train, bus, and highway is why we chose this place." (SBO 7)

Table 19.1 contains the measured walking time between each of the relocated stores and all of the other stores. It also provides the measured walking time to the nearest subway stop. The shortest walk is 5 minutes and the longest is 20 minutes. This supports the importance and influence of accessibility in the site selection process of these small relocated, Black immigrant small businesses. Accessibility, then, after availability, was the most important factor guiding the site-selection decisions of these displaced small ethnic businesses, which supports the findings of Teixeira's Canadian study (Teixeira 2001).

Most retail business models suggest the importance of the assessment of current and future competition when a location is considered. The small business model refers to this as "unfriendly competition" and, as part of organizational ecology, the ethnic business model urged an examination of existing stores and vacant premises that might be future competition. All of the retail models reviewed earlier also indicated the importance of retail affinity in site selection. The ethnic business model of the economic ecology theory suggests that clustering occurs among ethnic businesses because of dependency on social capital from one another and from the ethnic community, and the ecological literature argues that small business type and density influence the location of new ethnic small businesses (Fong et al. 2005). Conventional theory suggests, among other things, that cumulative attraction is important for walk-in traffic and the exchange of customers.

When we asked about competition, the majority of the relocated small businesses felt that they had strong competition at their new location. However, given the importance of shared customers and the reported high daily and weekend traffic in their businesses, this is not necessarily a negative. One owner expresses the balance between friendly competition and retail affinity in the relocation decision this way:

> "I don't think it is competition, but it compliments us. It was just like in the Bronx Market. If somebody comes here and I don't have a product, then I just show them to the Gold Coast. I don't see it as competition. It enhances our business." (SBO 7)

Thus, there seems to be a balance between friendly competition and retail affinity, or accumulative attraction, among these relocated small ethnic businesses.

POST SITE-SELECTION EXPERIENCES

We now address our final research question—how well the relocated businesses are doing at their new locations compared to their Terminal location. We were interested in what aspects of their businesses may have changed due to relocation. Approximately one year had elapsed between the opening of the relocated small businesses and our interviews with them. This period allowed for the formation of perspectives on what had changed for these ethnic business people. One of the obvious changes, previously mentioned, is that all of these small businesses have loans with the City. The majority of the respondents reported that relocation also had resulted in more square footage in the new location compared to their rental space at the Market. Of course, more space typically means higher rents. The majority also had the same number and mix of employees, family and non-family, as worked for them at their previous location. Their customer bases appear to have remained strong; the average daily traffic was estimated at 50 or more customers during weekdays and 200 or more on weekends. What did not change for all of these small operations was the socialization function shopping plays for their clientele. The merchants reported that this had not changed with the relocation to a new site, a finding similar to other ethnic studies that have illustrated the social value of ethnic small businesses to co-ethnics (e.g., Scott 2006).

Finally, these small businesses were asked to compare their current sales, one year after their relocation, to previous sales level at their former location. One African refused to answer the question. The remainder was equally split between "no differences," "lower," and "higher." Apparently, the results are mixed for these Black entrepreneurs. It is probably safe to say that after one year, the jury is still out for the majority and only time will tell us how this set of circumstances influences the survivors of the closing of the Bronx Terminal Market.

SUMMARY AND CONCLUSIONS

After many years of service to local ethnic consumers, the Bronx Terminal Market fell into disfavor with local officials because of its unattractive appearance and the desire to gentrify the area around it and adjacent to Yankee stadium. Redevelopment plans mandated the relocation of a number of small ethnic businesses from the Market to new locations. Initially, the small merchants fought City Hall but in the end found it too expensive to continue. Of the original 23 small ethnic businesses, only 8 survived and relocated; 12 ceased operation immediately or within a few months of the closing of the Market. Those who relocated did so under very tight time constraints due to their initial rejection of the City's mandate and then a threatened eviction. Although a real estate consultant was provided as part of the service package provided by the City, most small business operators felt the advice was inadequate, misinformed, or misleading. Specifically, the majority of these ethnic business people either misinterpreted the information provided by the consultant or felt misguided by him. It is impossible to ascertain from our analysis which is true. Most of the affected small businesses claimed that they were promised a grant because they had relocated into an Empowerment Zone. After relocation they found they had to repay the City.

Retail site selection theory provided some leading principles regarding the factors that influence the selection of a site. Our analysis showed somewhat different residential and income patterns for Afro-Caribbeans (West Indians) and Africans in the Bronx. Generally, more Afro-Caribbeans reside in the north-central area, which also is an area of relatively higher incomes compared to other areas of the Bronx. Africans were more highly concentrated in the south-central and south-east, which is an area of relatively lower income in the Bronx. We noted the potential importance of the African ethnic population due to the Ghanaian owners.

Our findings supported a number of the premises of small business site selection theory. Although it must be emphasized that availability of a site was a very important consideration, given the time pressure to relocate, other factors emerged as important too. Our findings suggest that retail affinity and customer access were the likely strongest factors in the site selection process under forced relocation. Specifically, these ethnic small business people cited the importance of being nearby other small ethnic businesses, which are seen less as unfriendly competitors and more as attracting a larger number of potential clients due to cumulative attraction. Also supporting theory was the importance of customer accessibility to their new store locations. Access to the modes of transportation that bring customers was a key factor in site selection.

NOTE

[1] We attempted several times to contact the real estate consultant for his perspective on the relocation process but he did not return our telephone calls.

Section 4:
Summary and Conclusions

Chapter 20

The African Diaspora in the United States and Canada at the Dawn of the 21st Century: Themes and Concluding Perspectives

JOE T. DARDEN, NORAH F. HENRY AND JOHN W. FRAZIER

The purpose of this final chapter is to revisit some of the key organizational themes and concepts of the text to underscore their relevance and to provide some additional perspectives about the African Diaspora in the U.S. and Canada at the dawn of the twenty-first century. We began with the premise that the origin and recent expansion of this Diaspora have been influenced by global forces. Historically, the international slave trade shaped the forced movements from Africa to the Western Hemisphere. The slave-based U.S. cotton economy and related technology resulted in the rapidly increasing demand for slaves. The socio-political ideology of the U.S. regulated the movements of slaves and later of African Americans to particular places, creating a new racial geography. Part of the Canadian Black legacy is tied to Blacks' efforts to escape American slavery. However, slavery also existed in Canada and developed its own associated legacy. Racism is embedded in Canadian ideology and has created racial inequalities. This is a history shared by these two nations, whose racial systems have persisted and influenced the well-being of Black immigrants and native-born Blacks in both countries.

Recent Black immigration to the U.S. and Canada is explained as part of a new globalization that has restructured national economies that resulted in changing patterns of labor supply and demand patterns. African and Afro-Caribbean migration to the U.S. and Canada are responses to these patterns. Institutional changes also were necessary to permit larger numbers of immigrant Blacks to migrate to their respective new countries. Changes in immigration law are paramount to understanding the increases of the African Diaspora in the U.S. and Canada. The policies and practices of both host nations and their local jurisdictions, controlled by the White majority, influence the experiences, choices, and well-being of members of the African Diaspora.

Although Black immigrants represent a small proportion of the total immigrants of both nations, they have profound impacts on their host nations. One impact is the provision of professional labor in a variety of economic sectors that are in demand in these two capitalist economies. Another is the reshaping of numerous specific places that attract them. In these cases, complex factors explain movements and settlement structures of Black Canadians and Americans. Both nations experienced restructuring of their economies in the latter part of the twentieth century. Thus, the role of economics in these capitalist frameworks is important to the movement and settlement of Blacks in both countries. However, other factors also emerge as explanations of destination and settlement patterns, including the role of culture and the desire of many Black immigrants to relocate to places that contain a large number of co-ethnics. Similarly, other characteristics at the potential destination, as well as distance from Black origins, influence the emerging patterns of the African Diaspora (chapter 12). In the end, place is important, not only because of the perceived opportunities it provides, but because it shapes the experiences of those who occupy it and becomes full of cultural meaning. Places not only express the presence of culture or ethnicity, they nurture occupants. This is why places and cultural landscapes provide attractive study areas. In this volume we have taken a place approach to studying the African Diaspora because, while valuing the role of theories, place enables a better understanding of how Black movements, experiences, and meanings are tied to and become somewhat unique in original and particular settings. For example, chapter 11 offers one example of the importance of cultural roots in New Orleans and the psychological "place shock" that occurs with sudden uprooting. Chapter 14 reports the creation of a new cultural center in Broward County, Florida, that has become a special landscape and place for a growing West Indian, particularly Jamaican, population that created "Jam Hill."

We identify two overarching themes and numerous sub-themes in this collective work. The first theme is the persistence of racism and its legacies in the U.S. and Canada, which negatively influences native-born and foreign-born Blacks in both nations. The second is the multidimensional diversity of the Black Diaspora. We summarize some of the sub-themes associated with these major topics, and provide some additional observations of these legacies.

PERSISTENT RACISM AND ITS LEGACIES IN THE U.S. AND CANADA

This volume presents common problems faced by people of African descent, and analyzes the importance of *place attributes* and the legacy of slavery in shaping the ideology of Whites towards Blacks. We explain the importance of immigration policy in determining why voluntary immigration of people of African descent is a recent phenomenon. Finally, the preceding chapters demonstrate how the experiences of people of African descent are shaped by differential incorporation, residential segregation, socioeconomic/neighborhood inequality, and overall racial inequality. This book continuously emphasizes that people of African descent are not homogenous, but are diverse ethnically, socioeconomically, and culturally. This concluding chapter summarizes, classifies, and reiterates the common experiences and examines the future prospects for achieving racial equality in both countries. We summarize the experience of each Black group separately within the context of the themes and concepts presented in chapter 1.

African Americans (Native-born Blacks) in the United States

The number of people who reported African-American ancestry increased by nearly 1.2 million, or 4.9 percent, between 1990 and 2000. With 8.8 percent of the total population, this group was the third largest ancestry group in the United States, exceeded only by Germans (15.2 percent) and the Irish (10.8 percent) (Brittingham and de la Cruz 2004). There were 33 million African Americans in the United States in 2000.

Geographic Distribution by State

The legacy of slavery contributes to the geographic distribution of African Americans. The African-American population in 2000 was still overrepresented in certain Southern and border states where slavery occurred prior to the American Civil War. Those states and their percent African-American population are Alabama (20 percent), Georgia (21.6 percent), Louisiana (25.5 percent), Maryland (20.5 percent), Mississippi (28.3 percent), North Carolina (16.6 percent), and South Carolina (22.8 percent). In 2000, in the cities of New York, Chicago, Philadelphia, Detroit, and Washington, DC, "African American" was the most-frequently-reported ancestry for people of African descent.

Comparative Socioeconomic Status

The socioeconomic status of African Americans is lower than that of Whites in general. However, according to certain socioeconomic indicators, the status of African Americans is also lower than that of other groups of African descent. Indeed, in 2000, African Americans (native-born Blacks) earned only $33,790 in median income, which was much lower than the $42,900 median income of Africans and $43,650 median income of Afro-Caribbeans (Logan and Deane 2003). African Americans also had a lower educational attainment level (12.4 years) compared to 12.6 years for Afro-Caribbeans and 14.0 for Africans. The lower educational level of African Americans results in their higher unemployment rate (11.2 percent) compared to 8.7 percent for Afro-Caribbeans and 7.3 percent for Africans. As a result, African Americans have a higher percentage of their population in poverty (30.4 percent) compared to 22.1 percent for Africans and 18.8 percent for Afro-Caribbeans. The higher socioeconomic status of Africans and Afro-Caribbeans is related to differential social capital (education and skills) that resulted from their selective immigration status.

Furthermore, there is the importance of birth place and the legacy of slavery, which resulted in the lack of intergenerational transfer of wealth among African Americans, thus reducing social capital accumulation. Moreover, while slavery was abolished in 1865 by the 13th Amendment to the Constitution of the United States, African Americans continued to experience residential, social, and economic segregation by law (*de jure*) and discrimination in practice until the 1960s in southern states that had held African Americans as slaves. They also experienced residential, social, and economic segregation and discrimination in practice (*de facto*) in the remaining states (see chapters 8, 9, and 10).

Although African Americans have a lower socioeconomic status than Afro-Caribbeans and Africans, they have a *lower level* of residential segregation from Whites. Based on the index of dissimilarity, African Americans had a segregation level in 2000 of 65.0 compared to 67.8 for Africans and 71.8 for Afro-Caribbeans (Logan and Deane 2003). Yet in terms of socioeconomic characteristics of neighborhoods, the average African American lives in census tracts (neighborhoods) that have lower median incomes than either Afro-Caribbeans or Africans. However, African Americans live in neighborhoods where the majority of residents own their homes (53 percent), which is a higher rate of home ownership than the rate for Afro-Caribbeans (49.8 percent), or Africans (47.2 percent) (Logan and Deane 2003). This higher homeownership rate may be related, in part, to the longer length of residence of African Americans in the United States, as homeownership rates usually increase with length of residence in a country (Logan and Deane 2003; Darden and Kamel 2000).

The Native-born Canadians of African Descent

In Canada, many native-born Blacks, similar to African Americans, trace their ancestry to slavery. These Blacks and their descendents are most represented in the Halifax Census Metropolitan Area (CMA) and the province of Nova Scotia (Milan and Tran 2004). Although slavery in Canada never appeared to be as extensive as slavery in the United States, and although there is a question as to whether it was even an institution recognized in law, it did in fact exist and is an important part of Canadian history (chapter 3). Black slaves helped build the City of Halifax (Smith 1899). When Halifax was founded in 1749, the census indicated that there were 104 slaves in a total population of 3,022 (Riddell 1920).

Like the United States, following the abolition of slavery in Canada, the legacy of slavery remained. The historical record shows that discrimination against Blacks in employment, housing, and education in Nova Scotia continued after the abolition of slavery (chapter 3). Blacks were viewed as a source of cheap labor and were often exploited (Walker 1992). Throughout the history of Black settlements in Nova Scotia, Blacks have occupied the lowest social and economic positions in the vertical mosaic (Pachai 1993). Over time, Black communities became geographically separate and distinct from White communities, as Blacks began to locate on the fringes of White communities or in all-Black neighborhoods (Rawlyk 1968; Walker 1992). Black schools were separate and unequal from White schools and Blacks were economically dependent on Whites, and marginalized (Clairmont and Magill 1999).

School segregation became official policy in 1865, when the legislative assembly of Halifax authorized separate Black and White schools by law (Saney 1998). This policy was not abolished until 1954 (Pachai 1993), the same year the U.S. Supreme Court ruled that separate and unequal schools were unconstitutional in the landmark case of Brown vs. the Board of Education (*Brown v. Board of Education*, Topeka 1954). As was the case in the United States, racial segregation of schools in practice continued after the decision. According to Pachai (1993), separate and unequal schools continued to provide Blacks in Nova Scotia with poor education long after *du jure* segregation had ended (Winks 1969, 1980).

Many native-born Canadians of African descent in Montreal can also trace their ancestry back to slavery (chapter 4). Many were domestic slaves for the White Canadian elites. Following the abolition of slavery, many Black women continued to work as domestic servants, while most Black men worked in the railway sector as porters and cooks (chapter 4). Both the labor market and the housing market were highly segregated by race until more contemporary times (chapter 3).

Unlike the United States, the native-born Black population in Canada represents a small percentage of the total Black population, and is geographically concentrated in Nova Scotia, a result of the long historical legacy of slavery. Most people of African descent in Canada are immigrants from the Caribbean and Africa. However, in comparing native-born Blacks with native-born Whites the preceding chapters have revealed that native-born Canadian Blacks have a lower income, lower educational attainment level, lower occupational status, and lower homeownership rate. Unlike African Americans, native-born Blacks in Canada in 2001 had much lower average homeownership rates (45.8 percent) compared to 53.1 percent. More important in assessing racial inequality, with a homeownership rate of 73.4 percent, native-born White Canadians were 1.6 times more likely than native-born Black Canadians to own their homes (chapter 3).

Caribbean Immigrants in the United States

After passage of the 1965 Hart-Celler Immigration Act (chapter 15), which reduced the restrictions on immigration from non-European countries, there were rapid increases in immigrants from the Caribbean and other non-European countries. As a result, The United States Census Bureau added the question "What is the person's ancestry or ethnic origin?" to the Census beginning in 1980. This question replaced the question on where a person's parents were born. The old question provided foreign-born-origin data only for people with one or both parents born outside the United States. The current ancestry question allows everyone to give one or two responses to their ancestry or ethnic origin. It allows respondents to indicate whether their own ethnic origin was, for example, Jamaican, African American, or Nigerian. Due to the option to identify ethnic origin or ancestry, nearly 12 million fewer people than those reported on the race question indicated "African American" as their ancestry or ethnic origin (Brittingham and de la Cruz 2004). One reason for the difference is that some people who reported Black or African American on the race question reported their ancestry or ethnic origin more specifically, such as Jamaican, Haitian, or Nigerian. Thus, they were not counted in the African-American ancestry category.

It is the more recent census question that allowed for a comparison of the different Black groups, i.e., people of African descent, to be made in the United States. The largest Caribbean immigrants, i.e., immigrant populations of 100,000 or more people, are Haitians, consisting of 548,199 or 0.2 percent of the total population; Jamaicans, consisting of 736,513, or 0.3 percent of the total population, and Trinidadian and Tobagonians, consisting of 164,738, or 0.1 percent of the total population, and Other West Indians consisting of 147,222, or 0.1 percent of the total population (Brittingham and de la Cruz 2004). As the preceding chapters have revealed, race, or "Blackness," is a strong factor in explaining the residential patterns of Afro-Caribbeans in general. Most reside closer to Black neighborhoods than to White neighborhoods.

West Indians are concentrated in both New York City and Miami. However, the residential pattern of West Indians in Miami (a more recent immigration process mainly since the 1970s) differ from the pattern in New York where West Indians have been arriving over a much longer period of time. In Miami, there are no West Indian (excluding Haitians) majority neighborhoods (census tracts). On the other hand, in New York City, there are a number of neighborhoods (census tracts) where West Indians comprise more than 50 percent of the population (chapter 13). Indeed, West Indian neighborhood dominance has served as a magnet attracting other West Indian immigrants to their neighborhoods. The West Indian community provides information to prospective immigrants about job opportunities, housing, health care facilities, and education, resulting in chain migration (chapter 13).

Within the socioeconomic structure, West Indians in the United States have enjoyed a higher socioeconomic status than native-born Black due in part to their greater emphasis on education, achievement and upward mobility (chapter 14). However, the color based racial stratification system prevents many West Indians from advancing based on merit. Thus, their mobility is blocked due to discrimination based on skin color (chapter 14). Therefore, Black neighborhoods provide West Indians security against racial discrimination, a built-in market for services, and the ability to compete with native-born Blacks. Also, because of their higher socioeconomic status, most West Indians are able to purchase or rent homes in the more upscale sections of Black neighborhoods (chapter 14). Such spatial and social distance from native-born Blacks has led some West Indians to perceive themselves as culturally different and superior to native-born Blacks. This perception is more prevalent in New York City than in Miami (chapter 14). Among the Caribbeans, Haitians appear to be the poorest group and also have a moderately different residential segregation pattern than other West Indians (chapter 14).

The lack of access of Afro-Caribbeans to White neighborhoods is similar to the lack of access to White neighborhoods experienced by African Americans (chapter 15). There is a pattern of residential segregation within the Black neighborhoods, however. West Indian neighborhoods are embedded within the better sections of racialized African-American neighborhoods (chapter 15). Moreover, because of their "Blackness," West Indians and other Afro-Caribbeans also experience barriers to upward and spatial mobility similar to the experiences of African Americans.

Caribbean Immigrants in Canada

Jamaicans were the first immigrants from the Caribbean to arrive in Canada. Prior to the lifting of Canada's racially restrictive immigration policy in 1967, most Jamaicans immigrated as contractual "live-in female domestics" workers (Darden 2004). In 2001 there were 122,340 Jamaicans in Canada, accounting for 0.2 percent of the Canadian population. Of this number, 93,315 resided in the Toronto CMA (Statistics Canada 2003). Some prospective Jamaican immigrants chose Canada over the United States because of differences between the immigration policies of the two countries. Canada's immigration policies favor immigrants who have the education and skills that would enhance employability, while the U.S. policies prioritize family reunification. Consequently, Canada is the preferred option for individuals who do not have family in the United States, but whose education, work experience, or other qualities enable them to qualify for entry under the Canadian Point System (chapter 7).

The Point System was established in 1967 with the objective of increasing the number of skilled immigrants to Canada by determining the employability of prospective immigrants and admitting them on this basis. Barring any serious health concerns or criminal offenses (determined by medical/criminal background checks), immigration candidates may be approved if they gain 67 of 100 possible points from six categories: education, language ability in French or English, work experience, age, arranged employment, and adaptability. Furthermore, applicants must have either an offer of employment or the financial means to support themselves (chapter 7). Often immigrants are admitted, however they are not immediately employed in a position to match their skills and education (Darden 2004). Thus many remain either underemployed or not employed at all, with a resulting decline in the social status they held in their country of origin. Jamaicans, like other immigrants from the Caribbean, represent a small percentage of most neighborhoods. They are, therefore, less visible and generally less segregated from Whites than Jamaicans and other Caribbeans in the United States (chapters 3 and 7).

Similar to the experience in the United States, "Blackness" is a factor. However, compared to the United States, West Indians in Canada's largest metropolitan areas are not as residentially segregated from Whites. There are however, identifiable West Indian commercial and residential neighborhoods. The residential location of West Indians is related in part to housing affordability and racial discrimination (chapters 6 and 3). There is considerable overlap among the West Indian and other Black communities. West Indians are overrepresented in the poorer neighborhoods. Similar to West Indians in the United States, it is more difficult for West Indians, compared to whites with comparable incomes and education, to translate their socioeconomic status into the higher-quality neighborhoods in Canadian metropolitan areas. Also similar to West Indians in the United States, West Indians in Canada face color based racial discrimination (chapter 3). Neighborhood quality is highly correlated with skin color, i.e., the higher-quality neighborhoods are occupied disproportionately by Whites, while the lower quality neighborhoods are occupied disproportionately by West Indians and other Blacks.

Finally, West Indians, as other immigrants from non-European countries, face a barrier in Canada that is a form of systematic discrimination. Canadian employers refuse to recognize West Indian education credentials and experience (chapters 3 and 6). This barrier has created a continuing problem of social mobility for West Indians. Due to Canada's point system, which requires education and skills for entry into Canada, many West Indians have the social capital, i.e., education and skills necessary for employment, however, they are prevented from using such skills in the job market. Such artificial barriers continue to delay the social mobility of the West Indians in Canada. Jamaicans and other Caribbean immigrants experience subtle racism and discrimination that prevents equal incorporation into Canadian society. Toronto and Montreal remain the two CMAs where most Afro-Caribbeans reside. Jamaicans are the largest group in Toronto and Haitians are more represented in Montreal (chapters 3, 4 and 7).

African Immigrants in the United States

Among people of African descent, African immigrants are the most recent group to arrive in the United States. Numbering over 600,000, Africans are dispersed geographically throughout the United States. The largest numbers are in Washington, DC and New York. In both places, the majority are from West Africa, especially Ghana and Nigeria. East Africa (including Ethiopia and Somalia) is also a major source region (Logan and Deane 2003). The smallest group among people of African descent consists of African immigrants. They constitute only 0.2 percent of the total United States population and 1.7 percent of the total Black population. Nearly 80 percent of the African population in the United States is foreign-born (Logan and Deane 2003).

Among the three groups of African descent, Africans have the highest level of educational attainment — 14 years, compared to 12.6 years for Afro-Caribbeans and 12.4 years for African Americans. This level of education exceeds that of Whites and even Asians (Logan and Deane 2003). It is clear that African immigrants are a highly selective group. However, the median income of Africans is slightly lower than the median income of Afro-Caribbeans ($42,900 compared to $43,650). A higher percentage of Africans also live below the poverty level (22.1 percent) compared to 18.8 percent for Afro-Caribbeans, and a lower percentage of Africans are unemployed (7.3 percent) compared to 8.7 percent for Afro-Caribbeans (Logan and Deane 2003).

Despite the higher educational level of Africans, they are more residentially segregated from Whites (with an index of dissimilarity of 67.8) than are African Americans (65). However, Africans (compared to Afro-Caribbeans and African Americans) are more likely to live in the higher socioeconomic status sections of African American neighborhoods (chapter 2).

Africans in the United States are more likely to be from a limited number of African countries due to the effects of the Immigration Act of 1990 (chapter 19). The act made possible the settlement of Ghanaians in Cincinnati, Liberians in Minneapolis-St. Paul, and Ethiopians in the District of Columbia (chapters 16, 18, and 19). Finally, the United States approved the resettlement of Somali refugees in 1996. Somalis, with a population of 65,000 (i.e., the largest group of African refugees) are a part of the more recent African Diaspora to the United States (chapter 17). These refugees have found themselves resettled in states such as Maine where very few other Africans reside. They have experienced not only racial and ethnic isolation but also have had to make difficult cultural adjustments (chapter 17).

African Immigrants in Canada

Immigrants from Africa are very recent in Canada as they are in the United States. Before 1961, immigrants from Africa represented only 0.5 percent of all immigrants. This was due to Canada's racially restrictive immigration policy (chapter 3). Even after the policy was changed, immigration from Africa tended to be low until the period from 1991–2001. During that period the number of immigrants arriving in Canada from Africa (139,770) exceeded the number of immigrants (84,005) entering from the Caribbean and Bermuda (chapter 3).

Indeed, Africa is now the number one source region for Black immigrants to Canada (chapter 3). However, many Africans in Canada have come as refugee claimants. Other African immigrants encounter longer delays in the process of immigration to Canada than immigrants from Europe or East Asia (chapter 6). The number of total African immigrants in Canada in 2001 was 282,600, representing 5.2 percent of all immigrants (chapter 3).

In general, African immigrants in Canada do not do as well socioeconomically as African immigrants in the United States. In 2007, African-born immigrants in Canada had the highest unemployment rates and lowest employment rates of other immigrants to Canada and the native-born population. This is true regardless of the year they arrived in Canada (Gilmore 2008). The unemployment rate was 9 percent for all African immigrants aged 25–54, a rate 1.3 times higher than the 6.8 percent unemployment rate for *all* immigrants in the same age range. The unemployment gap between African immigrants and the Canadian-born population was even wider. With a 4.4 percent unemployment rate for the Canadian-born population, African immigrants were twice as likely to be unemployed (Gilmore 2008).

African immigrants also experience strong barriers in their search for housing. Based on housing search studies involving Cape Verdeans, Angolans, and Mozambicans, barriers in the housing search are more difficult for Angolans and Mozambicans than Cape Verdeans (chapter 6). The difference in the degree of difficulty in the housing search appeared to be related to discrimination based on skin color (chapter 6), or "Blackness."

Summation and Future Prospects for Racial Equality

Based on the evidence presented in this volume, it is fair to conclude that whether people of African descent are native-born in the United States or native-born in Canada, or immigrants in the United States or immigrants in Canada, racial equality in comparison to Whites has not been a reality of life. In general, on every social and economic indicator, people of African descent remain at a disadvantage. The degree of disadvantage varies based on the amount of social capital that the group brings as immigrants, or transfers from one generation to the next. In recognition of the persistent racial inequality, governments of both the United States and Canada have responded to demands by people of African descent to develop public policies to address the inequality. This volume includes a comparison of those public policies (chapters 3 and 5), and the evidence seems to suggest that effective action to address the matter of racial inequality is probably more likely in the United States in the near future than in Canada. That is because Canada, unlike the United States, more often *denies* that barriers to equal social and spatial mobility of people of African descent are due to racial discrimination (Darden 2004) (chapter 3). Thus, future prospects for people of African descent to achieve racial equality are more likely to occur earlier in the United States than in Canada. It is only through a comparative assessment as presented in this volume that we advance our knowledge of the African Diaspora at the dawn of the twenty-first century. The achievement of racial equality will vary among people of African descent because of the great amount of diversity among the group.

THE MULTIDIMENSIONAL DIVERSITY OF THE BLACK DIASPORA AT THE DAWN OF THE 21ST CENTURY

Diversity comes in many forms, socio-economic (class), cultural, and ethnic settlement structures. All of these types of diversity apply to the current African Diaspora in the U.S. and Canada. There is no doubt that Blacks suffer from economic inequalities in both countries. However, it would be a mistake to ignore their gains during the second half of the twentieth century and their increasingly complex patterns related to these various forms of diversity.

Economic Diversity and Varied SES

Economic gains, although fleeting at times, have been made by native-born Blacks in both countries. The growth of the Black middle and professional classes that occurred during the late twentieth century contributed to economic diversity within these populations (Clark 1979; Frazier, Margai, and Tettey-Fio 2003). Foreign-born Blacks, overall, have generally better SES than the native-born Blacks. While millions of native-born Blacks have suffered long-term inequalities in educational, employment, and economic conditions, many foreign-born Blacks either have entered the U.S. with relatively higher SES or achieved it through higher education in the United States and remained in North America as permanent residents or citizens. This trend has contributed to Black economic diversity. At the same time, the Black immigrant streams to both nations, including the legal and undocumented, also contain individuals with low SES, which contribute to the substantial diversification of incomes and other SES variables among the overall Black populations. For the U.S., chapter 13 illustrates this among Caribbean Blacks, including the SES distinctions between West Indian immigrants and Haitians and, also, between West Indian SES and that of native-born Blacks. Similarly, chapter 14 illustrates the dramatic income range among Jamaicans in Broward County, Florida. These chapters provide substantial evidence illustrating the economic class differences between native-born Blacks and major immigrant Black groups, the variation within Black immigrant groups, and the broad range of incomes within particular Black ethnic groups. Blacks have clearly become very diverse economically.

Cultural, Ethnic Diversity and Racial Identity

The very fact that both nations attract Black immigrants from Africa and the Black Caribbean speaks to their cultural and ethnic diversity. This text has addressed various Black cultures and the social institutions that support them. These included origins from African nations, such as Angola, the Cape Verde Islands, Ethiopia, Liberia, Mozambique, and Somalia, and West Indian nations of the Caribbean. As with all cultural and ethnic groups, social institutions play significant roles in supporting their well being and cultural characteristics. Ethnicity is strong among first generation immigrants, and Blacks fit this pattern. This sometimes results in immigrant Blacks distancing themselves from native Blacks by emphasizing their cultural differences. However, there also is the case that racism and discrimination sometimes encourage a racial rather than an ethnic identity among immigrant Blacks, who after experiencing personal racism are more likely to identify and support the causes of native Blacks.

Diversity in Regional Settlement Patterns Among the Diverse Cultures

Like all immigrants, many recent members of the African Diaspora have been pushed out of their homelands and attracted to particular gateways, including Toronto, New York, Miami-Dade-Ft. Lauderdale-West Palm Beach, and Washington, DC. However, a number of other forces contribute to their broad regional settlement patterns. In this text, we examined the important support of resettlement organization (VOLAGS) in guiding African refugees to perhaps surprising locations, including the Liberians in Minneapolis-St. Paul (chapter 17) and Somalis in Portland, Maine (chapter 16). In addition to these forces, the pull of economic opportunity and the desire to locate in communities with co-ethnics, continue to pull secondary migrants to particular communities, gateways and other places. Among the examples were Jamaicans and Angolans to Toronto (chapter 5), Ghanaians to Cincinnati (chapter 18), and Jamaicans to Broward County, Florida (chapter 14).

Diversity in Metropolitan Settlement Structures and Integration: Culture and Class

There is a complex set of relationships between Black ethnicity and economic class status that have created a still-emerging set of spatial patterns of Black businesses and residential settlements within metropolitan areas. Chapter 19 reviews some of the Black ethnic business patterns present in Toronto and provides a case study of a few relocating Black businesses in the Bronx, New York. The Bronx case and the Canadian studies provide some insights into the links between culture, ethnicity, and class for business patterns.

Black residential patterns are equally complex in both nations, but this complexity is not unique to Blacks. Skop and Li have note the still emerging diverse and complicated ethnic settlements among various American immigrants in American metropolitan regions (Skop and Li 2003). This complexity goes beyond Black immigrants, however and is complicated by changes in native Black SES and settlement choices. On the one hand, there is plenty of evidence that the legacy of racism and perhaps other factors continue to create inequalities between Blacks and Whites. American inner cities and their adjacent suburbs continue to experience racial inequalities at the turn of the twenty-first century (Frazier, Margai, and Tettey-Fio 2003). This text illustrates current inequalities in cities such as Toronto (chapter 4), Atlanta (chapter 9), Austin (chapter 8), and New York City (chapter 19). On the other hand, there also is emerging evidence of neighborhood equity in suburban places within metropolitan regions, as illustrated in the Detroit region (chapter 10), and the relocation of Black families in exclusive White suburbs outside Ft. Lauderdale (chapter 14).

The Ft. Lauderdale situation also is a case of class trumping culture in certain situations and places. Other examples in this text include the Liberians in the Twin Cities of Minnesota (chapter 17) and Jamaicans in Toronto (chapter 6). Concerning Black Canadian settlements, chapter 6 reports the relationship between Jamaican immigrant residential distribution in different Toronto neighborhoods and their socioeconomic status. The Florida case provides an important example of the existence a persistent and well known type of Black immigrant settlement pattern involving West Indians residing on the periphery of predominantly native-born Black areas in better neighborhoods and embedded by ethnicity. Specifically, Jamaicans are embedded in West Indian neighborhoods that are parts of the larger Black settlement structure termed triple layering. This pattern is present in Broward County. However, it is but one type of Black settlement pattern there. Many wealthy Jamaicans prefer to mix with Whites in predominantly White exclusive suburbs, rather than in ethnic enclaves within larger Black regions of the metropolitan area. This heterolocal pattern allows them to preserve their ethnicity while enjoying the benefits of exclusive suburban locations.

Another important observation made in chapter 15 is that the type of involvement in ethnic institutions is related to time of immigrant entry and socioeconomic class. In the case of Ethiopians, churches appeal to immigrants throughout metropolitan Washington, DC. The same factors, time of entry and social status, also play roles in their social and political integration. Finally, Ethiopians, while maintaining cultural distinctiveness, reach out to other immigrants in common pursuits, such as affordable housing.

In summary, this book illustrates some of the similarities and differences of an increasingly complex African Diaspora in the U.S. and Canada, a daunting task, given the two different national histories, numerous subcultures, and different population sizes. Nonetheless, there are common ideologies that spawn long term racial inequalities and contemporary labor needs, which are embedded in capitalism and globalization, and result in a rapid increase in Black immigration from Africa and the Black Caribbean to both nations. We have collectively provided a perspective on the legacies of slavery and racism that underlie the continuing racial inequalities of these two important neighboring nations and expressed the prospects for greater equality in the future. We also provide snapshots of places in both nations that reveal both the persistence of racial inequality and the changes being brought by rapid immigration and secondary migration of Black people. The changing African Diaspora in the United States and Canada are evolving stories because culture, global and regional processes, and the places in which they occur, are dynamic. As attitudes and behaviors of the host cultures and the embedded subcultures change in response to various global, regional, and local forces, the African Diaspora in the two nations will also change. Therefore, this volume, like all volumes, is no more than an assessment, a stock taking, at a particular juncture in the evolution of the African Diaspora. It is an effort to capture some of the more pertinent aspects of the African Diaspora in two nations as expressed in particular places at the dawn of the twenty-first century.

Works Cited

Abbott, C. W. 2006. "Nigerians in North America: New Frontiers, Old Associations?" In *The New African Diaspora in North America: Trends, Community Building and Adaptation*, ed. K. Konadu-Agyemang, B. K. Takyi and J. A. Arthur. New York: Lexington Books, pp. 141–66.

Abler, R., J. S. Adams, and P. Gould. 1971. *Spatial Organization*. Englewood Cliffs: Prentice-Hall, Inc.

Abramson, D. and R. Garfield. 2006. "On the Edge: Children and Families Displaced by Hurricanes Katrina and Rita Face Looming Medical and Mental Health Crisis." Released April 17, 2006. National Center for Disaster Preparedness, Mailman School of Public Health, Columbia University.

Abt Associates of Canada. 1987. *Access to Trades and Professions in Ontario*. Toronto: Cabinet Committee on Race Relations.

Abu-Laban, Y. and C. Gabriel. 2002. *Selling Diversity: Immigration, Multiculturalism, Employment Equity, and Globalization*. Peterborough, Ontario: Broodview Press.

Adams, J. 2002. "Foreclosure Sales in Metro Atlanta Hit Record High." *The Georgia Real Estate Report* 3(3).

Afolayan, F. 2003. "Bantu Expansion and Its Consequences." In *Africa: African History Before 1885*, Vol. 1, ed. Toyin Falola. Durham, NC: Carolina Academic Press, pp. 113–36.

Agnew, J. 1981. "Home Ownership and Identity in Capitalist Societies." In *Housing and Identity: Cross-cultural Perspectives*, ed. J. Duncan. London: Croom Helm, pp. 60 97.

Agocs, C. and M. Boyd. 1993. "The Canadian Ethnic Mosaic Recast for the 1990s." In *Social Inequality in Canada: Patterns, Problems, Policies*, ed. J. Curtis, E. Grabb, and N. Guppy. Scarborough: Prentice-Hall Canada, pp. 330–60.

Agocs, C., C. Bird, F. Somerset, and D. Balkin. 1993. *Employment Equity*. Scarborough: Prentice-Hall Canada.

Ahmad, O. B. 2004. "Brain Drain: The Flight of Human Capital." *Bulletin of the World Health Organization* 82(10): 797–98.

Aimes, E., Professor, Bates College. 2007. Telephone Interview. 15 July.

Akokpari, J. 2006. "Globalization, Migration, and the Challenges of Development in Africa." *Perspectives on Global Development & Technology* 5(3): 125–53.

Alba, R. D. 1995. "Neighborhood Change Under Conditions of Mass Immigration: The New York City Region, 1970–1990." *International Migration Review* 29(3): 625.

Alba, R. D. and J. R. Logan. 1993. "Minority Proximity to Whites in Suburbs: An Individual Level Analysis of Segregation." *American Journal of Sociology* 98: 1388–427.

———. 1991. "Variations on Two Themes: Racial and Ethnic Patterns in the Attainment of Suburban Residence." *Demography* 28: 431–54.

Alba, R. D., J. R. Logan, and B. J. Stults. 2000. "How Segregated are Middle-class African-Americans?" *Social Problems* 47: 543–58.

Albelda, R. P. 1986. "Occupational Segregation by Race and Gender, 1958–1981." *Industrial and Labor Relations Review* 39: 404–11.

Aldrich, H. and R. Waldinger. 1990. "Ethnicity and Entrepreneurship." *Annual Review of Sociology* 16: 111–35.

Allen, J. P. 2006. "How Successful are Recent Immigrants to the United States and Their Children." *APCG Yearbook* Volume 68. (Presidential address delivered to the Association of Pacific Coast Geographers, 68th Annual Meeting, Phoenix, Arizona, October 22, 2005.)

Almanza, S. 2006. "Gentrification and Land use in Austin." Available from www.poder-texas.org (accessed October 12, 2006).

Al-Sharmani, M. 2006. "Living Transnationally: Somali Diasporic Women in Cairo." *International Migration* 44(1): 55–77.

American Community Survey. 2005. Factfinder. Last accessed January 5, 2007.

American Public Transportation Association. 2003. Table 1: Adult Single-Trip Base Fares. APTA Transit Fare Database. http://www. apta.com/research/stats/fares/documents/base.pdf (accessed December 12, 2003).

American Red Cross. 2006. "Challenged by the Storms: The American Red Cross Response to Hurricanes Katrina, Rita and Wilma." Washington, DC: American Red Cross.

———. 2005. "Foundations of Disaster Mental Health." ARC 3077 4A. Washington, DC: American Red Cross.

Anderson, K. 1987. "The Idea of Chinatown: The Power of Place and Institutional Practice in the Making of a Racial Category." *Annals of the Association of American Geographers* 77: 580–98.

Angus Reid Group. 1991. *Multiculturalism and Canadians: Attitude Study 1991 (National Survey Report)*. Ottawa: Multiculturalism and Citizenship Canada.

Antecol, H. D., A. Cobb-Clark, and J. Trejo. 2003. "Immigration Policy and the Skills of Immigrants to Australia, Canada, and the United States." *The Journal of Human Resources* 38(1): 192–218.

Apparicio, P. et al., 2006. *Atlas de L'immigration de la Region Métropolitaine de Recensement de Montréal en 2001*. Montreal: Université du Québec Institut national de la recherché scientifique.

Appleseed. 2006. "A Continuing Storm: The On-going Struggles of Hurricane Katrina Evacuees: A Review of Needs, Best Practices and Recommendations." Retrieved October 1, 2006 from http://www. hurricane-katrina.org/2006/08/appleseed_found.html.

Apraku, K. K. 1991. *African Emigres in the United States*. New York: Praeger Publishers.

Arnopoulos, S. 1979. *Problems of Immigrant Women in the Canadian Labour Force*. Ottawa: Canadian Advisory Council on the Status of Women.

Arthur, J. A. 2006. "The New African Diaspora in North America: Policy Implications." In *The New African Diaspora in North America: Trends, Community Building and Adaptation*, ed. K. Konadu-Agyemang, B. K. Takyi and J. A. Arthur. New York: Lexington Books, pp. 287–302.

———. 2000. *Invisible Sojourners: African Immigrant Diasporas in the United States*. Westport, CT: Praeger.

Ashabranner, B. 1999. *The New African Americans*. North Haven, CT: Linnet.

Association of Community Organizations for Reform Now. 2004. *Separate and Unequal: Predatory Lending in America*. Washington, DC: ACORN.

Association of Community Organizations for Reform Now (ACORN). 2003. "The Great Divide: Home Purchase Mortgage Lending in 115 Metropolitan Areas." Available: http://www.acorn.org

Atlanta Neighborhood Development Partnership. 2007. "Making the Case: For Housing Choices and Complete Communities: The Next Generation." Atlanta: ANDP, Spring.

Atlanta Regional Commission. 2007. *Metro Stats – Black History Month 2007*. Atlanta: ARC. Available at http://www.atlantaregional.com/cps/rde/xchg/arc/hs.xsl/metrostats_blackhistory2007_ENU_HTML.htm (Accessed September 28, 2007).

———. 2006a. *Population and Housing in the Atlanta Region*. Atlanta: ARC. Available at http://www. atlantaregional.com/cps/rde/xbcr/arc/mainreport.pdf (accessed September 28, 2007).

———. 2006b. *Envision 6: Envision Our Future*. Atlanta: ARC.

———. 2005. *Population and Housing 2005*. Atlanta: ARC.

———. 2004. *2000 Census: Foreign Born by Place of Birth; Ranked for the 10-County ARC Region*. November 17.

———. 2003. *Atlanta Region Transportation Planning: Fact Book 2003*. Atlanta: ARC.

———. 1998a. *Atlanta Region Outlook*. Atlanta: ARC.

———. 1998b. *Proposed 1998 Amendments to the Interim Atlanta Region Transportation Improvement Program FY 1999–FY 2001*. Atlanta: ARC.

Babington, C. 2005. "Some GOP Legislators Hit Jarring Notes in Addressing Katrina." *Washington Post*, Saturday, September 10, 2005, p. A04.

Backer, J. C. 1993. *Keeping to the Marketplace: The Evolution of Canadian Housing Policy*. Montreal: McGill-Queen's University Press.
Badenhause, K. 2003. "Wide Open for Business." *City and Community* 2(1): 3–19.
Balakrishnan, T. R. and K. Selvanathan. 1990. "Ethnic Residential Segregation in the Metropolitan Areas of Canada." *Canadian Review of Sociology and Anthropology* 19: 92–110.
Balakrishnan, T. and Z. Wu. 1992. "Home Ownership Patterns and Ethnicity in Selected Canadian Cities." *Canadian Journal of Sociology* 17: 389–403.
Ballay, P. and M. Bulthuis. 2004. "The Changing Portrait of Homelessness." In *Our Diverse Cities*, ed. C. Andrew. Ottawa: Metropolis Institute.
Bates, T. 1997. "Traditional and Emerging Lines of Black-Owned Small Businesses." In *Race, Self-employment & Upward Mobility: An Illusive American Dream*. Washington, DC: The Woodrow Wilson Center Press; Baltimore and London: The Johns Hopkins University Press, pp. 142–62.
Bauman, J. 1987. *Public Housing, Race, and Renewal*. Philadelphia: Temple University Press.
Bayer, P. and R. McMillan. 2005. "Racial Sorting and Neighborhood Quality." *National Bureau of Economic Research Working Paper* Number W11813.
Bendick, M. 1997. *Discrimination Against Racial/Ethnic Minorities in Access to Employment in the United States: Empirical Findings from Situation Testing*. Geneva: International Labour Association.
Bennett, D. L. 2001. "Losing a Home is So Easy, It's Scary." *Atlanta Journal-Constitution*, July 28. Page A1.
Benson, J. E. 2006. "Exploring the Racial Identities of Black Immigrants in the United States." *Sociological Forum* 21(2).
Benson-Rea, M. and S. Rawlinson. 2003. "Highly Skilled and Business Migrants: Information Processes and Settlement Outcomes." *International Migration* 41(2): 59–79.
Bernanke, B. 2005. "Technology and Economy." Speech Before the National Economics Club, October 11, 2005. New York.
Besteman, C. Professor, Colby College. 2007a. Internet Interview. 10 July.
———. 2007b. *Genocide in Somalia's Jubba Valley and Somali Bantu Refugees in the U.S.* http://hornofafrica.ssrc.org/Besteman.
———. 1999. *Unravelling Somalia*. Philadelphia: University of Pennsylvania Press.
Bigman, L. 1995. "Contemporary Migration from Africa to the USA." In *Cambridge Survey of World Migration*, ed. R. Cohen. New York: Cambridge University Press, pp. 260–62.
Billingsly, B. and L. Muszynski. 1985. *No Discrimination Here: Toronto Employers and the Multi-racial Workforce*. Toronto: Social Planning Council of Metropolitan Toronto and the Urban Alliance on Race Relations.
Binder, S. and J. Tosic. 2005. "Refugees as a Particular Form of Transnational Migrations and Social Transformations: Socioanthropological and Gender Aspects." *Current Sociology* 53(4): 607–24.
Blalock, H. 1967. *Towards a Theory of Minority Group Relations*. New York: Capricorn Books.
Blockson, C. L. 1987. "Sea Change in the Sea Islands: 'Nowhere to Lay Down Weary Head.'" *National Geographic* 172(6): 735–63.
Blunt, J., C. Frye, and B. Walker. *City of Austin Planning Project: Early Development*. Available from: http://www/ar.utexas.edu/Courses/parmenter/gis/spring/Austin/documents/planningfuntion.htm (last accessed October 26, 2006).
Bolaria, B. S. and P. S. Li. 1988. *Racial Oppression in Canada*, 2nd Ed. Toronto: Garamond Press.
———. 1985. *Racial Oppression in Toronto*. Toronto: Garamond Press.
Bollen, K. 1989. *Structural Equations with Latent Variables*. New York: John Wiley.
Bonacich, E. 1973, "A Theory of Middlement Minorities." *American Sociological Review* 38(5): 583–94.
Bonnett, A. 1997. "Geography, Race and Whiteness: Invisible Traditions and Current Challenges," *Area* 29: 193–99.
Borjas, G. J. 1993. "Immigration Policy, National Origin, and Immigrant Skills: A Comparison of Canada and the United States." In *Small Differences that Matter: Labor Markets and Income Maintenance in Canada and the United States*, ed. D. Card and R. B. Freeman. Chicago: University of Chicago Press.
———. 1986. "The Self-Employment Experience of Immigrants." *The Journal of Human Resources* 21(4): 485–506.

Bosch, G. R. 1997. "Eric Williams and the Moral Rhetoric of Dependency Theory." *Callaloo* 20(4): 817–27.

Boswell, T. D. 2007. *Profile of the Black Population in Miami-Dade County*. Office of Community Advocacy, Office of Black Affairs, Miami-Dade County Government.

———. 1983. "In the Eye of the Storm: The Context of Haitian Migration to South Florida." *The Southeastern Geographer* 23: 457–77.

Boswell, T. D. and T. A. Jones. 2006. "The Distribution and Socioeconomic Status of West Indians in the United States." In *Race, Ethnicity and Place in a Changing America*, ed. J. W. Frazier and E. L. Tettey-Fio. Binghamton, NY: Global Academic Publishing, pp. 155–80.

Bouchard, K. 2002. "A Thousand Miles." *Portland Press Herald*, June 30. http://bates.dailyjolt.com/johngaltforum/read.html?id=741.

Bourne, L. S. and D. Rose. 2007. "The Changing Face of Canada: The Uneven Geographies of Population and Social Change." In *The Changing Face of Canada: Essentials Readings in Population*, ed. R. Beaujot and D. Kerr. Toronto: Canadian Scholars' Press, pp. 255–68.

———. 2001. "The Changing Face of Canada: The Uneven Geographies of Population and Social Change." *The Canadian Geographer* 45: 105–19.

Bovenkirk, F. 1992. *Testing Discrimination in Natural Experiments: A Manual for International and Comparative Research on Discrimination on the Grounds of "Race" and Ethnic Origin*. Geneva: International Labour Organization.

Bovenkirk, F., M. Gras, and D. Ramsdedh. 1995. *Discrimination Against Migrant Workers and Ethnic Minorities in Access to Employment in the Netherlands*. Geneva: International Labour Organization.

Boyd, R. L. 1991. "A Contextual Analysis of Black Self-Employment in Large Metropolitan Areas, 1970–1980." *Social Forces* 70 (2): 409–29.

Boyko, J. 1998. *Last Steps to Freedom: The Evolution of Canadian Racism*. Toronto: J. Gordon Shillingford.

Breton, R. 1981. *The Ethnic Community as a Resource in Relation Problems: Perceptions and Attitudes*. Research paper no. 122. Centre for Urban and Community Studies, University of Toronto.

Breton, R., W. Isajiw, W. Kalbach, and J. Reitz. 1990. *Ethnic Identity and Equality: Varieties of Experiences in a Canadian City*. Toronto: University of Toronto Press.

Brittingham, A. and P. de la Cruz. 2004. *Ancestry: 2000*. Washington, DC: U.S. Bureau of the Census, Department of Commerce.

Broadway, B. 1998. "For Ethiopians, Church a Home Far from Home; Orthodox Christian Community Keeps Tradition Alive in DC Area." *Washington Post*, 2 May, D08.

Brown, L. A., T. E. Mott, and E. J. Malecki. 2007. "Immigrant Profiles of U.S. Urban Areas and Agents of Resettlement." *The Professional Geographer* 59(1): 56–73.

Brown v. Board of Education. 1954. 347 U.S. 483.

Brown, R. P. C. and J. Connell. 2006. "Occupation-Specific Analysis of Migration and Remittance Behavior: Pacific Island Nurses in Australia and New Zealand." *Asia Pacific Viewpoint* 47(1): 135–50.

Bullard, R. D. 2007a. *The Black Metropolis in the Twenty-First Century: Race, Power, and the Politics of Place*. New York: Rowman & Littlefield.

———. 2007b. *Growing Smarter: Achieving Livable Communities, Environmental Justice, and Regional Equity*. Cambridge, MA: MIT Press.

Bullard, R. D., J. E. Grisby III, and C. Lee. 1994. *Residential Apartheid: The American Legacy*. Los Angeles: University of California.

Bullard, R. D., G. S. Johnson and A. O. Torres. 2004. *Highway Robbery: Transportation Racism and New Routes to Equity*. Cambridge, MA: South End Press.

Bullard, R. D., G. S. Johnson and A. O. Torres. 2000. *Sprawl City: Race, Politics, and Planning in Atlanta*. Washington, DC: Island Press.

Burke, W. 2007. Marketing and Production Coordinator, and John Yanga, Outreach and Training Coordinator, New American Sustainable Agricultural Project. Interview. 19 July.

Busseri, M. A., S. W. Sadava and N. Decourville. 2007. "A Hybrid Model for Research on Subjective Well-Being: Examining Common- and Component-Specific Sources of Variance in Life Satisfaction, Positive Affect, and Negative Affect." *Social Indicators Research* 83: 413–45.

Butler, K. D. 2001. "Defining Diaspora, Refining a Discourse." In *Diaspora: A Journal of Transnational Studies*, Vol. 10, Issue 2, p. 189, 31p.

Cadwallader, M. 1992. *Migration and Residential Mobility: Macro and Micro Approaches*. Madison, WI: The University of Wisconsin Press.

Calliste, A. 1991. "Canada's Immigration Policy and Domestics from the Caribbean: The Second Domestic Scheme." In *Race, Class, Gender: Bonds and Barriers*, ed. J. Vorst et al. Toronto: Garamond Press, pp. 122–65.

Campbell, C. 2004. "Xpress Buses Overcrowd Already Busy Peachtree." *Atlanta Journal-Constitution*. June 8.

Canada Employment and Immigration. 1991. *Permanent Residents Years of Schooling by Country of Last Permanent Residence for Special Programs*. FDM January–December, 1989. Unpublished. Ottawa.

Canadian Human Rights Commission. 1998. *Annual Report, 1997*. Ottawa: A Report of the Commission.

Carey, E. 1999. "The 'City That Works' Could be Even Better." *Toronto Star*, May 1, A1, A10, A11.

Carney, J. A. 2001. *Black Rice: The African Origins of Rice Cultivation in the Americas*. Cambridge, MA: Harvard University Press, pp. 174–77.

Cashin, S. 2007. "Dilemma of Place and Suburbanization of the Black Middle Class." In *The Black Metropolis in the Twenty-First Century*, ed. R. Bullard. Boulder: Rowman and Littlefield Publishers, pp. 87–110.

Cassanelli, L. 1995. *Victims and Vulnerable Groups in Southern Somalia*. Research Directorate, Documentation information and research branch, immigration and refugee board, Ottawa, Canada, May.

Cebula, R. J. 1974. "Interstate Migration and the Tiebout Hypothesis: An Analysis According to Race, Sex and Age." *Journal of the American Statistical Association* 69: 876–79.

Cebula, R. J. and R. K. Vedder. 1973. "A Note on Migration, Economic Opportunity, and the Quality of Life." *Journal of Regional Science* 13: 205–11.

Center for Neighborhood Technology. 2004. *Making the Case for Mixed-Income and Mixed-Use Communities*. Chicago: CNT.

Chacko, E. 2008. "Washington: From Bi-racial City to Multi-ethnic Gateway." In *Migrants to the Metropolis: The Rise of Immigrant Gateway Cities*, ed. M. Price and L. Benton-Short. University of Syracuse Press, pp. 203–25.

———. 2003a. "Ethiopian Ethos and the Making of Ethnic Places in the Washington Metropolitan Area." *Journal of Cultural Geography* 20(2): 21–42.

———. 2003b. "Identity and Assimilation Among Young Ethiopian Immigrants in Metropolitan Washington." *Geographical Review* 93(4): 491–506.

Chacko, E. and I. Cheung. 2006. "The Formation of a Contemporary Ethnic Enclave: The Case of 'Little Ethiopia' in Los Angeles." In *Race, Ethnicity and Place in a Changing America*, ed. J. W. Frazier and E. L. Tettey Fio. Binghamton, NY: Global Academic Publishing, pp. 131–39.

Chaganti R. and P. G. Greene. 2002. "Who are Ethnic Entrepreneurs? A Study of Entrepreneurs' Ethnic Involvement and Business Characteristics." *Journal of Small Business Management* 40(2): 126–43.

Chappell, B. 2006. "The Barrio Moves: Lowriders and the Performance of Space." Paper presented at the American Anthropological Association, Washington, DC.

Chertoff, M. 2006. Testimony before Senate Homeland Security and Governmental Affairs Committee on the Hurricane Katrina: The Homeland Security Department's Preparation and Response on February 15, 2006.

Chikanda, A. 2006 "Skilled Health Professionals' Migration and its Impact on Health Delivery in Zimbabwe." *Journal of Ethnic and Migration Studies* 32(4): 667–80.

Chmelecki, L. 2003. "Immigrants Find Persistence Pays off with Jobs, Businesses." LEWISTON, 29 September (*Sun Journal*). http://www.somalilandtimes.net/2003/89/8912.shtml

Chui, T. 2003. *Longitudinal Survey of Immigrants to Canada: Process, Progress, and Prospects*. Ottawa: Statistics Canada.

Chusid, J. 2006. "Preservation in the Progressive City: Debating History and Gentrification in Austin." *Urban Conservancy*. Available from http://www.urbanconservancy.org/news/roundup/archive/786.php (last accessed October 15, 2007).

City of Lewiston, Maine. 2007. http://www.ci.lewiston.me.us/.

———. 2007. Lewiston, Maine: Setting the Pace (brochure).

Clairmont, D. H. and D. W. Magill. 1999. *Africville: The Life and Death of a Canadian Black Community*. Toronto: Canadian Scholars' Press.

———. 1973. *Nova Scotian Blacks: An Historian and Structural Overview*. Institute of Public Affairs, Dalhousie University, Working Paper No. 83. Halifax: Dalhousie University.

Clark, P. F., J. B. Stewart, and D. A. Clark. 2006. "The Globalization of the Labor Market for Health-Care Professionals." *International Labor Review* 145: 1–2.

Clark, T. A. 1979. *Blacks in Suburbs. A Natural Perspective*. New Brunswick: Rutgers University Press.

Clark, W. A. V. and F. M. Dieleman. 1996. *Households and Housing: Choice and Outcomes in the Housing Market*. New Brunswick, NJ: Center for Urban Policy Research.

Clark-Madison, M. 2006. "Use Only as Directed." *Austin Chronicle* 18:51; available from http://www.austin chronicle.com/issues/vol18/issue51/pols.neighborhood.html (last accessed May 3, 2006).

Cloud, A. 2006. "Uncovering Black Historical Spaces in Austin, Texas." Unpublished Manuscript.

CNN. 2005. "Reaction to Katrina Split on Racial Lines: More Blacks View Race as Factor in Federal Response, September 13, 2005." Retrieved 9/25/05 from http://www.cnn.com/2005/US/09/12/katrina.race.poll/index.html.

Cohen, R. E. 2006. "Project Seeks to Save Somali Culture Immigrants: UM Professors Collaborate to Preserve Old-country Stories." *Bangor Daily News*. 2 August. http://bangordailynews.com/news/t/city.aspx?articleid=138193&zoneid=176.

Columbus, D. 2006. "Depression and Suicide are Legacies of Katrina." New Orleans City Council, 6/20/06. Retrieved July 4, 2007 from http://www.nocitycouncil.com/shownews.asp?cid=77

Conservation Law Foundation. 1998. *City Routes, City Rights: Building Livable Neighborhoods and Environmental Justice by Fixing Transportation*. Boston: CLF, p. 18.

Conway, D. 1980. "Step-Wise Migration: Toward a Clarification of the Mechanism." *International Migration Review* 14(1).

Conway, D. and U. Bibgy, 1992. "Where Caribbean Peoples Live in New York City." In *Caribbean Life in New York City: Sociocultural Dimensions*, ed. C. R. Sutton and E. N. Chaney. Staten Island: Center for Migration Studies, pp. 70–78.

CQ Researcher. 2003. "Midwest is 'New Frontier' for Latinos." *CQ Researcher* 13(36): 881, October 17th.

Crary, D. 2007. "Africans in the U.S. Caught Between Worlds." *USA Today*, June 16.

Cromartie, J. and C. B. Stack. 1989. "Reinterpretation of Black Return and Non-Return Migration to the South, 1975–80." *Geographical Review* 79(3): 297–310.

Crowder, K. D. 1999. "Residential Segregation of West Indians in the New York City/New Jersey Metropolitan Area: The Roles of Race and Ethnicity." *International Migration Review* 33: 79–113.

Crowder, K. D. and L. M. Tedrow. 2001. "West Indians and the Residential Landscape of New York." In *Islands in the City: West Indian Migration to New York*, ed. N. Foner. Berkeley: Univ. of California Press, pp. 81–114.

Cultural Orientation Resource Center. 2007. U.S. Refugee Program. http://www.cal.org/co/refugee/statistics/index.html.

Cumming, P. A., A. L. Enid, and L. Dimitrios. 1989. *Access, Task Force on Access to Professions and Trades in Ontario*. Toronto: Ontario Ministry of Citizenship.

Curtis, A., J. W. Mills, and M. Leitner. 2007. "Katrina and Vulnerability: The Geography of Stress." *Journal of Healthcare for the Poor and Underserved* 18: 315–30.

Cushing, B. 2004. *Location-Specific Amenities, Equilibrium, and Constraints on Location Choices*. Morgantown: Research Paper Series 204-11, West Virginia University Department of Economics.

Daenzer, P. 1993. *Regulating Class Privilege: Immigrant Servants in Canada, 1940s–1990s*. Toronto: Canadian Scholars' Press, Inc.

Dannecker, P. 2005. "Transnational Migration and the Transformation of Gender Relations: The Case of Bangladeshi Labor Migrants." *Current Sociology* 53(4): 655–74.

Dannefer, R. 2004. "National Immigrant Farming Initiative: Helping Refugees and Immigrants to Succeed as Farmers." *Refugee Reports* 25(5).

Danso, R. K. and M. R. Grant. 2000. "Access to Housing as an Adaptive Strategy for Immigrant Groups: Africans in Calgary." *Canadian Ethnic Studies* 32(3): 19–43.

Darden, J. T. 2007. "Residential Apartheid American Style." In *The Black Metropolis in the Twenty First Century*, ed. R. Bullard. Boulder: Rowman and Littlefield Publishers, pp. 67–86.

———. 2006. "The Impact of Canadian Immigration Policy on the Structure of the Black Caribbean Family in Toronto." In *Inside the Mosaic*, ed. E. Fong. Toronto: University of Toronto Press, pp. 146–68.

———. 2005. "Black Occupational Achievement in the Toronto Census Metropolitan Area: Does Race Matter?" *The Review of Black Political Economy* 33(2): 31–54.

———. 2004. *The Significance of White Supremacy in the Canadian Metropolis of Toronto*. Lewiston: The Edwin Mellon Press.

———. 2003. "Residential Segregation: The Causes and Social and Economic Consequences." In *Racial Liberalism and the Politics of Urban America*, ed. C. Stokes and T. Melendez. East Lansing: Michigan State University Press, pp. 321–44.

———. 1990. *Racial Residential Segregation and Discrimination in Housing: The Evidence from Municipalities in Three Michigan Counties (Oakland, Wayne, and Macomb), 1970–1990*. Report submitted to the City of Southfield.

———. 1987a, January–April. "Socioeconomic Status and Racial Residential Segregation: Blacks and Hispanics in Chicago." *International Journal of Comparative Sociology* XXVII(1 & 2): 1–13.

———. 1981. *The Ghetto: Readings with Interpretations*. Port Washington: Kennikat Press.

Darden, J. T. and A. Tabachneck. 1980. "Algorithm 8: Graphic and Mathematical Descriptions of Inequality, Segregation or Concentration." *Environment and Planning A* 12: 227–34.

Darden, J. T., R. Hill, J. Thomas, and R, Thomas. 1987. *Detroit: Race and Uneven Development*. Philadelphia: Temple University Press.

Darden, J. T. and S. Kamel. 2000. "Black and White Differences in Homeownership Rates in the Toronto Census Metropolitan Area: Does Race Matter?" *The Review of Black Political Economy* 28(2): 53–76.

———. 2000a. "Black Residential Segregation in the City and Suburbs of Detroit: Does Socioeconomic Status Matter?" *Journal of Urban Affairs* 22: 1–13.

———. 2000b. "Black Residential Segregation in Suburban Detroit: Empirical Testing of the Ecological Theory." *The Review of Black Political Economy* 27(3): 103–23.

Dawson, W. W. 1955. Memorandum to A. H. Brown, "Jamaican Domestics." RG 76 Volume 838 File 553-36-644, part 1, May 10.

Davidson, B. 1994. *Modern Africa: A Social and Political History*. London: Longman.

Davies, R. L. and D. S. Rogers (eds.). 1984. *Store Location and Store Assessment Research*. New York: John Wiley and Sons.

Davis, S. 1994. Transportation and Black Atlanta. *Status of Black Atlanta 1994*. Atlanta: The Southern Center for Studies in Public Policy.

De Blij, H. J. 1993. *Human Geography: Culture, Society and Space*. New York: John Wiley.

Dear, M. and J. Wolch (eds.). 1990. *The Power of Geography*. Boston: Hyman Unwin.

Department of Homeland Security. *Profiles on Legal Permanent Residents: 2006*. http://www.dhs.gov/ximgtn/statistics/data/DSLPR06c.shtm (Last accessed on March 7, 2008).

Dewan, S. 2007. "Road to New Life After Katrina is Closed to Many." *New York Times*, Vol. CLVI 954,003. Thursday, July 12, 2007: A01.

———. 2006. "Gentrification Changing Face of New Atlanta." *The New York Times*, March 11. http://www.nytimes.com/2006/03/11/national/11atlanta.html?ei=5088&en=3f1cb81bbd4f4341&ex=1299733200&partner=rssnyt&emc=rss&pagewanted=all (accessed September 28, 2007).

Diatta, M. A. and N. Mbow. 1999. "Releasing the Development Potential of Return Migration: The Case of Senegal." *International Migration* 37(1): 243–67.

Dion, K. K. and K. L. Dion. 2001. "Gender and Cultural Adaptation in Immigrant Families." *Journal of Social Issues* 57(3): 511–21.

Dion, K. L. 2001. "Immigrants' Perceptions of Housing Discrimination in Toronto: The Housing New Canadians Project." *Journal of Social Issues* 57: 523–39.

Dixon, B. 2006. "Failure of the Black Misleadership Class." *The Black Commentator*, February 9. http://www.blackcommentator.com/170/170_cover_dixon_misleadership_class.html (accessed September 28, 2007).

Djamba, Y. K. 1999. "African Immigrants in the United States: A Socio-Demographic Profile in Comparison to Native Blacks." *African and Asian Studies* 34(2): 210–15.

Dobrev, S. D., T. Kim, and M. Hannan. 2001. "Dynamics of Niche Width and Resource Partitioning." *American Journal of Sociology* 106(5): 1299–337.
Dodoo, F. N. A. 1997. "Assimilation Differences among Africans in America." *Social Forces* 76: 527–46.
Dodoo, F. N. and B. K. Takyi. 2006. "Africans in the Diaspora: Black-White Earnings Differences among America's Africans." In *The New African Diaspora in North America: Trends, Community Building and Adaptation*, ed. K. Konadu-Agyemang, B. K. Takyi and J. A. Arthur. Boulder: Lexington Books, pp. 168–88.
———. 2002. "Africans in the Diaspora: Black-White Earnings Differences among America's Africans." *Ethnic and Racial Studies* 25: 913–41.
Donsky, P. 2006a. "MARTA Reports Surplus." *Atlanta Journal Constitution*, August 1. Page B1.
Dorkoosh, S. A. 1982. "Destination Choice of Interstate Family Migrants to Selected Areas in California." *Annals of Regional Science* 16(1): 57–74.
Dovidio, J. and S. Gaertner. 1996. "Affirmative Action and Unintentional Racial Biases, and Intergroup Relations." *Journal of Social Issues* 52(4): 51–75.
Doyle, S. 2007. "Civil Circles." *The Hill Times*, January 22.
Dreamcricketusa. 2007. "USA Get a Cricket Stadium in Lauderhill, Florida." November 12, 2007. ID 7900.
Dryburgh, H. and J. Hamel. 2004. "Immigrants in Demand: Staying or Leaving?" *Canadian Social Trends*.
Du Bois, W. E. B. 1997. "The Souls of Black Folk." In *Race, Class, and Gender in a Diverse Society: A Text-Reader*, ed. Diana Kendall. Toronto: Allyn and Bacon, pp. 48–53.
Duncan, J. and D. Ley (eds.). 1993. *Place/Culture/Representation*. London: Routledge.
Dupois, A. and D. Thorns. 1996. "Meanings of Home for Older Home Owners." *Housing Studies* 11(4): 485–501.
Dyer L. M. and C. A. Ross. 2000. "Ethnic Enterprises and Their Clientele." *Journal of Small Business Management* 38(2): 48–66.
Dymski, G. A. 1995. "The Theory of Bank Redlining and Discrimination: An Exploration." *Review of Black Political Economy* 23 (Winter).
Dyson, M. E. 2006. *Come Hell or High Water: Hurricane Katrina and the Color of Disaster*. New York: Basic Civitas Books.
Dwyer, C. 1999. "Migrations and Diasporas." In *Introducing Human Geographies*, ed. P. Cloke, P. Crang and M. Goodwin. London: Arnold.
Dwyer, O. J. and J. P. Jones, III. 2000. "White Socio-Spatial Epistemology." *Social and Cultural Geography* 1: 209–22
Eagan, J. V. 2002. "Predatory Lending and Black Atlanta." In *The Status of Black Atlanta 2002*. Atlanta: The Southern Center for Studies in Public Policy Clark Atlanta University.
Easthope, H. 2004. "A Place Called Home." *Housing, Theory and Society* 21(3): 128–38.
Eastwood, J. B., R. E. Conroy, S. Naicker, P. A. West, R. C. Tutt, and J. Plange-Rhule. 2005. "Loss of Health Professionals from Sub-Saharan Africa: The Pivotal Role of the UK." *Lancet* 365(9474): 1893–900.
Ebaugh, H. R. and J. Chafetz (eds.). 2000. *Religion and the New Immigrants*. Walnut Creek, CA: Altamira Press.
Economist. 2004. "Into the Suburbs." *The Economist* 379(8366).
Eilenberg, J. 1995. "Trauma in a Rural Setting," in CME Syllabus and Proceedings Summary, 148th Meeting of the American Psychiatric Association. Washington, DC.
El-Khawas, M. A. 2004. "Brain Drain: Putting Africa between a Rock and a Hard Place." *Mediterranean Quarterly* 15(4): 37–56.
Elliott, J. and A. Fleras. 1990. "Immigration and the Canadian Ethnic Mosaic." In *Race and Ethnic Relations in Canada*, ed. P. Li. Toronto: Oxford University Press, pp. 51–76.
Emerson, M., G. Yancey, and K. Chai. 2001. "Does Race Matter in Residential Segregation? Exploring the Preferences of White Americans." *American Sociological Review* 66: 922–35.
Emling, S. 1996a. "Black Areas in City Pay Steep Rates." *Atlanta Journal-Constitution*, June 30. Page A16.
———. 1996b. "Insurance: Is It Still a White Man's Game." *Atlanta Journal-Constitution*, June 30. Page A17.

Epstein, G. S. 2008: "Herd and Network Effects in Migration Decision-Making." *Journal of Ethic and Migration Studies* 34(4): 567–83.

Erickson, M., A. Tse, and J. Wilgoten. 2005. "Katrina's Diaspora." *New York Times*, October 2, 2005.

Esses, V. M. 2007. "Prejudice in the Workplace: The Role of Bias against Visible Minorities in the Devaluation of Immigrants' Foreign-Acquired Qualifications and Credentialism." *Canadian Issues,* Spring, pp. 114–18.

European Commission (EC). 2002. *European Commission Strategy for the Implementation of Special Aid to Somalia, 2002–2007*. Brussels: European Commission.

Fairlie, R. W. 1996. "The Ethnic and Racial Character of Self Employment." *Ethnic and Racial Entrepreneurship: A Study of Historical and Contemporary Differences*. New York & London: Garland Publishing, Inc., pp. 11–47.

Farley, J. E. 1995. "Race Still Matters: The Minimal Role of Income and Housing Cost as Causes of Housing Segregation in St. Louis, 1990." *Urban Affairs Review* 31(2): 244–54.

Farley, R. 1977. "Residential Segregation in Urbanized Areas of the United States in 1970: An Analysis of Social Class and Racial Differences." *Demography* 14: 497–518.

Feagans, B. 2007. "Jamaica Connection: Play Hits Home with Immigrants: In Decatur, a Surprising Encore to a One-Woman Show at the Academy Theatre." *The Atlanta Journal-Constitution*, May 27.

Feagin, J. R. 1999. "Excluding Blacks and Others from Housing: The Foundation of White Racism." *Cityscape: A Journal of Policy Development* 4(3): 79–91.

———. 1997. "The Continuing Significance of Race: Antiblack Discrimination in Public Places." In *Race, Class, and Gender in a Diverse Society: A Text-Reader*, ed. D. Kendall. Toronto: Allyn and Bacon, pp. 366–87.

Feeley, F. 2006. "Fight AIDS as Well as the Brain Drain." *Lancet* 368(9534): 435–36.

Federal Emergency Management Agency. 2006. *Hurricane Katrina: One Year Later*. Retrieved 10/21/2006 from http:// www.fema.gov/hazard/hurricane/2005katrina/index.shtm.

Fielding, E. L. 1990, May. "Black Suburbanization in the Mid-1980s: Trends and Differentials." Paper presented at the Annual Meeting of the Population Association of America, Toronto.

Finnegan, W. 2006. "Letter from Maine New in Town." *New Yorker*. 11 December. http://www.newyorker.com/archive/2006/12/11/061211fa_fact_finnegan.

Fischer, M. and D. S. Massey. 2000. "Residential Segregation and Ethnic Enterprise in the U.S. Metro Areas." *Social Problems* 47(3): 408–24.

Fischer, M. M. and P. Nijkamp. 1987. "Spatial Labor Markets Analysis: Relevance and Scope." In *Regional Labor Markets*, ed. M. M. Fischer and P. Nijkamp. Amsterdam, The Netherlands: Elsevier, pp. 1–33.

Fischer, W. and B. Sard. 2005. *Bringing Katrina's Poorest Victims Home: Targeted Federal Assistance will be Needed to Give Neediest Evacuees Option to Return to Their Hometown*. Center on Budget and Policy Priorities, November 3, 2005.

Florida, R. 2003. "Cities and the Creative Class." *City and Community* 2(1): 3–19.

———. 2002. *The Rise of the Creative Class*. Oshkosh, Wisconsin: Basic Books.

Flynn, K. 2004. "Experience and Identity: Black Immigrant Nurses to Canada, 1950–1980." In *Sisters or Strangers: Immigrant, Ethnic, and Racialized Women in Canadian History*, ed. M. Epp, F. Iacovetta and F. Swyripa. Toronto: University of Toronto Press.

Foley, M. W. and D. R. Hoge. 2007. *Religion and the New Immigrants: How Faith Communities Form Our Newest Citizens*. Oxford University Press.

Foner, N. 2001. "Introduction: West Indian Migration in New York." In *Islands in the City: West Indian Migration to New York*, ed. N. Foner. Berkeley: University of California Press, pp. 1–22.

———. 2000. *From Ellis Island to JFK: New York's Two Great Waves of Immigration*. New Haven and New York: Yale University Press.

———. (ed.). 1999. *New Immigrants in New York*. Also, see revised and updated edition (2001). New York: Columbia University Press.

———. 1998. "Towards a Comparative Perspective on Caribbean Migration." In *Caribbean Migration: Globalized Identities*, ed. M. Chamberlain. New York: Routledge, pp. 47–60.

———. 1992. "West Indians in London and New York City: A Comparative Analysis," In *Caribbean Life in New York City: Sociocultural Dimensions*, ed. C. R. Sutton and E. N. Chaney. Staten Island: Center for Migration Studies, pp. 108–20.

———. 1987. "The Jamaicans: Race and Ethnicity among Migrants in New York City." In *New Immigrants in New York*, ed. N. Foner. New York: Columbia University Press.

Fong, E. 2006. "Residential Segregation of Visible Minority Groups in Toronto." In *Inside the Mosaic*, ed. E. Fong. Toronto: University of Toronto Press, pp. 51–75.

———. 1996. "A Comparative Perspective of Racial Residential Segregation: American and Canadian Experiences." *Sociological Quarterly* 37: 501–28.

Fong, E., and M. Gulia. 1999. "The Attainment of Neighborhood Qualities among British, Chinese, and Black Immigrants in Toronto and Vancouver." *Research in Community Sociology* 6: 123–45.

Fong, E., C. Luk, and E. Ooka. 2005. "Spatial Distribution of Suburban Ethnic Businesses." *Social Science Research* 34(1): 215–35.

Fong, E. and K. Shibuya. 2000. "Suburbanization and Home Ownership: The Spatial Assimilation Process in U.S. Metropolitan Areas." *Sociological Perspectives* 43: 137–57.

Fong, E. and R. Wilkes. 1999. "An Examination of Spatial Assimilation Model." *International Migration Review* 33: 594–620.

Fonseca, M. L. 2005. "The Changing Face of Portugal: Immigration and Ethnic Pluralism." *Canadian Diversity/Diversite Canadienne* 4: 57–62.

Fortney, J. 1972. "Immigrant Professional: A Brief Historical Survey." *International Migration Review* 6: 50–62.

Frank, A. G. 1967. *Capitalism and Underdevelopment in Latin America. Historical Studies of Chile and Brazil*. New York: Monthly Review Press.

Frazier, J. W. 2006. "Race, Ethnicity, and Place in a Changing America: A Perspective." In *Race, Ethnicity, and Place in a Changing America*, ed. J. W. Frazier and E. L. Tettey-Fio. Binghamton, NY: Global Academic Publishing, pp. 1–23.

Frazier, J. W. and R. Anderson. 2006. "People on the Move. African Americans Since the Great Migration." In *Race, Ethnicity and Place in a Changing America*, ed. J. W. Frazier and E. L. Tettey-Fio. Binghamton, NY: Global Academic Publishing, pp. 83–96.

Frazier, J. W. and E. Tettey-Fio (eds.). 2006. *Race, Ethnicity, and Place in a Changing America*. Binghamton, NY: Global Academic Publishing.

Frazier, J. W., F. M. Margai, and E. Tettey-Fio. 2003. *Race and Place. Equity Issues in Urban America*. Boulder: Westview Press.

Freeman, H. 1984. *Introduction, in Mental Health and the Environment*. H. Freeman. London: Churchill Livingstone.

Freeman, L. 2002. "Does Spatial Assimilation Work for Black Immigrants in the U.S.?" *Urban Studies* 39: 1983–2003.

Frey, W. H. 2006. *Diversity Spreads Out: Metropolitan Shifts in Hispanic, Asian, and Black Population Since 2000*. Washington, DC: The Brookings Institution.

———. 2004. *The New Great Migration: Americans Return to the South, 1965–2000*. Washington, DC: Brookings Institution.

———. 2003. *Metropolitan Magnets for International and Domestic Migrants*. Living Cities Census Series. Washington, DC: Brookings Institution.

———. 2002. *Census 2000 Reveals New Native-Born and Foreign-Born Shifts Across US: Ann Arbor, MI*. Population Studies Center at the Institute for Social Research, University of Michigan.

———. 2002. *Metro Magnets for Minorities and Whites: Melting Pots, the New Sun Belt, and the Heartland*. Research Report No. 02-496. Ann Arbor: The University of Michigan Population Studies Center.

———. 2001. *Melting Pot Suburbs: A Census 2000 Study of Suburban Diversity*. Census 2000 Series. Washington, DC: Brookings Institution.

———. 2000. *The New Great Migration: Americans Return to the South, 1965–2000*. Living Cities Census Series. Washington, DC: Brookings Institution.

———. 1996. "Immigrant and Native Migrant Magnets." *American Demographics* 18(11): 36–41.

———. 1984. "Life Course Migration of Metropolitan Whites and Blacks and the Structure of Demographic Change in Large Central Cities." *American Sociological Review* 49: 803–27.

Frey, W. H. and D. Myers. 2002. *Neighborhood Segregation in Simple-Race and Multi-Race America: A Census 2000 Study of Cities and Metropolitan Areas*. Fannie Mae Foundations Working Paper.

———. 2001. *Analysis of Census 2000*. Social Science Data Network. Available: http://www.census scope.org.

Fried, M. 1963. *Greiving for a Lost Home, in the The Urban Condition: People and Policy in the Metropolis*, ed. L. J. Duhl. New York: Basic Books, pp. 151–71.

Friedman, S., A. Singer, M. Price, and I. Cheung. 2005. "Race, Immigrants and Residence: A New Racial Geography of Washington, DC." *Geographical Review* 95(2): 210–30.

Fullilove, M. T. 2005. *Root Shock: How Tearing Up City Neighborhoods Hurts America, and What We Can Do About It*. New York: One World Press.

———. 1996. "Psychiatric Implications of Displacement: Contributions from the Psychology of Place." *American Journal of Psychiatry* 153(12): 1516–23.

Gabe, T., G. Falk, M. McCarty, and V. W. Mason. 2005. *Hurricane Katrina: Social-Demographic Characteristics of Impacted Areas*. Congressional Research Service Report for Congress (Order Code RL33141), November 4, 2005.

Galabuzi, G.-E. 2006. *Canada's Economic Apartheid: The Social Exclusion of Racialized Groups in the New Century*. Toronto: Canadian Scholars' Press.

———. 2005. "Factors Affecting the Social Economic Status of Canadian Immigrants in the New Millennium." *Canadian Issues*, Spring, pp. 53–57.

Galligano, K. and J. W. Frazier. 2006. "Latinos in New York City: Ethnic Diversity, Changing Settlement Patterns, and Settlement Experiences." In *Race, Ethnicity and Place in a Changing America*, ed. J. W. Frazier and E. L. Tettey-Fio. Binghamton, NY: Global Academic Publishing, pp. 199–207.

Galster, G. 1992. "Research on Discrimination in Housing and Mortgage Markets: Assessments and Future Directions." *Housing Policy Debate* 3: 639–83.

Gavshon, A. 1981. *Crisis in Africa: Battleground of East and West*. New York: Penguin Books.

Georgia Stand-Up. 2007. *The Beltline and Rising Home Prices: Residential Appreciation Near the Beltline Tax Allocation District and Policy Recommendations to Minimize Displacement*. Atlanta: Georgia Stand-Up, September.

Geospatial and Statistical Data Center, University of Virginia Library, The. 1994. County Files, http://fisher.lib.virginia. edu/collections/stats/ccdb/county94.html#a.

Geschwender, J. and N. Guppy. 1995. "Ethnicity, Educational Attainment and Earned Income among Canadian-Born Men and Women." *Canadian Ethnic Studies* 27(1): 67–84.

Ghosh, A. and S. L. McLafferty, 1987. *Location Strategies for Retail and Service Firms*. Lexington and Toronto: Lexington Books: D.C. Heath and Company.

Gilbert, L. F. 2007. Mayor of Lewiston, Maine. Interview 20 July.

Gilmore, J. 2008. "The Canadian Immigrant Labour Market in 2007." *Immigrant Labour Force Analysis Series*. Ottawa: Statistics Canada.

Glaeser, E. L., M. Kahn, and C. Chu. 2001. *Job Sprawl: Employment Location in U.S. Metropolitan Areas*. Washington, DC: The Brookings Institution, Center on Urban & Metropolitan Policy.

Global Issues. 2007. www.globalissues.org accessed December 5th.

Goldberg, A., D. Mourinbo, and U. Kulke. 1996. *Labour Market Discrimination Against Foreign Workers in Germany*. Geneva: International Labour Organization.

Goldberg, D. 1999. "Deal Kills Money for 44 Roads But 17 Others Get Go-ahead as Environmentalists Drop Suit." *Atlanta Journal-Constitution*, June 21.

———. 1998. "Polls Say Suburbanites Aren't Hostile to MARTA." *Atlanta Journal-Constitution*, June 28.

———. 1998b. "A Guiding Hand: Does Metro Atlanta Need a New Agency to Handle Growth Problems? Many Residents Say Yes, But Making it Happen Could Be Tough." *Atlanta Journal-Constitution*. July 20.

———. 1997a. "Regional Growing Pains." *Atlanta Journal-Constitution*, March 10.

———. 1997b. "Atlanta Suburbanites Thinking Regionally." *The Neighborhood Works*, November/December 1997, p. 13.

Goldberg, D. and K. Pruitt. 1999. "GRTA Occupies Hot Seat." *Atlanta Journal-Constitution,* June 4. Page A1.

Golledge, R. G. and R. J. Stimson. 1997. *Spatial Behaviour: A Geographic Perspective*. New York: The Guilford Press.

Gomez, M. A. 1998. *Exchanging Our Country Marks: The Transformation of African Identities in the Colonial and Antebellum South*. Chapel Hill: University of North Carolina Press, pp. 27 and 155.

Gonzales, J. M. 2007. "Homeless on the Rise in New Orleans: Squat in Buildings Condemned After Hurricane Katrina." *The Boston Globe*, August 19, 2007.

Gordon, A. 1998. "The New Diaspora: African Immigration to the United States." *Journal of Third World Studies* 15(1): 79–103.

Goss, J. and B. Lindquist, 1995. "Conceptualizing International Labor Migration: A Structuration Perspective." *International Migration Review* 29: 317–51.

Goss, J. D. and T. Rheinbach. 1996. "Focus groups as Alternative Research Practice." *Area* 28(2): 115–23.

Government of Canada. 2007. *Foreign Credentials Referral Office: Frequently Asked Questions*. http://www.credentials. gc.ca/faq/index.asp (accessed July 21, 2007).

———. 2005. *A Canada for All: Canada's Action Plan Against Racism*. Ottawa.

———. 2003. *Diversity Survey: Portrait of a Multicultural Society*. Catalogue No. 89-593-X1E.

Graeber, D. 2006. "Turning Modes of Production Inside Out. Or, Why Capitalism is a Transformation of Slavery." *Critique of Anthropology* 26(1): 61–85.

Graham, M. 2006. "Preserving a Honky-Tonk Culture While Attracting New Buyers." *New York Times* (10 December). Available from http://www.nytimes.com/2006/12/10/realestate/10nati.html?_r=2&ei=5070&en=46fd372d3ccea673&ex=1168059600&pagewanted=all&oref=slogin&oref=slogin (last accessed April 11, 2007).

Grant, J. N. 1973. "Black Immigrants into Nova Scotia, 1776–1815." *Journal of Negro History* 58: 253–70.

Grant, R. and P. Yankson. 2003. Accra. *Cities* 20(1): 65–74.

Gravest, P. E. 1980. "Migration and Climate." *Journal of Regional Science* 20(2): 227–37.

Greenwood, M. J. 1985. "Human Migration: Theory, Models and Empirical Studies." *Journal of Regional Science* 25: 521–44.

Grieco, E. and B. Ray. 2004. "Mexican Immigrants in the U.S. Labor Force." *Migration Information Source*. 03/01/04. Migration Policy Institute. 10/07/04 www.migrationinformation.org.

Groot, M. C. and P. Gibbson. 2007. "Diasporas as Agents of Development: Transforming Brain Drain into Brain Gain? The Dutch Example." *Development in Practice* 17(3): 445–50.

Guarnizo, L. E. 1997. "The Emergence of Transnational Social Formation and the Mirage of Return Migration among Dominican Transmigrants." *Identities* 4(2): 281–322.

Gurack, T. D. and M. M. Kritz. 2000. "The Interstate Migration of U.S. Immigrants: Individual and Contextual Determinants." *Social Forces* 78(3): 1017–39.

Gyekye, K. 1997. *Tradition and Modernity: Philosophical Reflections on the African Experience*. New York: Oxford University Press.

Haan, M. 2005. *The Decline of the Immigrant Homeownership Advantage: Life-cycle, Declining Fortunes and Changing Housing Careers in Montreal, Toronto and Vancouver, 1981–2001*. Ottawa: Statistics Canada, Business and Labour Market Analysis Division.

Haapanen M. 2000. *Expected Earnings and Interregional Migration*. University of Jyväskylä, School of Business and Economics Working Papers, 221.

Haden, D. 1999. *The Power of Place. Urban Landscapes as Public History*. Cambridge: MIT Press.

Hairston, J. B. 2004. Express Buses Revved Up for Rollout. *Atlanta Journal-Constitution*, June 7.

Halter, M. 1993. *Between Race and Ethnicity: Cape Verdean American Immigrants, 1860–1965*. Urbana: University of Illinois Press.

Hamilton, J. 1990/91. "Exile in a Cold Land: Montreal's Haitian Community Faces a Double Barrier of Prejudice." *Canadian Geographic,* December/January: 34–42.

Hardwick, S. W. 2006. "The Geography of Whiteness: Russian and Ukrainian 'Coalitions of Color' in the Pacific Northwest." In *Race, Ethnicity and Place in a Changing America*, ed. J. W. Frazier and E. L. Tettey-Fio. Binghamton, NY: Global Academic Publishing, pp. 329–38.

Hardwick, S. W. and J. E. Meacham. 2005. "Heterolocalism, Networks of Ethnicity, and Refugee Communities in the Pacific Northwest: The Portland Story." *The Professional Geographer* 57: 539–57.

Hardy, Heck, Moore, & Myers, Inc. 2000. *City of Austin, Texas. Historic Resources Survey of East Austin.* Austin History Center, Austin, Texas, September 2000: 65.

Harris, J. (ed.). 1982. *Global Dimensions of the African Diaspora*. Howard University Press.

Harris, L. 2007a. "Roll Out the Red List: Changes Would Smooth Ride for MARTA, a New GM." *The Atlanta Journal-Constitution*, September 7.

———. 2007b. "Stuck in Traffic, Waiting on Answers: Despite Some Progress." *The Atlanta Journal-Constitution*, September.

Hart, A. 2007a. "'Grand Slam' Hire for Transit: MARTA Board Votes to Bring in Beverly Scott, CEO of Sacramento Regional Transit District, as General Manager." *The Atlanta Journal-Constitution*, September 11.

———. 2007b. "Advocates Fear Beltline Funding Cut." *The Atlanta Journal-Constitution*. August 7.

Hart, D. M. 2006. "From Brain Drain to Mutual Gain." *Issues in Science and Technology* 23(1): 53–62.

Hart, J. F. 1995. "Reading the Landscape." In *Landscape in America*, ed. G. F. Thompson. Austin: University of Texas Press, pp. 23–42.

Hass, H. 2006. "Migration, Remittances and Regional Development in South Morocco." *Geoforum* 37: 565–80.

Hawkins, F. 1988. "Multiculturalism in Two Countries: The Canadian and Australian Experience." *Journal of Canadian Studies* 17: 64–80.

Hayden, D. 1995. *The Power of Place: Urban Landscapes as Public History*. Cambridge, MA: The MIT Press.

Head, W. 1975. *The Black Presence in the Canadian Mosaic: Perceptions of Ethnic and Racial Discrimination*. Toronto: Ontario Human Rights Commission.

Heering, L., R. van der Erf, and L. van Wissen. 2004. "The Role Family Networks and Migration Culture in the Continuation of Moroccan Emigration: A Gender Perspective." *Journal of Ethnic and Migration Studies* 30(2): 323–37.

Hempstead, K. 2007. "Mobility of the Foreign-Born Population in The United States, 1995–2000: The Role of Gateway States." *International Migration Review* 41(2): 466–79.

Henry, F. 1999. "Two Studies of Racial Discrimination in Employment." In *Social Inequality in Canada: Patterns, Problems and Policies* (3rd ed.), ed. J. Curtis, E. Grabb and N. Guppy. Toronto: Prentice-Hall, pp. 226–35.

———. 1994. *The Caribbean Diaspora in Toronto: Learning to Live with Racism*. Toronto: University of Toronto Press.

Henry, F. and E. Ginzberg. 1985. *Who Gets the Work? A Test of Racial Discrimination in Employment*. Toronto: The Urban Alliance on Race Relations and the Social Planning Council of Metropolitan Toronto.

Hermanu, E. 2006. "Migration as a Family Business: The Role of Personal Networks in the Mobility Phase of Migration." *International Migration* 44(4): 191–230.

Hiebert, D. 2000. "Immigration and the Changing Canadian City." *Canadian Geographer* 44: 25–43.

Hill, D. 1960. *Negroes in Toronto: A Sociological Study of a Minority Group*. Unpublished Ph.D. dissertation. University of Toronto.

Hill, R. C. 1974. "Separate and Unequal: Governmental Inequality in the Metropolis." *American Political Science Review* 68: 1557–68.

Hirst P. and G. Thompson. 1996. *Globalization in Question. The International Economy and the Possibilities of Governance*. Cambridge: Polity Press.

Hobfoll, S. E., C. A. Dunahoo, and J. Monnier. 1995. "Conservation of Resources and Traumatic Stress." In J. R. Freedy and S. E. Hobfoll. *Traumatic Stress: From Theory to Practice*. New York: Plenum Press, pp. 29–47.

Hoelscher, S. 2003. "Making Place, Making Race: Performances of Whiteness in the Jim Crow South." *Annals of the Association of American Geographers* 93: 657–86.

Hollis, J. 2007. "MARTA Takes Over Clayton Transit Service." *The Atlanta Journal-Constitution*, October 4.

Holzer, H. and D. Neumark. 2000. "Assessing Affirmative Action." *Journal of Economic Literature* 38: 483–568.

Homeland Security. 2006. *Yearbook of Immigration Statistics: 2006*. www.dhs.gov/ximgtn/statistics/publications/YrBk06RA.shtm.

Hoogvelt, A. 2006. "Globalization and Post-modern Imperialism." *Globalization* 3(2): 159–74.

Hoskin, M. 1991. *New Immigrants and Democratic Society*. New York: Praeger.

Huffman, A. 2004. *Mississippin in Africa: The Saga of Slaves of Prospect Hill Plantation and their Legacy in Liberia Today*. New York, NY: Gotham Books, p. 159.

Hugo, G. 2006. "Population Geography." *Progress in Human Geography* 30(4): 513–23.

Hulchanski, J. D. 2007. *The Three Cities within Toronto: Income, Polarization among Toronto Neighborhoods, 1970–2000*. Toronto: University of Toronto Centre for Urban and Community Studies, Research Bulletin.

———. 2001. *A Tale of Two Canadas: Homeowners Getting Richer, Renters Getting Poorer*. Toronto: University of Toronto, Centre for Urban and Community Studies.

Hulchanski, J. D. and M. Shapcott (eds.). 2004. *Finding Room: Policy Options for a Canadian Rental Housing Strategy*. Toronto: Centre for Urban and Community Studies.

———. 2004. "Introduction: Finding Room in the Housing System for All Canadians." In *Finding Room: Policy Options for a Canadian Rental Housing Market*, ed. J. D. Hulchanski and M. Shapcott. Toronto: Centre for Urban and Community Studies, University of Toronto, pp. 3–12.

Humphrey, D. and W. W. Crawford. 1985. *Austin: An Illustrated History*. Austin, TX: Windsor Publications.

Ibrahim, H. 2007. Leader of Somali women farmers. Interview. 19 July.

IOE, Colectivo. 1996. "Discrimination Against Moroccan Workers in Access to Employment." In *Labour Market Discrimination Against Migrant Workers in Spain*, ed. IOE, Colectivo and R. M. Rerez. Geneva: International Labour Office.

In Motion: The African American Migration Experience: http://www.inmotionaame.org/migrations/

Institute for Cultural Partnerships. 1997. *A Profile of New Refugee Arrivals: The Rer Brava and Shangamas Tunnis from Somalia*. www.culturalpartnerships.org/ productspub/tunnisprofile.asp. 25 May.

International Labour Organization. 1997. "Combating Discrimination Against (Im) Migrant Workers and Ethnic Minorities in the World of Work." *Information Bulletin*, No. 4, May. Geneva.

Isajiw, W. W., A. Sev'er, and L. Dreidger. 1993. "Ethnic Identity and Social Mobility: A Test of the 'Drawback Model.'" *Canadian Journal of Sociology* 18(2): 177–96.

Itzingsohn, J. 2000. "Immigration and the Boundaries of Citizenship: The Institutes of Immigrants Political Transnationalism." *International Migration Review* 34: 1116–54.

Iwarere, S. 2004. "D.C. Based Center Reaches Out to African Immigrants." *Washington Informer* 40(41).

Jackson, P., ed. 1987. *Race and Racism: Essays in Social Geography*. London: Allen & Unwin.

Jargowsky, P. A. 2003. *Stunning Progress, Hidden Problems: The Dramatic Decline of Concentrated Poverty in the 1990s*. Washington, DC: The Brookings Institution.

Johnson, P. J. 1988. "The Impact of Ethnic Communities on the Employment of South-east Asian Refugees." *Amerasia* 14(1): 1–22.

Johnston, R., M. Poulsen, and J. Forrest. 2007. "The Geography of Ethnic Residential Segregation: A Comparative Study of Five Countries." *Annals of the Association of American Geographers* 97(4): 713–38.

Jokisch, B. and J. Pribilsky. 2002. "The Panic to Leave: Economic Crisis and the 'New Emigration' from Ecuador." *International Migration* 40(4): 75–99.

Jones, K. and J. Simmons, 1987. *Location, Location, Location. Analyzing The Retail Environment*. Toronto: Methuen.

Jones. T. A. 2007. *Jamaican Immigrants in the United States and Canada: Race, Transnationalism, and Social Capital*. New York: LFB Scholarly.

Justus, M. 2004. "Immigrants in Canada's Cities." In *Our Diverse Cities*, ed. C. Andrew. Ottawa: Metropolis Institute.

Kaniasty, P. and F. Norris. 1999. "The Experience of Disaster: Individuals and Communities Sharing Trauma." In *Response to Disaster: Psychosocial, Community and Ecological Approaches*, ed. R. Gist and B. Lubin. Philadelphia, PA: Bruner/Mazel.

Kantrowitz, N. 1973. *Ethnic and Racial Segregation in the New York Metropolis: Residential Patterns Among White Ethnic Groups, Blacks, and Puerto Ricans*. New York: Praeger Publishers.

Kaplan, D. H. and K. Woodhouse. 2004. "Research in Ethnic Segregation I: Causal Factors." *Urban Geography* 26: 579–85.

Karenga, M. 1993. *Introduction to Black World Studies*. The University of Sankore Press.

Kasadra, J. D. 1993. "Urban Industrial Transition and the Underclass." In *The Ghetto Underclass*, ed. J. Wilson. Sage Publications, pp. 43–64.

Kasinitz, P. 2001. "Invisible No More? West Indian Americans in the Social Scientific Immigration." In *Islands in the City: West Indian Migration to New York*, ed. N. Foner, pp. 257–75.

Kasozi, A. B. K. 1989. *The Integration of Black African Immigrants in Canadian Society*. Toronto: Canadian-African Newcomer Aid Centre of Toronto.

Kazemipur, A. and S. S. Halli. 2003. "Poverty Experiences of Immigrants: Some Reflections." *Canadian Issues* April: 18–20.

———. 2000. *The New Poverty in Canada: Ethnic Groups and Ghetto Neighbourhoods*. Toronto: Thompson Educational.

———. 1997. "Plight of Immigrants: The Spatial Concentration of Poverty in Canada." *Canadian Journal of Regional Science* 20:1(2): 11–28.

Kelley, K., B. Clark, V. Brown, and J. Sitzia. 2003. "Good Practice in the Conduct and Reporting of Survey Research." *International Journal for Quality in Health Care* 15: 261–66.

Kennedy, D. O. 1996. "Can We Still Afford to be a Nation of Immigrants?" *The Atlantic Monthly* November (56): 52–68.

Kent, M. M. 2007. "Immigration and America's Black Population." *Population Bulletin*, 62(4): Washington: Population Reference Bureau, December, pp. 4–5.

Kessler, R. 2006. *Overview of Baseline Survey Results: The Katrina Community Advisory Group*. Harvard University School of Medicine, August 29, 2006. www.hurrianekatrina.med.harvard.edu.

King, M. 2006. "Racial Shifts Speak Volumes and Metro Atlanta Will Have to Listen." *Atlanta Journal-Constitution*, March 9: Page A15.

King, R. and H. O'Connor. 1996. "Migration and Gender: Irish Women in Leicester." *Geography* 81(4): 311–25.

Kitchenham, B. and S. L. Pfleeger. 2002. "Principles of Survey Research, Part 4: Questionnaire Evaluation." *Software Engineering Notes* 27(3): 20–23.

Knowles, V. 1992. *Strangers at the Gate: Canadian Immigration and Immigration Policy, 1940–1990*. Toronto: Dundurn Press.

Kobayashi, A. and L. Peake. 2000. "Racism Out of Place: Thoughts on Whiteness and an Antiracist Geography in the New Millennium," *Annals of the Association of American Geographers* 90: 392–403.

Konadu-Agyemang, K. 1999. "Characteristics and Migration Experience of Africans in Canada with Specific Reference to Ghanaians in Greater Toronto." *The Canadian Geographer* 43(4): 400–414.

Konadu-Agyemang, K., B. Takyi, and J. A. Arthur (eds.). 2006. *The New African Diaspora in North America: Trends, Community Building and Adaptation*. Lexington Books.

Konadu-Agyemang, K. and B. K. Takyi. 2006. "An Overview of African Immigration to the U.S. and Canada." In *The New African Diaspora in North America: Trends, Community Building and Adaptation*, ed. K. Konadu-Agyemang, B. K. Takyi and J. A. Arthur. Lexington Books, pp. 2–12.

Krahn, H. J. G. S. and Lowe. 1998. *Work, Industry, and Canadian Society*. Scarborough, ON: ITP Nelson.

Kraly, E. P. and K. VanValkenburg. 2003. "Refugee Resettlement in Utica, New York: Opportunities and Issues for Community Development." In *Multicultural Geographies. The Changing Racial/Ethnic Patterns of the United States*, ed. J. W. Frazier and F. M. Margai. Binghamton, NY: Global Academic Publishing, pp. 125–48.

Kupfer, L., K. Hofman, R. Jarawan, J. McDermott, and K. Bridbord. 2004. "Strategies to Discourage Brain Drain." *Bulletin of the World Health Organization*. 82(8): 616–19.

Kwakye-Nuako, K. 2006. "Still Praisin' God in a New Land: African Immigrant Christianity in North America." In *The New African Diaspora in North America: Trends, Community Building and Adaptation*, ed. K. Konadu-Agyemang, B. K. Takyi and J. A. Arthur. Lanham, MD: Lexington Books, pp. 121–39.

Laccetti-Meyer, S. 1998. "Where Should MARTA Go Next." *Atlanta Journal-Constitution*, December 5. Page A18.

Lack, P. 1981. "Slavery and Vigilantism in Austin, Texas, 1840–1860." *Southwestern Historical Quarterly* 85 (July).

Laguerre, M. 1999. *Minoritized Space: An Inquiry into the Spatial Order of Things*. Berkeley: Institute of Governmental Studies Press.

Laitin, D. D. and S. S. Samatar. 1987. *Somalia: Nation in Search of a State*. Boulder, CO: Westview Press.

Lampkin, L. 1985. "Visible Minorities in Canada." In *Research Studies of the Commission on Equality of Employment*, ed. R. Abell. Ottawa: Supply and Services Canada.

Landry, B. 1987. *The New Black Middle Class*. Berkeley: University of California Press.

Ledford, J. 1999. "Beating Traffic Woes by Moving to Town." *Atlanta Journal-Constitution*, February 5.

Lee, D. O. 1995a. "Koreantown and Korean Small Firms in Los Angeles: Locating in the Ethnic Neighborhoods." *Professional Geographer* 47: 184–96.

———. 1995b. "Responses to Spatial Rigidity in Urban Transformation: Korean Business Experience in Los Angeles." *International Journal of Urban and Regional Research* 19: 41–54.

Lee, E. S. 1966. "A Theory of Migration." *Demography* 3: 47–57.

Lee, S. 2006. *When the Levees Broke: A Requiem in Four Acts*. New York: HBO Documentaries.

Leighton, A. H. 1959. "My Name is Legion: Foundations for a Theory of Man in Relation to Culture." *The Stirling County Study of Psychiatric Disorder and Sociocultural Environment*, Vol. 1. New York: Basic Books.

Leinberger, C. 1998. "The Metropolis Observed." *Urban Land* 57 (October): 28–33.

Ley, D. 1983. *A Social Geography of the City*. Harper and Row.

Ley, D. and H. Smith 1997. *Is There an Immigrant "Underclass" in Canadian Cities?* Vancouver: Vancouver Centre of Excellence, Research on Immigration and Integration in the Metropolis (Working Paper Series #97-08).

Levin, A. 2006. "New Orleans Sees Its Worst Violence Since Pre-Katrina." *USA Today*, June 19, 2006. Downloaded from http://www.usatoday.com/news/nation/2006-06-18-new-orleans-murder_x.htm.

Levinson, D. and M. Ember. 1997. "Ethiopians and Eritreans." In *American Immigrant Cultures: Builders of a Nation*, ed. D. Levinson and M. Ember. New York: Simon and Schuster Macmillan. Volume I, pp. 263–69.

Levy, L. F. 2003. "The First World's Role in the Third World Brain Drain." *British Medical Journal* 327(7407): 170.

Lewis, J. 1997. Foreword. In *Just Transportation*, ed. R. D. Bullard and G. S. Johnson. Gabriola Island, BC: New Society Publishers, pp. xi–xii.

Lewiston Public Library. 2004. Marsden Hartley Cultural Center. 21 May. Visioning Forum Report. http://www.lplonline.org/cultural/mhccvision.html.

Li, P. 1998. "The Market Value and Social Value of Race." In *Racism and Social Inequality in Canada: Concepts, Controversies and Strategies of Resistance*, ed. V. Satzewich. Toronto: Thompson Educational, pp. 115–30.

Lian, J. Z. and D. R. Matthews. 1998. "Does the Vertical Mosaic Still Exist?" *The Canadian Review of Sociology and Anthropology* 35: 461–81.

Liaw, K. and W. H. Frey. 2003. "Location of Adult Children as an Attraction for Black and White Elderly Return and Onward Migrants in the United States: Application of a Three-Level Nested Logit Model with Census Data." *Mathematical Population Studies* 10: 75–98.

———. 1998. "Destination Choices of 1985–90 Young Immigrants to the United States: Importance of Race, Education Attainment, and Labor Force." *International Journal of Population Geography* 4: 49–61.

Lieberson, S. 1980. *A Piece of the Pie: Black and White Immigrants Since 1880*. Berkeley: University of California Press.

Liebkind, K. 1996. "Acculturation and Stress: Vietnamese Refugees in Finland." *Journal of Cross-cultural Psychology* 27(2): 161–80.

Light, I. 2004. "Immigration and Ethnic Economies in Giant Cities." *UNESCO*: 385–98.

———. 1984. "Beyond the Ethnic Enclave Economy." *Social Problems* 41: 65–80.

Light, I. and S. Gould. 2000. *Ethnic Economies*. Academic Press: New York.

Listokin, D. and B. Listokin. 2001. "Asian Americans for Equality: A Case Study of Strategies for Expanding Immigrant Homeownership." *Housing Policy Debate* 12: 47–75.

Liu, B. 1975. "Quality of Life: Concept, Measure and Results." *The American Journal of Economics and Sociology* 34(1): 1–14.

Liu, B., T. Mulvey, and C. Hsieh. 1986. "Effects of Educational Expenditures on Regional Inequality in the Social Quality of Life." *American Journal of Economics and Sociology* 45(2): 131–44.

Lobo, A. P. 2006. "Unintended Consequences: Liberalized U.S. Immigration Law and the African Brain Drain." In *The New African Diaspora in North America: Trends, Community Building and Adaptation*, ed. K. Konadu-Agyemang, B. K. Takyi and J. A. Arthur. Lexington Books, pp. 189–208.

———. 2002. "The Impact of Hispanic Growth on the Racial Ethnic Composition of New York City Neighborhoods." *Urban Affairs Review* 37(5): 703.

Lobo, A. P. and J. J. Salvo. 2000. "The Role of Nativity and Ethnicity in the Residential Settlement Patterns of Blacks in NYC, 1970–1990," In *Immigration Today: Pastoral and Research Challenges*, p. 115, ed. L. F. Tomasi and M. G. Powers. New York: Center for Migration Studies, pp. 109–36. City of New York, Department of Planning.

Logan, B. I. 1999. "The Reserve Transfer of Technology from Sub-Saharan Africa: The Case of Zimbabwe." *International Migration* 37(2): 437–64.

Logan, J. R. 2006. "Who Are the Other U.S. Born Blacks? In Contemporary African and Caribbean Immigrants in the United States," In *The Other U.S. Born Blacks: Contemporary African and Caribbean Immigrants in the United States*, ed. Y. Shaw-Taylor and S. A. Tuch. New York: Rowman & Littlefield Publishers, Inc., pp. 49–68.

Logan, J., R. D. Alba, and S. Leung. 1996. "Minority Access to White Suburbs: A Multi-regional Companion." *Social Forces* 74: 851–81.

Logan, J. and G. Deane. 2003. *Black Diversity in Metropolitan America*. Albany, NY: Lewis Mumford Center. http://mumford1.dyndns.org/cen2000/BlackWhite/BlackDiversityReport/Black_Diversity_final.pdf

Logan, J. R. and M. Schneider. 1984. "Racial Segregation and Racial Change in American Suburbs, 1970–1980." *American Journal of Sociology* 89: 874–88.

Lohrentz, K. P. 2004. *Peoples of the Horn in the New African Diaspora: Eritrean, Ethiopian, Somali, and Sudanese Émigrés in the United States and Canada, A Bibliographic Survey*. University of Kansas Libraries. Presented to the Kansas African Studies Center, Fall 2004 Seminar, 14 September. http://www.kasc.ku.edu/~kasc/resources/ Publications_Transcriptions/.

Long, L. 1988. *Migration and Residential Mobility in the United States*. New York: Russell Sage Foundation.

Longbrake, D. B. and W. W. Nichols, Jr. 1976. *Sunshine and Shadows in Metropolitan Miami*. Cambridge, MA: Ballinger Publishing Company, pp. 18–19.

Lopez, G., J. G. Smith, and R. Pagnucco. 1995. "The Global Tide." *The Bulletin of Atomic Scientists*, July/August: 33–39.

Low, S. M. and I. Altman (eds.). 1992. *Place Attachment: Human Behavior and the Environment*. New York: Plenum.

Ludden, J. 2005. "Bantu Refugees Adjust to New Lives in America." *NPR All Things Considered*, March 20, 2005. www.npr.org/templates/story/story.php?storyId=4542221Maine.gov.2007. Office of Multicultural Affairs. www.maine.gov/dhhs/oma/.

MacAulay, L. 1998. Letter to the Right Honourable Romeo Leblanc, Governor General of Canada Presenting the Tenth Annual Report of Parliament on the Employment Equity Act.

Machado, F. L. 1994. "Luso-Africanos Nas Margens da Etnicidade." *Sociologia — Problemas e Praticas* 16: 111–34.

Mahler, S. J. 1999. "Engendering Transnational Migration: A Case Study of Salvadorans." *American Behavioral Scientist* 42(4): 690–719.

MaineToday.com. 2002. Mayor Raymond's letter to the Somali community. Blethen Maine Newspapers. http://pressherald.mainetoday.com/news/immigration/ 021005raymondletter.shtml.

Maraj, D. I. 1996. *Non-Accreditation: Its Impact on Foreign Educated Immigrant Professionals*. Unpublished master's thesis. University of Toronto, Toronto, Canada.

Martin, P. and E. Midgley. 2003. "Immigration: Shaping and Reshaping America." *Population Bulletin* 61(4): 5.

Markon, J. 2006. "Hunch Unravels Immigrant Wedding Scam." *Washington Post*, November 13th, Section A01.

Mason, C. and J. Preston. 2007. "Canada's Policy on Immigrants Brings Backlog." *New York Times*, June 27.

Massey, D. S. (ed.). 2008. *New Faces in New Places: The Changing Geography of American Immigration*. New York: Russell Sage Foundation.

Massey, D. 1999. "Why Does Immigration Occur? A Theoretical Synthesis." In *The Handbook of International Migration*, ed. P. Kasinitz and J. DeWind. New York: Russell Sage Foundation.

Massey, D. S. 1994. "An Evaluation of International Migration Theory: The North American Case." *Population and Development Review* 20: 699–751.

Massey, D. S. and C. Capoferro. 2008. "The Geography Diversification of American Immigration." In *New Faces in New Places*, ed. D. S. Massey. New York: Russell Sage Foundation.

———. 1993. In *Politics and Space/Time, in Place and the Politics of Identity*, ed. M. Keith and S. Pile. London: Routledge, pp. 141–61.

Massey, D., G. A. Condran, and N. Denton. 1987. "The Effect of Residential Segregation on Black Social and Economic Well-being." *Social Forces* 66: 29–57.

Massey, D. and N. Denton. 1993. *American Apartheid: Segregation and the Making of the Underclass*. Cambridge: Harvard University Press.

———. 1985. "Spatial Assimilation as a Socioeconomic Outcome." *American Sociological Review* 50: 94–106.

Massey, D. and B. Mullen. 1984. "Process of Hispanic and Black Spatial Assimilation." *American Journal of Sociology* 89: 836–73.

Mata, F. 1994. *The Non-Accreditation of Immigrant Professionals in Canada: Societal Impacts, Barriers and Present Policy Initiatives*. Ottawa: Citizenship and Immigration Canada.

Matthews, K. and A. Adams. 2007. "Gentrification Cuts with a Double Edge East of I-35." *The Daily Texan*, January 4.

Mayfield, M. 2005. Written statement. Washington, DC: National Hurricane Center.

McCosh, J. 2001. "MARTA Calls on Marketers for Image Air: Can Soft Drinks Fill Empty Seats?" *Atlanta Journal-Constitution*, February 11. Page A1.

McDade, K. 1988. "Barriers to Recognition of the Credentials of Immigrants in Canada." *Studies in Social Policy*. Ottawa: Institute for Research on Public Policy, April.

McHugh, K. E. 1988. "Determinants of Black Interstate Migration, 1965–70 and 1975–80." *Annals of Regional Science* 22: 36–48.

———. 1987. "Black Migration Reversal in the United States." *Geographical Review* 77(2): 171–82.

McHugh, K. E., T. D. Hogan, and S. K. Happel. 1995. "Multiple Residence and Cyclical Migration: A Life Course Perspective." *The Professional Geographer* 47(3): 251–67.

Mendez, P., D. Hiebert, and E. Wyly. 2006. "Landing at Home: Insights on Immigration and Metropolitan Housing Markets for a Longitudinal Survey of Immigrants to Canada." *Canadian Journal of Urban Research* 15: 82–104.

Menkhaus, K. 2003. "Bantu Ethnic Identities in Somalia." *Annales d'Ethiope* 19 (Fall): 323–39.

Mensah, J. 2005. "On the Ethno-Cultural Heterogeneity of Blacks in our EthniCities." *Canadian Issues*, Spring, pp. 72–77.

———. 2002. *Black Canadians: History, Experiences, and Social Conditions*. Halifax: Fernwood Publishing.

Metropolitan Atlanta Rapid Transit Authority. 2005. *Fiscal Year Annual Report: Metropolitan Atlanta Rapid Transit Authority*. Atlanta: MARTA.

———. 1999. *5th Annual Quality of Service Survey*. Atlanta: MARTA.

———. 1996. *Chronology*. Atlanta: MARTA.

Miami Herald.com. 2007. "USA Gets a Cricket Stadium in Lauderhill, Florida." Last accessed October 11, 2007. ID 7900.

———. 2001. "West Indians Lead Black Growth." November 21, p. 1A.

Michalos, A. C. 1997. "Migration and the Quality of Life: A Review Essay." *Social Indicators Research* 39: 121–66.

Michalos, A. C., P. M. Hatch, D. Hemingway, L. Lavallee, A. Hogan, and B. Christensen. 2007. "Health and Quality of Life of Older People: A Replication after Six Years." *Social Indicators Research* 84: 127–58.

Milan A. and K. Tran. 2004. "Blacks in Canada: A Long History." In *Statistics Canada. Canadian Social Trends,* Catalogue No. 11-008, pp. 2–7.

Miraftab, F. 2000. "Sheltering Refugees: The Housing Experience of Refugees in Metropolitan Vancouver, Canada." *Canadian Journal of Urban Research* 9: 42–63.

Mitchell, D. 1996. *The Lie of the Land: Migrant Workers and the California Landscape*. Minneapolis: The University of Minnesota Press.

Mock, J. 1993. "We Have Always Lived Under the Castle: Historical Symbols and the Maintenance of Meaning." In *The Cultural Meaning of Urban Space*, ed. R. Rotenburg and G. McDonogh. Westport, CT: Bergin, pp. 53–74.

Model, S. 2001. "Where New York's West Indians Work." In *Islands in the City*, ed. N. Foner, pp. 52–80.

Mohan, G. 2006. "Embedded Cosmopolitanism and the Politics of Obligation: The Ghanaian Diaspora and Development." *Environment and Planning A* 38(5): 867–83.

Monsho, K. 2004. "From East Austin to East End, Gentrification in Motion." *The Good Life Magazine*; available from http://www.goodlifemag.com/archives/2004/11-04/11-04_east.htm (last accessed October 11, 2007).

Morgan, W. J., A. Sives, and S. Appleton. 2005. "Managing the International Recruitment of Health Workers and Teachers: Do the Commonwealth Agreements Provide an Answer?" *Round Table* 94(379): 225–38.

Mott, R. E. 2006. *Pathways and Destinations: African Refugees in the U.S*. Dissertation: The Ohio State University.

Mullan, F. 2007. "Doctors and Soccer Players — African Professionals on the Move." *The New England Journal of Medicine* 356: 440–43.

Murdie, R. 1994. "Blacks in Near Ghettos? Black Visible Minority Population Metropolitan Toronto Housing Authority Public Housing Units." *Housing Studies* 9: 435–57. Chamber of Architects of Turkey.

Murdie, R. A. 2003. "Housing Affordability and Toronto's Rental Market: Perspectives from the Housing Careers of Jamaican, Polish and Somali Newcomers." *Housing, Theory and Society* 20: 183–96.

———. 2002. "The Housing Careers of Polish and Somali Newcomers in Toronto's Rental Market." *Housing Studies* 17: 423–43.

Murdie, R. A., A. Chambon, J. D. Hulchanski, and C. Teixeira. 1996. "Housing Issues Facing Immigrants and Refugees in Greater Toronto: Initial Findings from the Jamaican, Polish and Somali Communities." In *Housing Question of the Others*, ed. E. M. Komut. Ankara: Chamber of Architects of Turkey, pp. 179–90.

Murdie, R. A., and C. Teixeira. 2003. "Towards a Comfortable Neighborhood and Appropriate Housing: Immigrant Experiences in Toronto." In *The World in a City*, ed. P. Anisef and M. Lanphier. Toronto: University of Toronto Press, pp. 132–91.

Myles, J., and F. Hou. 2003. *Neighborhood Attainment and Residential Segregation Among Toronto's Visible Minorites*. Ottawa: Statistics Canada. Retrieved 7/29/07 from http://www.statcan.ca/bsolc/english/bsolc?catno=11F0019M 2003206.

Nadeau, P. 2007. Deputy City Administrator, Lewiston, Maine. Interview. 20 July.

———. 2005. "The Somalis of Lewiston: Effects of Rapid Immigration to Homogeneous Maine City." *The Southern Maine Review* 1(Spring): 5–46.

———. 2003. *The Somalis of Lewiston: Community Impacts of Rapid Immigrant Movement into a Small Homogeneous Maine City*. Brown University Center for the Study of Race and Ethnicity, Draft Paper, August 14.

———. 2002. Report to Governor Angus King: New Somali arrivals and other issues relative to refugee/secondary migrants/immigrants and cultural diversity in the city of Lewiston, May 9. www.ci.lewiston.me. us/cultures/files/ReportToTheGovernor5-9-02.pdf.

narbosa.com. 2007. July 17.

National Somali Bantu Project. 2007. A profile of Somali refugees in the United States: Introduction. 2006. http://paa.2006.princeton.edu. http://www.cal.org/co/bantu/sbhist.html.

N'Diaye, D. B. and G. N'Diaye. 2006. "Creating the Vertical Village: Senegalese Traditions of Immigration and Transnational Cultural Life." In *The New African Diaspora in North America: Trends, Community Building and Adaptation*, ed. K. Konadu-Agyemang, B. K. Takyi and J. A. Arthur. Lexington Books, pp. 96–106.

Neckerman, K., P. Carter, and J. Lee. 1999. "Segmented Assimilation and Minority Cultures of Mobility." *Ethnic and Racial Studies* 22: 945–65.

Newburger, H. 1995. "Sources of Difference in Information Used by Black and White Housing Seekers: An Exploratory Analysis." *Urban Studies* 32: 445–70.

Newcomb, M. and P. Bentler. 1998. *Consequences of Adolescent Drug Use*. Newbury Park: Sage.

New Orleans City Council. 2006. *Depression and Suicide are Legacies of Katrina*. Retreived 7/24/2007 from http:// www.nocitycouncil.com/shownews.asp?cid=77.

Niedomysl, T. 2006. "Migration and Place Attractiveness." *Geografiska Regionstudier, NR 68,* Dissertation University Uppsala; and How Migrants with "Choices" Choose Their Destination: Towards a Conceptual Framework of Place Attractiveness in a Migration Context, *Workshop 3 — Migration, Residential Mobility, and Housing Policy*. Paper presented at the ENHR conference; "Housing in an Expanding Europe: Theory, Policy, Participation and Implementation." Ljubljana, Slovenia 2–5 July 2006.

Norris, F. 2001. *50,000 Disaster Victims Speak: An Empirical Review of the Empirical Literature, 1981–2001*. Prepared for the National Center for PTSD and the Center for Mental Health Services (SAMHSA).

Norris, F., C. M. Byrne, E. Diaz, and K. Kaniasty. 2005. *Range, Magnitude, and Duration of the Effects of Disasters on Mental Health: Review Update 2005*. Hanover, NH: Dartmouth College NCPTSD.

Norton, I. 2006. "Integration, Urban Renewal Shaped East Austin." *The Daily Texan*, December 13. Available from http://media.www.dailytexanonline.com/media/storage/paper410/news/2006/12/13/TopStories/Integration.Urban.Renewal.Shaped.East.Austin-2551308.shtml (last accessed October 13, 2007).

Novac, S., J. T. Darden, D. Hulchanski, and A. M. Seguin. 2004. "Housing Discrimination in Canada: Stakeholder Views and Research Gaps." In *Finding Room: Policy Options for a Canadian Rental Housing Market*, ed. J. D. Hulchanski and M. Shapcott. Toronto: Centre for Urban and Community Studies, University of Toronto, pp. 135–46.

———. 2002. *Housing Discrimination in Canada: The State of Knowledge*. Ottawa: Canada Mortgage and Housing Association.

Obiakor, F. E. and P. A. Grant (eds.). 2002. *Foreign-Born African Americans: Silenced Voices in the Discourse on Race*. New York: Nova Science Publishers, Inc.

Office of Refugee Resettlement. 2006. United States Department of Health and Human Services.

Office on African Affairs, Washington, DC, http://www.dc.gov/agencies/2005.

Ogmundson, R. and J. McLaughlin. 1992. "Trends in the Ethnic Origins of Canadian Elites: The Decline of the BRITS." *Canadian Review of Sociology and Anthropology* 29: 227–42.

Okome, M. O. 2006. "The Contradictions of Globalization: Causes of Contemporary African Immigration to the United States of America." In *The New African Diaspora in North America: Trends, Community Building and Adaptation*, ed. K. Konadu-Agyemang, B. K. Takyi and J. A. Arthur. Lexington Books, pp. 29–48.

Oliveira, A. and C. Teixeira. 2004. Jovens Portugueses e Luso-Descendentes no Canada: Trajectorias de Insercao em Espacos Multiculturais. Oeiras, Lisboa: Celta Editora.

Olmstead, R. E. and P. M. Bentler. 1992. "Structural Equation a New Friend?" In *Methodological Issues in Applied Social Psychology*, ed. F. B. Bryant, J. Edwards, R. S. Tindale et al. New York: Plenum, pp. 135–58.

Ontario Human Rights Commission. 1999. Annual Report 1997–1998. Toronto: A Report of the Commission.

Ontario Ministry of Citizenship and Immigration. 2007, February 1. *McGuinty Government Announces $29 Million Investment to Expand Programs Province-wide for Skilled Newcomers*. News release.

Opoku-Dapaah, E. 2006. "African Immigrants in Canada: Trends, Socio-demographic and Spatial Aspects." In *The New African Diaspora in North America: Trends, Community Building and Adapta-*

tion, ed. K. Konadu-Agyemang, B. K. Takyi and J. A. Arthur. New York: Rowman & Littlefield, pp. 69–93.

Orfield, G. 1976. "Federal Policy, Local Power, and Metropolitan Segregation." In *Public Power and the Urban Crisis*, ed. A. Shank. Boston: Holbrook Press.

Orfield, M. 2002. *American Metropolitics: The New Suburban Reality*. Washington, DC: Brookings Institution.

Ornstein, M. 2000. *Ethno-racial Inequality in the City of Toronto: An Analysis of the 1996 Census*. Toronto: Access and Equity Unit.

Orum, A. 2002. *Power, Money, and the People: The Making of Modern Austin*. Portland, OR: Resource Publications.

Ossman, S. 2004. "Studies in Serial Migration." *International Migration* 42(4): 111–21.

Ovadia, S. 2003. "The Dimensions of Racial Equality: Occupational and Residential Segregation Across Metropolitan Areas in the United States." *City and Community* 2: 313–33.

Owusu, T. 2006. "Transnationalism Among African Immigrants in North America: The Case of Ghanaians in Canada." In *The New African Diaspora in North America: Trends, Community Building and Adaptation*, ed. K. Konadu-Agyemang, B. K. Takyi and J. A. Arthur. Lexington Books, pp. 273–86.

———. 1999. "Residential Patterns and Housing Choices of Ghanaian Immigrants in Toronto." *Housing Studies* 14: 77–97.

———. 1998. "To Buy or Not to Buy: Determinants of Home Ownership Among Ghanaian Immigrants in Toronto." *Canadian Geographer* 42: 40–52.

Paasi, A. 1991. "Deconstructing Regions: Notes on the Scales of Spatial Life." *Environment and Planning* 23: 239–56.

Pachai, B. 1993. *Blacks*. Tantallon: Four East Publications.

Palm, R. 1985. "Ethnic Segmentation of Real Estate Agent Practice in the Urban Housing Market." *Annals of the Association of American Geographers* 75: 58–68.

Palmer, H. 1976. "Mosaic versus Melting Pot: Immigration and Ethnicity in Canada and the United States." *International Journal* 3: 488–528.

Pamuck, A. 2004. "Geography of Immigrant Clusters in Global Cities: A Case Study of San Francisco, 2000." *International Journal of Urban and Regional Research* 28: 287–307.

Pandit, K. and S. D. Withers (eds.). 1999. *Migration and Restructuring in the United States: A Geographical Perspective*. Lanham: Rowman and Littlefield Publishers.

Pangi, R. 2002. "After the Attack: The Psychological Consequences of Terrorism." In *Perspectives on Preparedness*, No. 9. Cambridge, MA: Kennedy School of Governance.

Park, R. E. 1967. "The Foreign Language Press and Social Progress" (originally published in 1920). In *Robert E. Park on Social Control and Collective Behavior*, ed. Ralph H Turner. Chicago, University of Chicago Press, pp. 133–44.

Patterson T. R. and R. Kelley. 2000. "Unfinished Migrations: Reflections on the African Diaspora and the Making of the Modern World." *African Studies Review* 43(1): 11–35.

Pattillo-McCoy, M. 1999. "Middle Class, Yet Black: A Review Essay." *African American Research Perspectives* 5: 25–38.

Pendered, D. 2006. "Fourishing Intown Becomes the In Place to Live and Play," *The Atlanta Journal-Constitution*, August 20, page D13.

———. 1999. "MARTA Makes Its Move." *Atlanta Journal-Constitution,* March 29.

———. 1998. "MARTA Aims to Help Shape Development." *Atlanta Journal-Constitution,* October 19.

Pessar, P. R. 1999. "Engendering Migration Studies: The Case of New Immigrants in the United States." *American Behavioral Scientist* 42(4): 577–600.

Petrykanyn, J. 1989. "Foreign Domestic Workers and Misrepresentations: New Policy, Old Practices?" *Immigration and Citizenship Bulletin* 1(8): 3.

Pew Center for People and the Press. 2005. *Two-in-Three Critical of Bush's Relief Efforts: Huge Racial Divide Over Katrina and Its Consequences*. Released September 8, 2005. Washington, DC: Pew Research Center.

Piazza, T. 2005. *Why New Orleans Matters*. New York: Regan Books.

Pierre, J. 2002. "Interrogating Blackness: Race and Identity-formation in the African Diaspora." *Transforming Anthropology* 11(1): 51–53.

Pierre, R. E. and A. Gerhart. 2005. "News of Pandemonium May Have Slowed Aid." *Washington Post*, October 5, 2005: A8.

Pincock, S. 2006. "Papua New Guinea Struggles to Reverse Health Decline." *Lancet* 368(9530): 107–8.

Planning Services Division, Broward County, Florida. 2004. No. 1.

Porter, J. 1965. *The Vertical Mosaic: An Analysis of Social Class and Power in Canada*. Toronto: University of Toronto Press.

Porter, M. and N. Haslam. 2005. "Predisplacement and Postdisplacement Factors Associated with Mental Health of Refugees and Internally Displaced: A Meta-analysis." *Journal of the American Medical Association* 294(5): 602–12.

———. 2001. "Forced Displacement in Yugoslavia: A Meta-analysis of Psychological Consequences and Their Moderators." *Journal of Traumatic Stress* 14(4): 817–33.

Portes, A. 1997. "Immigration Theory for a New Century: Some Problems and Opportunities." *International Migration Review* 31(4): 799–825.

Portes, A., P. Fernendez-Kelly, and W. Haller. 2005. "Segmented Assimilation on the Ground: The New Second Generation in Early Adulthood." *Ethnic and Racial Studies* 28(6): 1000–1040.

Portes, A. and R. G. Rumbaut. 2006. *Immigrant America. A Portrait*. Second Edition. Berkeley: Univ. of California Press.

———. 2001. *Legacies: The Story of Immigrant Second-generation*. Berkeley, CA: University of California Press.

Portes, A. and A. Stepick. 1993. *City on the Edge: The Transformation of Miami*. Berkeley, CA: University of California Press.

Portes, A. and M. Zhou. 1993. "The New Second Generation: Segmented Assimilation and its Variants Post-1965 Immigrant Youth." *The Annals of the American Academy of Political and Social Sciences* 530: 73–96.

Possick, C. 2006. "Coping with the Threat of Place Disruption by Long-term Jewish Settlers in the West Bank." *International Social Work* 49(2): 198–207.

Preston, J. and C. Jones (eds.). 1954. *American Geography Inventory and Prospect*. Syracuse, NY: Syracuse University Press.

Preston. V. and A. M. Murnaghan. 2005. "Immigration and Racialization in Canada: Geographies of Exclusion?" In *Immigration and the Intersection of Diversity*, ed. M. Siemiatycki. Ottawa: Metropolis Institute, pp. 67–71.

Pruegger, V., D. Cook, and A. Hawkesworth. 2004. "Implications of Urban Diversity for Housing," ed. C. Andrew. *Our Diverse Cities*, Number 1, Spring. Ottawa: Metropolis Institute, pp. 124–25.

Pruitt, K. 1999a. "GRTA Clears Final Legislature Hurdles." *Atlanta Journal-Constitution*, March 24.

———. 1999b. Barnes: "GRTA No Miracle Cure." April 7. Page B1.

Pulido, L. 2006. *Black, Brown, Yellow, and Left: Radical Activism in Los Angeles*. Berkeley: University of California Press.

———. 2002. "Race, Class, and Political Activism: Black, Chicana/o and Japanese American Leftists in Southern California, 1968–1978." *Antipode: A Radical Journal of Geography* 34(4): 762–88.

———. 2000. "Rethinking Environmental Racism: White Privilege and Urban Development in Southern California." *Annals of the Association of American Geographers* 90: 12–40.

Qadeer, M. A. 2004. "Ethnic Segregation in a Multicultural City: The Case of Toronto, Canada." *CERIS, Policy Matters* 6: 1–6.

Raghuram, P. 2004. "The Difference that Skill Makes: Gender, Family Migration Strategies and Regulated Labor Markets." *Journal of Ethnic and Migration Studies* 30(2): 303–21.

Rapoport, A. 1969. *House Form and Culture*. Englewood Cliffs, NJ: Prentice Hall.

Ravenstein, E. G. 1889. "The Laws of Migration." *Journal of the Royal Statistical Society* 52: 241–305.

Rawlyk, G. 1968. "The Guysborough Negroes: A Study in Isolation." *Dalhousie Review* (Spring): 24–36.

Ray, B. K. 1998. *A Comparative Study of Immigrant Housing, Neighbourhood and Social Networks in Toronto and Montreal*. Ottawa: Canada Mortgage and Housing Corporation.

Ray, B. and E. Moore. 1991. "Access to Homeownership Among Immigrant Groups in Canada." *The Canadian Review of Sociology and Anthropology* 28(1): 1–27.

Rebhun, U. and A. Raveh. 2001. "The Spatial Distribution of Quality of Life in the United States and Interstate Migration, 1965–70 and 1985–90: Application of the 'Co-Plot' Method." In *Facet Theory: Integrating Theory Construction with Data Analysis*, ed. D. Elizur. Prague: Matfypress, pp. 211–27.

Redway, A. 1992. *A Matter of Fairness: Report of the Special Committee on the Employment Equity Act*. Ottawa: Ministry of Supply and Services Canada.

Reigon, S. D. Hoyt, and G. Ohland. 2004. "The Atlanta Case Study: Lindbergh City Center." In *Transit Town: Best Practices in Transit-Oriented Development*, ed. H. Dittmar and G. Ohland. Washington, DC: Island Press.

Reisinger, M. E. 2003. "Determinants of Latino Migration to Allentown, Pa." In *Multicultural Geographies. The Changing Racial/Ethnic Patterns of the United States*, ed. J. W. Frazier and F. M. Margai. Binghamton, NY: Global Academic Publishing, pp. 171–89.

Reitz, J. 2005. *Tapping Immigrants' Skills: New Directions for Canadian Immigration Policy in the Knowledge Economy*. Montreal: Institute for Research on Public Policy. http://atwork.settlement.org/sys/atwork_library_detail.asp? doc_id=1003784 (accessed July 20, 2007).

———. 2003. "Host Societies and the Reception of Immigrants: Research Themes, Emerging Theories, and Methodological Issues." In *Host Societies and the Reception of Immigrants*, ed. J. G. Reitz. La Jolla, California: Center for Comparative Immigration Studies, University of California at San Diego, pp. 1–18.

———. 1990. "Ethnic Concentrations in Labour Markets and Their Implications for Ethnic Inequality." In *Ethnic Identity and Equality: Varieties of Experience in a Canadian City*, ed. R. Breton, et al. Toronto: University of Toronto Press, pp. 135–95.

———. 1988. "The Institutional Structure of Immigration as a Determinant of Inter-racial Competition: A Comparison of Britain and Canada." *International Migration Review* 22: 117–45.

Reitz, J., and R. Breton. 1994. *The Illusion of Difference: Realities of Ethnicity in the United States and Canada*. Toronto: C. D. Howe Institute.

Renaud, J., K. Begin, V. Ferreira, and D. Rose. 2006. "The Residential Mobility of Newcomers to Canada: The First Months." *Canadian Journal of Urban Research* 15: 79–95.

Reuters. 2005. "Troops to 'Shoot to Kill' in New Orleans." *ABC News Online*, September 2, 2005. Retrieved 8/01/07 from http://www.abc.net.au/news/newsitems/200509/s1451906.htm.

Riddell, W. R. 1920. "The Slave in Canada." *Journal of Negro History* V: 261–377.

Roberts, S. 2006. "A Shift in the Income Divide Puts Blacks Ahead of Whites." *The New York Times,* Oct. 1.

———. 2005. "More Africans Enter the U.S. Than in Days of Slavery." *New York Times*, 23rd February, www.nytimes.com.

Robertson, R. 2007. *The Top Ten Big Demographic Trends in Austin, Texas, 2007*. Available from http://www.ci. austin.tx.us/census/downloads/top_Ten_Trends2.doc (last accessed October 15).

Rodney, W. 1974. *How Europe Underdeveloped Africa*. Washington, DC: Howard University Press.

Rodriguez, C. 2003. "Study Shows U.S. Blacks Trailing Immigrants from Africa." *The Boston Globe*, February 17.

Rodriguez, N. 2004. "Workers Wanted." *Work and Occupations* 31(4): 453–73.

Rogers, A. 1968. *Matrix Analysis of Interregional Population Growth and Distribution*. Los Angeles: University of California Press.

———. 1967. "A Regression Analysis of Interregional Migration in California." *The Review of Economics and Statistics* 68: 262–67.

Rogers, A. and S. Henning. 1999. "The Internal Migration Patterns of the Foreign-Born and Native-Born Populations in the United States: 1975–80 and 1985–90." *International Migration Review* 33(2): 403–29.

Rose, D. and B. Ray. 2000. *Landed Refugee Claimants' First Three Years in Québec: Their Housing Experiences*. Montreal: CERIS — Montreal.

Rose, E. J. B. et al. 1969. *Colour and Citizenship: A Report on British Race Relations*. London: Oxford University Press.

Rose, M. 1989. *Interstate: Express Highway Politics*. Knoxville, TN: The University of Tennessee Press.

Ross-Sheriff, F. and R. E. English. 2000. Conceptualizing Displacement Lecture. Fall 2000. "Social Work with Displaced Populations, II: Refugees, Immigrants and Internally Displaced."

Ruggles, S., T. Sobek, C. Alexander, A. Firch, R. Goeken, P. K. Hall, M. King, and C. Ronnander. 2004. *Integrated Public Use Microdate Series: Version 3.0* [Machine-readable database]. Minneapolis, MN: Minnesota Population Center.

Sako, S. 2002. "Brain Drain and Africa's Development: A Reflection." *African Issues* XXX(1).

Salt, J. and J. Stein. 1997. "Migration as a Business: The Case of Trafficking." *International Migration* 35(4): 467–28.

Sampson, R. J. and W. J. Wilson. 1995. "Toward a Theory of Race, Crime and Urban Inequality." In *Crime and Inequality*, ed. J. Hagan and R. D. Peterson. Stanford: Stanford University Press, pp. 37–54.

Sanders, J. and V. Nee. 1987. "Limits of Ethnic Solidarity in the Enclave Economy." *American Sociological Review* 52(6): 745–73.

Saney, I. 1998. "The Black Nova Scotian Odyssey: A Chronology." *Race and Class* 40(1): 78–91.

Saporta, M. 2004a. "Transit 'Catch-22' is Bad for Atlanta." *Atlanta Journal-Constitution*, August 16. Page E3.

———. 2004b. "Transit Funding in Mass. Opens Eyes of Atlantans." *The Atlanta Journal-Constitution*, May 17. Page E6.

———. 2003. "Transportation Funds Must Be Shared Fairly." *Atlanta Journal-Constitution*, February 24. Page E3.

Saravia, N. G. and J. F. Miranda. 2004. "Plumbing the Brain Drain." *Bulletin of the World Health Organization* 82(8): 608–15.

Sassen, S. 2000. "The Demise of Pax Americana and the Emergence of Informalization as a System Trend." In *Informalization: Process and Structure*, ed. F. Tabak and M. A. Crichlow. Baltimore: The Johns Hopkins University Press, pp. 91–117.

———. 1991. *The Global City: New York, London, Tokyo*. Princeton, NJ: Princeton University Press.

Satorra, A. and P. M. Bentler, 1988. *Scaling Corrections for Statistics in Covariance Structure Analysis*. Los Angeles: UCLA Statistics.

Satzewich, V. 1991. *Racism and the Incorporation of Foreign Labor*. London: Routledge.

———. 1989. "Racism and Canadian Immigration Policy: The Government's View of Caribbean Migration, 1962–1966." *Canadian Ethnic Studies* 21(1): 77–97.

Saulny, S. 2006. "Legacy of the Storm: Depression and Suicide." *New York Times*, June 21.

Saunders, P. and P. Williams. 1988. "The Constitution of Home: Towards a Research Agenda." *Housing Studies* 3(2): 81–93.

SBCMAA (Somali Bantu Community Mutual Assistance Association). 2007. www.sbcmaa.org.www.ci.lewiston.me.us/news/news2004 01 06.

Schacter, J. 2001. "Why People Move: Exploring the March 2000 Current Population Survey." *Current Population Reports*, pp. 23–204.

Schill, M. H., S. Friedman, and E. Rosenbaun. 1998. "The Housing Conditions of Immigrants in New York City." *Journal of Housing Research* 9: 201–35.

Schill, M. and S. M. Wachter. 1995. "Housing Market Constraints and Spatial Stratification by Income and Race." *Housing Policy Debate* 6: 141–67.

Schmidt, C. W. 1998. "The Specter of Sprawl." *Environmental Health Perspectives* 106 (June).

Schmidt, P. and R. Strauss. 1975a. "The Prediction of Occupation Using Multiple Logit Models." *International Economic Review* 16: 471–86.

———. 1975b. "Estimation of Models with Jointly Dependent Qualitative Variables: A Simultaneous Logit Approach." *Econometrica* 43: 745–55.

Schmitz, S., D. Williams, and P. Gabriel. 1994. "An Empirical Examination of Racial and Gender Differences in Wage Distributions." *Quarterly Review of Economics and Finance* 34: 227–39.

Schneider, M. and T. Phelan. 1993. "Black Suburbanization in the 1980s." *Demography* 30: 269–79.

Schrank, D. and T. Lomax. 2007. *The 2007 Urban Mobility Report*. College Station, TX: Texas Transportation Institute.

SCM (Somali Community Services of Maine), Inc. 2004. *Somali Families in Hillview: Assessing Needs, Setting Priorities, Building Consensus*. Prepared jointly by Somali Community Services Inc. and

Clark University in cooperation with the Hillview Action Committee with Assistance from the City of Lewiston.

Scott, E. P. 2006. "The New African Americans: Liberians of War in Minnesota." In *Race, Ethnicity and Place in a Changing America*, ed. J. W. Frazier and E. L. Tettey-Fio. Binghamton, NY: Global Academic Publishing, pp. 141–54.

———. 1997. "Home-Based Enterprises, Landscape and Human Well-being in Rural Zimbabwe." *Contemporary Development Analysis* 2(1): 111–53.

Sechler, A. R. 2002. *MDH Center for Health Statistics, Liberian Births by Zip Code*, 4/27/02.

Segal, U. A. and N. S. Mayadas. 2005. "Assessment of Issues Facing Immigrant and Refugee Families." *Child Welfare League of America*.

Selassie, B. 1996. "Washington's New African Immigrants." In *Urban Odyssey: Migration to Washington, DC*, ed. F. Carey. Washington, DC: Smithsonian Institution Press, pp. 264–75.

Semyonov, M., Y. Haberfeld, Y. Cohen, and N. Lewin-Epstein. 2000. "Racial Composition and Occupational Segregation and Inequality Across American Cities." *Social Science Research* 29: 175–87.

Shaw-Taylor, Y. and S. A. Tuch (eds.). 2007. *The Other U.S.-Born Blacks: Contemporary African and Caribbean Immigrants in the United States*. New York: Rowman & Littlefield Publishers, Inc.

Shelton, S. 2000. "MARTA Appoints New Chief." *The Atlanta Journal-Constitution*, December 1. Page D16.

Sheskin, I. M. 1992. "The Miami Ethnic Archipelago." *The Florida Geographer* (26): 40–57.

Shingadia, A. 1975. *Non-immigrant Foreign Workers in Canada — A Preliminary Look*. Report prepared for Canada Department of Manpower and Immigration. Ottawa: Department of Manpower and Immigration.

Shobo, Y. 2005. *African Immigrants: Patterns of Assimilation — Past Research and Present Findings*. Population Association of America Annual Meeting, Philadelphia, PA, March 31–April 2, 2005. http://paa2005.princeton.edu/abstractViewer.aspx?submissionId=50390.

Sibley, D. 1995. *Geographies of Exclusion: Society and Difference in the West*. London: Routledge.

Sierra Club. 1998. *The Dark Side of the American Dream: The Cost and Consequences of Suburban Sprawl*. College Park, MD: Sierra Club (August).

Silvey, R. 2004. "Transnational Migration and the Gender Politics of Scale: Indonesian Domestic Workers in Saudi Arabia." *Singapore Journal of Tropical Geography* 25(2): 141–55.

Singer, A. 2006. "The New Metropolitan Geography of Immigration: Washington, DC in Context." In *Race, Ethnicity and Place in a Changing America*, ed. J. W. Frazier and E. L. Tettey-Fio. Binghamton, NY: Global Academic Publishing, pp. 45–56.

———. *The Rise of New Immigrant Gateways*. Washington, DC: Center on Urban and Metropolitan Policy, The Brookings Institution.

Sjaastad, L. A. 1962. "The Costs and Returns of Human Migration." *The Journal of Political Economy* 70: 80–93.

Sjoquist, D. L. 2000. *The Atlanta Paradox*. New York: The Russell Sage Foundation.

Skaburskis, A. 1996. "Race and Tenure in Toronto." *Urban Studies* 33: 223–52.

Skop, E. 2008. *Saffron Suburbs: Lessons Learned from an Indian American Community*. Chicago: The Center for American Places.

———. 2007. *Austin City Limited: Race, Ethnicity and Place in a Dynamic Migrant Metropolis*. (Unpublished manuscript).

———. 2006. "Mapping Race and Ethnicity: The Influence of James A. Allen." *Yearbook of the Association of Pacific Coast Geographers* 68: 94–104.

Skop, E. and T. Buentello. 2008. "Austin: Immigration and Transformation Deep in the Heart of Texas." In *Twenty-First Century Gateways*, ed. A. Singer, C. Brettell, and S. Hardwick. Washington, DC: The Brookings Institute, pp. 257–80.

Skop, E. and W. Li. 2003. "From the Ghetto to Invisiburb: Shifting Patterns of Immigrant Settlements in Contemporary America." In *Multicultural Geographies of the United States. The Changing Racial/Ethnic Patterns of the United States*, ed. J. W. Frazier and F. M. Margai. Binghamton, NY: Global Academic Publishing, pp. 113–24.

Slevin, P. and P. Whoriskey. 2005. "Burdens of Past Limit New Orleans' Future." *Washington Post*, Thursday, November 10, A01.

Smedley, A. 1999. *Race in North America*. Boulder: Westview Press

Smith, C. 1957. Memo to G. McInnes, January 17. Ottawa: Public Archives of Canada, RG 76, Vol. 830, File 552-1-644.

Smith, G. M. 1999. "Atlanta's Working Solution to Smog." *Atlanta Journal and Constitution*, August 30. Page E1.

Smith, T. W. 1899. "The Slave in Canada." *Collections of the Nova Scotia Historical Society* X: 3–161.

Soflo.org/media. 2006. "Minorities become Majority in Broward: Caribbean, Latin American Populations Alter Demographics." August 4, 2006 Article ID = 17.

Sonfield M. C. 2005. "A New US Definition of 'Minority Business': Lessons From the First Four Years." *Entrepreneurship and Regional Development* 17(3): 223–35.

Southern Environmental Law Center. 1999. "SELC Scores Major Victory in Atlanta Lawsuit." *Southern Resources* (Summer). SELC.

Squires, G. 1996a. "Race and Risk: The Reality of Redlining." *National Underwriter* (*Property & Casualty/Risk & Benefits Management*), 100. September 16.

———. "Policies of Prejudice: Risky Encounters with the Property Insurance Business." *Challenge* 39, July.

Squires, G. and C. Kubrin. 2006. *Privileged Places: Race, Residence, and the Structure of Opportunity*. Boulder: Lynne Rienner Publishers.

Stack, C. B. 1996. *A Call to Home*. New York: Basic Books.

Stahura, J. 1988. "Changing Patterns of Suburban Racial Composition, 1970–1980." *Urban Affairs Quarterly*, March 23(3): 448–60.

Stasiulis, D. 1987. "Rainbow Feminism: Perspectives on Minority Women in Canada." *Resources for Feminist Research* 16(1): 5–9.

Statistics Canada. 2006a. *2001 Public Use Microdata Files (PUMF)*. Ottawa: Minister of Industry.

———. 2006b. C0-0857. *Target Group Profile — Population Born in Jamaica*.

———. 2006. *2001 Census Public Use Microdata Files (PUMF): Families*. Ottawa: Statistics Canada.

———. 2005. *The Daily*, March 22, p. 2.

———. 2003a. *2001 Census of Population*. Census of Canada: Catalogue No. 97F0010XCB 2001003.

———. 2003b. *Ethnic Diversity Survey: Portrait of a Multicultural Society*. Ottawa: Catalogue No. 89-593-XIE.

———. 2003c. *Canada's Ethnocultural Portrait: The Changing Mosaic*. Ottawa: Catalogue No. 96F0030XIE 2001008.

———. 2003d. *2001 Census: Analysis Series: Earnings of Canadians: Making a Living in the New Economy*. Ottawa: Minister of Industry.

———. 2002. *2001 Census Dictionary*. Ottawa: Ministry of Industry.

———. 2002. "Geographic Units: Census Metropolitan Area (CMA) and Census Agglomeration (CA)." *2001 Census Dictionary*. Catalogue Number 93-37 8-XIE.

———. 2001. Special Tabulation — Table 97f0009xdb2001002. Available from Statistics Canada web site at: http://ww12.statcan.ca/English/Census01/products/standart/themes/index.cfm.

———. 1998. *The Nation Series: 1996 Census: Immigration and Citizenship*. Ottawa: Supply and Services Canada.

———. 1997. *1996 Census Dictionary*. Ottawa: Ministry of Industry.

Stoller, P. 2001. "West Africans: Trading Places in New York." In *New Immigrants in New York: Completely Revised and Updated Edition*, ed. Nancy Foner. New York: Columbia University Press, pp. 229–49.

Stouffer, A. P. 1984. "A Restless Child of Change and Accident: The Black Image in Nineteenth Century Ontario." *Ontario History* LXXVI (2):128–50.

Strauss, A. and J. Corbin. 1998. *Basics of Qualitative Research: Techniques and Procedures for Developing Grounded Theory*. Thousand Oaks, CA: Sage Publications.

Suggs, E. 2000. "Complaint: MARTA Hike Based on Bias." *Atlanta Journal-Constitution*, December 7. Page D5.

SU LAIR 2007. *Africa South of the Sahara: Somalia/Somaliland on the Internet*. www-sul.stanford.edu/Africa/Somalia.html.

Sun Journal. 2002. Open letter from Lewiston, Maine, Mayor Raymond Laurier.

Sun, L. 1996. "At Soccer Event, a Field Day for Friendships: 30,000 Ethiopians Gather in Largo to Watch Tournament, Renew Acquaintances." *Washington Post*, 6 July: B01.

Swarns, R. L. 2003. "Africa's Lost Tribe Discovers American Way." *New York Times*, March 10.

Taeuber, K. E. and A. F. Taeuber. 1965. *Negroes in Cities: Residential Segregation and Neighborhood Change*. Chicago, IL: Aldine.

Takougang, J. 2002. *Contemporary African Immigrants to the United States*. www.africamigration.com/archive_02/j_takougang.htm.

Takyi, B. K. and K. Boate. 2006. "Location and Settlement Patterns of African Immigrants in the U.S.: Demographic and Spatial Patterns." In *The New African Diaspora in North America: Trends, Community Building and Adaptation*, ed. K. Konadu-Agyemang, B. K. Takyi and J. A. Arthur. Lexington Books, pp. 50–67.

Takyi, B. K. and K. Konadua-Agyemang. 2006. "Theoretical Perspectives on African Migration." In *The New African Diaspora in North America: Trends, Community Building and Adaptation*, ed. K. Konadu-Agyemang, B. K. Takyi and J. A. Arthur. Lexington Books, pp. 13–28.

Tator, C. and F. Henry. 2006. *Racial Profiling in Canada: Challenging the Myth of "A Few Bad Apples."* Toronto: University of Toronto Press.

Taylor, C. 1994. "The Politics of Recognition." In *Multiculturalism: Examining the Politics of Recognition*, ed. C. Taylor et al. Princeton, NJ: Princeton University Press, pp. 75–272.

Taylor, S. 2006. "A Multimedia Show Studies Somali Women's Lives in America." Lewiston. 10 September. *Sun Journal*. Reprinted in *The Somaliland Times*, 243. (http://www.somalilandtimes.net/sl/2005/243/11.shtml).

———. 2005. "From Border Control to Migration Movement: The Case for Paradigm Change in Western Response to Transborder Population Movement." *Social Policy and Administration* 39(6): 563–86.

Taylor Martin, S. 2005. *A Collision of Cultures Leads to Building Bridges in Maine: Somali Immigrants Are Finding a Haven in a Previously Homogeneous Enclave of Maine*. http://www.sptimes.com/2005/03/13/news_pf/Worldandnation/A_collision_of_cultur.shtml.

Teixeira, C. 2001. "Community Resources and Opportunities in Ethnic Economies: A Case Study of Portuguese and Black Entrepreneurs in Toronto." *Urban Studies* 38(11): 2055–78.

Teixeira, C. and L. Estaville. 2004. "Future Research Directions of North American Ethnic Geography." *International Journal of the Humanities* 2: 305–11.

Teixeira, C. and R. A. Murdie. 1997. "The Role of Ethnic Real Estate Agents in the Residential Relocation Process: A Case Study of Portuguese Homebuyers in Suburban Toronto." *Urban Geography* 18: 497–520.

Tettey, W. and K. Puplampu. (eds.). 2006. *The African Diaspora in Canada*. Calgary: University of Calgary Press.

The Economist. 2007. "Thirty-Year Retrospective: The Status of the Black Community in Miami-Dade County," Metropolitan Center, Florida International University. Sponsored by the Metro Miami Action Plan, pp. 89–96.

———. 2004. "Immigration: Into the Suburbs," March 13th, pp. 31–32.

———. 2002. "A Survey of Migration," November 2nd, p. 10.

Thomas, D. 1990. *Immigrant Integration and Canadian Identity*. A report of public affairs and strategic planning and research, immigration policy. Ottawa-Hull: Employment and Immigration Canada.

Thomas, W. 2000. "Mitigating Barriers to Black Employment through Affirmative Action Regulations: A Case Study." *The Review of Black Political Economy* 27(3): 81–103.

Thompson, C. 2005. "The New African Americans: African and Caribbean Immigrants Are Changing Black Identity in the United States." *AOL Black Voices*. December 7. Available at http://blackvoices.aol.com/black_news/canvas_directory_headlines_features/feature_article/_a/the-new-african-americans-african-and/20051205120309990001 (Accessed 8/22/2007).

Tiebout, C. M. 1956. "A Pure Theory of Local Expenditures." *Journal of Political Economy* 64: 416–24.

Tilove, J. 2002. "Nomads in America: Somali Migration Transforms a New England City." Lewiston. 8 September. *Sun Journal*. http://www.centralmaine.com/news/stories/020908somalis. shtml.

Tobler, W. 1995. "Migration: Ravenstein Thornwaite and Beyond." *Urban Geography* 16: 327–43.

Tolbert, E. J. 2001. "Extract from The Autobiography of Kwame Nkrumah." In *Perspectives on the African Diaspora* Volume Two. New York: Houghton Mifflin, p. 344.

Torpy, B. 2002. "Foreclosures Set One-Month Record for State." *Atlanta Journal-Constitution*, March 28, p. J1.

Tremblay, C. 1996. "Enforcement Mechanisms in Employment Equity Assessment and Direction for the Nineties." In *Racial Discrimination: Law and Practice*, ed. E. Mendes, chapter 6. Toronto: Carswell Publishing.

Trivedi-St. Clair, R. 2007. "Study Shows Racial Disparity in Home Loans." *St. Louis Post-Dispatch*, September 9.

Tuan, Yi-Fu. 1996. "Space and Place: Humanistic Perspectives." In *Human Geography: An Essential Anthology*, ed. J. Agnew, D. N. Livingstone and A. Rodgers. Cambridge, MA: Blackwell, pp. 444–57.

———. 1991. "A View of Geography." *The Geographical Review* 81(1): 99–107.

———. 1979. "Space and Place: Humanistic Perspectives." In *Philosophy in Geography*, ed. S. Gale and G. Olsson. Dordrecht, Holland: D. Reidel Publishing Company, pp. 89–102.

———. 1979. "Thought and Landscape: The Eye and the Mind's Eye." In *The Interpretation of Ordinary Landscapes*, ed. D. W. Meinig. Oxford University Press, Inc.

———. 1974. *Topophilia: A Study of Environmental Perception, Attitudes, and Values*. Englewood Cliffs: Prentice-Hall, Inc.

Turner, M., S. Ross, G. Galster, and J. Yinger. 2002. *Discrimination in Metropolitan Housing Markets: National Results from Phase I HDS 2000*. Washington, DC: The Urban Institute. http://www.huduser.org/publications/asgfin/ hds.html.

Turner, M., S. Ross, G. Galster, and J. Yinger. 2002. *Discrimination in Metropolitan Housing Markets: National Results from Phase 1 HDS 2000*. Washington, DC: The Urban Institute.

Turner, M. A. and R. Wienk. 1993. "The Persistence of Segregation in Urban Areas: Contributing Causes." In *Housing Markets and Residential Mobility*, ed. G. T. Kingsley and M. A. Turner. Washington, DC: Urban Institute Press, pp. 193–216.

Unfinished Migrations: Reflections on the African Diaspora and the Making of the Modern World. Preview by: Patterson, Riffany Ruby, Kelley, Robin D. G. *African Studies Review*, April 2000, Vol. 43, issue 1, p. 11.

Ungar, S. 1995. "Getting Down to Business: The Ethiopians and Eritreans." In *Fresh Blood: The New American Immigrants*, ed. S. Ungar. New York: Simon and Schuster, pp. 247–72.

United Nations Development Program. 2007. http://siteresources.worldbank.org/INTSOMALIA/Resources/conflictinsomalia.pdf.

University of Maine News. 2007. http://www.umaine.edu/news/default.asp.

U.S. Bureau of the Census. 2007. *American Community Survey 2006*. Washington, DC.

———. 2006. *American Community Survey*. "Selected Social Characteristics in the United States: 2006."

———. 2005. *American Community Survey* (ACS). http://factfinder.census.gov/servlet/DatasetMainPage Servlet?_program=ACS&_submenuId=&_lang=en&_ts= (Last accessed September 14, 2007).

———. 2002. "Statiscal Abstract of the United States: 2000." 117th Edition. Washington, DC: U.S. Government Printing Office.

———. 2000. http://factfinder.census.gov/servlet/DatasetMainPageServlet?_lang=en (Last accessed September 14, 2007).

———. *2000 Census of Population and Housing*. Summary File 1, Tables P8 and P10.

———. *2000 Census of Population and Housing*. Summary File 3, Table PCT18, "Ancestry (Total Categories Tallied) for People with One or More Ancestry Categories Reported."

———. *2000 Census of Population and Housing*. Summary File 3, Table PCT 19.

U.S. Census Bureau. 2006. *Estimated Daytime Population*. Washington, DC: Population Division, Journey to Work and Migration Statistics Branch, December 6, 2005, http://www.census.gov/population/www/socdemo/daytime/daytimepop.html (accessed April 17, 2006).

———. 2004. "Percent of Children Under 18 Years Below Poverty Level in the Past 12 Months (For Whom Poverty Status is Determined): 2004." *American Community Survey*. Washington, DC: U.S. Census Bureau.

U.S. Department of Homeland Security. 2005. *Yearbooks of Immigration Statistics*.

U.S. Department of Justice. 2000. *Statistical Yearbook of the Immigration and Naturalization Service*. Washington, DC: The Immigration and Naturalization Service.

U.S. Department of Transportation, Federal Highway Administration. 1999. Assessment of Environmental Justice Issues in Atlanta Proposed Work Plan. June 28. Washington, DC: USDOT.

———. 1998. Certification Report for the Atlanta Transportation Management Area, Washington, DC: USDOT.

U.S. Department of State. 2003a. Bureau of Population, Refugees and Migration: Somali Bantu http://www.state.gov/g/prm/rls/fs/2003/17270.htm.

———. 2003b. The United States Refugee Admissions Program: Reforms for a New Era of Refugee Resettlement. http://www.state.gov/g/prm/ refadm/rls/rpts/36057.htm.

U.S. Department of State. 2007. Bureau of African Affairs. Background Note: Somalia http://www.state.gov/r/pa/ei/bgn/2863.htm.

———. 2006. Bureau of Population, Refugees and Migration: Refugee Admissions Program for Africa. http://www.state.gov.g/prm/rls/fs/2006/66017.htm.

———. 2006. Bureau of Population, Refugees, and Migration. Summary of Refugee Admissions for Fiscal Year 2006. www.state.gov/g/prm/refadm/rls/85970.htm.

U.S. House of Representatives, 2006. Select Bipartisan Committee to Investigate the Preparation for and Response to Hurricane Katrina. A Failure of Initiative: Final Report of the Select Bipartisan Committee to Investigate the Preparation for and Response to Hurricane Katrina. U.S. Government Printing Office: Washington, DC. February, 15.

van Dalen, H. P., G. Groenwood, and J. Schoorl. 2005. "Out of Africa: What Drives the Pressure to Migrate?" *Journal of Population Economics* 18: 741–78.

Vertovec, S. 2006. "Diasporas good? Diasporas bad?" *Metropolis World Bulletin*, September 6: 5–8.

Vesely, M. 2005. "Africans in the U.S.: Second Wave Migrants Outdo African Americans." *African Business* 309: 38–40.

Vickerman, M. 2001. "Tweaking a Monolith: The West Indian Immigrant Encounter with 'Blackness.'" In *Islands in the City*, pp. 237–56.

Vigdor, J. L. 2006. *The New Promise Land: Black-White Convergence in The American South, 1960–2000*. Working Paper 12143. Cambridge: National Bureau of Economic Research.

———. 2001. *The Pursuit of Opportunity: Explaining Selective Black Migration*. Working Paper Series SAN01-08. Durham: Terry Sanford Institute of Public Policy, Duke University.

Villa, R. 2000. *Barrio-Logos: Space and Place in Urban Chicano Literature and Culture*. Austin: The University of Texas Press.

Village Voice. 2006. March 22.

Walen, B. 2002. Lutheran Social Services, Refugee Services and Employment Programs. Provided data on LSS Resettlement Program-Liberians in MN, 6/12/02.

Waldinger, R. 1987. "Beyond Nostalgia: The Old Neighborhood Revisited." *New York Affairs* 10: 1–12.

Walker, J. W. 1999. "African Canadians." In *Encyclopedia of Canada's Peoples*, ed. P. R. Magocsi. Toronto: University of Toronto Press, pp. 139–76.

———. 1992. *The Black Loyalists*. Toronto: University of Toronto Press.

———. 1980. *A History of Blacks in Canada*. Ottawa, Minister of State and Multiculturalism.

Wallerstein, I. M. 2005. "After Developmentalism and Globalization, What?" *Social Forces* 83(3): 1263–78.

———. 2004. *World-Systems Analysis: An Introduction*. Durham: Duke University Press.

Walton-Roberts, M. G. and G. Pratt. 2005. "Mobile Modernities: A South Asian Family Negotiates Immigration, Gender and Class in Canada." *Gender, Place and Culture* 12(2): 173–95.

Washington Post, The. 2006. "Five Years After Somalis Migrated to Lewiston, Maine USA." 2 March.

———. Kaiser Family Foundation & Harvard University. 2005. Survey of Hurricane Katrina Evacuees. Kaiser Family Foundation, September, 2005. Retrieved June, 1, 2006 from http://www.kff.org/newsmedia/upload/7401. pdf.

Waters, M. C. 2001. "Growing Up West Indian and African American: Gender and Class Differences in the Second Generation." In *Islands in the City: West Indian Migration to New York*, ed. N. Foner. Berkeley: Univ. of California Press, pp. 193–215.

———. 1999. *Black Identities: West Indian Dreams and American Realities*. Cambridge: Harvard University Press, pp. 44–93; 242.

Watson, T. 2007. *New Housing, Income Inequality, and Distressed Metropolitan Areas*. Washington, DC: The Brookings Institution.

Webster's New Universal Unabridged Dictionary, 2nd ed. 1983. New York: Dorset & Baber.

Welch, S., M. Combs, L. Sigelman, and T. Bledsoe. 1997. "Race or Place? Emerging Public Perspectives on Urban Education." *Political Science and Politics* 30(3): 454–58.

West, R. C. and J. P. Augelli (eds.). 1989. *Middle America: Its Lands and Peoples*. Englewood Cliffs: Prentice Hall, pp. 103–14.

Wettlaufer, K. 2007. Executive Director, and Gure Ali, After School Director, of Trinity Jubilee Center. Interview. 19 July.

Wiese, A. 2004. *Places of Their Own*. Chicago: University of Chicago Press.

Williams, D. W. 1997. *The Road to Now: A History of Blacks in Montreal*. Montreal: Vehicule Press.

———. 1989. *Blacks in Montreal, 1628–1986: An Urban Demography*. Cowansville, Quebec: Yvon Blais Inc.

Williams, E. E. 1944. *Capitalism and Slavery*. Chapel Hill: University of North Carolina Press.

Williams, W. L. 1980. "Ethnic Relations of African Students in the United States, with Black Americans, 1870–1900" in *The Journal of Negro History* 65(3): (Summer, pp. 228–49).

Wilson, C. 1992. "Restructuring and the Growth of Concentrated Poverty in Detroit." *Urban Affairs Quarterly* 28: 187–205.

Wilson, T. D. 1999. "Anti-immigrant Sentiment and the Process of Settlement among Mexican Immigrants to the United States: Reflections on the Current Race of Mexican Immigrant Bashing." *Review of Radical Political Economical* 17: 147–91.

Wilson, W. J. 1995. "The Declining Significance of Race." In *Sources: Notable Selections in Race and Ethnicity*, ed. A. Aguirre, and D. Baker. Dushkin Publishing Group.

Winant, H. 1997. "Where Culture Meets Structures: Race in the 1990s." In *Race, Class and Gender*, ed. D. Kendall. Toronto: Allyn Bacon, pp. 27–38.

Winks, R. W. 1980. *The Blacks in Canada: A History*. Montreal: McGill-Queens University Press.

———. 1971. *The Blacks in Canada: A History*. Montreal: McGill-Queens University Press.

———. 1969. "Negro School Segregation in Ontario and Nova Scotia." *Canadian Historical Review* Vol. L: 164–91.

Winnemore, L. and J. Bills. 2006. "Canada's Two-way Street Integration Model: Not Without its Stains, Strains, and Growing Pains." *Canadian Diversity* 5(1): 23–30.

Winsberg, M. D. 2006. *Atlas of Race, Ancestry and Religion in 21st-Century Florida*. Gainesville, FL: University Press of Florida, pp. 73–89.

Woldemikael, T. M. 1996. "Ethiopians and Eritreans." In *Refugees in America in the 1990s: A Reference Handbook,* ed. D. W. Haines. Westport, CT: Greenwood Press, pp. 147–169.

Wolpert, J. 1965. "Behavioral Aspects of the Decision to Migrate." *Papers and Proceedings of the Regional Science Association* 15: 159–69.

Wong, D. F. K. and H. X. Song. 2006. "Dynamics of Social Support: A Longitudinal Qualitative Study of Mainland Chinese Immigrant Women's First Year of Resettlement in Hong Kong." *Social Work in Mental Health* 4(3): 83–101.

Wong, M. 2006. "The Gendered Politics of Remittances in Ghanaian Transnational Families." *Economic Geography* 82(4): 355–82.

———. 2000. "Ghanaian Women in Toronto's Labor Market: Negotiating Gendered Roles and Transnational Households." *Canadian Ethnic Studies* 32(2): 45–77.

Woodlee, Y. 2005. "Activists Call for African Affairs Office." In *Washington Post*, December 29.

Wortley, S. and J. Tanner. 2004. "Discrimination or 'Good' Policing? The Racial Profiling Debate in Canada." *Our Diversity City*, (Spring): pp. 197–201.

———. 2003. "Data Denials and Confusion: The Racial Profiling Debate in Canada." *Canadian Journal of Criminology and Criminal Justice* 45(3): 367–89.

Wright, D. R. 1993. *African Americans in the Early Republic, 1789–1831*. Arlington Heights: Harlan Davidson.

Wright L. T., M. L. Martin, and L. Stone. 2003. "Exploring the Characteristics, Attitudes to Targeting and Relationship Marketing of Small Ethnic Minority Businesses." *Journal of Targeting, Measurement & Analysis for Marketing* 12(2): 173–84.

Wright, R. and M. Ellis. 2001. "Immigrants, the Native-Born, and the Changing Division of Labor in New York City." In *New Immigrants in New York*, ed. N. Foner. New York: Columbia University Press, pp. 81–110.

Yeboah, I. E. A. 2008. *Black African Neo-Diaspora: Ghanaian Immigrant Experiences in Greater Cincinnati Area*. Lanham, MD: Lexington Books.

———. 2003. "Historical Geography of Sub-Saharan Africa: Opportunities and Constraints." In *Geography of Sub-Saharan Africa*, ed. Samuel Aryeetey-Attoh. New Jersey: Prentice Hall, pp. 78–104.

———. 2000. "Structural Adjustment and Emerging Urban Form of Accra, Ghana." *Africa Today* 47(2): 61–89.

Yinger, J. 1998. "Housing Discrimination is Still worth Worrying About." *Housing Policy Debate* 9: 893–927.

———. 1995. *Closed Doors, Opportunities Lost: The Continuing Costs of Housing Discrimination*. New York: Russell Sage Foundation.

Yomoah, C. S., State Refugee Coordinator. 2007. Interview. 19 July.

Young, D. 1992. *The Donna Young Report: The Handling of Race Discrimination Complaints at the Ontario Human Rights Commission*. Toronto: Report of the Commission.

Zeleza, P. T. 2002. "Contemporary African Migrations in a Global Context." *African Issues* 30(1): 9–14.

Zelinsky, W. and B. A. Lee. 1998. "Heterolocalism: An Alternative Model for Sociospatial Behavior of Immigrant Ethnic Communities." *International Journal of Population Geography* 4(4): 281–98.

Zweig, D. 2006. "Competing for Talent: China's Strategies to Reverse the Brain Drain." *International Labor Review* 145(1–2): 69–90.

About the Authors

Fenda A. Akiwumi is an Assistant Professor of Geography at the University of South Florida, where she is a resource geographer. Her holistic research covers varied aspects of resources such as resource sectors, resource topics, resource problems, equitable distribution, and public involvement. Her research also incorporates environmental change and impact assessment and resources and cultural diversity. Fenda has ongoing research projects in the United States, Guyana and Sierra Leone. Her recent work has appeared in journals such as the *Journal of Geography*.

Nemata Blyden is an Associate Professor of History and International Affairs, and is the Director of the Africana Studies Program at The George Washington University, Washington, DC. She received her PhD from Yale University and specializes in the history of African Studies and the African Diaspora. Nemata is the author of *West Indians in West Africa, 1808–1880: A Diaspora in Reverse* (2000).

Thomas D. Boswell is Professor of Geography, University of Miami, Florida and former chair of the Department. His research and teaching interests are in world population problems, migration, ethnicity, housing segregation and discrimination and poverty. He has published more than 40 articles in refereed journals including: *Geographical Review, Urban Geography,* and *The Professional Geographer*. He also has co-authored or edited six books. He is currently working on research dealing with immigration from the West Indies to the United States.

Robert D. Bullard is the Ware Distinguished Professor of Sociology and founding director of the Environmental Justice Resource Center at Clark Atlanta University. He has written 15 books, including *Growing Smarter* (2007), *The Black Metropolis in the Twenty-First Century* (2007), *Race, Place, and Environmental Justice After Hurricane Katrina* (2009) and numerous articles.

Elizabeth Chacko is Associate Professor of Geography and International Affairs at The George Washington University. Her research interests include immigration from the Horn of Africa to the United States and return migration of Asian Indians living in Canada and the United States. Elizabeth has published on immigrant identity, ethnic space and ethnic entrepreneurship particularly among Ethiopian immigrants in various scholarly journals, including *Geographical Review* and the *Journal of Cultural Geography*. She also is co author of the book *Contemporary World Geography: Global Connections, Local Voices* (2006).

Joe T. Darden is Professor of Geography at Michigan State University and former Dean of Urban Affairs Programs. He is a former Fulbright Scholar, Department of Geography at the University of Toronto, 1997–98. Joe also is a faculty Fellow in the Centre for Urban and Community Studies at the University of Toronto. His research interests are urban social geography, residential segregation, and socioeconomic neighborhood inequality in multi-racial societies. He is the author of several books, including *The Significance of White Supremacy in the Canadian Metropolis of Toronto* (2004).

Lawrence E. Estaville is a Professor in and former chair of the Department of Geography at Texas State University-San Marcos. He is an award-winning author and teacher specializing in ethnic geography research and teaching. Lawrence's recent works include the editorship of a special issue of the *Journal of Geography,* which focuses on race and ethnicity.

David Firang is a PhD Candidate at the Faculty of Social Work, University of Toronto, and a Child Welfare Officer at the Children's Aid Society of Toronto. His research focuses on race, social capital, housing, and the settlement and integration process of immigrants. David held a Royal Bank Research Fellowship at the Faculty of Social Work during the 2005–06.

John W. Frazier is a Professor of Geography at the State University of New York at Binghamton. His research and teaching focus on applied urban geography and race, ethnicity, and place issues. John has authored or edited six volumes, including *Race, and Place* (2003) and *Race, Ethnicity, and Place in a Changing America* (2006).

Norah F. Henry is an Associate Professor and former chair of Geography, and former Associate Dean of Harpur College of Arts & Sciences, at the State University of New York at Binghamton. Norah has published widely on the geographic dimensions of social problems in journals such as *The Professional Geographer* and *Social Science and Medicine*.

Milton E. Harvey is Professor and former chair of Geography at Kent State University. He is the author of two books and numerous articles in scholarly journals in Geography and Marketing. His research has focused on the application of spatial statistics in human geography. Milton has published in leading journals such as *Economic Geography*.

Terry-Ann Jones is an Assistant Professor of Sociology at Fairfield University. Her areas of research and teaching interest are in migration, both within the region and between Latin America and the Caribbean and North America. Her book, *Jamaican Immigrants in the United States and Canada: Race, Transnationalism, and Social Capital*, was published in 2008. She is currently working on domestic labor migration in Brazil.

Joseph Mensah is an Associate Professor of Geography at York University in Toronto. He is the author of the *Black Canadians: History, Experiences, and Social Conditions* (2002); editor of *Understanding Economic Reforms in Africa: A Tale of Seven Nations* (2006); and editor of *Neoliberalism and Globalization in Africa: Contestations on the Embattled Continent* (2008). Joseph also is Project Manger of the SSHRC-sponsored Ghanaian Immigrants' Religious Transnationalism (GIRT) project at York University.

Esther Ofori grew up in Ghana, West Africa, and moved to the United States at age 16 to live with her mother in the Bronx, NY. She received her graduate degree in Geography from Binghamton University. Esther is a member of the Ronald E. McNair Scholars Program and the International Geographic Society (Gamma Theta Upsilon). She currently resides in Cincinnati, Ohio, and works as a retail location analyst for Macy's Inc.

Lisa Renee Rawlings received a PhD from Howard University in Social Work with a concentration in Displaced Populations. Her dissertation examined the psychological functioning of Hurricane Katrina survivors. Lisa recently has been overseeing two federally funded international exchange programs for graduates. They focus on socio-economic inequality and migration in Brazil and Europe.

Earl P. Scott is a Professor (Emeritus) of Geography and African American and African Studies at the University of Minnesota. He acquired his academic training at Southern University, Louisiana State University, and the University of Michigan. His research, publication and teaching on Africa spanned more than thirty-five years. As Chairman of the Department of African American and African Studies, Earl expanded its staff and restructured its undergraduate degree program, which included opportunities for study abroad and access to three major African languages.

Ira M. Sheskin is an Associate Professor of Geography and Regional Studies and directs the Jewish Demography Project of the Sue and Leonard Miller Center for Contemporary Judaic Studies at the University of Miami, FL. Ira has served as chair of the Ethnic Geography Specialty Group of the Association of American Geographers. His research centers on the geography and demography of the American Jewish community and the manner in which ethnic groups adapt to American society.

Emily Skop is an Assistant Professor of Geography in the Department of Geography and Environment Studies at The University of Colorado at Colorado Springs. At the center of her research and teaching is attention to the role that race, ethnicity, and other social differences play in shaping unequal geographies of mobility, belonging, exclusion, and displacement. Emily has published widely in scholarly journals such as the *Geographical Review, Urban Geography, The Professional Geographer*, and the *International Migration Review*. Her recent book is titled *Saffron Suburbs: Lessons Learned from an Indian-American Community* (2008).

Carlos Teixeira is an Associate Professor of Geography at the University of British Columbia-Okanagan. His research interests include urban and social geography, with an emphasis on migration processes, community formation, housing and neighborhood change, ethnic entrepreneurship and the social structure of North American cities. Carlos has published widely in Canadian and U.S. scholarly journals, including *Housing Studies, Environment and Planning, GeoJournal, and Canadian Ethnic Studies.*

Eugene L. Tettey-Fio is an Associate Professor of Geography at the State University of New York at Binghamton. His research has focused on Hispanic and African settlements in the United States and on social inequalities in the U.S. He is co-author of *Race and Place* (2003) and co-editor of *Race, Ethnicity, and Place in a Changing America* (2006).

Ian E. A. Yeboah is a Professor of Geography at Miami University, Oxford, Ohio. His teaching and research focus on globalization and African urbanization, globalization and African migration, and globalization and African poverty. Ian has published in journals such as *Area*, *African Geographical Review*, *Canadian Geographer*, *GeoJournal*, *The Geographical Journal*, *Africa Today*, and *Social Science and Medicine*. His recent book is titled *Black African Neo-Diaspora: Ghanaian Immigrant Experiences in the Greater Cincinnati, Ohio, Area* (2008).